THE CHURCH IN LATIN AMERICA: 1492–1992

A HISTORY OF THE CHURCH IN THE THIRD WORLD

Under the General Direction of EATWOT
Working Commission on Church History in the Third World

General Editor: Enrique Dussel

Volume I: The Church in Latin America: 1492–1999

Edited by Enrique Dussel

Forthcoming volumes:

Volume II: The Church in Asia and the South Pacific

Edited by Teotonio de Souza

Volume III: The Church in Africa

Edited by Ogbu Kalu

Indians obliged to learn about Christianity and perform baptisms
Source: Felipe Guamán Poma de Ayala, *El primer neuva corónica y buen gobierno.* Mexico City, Siglo XXI, 1980, vol. II.

CEHILA
Commission for the Study of Church History in Latin America

THE CHURCH IN LATIN AMERICA 1492–1992

Edited by

ENRIQUE DUSSEL
President of CEHILA

BURNS & OATES

First published 1992
BURNS & OATES, Wellwood, North Farm Rd,
Tunbridge Wells, Kent TN2 3DR

Published in the United States of America by
ORBIS BOOKS, Maryknoll, N.Y. 10545

The Catholic Foreign Mission Society of America (Maryknoll) recruits and trains people for overseas missionary service. Through Orbis Books Maryknoll aims to foster the international dialogue that is essential to mission. The books published, however, reflect the opinions of their authors and are not meant to represent the official position of the Society.

ISBN 0 86012 180 1 (U.K.)
ISBN 0 88344-820-3 (U.S.A.)

Library of Congress Cataloging-in-Publication Data

The Church in Latin America, 1492-1992 / edited by Enrique Dussel.
   p. cm. − − (A History of the Church in the Third World; v. 1)
At head of title: CEHILA, Commission for the Study of Church History in
Latin America.
  ISBN 0-88344-820-3: $49.95
  1. Latin America−Church history. 1. Dussel, Enrique D.
II. Comisión de Estudios de Historia de la Iglesia en Latinoamérica.
III. Series.
BR115.U6H56 1992 vol. 1
(BR600)
270'. 09172'4 s−dc20
[278]   92-21631
                                               CIP

Acknowledgement
CEHILA would like to express special thanks to Paul Burns, without whose
collaboration this publication would not have been possible.

Composition by Genesis Typesetting, Rochester, Kent
Printed and bound in the United Kingdom by
Staples Printers Rochester Limited, Rochester, Kent

CONTENTS

PART TWO
REGIONAL SURVEY

PART THREE
SOME SPECIAL SUBJECTS

MAPS AND DIAGRAMS

GLOSSARY

AUDIENCIA – The highest court in the Indies, made up of a President with auditors, scribes, judges, bailiffs, translators, etc. They existed in Santo Domingo, Mexico City, Guadalajara, Guatemala, Panama, Lima, Santa Fe de Bogotá and elsewhere.

CACIQUE – Appellation extended by Spaniards and Portuguese to Indian leaders of clans, tribes, peoples or nations.

CANDOMBLE – Rites and beliefs of African origin widespread in Brazil, to be distinguished from Macumba and Voodoo.

CAPITULATION – Contract signed by monarchs of Spain or Portugal with discoverers, conquistadors or colonizers. The name derives from the "chapters" (*capítulos*) or articles of the contracts.

CRIOLLO – Persons of Spanish or Portuguese descent, without mixed blood, but born in America.

ENCOMIENDA – Grant of land to colonizers, together with right to employ Indian labour. The grantees were *encomenderos*.

INTENDENCIES – The Bourbon kings who came to the throne of Spain in the eighteenth century organized this new colonial institution to control the collection of tributes, reorganize military dispositions and administer justice.

JUNTA – Equivalent of English "council" used to designate various bodies, such as of religious, bishops, etc. Later used of military governments.

LADINOS – Name given by the Indians to persons of mixed Spanish/Portuguese and Indian blood, i.e. *mestizos*.

MANIFEST DESTINY – The "Monroe doctrine" propounded by the U.S. President in 1823 of "America for the Americas" was soon interpreted as meaning that the United States had a "manifest destiny" to occupy the lands to the South and West of its then territory.

MESTIZOS – Children of mixed Spanish/Portuguese and Indian parentage, nearly always of white men and Indian women, born in America.

WESTERN DESIGN – When Cromwell sent an expedition to take Santo Domingo in 1665, he proclaimed that England had a divine mission to save the Caribbean from the "Papists," and this mission became known as the Western Design.

VOODOO – Religion of African origin much practised in Haiti, where it has a marked influence on the people.

GENERAL INTRODUCTION

Enrique Dussel
President of CEHILA

Every historical *event* is unrepeatable, unique. No description of a historical *fact* can be obvious, neutral, immediate. Every account supposes an "interpretation," whether conscious or not, willed or involuntary. So every history of the church supposes a certain way of handling ecclesial facts. The concept one has of the church (based on daily experience or a theological construct) will determine one's account of its history. In Latin America, we are trying to produce a history of the church on the basis of a particular *experience* we have of the institutional community founded by Jesus Christ.

The programme of the historical mission of the founder of Christianity is at the same time the mission or essence of the church. This programme was set out by Jesus when he unrolled the scroll containing the book of Isaiah:

> When Jesus came to Nazareth . . . he entered the synagogue . . . stood up to read and they handed him the book of the prophet Isaiah. Jesus then unrolled the scroll and found the place where it is written: *The Spirit of the Lord is upon me. He has anointed me to bring good news to the poor, to proclaim liberty to captives.* . . . Then he said to them: "Today these prophetic words come true even as you listen" (Luke 4:16–21).

If "bringing good news to the poor"[1] was his specific historical purpose and that of his church, this must also be the absolute and primary criterion of a *Christian* interpretation of the history of that church – a scientific interpretation, certainly, but also Christian (based on faith). The "meaning" of an event, then, is deduced from the effect (positive or negative) it has on the poor, the oppressed, the ordinary people. The criterion for writing the history of the church is not the triumphalism of the great cathedrals or the splendour of papal coronations of emperors, but the mutual love in the "breaking of bread" in persecuted, poor, missionary, prophetic Christian communities. It has to be a history from the people, for the people, of the people in their pastoral, catechetical and evangelizing role.

To do this, we need to *construct* the biblical category of "poor," oppressed, dispossessed, as a category with historical validity. This means studying the social totality of a period as determined by an overall practical-productive relationship (feudal, capitalist, etc.) which in turn enables one to define social classes. The different ways these classes interact in historical conjunctions, "historical blocs," will shed light on the meaning of an era, period, phase or event. So the *Christian* meaning of these can be discovered from the poor, seen as dominated race, sex, class, ethnic group or nation.

In the same way, the church, in its institutional history, can be meaningfully described by discovering its interaction as a community in history with the

1

overall structure of society. In the first three centuries of its existence, the church found its place in society, organized its structures and counted its faithful only among the dominated (peripheral nations and oppressed classes). It was a church of the poor, a persecuted church, the church of the martyrs. It was a "model" of church that could not be confused with the state and did not depend on the power of the ruling classes.

In the fourth century, another "model" appeared, that of *Christendom*, as Kierkegaard was to call it. The church now justified the coercive action of the state, and the state fulfilled church functions – building places of worship, protecting its missionaries, forcing obedience from those who dissented from church authority, and so forth.

So "models" of church of the poor or of Christendom become hermeneutical categories operating as interpretative principles. We need to try to write, above all, the history of the church *from* the poor, *for* the poor and – the ideal to which we are still aspiring[2] – *by* the poor themselves. We are still a long way from achieving this, as this book shows.

This epistemological question could be the subject of lengthy debate. Here we can only note its importance and, above all, its deep methodological implications, which we are just beginning to glimpse.

1. LATIN AMERICA IN WORLD HISTORY

As historians of the church in Latin America, we find ourselves faced with two problems: first, the need to write a history of the church; second, the task of reinterpreting the history of Latin America in such a way that it can serve as an adequate basis for our proposed history of the church. We need to re-situate Latin American history in world history, in order to revalue the oppressed peoples – the Indians first, then the African slaves, and finally the peasants and workers, with women as doubly oppressed in all periods and classes.

(a) Amerindia as Primary History

Amerindia was not solely or principally the context of the discovery and conquest by Spain and Portugal, by Europeans, as though it came on the scene of world history after Columbus set sail from Europe. It is an assembly of cultures derived from north-eastern Asian emigration through Bering. Its Neolithic focus is the Pacific Ocean, so American cultures come from the East.

The Neolithic revolution reached its culmination in the confederation of cities in Mesopotamia in the the fourth millenium BCE, in Egypt and the cultures of the Indus Valley in the third, and in China in the second. So the great urban cultures of America have to be situated within this vast current of civilization moving Eastward, from the Middle East to the Far East and then through the Polynesian cultures to America. In the first millenium CE (from 300 to 900 approximately), two great classical cultures flourished in America, centred on Tiahuanaco near Lake Titicaca (in modern Bolivia) and Teotihuacan not far from Lake Texcoco in the vale of Mexico. The splendour of these cultures, which reached their apogees with the Inca and Aztec empires in Peru and Mexico in the fifteenth century, gives Amerindia a distinguished place in world history.

The American peoples, whether *nomads* from North or South, *planters* from the valleys of the Mississippi and the Antilles down to the Orinoco, Amazon and Plate, or *city-dwellers* from Inca and Aztec, Maya and Chibcha cultures, were then the makers of high cultures, producers of original civilizations and of a religious world of prodigious riches and meaning.[3]

It was on these peoples, on their races, cultures and religions, that the Christian-European "invasion" was launched as by "wolves and tigers and lions that have been hungry for many days," as Bartolomé de las Casas was to put it. The dignity, numbers and beauty of the Amerindian peoples was the fertile and positive soil on which the history of Latin America was built – a soil today despised, forgotten, exploited.

(b) The Proto-history of the Latin American Church

One source that must feed into a history of the church in Latin America is the previous history of American religions and cultures; another, equally relevant, is the whole history of Christianity, from its origins, through its experience and assimilation of Mediterranean culture, to its arrival in the Iberian peninsula. This history of Germano-Latin Christendom would be the proto-history of the church in Latin America, its main source and determinant, with all its faults and virtues. We need a *complete* re-reading of the history of the church as a whole and from its beginnings in order to understand the history of Latin America.

In effect, the ability of historians of the Latin American church to interpret the Christianity that "reached us" from Europe in the fifteenth century *critically* depends largely on their particular view – starting from the criterion of "bringing the good news to the poor" – of the overall course of the Christian event in world history. So a complete re-reading of the history of Christianity is a task facing Christian historians in the Third World.

The Semites – starting with Akkadians, Assyrians and Babylonians, Phoenicians and Amorites, then the Hebrews and centuries later the Arabs – burst into the Indo-European cultures and states – Phrygian, Hittite, then Greek and Roman, Medean and Persian, down to Aryan and others. The history of Israel belongs in that of the Semites, especially to its struggles against the kingdoms of Mesopotamia and Egypt, against Greeks and Romans. The relevant point here is that the "religious community" of Israel, from the patriarchs and prophets down to the synagogues of the diaspora, is a very different "model" from that of the monarchy, in which the state was confused with the chosen people.

In the same way, the early Christianity of the the first three centuries, of the martyr church, presents a very different church "model" from that of post-Constantinian Christendom. Armenian, Georgian, Byzantine, Latin and later Russian, Moravian, Polish and other *Christendoms* became historical absolutes which inevitably identified Christianity with their Western, European cultures. So Iberian Christendom, which went through an early Roman phase, then turned in on itself during the Visigothic period, the Moorish occupation and the long process of reconquest, which ended in 1492 with the taking of Granada, was the immediate context for the expansion of Christendom into Latin America.

This Spanish-Portuguese Christianity came formed by a long history of Christendom, which meant that the process of evangelization was at the same time, and equivocally, a "civilizing" process: one which in fact meant the political and cultural annihilation of the Amerindian peoples. The cross came together with the oppressing, violent, conquering sword. America then had to bear a church identified with the state. Americans came to know Christianity through the "model" of Latin, Iberian Christendom.

2. FIRST ERA: COLONIAL CHRISTENDOM (from 1492)

The history of the church in Latin America can be divided clearly into three eras:[4] (1) Indian Christendom under Spanish-Portuguese rule, mercantile capitalist and exclusively Catholic; (2) the crisis of the Christendom of the Indies and the new situation of the neo-colonial pact under Anglo-Saxon (first English and then North American) rule, dependent on industrial capitalism, first free-market and then imperialist, and with a growing Protestant presence (first from Europe and then almost exclusively from North America, ending with Pentecostalism and fundamentalist sects); (3) the long crisis of capitalist dependency, at present marked by the further turning of the screw of North-South domination.

(a) First Period. The Caribbean (1492–1519) and the Brazilian Coast (1550–1549)

Columbus' companions seem to have included a priest, who celebrated the first mass on the Continent in 1492 on the "isle of the Lucaios" (Pedro de Arenas). In any event, the "discovery" (*invasion* of conquest for the inhabitants of America), carried out by a merchant and seamen from the Mediterranean, was a phase in the expansion of Iberian Christendom. Spain and Portugal were then the centre of the "empire-world" – as Emmanuel Wallerstein was to call it.

The time of Isabella (1492–1504) and then Ferdinand (1506–16) gave the Christendom of the Indies its structure, extending the royal patronage (power of appointment of bishops) over the Canary Isles and Granada to the newly conquered lands. With the establishment of the Council of the Indies in 1524, this patronage over the church was consolidated till the nineteenth century. The first economic cycle in the Antilles was devoted to gold and marked by the *encomiendas* of Indians, by which they were "granted" to conquistadors as personal property. This process was completed in 1514, but by 1518, after the smallpox epidemic, there were scarcely 3000 natives left in Santo Domingo. This brought the gold cycle to an end, to be replaced by that of sugar plantations and African slaves.

Under Friar Bernal Boyl, the ecclesiastical power was separated from the civil power, over which Columbus held the regency from 1493, under the Bull *Piis Fidelium*. Franciscan brothers arrived and the evangelization of Latin America began. The Dominicans arrived in 1510, and the following year one of their number, Antón de Montesinos, launched the first prophetic cry: "I am the voice of one crying out in the desert of this island."

On 15 November 1504, Pope Julius II founded the first three dioceses in America: Baynua, Magua and Yaguata. Ferdinand objected and was granted

Patronage over the church in the Indies, under the Bull *Universalis Ecclesiae* of 28 July 1508. This was the formal introduction of Christendom. He nominated three bishops, to Santo Domingo, San Juan and Concepción de la Vega, in 1511. At the Burgos Junta of 1512, the products of their tithes were handed over to the king.

Whether consciously or not, the church, through its ruling hierarchical structures, was becoming part of the conquering power. Missionaries and clergy, in the eyes of the natives, were part of the same class as conquistadors, traders and *encomenderos*. There were to be notable exceptions.

The same was true of the missionary endeavours on the Brazilian coast in the first phase of its conquest (1500–1559), a period marked by chaotic exploitation of the natives, the time of *pau brasil* and division of the territory into Captaincies. A few Franciscans were not enough to ensure an exemplary Christian presence. Brazil was simply a port of call on the way to Africa, the "Arabian sea," (Indian Ocean) and the Far East (Goa, Cochin, etc.).

(b) Second Period. The Great Missions (1519–51) and the Jesuits in Brazil (from 1549)

The process of overall evangelization began in 1519, when Hernán Cortés set out from Cuba to conquer the Aztec empire. The first missionary cycle (the Caribbean) was followed by those embracing Mexico, Central America and the Inca and Chibcha regions, thus reaching out to the major centres of pre-Hispanic American population. The arrival of Tomé de Souza in Brazil in 1549, accompanied by the first Jesuits, likewise marked the systematic beginning of evangelization on the coast of Portuguese America.

The Spain of Charles V, who succeeded to the throne under a regent in 1516 and reigned till his abdication in 1556, and the Portugal of the great naval empire were at the height of their splendour. Even before the full financial benefits of the mining boom in the colonies, they were the centre of the "empire-world." This was the time of "warrior Catholicism," in which evangelization by *tabula rasa* produced the model of Christendom in the Indies. The Dominicans Bartolomé de Olmedo and Vicente Valverde went respectively with Cortés to Mexico and Pizarro and Almagro to Peru. Our Lady "of the Remedies" defended Cortés against the Aztecs, as Our Lady of Victories was to aid Alvaro de Castro against the natives of Brazil in 1555. Conquest was upheld by the Christian religion.

Systematic evangelization began with the arrival of the Franciscan "twelve apostles" in San Juan de Ulúa on 14 May 1524, followed by twelve Dominicans on 2 July 1526 and the Augustinians on 22 May 1533. The missionaries progressed rapidly from preaching through interpreters to learning large numbers of native languages, in which they went on to produce dictionaries, grammars, catechisms, confessionals and books of sermons. Dioceses were founded in major centres from Mexico in the North down to Asunción in the South. A "Christian people" was taking shape.

At the same time, against the will of Spanish and Portuguese Christians, an *original and creative reception* of the gospel message began to form among the mixed population of Latin America: native peoples, *mestizos*, African slaves, impoverished Spaniards and Portuguese. And the first uprisings – particularly

among the Incas who were never completely conquered – were the beginning of
the long march of liberation. In contrast to the ruling Christendom model,,
another model of church was emerging: a church "of the poor people," those
who lived beyond the "republic of the Spaniards," in the countryside and the
poor quarters of the cities, who identified with the patient, suffering, bleeding
Christ shown in the violently bloody images in churches in the popular
quarters, the Christ of the "*tremendismo*" of the people of Latin America
awaiting their liberation.

The "New Laws" of 1542 also produced the beginnings of struggles for
justice to the Indians, and though Las Casas' position was to lose out all down
the line, he remains an inspiration to the present time. The Christendom of the
Indies was being built on the blood of the natives and of black slaves.

(c) Third Period. Church Organization (1551–1620)

In 1551 the first diocese of Brazil, San Salvador de Bahía, was founded, and the
first Latin American Provincial Council was held in Lima. In 1546, the first
three archdioceses, Santo Domingo, Mexico and Lima, were established. In
1556 Charles V abdicated and retired to a monastery and the rapacious Philip II
ascended the throne of Spain. In 1548 silver was discovered in Northern
Mexico, giving rise to the third cycle of evangelization, and at about the same
time in Peru, producing the fourth.

"Warrior Catholicism" began to give way to a settled ruling class, an
oligarchy of landowners, sugar mill owners and mine owners: the "patriarchal
Catholicism" of the "Lord of the manor" ruling over the *senzala* (slave
quarters). The "Great Junta" of 1548 gave control of the church entirely over
to the state, through a system of patronage under which the civil and political
powers produced nominees for all church appointments, from the lowliest
sacristan to the grandest archbishop.

This period also saw eleven provincial councils, more than seventy diocesan
ones, the founding of the universities of Lima and Mexico in 1553, plus more
than thirty centres granting diplomas in theology, and the establishment of
major seminaries. The dioceses of Vera Paz and Yucatán were founded in the
North, Charcas, Santiago, Bogotá, Concepción, Córdoba del Tucumán,
Arequipa, Trujillo, La Paz, Santa Cruz and Huamanga in the South. The
Jesuits arrived, and the Inquisition was established in Mexico, Cartagena and
Lima. When the dioceses of Durango in Mexico and Buenos Aires were added
in 1620, the organization of Spanish colonial Christendom was complete.
"Popular Catholicism" was also progressing with lay confraternities, charitable
organizations, hospitals, assistential and loan systems, associations and Third
Orders, also the first "doctrines" (residential schemes) for the Indians. It was
also the time of the first *quilombos* (villages founded by runaway slaves) and their
resistance to oppression. Native Christian rebellions multiplied; the "Christian
people" were refusing to accept the rule of the Christendom of Europeans and
white *criollos* (persons of European descent born in America).

One way and another, the Catholic Church was, through its hierarchical
structures (but with honourable exceptions), becoming the state apparatus for
creating consensus in civil society. The hegemonic ruling classes needed the

church in order to achieve their coercive objectives within the Christendom of the Indies.

(d) Fourth Period. The Church in the Seventeenth Century

Philip IV was crowned in 1621, and in 1623 Rome launched *Propaganda fide* as an organ to counter Spanish patronage. This was the end of Spanish hegemony, the beginning of Spain's decline and the rise of Holland, followed by England. The Treaty of Westphalia marked the end of Spain and Portugal, of mercantile capitalism and of the mining boom.

In Brazil, this was the time of the "entries" (*bandeiras*) up the rivers towards Minas Gerais, Mato Grosso and Goyás; also of the first missions in Maranhão and Pará. In Spanish America, it was the century of the "reductions," missionary settlements of Indians, extending from the Orinoco and the plains of Colombia in northern South America down to Paraguay, where the Jesuit reductions became prototypes of socialism in their way.

It was the age of the baroque culture favoured by the Jesuits, complex and gilded, subjective and emotive, producer of impressive churches, statues, altars and works of literature. It was a time of growing *criollo* autonomy in relation to Spain – forerunner of independence – with the "native American" church joining the "church of the poor," the church of those who had been oppressed for almost two centuries, against Spaniards, Europeans, those not born in Latin America.

It was also the time of provincial quarrels – between Franciscans and Dominicans, the latter and the Jesuits and their universities; between religious and secular clergy, between the church in general and the civil powers. Disputes raged over tithes and first-fruits, crown donations and *encomenderos*, parish tariffs and priests' way of life: the "daily life" of an imposed, enclosed, remote American Christendom. It was, too, a time when the church became enormously wealthy through bequests; when huge estates were created, cities built and money amassed in state-owned pawnshops – the banks of the day.

There was not a single year of the seventeenth century that did not see a rebellion of natives, blacks or *mestizos* in either Spanish or Portuguese America. When Good Friday was being celebrated on 22 March 1660, thousands of Indians rebelled in the province of Tehuantepec, in which more than 150,000 men paid tribute. Within the space of five hours, more than two hundred villages were in arms. Only the efforts of the *criollo* bishop Cuevas Dávalos de Oaxaca prevented full-scale war. The "Christian people" were still a force to be reckoned with, waiting for their liberation.

In Spanish America, Protestantism had made its appearance and was attracting the attention of the Inquisition. The crime of being a "Lutheran" was one of the most heavily punished – with flogging, imprisonment and exile from the Indies. Apart from the brief presence of the German colony of the Weslers in the conquest of Colombia, Protestantism took root mainly in Brazil. There was a Huguenot colony founded by Nicholas Durand de Villegaignon in Rio de Janeiro in 1555, and the Dutch colony of Pernambuco lasted till 1654, when the North East of Brazil was reconquered by the Portuguese.

Protestantism was to take firm root in the Caribbean. England occupied Barbados in 1625, and Jamaica in 1655, bringing the theology of Cromwell's

"Western Design," which was centuries later to be translated into the "Manifest Destiny." In 1694 the English occupied the Bahamas. Holland took Surinam in 1625, then Curaçao in 1634. France took Guadaloupe and Martinique in 1635, Haiti in 1659 and Cayenne in 1664. So if Catholicism came to America with the conquering violence of mercantile capitalism, Protestantism came with the expansion of the dawning Anglo-Saxon industrial capitalism. Neither of the two can be exonerated from blame and responsibility. Both brought a mental model of Christendom: Catholic Spanish-Portuguese Christendom; Anglican, Calvinist and other central European Christendoms. Again an oppressed "Christian people," this time made up of black slaves, began to make an original and creative reading of the gospel, now in opposition to the ruling Protestant capitalism.

(e) Fifth Period. The Christendom of the Indies in Crisis (Eighteenth Century)

The year 1700 saw the beginning of the War of Spanish Succession, which ended with a French Bourbon on the Spanish throne. The Treaty of Methuen in 1703 made Portugal an English dependency. From the "centre of the empire-world," the Iberian peninsula had moved to the semi-periphery of the central nations of industrial capitalism. The rise of a business middle-class in Spain and Portugal (dependent on the Anglo-Saxon industrial middle-class) shifted the "historical bloc" in power, and this applied equally in the Indies, where the Habsburg oligarchies and bureaucracies gave way to a commercial bourgeoisie dependent on Cadiz (as opposed to Seville). On other fronts, the renaissance of gold and silver mining in Mexico and Brazil, administrative reorganization, and the agricultural revolution begun in Britain and now exported to the Spanish world, produced a century of enormous growth for America, but also one of crisis.

The first half of the century brought the most significant religious development in Brazil, with the "mining Catholicism" based on Ouro Preto, and the fourth, and then fifth, cycles of evangelization in Portuguese America, ministering to a population increased many times over by the rise in mining activity. But this was largely a lay evangelization, virtually without religious, based on confraternities and local saints. The dioceses of Olinda, Rio and São Luis de Maranhão were founded in 1676, the archdiocese of Bahía in the same year, followed by Pará in 1719 and Mariana and São Paulo in 1745. The first synod of Bahía was held in 1707. This was the beginning of "greater Brazil." The period came to an end in 1757 with the expulsion of almost five hundred Jesuits from Brazil and Maranhão on the orders of the Marquess of Pombal, representing the Catholicism of the Enlightenment. This was a real break with history.

In Spanish America, on the other hand, the second half of the century was more significant. In 1757 Charles III came to the throne, with Aranda as his chief minister, whose policies coincided with those of Tanuci in Naples and Choiseul in France. The Jesuits were expelled from the Spanish territories in 1767, thus bringing the prototypical missionary experiment of the reductions to an end. Indian Christendom was henceforth defined as a colony. Taxes were increased and *criollos*, native peoples and slaves all felt the weight of oppression grow heavier. On 20 November 1761, the Maya chief of Cisteli, Santos Canek, exclaimed at the outset of his rebellion:

> Most beloved sons of mine: I know not what you expect of the heavy yoke and burdensome servitude laid on you by subjection to the Spaniards. I have journeyed through the whole province and asked in all its villages, and considering with due attention what use or benefit subjection to Spain has brought us, I find nothing other than a painful and unbreakable servitude.

The "Christian people" oppressed by Bourbon Christendom was by now made up not only of natives, slaves and *mestizos*, but included the *criollo* middle classes. The Virgin of Guadalupe, previously an exclusively Indian devotion (like the Virgin of Copacabana on Lake Titicaca), was now invoked by the *criollos* against the Spaniards. In the struggles for emancipation the Spaniards carried the banner of the Virgin of Remedies and the Americans that of the Virgin of Guadalupe: a struggle of Virgins, a class struggle.

"Enlightenment Catholicism" sought to reform the church, and the religious orders, by means of the "*Tomo regio.*" The royalist episcopacy was strengthened at the expense of the religious orders, scripture reading was favoured above scholasticism, there was a return to the Fathers of the church and support given to the secular clergy. Provincial councils were used in the 1770s as an aid to Bourbon policies.

Internal tensions in the Catholic Church increased: the higher ranks owed allegiance to royal patronage, while the lower clergy, the *criollos* and the oppressed "Christian people" moved increasingly towards autonomy. In keeping with the traditions of "popular Catholicism," emancipation became a shared aspiration. The rebellion of thre "*comuneros*" in New Granada and the uprising led throughout the Viceroyalty of Peru by the Inca Tupac Amaru, who was executed in 1781, were to destroy the model of Christendom patiently constructed over three centuries.

3. SECOND ERA: THE CHURCH IN NEO-COLONIAL DEPENDENCY (FROM 1807)

While Latin America emancipated itself from Spain and Portugal in the early nineteenth century, it actually moved into a neo-colonial position of dependency on Anglo-Saxon industrial capitalism, first English and then North American. This is why, when Latin Americans talk of "liberation" today, they mean, strictly speaking, liberation from dependence on Anglo-Saxon capitalism, something they suffer from in a very special sense, in a way that Africa and Asia do not, since Anglo-Saxon aggression toward Latin America has been quite *sui generis* – with the invasion of Panama in 1989 being the latest instance.

(a) First Period. The Church in National Emancipation (1807–31)

The struggle for the emancipation of the new Latin American nationalities covers the period from Napoleon's invasion of Portugal in 1807 and then Spain, which triggered the process, to the appointment of six residential bishops by Pope Gregory XVI on 28 February 1831. In the process, a conflict appeared within the core of Christendom: the royalist bishops were on one side and the minor clergy were on the other – patriotic and anti-Spanish. Religious, priests and lay people took up arms and produced, in a way, a sort of theology of liberation. Within this process, however, five different cycles of independence struggle can be distinguished, covering three stages in time.

In the first stage (1807–14) the uprising was against Napoloeon and in support of Ferdinand VII. *Criollos* seized power in several places and expelled royalist bishops. In the second stage, Ferdinand returned to power in Spain and re-imposed royal authority over the colonies. Pope Pius VII condemned emancipation in his encyclical *Etsi longissimo* of 30 January 1816. The third stage was a struggle against the king and led to definitive independence around 1821. Again the Pope issued an encyclical, *Etsi iam diu* of 24 September 1824, demanding obedience to the Spanish throne. Both were grave historical errors, which were to produce an irreversible crisis in the Christendom of the colonies.

The cycles of emancipation in the River Plate (first) and New Granada (second) followed a similar pattern. From the River Plate, General San Martín, supported by the minor clergy and religious orders, but not by most of the bishops, emancipated Argentina, Chile and Peru. Moving southward from Venezuela, Bolívar emancipated Colombia, Ecuador and Bolivia between 1810 and 1821. The third cycle covered Mexico and Central America, where first one priest, Miguel Hidalgo, and later another, Morelos, fought against *criollos* and Spaniards but were defeated; then, in 1821, independence was gained under Iturbide.

Brazil followed a different course (fourth cycle). Since the king of Portugal fled from Napoleon and established the capital of his empire in Rio, Brazil did not have a war of independence as such – though heroes such as Tiradentes anticipated the struggle for popular emancipation. When Pedro I declared his *fico* in 1822, Brazil was independent of Portugal, and retained a monarchical system till 1889 when the Republic was established. Compared to the Spanish-speaking region, the Church suffered less in the process and was not so violently divided against itself.

The fifth cycle, in the Caribbean, is more complex, and, begun in the early nineteenth century, is still incomplete, since there are still colonies needing to become free nations. Haiti gained its independence in 1804, the first of all the Latin American countries. Santo Domingo won independence from Spain, but was then occupied by Haiti, from 1822–44. Cuba and Puerto Rico remained Spanish colonies till 1898, when they came under the control of the United States. The other islands of the Caribbean still had to endure long periods of English, French or Dutch rule, as did Surinam and the Guyanas.

Newly independent governments immediately claimed patronage over the Church, and in most cases succeeded in this, even against the will of Rome. The wars of independence shattered the structure of Christendom: seminaries were closed, libraries burned, convents emptied, new missionaries prevented from arriving. The "Christian people" identified the struggle for national independence with their own faith and the habits of popular Catholicism. They felt no conflict in their conscience. This was not the case with the new *criollo* class that rose to power: the liberals, a business class linked with Anglo Saxon industrial capitalism.

(b) Second Period. The Church and National Organization (1830–80)

The liberals, mainly the commercial oligarchy that had brought independence about, and the conservatives, mainly landowners who exported tropical foodstuffs and mining products, were jointly responsible for the neo-colonial status of the emergent nations: selling raw materials and importing manufactured goods.

In Brazil, this was the time of Pedro II (1840–89); in Mexico, of Santa Ana and other transitory governments (1824–57); Central America saw the destruction of its unity in 1831; Colombia went through a period of instability after the death of Bolívar in 1830; Venezuela was ruled by José Antonio Pérez from 1829 to 1846, Argentina by Rosas from 1835 to 1852, Ecuador by Flores and then Rocafuerte and Gabriel García Moreno (1860–75); Chile went through the period of "*pipiolos*" (youngsters) till 1861; Paraguay had its dictator in Franciq (d. 1840).

In the Catholic Church, Tejada's embassy from Great Colombia made contact with Rome, Rome took its first initiative in contacting Latin America with the Muzi mission in 1823 (which failed); residential bishops were later appointed, but the situation became increasingly problematic. It was generally allied to the conservatives, defending the fortunes made in the countryside ("dead hand" goods acquired through traditional non-capitalist means), while liberals, proponents of a free-market, capitalist approach to national development, pursued a policy of secularization and expropriation of church goods.

The liberals generally clung to power in this period: from 1849 to 1866 in Colombia, throughout the 1870s in Brazil, from the coming of Mitre and the ascendancy of Buenos Aires in 1860 in Argentina, under Juárez in Mexico from 1857, Pérez in Chile from 1861, the "reds" in Uruguay from 1852. So the state did not allow the church to pursue the Christendom model: quite the contrary, it sought to impose an anti-church ideological hegemony through education.

At the same time, the growing social revolution in Europe had led to a missionary crisis, which was ended only at the Restoration. In 1859 Pius IX founded the Latin American Pius College in Rome, in which many of the influential bishops of the latter part of the century were to be educated. The teaching religious orders also began to send their members out to Latin America around the middle of the century. In this way, a process of "Romanizing" the Catholic Church in Latin America – which had been more Iberian than Roman till then – was begun.

In 1848 the northern part of Mexico (Texas, New Mexico, Arizona and California) was violently annexed by the United States as part of its drive to the Far West. This gave rise to a "*chicano*," "Hispanic" Church dominated by Anglo-American Catholicism: French- and English-speaking bishops were appointed, its Mexican priests were excommunicated, and it was not allowed to express itself through its own language or culture till the end of the 1960s.

(c) Third Period. The Church and Dependence on Imperialism (1880–1930)

Between 1870 and 1880 a basic change took place in the central capitalist powers, which was to realign Latin American society and affect influences on the church, one of its effects being a growing Protestant presence.

Imperialism, a new phase in the development of capitalism distinguished by monopolistic concentration of financial and industrial capital, moved into Latin America systematically. The new "entrepreneurial spirit" followed the railways. The liberals, a basically dependent class, gained an unshakable hold on power and set up neo-colonial states. The masses of the people, the conservative landowners and the "internal market" liberals (who opposed an economy based on imports and enjoyed a brief success only in Paraguay up till 1870), together with the Catholic Church itself, went on the defensive, set up resistance and waited for the tide of history to turn.

The new ruling class used "Positivism" – as preached by Comte, Darwin and Spencer – as its fighting ideology. The Church had no adequate pastoral or theological defence against the advance of this new ideology, though in Mariano Soler, bishop of Montevideo, it produced one intellectual who could debate with it.

These were the years (in the three countries most closely tied to Anglo-Saxon expansion) of the "Porfiriate" in Mexico (1876–1910), the government of Roca in Argentina (1880 onwards), and the liberal Republic in Brazil (from 1889). In Rome, the first Plenary Latin American Council was held in 1899, attended by thirteen archbishops and forty-one bishops. A combination of the place in which it was held, the excessive influence of Roman Canon Law and the fact that it was prepared by exclusively European theologians, made this major event into more of a formal act than an effective spur to pastoral action. Its spirit was one of "keeping the faith," defending it, protecting it: a conservative, rearguard approach.

It was, however, a time of renewed missionary outreach. The Franciscans and Capuchins began evangelizing in the Amazon region in 1860, followed by the Dominicans in 1880 and the Salesians in 1895. Pope Leo XIII established missions to the Andean regions of Peru. The Salesians came to Argentina in 1879 to evangelize Patagonia – at the time when Roca's "invasion of the desert" was advancing with mass slaughter of Indians. In Colombia, missionary renewal had begun back in 1840; the Augustinians arrived in 1890, the Montfortians in 1903, Lazarists in 1905, Claretians in 1908, Carmelites and Jesuits in 1918.

Protestantism also took a firm hold during this period, progressing in three stages: scattered groups up to 1880; growing settlement from 1880 to 1916; taking deep root from 1916 to 1930. Diego Thomson had celebrated the first Protestant worship in Latin America in Argentina in 1820; several Anglican chapels were opened in Buenos Aires when 250 Scots settled there in 1825. In 1836, the Methodists arrived, this time from the United States. The first Anglican church in Brazil was opened in 1819, followed by German Lutheran communities who settled in Santa Catalina. Shortly afterwards, the Waldensians came to Uruguay. So the various denominations gradually spread throughout Latin America.

It was, however, the first Missionary Societies, such as the Methodist, which reached Mexico in 1871, Brazil in 1876, the Antilles in 1890, then spreading to all the other countries, that brought about the real expansion of Protestantism. The Presbyterians came to Brazil in 1860, Argentina in 1866, Mexico in 1872, Guatemala in 1882; the Baptists to Brazil in 1881, to Argentina in 1886, to Chile in 1888, and counted over 100,000 members by the beginning of the twentieth century. With the Congresses of Panama in 1916, Montevideo in 1925 and Havana in 1929, Protestantism became a major factor on the Latin American scene.

(d) Fourth Period. The Church and Populism (1930–55)

The great crash of 1929 and the struggle for hegemony at the capitalist centre (USA versus Britain, even though the Axis powers started the two World Wars) partly destroyed the neo-colonial "pact" and weakened the importing liberal class. This led to the rise of a new class: the nationalist industrial bourgeoisie, who became the heirs of the "internal market" liberals, of the craft unions and the non-exporting conservative landowners. A new "historical bloc" had come to power: Latin American populism.

This nationalist bourgeoisie was not anti-church, since its structural enemies were the Anglo-Saxon industrial powers. This led them to see the Catholic Church as a natural ally, since this Church had been anti-liberal and nationalist. Latin American populist regimes (Vargas in Brazil from 1930, Irigoyen from 1918 and Perón from 1945 in Argentina, with the exception of Cárdenas in Mexico from 1934, where the "Cristeros" uprising in 1926 set the Church in opposition to the Mexican state) once more set a model of Christendom before the Catholic Church. So this period can be called one of "new Christendom." In practice, the populist state (so called because despite its capitalist programme it stands for national autonomy and advancement of workers and peasants) allowed the Catholic Church to "go forth" with huge Eucharistic Congresses, and to teach the Catholic faith in state schools, forbidden by the liberals since the "lay teaching" of the 1880s.

The salient feature of the "new Christendom" was the spread of Catholic Action (founded in Italy in similar circumstances under Mussolini's populist regime). It was established in Cuba in 1929, in Argentina in 1930, in Uruguay in 1934, in Costa Rica and Peru in 1935 and in Bolivia in 1938. The Church concentrated its energies on the petty bourgeoisie, which played a central role in Latin American populist regimes, as it did in European fascist ones.

Catholic Action produced a major intellectual renewal, partly inspired by Jacques Maritain. In Brazil this led to the rise of Tristão de Atayde (Amoroso Lima), who took the place of Jackson de Figueiredo who died in 1930. In Argentina, the tradition of anti-positivist intellectuals such as Manuel Estrada (1842–94) produced an elite generation, typified by Martínez Villada (1886–1959) which opened the way for new post-war groups to make Christian thinking a factor in the intellectual life of the country. In Mexico, Vasconcelos and Antonio Caso were responsible for a similar process. New Catholic universities were founded – the colonial ones having been nationalized by the liberals in the last century: the Xavieran in Bogotá in 1937, Medellín in 1945, São Paulo in 1947, Porto Alegre in 1950, Campinas in 1956, Buenos Aires and Córdoba in 1960, Valparaiso in 1961, along with scores of other educational establishments.

The social struggle was also assuming a new profile, with the growth of Christian trade unionism and the establishment of centres for social studies after the Second World War. Particularly significant were the foundation of JOC (Young Christian Workers), which had five hundred branches and almost

100,000 members in Brazil alone by 1961, and JAC (Young Agricultural Workers).

(e) Fifth Period. The Church, "Developmentism" and National Security (since 1955)

This period, being the most recent and of particular importance, will be treated here in greater detail, considered under three phases. The first of these, from 1955 to 1964, is that of "developmentism" proper, the model of development dependent on the introduction of North American and European capital and technology. The second, from 1964 to 1976, is that of the most brutal dictatorships, brought in by military coups for reasons of "National Security." The third, since 1976, is marked by the crisis of these dictatorships (and the economic crisis of the United States), together with the phenomenon of foreign debt, leading to the slow emergence of a degree of "democratization," under the varying guises of neo-populism, social democracy, neo-liberalism, and so forth.

(i) Developmentism, Christian Democracy and church renewal. The ten years following the Second World War sufficed for the United States to impose its hegemony over Europe (the German "economic miracle") and Asia (the rise of Japan). Turning its attention to "the periphery," it found nationalist capitalist governments in Latin America. "Nationalism" was regarded as the prime enemy of the dawning expansion of what were to become the "transnational corporations." The populist regimes fell: Vargas in 1954, Perón in 1955, Rojas Painilla and Pérez Giménez in 1957, Batista in 1959, etc. Their place was taken by *developmentist* governments which brought about dependence on North American and European capital: Kubitschek in Brazil in 1956, Frondizi in Argentina in 1957, López Mateos in Mexico in 1958, Betancourt in Venezuela in 1959, and the Christian Democrats Eduardo Frei in Chile in 1964 and Calderas in Venezuela in 1969. All these governments were *formally* democratic.

The Catholic Church had begun its post-war renewal and had a model to put forward: liturgical, pastoral and catechetical renewal; the new European theology; Catholic Action for lay affairs; Christian Democracy in the political sphere. The Church in Chile was the exemplar and guide; Manuel Larraín the prototypical bishop. It was a time of growth and organization. The first General Conference of Latin American bishops was held in Rio de Janeiro from 25 July to 4 August 1955, and CELAM (the Episcopal Council of Latin America) was founded.

A series of other foundations also belong to this phase: CLAR, the Latin American Confederation of Religious, in 1958; OSLAM, the Organization of Latin American Seminaries, also in 1958; The Conference of the International Federation of Catholic Youth, in 1953; the JOC Information Centre, in 1959; UNIAPAC, the Delegation of Latin American Employers, in 1958; the Family Christian Movement in 1951; the Latin American Catechetical Institute in 1961; ULPAC, the Latin American Catholic Press Union, in 1959, CLASC, the Latin American Confederation of Christian Trade Unionists, in 1954; ODUCAL, the Organization of Catholic Universities of Latin America, in

1953; the American Christian Teachers' Union in 1955. . . . So it was a time when the continent looked forward with hope in development and also in the possibility of Christian intervention in it. The bishops of Latin America took part in the Second Vatican Council of 1962–5, though the part they played was more that of spectators, "observers," not yet that of creative players. The fact that 186 million Catholics had only 39,000 priests (one for every 4,700) was realized. The burning questions (for Catholics) were the priest shortage, the advance of communism, and the spread of Protestant evangelism. Protestants, for their part, had also seen impressive growth since 1930. In 1936, the various churches and other groups numbered around 2,400,000 members; by 1960 this figure had risen to ten million. Protestantism also developed an ecumenical dimension in this period and several co-ordinating bodies covering Latin America came into being.

(ii) *The church under National Security dictatorships.* The formally democratic "developmentist" governments found it impossible to control the people who were increasingly repressed by dependent (on North America) capitalism, so a new model of government was applied: military dictatorship, which would allow capitalism to flourish without democracy. On 31 March 1964 there was a military coup in Brazil; Bolivia succumbed in 1971; the Uruguayan Congress was dissolved in 1973; on 11 September of the same year Allende was assassinated and Pinochet came to power in Chile; in 1975 Francisco Morales Bermúdez took power in Peru; in 1976 the nationalist government fell in Ecuador; the same year saw the military take over in Argentina. Latin America was sunk in repression and persecution; for the people it was a time of captivity. For its part, the Catholic Church went through one of its deepest experiences since its implantation in America. In 1968 the bishops held their Second General Conference in Medellín, and this produced a dividing line: between a developmentist Church and one committed to liberation. The theology of liberation was born at the same time as a widespread acceptance of political commitment to the cause of the "oppressed" – oppressed by "development-ism," by dependent capitalism, and now by cruel and bloodthirsty dictatorships.

The years 1964/5 to 1968 were a time of preparation and growth. The years from 1968 to 1972 (the Fourteenth Assembly of CELAM in Sucre in Bolivia) were a time of deep creativeness, with many Christians making a commitment to the people and prophetic movements demonstrating new ways of living Christianity. The base church communities came into being and spread; CELAM's Pastoral Institute (IPLA) flourished. 1969 brought the first experience – to be followed by hundreds and hundreds of such witnesses to the gospel – of martyrdom: Antonio Pereira Neto was murdered in Recife, Brazil – tortured, riddled with bullets and hung from a tree by right-wing paramilitaries. He was the first priest so to die. On 24 March 1980, Oscar Romero was shot saying mass; it had gone beyond lay people and priests; this time it was an archbishop. The lay Christian workers and peasants who have been killed cannot be counted. Slowly, a new church model was taking shape.

In 1973 the bishops of North-East Brazil produced a document entitled "I have heard the cry of my people!" This was the formulation of a church of the poor, a church born of the people through the action of the Spirit. Now the people had seized the word, and had their pastoral action, their theology, their bishops, their pastors.[5]

This is why, in the harshest political period (from Sucre to the election of President Carter in 1976), the church went through a conversion experience, in which a spirituality of martyrdom went hand in hand with realism. At the Rome Synod of Bishops in 1971, and again in 1974, the Church of Latin America appeared as such, and spoke with its own voice. But it was, at the same time, following a long Way of the Cross.

(iii) The church and new "democratic" models of dependent capitalism. Since the fall of the populist regimes (around 1955), Latin American capitalism has inevitably been dependent and repressive. The "hard" dictatorships (in Brazil, Argentina, Chile and elsewhere) were running out of steam. Carter proposed a "softening," with stress on human rights, and a return to democracy. This, however, was short-lived, with the presidency of Ronald Reagan (1980–88) marking a return to repression of the people. Types of regime varied during a period when capitalist dependency prevented the people from developing through the continual outflow of capital, which in turn mobilized popular unrest. The presidency of George Bush brought the invasion of Panama (not to mention the Gulf War), showing that the post-cold war "New World Order" meant the total hegemony of the North over the South. The problem of the right to work, of the right to *life* – a central theological preoccupation at present – shows a structural crisis within Latin American capitalism, which is producing growing poverty for the mass of the people. The Catholic Church is divided: on one side is the "developmentist" model of New Christendom, intent on renewing the Latin American Church through Christian or Social Democracy on European lines, with European theology, pastoral approaches, and so on; on the other is the church-of-the-poor model, intent on committing itself to the people themselves, being with the poor, oppressed and starving people, and with them creating a new theology, a new pastoral strategy. These two sides were clearly in evidence at the Third General Conference of Latin American Bishops held at Puebla in Mexico in 1979, and each is still following its own course for the Fourth Conference in Santo Domingo in 1992.

Since the death of Archbishop Manuel Larraín in Chile in 1966 and the appointment of Archbishop Aloisio Lorscheider as President of the Brazilian Bishops' Conference in 1968, the Brazilian Catholic Church has been at the forefront, with its over 100,000 base communities, its bishops committed to the defence of peasants' land rights, of indigenous peoples' rights, supporting strikes and workers' claims (particularly in São Paulo), allowing space for political organization and intellectual discussion. The Catholic Church in Brazil is carrying out a special prophetic work. The Protestant churches too – through organizations such as ISAL, ULAJE and CELADEC – reached a decisive point in 1969, at the Latin American Congress for Evangelization (CLADE) in Bogotá, with its call to responsibility in the face of the crisis of poverty. The Third Latin American Evangelical Conference (CELA III) produced a clear definition of aims in the political, economic and social spheres. Protestantism is now Latin American, with its own personality within world Protestantism. However, the move away, at the 1978 Assembly of

Churches held at Oaxtepec in Mexico, from the Latin American Evangelical Union (UNELAM) to the Latin American Conference of Churches (CLAI), was an indication that a new stage has been reached in the prophetic stance of the ecumenical movements.

4. THIRD ERA. THE CRISIS OF PERIPHERAL CAPITALISM (from 1959)

Historical processes take time to work themselves out: that of national independence began in Haiti at the beginning of the nineteenth century and ended in Belize in the 1980s. So the introduction of the second era ended in Belize. In the same way, the situation in which Christians, and the Churches, are beginning to live is that of the crisis of dependent capitalism, but in some cases this is already frankly post-capitalist, with new, disconcerting problems, situations and structures unknown till now, so that it seems reasonable to talk of a third era.

In effect, Christians in Latin America share in the continent-wide crisis, a slow, sporadic and hidden process, which has frankly been set back by the collapse of socialism in the USSR and Eastern Europe. This is felt most keenly in the Caribbean and Central America, so I should like to take two final examples as prototypical of this third era.

(a) The Church in Cuba

This Caribbean island was discovered by Columbus on 27 October 1492, and remained a Spanish colony till 1898. In 1954, Fulgencio Batista, who had been *de facto* ruler since 1933, was elected President. In 1956 the lawyer Fidel Castro began the struggle against the dictator, in the Sierra Maestra. Mgr Pérez Serrantes, Archbishop of Santiago de Cuga, interceded for the the fugitives who had attacked the Moncada barracks. On his deathbed, referring to the triumphant revolution led by Castro, he exclaimed: "All that is happening to us is providential. We believed more in our institutions than in Jesus Christ."

Castro had entered Santiago on 2 January 1959 and on the 8th he was welcomed in triumph in Havana. The same year, Pope John XXIII announced the calling of a Council. The Catholic Church in Cuba certainly had no idea that it was – without adequate preparation – being immersed in a new *historical era*.

The first phase of the revolution might be called "democratic and humanist." The Archbishop of Santiago issued a strong circular "against the shootings" on 29 January. On 17 March the Agrarian Reform Law was passed, affecting private property of US citizens, who owned more than 40 percent of Cuba's cultivatable land. By November 1959 the Catholic Congress convoked in Havana was chanting: "We want a Catholic Cuba," and "Cuba Yes; Russia No." The direct confrontation was beginning.

On 27 June 1960 Castro made his decisive speech: "Those who are anti-communist are anti-revolutionary." The following 17 April brought the Bay of Pigs invasion, carried out by anti-Castro exiles supported by the CIA and approved by John F. Kennedy. The Church aligned itself solidly with the anti-socialist side. Castro declared: "The priests are allies of theft, crime, lies; they are now the fifth column of the counter-revolution."

1961–8 was a period of complete break, total misunderstanding, on both sides. The Catholic Church was an unjustifiable bastion of capitalist conservatism. Much of the ruling party was made up of equally unjustifiable, imported, dogmatic Marxism. The Apostolic Delegate, Mgr César Zacchi, began to try to build bridges. In the meantime, the Council and then Medellín had given the Catholic Church a different face. Fidel himself was to say, addressing five hundred intellectuals in Havana in 1968: "There is no doubt that we are faced with new events. These are the paradoxes of history: so when we see sectors of the clergy become revolutionary forces – I am thinking of Camilo Torres among others – are we going to resign ourselves to seeing sectors of Marxism become conservative forces?" Mgr Zacchi declared: "The Church should begin to think out the place it should occupy in the new socialist society."

On 10 April 1969, the bishops criticized the US blockade of Cuba: "Seeking the good of our people and faithful to the service of the poorest, in conformity with the commandment of Jesus Christ and the commitment newly proclaimed in Medellín, we denounce this unjust situation of blockade which is contributing to an increase in suffering." And on 3 September the same year, they issued another communiqué: "This is a time when, as at all times, we have to be able to discern the presence of the Kingdom of God in the positive aspects of the crisis . . . (There is therefore) a huge field of endeavour common to all and involving the whole person, whether atheist or believer."

After this came a period of gradual maturing, of renewal on the basis of an opened dialogue between bishops and government. Now the crisis of *perestroika* has led to a particularly critical moment in Cuba – for Christians too.

(b) The Church and the Religious Question in the Central American Crisis

Central America, violently conquered in the sixteenth century, exploited throughout its history, divided by Anglo-Saxon capitalist interests, occupied and lately abandoned by the transnationals and a land-owning oligarchy with no social conscience, has risen up, with Christians taking part in the process. From the time of the holy Dominican bishop Antonio Valdivieso, martyred in February 1550 for defending the Indians against the conquistador Carreras in León in Nicaragua, down to the thousands and thousands of martyrs of our own days, Central America is now an example of Christianity committed to the people's liberation struggles.

The early 1970s produced a movement that was kept hidden from the eyes of the keenest observers. A group of young people, including the *comandantes* of the "Proletarian" Sandinista group (Luis Carrión, Joaquín Cuadra and many others, including *comandante* Mónica Baltodano), then students doing committed Christian work in the suburban Managua parish of Santa María de los Angeles, joined the Sandinista Front for National Liberation (FSLN). The incorporation of Christians in the liberation struggle was a new event. They joined in the triumph of 19 July 1979. The base communities, the bishops themselves and the Catholic Church in general had openly fought against the Somoza dictatorship – even if the Papal Nuncio had toasted the bombing of León with the dictator a few days before the triumph of the revolution.

On 17 November 1979, the Bishops' Conference of Nicaragua issued a historic Pastoral Letter on "Christian Commitment to a New Nicaragua." In it they declared:

> If socialism means, as it should mean, pre-eminence given to the majority of the Nicaraguan people and a nationally planned economic model marked by solidarity and progressive participation, we have no objections to make . . . If socialism supposes power exercised from the standpoint of the majority of the people and increasingly shared by the organized people, then again it will find in the faith nothing but motivation and support. If socialism leads to cultural processes that awaken the dignity of our people, this is a process of humanization convergent with the human dignity our faith proclaims. We are confident that the revolutionary process will be something original, creative, deeply national and in no way imitative."

A year later, on 7 October 1980, the National Directive of the Sandinista Front released an "Official Communiqué of the National Directive of the FSLN on Religion," whose central message was:

> We Sandinistas state that our experience shows that when Christians, taking a stand on their faith, are capable of responding to the needs of the people and of history, their very beliefs impel them to revolutionary militancy. Our experience has shown us that one can be a believer and a revolutionary at the same time and that there is no irreconcilable contradiction between the two.

It was the end of one era and the opening of another, the first time that a post-capitalist revolutionary movement had spelled out such an attitude to religion in both theory and practice, and its repercussions were not slow to spread to Cuba, Mozambique and other socialist countries.

The Nicaraguan experience, but also the presence over the years of Christians – priests, religious, lay people and the martyr figure of Archbishop Romero, hero of the people and already proclaimed a saint by the masses – in the liberation struggles of El Salvador, Guatemala and Honduras, shows that the church of the poor has been growing uncontainably from the people themselves.

In El Salvador, the population of the countryside had lived a scattered existence since the peasant massacre of 1932. It was the Catholic Church, through its base communities – the first apostle of which was Fr Rutilio Grande, martyred like Archbishop Romero and more than twenty other priests in Central America in recent years – that gave the peasant community self-understanding, a sense of purpose and organization. So the Church was at the base, the start of the liberation process itself; not a guest invited at the hour of triumph, but a midwife at the very birth of the people's advance.

Evangelization, through the blood of the martyrs and the day-to-day work of ordinary Christians, has progressed even despite the actions of many of those responsible for church structures. It is now the people themselves, the same humble, simple, poor people violently dominated during the conquest, oppressed by estate and mine owners, by oligarchs and liberals, by absentee landlords and transnational corporations, this Christian people who are the agents of their own liberation, identified with the carpenter Christ, tortured and crucified, bleeding before the soldiers of the Empire.

The FSLN's loss of the elections in Nicaragua in February 1990 has radically changed the situation in the region. The church, however, though divided by its previous history, will continue on its way much as before, having reaped an enormous harvest of historical experience in the process. Here and elsewhere, it can draw on the positive values of its past: the generosity of thousands of missionaries in the colonial period; the emergent church of the poor in the nineteenth century. The memory of the people, of the presence of at least part of the church in the people's resistance struggles, forms the basis for the active Christian agency in the liberation struggles of today.

Translated from the Spanish by Paul Burns

NOTES

1. *The concept of "poor" (ptokhois* in Luke, *hanavim* in Isaiah) was defined as the key interpretative concept in CEHILA's 1973 proposal to write a "General History of the Church in Latin America" (cf CEHILA, *Para una historia de la Iglesia en América Latina,* Barcelona, 1975, pp. 23ff). This initiative derived from my conversations with Paul Gauthier in Nazareth in 1959 (see *Jésus, l'église et les pauvres,* Tournai, 1962), which led me to the idea of writing a history of the church "upside down," from the poor (cf Dussel, *Hipótesis para una historia de la Iglesia,* Barcelona, 1967). Over the years, however, the hermeneutical difficulty of making the concept of "poor" into a usable scientific historical category became apparent. In 1979 CEHILA's seventh meeting, a symposium in San Juan in Puerto Rico, discussed this methodological problem. On this see my *Historia general de la Iglesia en América Latina,* vol. I/1, ch. 1 (Salamanca, 1983). This eleven-volume work contains full bibliographies on the history of the church in Latin America.

2. At its ninth annual symposium held in Manaos, CEHILA organized an experimental "historico-popular production workshop," in which a historian provided the basic elements (often images, or simply the context of events known to the popular memory handed on by "ancients," "sages" or popular poest) on which the people themselves could construct a history of the church in their own categories, language and symbols. So the people redefined the "discovery" of America by Columbus and the Christians as the "invasion" of America (from the point of view of the Amerindian inhabitants). The same happened at a workshop held in Recife in Brazil. Cf E. Hoornaert, "A questão do destinador e do destinatario," *Boletín CEHILA* 14–15 (1978), pp. 19ff.

3. Cf W. Krickeberg, H.Trinmborn, W. Müller, O. Zerries, *Die Religionen des alten Amerika* (Stuttgart, 1961).

4. My division into periods does not necessarily coincide exactly with that of the chapters in part one of the present work. It aims to give an overall view, drawing the following chapters together.

5. See my *De Medellín a Puebla. Una década de sangre y esperanza (1968–1979)* (Mexico, 1979). For a bibliography on Protestantism in the period, see J. Sinclair, *Protestantism in Latin America: a Bibliographical Guide* (South Pasadena, 1976); on Catholicism, there is a select bibliography in my *History and Theology of Liberation* (Maryknoll, N.Y., 1976, pp. 183–9).

PART ONE

CHRONOLOGICAL SURVEY

1. Río Pinturas (Cave paintings of ancient hunters).
2. Zona de Lagõa Santa (Cave paintings of ancient hunters).
3. Zona de São Raimundo Nonato (Piaui)
4. La Aguada (Diaguita Area, N.W. Argentina)
5. Tiahuanaco
6. Cuzco
7. Pachacámac
8. Kotosh
9. Chavín
10. Sechín Alto and Cerro Sechín
11. Moche (Mounds of the Sun and Moon)
12. Valdivia
13. San Augustín
14. Tikal
15. Copán
16. Palenque
17. Uxmal
18. Chichén-Itzá
19. La Venta
20. San Lorenzo
21. Monte Albán
22. Tenochtitlán (present day Mexico)
23. Teotihauchan
24. Tula
25. Chaco Canyon (Anasazi Area, S.W. United States)

1. Amerindian America: principal sites mentioned in chapter 1.

Chapter 1

THE AMERINDIAN RELIGIONS

Juan Schobinger

Five hundred years after the official "discovery" of America by south-western Europeans (northern Europeans had found it five hundred years earlier, but left little trace), no one doubts the significance of the event, but interpretations of it differ. The *viewpoint of the conquered*[1] obviously differs from that of the conquerors, who, by the mere fact of being so, saw themselves as superior and in no need of getting to know and understand the conquered. Was not this, still, our grandparents' attitude? In the sixteenth century, though, the disciplines now collected under the heading "anthropology" did not exist. We had to wait till the late nineteenth century for this, and in America old theories and speculations had to be painfully superseded. It was not till the 1950s that an ethno-history of the high cultures of the American West was developed, capable, in conjunction with the great progress made in archeology, of glimpsing the complexity and depth of the pre-Columbian mind. It is only gradually that we are succeeding in eliminating distorted images of the American "Indians."

In general terms, pre-Columbian religious ideas and practices can be said to be closely connected to a cosmovision diametrically opposed to our own: intuitive, open to nature and the cosmos rather than shut up in the ego, communitarian rather than individualistic, seeing everything visible as a symbol of something greater, on which they depended. America – particularly in its high cultures – represents a notable conservation of the magical-mythical mentality that forms one of the great steps in the cultural evolution of the human race. So the collision that occurred in the sixteenth century was not just between opposing cultures, or betwen races, or between different historical products; it was not between "more advanced" and "backward" cultures, or "civilized" people and "barbarians." It was, essentially, between two states of consciousness, and this is perhaps why it was so painful.

1. THE HUNTER CULTURES

Going back to pre-history, we have to admit to knowing nothing of the religions of Paleolithic hunters in America. Different types of arrow-head can be dated back to some 11,000 BCE, and two or three thousand years later, after the Ice Age, some groups began to produce cave paintings in the rocky valleys of East and North-East Brazil and South Patagonia. One of their designs, hands painted in "negative," is identical to those in the High Paleolithic cave paintings of France and Spain, and leads one to suppose that they reflect rites similar to those practised by the hunters of Western Europe five or six thousand years earlier. Paintings of animals and hands persist almost to the beginning of the Christian era, when they give way to drawings with biomorphic symbols (mainly based on the prints of different animals and the human foot) and geometric paintings of varying complexity. These latter persist almost to ethnographic times, and their magical significance has been shown (as has that of all cave paintings to some degree).

In this age – characterized by what has been called the "magical mentality"[2] – ritual practices must have been relatively simple, with a proto-shamanism and "hunting magic." This would explain the human figures chasing or encircling "little camels" (llamas or alpacas), found in the Río Pinturas region of Santa Cruz in Argentina, and also in mountain sites in Peru and Northern Chile, the home of the Andean hunter-gatherers who spread through there and the Bolivian *altiplano* (high plateau) betwen 8000 and 4000 BCE.[3]

In other cases, the idea of fertility must have played a part, giving us another analogy with the prehistoric hunters of the Old World. We do not know if true totemism (which is in any case a social system rather than a religion) developed in America, though ethnographic survivals indicate that a variant of it developed in parts of North America and perhaps in northern Patagonia. There is the same evidence of a rich animism on Tierra del Fuego, expressed in ritual dances by masked men, initiation rites, body painting and the like. There are no other signs here of an "animalistic" cult such as that expressed in the *loncomeo* (ostrich dance) of the tribes of Northern Patagonia, also adopted by their Araucanian neighbours.

This desire to identify with or embody superior beings ("spirits") shows the hunter cultures prefiguring something that took more definite form among the paleo-farming cultures: the characteristic American shamanism.

2. FARMER-POTTER CULTURES

While shamanism in its prototypical form appeared among hunter peoples of Central and North-East Asia, forms or variants of it also appear among American peoples who had reached the agricultural stage. This suggests that shamanism is associated not so much with an outer form of culture or economy as with a type of mentality. American religiosity has been said to be essentially shamanistic, and this would explain the persistence of rites of this type even in the high cultures, at least in their early stages.

Shamanism in Asia and America arose, in my view, as an attempt, using more or less artificial techniques, to recapture the intimate contact with the world and its immanent forces (seen as divine) that was natural in humanity's earliest stages. Though on a more "primitive" level than the initiation rites found in Mediterranean and Middle Eastern cultures, American shamanism also gave rise to a particular type of esoterism, whose signs can be found in the "temple" cultures of Central America and Peru, and in some "middle-level" (farmer-potter) cultures of the Southern Andes and the Amazon basin.

As in Western Asia, America had several millenia of "incipient agriculture," pre-ceramic, traces of which have been found in Central America and the Andean region. We know nothing of their religious practices before the period around 2300 BCE, when ceremonial constructions first appear, mainly on the coast of central Peru and shortly after in the mountain ranges of the interior. A thousand years earlier, however, there were settled, ceramic-producing communities in Colombia and Ecuador. The Pacific coast region, spreading some way into the interior, produced the first relatively well-known culture: the Valdivia, radiocarbon dated between 3300 and 1500 BCE. After a period of local ceramics, there came one of richly decorated ceramics with carved motifs that bear a remarkable similarity to the decorative patterns used by a contemporary culture from the southern islands of Japan, called Jomon.[4] This was more than a modest fishing culture, as was thought thirty years ago when it was first studied. These early Neolithic comunities traded actively, multiplied and developed growing religious activity. In the third millenium BCE some villages of the Valdivia culture became ceremonial centres, with mounds surrounding a central square. Their principal artistic product was lovely female statuettes, the oldest evidence of a symbolism indicating fecundity as a divine power, which they share with many other Neolithic culture of the Old World, and with later American cultures. Some are slim, serenely realistic figures, with the headgear emphasized; others are pregnant, virtually in a birthing position. These are evidence of an old and persistent concept that can be classified as religious, even though we do not know the actual rites with which these statuettes were associated.

Neolithic (often wrongly called "Formative") cultures developed and spread over wide central zones of the continent, including the south-eastern United States, during the third and second millenia BCE. Shamanism appears to have been an integral part of this development. At some stage the shamanic initiation process began to include the use of vegetable substances with psychotropic or "hallucinogenic" properties. Up to eighty different such species have been used in America, while the Old World has known only six or seven. Why should this be? In my view, the most convincing explanation lies in their importance in the broad paleo-psychological context mentioned in my introduction: as the general process of individuation progressed (completed more or less at the end of the pre-Christian era), there was growing recourse to hallucinogenic substances of vegetable origin as a means of renewing contact with divine powers. They are a means of strengthening the "archaic techniques of ecstasy," in Mircea Eliade's phrase.[5]

Archeological evidence of the religious practices of all these peoples is scanty, so I propose to examine some peoples from marginal areas (in relation to those of the high cultures), who represent survivals, in more or less modified form, of the paleo-agricultural cultures.

(a) The Anasazi

This group, from the semi-arid regions of the south-western United States, had an initial period known as the Basketmakers, at the beginning of the Christian era. Their tombs contain little "gaming disks" of wood and bone with incised lines, perhaps used for purposes of divination. Shamanistic rites are evidenced by tubular stone pipes, and cave drawings and paintings from this and the following period, particularly abundant in the upper Colorado River plateau in Utah. In the Basketmaker III period (400–700 CE) settlements arose made up of semi-subterranean rooms with an entrance passageway. An interesting example is the village of Shabik'eshee in north-western New Mexico, made up of eighteen rooms grouped round a *kiva*, a circular ceremonial enclosure with stone walls, which was to become a typical element of the later *Pueblo* periods.

In *Pueblo* I and II, characterized by pottery with geometric patterns, the semi-subterranean houses persist, but now in larger groups backing on to one another. The most salient new feature is deliberate deformation of the skull by binding the rear portion of infants' skulls to the base of their cot, a custom widespread in the Andean region and less so in Central America. With its implicit symbolism, this seems be of shamanic inspiration, linked to the growing importance of the *kiva* as a place for masculine initiation and trance rites. In the *Pueblo* III period (1050–1300) large groups of inter-connected settlements were built, like that in Chaco Canyon in north-western New Mexico. Some of these had hundreds of enclosures, with the smallest *kivas* inside these and larger ones in a big open crescent towards which the dwellings looked. In the centre, immediately behind the boundary wall, was the "Great *Kiva*," surrounded by rectangular rooms; this was undoubtedly the main religious and probably also political centre, suggesting the existence of a proto-priesthood.

(b) The Diaguitas

This is what the Spaniards called agro-potter tribes who lived in the valleys and mountains of north-eastern Argentina. In their early and middle periods they lived in more or less autonomous villages, strictly controlled by shamans. This is reflected in their usage of long pipes and hollowed-out mortars for preparing psychotropic vegetable substances, in their feline symbols (of jaguars, sometimes taking on dragon-like forms), and cave paintings of priest-warrior-sacrificers. These are seen mostly in the period or culture of La Aguada (600–900), when the first ceremonial structures were built in the form of small pyramids with three levels and an access ramp, facing a rectangular open space. The first forts on the sides of some mountains also date from this time.

In late Diaguita culture (900–1550) the feline symbols disappear, though birds and serpents remain (the latter sometimes S-shaped, with a head at each end, the symbolism of which is unknown), and toads, ostriches, human figures and various geometric patterns appear. A strong belief in the Beyond is shown by the burial of children in medium-sized or large urns, on which these symbols are especially prominent. At this time, settlements grew larger, often placed on summits and fortified (known as "*pucará*"). Each major valley seems to have formed a "Manor" ruled by the principal chief; so social behaviour was controlled not by shaman-priests, but by political-military powers.

Ethno-historical data on the religious practices of these peoples is scarce, and it is also difficult to separate native customs from those derived from the influence of the Incas, to whom these tribes were subject from around 1475 to 1532. Fr Lozano claims that they worshipped thunder and lightning, to which they dedicated "small houses in whose inner circumference they hung rods sprinkled with the blood of the sheep of the land (llamas) and adorned with feathers of various colours." He also states that in these places they paid homage to "other idols which they called *caylles*, whose images they worked in copper sheets, and which they carried with them to crops, houses and other places they wished to protect from disease or ill luck. The places in which they worshipped were called *zupca*, which Lozano says means "place of sacrifice."

Missionary reports often speak of these houses with their many plumed rods, which they claimed were for drinking bouts and sacrifices. They were set apart from the dwellings and in the charge of witchdoctor-shamans, whom the missionaries generally referred to as "fathers of lies" since they used to converse with their divinities and act as their messengers.[6]

What the Spanish called drinking bouts were really shamanic sessions involving ingestion of hallucinogens, either by smoking them in pipes, or grinding them to powder and sniffing them through tubes. The substance most used was *cebil* (*Anandenanthera*) which grows on the eastern slopes of the Andes. This was ground on wooden or stone tablets, often richly carved.[7]

Like most peoples of the Andean regions, the Diaguitas worshipped Pacha-Mama, the old earth goddess, equivalent to the Magna Mater of Asia and the Mediterranean. She gave fertlity to plants and animals, and still today on the *altiplano* "she is begged to give fertility to the fields, safe journey to travellers, safe childbirth to women and success in all undertakings. Her cult is blood sacrifice and the offering of first fruits of the harvest, the first mouthful of food or drink."[8] Like most "formative" (agro-potter, pre-urban) peoples of America, the Diaguitas made clay statuettes (and sometimes stone "idols") which probably have to do with the cult of this great female archetype.

3. ANCIENT TEMPLE CULTURES

(a) Peru (approx. 2200–300 BCE)

The extremely dry conditions of the coastal strip and consequent exceptional conservation of remains mean that our knowledge of the initiation and development of cultures here can go back to the centuries spanning the "pre-ceramic cotton-weaving" and "first ceramic" periods. The region in the centre and north of the coast, from Las Haldas down to the site of Asia south of Lima seems to have where various elements typical of later periods originated: pyramidal temples and platforms, varied stone, adobe and clay constructions, funerary bundles, multiple burials in which others were sacrificed to accompany an important personage on his journey to the Beyond. . . .

The earliest temple constructions of the central coastal strip are those of Río Seco and Chuquitanta, dating from between 200 and 1800 BCE, the latter much added to in subsequent centuries. The population here was sparser than in the north, so people living in surrounding areas would have been brought in to help in their construction. Society was already organized into hierarchical division of labour. As in Central America and other parts of the world, the building of the earliest temples implies the existence of an incipient priestly *élite* controlling society.

Ceremonial centres became progressively more monumental and complex during the centuries of the "first ceramic" or "early formative" period, indicating that priestly groups were increasing their prestige and power. Villages spread over the central Andean region; temple structures appeared on the north coast and in the high mountain valleys, while some central ones were enlarged, such as Las Haldas and La Florida in the suburbs of present-day Lima. This is a large stepped pyramid, not built of adobe as was usual on the coast, but of stones held together with a stucco mortar. It was surrounded by other buildings and open squares, and was undoubtedly the focal point for the village communities scattered along the Rimac river.

Some sites, such as Río Seco, were abandoned; new ones arose, such as Ancón, which has a series of superimposed platforms running along a coastal ridge. Others made use of the tops of hills, with a series of buildings and open places following the contours, as at Las Haldas, which also has a curious lower oval structure. This ceremonial complex measures some 650 × 200 metres, excluding a long levelled access road. Its situation, on a rocky promontory facing towards the sea, suggests an early cult of "Mama-Cocha" – the primordial water, materialized in the ocean and in some lakes, especially Titicaca – which was still extant at the time of the conquest.

The structure and evolution of temple nuclei was not uniform, which indicates that there were divergent ideological and ritual traditions. In the coastal region, there are two types: one has platforms of varying heights, with a "sunken courtyard" (circular or rectangular) facing it; the other, more usual, is U-shaped, composed of two or three superimposed platforms, with the space enclosed by the arms of the U generally facing east or north-east, i.e. towards the mountains, the source of the water that gives life to the valleys. In the interior, there is a group made up of five sites discovered till now, rising from the lowest at La Galgada, one thousand metres above sea level, through Huaricoto at 2750 metres to Piruru, east of the Marañón river, at 3800 metres. This group includes Kotosh, the best-known and most excavated site, at 2000 metres, on a tributary of the Huallaga river, which has three superimposed temples from the period 2000 to 1800 BCE and two from the first ceramic period. The basic characteristic of this group is a rectangular chamber with its floor on two levels: the lower, also rectangular, is in the centre, and served as a ceremonial fireplace, in which offerings were burned. This group is considered to represent a "Kotosh religious tradition," with a cult of wood as opposed to the cult of water on the coast.

The site of Sechín Alto in the Casma valley represents a new stage in the socio-religious evolution of Peru. Built around 1400 BCE, the structure consists of a platform some three hundred metres long by 250 wide, forty metres high. On top of this is a ceremonial centre, U-shaped, opening to the north-east, so a larger and more complex version of earlier structures in the coastal region. Some fifty years later, another complex was built at the foot of Sechín hill, about 1500 metres South of Sechín Alto. This is a rectangular structure with numerous subdivisions, built of adobe in four stages. The north stairway is flanked with carvings and paintings of fishes, some twelve feet long. There were other figurative works in the interior, but these have been mostly destroyed.

The building was enlarged around 1300 BCE with the "platform of carved stones," a strange series of carvings on big and small stone blocks, fixed to the outer wall. Warriors armed with clubs alternate with heads with their eyes closed, parts of bodies and what appear to be bones and entrails. This has been interpreted as the commemoration of a bloody invasion by people from the mountains, but is more probably related to the inauguration of greatly increased agricultural works in the valley with the attendant fertility rites, which included human sacrifice. Whatever its origin, this long frieze, which would seem to have continued along the side walls, was designed to instill terror (in the non-initiated?), and marks the beginning of Andean monumental stone art with this main characteristic.

Cerro Sechín precedes the famous site of Chavín de Huántar by several centuries, and carries on a tradition of ceremonial architecture on the Peruvian coast and in the interior lasting at least a thousand years. So Chavín cannot be seen as a sudden explosion of the first great Andean artistic style (as it was till recently thought to be). It is a late centre building on, extending and amplifying earlier experiences, a brilliant synthesis developing, in imaginative, profound, monumental and highly baroque fashion, ideas and pratices of shamanic origin which originated in the late pre-ceramic period.

Chavín, some three thousand metres above sea level in the Andes of north-central Peru, sits on an old route from the coast to the high valley called Callejón de Huaylas and the valley of the Marañón river, which marks the beginning of the Amazon rainforest region. Towards 900 BCE an unknown group built a U-shaped temple, opening eastwards, with stones dragged from the surrounding hills. Including the base of the side walls, it was more than a hundred metres wide, making it the first monumental structure in the mountain regions of Peru. A circluar "sunken courtyard" faced the opening of the U.

Two centuries later, when the power of the priestly group responsible had been consolidated, a proto-state seems to have been established, with Chavín becoming an open city (a ceremonial and administrative centre with craft, trade and peasant "suburbs" grouped round it). This phase is marked by a major extension of the temple to the south, forming what the Spaniards called "the castle" and archeologists refer to as "the recent temple."

The principal monument in the Old Temple is a great monolith "set" at the intersection of two galleries, known from its shape as the "great lance." This is an impressive anthropomorphic figure carved on a granite block fourteen feet high, a sort of column or menhir (*huanca* in native terminology), with its pointed base set in a space left between paving stones, and its top holding up the gallery roof. The roughly square head of the figure is basically human-featured; the corners of the mouth are drawn upwards, producing the effect of a "smiling deity," contradicted by two large downward-pointing canine teeth. Around the eyes, two vipers outline the eyebrows, and the hair is also made up of snakes. Circular earrings hang from the ears. An arm and a foot are carved on each side, with five fingers and toes whose nails are between human, bird and cat. The only asymmetry between each side is that the right arm is raised and the left lowered.

It is not easy to interpret this figure. Certain resemblances suggest a divinity: as in pre-classic Central American art, there is a triad – bird of prey (modelled on the harpy eagle of the forest zone), cat (jaguar, also of the forest) and serpent (tropical zones in general) – separate from or associated with the human figure. This would make it a great cosmic-nature-human symbol, but with – to my mind – monstrous elements too. Its siting at the intersection of two galleries at the back of the Old Temple suggest that it was the image priests had to confront at the final stages of their initiation process.

Details of the rites and religious ideas of Chavín culture are unknown, but archeological and comparative indications suggest that cat *symbolism* played an important part. This has recently been studied in ethnographic peoples such as the Tukano of the Colombian Amazon region, with some interesting parallels emerging.[9] The Tukano wise man or shaman swallows or inhales the drug called *yapé* and "changes" into a jaguar, acquiring superhuman powers. Something similar, though in a far more complex context, was probably done by the priests of Chavín. Two later Andean cultural centres that produced major megalithic art, San Agustín in Colombia and Tiahuanaco on the Bolivian *altiplano*, also show cat and human features combined; so does the La Aguada culture in north-western Argentina, the southernmost example of this manifestation, whose ceramic, stone and cave painting art has shamanic roots.

What is beyond doubt is that the cultural complex of Chavín contained some of the fundamental beliefs that made up the overall "Formative horizon" of early America and provided the basis for its great civilizations, whose classic phases began in the early years of the common era.

(b) Central America (approx. 1300–0 BCE)

Toward the middle of the thirteenth century BCE, a group of people began to infill a terrace some 1200 metres long in the area of the present-day town of San Lorenzo, and so laid the basis of Olmec culture, and of Central American civilization. The site is in the humid forest region of the south-east of the Mexican state of Veracruz, at the foot of a group of extinct volcanoes known as the Tuxtlas. On the infill they built mounds and platforms spread along a north-south axis, with rectangular courtyards, underground channels and artificial lakes. During a space of three hundred years an élite with priestly characteristics, of unknown origin, managed to bring together and direct the natives of the area to produce these works, to transport and carve stones for altars, stelae and the first huge heads, more than six feet high and weighing up to twenty-five tons. Besides this monumental art they produced statuettes and instruments in serpentine, flint, obsidian and other minerals, the raw material for which was brought from the interior, and the finished products in turn taken to Tlatilco and other sites in central Mexico. This is the origin of the first great art style of Central America, based on the first great religious cult whose principal symbol was the cat, and the jaguar in particular. Similarities with the Chavín "feline transformation" process are dramatically illustrated in Olmec statuettes.

The next phase of this culture is represented by the La Venta site, some sixty miles north-east of San Lorenzo towards the Gulf of Mexico, which flourished between 900 and 400 BCE. La Venta is also made up of a series of "ceremonial complexes" with earthern structures rectangular in shape, of varying lengths, the whole crowned by the oldest "pyramid" known in Central America. This is a truncated cone, over one hundred feet high, set on a rectangular platform, all built of compressed earth. Its surface is shaped with ten humps and depressions, like the folds of the flank of a volcano.

Ceremonies must have taken place in two rectangular spaces surrounded by basalt columns sunk in adobe bases. Here and at another site further south, basalt, which had to be brought from far off, was used for many monumental carvings: altars, stelae and the colossal heads whose meaning is still debated. There is also a green serpentine mosaic pavement in three parts, which, seen from above, forms a great formalized jaguar mask.

The prehistoric Olmec culture is generally recognized as the chief basis of Maya civilization. The environment (humid forest) is the same; the Olmec language probably belonged to the Maya family; there is the same ceremonial activity expressed in "open cities"; the Jaguar symbolism was retained, though in attenuated form, by the Mayas. Artistic details also overlap: monolithic stelae and altars decorated with scenes, human statues that seem to have come from niches, nooks containing jade offerings, the use of cinnabar in burials. Above all, the Olmecs invented the system of numbering and calculating the calendar which the Mayas used. All these suggest a genetic connection.

Olmec influences in central Mexico also provided a major impetus in the formation of ceremonial centres such as those of Totimehuacán in Puebla, Tlapacoya and Cuicuilo near the present capital, and later, in the early years of our era, the first great planned city of America, Teotihuacan.

4. RELIGIOUS IDEAS AND PRACTICES OF THE HIGH STATE CULTURES

(a) Central America (0–1521 CE)

(1) The Maya region. This civilization was at its height in the Classic Maya period, from 300 to 900. Its splendours are best seen in the city-states of the low-lying Chiapas and Petón areas of Guatemala: Palenque, Tikal, Copán and others. These were governed by a priestly élite in the name and under the inspiration of the divinities. This élite was headed by the *Halach Uinic* ("the true man"); the office was hereditary, though changes of dynasty did occur. The system was respected by the lower classes (craftsmen, traders and peasants), and the élites of separate cities also respected one another, since there were generally no wars between them. There were warriors, it is true (armed with wood and stone weapons, since the Classic Maya culture, like that of Teotihuacan, was ignorant of metallurgy), but their function seems to have been mainly a public order one, and to repel invasions from the east of the territory – as they are shown doing in the impressive paintings from Bonampak, in Chiapas.

This highly stratified society eventually fell into decline.[10] A series of factors still being studied (climatic change, exhaustion of the soil through excessive cultivation?) combined with a probable intellectual and moral decline in the Maya élite to produce a situation of rebellion (a sort of "civil disobedience") in the craft and peasant population. This interrupted the building and commemorative programme and eventually led to the abandonment of the great ceremonial centres of the region. The last recorded date, on a stele in Uaxactún, corresponds to our 889.

The post-classical period saw some kind of cultural renaissance, centred on the cities of the Yucatán peninsula, though influenced by Toltec culture as found above all in Chichén Itzá. Religious culture divided into popular religiosity – which in some form or another survived in folklore – and the "official" religion of the upper classes, reflected in architecture and associated arts. As in most of the American high cultures (and ancient Asiatic ones), there was also one form of external cult, ceremonial and rich in symbolism, associated with feast days, agricultural cycles and the like, and an esoteric form, with initiation rites to which the chief priests and the *Halach Uinic* of each city had to submit.

The stepped pyramids represented a symbolic form of coming closer to Heaven, to the cosmic world, that is. The ancient Mayan religion can be supposed to have been fundamentally a cult of the stars, without this excluding a naturalist or earthly counterpart. Hence the importance given to astronomy and the computation of time. Cosmogony was another aspect, which survived in late stories such as that of *Popol Vuh*. The basic idea was that there had been four ages previous to the one they were then living in, each brought to an an end by a great cataclysm, ordained by the gods who were dissatisfied with the imperfections of their earlier creations. Only once earlier beings had been set aside (changed into monkeys and the like) could present man emerge, with the mission of invoking and serving the gods (and even of "feeding" them through various offerings, including blood sacrifices). But present creation can also be annihilated; hence the special liturgies that took place every New Year and at the end of each calendar cycle of fifty-two years, designed to prevent this from happening. This idea finally became an obsession and contributed to bringing in the practice of human sacrifice, originated by the Toltecs and adopted by the Mayas under their influence.

Their cosmovision was expressed as a universe made up of thirteen superimposed heavens, called *Oxlahuntikú*; our earth was the lowest heaven; below it were nine subterranean worlds called *Bolontikú*, the deepest of which belonged to the Lord of Death. Each of these worlds had its own god, as did the days (*kin*), the *uinal* (months of twenty days) and *katún* (twenty-year periods, at the end of which a commemorative stele was generally erected). The Maya pantheon was numerous and complex, and, like the Aztec, contained a dualism: divinities such as those of rain, thunder and lightning were well disposed toward human beings and opposed to another series of harmful gods – those of drought, tempest, war, which were harmful to human beings.

The creator of the world was Hunab; his son Itzamná, Lord of the Heavens, was also the civilizing hero, since it was he who had given the Mayas writing and their calendar; he was invoked at propitiatory New Year ceremonies so as to avoid public disasters. His cult was often associated with that of Kinch Ahau, god of the sun. Chaak, god of rain, played an important role because of the climate, particularly in the Yucatán where rivers are lacking. He was generally shown, in written codices and in sculptures, with a long nose, and was associated with Kukulkán, the Plumed Serpent, who in one of his manifestations was god of the wind. The god of maize or of agriculture was shown with the features of a young man, carrying a stalk of maize. The god of death was called Ah Puch; by way of a head he had a fleshless skull and carried a number of bells. As a maleficent deity he was associated with Ek Chuah, god of war.

Each of these gods was the object of a very complex cult, whose ritual was strictly observed. Ceremonies were preceded by fasts or strict abstinences. Sacrifices played an important part: one of them consisted in making one's own blood flow by piercing the lobe of one's ear or one's tongue with a thin silica blade or fishbone. Sacrifices portrayed in the classic period were nearly always peaceful: offerings of food, animals or precious objects. Human sacrifices,

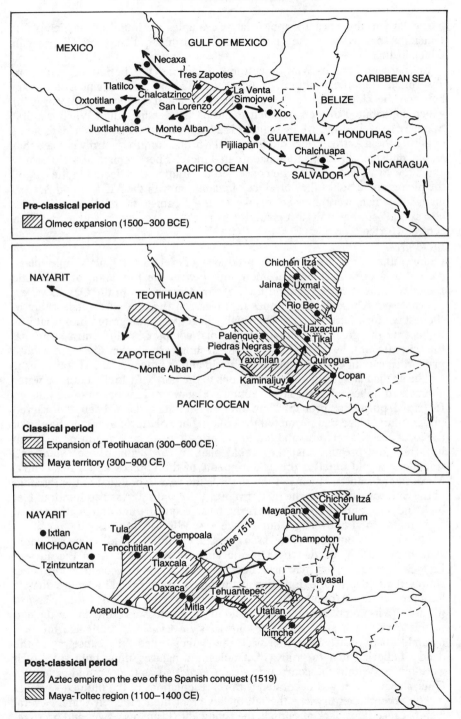

2. Pre-classical, Classical and Post-classical periods in the Mexican Empire
Source: Il nuovo Atlante storico Zanichelli. Zanicchelli, Bologna, 1987. (Zanichelli)

particularly in the Yucatán, appear later: examples are found in the Temple of Jaguars associated with the "Ball Game," and in the Temple of Warriors in Chichén Itzá.

In the later age of Mayan culture, known as the period of "Mexican absorption," another cultural decline set in. There were alliances and wars between the chief cities of the Yucatán (Chichén Itzá, Uxmal and Mayapán) which contributed to their decadence and partial depopulation. When the first Spaniards reached the Maya region (1524–7), there was no power capable of opposing them as the Aztecs did in central Mexico, and they hardly noticed that an old and splendid civilization had existed there. There remained the peasants and a few lords and priests who conserved the traditions reflected in the *codices*, the pictographic books they produced in common with the Mixtecs and Aztecs, many of which were burned thanks to the Spanish friars' "anti-diabolical obsession," so that only three survive from the Maya region and a few from central Mexico.

(b) Central Mexico

Olmec influence, as we have seen, produced a development from simple village society to a growing hierarchization and then to the formation of theocratic societies. This occurred around the Lake of Mexico and in the Oaxaca valley, but most notably some thirty miles north-east of the present capital, where in the last centuries BCE, the existing small villages were integrated into what was to become the greatest symbolic-ceremonial complex in all Central America, the city (*tollan*) by definition, raised in homage to the divinities whose primordial sacrifice had produced the world and the human race: Teotihuacan.

The site is flat, closed off by mountains to the north. In ancient times a water course had hollowed out a cavern running east-west. This began to be utilized for ritual purposes, probably initiation rites. It may have been this sacred underground place that prompted the building of a platform over it at the end of the local pre-classical era, and led to the priestly caste here acquiring so much influence and prestige that they could plan an *élite centre* whose extent and splendour would outclass the achievements of the Olmecs and other central Mexican civilizations. In any event, towards the year 0, building of the Pyramid of the Sun was started on the platform over the cavern. It was two hundred feet high and seven hundred feet across the base, requiring not only mathematical and architectural knowledge, but a huge and well organized labour force.

How was this done, since (as far as we know) there was still no consolidated state organization, headed by a divine king, as was the case in the ancient Egyptian empire? This may have been the reason for the construction being slower than that of the Egyptian pyramids, apparently taking more than a hundred years. Around the middle of the period called Proto-classical (0–300 CE) its complement, the Pyramid of the Moon, was built, and at the end of this period, the great complex known as *La Ciudadela*, built like the first pyramid on the Eastern side of what the Aztecs called "the causeway of the dead," believing that the ruins of temples and palaces along both sides of it were tombs. Within the courtyard of the *Ciudadela* was the pyramid called "of Quetzalcóatl," as it was decorated with representations of the plumed serpent.

The seventh century saw the fall of this great theocratic city-state. Several factors caused this: lack of rainfall, the ruling élite losing its power and prestige, often violent inroads by barbarian tribes from the north. Its culture, however, lived on in other centres such as Atzcapotzalco, Xochicalco and Cholula, whose high pyramid inspired by those of the Sun and the Moon remained an active religious centre for a long time. (The church built on its summit in colonial times reflects a cultic continuity common in America: one religion is replaced by another, but the *sacred place* remains.)

The expansion of Teotihuacan culture – through trade and industries based often at a great distance – brought the first political-cultural unification of the region on the level of "civilization" (in the sense of urban culture). Without it there would not then have been a Toltec kingdom, nor later an Aztec empire. Both were more or less direct heirs of Teotihuacan.

This is particularly true in the area of mythical-religious concepts. The prestige of the priestly caste of Teotihuacan lasted down the centuries and is reflected in the attribution of "giant" status to the builders of the two great pyramids (already in ruins at the time of the conquest), at a time before the birth of the "Fifth Sun," the one that lights us at present. It was in Teotihuacan that the gods met to originate this new era after an epoch of darkness; it was there that, led by the "pustulent" Nanahuatzin (who first threw himself into the fire and was changed into the sun), they created the present world and the human race through his sacrifice.

The name Teotihuacan means "city of the gods," but also "city where men become gods." The native tradition held that ancient kings and lords whose spirits had ascended to the divine world were buried in the supposed tombs along the "causeway of the dead." In my view, this reflects the importance accorded to initiation rites in Teotihuacan culture – as in the Olmec culture that preceded it. (Think of the cavern placed under the Pyramid of the Sun in this regard.) It was in experiences of this type that the myths and ceremonies inherited by later Central American groups took root. They produced figures such as Huehuetéotl, the old god of fire; Xipe-Tótec ("our lord the flayed one"), who symbolizes the annual renewal of vegetation; cosmic gods (the Sun and Moon to whom the pyramids were consecrated), and a duality shown in the pyramid of *La Ciudadela*: Quetzalcóatl the plumed serpent and Tlalóc the god of rain, so of life-bringing water.

It is not known whether Quetzalcóatl was already identified with a historical or mythical personage, as happened after the Toltec period; for the inhabitants of Teotihuacan, he was probably the civilizing god recounted in later traditions. If the *Ciudadela* functioned partly as a royal palace (as some believe), there could have been a court cult of Quetzalcóatl, considered the tutelary god of the city and inspiration to its rulers. "Conceived as the eternal duality of things – life and death – , he is the serpent who from the ground, the place where life is based, tries to reach heaven in the shape of a bird; he is the sun who dies in the evening, and Venus, the evening star who carries the sun to its rest, and the morning star who proclaims the return of life. The deities of this period were taken into the Toltec, and consequently the Aztec, pantheon. Their underlying philosophy of life (union of opposites, death as transformation and seed of new life, etc.) lasted till well into the Spanish conquest and helped to give Mexico its overall "toltequistic" characteristics, the roots of which are found in Teotihuacan."[11]

The burning of the main buildings of Teotihuacan was the first step in a series of disasters that affected all Central American cultural groups during the eighth and ninth centuries. New cities arose or grew, such as Cholula and Xochicalco, where Quetzalcóatl was venerated; then Tula, some fifty miles north of present-day Mexico City, which became the capital of a major kingdom, and has left traditions, including mention of a pious priest-king of the tenth century called Topiltzin Quetzalcóatl, said to have been expelled from the city by his enemies. Tula fell to attacks from new "barbarian" (*chichimeca*) groups from the north, but a large number of its inhabitants moved to Yucatán and there revitalized the city of Chichén-Itzá.

Various lordships vied for power, including a new group from a mythical place of origin known as Aztlán; these were the Mexics, better known as Aztecs, who founded Tenochitlán in the fourteenth century on an island on the lake of Mexico. They took over the Toltec culture, and saw themselves as its heirs. Their religion developed an element that had been present in limited form in earlier cultures: human sacrifice, to feed the gods and in particular the Sun with precious human blood, and to atone in a certain measure for the the Sun's original sacrifice that gave life to human beings. They obtained prisoners to sacrifice through the "*guerra florida*" ("flower war"). This showed that they gave predominance to the sun warrior Huitzilopochtli over the peaceful and suffering Quetzalcóatl. But something of the wisdom of the latter survived, and after the conquest he was – to varying degrees and more or less syncretically – amalgamated into Hispanic Christianity. And so three thousand years of Central American cultural tradition came to an end.[12]

(b) The Central Andean Area (Peru and North-west Bolivia) (0–1532)

(i) Pre-Inca cultures. At the end of the pre-Christian era, the cultures derived from Chavín gave way to several brilliant regional sub-cultures. Their artistic styles, shown above all in ceramics, but also in other products such as textiles, are very distinctive. Architecture was mainly religious or funereal, but showed the formation of true states governed by a priestly-warrior élite. These regional groups led a relatively stable existence for seven or eight centuries, then rapidly declined or were more or less completely subsumed in the "second pan-Peruvian horizon" which originated in Tiahuanaco. Very little is known of their religious beliefs, which have survived only in archeological remains. Some of these are outstanding, such as the mortuary practices of the Paracas culture, with the complex symbolism of textiles found on the "mummies" preserved in the dry climate of the southern coast, or the great "geoglyphs" known as the "Nazca lines", made up of furrows cut in the Pampa, straight lines, sometimes crossing each other, and figures of birds and other beings, perhaps suggesting a cult of the heavens. On the northern coast of Peru, the major ceremonial constructions are the "mounds" of the Sun and Moon near the present-day city of Trujillo, huge platforms built of adobe blocks, belonging to the Mochica culture, famous for its "portrait vases."

Another great Andean civilization flourished between the third and twelfth centuries in a completely different environment: the *altiplano* around Lake Titicaca, some 12,000 feet above sea level. After many centuries of adapting to the harsh climate and economic possibilities – suitable crops and herds – , the village communities saw a planned metropolis, known as Tiahuanaco, arise in their midst. Priest-shamans again led this process, giving it a character of combined commercial and manufacturing centre and sacred place, where social life was ordered and directed under divine inspiration. As happened in Chavín and several Central American sites, a priestly élite gathered power and prestige, expressed in monumental constructions and their associated arts. Imbued with mystical attributes, especially those of the jaguar, and exceptional powers, the shamans must have exercised considerable influence over the population, particularly through "sanctification rites." The community saw its deepest intuitions and beliefs reaffirmed through the intense religious experience these generated. It is likely that, when the interests of proto-priests and secular leaders came together, the former began to practise "sanctification rites" to confer authority on more arbitrary matters, such as transmission of offices of authority solely through certain families. In this way, the ideology derived from shamanic initiation rites seems to have been instrumental in forming lordships, providing the religious underpinning for a virtually perpetual ruling élite acting as sole mediator between society and divine resources.

In their capacity as chroniclers or sages of the community, the priest-shamans were the only persons empowered to determine the calendar of rites and other activities associated with agriculture and the herding of llamas and alpacas. They "spoke" to the peaks, the springs, the caves, and surely also to the Sun and Moon and any other sources that controlled the phenomena associated with productive activity. So they alone could control droughts, frosts, torrential rains and floods. They doubtless stood behind the first lords who organized the population of the Tiahuanaco region in terracing and draining areas subject to annual flooding. These and other factors led to the establishment of Tiahuanaco first as a "sacred place," then as "centre of the world" and finally as capital of a theocratic state, boasting impressive monumental architecture in stone (erected between 200 and 700 CE).

The seventh to ninth centuries saw an imperial expansion of this culture. The political centre moved to Huari (near Ayacucho in southern Peru), while Tiahuanaco remained the economic and above all ceremonial centre, much visited by pilgrims. Then suddenly – as happened to other Andean and Central American cultural and religious centres – it declined in the twelfth century and was virtually abandoned, for reasons that are still debated.

The Huari empire was split into several local kingdoms, one of which was based in Cuzco. This was to become the centre of a new and final Andean expansion, in the form of the Inca empire. Starting in 1438, in a few years this engulfed all these kingdoms (including the biggest, the Chimu of the northern coast), as well as more distant regions such as Ecuador and north-eastern Argentina. But the coming of Pizarro and his troops in 1532 overthrew this notable example of social and economic organization, which has been called the "Pax Incaica."

When the Spanish invaders of Cuzco enquired into the origin of "Andean Man," they were told that the first men had come from the land of the mountains, the altiplano. First, the god Con-Ticsi Huira-Cocha had emerged from the waters of Lake Titicaca. He made the sun and the moon come out, and dried out some beings who had existed in the previous era, till they turned to stone. He created the present generation in Tiahuanaco, giving them clothes and naming the nations. Then he ordered them to return underground and emerge in different places, so as to re-populate the world. Among these men, the legend continues, were the ancestors of the Inca monarchs, the four Ayar brothers with their wives. The "officialized" legend told that they had emerged from a place some twenty-five miles south-east of Cuzco: the *Tamputoco*, the cave "of the three windows." By divine command, one of them established himself in a high (11,000 feet) valley, founded the city of Cuzco (whose name means "navel" so "centre" of the world) and had himself recognized as Son of the Sun. He, Manco Cápac, in this way initiated the dynasty of the Inca sovereigns. (Some say he could have been a high Aymara chief who left Tiahuanaco when it was de-populated.)

This account illustrates the sacred character of Lake Titicaca, and at the same time shows the prestige the civilization of Tiahuanaco retained in the Andean region, long after its former splendour was extinguished. By linking their royal lineage with those who built the by then legendary city, the monarchs of Cuzco were claiming the right to found their own empire.

(ii) The Inca empire (Tahuantinsuyu, *"The Four Regions"*). The great period of imperial expansion began with the ascent to the throne of Prince Yupanki in 1438. His successful martial exploits and his reforms in the area of state organization earned him the title of *Pachacuti* ("he who overturns things," "the renewer"). With him, we come to the ethno-historical period, which means we have more and more trustworthy data on the political and socio-cultural history of the central Andes. It is generally agreed that the Incas were the heirs of more than three thousand years of cultural development in the Andean region, and, more directly of Tiahuanaco-Huari.[13]

This led the Incas to recognize the old creative divinity Huira-Cocha (also written Viracocha) as Supreme Being and father of gods and human beings. In reality, he had no proper name, and his complete qualification, Con-Ticsi-Huira-Cocha, was originally a cosmological symbol alluding to the four elements, fire, earth, air and water: "the same that determine the four successive destructions of the world, placed at the end of each of the Suns or great solar years, the *Intipwata*, which are in turn unities characteristic of Peruvian cyclography, which is closely linked to that of Central America".[14]

By the time the Spaniards made contact, Viracocha had been relegated to a somewhat distant role, leaving the care of creation to a series of of hierarchically lower gods, headed by the Sun (*Inti*, father in his turn of the legendary Manco Cápac and his wife Mama Ocllo), legitimation of the *divine right* of the Cuzco monarchy. Pachacuti and his successors claimed the Sun as their imperial god, justifying their conquests by the need to impose his worship in the four regions (*Tahuantinsuyu*) of the known world.

The Sun's wife was the Moon (*Mama Quilla*), who presided over the night sky with her stars and constellations. A special veneration was accorded to *Illapa*, whose manifestation was thunder and lightning, precursors of rain. These divinities "on high" (somehow connected with *Hanan-pacha*, the "world above" to which the virtuous went after death) had their counterpoise in in the ancient earthly divinity *Pacha-Mama*, the *Magna Mater* of America (called

Coatlicue by the Aztecs), with whom was associated the *Mama-Cocha*, the sea divinity, among the coastal peoples. Supernatural power was also attributed to certain places and objects known generically as *huacas* (mounds): certain peaks, rocks used as markers or with a special shape, tombs, shrines set in sacred places or along roads. . . .

The Inca state can be described as theocratic-militarist, backed by an efficient economic organization including an extensive trade and distribution network, with many roads branching out from the capital. The priesthood occupied a prominent place in its iron social order; its members formed part of the ruling class (the *orejones*, "big ears"), and they were in charge of the numerous ritual acts spread over the year, with the solstices and equinoxes the most important times.

There is no space here for details of these ceremonies, but the deep symbolic value attached to things is worth pointing out. Gold, for example, had no "material value" nor was it anyone's "private possession." The *Sapa Inca* ordered it to be brought and administered it as a direct manifestation of the solar divinity. The Inca religious spirit seems to have lost the particular mysticism of shamanic origin that characterized preceding cultures, and to have concentrated instead on ceremonial. This reflects a certain change of mentality, but also the the placing of religion at the service of the state.

Individual and social morality, both in Central America and in the Andes, was controlled by family and community tradition, and by the state, rather than by religion, which was more concerned with what might be called "metaphysical" affairs, and with teaching and directing ritual acts, which included vegetable, animal and – in special cases – human offerings. This has been proved recently by the discovery of evidence of child sacrifices in high areas of the south-central Andes. These were related to veneration of the sacred mountains as sources of life and centres of power, a belief originating in the *altiplano*, which the Incas assimilated and to a degree made "official," as they did with other beliefs and customs.

CONCLUSION

The preceding pages have been able only to sketch an idea of the variety and riches of religious ideas and practices in pre-Columbian America. I have said that religions were intimately linked to cultures, "informing" them from within. There are obvious parallels with the religions of ancient Asia, and, regardless of the old problem of whether this is due to a process of diffusion, it points to a basic conservation of an archaic *forma mentis* in the Amerindian peoples, with intuition predominating over rationalization, and a sense of community over individualism. Would the "clash of cultures" in the sixteenth century have been so painful if the Europeans had appreciated this and been able to respect it? Would they, for example, have classed the natives as "primitive" for not making practical use of the wheel and for using only sticks to work the soil, if they had realized that this was not for lack of ability, but for symbolic reasons connected with the veneration of the Sun and Mother Earth? Would they have condemned many beliefs and practices as mere "idolatry" if they had understood their underlying deep symbolism, whose distant roots were connected in some way to those of their own religious outlook?

As Christians, we have to be glad that Christianity, though in imperfect form and wearing the clothes of the time, came to America. But as historians and anthropologists, we have to recognize that it came "in bad company" and, therefore, lament its quota of responsibility for the unnecessary process of destruction of the high American cultures. Was this process inevitable? Perhaps. The "discovery" had to happen some time; need the *conquista* and all it implied have followed? There is no way of answering this. We have to live with the question, and for those of us who are Americans of European origin, it is more of an existential dilemma than a matter of historical speculation.

Translated from the Spanish by Paul Burns

NOTES

1. See M. León-Portilla, *La visión de los vencidos. Relaciones indígenas de la conquista* (Mexico, 1972).
2. See J. Gebser, *Ursprung und Gegenwart*, vol. 1 (Stuttgart, 1949).
3. See J. Schobinger, *Prehistoria de Sudamérica: culturas precerámicas* (Madrid, 1988).
4. Since men learned to navigate by the stars, there could have been occasional landings by fishermen and others in the New World. The question is whether these had any influence on the development of American culture. While possible landings from across the Atlantic had no effect, landings from south and south-east Asia across the Pacific may well have done. Contact from Jomon would be the first of four instances that can be detected archeologically; others are: China and the megalithic culture of Indonesia to Central America, second to first millenia BCE; Hindu-Buddhist influences on Central America, first millenium BCE; Polynesian influence on western South America, first millenium BCE.
5. Eliade objects to the use of these substances as being a distortion of "pure trance." He considers it a "decadent" form in comparison to initiatory practices in Asia and the ancient Mediterranean. But such an absolutist judgment is more that of a historian of classical religions than an anthropologist, who would accept the validity of hallucinogenic techniques to the extent that they form an authentic part of any culture and/or social group, and represent a positive means of satisfying their needs (which of course they do not in our own culture).
6. Cf A. Serrano, *Los aborígines argentinos. Síntesis etnográfica* (Buenos Aires, 1947), pp. 37–8.
7. There is a description, related to the Huarpes of the southern Andean provinces of Mendoza and San Juan (and possibly inaccurate), of a late form of the ceremony of transformation into a cat which long characterized American shamanism in various places. Toward 1625, a Jesuit missionary recounted the following: "The Indians among whom I was invite each other to bacchanalia, to which they come from several villages. The headman of the village in which the banquet is held builds a round straw hut with various openings. There the men dance and drink for three or four days without stopping. The women stay outside and only go in with their heads turned away and their eyes closed to give wine to their husbands; if they are careless and see them, they are condemned to death. They justify this inhumanity by saying that while they are engaged in dancing and feasting the devil kills them if their women look at them. The demon comes to their drinking bouts, whose infernal beast they summon in this manner: an old man surrounded by dancers beats a drum till Satan appears in the form of a man, a fox or a dog, with great howls and not forbearing to drink; then he addresses a discourse to the assembly; he scratches children presented by their fathers with his claws, and by making them bleed initiates them into deadly rites" (cited in Serrano, *Los aborígines*, pp. 157–8). What the Spaniards believed to be bouts of drunkenness induced by wine were in fact, as we have seen, shamanic practices involving the ingestion of hallucinogenic preparations in liquid form. Serrano comments that this ceremony, apparently an initiation rite for young men, recalls those of the southern hunters, the Onas and Yámanas, from Tierra del Fuego.
8. Serrano, *Los aborígines*, p. 41.
9. See G. Reichel-Dolmatoff, *The Shaman and the Jaguar. A Study of Narcotic Drugs among the Indians of Colombia* (Philadelphia, 1975).

10. Seen from our secularized viewpoint, it can be said that here "religion was the chief tool for maintaining the cultures that developed in the pre-Cortés era. In general, religion has always been an element of control which comes to play a part in the division between manual and intellectual work. It is highly likely that in Maya social organization those responsible for art, religion and politics collaborated very closely to institute a cohesive set of symbols of power. Law, art and literature functioned together as a range of knowledge, objects and maxims against which there was no appeal, and which could not be changed or replaced. Naturally the lower strata of the population (those engaged in manual work) were buried under the weight of this monolithic power manifested to them through these super-structural manifestations. The individual was, on one hand, minimalized, but on the other felt integrated as a part – even if a lower part – of this cosmic totality, whose secrets could be deciphered only by the lords of the nobility. So the fact that power was restricted to a few was justified by the fact that they alone seemed to be the chosen ones who guarded the relationship between the official group and the gods. It is not surprising, then, that the official message was always one of submission to one or several gods. In the final analysis, this meant submitting to work laid on by the social group that looked after the interests of the gods on this earth" (D. Scavelzon and I. Zatz, "El derecho y los mecanismos de justificación ideológica del poder: la sociedad maya prehispánica," *Memoria del II Congreso de Historia de Derecho Mexicano* [Mexico, 1980], p. 117). I should say that in reality Americans of the "classical" cultures, in Central America as well as Peru, still felt immersed in cosmic-human order, in a harmonious rhythm of the Universe whose representatives and interpreters were the priests. Therefore, they would not have felt this domination as an unjust burden, as long as the priests retained the "divine spark," as long as their wisdom did not lessen. (There were, as we have seen, several crises due to this cause.)

11. See O. Silva, *Prehistoria de América* (5th ed., Santiago, 1983), p. 96.

12. Given the impossibility of summarizing Aztec mythology, ritual and priestly organization in the space available, I refer the reader to works by Séjourné, Piña Chan, González Torres, Nebel, Davies and Matos Moctezuma listed in the Select Bibliography below.

13. The name Cuzco, meaning navel or centre of a universe divided into four cosmic-earthly quarters, was also derived from the old appellation given to the ceremonial centre of Tiahuanaco: the Aymara word *Taipicala*, meaning "the stone in the middle."

14. See J. Imbelloni, *La segunda esfinge indiana* (Buenos Aires, 1956), p. 403; idem, *Religiosidad indígena americana* (Buenos Aires, 1979).

SELECT BIBLIOGRAPHY

Baudin, L. *La vie quotidienne au temps des derniers Incas*. Paris: Hachette, 1955.

Davies, Nigel. *The Aztecs. A History*. London: Macmillan, 1973.

Gebser, Jean. *Ursprung und Gegenwart*, vol. 1. Stuttgart: Deutsche Verlags-Anstalt, 1949; vol. 2, 1953.

González Torres, Yólotl. *El sacrificio humano entre los Mexicas*. Mexico City: INAH and Fondo de Cultura Económica, 1985.

Imbelloni, José. *La segunda esfinge indiana*. Buenos Aires: Hachette, 1956.

—. *Religiosidad indígena americana*. Buenos Aires: Castañeda, 1979. A collection of eight pieces, originally published between 1939 and 1950, on the theme of what the author calls "templar thinking," or the "tetractic concept" of time and space.

Ivanoff, Pierre. *Città Maya*. Series *Le Grandi Civiltà*. Milan: Mondadori, 1970.

León-Portilla, Miguel. *La visión de los vencidos. Relaciones indígenas de la conquista*. Mexico City: Universidad Nacional Autónoma de México, 1959, 6th ed. 1972.

Matos Moctezuma, Eduardo. *Aztechi*. Series *Corpus Precolombiano*. Milan: Jaca Book, 1989.

—. *Teotihuacan, la metropoli degli Dei*. Milan: Jaca Book, 1990.

Mason, J. Alden. *The Ancient Cultures of Peru*. Harmondsworth: Penguin, 1957.

Métraux, Alfred. *Les Incas*. Paris, 1962. Eng. trans. *The Incas*. New York: Schoken, 1970.

Nebel, Richard. *Atlmexikanische Religion und cristliche Heilsbotschaft. Mexiko zwischen Quetzalcóatl und Christus*. Immensee: Neue Zeitschrift für Missionswissenschaft, 1983.

Piña Chan, Román. *Gli Olmechi. La cultura madre*. Milan: Jaca Book, 1989.

Ponce Sanginés, Carlos. *Tiwanaku: espacio, tiempo y cultura*. Cochibamba and La Paz: Los Amigos del Libro, 1977.

Reichel-Dolmatoff, Gerard. *The Shaman and the Jaguar*. Philadelphia: Temple Univ. Press, 1975.

Reinhard, Johan. *Chavín y Tiahuanaco. Una nueva perspectiva de los centros ceremoniales andinos. Boletín de Lima*, nos. 50 and 51. Lima, 1987.

Schavelzon, Daniel and Iván Zatz. "El derecho y los mecanismos de justificación ideológica del poder: la sociedad maya prehispánica." *Memoria del II Congreso de Historia del Derecho Mexicano*, pp. 109–22. Mexico, 1980.

Schobinger, Juan and others. *La momia del Cerro El Toro. Investigaciones arqueológicas en la Cordillera de la Provincia de San Juan (Argentina)*. Supplement to *Anales de Archeología y Etnología*. Mendoza: Universidad Nacional de Cuyo, 1966.

—. *Prehistoria de Sudamérica: culturas precerámicas*. Madrid: Alianza Editorial, 1988.

Séjourné, Laurette. *Pensamiento y religión en el México antiguo*. Mexico City: Fondo de Cultura Económica, 1957.

—. *El universo de Quetzalcóatl*. Mexico City: Fondo de Cultura Económica, 1962.

Serrano, Antonio. *Los aborígines argentinos*. Síntesis etnográfica. Buenos Aires: Nova, 1947.

Silva, Osvaldo. *Prehistoria de América*. Santiago, Ed. Universitaria, 5th ed., 1983.

Soustelle, Jacques. *Les Olmecs. La plus ancienne civilisation du Mexique*. Paris: Arthaud, 1979. The same author also has books on the Aztecs and Mayas.

Chapter 2

INVASION AND EVANGELIZATION IN THE SIXTEENTH CENTURY

Mario A. Rodríguez León

The period between the arrival of Christopher Columbus and the first Christians to reach the Caribbean and about the year 1550 marks the first stage of evangelization in Latin America.

The violent cultural clash between the the European world and the societies and civilizations of the "New World" brought about a profound change that was to have drastic consequences in the history of the Amerindian peoples. The military superiority of the Europeans led to the rout of the indigenous peoples, despite their revolts against the conquistadors. While it is true that the Crown of Castile had a genuine evangelizing intent with regard to the new lands, it is no less true that conquest of America was inspired by commercial gain. This dichotomy between evangelization and greed for gold is clearly evidenced in the work known as the *Parecer de Yucay* (Yucay Outlook) of 1571, which tacitly declared that "if there is no gold there is no God in the Indies."[1] For the author, Fray García de Toledo, whose memoir was written as an attack on Las Casas, gold had become the very mediator of the presence of God in the Indies. As Gustavo Gutiérrez has written, his position "is a sort of back-to-front Christology. In the final analysis, gold takes the place of Christ as intermediary of the Father's love; it is thanks to gold that the Indians can receive the faith and be saved; without it they would be condemned. This is the heart of the theology informing the *Parecer de Yucay*."[2]

This insatiable desire for gold, so strongly condemned by Las Casas, has to be seen in the broad framework of the mercantilist economy of the sixteenth century, a time of great social and economic change in Europe. The rise of national monarchies in the Old World led to the imposition of central authority in strong, organized states. In the particular case of Spain, this political situation greatly facilitated the invasion of America. The development of commercial mercantilism was the driving force behind Columbus' discoveries. The Spanish, seeking to increase their holdings of gold and silver, found the easiest ways to obtain these in the Antilles during the first three decades of the sixteenth century. Mercantilism, consisting of a series of economic theories designed to increase trade and expand European markets, was in its early American phase closely tied to the history of the Caribbean region. Christianity, established in the Antilles on the basis of this mercantilist, agrarian and medieval socio-economic system, spread from there to the rest of the continent.

1. HISPANIOLA

On 27 November 1493, the expedition organized by Columbus to begin the process of settling the new territories reached the island of Quisqueya. It was made up of more than three hundred volunteers, including minor nobility, craftsmen and labourers. This motley crew of Christians came upon the Tain Indians, whose territory extended along the Cibao valley and the South coast of the island. They lived in families grouped into tribes governed by a chieftain who could be either a man or a woman. Their religion was animistic and totemic. Friar Ramón Pané, in his *Relación acerca de las antiguedades de los indios* (Account of Indian Antiquities), tells that the natives of Quisqueya and other Caribbean islands believed in *cemíes* (idols) which they fashioned from stone or wood. They had a Supreme Being, who "they believe lives in heaven and is immortal, and that no one can see him, and that he has a mother, but has no beginning, and they call him Yocahu Baque Maórocoti, and his mother they call Atabey."[3] That is, the Tain Indians believed in God; the only new elements the Spaniards introduced were Christ and the gospel. Religion played a major role, giving their culture its cohesion and direction. It came into conflict with the religion of the Spanish conquistadors. Bartolomé de Las Casas, who came to Hispaniola in 1502 and saw the results of the cultural clash between Indians and Spaniards for himself, wrote: "The Christians hit them with their fists and with sticks, even laying hands on the rulers of the peoples. And such was their temerity and effrontery that a Christian captain even violated the wife of the senior king, lord of the whole island. From this point, the Indians began to seek ways of ejecting the Christians from their lands."[4]

The violence of the invasion and conquest was continued in the *encomienda* system, legalized in 1503, which added greatly to the exploitation of the natives. Originally, the *encomienda* was the act of sharing out or "charging" Indians to Spanish residents in the name of the king. The practice was later made hereditary, thereby becoming virtual slavery. It was severely criticized by the Dominican friars working in Hispaniola, as being "against divine, natural and human law."[5] This was the setting for the approach to evangelization taken by the Dominicans.

On 21 December 1511, the fourth Sunday of Advent, by order of the Superior, Fray Pedro de Córdoba, and with the approval of the whole community, Fray Antón de Montesinos, renowned as a fine preacher, mounted the pulpit and began to preach: "I am the voice of one crying out in the desert. . . . " Firmly and authoritatively, he denounced the enslavement of the Indians as sin and energetically attacked the *encomenderos*, those "in charge" of the Indians.[6] The Spaniards and civil authorities present were indignant at the charges laid against them and demanded that he retract them. The following Sunday, Montesinos reaffirmed all that he had said in his first sermon: "What I preached to you last Sunday was true, and I shall prove that those words of mine, so bitter in your ears, were true words."[7] This prophetic denunciation by Montesinos and his community made a great impact in the colonial society of Santo Domingo, and also in Spain itself. The *encomenderos* turned against the Dominicans and laid accusations against them before the king. Pedro de Córdoba and Antón de Montesinos journeyed to Spain to defend their position. Their stay in the mother country produced the legal document known as the *Leyes de Burgos* of 1512, the first formal piece of legislation dealing with the Indians.

The evangelization undertaken by the Dominicans was not aimed at mass baptism: they were more interested in quality than quantity, and sought to give those converted a solid grounding in the new faith. The methods of this first community rested on four pillars: understanding of Indian languages and religion, doctrinal teaching in the form of stories rather than theological abstactions, frequent preaching from the scriptures and the witness of the missionary's own poverty and life of prayer.[8] The community produced its own material for evangelization, in the form of the first catechism written in America, Fray Pedro de Córdoba's *Doctrina cristiana*. This was a methodically organized treatise of pastoral and catechetical practice. Armed with this, the members of this first religious community in the Caribbean went out to preach the Kingdom of God and its justice, distinguishing themselves as men of vision and talent who devised and put into effect a programme of evangelization based on the actual situation in which the Indians were living. Their direct contact with the reality of the oppression and injustice to which the Indians were subjected moved them to commit themselves to the Indian cause and become their spokesmen through their preaching, denouncing the ruling economic system.

2. PUERTO RICO

When the Spaniards landed at Boriquén, they again destroyed the Tain culture of the island. Through forced labour, malnutrition, diseases contracted from the Spaniards and flight to other islands, the Indian population declined dramatically.[9]

The warlike expedition of Juan Ponce de León and his companions in 1508 brought a new twist to the history of Puerto Rico with the introduction of Christianity to the island. Here too, it was brought in under the aegis of violence and oppression. In 1511, after the death of the Tain leader Agueybana I and the enslavement of his subjects, the Indians rose up under their new *cacique* Agueybana the Brave.

This uprising was suppressed, and the Spaniards began to impose their political and religious institutions. On 8 August 1511 the diocese of Puerto Rico was established by Pope Julius II through the bull *Romanus Pontifex*. The same bull also established the dioceses of Santo Domingo and Concepción de la Vega.[10] San Juan de Puerto Rico was the first diocese to have a resident bishop: Alonso Manso, who reached his see in December 1512.[11] These first three dioceses of the New World were suffragans of the episcopal see of Seville. 1515 saw the establishment of the Abbey of Jamaica, whose mitred abbot was given the privileges of a bishop's crozier and jurisdiction.

Once settled in his diocese, Alonso Manso had to tackle the problems of shortage of priests and the poverty of the island. His first cathedral, in Caparra, was built of wood and thatch, and the diocese had only three parishes: San Juan, San Germán and the island of Cubagua. The islands of Trinidad and Margarita, and Barcelona, Cumaná and Guayana on the Eastern coast of Venezuela were added in 1518. In 1515 Manso returned to Spain, where he stayed till 1519, returning with the proud title of Inquisitor General of the Indies.[12] He set about introducing slaves from Hispaniola, and in 1521 applied to Charles V for a licence to buy more, whom he employed in sifting the gold-bearing sands and building a new cathedral.[13] Manso had both black and Indian slaves in his charge, some of the Indians *encomendados* and some formally slaves. It cannot be said that the first bishop in America was distinguished by his championing of the Indians and blacks, as some other early prelates were.

3. CUBA

Christianity arrived on 27 October 1492 with Columbus, who called the island Juana. On the Admiral's second voyage, the first eucharist in the New World was celebrated there. The native population of Cuba was made up of Siboyene Indians and a people called Guanahatahibe, as well as Tains. When the Spaniards came, the population was around 100,000; by 1532, the Indian numbers had been reduced to 14,000.

The conquest of Cuba was effected under the command of Diego Velázquez, who reached the island in 1510 with some three hundred men. The occupation was carried out in three stages. The first base was set up near Guantánamo, where the Spaniards had to tackle Indian resistance under the leadership of Hatuey, who had fled to Cuba from Hispaniola to escape the harsh treatment meted out to the Indians there. After a bloody campaign, many Indians were taken prisoner and many more killed, Indian resistance being unable to stand up to the superior military prowess of the Spaniards. Hatuey himself was taken prisoner, tried as a heretic and rebel and condemned to be burned alive. The cruel fate of the indomitable Hatuey was witnessed by Bartolomé de las Casas, and led to his radical change of attitude to the conquest and evangelization of the Indies.[14]

With Hatuey dead, Diego Velázquez concentrated all his forces on subduing the Eastern end of the island. This second stage of the conquest was entrusted to Francisco Morales and Pánfilo de Narváez, who ocupied the regions of Maniabón and Bayamo.[15] Both treated the Indians with cruelty and violence, provoking another uprising.

The third stage brought about the occupation of the whole island. On 2 February 1517 the bishopric of Baracoa was established. Its first bishop was the Dominican Bernardo de Mesa, who was severely criticized by Las Casas. The second was the Flemish Dominican Jan Witte, who never set foot in his episcopal see, but who in 1522 had it moved from Baracoa to Santiago de Cuba. He resigned in 1525, to be succeeded by yet another Dominican, Miguel Ramírez, who came to Cuba in 1529, but showed no interest in standing up to the injustices the Indians were suffering at the hands of the Spaniards.[16]

Evangelization in Cuba in the first half of the sixteenth century was shared among Dominicans, Franciscans, Jesuits and diocesan clergy. They had to face a large number of problems: conflicts and differences between conquistadors and governors, native rebellions, attacks by pirates, hurricanes, lack of clergy.

4. MEXICO AND CENTRAL AMERICA

Setting out from Havana, Hernán Cortés embarked on the conquest of the Aztec Empire in 1519. He took the Mercedarian friar Bartolomé de Olmedo on his voyages of conquest as chaplain. When he was confirmed as governor of New Spain in October 1522, he petitioned the Spanish king to send religious for the work of evangelization. The first church in Mexico was built at Tlaxcala in the same year. Cortés himself always showed great interest in the conversion of the Indians, declaring that "the aim of his expedition was the extirpation of idolatry and the conversion of the native people to the Christian faith."[17] Evangelization was of such concern to him because he envisaged the establishment of an autonomous kingdom to replace the old Aztec Empire, and religious and political unity were essential to the realization of this ambition. The Mexico Cortés found was a heterogeneous collection of peoples, and he was quick to capitalize on the internal dissensions among the various peoples subjected by the Aztecs. Moctezuma vacillated and compromised in the face of the cruelties committed by the conquistadors; his successor Caunhtemóc, on the other hand, offered valiant resistance.

The systematic and methodical evangelization of Mexico began with the arrival of the first twelve Franciscan friars in 1524. These Franciscan missionaries were given apostolic authority in all parts where there was no bishop. The first bishopric was established by Clement VII on 11 October 1525 in Tlaxcala, with the Dominican Juan Garcés appointed first bishop. This see was moved to Puebla de los Angeles in 1539. The diocese of Mexico City was set up on 2 September 1530, its first bishop being the Franciscan Juan de Zumárraga; the see was elevated to the status of archbishopric in 1546.

In 1526 twelve Dominican missionaries arrived in Mexico City and, having nowhere to live, were fraternally housed in the Franciscan convent. The Augustinians established themselves in 1532. By the year 1559, the Franciscans had eighty houses with 380 religious in Mexico; the Dominicans had forty houses and 210 religious; the Augustinians forty houses and 212 religious.[18]

The propagation of Christianity among the Mexican Indians was of course given a great boost by the appearance of the Virgin of Guadalupe to the Indian Juan Diego on the hill of Tepeyac in 1531.[19]

The first stage of the conquest of Central America began in 1523 when Cortés sent Pedro de Alvarado to subdue the Guatemala region, which he reached the following year, with three hundred Spaniards and a number of Tlaxcaltec, Texcoan and Aztec Indians. The Mayas resisted, but Alvarado overcame them and continued his advance southwards, down the Pacific coast. Further south, the Spaniards had begun the conquest and evangelization of Panama when they reached the isthsmus in 1501. In 1514 the Spanish king appointed Pedroarias governor of the region and named it Castilla de Oro, Panama being the Indian name. There, Pedroarias founded the city of Panama on 15 August 1519.[20] Santa María la Antigua of Darien was the first episcopal see on the continental mainland, founded in 1513, and formally established on 1 December 1521.

In Central America, the imposition of Christianity had to contend with endless problems and difficulties, not least the frequent rivalries among conquistadors and resistance from the Indians. The first phase of evangelization in Guatemala, from 1524 to 1529, was marked by the active intervention of lay people, the clergy being few and lacking in religious formation. The second phase of the process of Christianization can be dated from 1530 to 1541, when Spaniards began to settle in Guatemala. The third phase runs from 1541 to the death of Bishop Francisco de Marroquín in 1563. Throughout all three, the bulk of the work of evangelization was carried out by the Dominicans, who laid the foundations of their first convent in 1529. Bartolomé de Las Casas and Luis Cáncer, among others, succeeded in attracting the Indians of the region that became known as Vera Paz by pacific means.[21] But as Rodolfo Cardenal says: "Many regions were conquered, then abandoned and later attacked again and reconquered. This period of instability and arbitrariness lasted till 1540 , when the military phase of the conquest of Central America was officially closed."[22]

The passing of the *Leyes Nuevas* (New Laws) in 1542, which partly suppressed the *encomienda* system and prohibited the enslavement of Indians, led to intense conflicts between civil and religious authorities when they were applied to Central America. The Dominican bishop of Nicaragua, Antonio de Valdivieso, who maintained close links with Bartolomé de Las Casas, then bishop of Chiapas, found himself in a major dispute with those *encomenderos* who were not prepared to comply with the stipulations of the New Laws. Bishop Valdivieso earned the enmity of the governor, Rodrigo de Contreras, who persisted in exploiting the Indians, and his ardent defence of the native peoples led to his assassination, stabbed to death by a gang of Contreras' supporters on 26 February 1550.[23]

His tragic death, however, did not hold back missionary progress, nor the defence of the natives of Central America by the religious. On 6 September 1531, the bishopric of Trujillo was set up in Honduras, the see being later moved to Camayagua, in 1561. The progress of evangelization in the Honduras region was slow and beset with problems caused by frequent skirmishes among the conquistadors, economic hardship, Indian resistance and the paucity of Christians. The Indians lived in scattered groups, which put a considerable brake on the process of Christianizing them.[24] The situation was similar in what is today Costa Rica, which was first explored and evangelized from the Pacific coast, with relative success, though it was not till 1561 that the Spaniards penetrated to the central valleys of the region.[25]

5. THE COAST OF SOUTH AMERICA

The first evangelizing expedition to the Piritu region was composed of the Dominicans Antón de Montesinos, Francisco de Córdoba and Juan Garcés. They sailed from Hispaniola to Puerto Rico, where Montesinos fell seriously ill and had to stay there to recuperate, while his two companions continued their journey to the coast of the mainland. Though it is difficult to establish the exact date of their arrival in Piritu, the indications are that it was some time in 1514.[26]

The two friars devoted themselves to preaching to the Indians, and applied to Fray Pedro de Córdoba to send more friars. A Spanish man-of-war, captained by Gómez de Ribera, captured the chieftain Alonso and his family, who were held prisoners. This action led to protests on the part of the Indians, who appealed to the friars for the release of their chief. But protestations from the Dominicans on their behalf proved vain and the prisoners were not released. The Indians took their revenge and Juan Garcés and Francisco de Córdoba were martyred in 1515, thereby putting an end to attempts at peaceful evangelization on the mainland.[27]

Fray Pedro de Córdoba did not lose heart with the martyrdom of his friars, but applied to the crown to be allocated two hundred leagues of territory on the mainland, which would be kept free of any Spanish presence except for that of his friars and individuals selected by them. Antón de Montesinos was entrusted with obtaining this concession at Court. This was the origin of the native "reductions," later developed more extensively by the Jesuits in Paraguay.

A situation very similar to that of the Piritu missions on the coast of Venezuela obtained in the evangelization of the Indians of present-day Colombia. Hardly any of them became Christians in the first half of the sixteenth century. The repeated expeditions to capture the Indians and sell them as slaves increased their hostility and resistance to being converted to Christianity. Fernández de Angulo, bishop of Santa Marta, made a diocese in 1534, wrote to the king in 1541: "And know too that in these parts there are no Christians, but only demons; nor are there servants of God or of the king, but only traitors to his law and his king. Because in truth the greatest impediment I find to turning Indians from war and pacifying them, and bringing the pacified ones to knowledge of our faith, is the harsh and cruel treatment that the pacified ones receive from the Christians."[28]

6. THE ANDEAN ZONE: THE INCA EMPIRE

The evangelization of the ancient Inca Empire began in 1531 with its conquest by Francisco Pizarro, who was accompanied by Vicente Valverde, a Domincan friar, and Juan de Sosa, a secular priest. Responsibility for evangelization was then entrusted to religious in the mission areas inhabited by Indians, while the secular clergy were generally established in areas settled by Spaniards. The progress of evangelization was considerably hampered in the early years by shortages of both religious and secular clergy. In the meantime, the conquistadors took advantage of divisions between the Inca brothers Huáscar and Atahualpa to consolidate their gains.

Cuzco, the capital of the Inca Empire, was established as a diocese in 1537, with Vicente Valverde being appointed as its first bishop. It originally covered a vast area, extending from New Granada down to Chile and the River Plate. On 13 May 1541, Pope Paul III established the see of Ciudad de los Reyes, whose first bishop was the Dominican Jerónimo de Loaysa (1543–75). In 1551–2 he held the First Council of Lima, which gave major impetus to the process of catechesis and evangelization. The Second Council of Lima was held in 1567, and the Third, one of the most important to be held in the New World, in 1582–3, under the second archbishop of Lima, St Toribius of Mogrovejo.[29]

Unlike Mexico, Peru, in the early stages of missionary activity, lacked a good number of religious familiar with the native languages. This held back progress in converting the natives to Christianity in no small measure, a situation reflected in the book written by a priest called Pedro de Quiroga in the mid-sixteenth century, entitled *Coloquios de la Verdad que trata de las causas e inconvenientes que impiden la doctrina e conversión de los indios en los reinos del Perú y de los daños* (Colloquies on the Truth concerning the causes and impediments that hinder the teaching and conversion of the Indians in the kingdoms of Peru and the harm resulting).

The Inca Felipe Guaman Poma de Ayala, describing the behaviour of priests toward the Indians of Peru, pointed out that: "As the priests and curates who teach doctrine are very choleric and absolute lords and proud, and have so much seriousness, that the said Indians flee from them in fear; and that the said priests do not agree that our Lord Jesus Christ became poor and humble to attract and draw poor sinners to him, to bring them into his Holy Church, and thence to lead them to his kingdom of heaven."[30]

Once Indian resistance had been put down, Sebastián de Benalcázar founded the city of Santiago de Quito. The first Franciscans arrived there almost immediately, in 1535, followed by the Mercedarians in 1537 and the Dominicans four years later. In 1545 Quito became a diocese, as a suffragan see of Seville and later, in 1546, of Lima. In 1542 the governor of Peru, Cristóbal Vaca de Castro sent out an expedition, which three years later discovered the silver mines of Potosí, a place that was to become the scene of one of the worst instances of exploitation of native labour in mining. The Viceroy Hurtado de Mendoza called it "the main nerve-centre of the kingdom." The Uruguayan writer Eduardo Galeano describes it like this: "In Potosí silver raised up temples and palaces, monasteries and gaming dens, gave rise to tragedy and festival, spilt blood and wine, awakened envy and unleashed extravagance and adventure. The sword and the cross marched together in the conquest and colonial plunder."[31]

7. THE SOUTHERN CONE

Evangelization in the River Plate area began in 1536 with an expedition of sixteen ships carrying fifteen hundred men and women, under the command of the Spaniard Pedro de Mendoza. Eleven secular clergy, two Mercedarian and four Jeronymite friars were part of the expeditionary force.[32] Mendoza established the fort of Nuestra Señora del Buen Aire, which later became Buenos Aires, though the actual city was not founded till 1580. The missionaries who accompanied the conquistadors originally took charge of local evangelization; more, mainly Franciscans, followed, working in the broad expanses that were to become Argentina. Outstanding among them was St Francisco Solano (1549–1610), who in the space of twenty years covered the lands of Tucuman, El Chaco, Paraguay and the shores of the Plate. Four major religious orders established themselves in Argentina during the sixteenth century: the Mercedarians in 1536, the Franciscans, who came from the East in 1549, the Dominicans from the North in the same year, and later the Jesuits, in 1585.[33]

In Uruguay, the history of the church started with a fruitful and unusual evangelizing effort. In 1538, two Franciscans, Bernardo de Armenta and Alonso de Lebrón, abandoned Alonso de Cabrera's expedition and set foot in the Eastern region of Uruguay, accompanied by three lay people, where they began to preach the gospel. This little community eventually Christianized a stretch of 480 kilometres and organized a Christian lifestyle based largely on Indian models. Unlike other parts of Latin America, where evangelization went hand-in-glove with a violent process of colonizing, this early Christianity in Uruguay produced fine fruits without any notable cultural clash. During this period the bases of church organization were laid, without any direct input from the political or economic authorities, and without a bishop. It was the Indians themselves who became active agents of evangelization.[34]

The expedition which set out from Cuzco under the leadership of Diego de Almagro (1475–1538), reached the valley of Copiapó, but there divisions broke out and the project of colonizing Chile was abandoned. Almagro's successor

Pedro de Valdivia (1500–54) reached the Mapocho valley after eleven months of arduous journeying, and there on 12 February 1541 founded the city of Santiago. This became a diocese in 1561, as a suffragan see of the archdiocese of Lima. Mercedarians and Dominicans began intense evangelization of the area around the middle of the century, but in 1533 the "heroic Araucanian war" broke out, which was to keep the Spaniards in check for two whole centuries.[35]

8. BRAZIL

There are two clear phases in the early evangelization of Brazil. The first began with Pedro Alvarez de Cabral, who reached the Brazilian coast in 1500 at the head of a fleet of thirteen vessels. Diocesan priests and fifteen Franciscans made up part of the expedition. During this phase, there was a great deal of questioning as to whether the Indians could be called human or not, largely because the Portuguese found peoples living on subsistence farming only, and not the great civilizations which the Spaniards had found in Mexico and Peru. Colonization as such began in 1530 with the arrival of the expedition led by Martím Afonso de Souza and the introduction of sugar cane. At the same time, slaves from Africa began to be disembarked in large numbers, gradually leading to the creation of a society of masters and slaves. The secular clergy came to Brazil largely to look after the religious needs of the Portuguese there, and paid scant attention to evangelizing the Indians and blacks. In 1543 the king of Portugal divided the territory of Brazil into fifteen Captaincies, of which the Captains were effectively feudal lords, exercizing absolute power. The Portuguese crown kept the right of patronage, under which the monarch was responsible for the designation of parishes and dioceses, the building of churches and convents, the appointment of parish priests and bishops, and the maintenance of colleges, amongst other things.[36]

Effective evangelization of the vast lands of Brazil was in the hands of missionary orders, in particular the Jesuits, who landed in the bay of All Saints (now Bahia) on 29 March 1549. This date marks the beginning of the second phase of the propagation of Christianity in Brazil. The Captaincy system had proved a failure, and a central government had to be organized. The first governor-general, Tomé de Souza, arrived in March 1549, and established himself in Bahia. He was accompanied by several Jesuits, who undertook the task of catechizing the Indians. Led by Manuel de Nóbrega, this group of six Jesuits soon made an impact on Brazil; four more came in 1550, and three years later saw the arrival of the illustrious José de Anchieta, a native of the Canary Isles, who soon produced a rough grammar in Tupí-Guaraní, and set Christian teachings to Indian tunes[37]. His evangelizing actions were an excellent example of an indefatigable apostolate, immersed in Indian cultures.

The Jesuits' fruitful missionary work was, however, hampered by Bishop Pedro Fernández Sardinha, whose bishopric had been established in Bahia in 1551. He forbade the Jesuits to catechize in native languages, telling them that the gospel had to be preached in Portuguese.[38]

The Jesuits tried to establish reductions in Brazil; the first was set up in Bahia by Diego Alvares, but opposed by Bishop Sardinha. In view of his opposition, Fr Nóbrega chose another site on the shores of the river Tieté and convinced the Indians to move there. This was the origin of what was to become the city of São Paulo. After 1553, with the creation of the Jesuit Province of Brazil, the Jesuits operated without reference to the bishop.[39]

Development of ecclesiastical structures was slow in Brazil, unlike in the Spanish colonies. According to José Oscar Beozzo: "The bishops played a minor and timid role in the whole history of the implantation of the faith in Brazil, as can be seen from the mere fact that till 1675 there was only one bishop, of Bahia, and often none, since the see was often vacant for long periods, its prelate having either resigned or died."[40]

CONCLUSIONS

The foregoing brief account of the first period of evangelization in the different regions of Latin America sheds light on some aspects and circumstances that define the type of church established in the newly conquered lands. The splitting apart and disintegration of the social, political and economic structure of Indian life was the prime reality confronting the missionaries in their great task of evangelization. But not all the missionaries understood the Indian religious world. As Hans-Jurgen Prien states: "Everything Indian was condemned *en bloc* as the work of the devil, which in practice meant that the Indians were stripped of their identity and downgraded to second-class beings, whose very humanity depended, in the judgment of the conquistadors, on the degree to which they absorbed Iberian religion and civilization."[41] The situation of the native peoples, "disintegrated and dispersed elements," made true catechesis and effective evangelization considerably more difficult. And the same problem was repeated with the arrival of uprooted and exploited blacks from Africa.

This brutal situation, the product of the conquest, was condemned by some missionaries, who saw that the cross and the sword could not go hand-in-hand, if there was a real desire for genuine evangelization. This gave rise to the prophetic community of the Dominicans in the Caribbean. The illustrious figure of Bartolomé de Las Casas, defender of Indians and blacks, was to become the voice of those whom the European conquest had silenced. And so a constellation of missionaries – Dominicans, Franciscans, Augustinians, Mercedarians and Jesuits – formed with an evangelizing outlook very different from that promoted by the crowns of Spain and Portugal with their system of Royal Patronage. Two evangelizing prorammes were on collision course. That of the crown, on one hand, was supported by eminent scholars who legitimized imperialism and war against the Indians, such as Juan Ginés de Sepúlveda, who, taking his stand on Aristotle, upheld the inferiority of the Indians and declared that it was right for them to be governed by Spaniards.[42] That of a number of religious, on the other hand, was different: Las Casas' evangelizing programme, for example, consisted in setting up "communities of free Indians" on the coast from Paria to Cumaná in Venezuela, and in Vera Paz in Guatemala. Las Casas maintained that an atmosphere – and an order – of freedom were an essential condition for preaching the gospel, and upheld a form of community in which preaching and spiritual growth would be possible. As he wrote: "Christ granted to the apostles only the licence and authority to preach the gospel to those who voluntarily wished to hear it, but not that to force or cause any molestation or inconvenience to those who might not want to listen."[43]

In the event, however, the model of catechesis, peaceful evangelization and inculturation put forward by the Dominicans and other religious orders was defeated by the evangelizing programme of the crown, which was to convert the Indies into a colonial Christendom. The church of the time, born from this model of Christendom united to the system of Royal Patronage, was to leave a deep mark on Latin American Christianity. What emerged was a peripheral Christendom, dependent on the European church, even though a flourishing popular Catholicism also developed. The institutional church in Latin America established its economic bases on exploitation of the Indians in the mines and in an agriculture carried out by slave labour, mainly that of blacks brought over from Africa.

During the period under review, there was no indigenous or black clergy as such, either secular or regular. In America, only Spaniards, Portuguese or white *criollos* could be ordained. In 1550 the Franciscan Jacobo Daciano warned his order that the church in Mexico had still not been properly established, since it included not a single indigenous priest.

Not everything in the conquest and evangelization of the New World should be seen as negative, however. Alongside cruel and unjust conquistadors came good Christians too, men and women of upright conscience who made America their second homeland. In less than a century a wide-ranging process of settlement was accomplished which gave rise to a new culture and civilization. This was a renewing process that changed the political concept of the world held till then. The intervention of the religious orders in the way cities in Latin America were organized, for example, was of major importance.

The rich debate unleashed among theologians and jurists concerning the justice of the conquest stands as "one of the most glorious pages of spiritual life in modern times." As Lewis Hanke writes: "Other powers that had colonies in the New World were not greatly exercised by theoretical questions. No protector of the Indians appeared in English or French colonies in America. The Puritans regarded the Indians as benighted savages who could justly be destroyed or subjugated."[44]

This first phase of the complex historical process of evangelization in Latin America has its lights and its shadows. It is a dense and complex history, and its development is continuing in our own days. Latin American Christianity is the inheritor of this past; studying it from a critical standpoint should enable us not to repeat the errors of the past: it should be a contribution to a turn of the wheel of history – starting from the preferential option for the poor and moving on to the Kingdom of God and its justice.

Translated from the Spanish by Paul Burns

NOTES

1. G. Gutiérrez, *Dios o el oro en las Indias* (Salamanca, 1989), p. 113.
2. Ibid., p. 115.
3. R. Pané, *Relación acerca de las antiguedades de los indios* (Mexico City, 1974), p. 21.
4. B. de Las Casas, *Brevísima relación de la destrucción de las Indias* (Madrid, 1985), p. 72.

5. Gutiérrez, *Dios o el oro*, p. 41.

6. Las Casas, *Historia de las Indias*, vol. II (Santo Domingo, 1985), p. 441.

7. Ibid., p. 444.

8. M. A. Medina, "Metodología evangélica de fray Pedro de Córdoba," *CIDAL* 4 & 5, May-Dec. 1982, p. 39.

9. L. Fifueroa, *Historia de Puerto Rico*, vol I (Río Piedras, Puerto Rico, 1979), p. 60.

10. L. Lopetegui and F. Zubillaga, *Historia de la Iglesia en la América Española*, (Madrid, 1965), p. 248.

11. V. Murga and A. Huerga, *Episcopologio de Puerto Rico, I. D. Alonso Manso, Primer Obispo de América* (1511–1539, (Ponce, Puerto Rico, 1987), p. 89.

12. Ibid., p. 170.

13. L. Díaz Soler, *Historia de la esclavitud negra en Puerto Rico* (San Juan, 1970), p. 57.

14. Cf Las Casas, *Brevísima relación*, p. 81.

15. R. Guerra, *Manual de Historia de Cuba* (Madrid, 1975), p. 28.

16. On the first two bishops in Cuba, see I. Testé, ed., *Historia Eclesiástica de Cuba*, vol. I (Burgos, 1969), pp. 65–72.

17. D. Ulloa, *Los predicadores divididos. Los dominicos en Nueva España*, siglo XVI (Mexico City, 1977), p. 88.

18. E. Dussel, *Historia de la Iglesia en América Latina* (Barcelona, 1974), p. 93.

19. Cf P. F. Velázquez, *La aparición de Santa María de Guadalupe* (Mexico City, 1931). Cf also I. Gebara and M. C. Bingemer, *Mary, Mother of God and Mother of the Poor* (Maryknoll, N.Y. and Tunbridge Wells, 1989), pp. 144–54 (TRANS).

20. A. Ariza, *Los dominicos en Panamá* (Bogotá, 1963), p. 11.

21. L. Hanke, *Estudios sobre Fray Bartolomé de Las Casas y sobre la justicia en la conquista española de América* (Caracas, 1968), pp. 117–26.

22. CEHILA, *Historia General de la Iglesia en América Latina* (Salamanca, 1985), p. 21.

23. F. Ximénez, *Historia de la Provincia de San Vicente de Chiapas y Guatemala*, vol. IV (Guatemala, 1965), pp. 1029–40.

24. M. Carías, "Honduras," CEHILA, *Historia General. Vol. IV: América Central*, pp. 61–3.

25. M. Picado, "Costa Rica," Ibid., pp. 70, 72.

26. D. Ramos, "El P. Córdoba y Las Casas en el plan de conquista pacífica de Tierra Firme," *Estudios de Historia Venezolana* (Caracas, 1988), pp. 126–30.

27. M. Angel Medina, *Una comunidad al servicio del Indio. La obra de Fr. Pedro de Córdoba, OP (1482–1521)* (Madrid, 1983), pp. 107–9.

28. Las Casas, *Brevísima relación*, p. 114.

29. Cf *Tercer Concilio Limense*, 1582–3 (Lima, 1982).

30. F. Guaman Poma de Ayala, *Nueva Coronica y Buen Gobierno*, vol II (Caracas, 1980), p. 10.

31. E. Galeano, *Las venas abiertas de América Latina* (Mexico City, 1975), p. 31. Eng. trans. *The Open Veins of Latin America* (London, 1976).

32. Cf B. Cayetano, *Historia de la Iglesia en la Argentina*, vol. I, 16th century (Buenos Aires, 1966).

33. R. González, "La Orden Dominica en la Argentina," *Communio. Commentarii internationales de Ecclesia et Theologia*, vol XVIII (Seville, 1985), p. 271.

34. Instituto E. Florez, *Diccionario de Historia Eclesiástica de España* (Madrid, 1975), p. 2680.

35. Cf F. Araneda Bravo, *Breve Historia de la Iglesia en Chile* (Santiago, 1968).

36. P. Richard, ed., *Historia de la Teología en América Latina* (San José, Costa Rica, 1981), pp. 43–4.

37. W. V. Bangert, *Historia de la Compañia de Jesús* (Santander, 1981), pp. 53–4.

38. J. O. Beozzo, "La evangelización y su Historia Latinoamericana," *Medellín* Extracts, vol. IV, nos. 15–16, Sep.–Dec. 1978, p. 340.

39. H. J. Prien, *La Historia del Cristianismo en América Latina* (Salamanca, 1985), p. 210.

40. Beozzo, "La evangelización," p. 340.

41. Prien, *Historia del Cristianismo*, p. 70.

42. On the debate between Juan Ginés de Sepúlveda and Bartolomé de Las Casas, see L. Hanke, *Aristotle and the American Indians* (Philadelphia and London, 1959) (TRANS).

43. Cited in J. A. Barrera, "Primera anunciación y bautismo en la obra de Bartolomé de Las Casas," *Ciencia Tomista*, no. 379, May-Aug. 1989, p. 303.

44. L. Hanke, *The Struggle for Justice in the Spanish Conquest of America* (Philadelphia, 1949).

Chapter 3

THE ORGANIZATION OF THE CHURCH

Johannes Meier

"So I went on shore and at the entrance to the harbour, on a clearly visible eminence situated to the west, I erected a large cross, to show that this land belonged to your Majesties, under the banner of Jesus Christ our Lord, and to the glory of all Christendom."[1] This entry in Christopher Columbus' log-book is dated Wednesday, 12 December 1492, and refers to a location on the northern coast of Haiti, opposite Turtle Island. It shows the intimate relation to the religious dimension of the Spanish Crown's political claim to sovereignty over the new-found territories. The cross is the symbol of the political and religious unity which the Catholic monarchs sought to establish in their realms by abandoning the greater tolerance of former years, by introducing the Inquisition (1480), and by expelling the Jews (1492) and later the Moors (1502).[2]

The cross which Columbus set up also indicates how surely he took for granted the future Christianization of the indigenous Indians if they were to become obedient subjects of the Catholic monarchs. It scarcely proves, however, that his voyage was inspired mainly by religious intentions or by the prospect of evangelization. The missionary impulse nevertheless surfaced in the five papal bulls of 1493 which confirmed the Spanish monarchs' title to the territory which Columbus had discovered.[3]

King Ferdinand and Queen Isabella requested the bulls when bad weather on Columbus' return to Europe forced him to put in at Lisbon. As a result, John II of Portugal was the first to learn of the recently discovered lands. He promptly claimed them himself by recourse to the Treaty of Alcáçovas (1479). The Spanish monarchs used the same means that the Portuguese Crown had often applied to confirm its dominion over African shores and Atlantic islands. As a reciprocal measure, through their ambassador in Rome the Catholic monarchs pressed Pope Alexander VI for a speedy confirmation of their claims. The pope, born in Valencia, was indebted to them in several ways. The main content of the papal bulls was a recognition of the Castilian throne's rights of possession of islands and mainland already discovered by Columbus, and of any still to be found beyond a line 100 miles to the west of the Azores and of Cape Verde. The acknowledgement also referred to the missionary intentions of the Catholic monarchs in that area. At the same time, other "persons irrespective of rank" were forbidden "on pain of excommunication" to despatch expeditions to the region.

With the bull *Piis fidelium* of 25 June 1493 the pope appointed Friar Bernal Boyl vicar apostolic of the newly discovered territories in the West Indies. In person and with the help of other priests Boyl was to preach the word of God in those lands, in order to bring the natives to the Christian religion and to induce them to behave as God had commanded. Originally Bernal Boyl had been a member of the Catalonian Benedictine monastery of Montserrat. In 1492 he had joined the Order of Minims, founded by St Francis of Paola. He had chanced to meet the founder of the order when travelling in the diplomatic service. In accordance with the papal nomination, Boyl and twelve other "*eclesiásticos*", priests from various orders, took part in Columbus' second expedition, when the explorer started for the West Indies on 25 September 1493 with seventeen ships and a total of 1500 men on board.[4]

At the end of November 1493 Columbus arrived off Haiti. A few weeks later he founded "La Isabella", the first Spanish town in the New World. "On the day when we celebrate the feast of the Three Kings, 16 January 1494, mass was said there in accordance with our use, and celebrated by thirteen priests so to speak in another world, far away from all civilization and religion."[5] Nevertheless the group did not follow up this festive occasion with any prosperous missionary activity. Before long there were disputes and plotting among the settlers, and Boyl too was caught up in it. At the end of 1494, after quarrelling with Columbus, Boyl returned to Spain and on 16 February 1494 a letter from the Catholic monarchs relieved him of his office. Apart from three lay brothers, the other members of his group also returned to Europe in 1494–5. Boyl turned to other tasks, but no successor was appointed. At first, as the voyages to the West Indies continued, no attention was paid to missionary endeavours. To be sure, in their letter to Columbus before his third crossing to America, the Catholic monarchs stressed the importance of "converting . . . the natives of the said Indies to our holy Catholic faith,"[6] and also decreed that "some religious and clergy should travel to the said Indies . . . in order to administer the holy sacraments there; and , that they should remain there, and obtain the conversion of the said Indians."[7] But there would seem to have been no priest on board on 30 May 1498, when the admiral reached the West Indies for the third time. According to Las Casas, on arriving in America they said prayers and sang the "*Salve Regina*," but mass was not celebrated.[8]

The Crown cancelled Columbus' viceregal powers (1500) and appointed Francisco de Bobadilla (1500–1502) and Nicolás de Ovando (1502–1508) as directly dependent governors, thus completing the ideological breakthrough to territorial colonization by settlement. The royal interest in missionary activity was reawakened with this approach. The inhabitants of the new overseas possessions were to be included in Spanish "Christendom." Accordingly, the monarchs now concentrated on building up a church organization in the West Indies.

In view of the considerable costs of such an enterprise, they succeeded in persuading Pope Alexander VI to issue the bull *Eximiae devotionis sinceritas* of November 16th 1501. The pope awarded the Crown the tithes from the newly discovered islands and mainlands on condition that the monarchs established churches there and funded them adequately.[9] Having achieved this concession, the Crown supervised the foundation of the first dioceses in America. Then, on 15 November 1504, the bull *Illius fulciti praesidio* was approved by the new Pope Julius II. Three dioceses were provided for "La Española": the archdiocese of Yaguata (Santo Domingo) and the suffragan dioceses of Magua (Concepción de la Vega) and Baynua (Lares de Guahaba).[10] Queen Isabella of Castile did not live to see this fulfilment of the Crown's plans, for she died on 26 November 1504.

After her death, progress in this respect slackened. Only on 20 March 1505 was ambassador Francisco de Rojas able to send the news from Rome that the bull was complete, and despatched it to Spain as late as 8 July 1505. King Ferdinand found the text of the bull unsatisfactory, for it did not take into account his claim to patronage. He wrote to ambassador Rojas about this on 13 September 1505. He wanted the new dioceses to be subject to royal patronage to the same extent as in the kingdom of Granada. Until that was guaranteed, he refused to issue letters of appointment to the bishops allocated to the new dioceses.

Little happened on the American front in the next few months, for Ferdinand left Castile. The new ruler was Philip the Handsome of Burgundy, his son-in-law, but he died on 25 September 1506. Ferdinand returned to Castile, and on 21 October 1507 he assured Governor Nicolás de Ovando on "La Española" that they could soon count on Rome issuing the bulls revised in his favour, so that the people on the island could prepare for the bishops' arrival.[11] A further letter of 30 April 1508 yet again declared that they were awaiting the issue of the bulls. The King also said that he had told the "Casa de la Contratación" in Seville to send competent master builders to Santo Domingo, who would see to the erection of churches "*de obra durable*" (that would last), and that "*á costa de los diezmos é primicias desa ysla*" (covered by the tithes and primacies of the island).[12]

The bull *Universalis Ecclesiae Regimen* was issued on 28 July 1508. Pope Julius II bestowed upon the kings of Castile and Leon the "*ius patronatus et prestandi personas idoneas ad . . . quascumque Metropolitanas ac Cathedrales Ecclesias et monasteria ac dignates . . . ac quecumque alia beneficia ecclesiastica et pia loca in dictis insulis et locis pro tempore vacantia*".[13] Ferdinand's dream was realized. He and his successors were accorded full patronage over the Church as it came into being in "Las Indias." He was to propose candidates to the Pope for all spiritual honours and offices in America; co-determine the establishment and delimitation of dioceses; and influence the allocation of lesser ecclesiastical offices by the local ordinaries who were obedient to him.

From now on Ferdinand worked resolutely toward the foundation of efficient dioceses in the West Indies. On 3 May 1509 he recommended Diego Columbus, the new governor of "La Española", to treat "*las cosas del servicio de Dios, Nuestro Señor*" (matters to do with the service of God our Lord), with special care.[14] On 14 August 1509 he urgently requested the "Casa de la Contratación" to send him the "*pintura de la divisyón de los obispados de las Yndias*" (account of the demarcation of the dioceses of the Indies) , which had been the subject of one of Diego Columbus' letters to him.[15] On 13 September 1509 Ferdinand informed his ambassador in Rome of new thinking about the boundaries of the West Indian dioceses.

An appraisal, which is undated but presumably originated in 1510, makes a case, in regard to the minimal population and the only moderate economic prosperity of "La Española", for the establishment of merely one bishopric on the island, at Santo Domingo (Yaguata). The two other dioceses of Magua in Concepción de la Vega and Baynua in Lares de Guahaba, which had been provided for since 1504, were to be dissolved. Moreover Yaguata should not become an archdiocese but a suffragan diocese of the ecclesiastical province of Seville.[16] The problem with this plan was that in 1504 the Holy See had already appointed bishops for the three planned dioceses, even though they had not yet been consecrated and remained in Spain. Nevertheless, the idea prevailed that no new ecclesiastical province should be established in the West Indies, but that the new dioceses should be subject to Seville.

With the successful acquisition of Puerto Rico in 1508–9 it was suggested that one of the three planned dioceses should be transferred to those islands. Accordingly, the bull *Romanus Pontifex* of 8 August 1511 announced the abolition of the dioceses of Yaguata, Magua and Baynua which had been founded in 1504, and the elevation of Santo Domingo, Concepción de la Vega and San Juan to the status of bishoprics.[17] With the consecration of Bishops Francisco García de Padilla, Pedro Suárez de Deza and Alonso Manso, who had been appointed in 1504, their *"capitulación"* before King Ferdinand in Burgos, and their acceptance of the canonical constitution of their dioceses, the first ecclesiastical structures in Latin America were established in the course of the year 1512.[18]

Even when the first steps in the foundation of the Church in America had been taken almost wholly in accordance with its wishes, the monarchy continued to extend its writ. As early as 26 July 1513 Ferdinand wrote to his ambassador at the Holy See, Jerónimo de Vich, asking him to represent to the pope the case for the establishment of a patriarchate for the overseas territories. The king already had a patriarch in mind: Juan Rodríguez de Fonseca, Bishop of Palencia, who had long been his indispensable support as unofficial minister for American affairs.[19] But the Holy See did not agree, and it was only in 1524 that Clement VII bestowed the title of patriarch on Antonio de Rojas, archbishop of Granada; the office, however, was honorary, and implied no practical duties.[20]

In the meantime, after the death of Ferdinand and the provisional regency of Cardinal Jiménez de Cisneros, the young heir Charles succeeded to the throne. Over the years, his firm and profoundly religious sense of mission led him to interfere even more directly in the affairs of the Church in America than had been customary hitherto. The "Consejo Real y Supremo de las Indias" became a decisive instrument in the process. Its origins went back to Bishop Fonseca, and since 1519 the committee had operated as an independent section of the "Consejo Real de Castilla". On 1 August 1524 new statutes raised it to the level of fourth central council – alongside the councils for Castile, Aragon and Navarre. The first president of this institution, which consisted of eminent jurists, was the king's confessor, Bishop García de Loaisa OP. The Council for the Indies was able to prevent almost all direct connections between the Roman curia and the American Church, and to keep a close watch on the entire correspondence of the Hispanic American episcopate and other ecclesiastics. The ordinances of the Council for the Indies were revised several times (1542, 1571, 1636 and 1681) and offered conclusive and detailed answers to all conceivable questions which might arise for the Church or between Church and state in the New World.[21] Though there were occasional direct contacts between Rome and the Church in Hispanic America, as in the case of the transmission of Paul III's famous bull *Sublimis Deus* (1537), this caused considerable ill-feeling at the Spansh court and among the members of the Council for the Indies, because it was seen as contrary to the customary exercise of the right of patronage. In this respect, there was at that time even an attempt to unite the supreme secular and spiritual powers in America in one individual. To this end, in 1527 Sebastián Ramírez de Fuenleal was appointed bishop of Santo Domingo and shortly thereafter president of the local *audiencia*. In 1531, when Fuenleal was translated to the "audienca" of Mexico, he remained the spiritual head of the see of Santo Domingo and ensured that the provisor Francisco de Mendoza represented him in his pastoral office. At the same time it was assumed that the provisor would be accountable to the new president of the *audiencia* of Santo Domingo, Alonso de Fuenmayor (appointed in 1533), who was also a priest and who, in 1538, on the appointment of Fuenleal as bishop of Tuy, also became bishop of Santo Domingo.[22] Nevertheless, after a time the Council for the Indies abandoned the idea of combining secular and spiritual offices in one person, for Charles V found it disagreeable.

In view of the "Conquista", which gathered force in the 1520s and 1530s, the Council for the Indies was faced with the task of endowing the vast territories with not only secular but ecclesiastical structures. Several new dioceses were created with astonishing speed. The first three foundations on "La Española" and Puerto Rico were followed by another fourteen by 1540, in the Caribbean area, in Mexico, in Central America and Cuzco, the site of the first South American see. Another eleven dioceses were established between 1540 and 1570, now for the most part in South America. Finally, another seven were added by 1620, when with the foundation of the sees of Durango in Northern Mexico and Buenos Aires at the mouth of the Río de la Plata, the ecclesiastical organization of Hispanic America took the form it was to retain until the late eighteenth century. Each of these dioceses received a papal "*bula de erección*", the content of which was nevertheless largely decided in advance by the Council for the Indies. This later caused the court lawyer Solorzano to opine that formulation of the decree of establishment of dioceses was part of the monarch's right of patronage.[23] In the first few decades the boundaries of the new dioceses were very vaguely drawn. The Indies legislation features two modes of demarcating boundaries: 1. a radius of fifteen "*leguas*" roundabout the see in question; 2. half of the distance between two sees.[24] Before 1570 it was not the practice to define diocesan boundaries more precisely; that happened only in 1577[25], when the Peruvian dioceses of Arequipa and Trujillo were established. In the Caribbean at the same time the spiritual authority settled in favour of Santiago de Cuba an old dispute between the dioceses of Santo Domingo and Santiago de Cuba regarding the island of Jamaica.[26]

Up to 1546 all American dioceses were subject to the archdiocese of Seville. As early as 1536 the Council for the Indies had proposed that the emperor should ask the pope to establish two American archdioceses (Santo Domingo and Mexico), because the great distance from the metropolitan see of Seville considerably disadvantaged the spiritual governance of the Church in the New World. Initially, however, Charles V did nothing in this regard. It was not till 1544 that a petition from the council of the city of Mexico, and most likely the visit to Spain of the bishop of Santo Domingo, Alonso de Fuenmayor, elicited any new action in this respect.[27] On 20 June 1545 an imperial brief to the Spanish ambassador to the Holy See instructed him to ask the curia to found three archdioceses in Spanish America. The consistory of cardinals realized the expectations of the Spanish crown. With the bull *Super universas orbis ecclesias* of 12 February 1546, Paul III elevated the cathedrals of Santo Domingo, Mexico and Lima to the status of metropolitan churches.[28] In Santo Domingo the suffragan dioceses were determined in accordance with a maritime criterion; the bishops of the adjacent islands of Puerto Rico and Cuba and of the coastal towns of Coro, Santa Marta, Cartagena and Trujillo were subject to the archbishop of Santo Domingo. Mexico acquired Puebla, Michoacán, Oaxaca, Chiapas and Guatemala. The greatest distances were to be found in the ecclesiastical province of Lima, which extended from Nicaragua through Panama and Quito to Cuzco.[29] Cardinal García de Loaisa OP, for many years archbishop of Seville and president of the Council for the Indies, had lived to see the independence of the American hierarchy. On 18 February 1546 he was appointed inquisitor general, but died on 22 April of the same year.[30]

Of the four dioceses on the mainland, only Venezuela, where the see was transferred from Coro to Caracas in 1637, remained permanently in the ecclesiastical province of Santo Domingo. Santa Marta was abolished in 1562, when in the highlands to the south, where a new centre of settlement had arisen, the diocese of Santa Fe de Bogotá was established and elevated to the status of archdiocese as early as 1564. America's fourth ecclesiastical province was accorded the suffragan dioceses of Cartagena, Popoyán and Santa Marta, which was re-established in 1577.[31]. The colonization of the Philippines began in 1565. It was clear from the start that the islands offered scant economic advantages; in the religious domain, however, the Spanish presence proved very effective, and evinced the "quasi-theocratic nature of the Spanish régime".[32] The first episcopal see of Manila was established in 1579 and by 1595 had become an archdiocese with the suffragan dioceses of Nueva Segovia, Nueva Cáceres and Nombre de Jesús on the islands of Cebú.[33] In 1609 a fifth metropolitan see for Hispanic America was founded in Charcas de la Plata (now Sucre). This province covered the south-eastern part of the continent, approximating to the territory of the present-day states of Bolivia, Argentina and Paraguay.[34]

Local ecclesiastical structures came into being promptly in all these dioceses of Spanish America. In addition to the chapters established by the bishops in the cathedral churches, individual parishes were set up in the episcopal town and in those places where Christian Spaniards predominated, whereas mission stations were founded for the Indian population living for the most part in country areas and not yet or only just christianized; these missions, or *doctrinas*, were almost exclusively in the charge of religious orders.[35] The secular right of patronage which decided the bestowal of these subordinate ecclesiastical centres belonged to the organs of state administration, the presidents of the *audiencias*, the captains general and governors. Nevertheless, as long as the civil administration itself was still in the process of formation, the Church retained a considerable degree of autonomy in this area. The situation changed under Philip II. In 1568 the king summoned the "*Junta Magna*", an assembly which

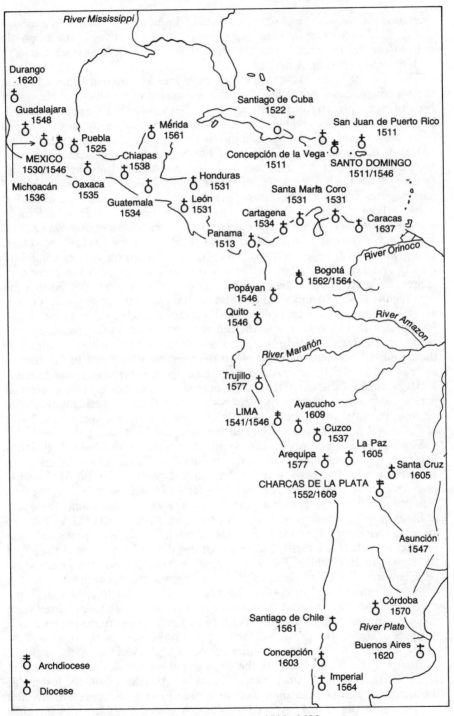

Durango
.1620

Guadalajara
1548

Puebla
1525

MEXICO
1530/1546

Chiapas
1538

Michoacán
1536

Oaxaca
1535

Guatemala
1534

Mérida
1561

León
1531

Honduras
1531

Panama
1513

Santiago de Cuba
1522

Concepción de la Vega
1511

SANTO DOMINGO
1511/1546

San Juan de Puerto Rico
1511

Santa Marta
1531

Coro
1531

Cartagena
1534

Caracas
1637

River Orinoco

Bogotá
1562/1564

Popáyan
1546

Quito
1546

River Amazon

River Marañón

Trujillo
1577

LIMA
1541/1546

Ayacucho
1609

Cuzco
1537

La Paz
1605

Arequipa
1577

Santa Cruz
1605

CHARCAS DE LA PLATA
1552/1609

Asunción
1547

Córdoba
1570

River Plate

Santiago de Chile
1561

Buenos Aires
1620

Concepción
1603

Imperial
1564

☿ Archdiocese

☿ Diocese

River Mississippi

3. Archdioceses and Dioceses in Spanish America: 1511–1620

examined the consequences of the Council of Trent for the Church in America and decided on several fundamental reforms. It also so changed the emphasis as to ensure that in future the secular right of patronage could be extended to all ecclesiastical offices in America.

This was not to the liking of the then Pope Pius V, who had allocated to the curia a congregation of cardinals for the conversion of unbelievers. He would certainly have preferred to create a nunciature in order to ensure a direct link between the Holy See and the ecclesiastical provinces and missionary territories of the New World. But the Spanish throne firmly rejected any such idea.[36] The efforts of the monarchy to make its authority prevail in ever greater areas of ecclesiastical life in America met with less resistance from the next pope, Gregory XIII. On 1 June 1574, therefore, Philip II defined the royal right of patronage in very inclusive terms: "... *ninguna persona secular ni ecclesiástica, orden, convento, religión, comunidad de cualquer estado, condición, calidad y preemencia que sean ... por cualquer ocasión y causa sea osado a se entremeter en cosa tocante a nuestro real patronazgo*" (... no secular or ecclesiastical individual, order, monastery, religious body, community of whatever estate, condition, quality and rank it may be ... for any occasion or reason whatsoever may venture to interfere in matters which affect our royal patronage).[37] At first the new regulations regarding the presentation and appointment of parish priests, as might have been expected, evoked vehement episcopal protests. Many bishops felt that their most specific duties were subject to the inspection and control of the secular administration. Far from all of them were so realistic as the Bishop of Santiago de Cuba, Juan del Castillo, who wrote to the king as early as 14 June 1570: "*Y en estas partes tanta authoridad tienen los prelados, cuanta V. Mag.t. les da*" (And the prelates have only as much authority in those areas as your majesty allows them).[38] But the crown proved the more resilient of the two parties. In time the initial exasperation died down, and once the lesser ecclesiastical positions were occupied the new practice became the norm.

Since 1524 a bishop resident in Spain, often based at the court, had always held what was therefore the honorary title of Patriarch of America. In accordance with its ecclesiastical politics based on the exercise of the royal prerogative, the crown now renewed its efforts to make the title effective as a supreme office of the Hispanic American hierarchy. Rome found the going arduous when it tried to oppose this policy; its attempt in 1582 to have an apostolic visitator appointed for the American church provinces was unsuccessful. Sixtus V finally had to accept that this office too was in the gift of the crown. In 1588 Philip II gave it to the bishop of Mexico, Don Pedro Moya de Contreras.[39] Nevertheless, in the same period the curia insisted on the "*visitatio liminum*" and compelled the bishops of America to appear in Rome every ten years. Because the journey required a very long absence from their dioceses, in practice the Holy See agreed to the bishops' representation by a delegate or agent who presented their report on the state of the diocese.[40]

To undermine the excessive interpretation and exercise of the right of patronage by the Spanish crown, theologians and lawyers developed the theory of the vicariate of the Spanish monarch over the American Church. Just as (so the argument went) Christ appointed the apostle Peter as his representative and since then the popes had governed the Church as vicars of Christ, by the bulls of 1493 Alexander VI had entrusted the Catholic monarchs and their successors with the office of mission to the heathen, and with the foundation and endowment of churches in the overseas territories. Accordingly it was permissible to describe the Spanish king as a papal vicar or even as a vicar of Christ. This theory, which accorded with Philip II's well-documented conception of himself as a kind of vice-pope for America (and for his other territories), was first formulated by the Franciscan Juan de Focher around 1570. At the beginning of the seventeenth century it was also adumbrated by other Franciscans such as Manuel Rodríguez, Juan Bautista and Luis de Miranda. Its most emphatic proponent, however, was the jurist Juan de Solórzano y Pereyra, a member of the Council for the Indies, whose work *De Indiarum jure*, published in 1636, expressed such an uncompromising secular-ecclesiastical form of regalism that in 1642 Rome placed it on the *Index of Forbidden Books*.[41]

On 6 January 1622, Gregory XV established in the curia a central authority for missionary activity, the *"Sacra Congregatio de Propaganda Fide"*. Because of growing dissatisfaction with the Spanish and Portuguese system of patronage, and because of the new colonial activities of France and other countries, the pope thereby established the right and duty of spreading the faith as the main task of his pastoral office. As far as possible, all forces active in the mission field were to be directly subordinated to the new congregation. To ensure this, the first secretary of the *Propaganda*, Cardinal Francesco Ingoli (1622–49), established agencies of his department in Seville and Lisbon. In three major memoranda of 1625, 1628 and 1644 Ingoli set forth his concept of the missions, and was not reluctant sharply to criticize the powers exercising the right of patronage.[42]

Whereas in time Rome did to some extent obtain a say in the affairs of the local churches in Asia and Africa, its claim in this respect was unavailing in America. The Spanish Cardinal Egidio Albornoz informed Madrid in 1636 that America had been assigned to him within the Congregation as his sphere of responsbility. He now desired the Crown's support for his work. The answer was somewhat curt: the Crown rejected any kind of curial interest in the work of the missions. It stressed moreover the exclusive responsibility of the Council of the Indies for correspondence with the staff of the missions in America. In addition, since 15 March 1629 the crown had required from all bishops in Spain a formal oath of recognition of the state right of patronage.[43] In subsequent decades the Crown and the Council for the Indies retained this precisely demarcated boundary between them and the *Propaganda*.[44]

In the exercise of its right of patronage, over some two centuries the state passed legal ordinances regarding all the numerous questions which arose in connection with the foundation and development of the Church in the New World. This gave rise to a finely-wrought network of secular church laws which derived from canon law but went far beyond it in matters of detail.[45] In 1680 a cohesive delineation of this Spanish state law of the Church for America appeared in the first book of the *Recopilación de leyes de los Reynos de las Indias*.[46] The prologue to this legal code states: "It has pleased God our Lord in his infinite mercy and loving-kindness to accord us through no merit of our own so great a share in the governance of this world . . . He has enjoined us more than any other prince in the world to bear the burdens of concern for his service and the proclamation of his name, and to use all those powers and all that might which he has given us so that he may be known and worshipped throughout the world as the true God, which he is, and as the creator of all things visible and invisible. Desiring thus to glorify our God and Lord, happily we have been able to bring to the bosom of the holy Roman Catholic Church the innumerable peoples and nations that inhabit the West Indies, islands and mainland beyond the ocean, and other territories subject to our rule".[47]

It was in this very context, justified so to speak by salvation history, that the crown discerned the ground of its right of patronage over the church. With reference to Philip II's definition of 1 June 1574, the *Recopilación* explains "*que este derecho de Patronazgo de las Indias único e insolidum siempre sea reservado á Nos y á nuestra Real Corona, y no pueda salir della en todo ni en parte, y por gracia, merced, privilegio o qualquier otra disposición, que Nos o los Reyes, nuestros Successores, hicieremos o concedieremos, no sea visto, que concedemos derecho de Patronazgo a persona alguna, Iglesia ni Monasterio, ni perjudicarnos en el dicho nuestro derecho de Patronazgo. Otrosi por costumbre, prescripción, ni otro titulo ninguna persona o personas, comunidad ecclesiastica ni seglar, Iglesia ni Monasterio puedan usar de derecho de Patronazgo, si no fuere la persona que en nuestro nombre y con nuestra autoridad y poder le exerciere*" (. . . that this sole and inviolable right to patronage over the Indies is perpetually reserved to us and to our royal Crown and may not be surrendered entirely or in part, whether for favour, reward, privilege or any other provision, that we or the kings our successors may make or grant; it is inconceivable that we would concede the right of patronage to any person, church or convent, or prejudice the same right of patronage. Whether by custom, prescription, or by any other title no person or persons, ecclesiastical or secular community, church or monastery may exercise the right of patronage, unless it is that person who in our name and by our authority can exercise it).[48] Thus the Spanish monarchy succeeded in controlling and supervising the affairs of the Church in America as far as possible to the exclusion of the papacy.

In Brazil, as in Hispanic America, colonization and missionary activity were closely connected. Here, too, the Portuguese monarchs could rely on the right of patronage, which they had received in 1522 and 1551 as grand masters of the three orders of knighthood (Ordem de Cristo, Ordem de São Bento [de Aviz] and Ordem de São Tiago da Espada). The right of patronage brought with it the task of promoting the evangelization and organization of the Church in the overseas territories, which considerably reduced the influence of Rome in Brazil too. The "*Conselho Ultramarino*" formulated ecclesiastical policy, and the "*Mesa da conciência e Ordens*" prepared the episcopal appointments. In 1551 Bahia received a bishop, and as a suffragan diocese was subordinated to the archdiocese of Funchal on Madeira. Like the bishops of Hispanic America, the Bishop of Bahia was dispensed from taking part in the Council of Trent.

From 1580 to 1640 Spain was responsible for political rule in Portugal. In this period the bishops of Bahia were proposed by the Spanish monarch and appointed in accordance with the right of patronage. The Calvinist Dutch, who were at war with Spain, occupied north-eastern Brazil from 1630 to 1654. Consequently the episcopal see of Bahia remained vacant for three decades.

After the expulsion of the Dutch and the conclusion of peace between Spain and Portugal, church affairs in Brazil were reorganized. In Olinda (Pernambuco), where there had been a prelature since 1614, and in Rio de Janeiro, dioceses were established in 1676 and placed under Bahia, which became an archdiocese in the same year. In 1677 a further diocese was established in São Luis de Maranhão, which was however directly dependent on Lisbon. Gradually the organization of the church grew stronger as the colonial population increased. In the eighteenth century further dioceses were set up in Belem do Para (1719), Mariana and São Paulo (both in 1745), and two prelatures in Goias and Cuiaba (both also in 1745). Overall, the extension of the ecclesiastical organization in Brazil was essentially slower and less systematic than in Hispanic America.[49]

From the beginning of its history the Church in Latin America entered into a close relationship with the Spanish or Portuguese state because of the right of patronage. Consequently, at least as far as hierarchy and clergy were concerned, it had a largely European countenance. This impeded the enculturation of the Christian faith among the peoples of Latin America. The same historical encumbrance is still discernible in our own times.

Translated from the German by John Cumming

NOTES

1. Christoph Kolumbus, *Bordbuch – Briefe – Berichte – Dokumente*, ed. E.G. Jacob (Bremen, 1957), p. 133.

2. H. Jedin, "Weltmission und Kolonialismus," *Saeculum* 9 (1958), pp. 393–404, cf 394; R. Konetzke, "Forschungsprobleme zur Geschichte der Religion und ihrer Bedeutung in den Kolonisationen Amerikas", *Saeculum* 10 (1959), pp. 82–101, cf 97–100.

3. The following are the relevant documents:

a. The brief *Inter cetera* of 3 May 1493 (ed. M. G. Fernández, "Nuevas consideraciones sobre la historia y el sentido de las letras alejandrinas de 1493 referentes a las Indias," *Anuario de Estudios Americanos 1* (1944), pp. 171–429, cf 205–7 and 341–69;

b. The bull *Inter cetera* of 4May and 28 June 1493 (M. G. Fernández, "Nuevas consideraciones," pp. 209–12 and 341–69);

c. The bull *Piis fidelium* of 25 June 1493 (Fernández, pp. 207–9 and 371–9);

d. The brief *Eximiae devotionis sinceritas* of 3 July 1493, back-dated to 3 May 1493 (Fernández, pp. 212ff and 341–69.

e. The bull *Dudum si quidem omnes* of 26 September 1493 (Fernández, pp. 213–5 and 381–7).

4. F. Frita, "Fray Bernal Buyl y Cristobal Colón. Nueva colección de cartas reales, enriquecida con algunas inéditas," *Boletín de la Real Academía de la Historia* (1891), pp. 171–233.

5. Peter Martyr von Anghiera, *Acht Dekaden über die Neue Welt*, ed. H. Klingelhöfer: Vols I-II (Darmstadt, 1972–5), cf first decade II/11[46].

6. *Real cédula* of 23 April 1497: *Colección de documentos inéditos relativos al descubrimiento, conquista y organización [colonización] de las antiguas posesiones españolas de América y Oceania . . . .* (CDIA), 1–42 (Madrid, 1864–84), cf 38, pp. 358–64, quotation on p. 359.

7. *Real cédula*, undated of 1497: CDIA 30, pp. 457–64, cf 462.

8. Bartolomé de Las Casas, *Historia de las Indias: Obras escogidas*, I-II, ed. J. P. de Tudela Bueso in BAE 95 and 96 (Madrid, 1957 and 1961), cf I, p. 131 (N. 95, p. 352).

9. F. J. Hernáez, *Colección de bulas, breves y otros documentos relativos a la iglesia de América y Filipinas*, vols I-II (Brussels, 1879), cf I, pp. 20f.

10. *Colección de documentos*. Second series (= CDIU), 1–25 (Madrid, 1885–1932), cf 5, pp. 86–91.

11. W. E. Shiels, "King and Church. The Rise and Fall of the Patronato Real", *Jesuit Studies* (Chicago, 1961), pp. 105–7.

12. F. Fita, "Primeros años del episcopado en América," *Boletín de la Real Academia de la Historia*, 20 (Madrid, 1892), pp. 261–300, cf 276–9.

13. CDIA 34, pp. 25–9, cf 28.

14. CDIA 23, pp. 290–309, cf 290.

15. Fita, "Primeros años" (n. 12), p. 285.

16. Ibid., pp. 292–4.

17. CDIA 34, pp. 29–35; Fita, "Primeros años" (n. 12), pp. 295–300.

18. E. W. Loughraan, "The first episcopal sees in Spanish America," *The Hispanic American Review*, 10 (1930), pp. 167–87, cf 177–80 and 184–7.

19. CDIU 15, pp. 43–9; W. J. Shiels, "King and Church" (n. 11), pp. 127–30.

20. Hernáez, *Colección de bulas* (n. 9), II, p. 6.

21. E. Schäfer, *El Consejo Real y Supremo de las Indias*, vols I and II (Seville, 1935 and 1947), cf I, pp. 26f and 33–70; P. B. Morán, "La Santa Sede y América en el siglo XVI," *Estudios Americanos* 21 (1961), pp. 141–68, cf 148–52.

22. *Real cédula* to Fuenmayor of October 26th 1536, *Archivo General de Indias, Sevilla, Santo Domingo*, p. 868, 1, f.6.

23. J. de S. y Pereyra, *Política indiana*. Estudio preliminar por M. A. Ochoa Brun, BAE 252–6 (Madrid, 1972), cf lib. IV, cap. IV, n. 1 (254, p. 42).

24. *Recopilación de leyes de los Reynos de las Indias*. Prólogo por R. M. Pidal, estudio preliminar de J. M. Manzano, vols I-IV (Madrid, 1973), cf lib. I, tit. VII, ley 3 (I, ff. 31 v.).

25. A. C. van Oss, "Comparing colonial bishoprics in Spanish South America," *Boletín de Estudios Latinoamericanos y del Caribe* 24 (1978), pp. 27–66, cf 33.

26. F. X. Delany, *A History of the Catholic Church in Jamaica BWI 1494 to 1929* (NY, 1930), p. 11.

27. Letter of 12 July 1544, the day of arrival in San Lúcar de Barrameda, to the emperor: *Archivo General de Indias, Sevilla, Santo Domingo* 993, No. 12.

28. B. de Tobar, *Compendio Bulario Indico*, vols. I-II, ed. M. G. de Arce, PEEH 82 and 167 (Seville, 1954 aand 1965), cf I, pp. 275–7.

29. Schäfer, *El Consejo Real* (n. 21), II, p. 201.

30. Ibid., p. 351.

31. Ibid., II, pp. 207–10, 568–70, 590f and 594–6.

32. D. M. Roth, *The Friar Estates of the Philippines* (Albuquerque-New Mexico, 1977), p. 25.

33. M. Mananzan, "A History of the Church in the Philippines," M. D. David (ed.), *Asia and Christianity* (Bombay, 1985), pp. 53–66.

34. E. Dussel, *Historia general de la iglesia en América Latina*, I/1: Introducción general a la historia de la iglesia en América Latina (Salamanca, 1983), pp. 446–9.

35. *Recopilación* (n. 24), lib. I, tit. II, ley 3 (I, f. 7 vv) and ley 6 (I, f. 8 r.).

36. H. Jedin, *Weltmission und Kolonialismus* (n. 2), p. 396.

37. R. C. Padden, "The *Ordenanza del Patronazgo* 1574. An interpretative essay," *The Americas* 12 (1955–6), pp. 333–54, cf 352.

38. *Archivo General de las Indias, Sevilla, Santo Domingo*, p. 115, f. 245 r.

39. P. B. Morán, *La Santa Sede y América en el siglo XVI* (n. 21), pp. 165–7.

40. R. R. Lluch & V. C. Maiques, "La visita 'Ad Limine' durante el pontificado de Sixto V (1585–90). Datos para una estadística general. Su complimiento en Iberoamérica," *Anthologica Annua* 7 (1959), pp. 147–213.

41. A. de Egana, "La teoría del regio vicariato español en Indias," *Analecta Gregoriana* 95 Series Facultatis Historiae Ecclesiasticae, Sectio BB, No. 17 (Rome, 1958).

42. E. Burrus, "Un programa positivo: La actuación misionera de Propaganda Fide en Hispanoamérica," ed. J. Metzler, *Sacrae Congregationis de propaganda fide memoria rerum*, vol. I/2: 1622–1700 (Freiburg, 1972), pp. 648–66, cff 655f.

43. *Recopilación* (n. 424), lib. I, tit. VII, ley 1 (I, f. 30 v. - 31 r).

44. After the formation of the Propaganda congregation, 155 years passed before two new dioceses were again founded in Hispanic America: Nerida amnd Linares (1777). Sonora followed them, also during the pontificate of Pius VI, in 1779. Another six dioceses were established – again under Pius VI – before the end of Spanish colonial rule: Cuenca (1786), Havana (1787), as well Santo Tomé de la Guayana (1790), and under Pius VII, Mainas (1803), Antioquia-Medellín (1804) and Salta (1806), the last foundation of a diocese in the Spanish period. In addition, Santiago de Cuba and Caracas became archdioceses in 1803; Guatamela had been similarly elevated in 1743.

45. B. Biermann, "Das spanisch-portugiesische Patronat als Laienhilfe für die Mission," J.

Specker & W. Bühlmann, eds, "Das Laienapostolat in den Missionen," *Neue Zeitschrift für Missionswissenschaft*, Supplementa 10 (Schöneck-Beckenried, 1961), pp. 161–79, cf 171–3.
   46. *Recopilación* (n. 24), lib. I, tit. I – XXIV (I, f. 1 r – 125 v).
   47. *Recopilación* (n. 24), lib. I, tit. I, ley 1 (I, f. 1 r.).
   48. *Recopilación* (n. 24), lib. I, tit. VI, ley 11 (I, f. 21).
   49. R. Azzi, "A instituição eclesiástica durante a primeira época colonial," E. Hoornaert (ed.), *Historia da Igreja no Brasil. Ensaio de interpretação a partir do povo. Primeira Epoca 1500–1808)*: *Historia General da Igreja na America Latina* II/1 (Petrópolis, 3a ed. 1983), pp. 153–242.

CHRONOLOGY

1493 In five documents Alexander VI confirms the Spanish crown's possession of the territories discovered by Columbus. He appoints Fr Bernal Boyl vicar apostolic of these lands.
1501 Alexander VI assigns to the Spanish crown the tithes from these territories, enjoining it to found churches there and endow them appropriately.
1508 Julius II bestows on the Spanish crown the right of patronage over the church in the course of establishment in *Las Indias*.
1511 Julius II founds the first dioceses in *Las Indias*: Santo Domingo and Concepción de la Vega on "Hispaniola" and San Juan on Puerto Rico; as suffragan dioceses they are subordinated to the archdiocese of Seville.
1524 The *Consejo Real y Supremo de las Indias* is set up as the central council of the Spanish crown for all Spanish-American – including ecclesiastical – affairs.
1525 The first diocese in Mexico is founded in Tlaxcala. The see is transferred to Puebla in 1539.
1537 The first diocese of South America is established in Cuzco.
1546 Three ecclesiastical provinces are established in America: Santo Domingo (with Cóncepcion de la Vega, San Juan de Puerto Rico, Santiago de Cuba, Coro, Santa Marta, Cartagena and Trujillo/Honduras); Mexico (with Puebla, Michoacán, Oaxaca, Chiapas and Guatemala); Lima (with León/Nicaragua, Panama, Quito and Cuzco).
1551 The first diocese of Brazil is founded in Salvador da Bahia.
1564 Santa Fe de Bogotá becomes the fourth ecclesiastical province in America (suffragan dioceses: Cartagena, Popayán and Santa Marta).
1568 Philip II summons the *Junta Magna*; decrees and reforms of the Council of Trent are applied to the church in Hispanic America, and the crown's right of patronage is intensified.
1609 A further ecclesiastical province is established in South America: Charcas de la Plata (with Asunción, Santiago de Chile, Concepción, Córdoba, Santa Cruz and La Paz).
1620 The number of dioceses in Hispanic America rises to 35 with the establishment of Durango in Mexico and Buenos Aires.
1622 Gregory XV founds the *Sacra Congregatio de Propaganda Fide* as the central curial authority for the missions. The Council of the Indies refuses to allow the curia any part in the ecclesiastical affairs of Latin America. For 155 years no new dioceses are founded in Hispanic America.
1676 Reorganization of ecclesiastical affairs in Brazil: Bahia becomes an archdiocese; the new dioceses of Olinda and Ro de Janeiro are subordinated to Bahia.
1680 Spanish state ecclesiastical law is presented in the first book of the *Recopilación de leyes de los Reynos de las Indias*.

SELECT BIBLIOGRAPHY

Borges Morán, Pedro. *El envío de misioneros a América durante la época española*. Bibliotheca Salmanticensis, Estudios 18. Salamanca, 1977.
Paulo Florêncio, Camargo da Silveira. *Historia eclesiástica do Brasil*. Petrópolis, 1955.
Driesch, Wilhelm von den. *Grundlagen einer Sozialgeschichte der Philippinen unter spanischer Herrschaft 1565–1820*. Frankfurt a.M., 1984.
Dussel, Enrique. *Les Evêques Hispano-Américains, défenseurs et évangelisateurs de l'indien (1504–1620)*. Institut für Euopäische Geschichte, Mainz, vol. 58. Wiesbaden, 1970.

Dussel, Enrique. *Introducción general a la historia de la iglesia en América Latina: Historia general de la iglesia en América Latina I/1*. Salamanca, 1983.

Egaña, Antonio de. *Historia de la iglesia en la América española desde el descubrimiento hasta comienzos del siglo XIX. Hemiferio Sur*. Biblioteca de Autores Cristianos 256. Madrid, 1966.

Hoornaert, Eduardo. *Formação do catolicismo brasileiro 1550–1800. Ensaio de interpretação a partir dos oprimidos*. Petrópolis, 1974.

Konetzke, Richard. "Die Indianerkulturen Altamerikas und die spanisch- portugiesische Kolonialherrschaft: Süd- und Mittelamerika", I. *Fischer-Weltgeschichte* vol. 22. Frankfurt a.M: 6th ed., 1977.

Leturia, Pedro. *Relaciones entre la Santa Sede e Hispanoamérica 1493–1835. I: Epoca del Real Patronato 1493–1800*, ed. Antonio de Egaña. Rome & Caracas, 1959.

Lopetegui, León and Felix, Zubillaga. *Historia de la iglesia en la América española desde el descubrimiento hasta comienzos del siglo XIX. Mexico, América Central, Antillas*. Biblioteca de Autores Cristianos 248. Madrid, 1965.

Sousa Montenegro, João Alfredo de. *Evolução do catolicismo no Brasil*. Petrópolis, 1972.

Tormo, Leandro. *Historia de la iglesia en América Latina. I: La evangelización de la América Latina*. Estudios Socio-Religiosos Latino-Americanos 8. Fribourg & Bogotá, 1962.

Chapter 4

DAILY LIFE IN THE INDIES
(Seventeenth and early Eighteenth Centuries)

Manuel María Marzal, SJ

This chapter is concerned with the *daily life* of baptized people in the Church in Latin America. A study of daily life is relevant at this point, since it is a necessary complement to that of the evangelizing process and the workings of the institutional Church, made in the preceding chapters. Such a study should analyze all aspects of colonial Catholicism: belief in God, in Jesus Christ, in the Virgin Mary, in saints and devils; the ritual practice of prayer, the sacraments and sacramentals; the organization of parishes and confraternities, and the particular mode in which Indians and blacks belonged to a Church so closely tied, through the system of royal patronage, to the state that oppressed them. Finally, it should look at how the commandments were observed in a society shot through with the contradictions of colonial rule, but still capable of producing true saints in all sectors of society. This is shown by seventeenth-century Lima (though one cannot generalize from this example): this produced the archbishop Toribius of Mogrovejo, the Franciscan Francisco Solano and the Dominican Juan Macías – Spaniards; the laywoman Rose of Lima, the Jesuit Francisco del Castillo and the Mercedarian Pedro de Urraca – *criollos*; the Dominican Martín de Porras – black, and the layman Nicolás de Ayllón – Indian. All have had the cause of their canonization put forward and most have been canonized.

It is not, however, possible to detail all this information, covering the whole of Spanish and Portuguese colonial America, in the space of a chapter. So, after setting out my approach and a typology of Latin American colonial Catholicism, I propose to examine its daily life in two of its aspects: the rites of patronal festivals and pilgrimages, which can both be considered "complete social happenings" and reveal the foundational religious experience of the Church in Latin America. So there are four sections to this chapter: 1. Approach and qualifications; 2. Typology of Latin American colonial Catholicism; 3. Patronal festivals and pilgrimages; 4. Foundational religious experience.

1. APPROACH AND QUALIFICATIONS

There is no doubt that a better understanding of history can be achieved through shuffling different viewpoints. So a view of history from the standpoint of ruling groups and based on great events is usefully complemented by a view from the "base" of society and rooted in "daily life." This is what CEHILA's recent *Historia General de la Iglesia en América Latina* sets out to do. There Enrique Dussel writes:

> This part, the most important in this work, is nevertheless the most difficult, and, given the state of research in Latin America, it can be said that it will be

a long time before the matter can be dealt with adequately. . . . In [American] Christendom a kind of dualism was produced between the hierarchical church institution, which was linked to the state structures in political society, and the "Christian people" . . . . [These] are civil society hegemonized by the ruling *bloc* in power, but at the same time members of the Church. So to speak of the "daily life" of the Christian people is simply to speak of the *life* of the Latin American people in the colonial epoch.

This *life* was Christian, or at least religious, in its deepest structures. The matter is not one just of "spirituality" or "confraternities," but of the whole of life, of everyday life, as it related to the absolute. And the *life* of our people – the Amerindians themselves, the Spaniards, *criollos*, slaves – was wholly made up of their *religious* attitude. The daily field of their lives was the "*religious field*."[1]

This approach is followed in this chapter, which takes account of the separate chapters on daily life in various parts of the continent in the *Historia General*.[2] Two preliminary qualifications:

First, I am confining myself to daily life *in the religious field*, taking "religion" in both its objective dimension of "a system of beliefs and ritual and ethical practices, which refer to the sacred world and group their adepts in a church" (Durkheim), and its subjective dimension of "a system of symbols which produces deep and lasting attitudes and motivations in believers, through an overall conception of the meaning of life, manifested as completely real" (Geertz). And let us not forget that in Latin America everyday Catholicism developed, for historical and social reasons, into something expressed above all in rites and emotions.

My second qualification relates to time limits. I deal not with daily religious life throughout the colonial era, but only in the period consisting of the seventeenth century and the first half of the eighteenth. The limits are, of course, not arbitrary: the period begins with the seventeenth century because this is when evangelization was consolidated, even though in the previous century missionaries baptized large numbers of the indigenous peoples and established the main lines of pastoral policy through the provincial councils (the Third Council of Lima in 1582–3 and the Third of Mexico in 1585). It ends with the first half of the eighteenth century because the second half brought major changes under the influence of the Enlightenment. As I have written elsewhere on the consolidation of Christianity in Peru:

> I consider the religious transformation of the indigenous population of Peru through the action of the Church towards the end of the seventeenth century sufficiently proved. This transformation took place in the population of the Tawantinsuyu as a whole, though not in the same way or to the same extent in each or all of the ethnic groups of the coastal or mountain areas, through acceptance of an overall system of beliefs, rites, forms of organization and ethical norms of Christian origin, even though many Indians, especially in the Southern Andean region, still kept and integrated elements of their old Andean system, thereby producing a more or less syncretic system.[3]

Similar studies have been made of Mexico, and the authors of the chapters on daily life in the *Historia General* all, in one way or another, agree that the majority of the population both felt themselves to be and were truly Christian.

2. TYPOLOGY OF COLONIAL CATHOLICISM

Although Latin American colonial Catholicism was and still is fairly homogeneous, so that most Catholics on the continent would recognize themselves in the synthesis the bishops make of the "people's religiosity" in the Puebla document (nos. 454–6)[4], it is also true that different versions of this Catholicism appeared in various parts of the vast continent. This diversity is due to several factors: the missionary approach employed, the degree of resistance by the native or black population and the numbers of Catholics transplanted from the homelands. A good analysis of the diversity of popular Catholicism has been made by the Brazilian anthropologist Darcy Ribeiro. He maintains that the present non-European peoples "can be classified in four main historico-cultural groups . . . each sufficiently homogeneous as to their basic ethnic characteristics and in relation to the problems of development they face." He calls these groups *witness*, *new*, *transplanted* and *emergent* peoples, and of them he writes:

> [The *Witness Peoples*] are made up of the modern representatives of the old autonomous civilizations on which European expansion descended. The second group, called *New Peoples*, is represented by those American peoples formed over recent centuries as a sub-product of European expansion by the fusion and acculturation of indigenous, black and European matrices. The third, *Transplanted Peoples*, is made up of the nations constituted by the implantation of European expatriate contingents who retained their original ethnic profile, language and culture. Finally, the *Emergent Peoples* group is made up of the new nations from Africa and Asia, whose populations have risen from tribal level or the condition of mere colonial forced labour to form national ethnic groups.[5]

Applying this typology to Latin America, Mexico and Peru must certainly be classified as *witness peoples*, Brazil and Colombia as *new* and Argentina and Uruguay as *transplanted*. And the same can be said of their respective Catholicisms. But we need to bear in mind that this typology also serves to analyze regional differences within each country produced by the colonizing and evangelizing processes carried out by Spain and Portugal.

The various Spanish colonies in America are known to have been "kingdoms with two republics," in the classic formula of Solórzano Pereyra, meaning a "republic of Spaniards" in the cities, many of which soon acquired a surrounding belt of black slave population, and a "republic of Indians" in the rural communities, where the scattered native populations were collected so as to ensure their Christianization and insertion in the colonial system through tributes and enforced service, particularly the *mita* in the mines, which were the real engine of the colonial economy. Both republics kept a certain cultural and even political autonomy, the matrix in which their particular Catholicism was forged, but complete separation between the two was rendered increasingly impossible with the spread of *mestizaje* (racial interbreeding),[6] and because the Spaniards increasingly settled in the villages/reductions and used various methods of attracting native workers to their estates.

In the Portuguese colonies, the situation was fairly similar, with cities/workplaces peopled by Portuguese with black or native slave populations, and indigenous "village settlements." *Mestizaje* was also a daily occurrence, and even officially encouraged at the end of the period under review, when the Marqués de Pombal tried to "lusitanize" the native village settlements of Pará and Maranhão, which had been under the control of the Jesuits.[7]

We can now specify four types of Latin American popular religion, corresponding to Ribeiro's four groups. I propose to call these syncretic, mestizo, transplanted and emergent popular religion.

(1) *Syncretic Catholicism.* This is found in those regions where evangelization, though it brought about a true religious change, met most resistance, owing to the tenacity and complexity of native religious traditions, as in the high cultures of the Andes and Mesoamerica, particularly the Southern Andean region of Peru, the *altiplano* of Bolivia and the high Mayan regions of Mexico and Guatemala. Perhaps this first type ought also to include regions with a high black slave population, such as Haiti and the central coast of Brazil, even though evangelization there did not produce a real religious transformation, but simply acceptance of baptism and feasts and confraternities of the "saints."

(2) *Mestizo Catholicism.* This belongs to those parts of the continent where evangelization met with less resistance and where the native or black religious traditions, belonging to fewer people or being less deeply rooted in their cultures, were assimilated by a Catholicism of worship and catechesis, though not without leaving their mark on the new religious system. This was the outcome of evangelization among many American ethnic groups which had not achieved a "high culture," such as those of Chile and Paraguay, where a notable example of inculturated evangelization flourished in the Jesuit reductions, as recounted by Ruiz de Montoya.[8] Mestizo Catholicism also arose in places where there had been a high culture, such as the coastal regions of Peru, or the Mexican meseta, where evangelization was more effective or the population became mixed. This second type should also include the black population of the Pacific region (Mexico, Peru, Ecuador and Colombia), who do not celebrate ancestral forms of worship such as *Candomblé* in Brazil or Voodoo in Haiti.

(3) *Transplanted Catholicism.* This belongs to those parts of the continent occupied almost exclusively by emigrant Europeans, coming either as colonizers during the colonial period or later as emigrants to already independent countries. They *transplanted* their old culture and with it their Catholicism to their new habitat. This happened in the early Spanish cities (so St Rose of Lima was called St Rose of Seville), and later in Uruguay, the greater part of Argentina and Southern Brazil. One must, however, bear in mind that in these parts there was also a transplanted Italian or German Catholicism, which became more or less assimilated to the matrix of Iberian Catholicism which had arrived earlier.

(4) *Emergent popular religion.* As we saw, Ribeiro had a fourth group in his typology, though he could not use it to analyze the American cultural sphere. But it does work in the religious sphere, and so I am adopting it. The history of Latin America is full of *emergent* popular religions. They begin as informal or salvationist cults, but always form part of the religious scene on which the daily

life of the Christian people unfolds. An example from the Mayan region is the "*María candelaria*" movement in Chiapas in 1712, to which the Dominican chronicler Francisco de Ximénez, writing in 1722,[9] devotes twenty chapters, and which I have studied on the basis of detailed information culled from the Archive of the Indies.[10] David Gow, in a 1979 issue of the review *América Indígena* devoted to indigenous religious movements, compares the saving movements of Chiapas in 1712 and 1868–70 with those of Taki Onqoy in 1565 and Lircay (Huancavelica) in the Peruvian Andes in 1811.[11]

There are also numerous modern examples, which confirm the existence of a Latin American matrix behind the frequent emergence of new religions. An example from Peru is the "Crossed Catholic, Apostolic, Evangelical and Peruvian Church," founded by a Brazilian, Brother José Francisco de la Cruz (of the Cross), who carried out healings and preached revivalist religion in the 1960s in the Ucayali and Amazon river valleys.[12] Another example, from Mexico, is the New Jerusalem organization, a religious centre and destination of many pilgrimages in the town of Puruarán (Michoacán), founded by a priest, Nabor Cárdenas, on the basis of a supposed apparition of the Virgin to a Tarasca girl[13]. A final example comes from Peru in 1968: a Quechua peasant, Ezequiel Ataucusi Gamonal, who claimed to have been taken up into heaven and to be the incarnation of the Holy Spirit, founded the "Evangelical Association of the Israelite Mission of the New Universal Pact," which reintroduced Jewish Old Testament worship and attracted many adherents of Andean origin, in rural areas and the peripheral *barrios* of the cities.[14] A consideration of emergent Latin American popular religion should also take account not only of new churches, but also of plain cults, such as that of Sarita Colonia in Peru, "The Defunct Correa" in Argentina or María Lionza in Venezuela.

3. PATRONAL FESTIVALS AND PILGRIMAGES

There is no doubt that, throughout the seventeenth century and the first half of the eighteenth, daily life was strongly marked by the Church. With its pastoral aims well planned in the provincial Councils and Synods, an adequate number of parish priests and large numbers of religious in convents, the Church took care of worship and most of education and charitable works in a fairly stable colonial society, to which it was thoroughly tied through the system of royal patronage. Most of the population of the Iberian cities and – to a lesser but still significant extent – of the native reductions and estates or plantations received baptism, went to mass with reasonable regularity, made their Easter duties (confession and communion), took part in patronal festivals and went on pilgrimages to regional sanctuaries, and received the Church's final benediction in the sacrament of extreme unction or burial rites. It is true that this religious practice was backed up with a certain amount of pressure and canonical sanctions (people were called for annual confession, for example, from the tax-list, and those who failed to comply could be excommunicated). The same sanctions were also largely operative in Spain and Portugal, but could more easily be applied to Indians and blacks, who were a conquered or slave population and "new Christians."

As I have said, there is no space here to examine the whole of daily religious life, and I propose to confine myself to patronal festivals and pilgrimages; despite being mere "sacramentals," these were the two most important collective rites, and can be called "complete social happenings," since they reveal so many elements, not just of Latin American society, but above all of its spirituality. I think these two rites lead us to the religious personality – Iberian, Indian, black, mestizo and mulatto – of the colonial world, which is still present in the hearts and minds of our people today.

Before proceeding to analyze each in turn, let me recall what I mean by "rite." By this I mean a form of communication with the sacred, made up of gestures and words, socially accepted and handed down from generation to generation, which is both a reflection of faith held and a symbol through which to express this, which identifies the believing group and which can be reinterpreted, changing its original significance.

(a) Latin American Patronal Festivals

Patronal festivals were at once something brought deliberately by the missionaries as an effective pastoral instrument of mass evangelization, and the most visible religious expression of the colonists in the "republics of Spaniards." While transmission of Christian beliefs to the native population proved a slow and difficult process, transmission of rites – as always happens through the very ambiguity of their language, which lends itself to reinterpretation to suit those who carry out the rites – was easier and fairly quick. The Inca Garcilaso has left us an early account of the feast of Corpus Christi as he saw it during his adolescence in Cuzco:

> Each one of them [the *encomenderos* from around Cuzco] had taken care to decorate the floats which their vassals had to carry in the festival procession ... And inside the floats they placed an image of Our Lord or Our Lady or another saint ... The floats looked like those carrried by the confraternities on such feast days in Spain ... [The Indians] carried all the decorations, ornaments and instruments which they used to celebrate their principal feasts in the time of their Inca kings ... Some wore lion skins ... , others carried the wings of a very large bird which they call *cuntur* [condor] ... And so others came with other painted emblems, such as fountains, rivers, lakes, mountains, caves, because they said that their first fathers came from such things ... With these things those Indians solemnized the feasts of their kings, with the same things (adding to them as much as they were able) they celebrated in my times the feasts of the Most Holy Sacrament ... as people now disabused of their gentile past.[15]

Although this last phrase is debatable and perhaps more a reflection of what the old chronicler, writing in distant Córdoba, would have liked to be true, than of the religious reality of Cuzco in the fifth and sixth decades of the sixteenth century, his account undoubtedly confirms full participation in the festival, in which each *ayllu* carried the symbol of his own *pagarina*, and the solemn celebration of which has continued to the present. The feast of Corpus Christi in Cuzco was no exception, but rather an example of a fairly generalized situation. It seems proven that such celebrations were held in both the two "republics" of Spaniards and Indians. This is fully valid at least for feasts from the calendar of saints, for each "saint" belonging to a church with the appropriate confraternity. I doubt whether the liturgical cycle, based on the history of salvation, made much impact on many native peoples, not so much because catechesis and preaching were non-christocentric, as because many festivals from the cycle were celebrated only in the main church of a widespread parish, whereas many Indians still lived scattered about its territory. This fact became more evident with the gradual decline in clergy numbers throughout the nineteenth century, so leading to the present situation in which many Indian peoples celebrate only the feast of their patron saint.

This, however, took root with incredible force, owing to the fact that the cult of the "saints" and its most typical expression, the patronal festival, became the catalyzing agent of dawning colonial society. Though this festival sprang from the Church's pastoral need to establish "strong times" in Christian daily life, and also resulted from the transplantation of the same cycle in Spain, as it arrived at the time when the "republics of the Indians" were coming into being, it turned into a catalyst for the concerns of the priests, who sought to evangelize, of the colonial officials, who sought to found stable settlements so as to control the Indians, and of the Indians themselves, who, faced with the overthrow of their own gods, sought to restore the religious base of their world view and that of their social solidarity. This process, which I have analyzed elsewhere as it applied in Peru,[16] was carried out almost universally among the Indian peoples of colonial America. Eric Wolf, who has studied the process in Mesoamerica, writes: "In our day it is still possible to refer to a community and to see it as a direct descendant of one rebuilt in the seventeenth century," and whose motive centre is the religious festival.[17]

The celebration of colonial festivals was organized by confraternities, which were lay organizations devoted to the cult of a particular image and to promoting various forms of assistance among their members. They owned land, herds and money, the fruit of donations, and flourished greatly on American soil. One significant point is that the provincial Councils acted not to promote confraternities, but rather to put a brake on their growth. For example, the First Council of Lima, as early as 1551, laid down that "in future in the whole of our archbishopric and province no new confraternities shall be formed without our express approval or that of the bishop," and the Third Council of Lima, in 1582, added that confraternites should "as far as possible be reduced to a smaller number," with the express prohibition of "giving the title of confraternity to bands and conventicles of dark-skinned persons or slaves." Leaving this last observation aside for the moment, there is no doubt that the confraternities, during the period under review, were enormously important throughout Spanish and Portuguese America. To take two examples: (1) Bishop Mollinedo y Angulo of Cuzco made wide pastoral visits to his diocese in 1674–5 and again in 1687, and also asked his priests for detailed statistics of their parishes. The reports of his visits, which I have found in the Archives of the Indies, and the accounts from the priests, which have been published,[18] fully confirm their importance. Another bishop, Cortés y Larraz, visiting his diocese of Guatemala in 1772, left detailed information on the confraternities there, of which he found "1963 in number, corresponding to 145 different advocations with a capital of 390,035 pesos and 3 reals, with 41,829 heads of cattle and 10,414 of horses and mules."[19]

The great number of confraternities is explained by the function they served in American colonial society. In effect, they were functional for the priests, who saw them as useful instruments in evangelization, devotion to the saints, sacramental practice, mutual solidarity and charity to the needy. And they were functional in strengthening group solidarity in a caste society, since there were confraternities of "Spaniards," of "blacks" and of "Indians." Good studies have been made of how the confraternities helped in restoring old solidarities, broken by the conquest and by the colonial policy of "reductions."

What is clear, however, is that Indians and blacks used the confraternities not only to rebuild their ethnic identities, but also to carry on practising their ancestral worship in a clandestine manner. In the Andes and Mesoamerica this was particularly true in the sixteenth century, as many witnesses testify, but it seems to have happened too among the slave populations of Brazil and Haiti throughout the seventeenth and eighteenth centuries. For Brazil, Eduardo Hoornaert has described how many slave confraternities, after taking part in the festival of the saint, "held their dances in the evening in front of the churches, and at night practised their worship."[20] And for Haiti, Alfred Metraux maintains that in the *Description de la partie française de Saint-Domingue* (1792), there is a detailed description of Voodoo with "rites and practices that have not changed down to our days. The authority of the priest, his robes, the importance of trance, the patterns traced on the ground, are all familiar elements."[21]

To return to festivals, social scientists have analyzed the various functions they perform today: a religious function, since devotion is paid to the "saints" and their protection sought; a festive function, a break from the daily monotony and an affirmation of life even to excess, through a symbolic language that refers back to the normally hidden, deep side of life and gives reasons for living; a prestige function, since it promotes social recognition of those who "carry the burden," even though in most places there is no longer a "scale of burdens," nor are these strictly obligatory; an integrating function, binding members of a community who live outside the economy of self-sufficiency together among themselves, with the emigrants who return for the festival, and with the dead, who celebrated it for so many years. They also perform an economic function, since the high cost of the festival contributes, through expenditure that benefits everyone, to a certain levelling-out of income, or at least a justification of different levels of income. These multiple functions of festivals explain their persistence, despite the fact that many priests, who were their chief promoters in colonial Christendom, now have little interest in encouraging them, seeing little pastoral value in them.

(b) Pilgrimages

Just like patronal festivals, pilgrimages took deep root in America. They did this because they embodied not only an Iberian tradition, but also a native one, at least in the high cultures and among the Tupí-Guaranís, who undertook messianic migrations in search of the "land without evil." Bernabé Cobo, writing in 1653, describes the pre-Hispanic Andean world as having "rich and most sumptuous temples, like sanctuaries of general devotion, to which people went on pilgrimage from all parts of Peru, just as Christians used to go to"

Jerusalem, Rome and Santiago de Compostela, the three major pilgrimage centres of the Middle Ages; these were Coricancha in Cuzco, Pachacamac on the central coast and Copacabana on Lake Titicaca.[22]

It is this convergence of traditions that explains the proliferation of sanctuaries on the continent. All countries have them, but to take the case of Bolivia as an example, Josep Barnadas has described the three great sixteenth-century sanctuaries. These were: *Nuestra Señora de la Gracia de Pukarani* (La Paz), where pilgrims venerated an image carved in 1589 by the Indian Francisco Titu Yupanki, of which Calancha wrote: "no great sculptor could have made it as beautiful, as devout or as majestic"; Our Lady of *Qupakhuwana*, whose image was also carved by Yupanki, and whose cult, as Cobo describes, was linked to the Inca sanctuaries of the Moon and the Sun; and The Cross of *Q'araphuku* (or Carabuco), also linked to the Andean religious substrate through an Aymara oral tradition of Thunupa, who became identified with one of the apostles (Bartholomew or Thomas), whose cross it was that was "found" in 1599. Barnadas continues:

> During the seventeenth and eighteenth centuries, the number of Christian and Marian sanctuaries in Charcas went on increasing: Our Lady of the Nativity (in Peñas), Our Lady of the Candlestick (in Potosí), Our Lady of the Cherry Tree (in Chirka), Our Lady of the Star (in Chuchulaya), Our Lady of the Snows (in Irupana), Our Lady of Apumalla (in La Paz), Our Lady of the Cavern (in Oruro) among those of Mary; those devoted to Christ included The Lord of Killakas (in Killakas), The Lord of the Holy True Cross (in Cochabamba), The Lord of Mankiri (in Mankiri), all of which have remained centres of mass pilgrimage.[23]

Colonial Ibero-american sanctuaries all had certain features in common. The first is that, as in confraternities, lay people played the major role. This was true of Spaniards and Indians: among the latter were Juan Diego in Guadalupe (Mexico), Titu Yupanki in Copacabana (Bolivia) and Sebastián Quimichi in Cocharcas (Peru). The second feature is their inter-ethnic character, which meant that they became supports for the growing *mestizo* consciousness. For example: in 1675 the Lord appeared in Huanca (Cuzco) and rescued a fugitive Mitaya Indian, Diego Quispe; a century later he appeared to a sick *criollo* miner, Pedro Valero, as though to point out that the great racial divide of the colonial system was negated before God.[24] And the third feature is that the sanctuaries did not simply transplant Iberian pilgrimage piety, of vows and promises, receiving the sacraments, etc., but re-elaborated many Indian contributions, as Michael Sallnow has proved in his study of sanctuaries of the Cuzco region.[25]

4. A FOUNDATIONAL RELIGIOUS EXPERIENCE

Both patronal festivals and pilgrimages were expressions of "devotion to the saints," which became a *foundational religious experience* in Latin American Christendom. But why did devotion to the saints strike such a deep chord in the daily life of the continent? In the first century of evangelization, there was undoubtedly a convergence of interests between evangelizers and evangelized. On the one hand, the majority of missionaries practised medieval devotion to the saints and transplanted this, with all its ritual richness and complex organization of contraternities, since they judged it to be an excellent instrument of pastoral work. (Remember that, despite the harsh criticism of Protestant reformers, this devotion emerged strengthened from the Council of Trent, which upheld both the cult of *images* and the actuation of sacred *intermediaries*: images and intermediaries – two concepts that in Latin America came to be expressed in the single word "saints.") On the other hand, the Indians, through their own religious traditions, were already familiar with sacred intermediaries, who granted favours in exchange for the cult rendered by their devotees, and with complex systems of ritual and organization that upheld these cults. For both these reasons, the missionaries' propagation of devotion to the saints was an increasing success.

In the sixteenth century there must have been a certain pressure to encourage these devotions, but as time went by the Indians began to have recourse to the saints in the same way as they did to their ancestral intermediaries and, eventually, they felt that the saints too listened to their supplications, and began to discover true "hierophanies" in them. This attitude must have been fully established by the seventeenth century. These miraculous hierophanies were attributed not only to the most venerated images of Jesus Christ, the Virgin Mary and the saints, whose sanctuaries were pilgrimage centres (the Virgin of Guadalupe and the Cross of Carabuco being two early examples), but also to images venerated in virtually unknown towns. A typical case is the "miraculous apparition" of the Virgin Mary in 1687 in Anan Cusi, in the "doctrine" of Acoria (Huancavelica, Peru), the account of which is preserved in the archive of the archdiocese of Ayacucho.[26]

The result of all this was that devotion to the saints became very deeply rooted in the people of Latin America. Eventually, due to the scant attention paid to the people by a clergy that was gradually vanishing from rural areas, this devotion became their basic religious mediation. For the people, devotion to their saint is a form of faith-trust, through which an ever-deepening relationship is established between the saint and the devotee. This relationship starts from cultural motives, such as that of the saint being the patron of the locality, but develops into a steadily more personal relationship, demanding its quota of acceptance of mystery, since the saint belongs to the world of the sacred, but benefiting from the visible and tangible character of the saint, and nourished by his/her miracles. This devotion involves a certain amount of reinterpretation of the concept of *saint* in Catholic theology, since the people classify Jesus Christ and the Virgin Mary among the saints, as well as those canonized and certain "emergent saints"; also because ignorance of the lives of the saints leads them to see them more as intercessors before God than as models for living. However, if the saints do not function as models, they do function as myth and are important motivators of the Christian attitudes and values of the people.

The people, however, also reinterpret the theological category of miracle and call a *miracle* anything that goes beyond their actual capabilities, which are often severely limited. So they make a religious reading of their lives, one that allows them to discover the numinous presence of the saints and to feed their faith to ask for new miracles. Then their faith is also fed by the *punishments* meted out by the saints, through which these cease to be simply benevolent protectors and become demanding and jealous friends, who will not tolerate indifference or forgetfulness on the part of their devotees. Such punishments, especially when they appear to be deserved, are the other face of miracles and strengthen the faith of the pious more than the silence of God characteristic of the secularized world; when all is said and done, such punishments, like miracles and revelatory dreams, prove that the saints are alive and concerned for their devotees.

The counterpart of miracles and punishments from the saints is the *promises* made by the devotees. These, though they may appear self-interested, being often associated with prior conferment of favours, do not necessarily have a utilitarian purpose, but express, above all, a sacred commitment, like the vows taken by religious. Ultimately, though, the most characteristic expression of the people's devotion to the saints is their organization of and taking part in festivals and pilgrimages.

Such a constellation of terms – "devotee," "saint," "festival," "pilgrimage," "promise," "miracle" and "punishment" – can be said to provide the words that *generate* the foundational religious experience of Latin America. And therefore most Catholics from the people of the continent use this experience to live out their very faith in Christ. Such people should certainly be classed as Christians, since they believe that Jesus is the Son of God, who died on the cross to save us. But, starting as they do from their foundational religious experience of hierophany of the "saints," they express this faith in Christ in ways different from other sectors of the church, who start from a hierophany of "the book" (the Bible) or of "the poor." This means that Catholics of the people live their Christian faith through the mediation of devotion to the "Saint" Christs of miracles and festivals. This is an inheritance from the daily life of the colonial church, and is perfectly valid, even if it should be rounded out by other mediations.

Translated from the Spanish by Paul Burns

NOTES

1. E. Dussel, *Historia General de la Iglesia en América Latina (HG): Introducción General* (Salamanca, 1983),p. 561.

2. F. Aliaga Rojas, "La vida cotidiana en el Perú," *HG: Perú, Bolivia y Ecuador* (1987), p. 11–36; J. E. Arellano, "La vida cotidiana en Nicaragua," *HG: América Central* (1985), pp. 222–5; J. Barnadas, "La vida cotidiana en Bolivia," *HG; Perú, Bolivia y Ecuador*, pp. 137–45; R. Bendaña, "La vida cotidiana en Guatemala," *HG: América Central*, pp. 150–78; R. Cardenal, "La vida cotidiana en El Salvador," ibid., pp. 179–92; J. Martín Rivera, "La vida cotidiana de la cristiandad en la Nueva España," *HG: México* (1984), pp. 95–164; J. M. Pacheco, "La vida cotidiana de la cristiandad en Colombia," *HG: Colombia y Venezuela* (1981), pp. 185–216; M. Picado, "La vida cotidiana en Costa Rica," *HG: América Central*, pp. 241–2; J. Vargas, "La vida cotidiana en Ecuador," *HG: Perú, Bolivia y Ecuador*, pp. 146–50.

3. M. Marzal, *La transformación religiosa peruana* (Lima, 1983).

4. *Evangelization at present and in the Future of Latin America: Conclusions*. Final document of the Third General Conference of Latin American Bishops, held at Puebla, Mexico, 1979. The text of the document is in J. Eagleson and P. Scharper, eds., *Puebla and Beyond* (Maryknoll, N.Y., 1979); also in *Puebla* (London and Slough, 1980). (TRANS.)

5. D. Ribeiro, *Las Américas y la civilización* (Buenos Aires, 1972), p. 80.

6. C. Esteva Fabregat, *El mestizaje en Iberoamérica* (Madrid, 1988).

7. C. Moreira Neto, *Indios de Amazonia: de majoria a minoria* (1750–1850) (Petrópolis, 1988), p. 26.

8. A. Ruiz de Montoya, *La conquista espiritual del Paraguay* (1639, Bilbao, 1892).

9. F. Ximenez, *Historia de la provincia de San Vicente de Chiapa y Guatemala* (1722, Guatemala, 1929–31).

10. Marzal, *El sincretismo iberoamericano* (Lima, 1985), pp. 144–54.

11. D. Gow, "Símbolo y protesta: movimientos redentores en Chiapas y en los Andes peruanos," *América Indígena*, (Mexico, 1979), pp. 47–80.

12. J. Regan, *Hacia la Tierra sin mal: estudio de la religión del pueblo en la Amazonia*, 2 vols (Iquitos, 1983), vol. 2, pp. 229–46.

13. J. M. del Val, "La nueva Jerusalén michoacana: ¿una experiencia revolucionaria?," *Hacia el nuevo milenio* (Mexico, 1986), vol. 1, pp. 125–48.

14. Marzal, *Los caminos religiosos de los inmigrantes en la Gran Lima* (Lima, 1988), pp. 342–73.

15. (Inca) Garcilaso de la Vega, *Comentarios reales de los Incas* (1609, Buenos Aires, 1943–4), vol. 3, pp. 185–6.

16. Marzal, *La transformación religiosa peruana*.

17. E. Wolf, *Pueblos y culturas de Mesoamérica* (Mexico City, 1967), p. 192.

18. H. Villanueva, ed., *Cuzco 1689* (Cuzco, 1982).

19. P. Cortés y Larraz, *Descripción geográfico-moral de la diócesis de Goathemala*, 2 vols. (1772, Guatemala, 1958); Bendaña, "La vida cotidiana en Guatemala," p. 175.

20. E. Hoornaert, ed., *Historia da Igreja no Brasil*, 2 vols (Petrópolis, 1979–80), p. 45.

21. A. Metraux, *Vodú* (Buenos Aires, 1963), pp. 26–8.

22. B. Cobo, *Historia del Nuevo Mundo en obras*, 2 vols (1653, Madrid, 1964), p. 167.

23. Barnadas, "La vida cotidiana," p. 144.

24. Marzal, *La transformación*, pp. 282–3.

25. M. Sallnow, *Pilgrims of the Andes: Regional Cults in Cusco* (Washington, 1987).

26. Marzal, *La transformación*, pp. 204–10.

Chapter 5

THE CHURCH IN THE EMANCIPATION PROCESS (1750–1830)

Ana María Bidegain

I use the term "emancipation" rather than "independence" because the disintegration of the Spanish and Portuguese colonial empires ended in a transformation, but not a dissolution, of the ties between the former colonies and Europe. This transformation was the result of the interrelationship between international events and the reaction to them in colonial society. Within this process, the historical presence of the Church can be divided into two main phases: (1) The repercussions of Enlightenment reforms on church life and the reactions of secular society (1750–1804); (2) The Church and Christians in the consolidation of emancipation and the transformation of ties with Europe (1804–30).

1. THE REPERCUSSIONS OF ENLIGHTENMENT REFORMS ON CHURCH LIFE AND THE REACTIONS OF CIVIL SOCIETY (1750–1804)

In both Spain and Portugal, the reforms introduced under the influence of the Enlightenment were an attempt to avoid the dissolution of their empires under the pressure of a new international order, the cultural hegemony of science and technology and the difficulties stemming from the actual situation of the American colonies; they can be seen as a supreme Iberian effort to recover their prosperity at the expense of the colonies. These reforms have therefore been seen as a second conquest of America: a great effort to take America back into Spanish and Portuguese hands, involving a profound restructuring that affected the Church itself. The greatest repercussion of the Enlightenment reforms on the organization of the Church in Latin America was undoubtedly the expulsion of the Jesuits, along with the weakening of the religious orders and the systematic subjection of the Church to the authority of the state, in accordance with the regalist spirit of the age. These measures provoked a series of social movements nourished by social programmes upheld and spread in America by sectors of the Church itself. Whatever their objectives, the Enlightenment reforms were in fact the prelude to emancipation.

(a) The Jesuits and Enlightenment Reforms

(i) The economic background to their expulsion. In the sixteenth and seventeenth centuries, the Iberian empires had commonly handed over estates and *encomiendas* to the religious orders and the secular clergy, so that their produce could sustain hospitals, hospices and educational establishments; furthermore, they had sponsored the setting up of missions in the furthest confines of imperial territories in order to establish frontiers. The economic changes of the eighteenth century gave new value to labour and land, and so the riches of the

81

Church came under fresh scrutiny. Reformist currents affecting the economic interests of the Church based their arguments on the corrupting influence of accumulated wealth on the clergy. In fact there were more specific reasons for looking at the properties held by the Jesuits and the Church in general. In Portugal, there was a causal link between the financial crisis of the Portuguese crown and the confiscation of the fortunes of the richest noble families in Portugal and those of the Society of Jesus.

The missions authorized by the empire as a means of establishing frontiers had, under the religious orders, developed into community projects outside the control of the colonial adminstration and private ownership. The productive efficiency of these projects provided a sharp contrast to the low returns achieved by Spanish and Portuguese colonists. The economic strength of the Guaraní missions, the labour force they absorbed, and their closure of large areas to outside trade, finally led to uniting Spanish and Portuguese with British, French and Dutch traders against the activities carried on by the missionaries. What most annoyed the European bourgeoisie of the Enlightenment, dedicated to the defence of private property, was the success of experiments in holding goods in common within the communities.

Denunciations of the economic power of the Jesuits through their missions flowed in to the King of Spain throughout the first half of the eighteenth century. In 1723, the wealthy landowners and *encomenderos* of Paraguay rebelled, petitioning the king to expel the Jesuits as soon as possible for the sake of peace in the province. In 1750 the Madrid Treaty was signed, by which Spain set limits on Portuguese expansion in the interior of the continent but in return ceded an immense tract of mission territory affecting 30,000 Guaranís living in Jesuit reductions. Despite Jesuit protests, the demarcation commission began its work in 1753. The Guaranís took up arms and threw back the Portuguese-Spanish forces in 1754, but were finally overcome by the combined forces of the Iberian powers in 1756.

Even though the Jesuits did not mobilize the reductions' powerful armed forces, the fact that they resisted the new demarcation was sufficient protest for seeking their expulsion. The Jesuits also opposed the innovations brought in by the Portuguese authorities in 1755 in Maranhão, where through its mission activities, the Society had achieved economic as well as spiritual ascendancy. Its mission policy was incompatible with that proposed by the "enlightened" governors for the natives. They sought to incorporate the natives quickly into the colonial economy and society, which meant removing the barriers the Jesuits had set up to prevent the native population being enslaved and exploited as a cheap labour force.

Echoes of this offensive by the European Enlightenment against the Society of Jesus, its vast involvement in the state affairs of Spain and Portugal and inherited wealth in the colonies, and above all its controversial policy for the native population were all fundamental to the crisis that produced, in Portugal, the expulsion of the Jesuits from the kingdom and its colonies in 1759. Eight years later, they were expelled from all Spanish territories as well. Their expulsion was carried out in an inhumane and brutal fashion, often under threat of death, and involving physical sufferings often leading to their premature death in exile.

4. America in the Eighteenth Century
Source: Ana María Bidegain, *Así actuaron los cristianos en la historia de América latina*.
Bogotá, CIEC, 1985.

The persecution also extended to sectors of the church hierarchy and secular clergy who did not unconditionally give way to the demands of absolutism. In 1760 the archbishop of Bahía, Jose Bolthos Matos, was deported to Portugal and imprisoned in a convent, and in 1764 the bishops of Para and Maranhão, along with Oratorian, Augustinian, Carmelite and Franciscan religious suffered the same fate.

Naturally, the expulsion was welcomed in certain landowning and mercantile sectors in Paraguay, and by some bishops, notably in Mexico, who had complained about the loss of revenue resulting from the fact that the reductions paid no tithes. The general feeling among the population, however, was quite the reverse of this. The Governor of Buenos Aires, who was responsible for expelling the Jesuits from Paraguay, had to be very cautious in revealing his true intentions. There was an explosion of popular anger among the miners of San Luis Potosí against the commandant, who was forced initially to free the Jesuits he had arrested, as they were much loved by the miners as their advocates against the high taxes to which they were subjected. The upper classes had mostly been educated by the Jesuits, but they had to submit to the despotic will of Charles III. The simplest expression of opposition to the coercive measures was severely punished with exile, as happened in several of the main cities of Spanish America, where the people and the religious orders regarded the bishops and all who collaborated in the expulsion of the Jesuits as heretics and excommunicated. The *criollos*, educated by the Jesuits, regarded the expulsion as an act of violence on the part of the Spaniards, and this, along with other factors, fanned the flames of the independence movement.

(ii) Asserting a new cultural hegemeony. The conflict over the missions was not the basic aspect of the confrontation between the enlightened despots and the Jesuits, which was really broader than both the confines of the Americas and the Society of Jesus itself. The bourgeois élite was in fact trying to create a new ideological hegemony, and to do so, had to take on the religious orders, the Jesuits, the papacy and the whole Counter-Reformation culture.

The Society of Jesus was undoubtedly the militant wing of the Council of Trent and had played an outstanding part in the Hapsburg programme. But in the context of European Enlightenment a contradiction sprang up between the type of church-state relationship supported by the Jesuits and the state cause of the enlightened despots. Both in America and Europe, the Jesuits had espoused the humanist outlook of neo-scholasticism. The juridical thought of the Salamanca school and the legacy of Las Casas in the native church had posed basic problems from the American perspective, such as freedom, democracy and the right of some kingdoms to prosper by exploiting the riches of others. In the eighteenth century, the Jesuits and Dominicans were still upholding some of these theses through their network of schools and universities in Spanish America.

These propositions gave individuals the right to act in their own interest against laws currently in force when there was good reason to do so; they defended the right to resist, to put a tyrant to death; they upheld the view that royal power was legitimated by popular sovereignty; in short, they asserted the supremacy of liberty over authority, thereby setting limits to monarchical power and in the final analysis not excluding revolution. Such an ethical stance was in marked contradiction to the interests of an absolutist state seeking greater control over its subjects. And yet the bourgeoisie was raising the standard of individual freedom. But their freedom was confined within the consensus required by capitalism: that is, the freedom that implies consent to change oneself from a slave into a free wage-earner, selling one's labour in freedom, that is with inner assent, "as is natural, as follows from the natural order of things."[1] Individual freedom within the consensus necessarily implies that there be no dissension, that order be maintained.

The universal claims and structure of Catholicism were a major cause of controversy. The proponents of enlightened despotism distinguished the moral presence of the Church from its institutionalization of its mission as receiver and administrator of revelation. While they were in favour of the first, where and whenever the Church supported and legitimized state purposes, they saw the existence of an institution such as the Catholic Church under the direction of a pope as contrary to the interests of the state. The Jesuits on the other hand, proposed the independence of the Church in relation to the state, which automatically implied a strengthening of the papacy. While enlightenment and progressive theorists clamoured for the secularization of politics, they nevertheless clung to the sacrality of three categories: modern scientific knowledge, private property and economic development. These three led to an increasing marginalization of the papacy from international politics and the secularization of intellectual life, dominated by the royalist capitalist centres of the New Learning.

(iii) Education, Church and enlightenment. Enlightened Spaniards held that the world would be changed through education; they saw the reconstruction of Spain as depending on all (boys and girls, men and women) having access to elementary education, which they were determined to use as an instrument of social reform. Learning was considered the chief source of happiness and the prime mover of social prosperity. So the right of citizens to education became an absolute duty on the state to provide it, which fitted in neatly with their aim of achieving ideological hegemony over the Catholic Church – and naturally brought them into conflict with the Society of Jesus, the main providers of education in colonial America. When the Jesuits were expelled, education in America, with all its faults, was dealt a massive blow. This was true in Brazil, where Jesuit responsibilities had been huge, and also in the Spanish colonies, where many colleges remained empty, despite the efforts of the Franciscans and Dominicans to make good the deficiency.

The new educational goal was to produce citizens useful to the nation; the expansion of capitalism required literacy, and at secondary level more emphasis was placed on the sciences, with some "vocational" schools also being opened. Interest grew in educating girls "as future mothers and housewives," and American women took advantage of this current of modernization. The two best examples are Doña Clemencia de Caycedo y Vélez in Colombia and Doña Ignacia de Alzor in Mexico, who both put all their efforts and personal fortunes into schools for girls, the one in Mexico opening its doors in 1755 and that in Bogotá in 1783.[2]

In Brazil, the educational system had not progressed beyond imparting literacy, catechism and good manners. The school system existed entirely for the benefit of Portuguese immigrants and their children. In Spanish America, illiteracy among the white population was probably hardly higher than in the mother country; Indians, mestizos, blacks and mulattoes, who made up the great bulk of the population, had some access to primary education, but not to the higher grades, and those living in rural areas were virtually cut off from the colonial educational system. In this way the colonial institutions kept their ideological influence even after emancipation – not by casting the educational net wide, but by educating the ruling class. By doing this they stabilized colonial society, encouraging dependence on the Iberian mother countries first, on Franco-British Europe later. The Latin American educational system hardened into one of private schools kept going by the ability of parents to pay fees: education became a privilege of the wealthy and laid the base for a strongly class-structured society.

(iv) The Enlightenment in America and new forms of piety. The Catholic Enlightenment in America had a particular impact on piety, as reaction and protest against the baroque, which it saw as Jesuitical and Counter-reformation. It inveighed strongly against elaborate liturgy, veneration of saints and the excessive clutter of sacred ornaments in churches. Where the Counter-Reformation had ushered in the baroque, the Enlightenment brought neo-classicism. Images, pictures, reliquaries were all cleared out of churches without regard to the feelings of the faithful. Practices that were considered to verge on superstition were abolished; fortunately these included belief in witches, and the struggle against this reduced repression of female folk wisdom, one of the better consequences of enlightenment. In general, however, it was against popular religious practices, which were strongly influenced by the baroque.

The Enlightenment in America was a movement that basically affected men of the economically privileged élite. They were the ones who had access to European literature and flocked to the universities, where enlightened ideas circulated without difficulties up to the French Revolution. Devotions and piety declined among the male élite, while women and the popular classes clung to a baroque spirituality. So the Enlightenment produced a religious gap between élite men on one hand and women and the rest of the people on the other.

(b) Religion in the Prelude to Emancipation. Secular Society's Reaction to Reforms

During the whole period of colonial rule, uprisings were continually taking place wherever the slave system was imposed, leading to the creation of enclosures and *quilombos* in which Africans tried to re-create the structures they had known in their homelands. Nor could the Amerindians be controlled without force of arms and permanent politico-military subjection. The *criollos* and poor Europeans often joined the Amerindians in their struggles for their rights; those of the wealthier classes adopted an ambiguous stance that became clearer as the process of dissolution of the Iberian empires advanced. Among major uprisings in the second half of the eighteenth century, two stand out: that of "Tupac Amaru II" in Peru in 1780, and the *comuneros* in New Granada in

1781.[3] Both, sparked off by tax reforms, illustrate the different attitudes taken to independence movements within the Church.

(i) Clergy reactions to religious reforms and clerical involvement in the popular movement. The rebels of Peru and New Granada showed their dislike of enlightened reforms with shouts of "Long live the king and death to bad government!" The church hierarchy saw itself caught for the first time between opting to support the just demands of the people and remaining loyal to crown officials. For such a man as Antonio Caballero y Góngora, archbishop of Bogotá and later (1782–9) Viceroy, there could be no doubt where his duty lay and his presence was decisive in neutralizing and dispersing the rebel movement. Other hierarchs, though, used to the greater independence that went with their more routine functions, helped either the reforms or the resistance, both with mixed feelings. In cases such as Peru and New Granada, the lower orders of clergy were certainly with the rebels.

Once the Jesuits had been expelled, the authorities of the Viceroyalty gave themselves the right to inspect all convents, and any protest was brutally repressed. These actions were the result of the so-called religious reforms, which were designed to assure fidelity to the monarch and his officers, re-establish monastic discipline, ensure doctrinal purity through educating the clergy, and remove conflicts between religious and secular clergy. To carry these out, posts of Visitators General were created and to separate the Church in the Americas completely from the papacy, religious orders were forbidden to send their own superiors out from Europe. The provincial church councils held in the eighteenth century were controlled by royal instructions down to the smallest details and high crown officials with fiscal powers attended them.

The only object of "religious" reform was to make the Church dependent on the state. Any protest was met with violence and in this way Spanish imperialism fused clerical opposition and that of the most oppressed sectors of the population together in a single melting pot. The Dominican friar Ciriaco de Archila expressed this fusion of interests between clergy and people most clearly:

Otro demonio que hay, que lo es Moreno,
perturbador del vulgo y de la paz,
en caso que no mude de tereno,
no faltará otro arbitrio muy sagaz
para acabar con tal mortal veneno,
que en nuestra destrucción es pertinaz,
y caso que no baste arbitrio nuevo
muy fácil es que le pegue fuego.
¿Qué hizo con los estudios? ¡Confundirlos!
¿Qué intentó con los frailes? ¡Acabarlos!
¿Qué piensa de los clérigos? ¡Destruirlos!
¿Qué con los monasterios? Destrozarlos!
¿Y qué con los vasallos? ¡El fundirlos!
ya que por aquí no puede degollarlos;
pero no hay que admirar que esto le cuadre
cuando gustoso enloqueció a su padre.

[There's another devil, called Moreno,/upsetting the people and the peace;/if he doesn't shift his ground/another wiser power will do it for him/to put an end to such a deadly poison/bent on destroying us,/and if a new power is not enough/he may well be set on fire./What has he done to studies? Confounded them!/What has he tried with the friars? To get rid of them!/What does he think of priests? They should be destroyed!/What would he do to monasteries? Pull them down!/And what with his vassals? Ruin them!/since he can't cut their throats round here;/but none of this is surprising/in a man who happily drove his father mad.][4]

His call was to the unity of all the least favoured classes in the kingdom: Indians, peasants, artisans, the poor; he attacked the situation of foreign dominion which split law from religion, particularly in the economic sphere, which most affected the people's concerns. He asserted the sovereignty of the people against a despotic government:

A mas de que estos dominios
tienen sus propios dueños
señores naturales, por qué razón a gobernarlos vienen
de otras regiones malditos nacionales.
De esto nuestras dichas nos previenen,
y así par excusar fines fatales,
Unámonos por Dios, si les parece,
y veamos el Reino a quien les pertenece.

[Besides, these dominions have their own, natural masters, so why do cursed nationals come from other parts to rule them? Our luck saves us from this, and so, to avoid a fatal outcome, let us unite for God, if you will, and let's see who the Kingdom belongs to.]

Many of his arguments are based on Spanish neo-scholastic codes of law. These doctrines, widely diffused and much discussed in relation to the expulsion of the Jesuits, had taken root among the people and were invoked in defence of their rights.

For its part, the imperial power expected the clergy, as part of the Church, which in turn was considered a state appendage, to help in applying fiscal policy. The terms of the Royal Decree of 17 August 1780, besides ordering all free vassals of America to contribute to the war against England, expressly ordered the regular and secular clergy to help through "their effective persuasions and authorized examples"[5] in collecting the dues. But not all the clergy were prepared to see their pastoral practice reduced to carrying out official policy, and religious and parish priests charged with spreading official ideology among the people tended instead to side with them rather than with the dictates of a hierarchy allied to the political authorities.

(ii) Religion as political utopia. The people flatly rejected the governmental absolutism of the eighteenth century and sought an agreement between subjects and monarch as proposed by Spanish neo-scholastic jurists. They rejected the arguments for fiscal oppression and the regulations imposed by Spanish

dominion, but not the world view spread by religious principles. So there was a struggle against the absolute governments of the Spanish state, but not against religion or faith, as is shown by the last slogan of the *comuneros* led by Galán: "Long live God, long live our Faith, long live Our Sovereign Lord and death to bad government!"[6]

So the people went on affirming the truths of a religion that had been imposed on them but nevertheless expressed the religious needs of another oppressed people – the poor of Spain. The *comuneros* proclaimed the gospel demands of justice and equality alongside the affirmation of the right to popular sovereignty. These became a popular self-understanding that brought cohesion to different social groups. Lacking a defined ideology, the *comuneros* found these ideas welling up as a requirement of the popular will to find a rationale for the world and life that they could use in opposing Spanish rule.

In such a colonial situation, where the state was in total control of the political apparatus and prevented the formation of any political organizations, and where there was no autonomy of political from religious thought, the only form of expression open to the people was affirming fundamental religious principles as a basis for a political utopia. In this situation, where religion presented itself as a cohesive and dynamizing element, the Church appeared to be the only vital element in the imperial system that the popular classes saw as not foreign and alien to them. This means that when the *comuneros* or *Tupamaros* (supporters of Tupac Amaru II) vented their rage against clerics and church buildings or symbols, it was not doctrine they were attacking, but the support the church institution gave to a hated system. The popular classes had not broken with God, or the Church, and this, paradoxically, is ultimately why the archbishop of Bogotá could neutralize the movement and immediately set out on a pastoral mission designed to redirect the religious ideas of the people, the source of their dreams of a political utopia.

In *El Vasallo ilustrado* (The Enlightened Vassal), the Capuchin friar Finestrad, who accompanied the archbishop on this mission, stressed the need for a real reform of popular religion, since otherwise "the throne will be quite unsafe and there will soon be civil wars and public disturbances which will destroy the throne."[7] Finestrad held that the people had to be re-educated in their religious ideas – which in effect meant that they had to be redirected ideologically. He argued that while it was true that authority comes from God through the intermediary of the people, once they have given their consent to the king, this binds them in perpetuity and removes their right to rebel. Once power has been conferred on the king and the royal dynasty, this includes the power to make the law, which is normally absolute. Religion should not do anything other than instruct vassals in faithful and total obedience to the king – a thesis totally opposed to that of the Jesuits. This "enlightened" view links two functions, one pastoral and the other political-repressive, in a confusion of powers that was a central plank in the politics of enlightenment tied to regalism, Jansenism and Josephism: all varieties being, of course, totally opposed to the ideas deriving from Suarez that inspired the *comuneros* and were later to resurface behind the independence movements.

In this same year, 1781, one of the Jesuits expelled from Peru, Juan Pablo Viscardó, wrote a "*Lettre aux Espagnols-Américains*" from Philadelphia, demanding independence for Peru, which he called "my country." He was an active champion of the cause of Peruvian independence and tried to persuade the British government to send a military expedition in support of Tupac Amaru II. The letter, a call to support the popular movements, circulated among elements of the *criollo* élite but failed to mobilize the wealthy *criollos*. It was published only in 1799 by Francisco de Miranda, forerunner of Venezuelan independence, to demonstrate the complaints of the colonial population and the reasons for independence. The ecclesial and educational reforms of the Bourbons failed to achieve an ideological hegemony and their new world view spread only to the intellectuals of the regime. It failed to spread among the people because collective mentalities change only very slowly and the people's world view continued to express, in a form both stereotyped and chaotic, the old ideas of representative popular Spanish tradition and the juridical philosophy of the Counter-Reformation.

2. THE CHURCH AND CHRISTIANS IN THE CONSOLIDATION OF EMANCIPATION AND THE TRANSFORMATION OF TIES WITH EUROPE (1804–30)

(a) The International Situation

The rapid industrial development of the late eighteenth and early nineteenth centuries forged power bases for the ascendant European bourgeoisie, and gave them new possibilities for imposing their views on social organization. It also sharpened the struggle between France and England for hegemony of the commercial world and primacy in industrial development.

The French Revolution, the continental blockade and the expansion under Napoleon were an expression of the efforts of the French bourgeoisie to break the last links with the *ancien régime*, make France the industrial centre of the world and seize the primacy from England. For the blockade to succeed, any cracks on the continent through which English goods might penetrate had to be sealed. This was largely the reason behind the occupation of the Papal States belonging to Spain and Portugal in 1808.

Pius VII tried to maintain a neutral stance, but Napoleon saw this as a crack in the blockade and on 2 February 1808 French troops occupied Rome; in Spring 1809 the Papal States were annexed to the French empire. Pius VII was finally arrested.

France, under Napoleon, became the supplier of industrial goods to Europe, while Britain, winner of the batttle of Trafalgar, consolidated its position as mistress of the seas. Spain found itself caught between the two powers deciding the course of international politics. Its weakness at sea forced it to bend to British demands, while its weakness on land forced it to bow to French. It lost everything, first its fleet at Trafalgar, and then its king, when Napoleon imprisoned the whole royal family in 1808, forcing them to abdicate in his favour and installing his brother Joseph as king.

Under the threat of an imminent French invasion of Portugal, the British proposed – and arranged – for the Portuguese royal family to move to Brazil. The Braganzas eventually set up court in Rio de Janeiro.

Europe was the main market for goods, and Britain underwent a crisis of over-production owing to the French commercial blockade. During the course of the eighteenth century, Britain had forced cracks in the rigid Spanish monopoly on trade with the rich Spanish-American market; it had access to and influence in Latin America and decided to instigate movements against the Spanish empire. It seized the island of Trinidad and told all British colonial officials in the Caribbean to be on the watch for any movement in America directed against the Spanish crown. It was the need for new markets that also drove them to invade parts of the River Plate States in 1806 and 1807. The British were well aware of the importance of this continent, capable of absorbing more manufactured goods than the United States or India, but had to break the last, even though fatally weakened, links between these colonies and Spain. The *criollos* of the River Plate twice repulsed British expeditions and this filled them with optimism, since if they were capable of repelling a fleet as powerful as the British, what could they not do to the Spanish?

(b) Religious Participation in Popular Mobilization in Spain

The enlightened sectors of Spanish society supported the French occupation, seeing Napoleon as a modernizing force, and though the French behaved as though in a conquered country, the Spanish authorities offerd no resistance. This was not true of the people, who mutinied in Madrid on 2 May 1808 and with some Spanish army officers, sectors of the clergy and the petit bourgeoisie, pledged resistance. Organs of government known as *Juntas* (councils) were set up all over Spain, which organized militias, who fought with the first "guerrilla" techniques.

The uprising was organized in the name of Nation, King and Faith, conferring a "holy war" status on it. The struggle was legitimated by reference to scholastic juridical teaching on usurping monarchy and popular sovereignty, mixed in with some eighteenth-century liberal theories. By these criteria, the abdication of the Spanish monarchs was null and void, even if made of their own free will, since the social contract between monarchs and people could be transmitted only through inheritance. To give up the crown in favour of another dynasty, therefore, the Spanish monarchs should first have ascertained the will of the people. As they had not, the abdication in favour of Napoleon was invalid and the throne vacant, in which case sovereignty reverted to the people and it was therefore the people who, through their councils, should govern the nation. In their struggle, the Spanish people discovered and exercised the principle of popular sovereignty; the War of Spanish Independence, fed partly by eighteenth-century revolutionary ideas and partly by seventeenth-century scholastic legal principles, in effect legitimized and created the conditions for Spanish American struggles for independence from Spanish rule.

One of the features of this war was participation by the clergy in it – the first appearance of the guerrilla-fighter priest. The greatest services the clergy could provide for the "holy cause" were to supply an ideology, raise spirits, inflame feelings and impart the soul and *raison d'être* of the sacrifices involved in resistance. Many parish priests, religious and even bishops fanned the struggle with their possessions and exhortations, some taking a direct part in the fighting; every council had a priest, friar or bishop member. Calls to arms were accompanied by liturgical ceremonies, processions, rogations and missions. Death in battle was the equivalent of martyrdom. All this was to have deep ideological repercussions in Spanish America, where the "conciliar" movement began to organize in 1808.

(c) From the Conciliar Movement to American Independence

The Spanish *juntas* sent out requests to the colonies for them to form similar councils, and between 1808 and 1810 all Spanish America swore fidelity to Ferdinand VII. The process unleashed in Spain had deep repercussions in America, effectively changing the course of its history. The American concillar movement was a direct consequence of the events taking place in Spain, with the same doctrinal underpinning and the same aims proclaimed. Between 1808 and 1810 a wave of dynastic legalism and Spanish patriotism swept the Indies. Despite oaths sworn to Ferdinand VII and his representatives, however, the process of decline of Spanish power, begun in the eighteenth century, was gathering pace. Revolutionary movements gathered round town councils, old colonial legislative bodies, which called insurgents together and then used their legal status so as not to be classified as rebels. On all sides this new regime, though it detested the old one, invoked its legitimate descent from it.

This concentration of power in the town councils had the advantage that they were constituted not by the crumbling Spanish authorities, but by the populations installed in the colonies. The institution of "open council" (a meeting of all the population of a town considered citizens) assured the supremacy of the *criollos*, who could thereby form governing councils and place their militant revolutionaries on these.

Napoleon's expedition to Spain to put down the popular uprising in 1810 changed the situation. Britain was then Spain's ally; preventing the modernization of Spain under Napoleon became for the moment far more important than freeing South American markets. Britain sent troops to Spain to fight for its independence alongside the Spanish guerrilla forces – though this did not stop it from pursuing its contraband trade with Spain's colonies, where Spanish power was more precarious than ever. Meanwhile, in Spain, the Central Council, in desperate straits, called on the Parliament for Spain and the Indies to assume constituent authority over whatever territory it controlled. The ensuing parliamentary debates convinced their American participants that not even victory for liberalism over absolutism in Spain would give full equality to America in the framework of a common nationhood. Spanish deputies, both liberal and conservative, refused to give the Americans full equality of rights, except in pompous general statements.

In 1810 the collapse of anti-Napoleonic Spain seemed certain with the loss of Andalusia and resistance confined to an island in the Bay of Cadiz. The Council of Seville had been dissolved in a bloodbath, and only that of Cadiz retained a precarious sovereignty and legitimacy. This gave America ground on which to define itself in relation to the situation in the mother country.

On 19 April in Caracas, 25 May in Buenos Aires, 20 July in Bogotá and 18 September in Santiago, the *criollos*, using Spanish institutions (the open councils), took over regional government and declared independence. Throughout Spanish America the Spanish officials, bishops and army officers in particular, used their power to put the movement down, since despite its cloak of legality, they knew that it was directed against them and their privileges. Spaniards resident in America identified defence of the empire with defence of their personal positions within the imperial system against the white *criollo* leaders, who saw their opportunity to take over these positions, rather than to replace colonial rule itself. So at first there was a civil war between elite groups over who should run colonial society. Each faction then sought recruits from other social classes and so the people of Latin America were eventually caught up in the struggle for independence.

(d) Church Participation in the Emancipation of Spanish America

Just as in Spain, the Church did not adopt a unitary stance with regard to the struggle for emancipation. The crisis was above all political, not religious, and it was only natural for the social and political divisions affecting Spanish American society to be echoed within the Church. The various layers of clerical structure opted in favour of one or other faction, as they did in Spain. Most of the bishops, however, stuck firm to rejecting independence movements and supporting the Spanish remnant that waited in hope for the return of Ferdinand VII to the throne. The lower clergy split into royalists and revolutionaries, with the latter in the majority, since priests were most familiar with the needs and problems of the *criollo* classes who sought emancipation, while the bishops, through their oath of allegiance to royal patronage, had more ties to break if they were to espouse the cause of independence.

(i) Independence begins with a clerical revolution. As the clergy were the intellectual class of the colonial regime, the decisive role they played in the emancipation process is understandable, especially in view of their close connection to all social strata. In some parts, their participation was decisive: so Jorge Tadeo Lozano, in his opening address to the Electoral College of Cundinamarca in Colombia in 1813 could say:

> You have all been witnesses to the enthusiasm with which the clergy promoted and prepared the memorable revolution of 20 July . . . [and to the fact that] the Supreme Council that was installed and which, throwing out the authorities unknown to the Regency, declared our perpetual emancipation, included among its numbers many members of the lower ranks of the church hierarchy. Señor Rosilio was accompanied on his recruitment drive by a cortège of more than two hundred priests, who captained the people from Bosa and Choachi, and it was priests who directed the people's uprising, not only in the capital, but in El Socorro, Pamplona and, in a word, throughout the whole kingdom. Even our most distant progeny will recall with gratitude that the revolution that emancipated us was a clerical revolution."[8]

This active participation by the clergy was repeated throughout virtually the whole of Spanish America. Of eight thousand priests in Mexico, six thousand supported independence, led by Frs Hidalgo and Morelos. In the River Plate, the action of the clergy was decisive; in the petition presented to the Buenos Aires town council for the nomination of a new council, there were seventeen clerical signatures. In Uruguay, most of the clergy declared for independence; in Caracas, there were nine priests in the Congress that declared independence; Fr José Matías Delgado inspired the movement in El Salvador, which lit the spark of independence throughout Central America. So clergy participation was decisive, and not all were simply animators: there were even army engineers among them, such as Friar Luis Beltrán, who melted down convent bells to make cannons for the liberating army of San Martín which set Chile and Peru free.

(ii) The clergy as the intellectuals of independence. As in Spain, the greatest service the clergy lent to the revolutionary cause was to breathe a revolutionary spirit into the people. Popular catechisms, novenas, homilies and all kinds of devotions were used to this end. Fernández de Soto Mayor, parish priest of Mompox (now in Colombia), produced a "People's Catechism or Instruction" in 1814. In his introduction he signalled the need to teach the rights and duties of a citizen since ignorance of these is, he maintained, the basis of domination; he recommends this work above all to parish priests, and states that Spanish rule has no legal basis: "Neither is conquest a legitimate title since it is nothing other than the right of might. If it were, the Spaniards would have been criminals to resist the French. Resistance is not a crime, since men cannot leave their children and descendants servitude and oppression as their inheritance. [So the war of independence is] a just and holy war, perhaps the most just and holy the world has seen for many centuries."[9] About the same time José Amor de la Patria published a Politico-Christian Catechism in Chile, with the same aim of spreading pro-emancipatory ideas, but based more on the juridical and philosophical tenets of scholasticism.[10]

The intellectual efforts of the clergy also bore fruit in newspaper publishing. Here too there was a divide between those who based their support for independence on the philosophical foundations of the Enlightenment and those who did so on Thomism. So the Franciscan Fr Padilla, who founded the newspaper *El Aviso al Público* of Bogotá, invoked the common good as the objective of the new independent government. Basing himself on St Thomas and St Augustine, he refuted a royalist who denied the legality of the people taking back their rights even when the sovereign was tyrannical. The Chilean friar Camilo Henríquez, an Enlightenment follower, used the Press in the cause of emancipation through a series of articles in the *Aurora de Chile*, the first newspaper in Chile, which he himself had founded.

(iii) The clerical contribution to armed struggle. Priests were found not only in intellectual exercises or as council members: many served as soldiers in armies of liberation, which were then not regular armies but rather armed groups fighting guerrilla-style campaigns. Examples of priests taking up arms can be found from Mexico down to the River Plate. In Mexico, Frs Hidalgo and Morelos, two parish priests, were among the first to call for an independence struggle. Priests who led or joined militias made no real distinction between care of souls and their political ideals. Whether as chaplains or as fighting men, they joined fully in the life of the roaming armies. Those who did not go to the front stayed behind to work for the resistance, and the deposed royalist authorities complained of their effectiveness in this work.

The fact that religious and secular clergy played such a part in the struggle for independence is easy to understand in view of the religious monism of colonial times since the beginning of evangelization. This monism was reaffirmed by the Bourbon laws which tried to change the Church into an arm of the absolutist state. Once religious had learned that religion had to be at the service of politics, it was quite logical for them to place it at the service of the politics they believed to be a just and holy cause, God's cause – which some saw as the independence struggle and others as defence of the Spanish regime.

(iv) Toward a theology of American independence. The theological underpinning for this war – which patriotic religious saw as holy and just, as the Spanish did their war against France – was provided in the form of writings, homilies and sermons by clerics who believed in the cause of independence. They were not trying to work out a new theology, but merely to situate this war within the history of salvation, as the Spaniards were doing with theirs. For American patriots, Spanish oppression was unjustified and was being brought to an end through the independence struggle, in which the action of God in human history could be discerned. The importance of this theological argument lies in the fact that the Americans were convinced they were fighting a holy war, carried on by the hand of God, and that victory had to be God's.

The Virgin Mary also had to be on the side of independence, since Latin Americans were above all Marian Christians, and since this was a holy war, they had not only to fight on the battlefields, but pray to and petition the ever venerated Virgin Mary to protect her American children, who were dearer to her than all other peoples. Every kind of prayer, rogation and procession was organized by different groups to implore Mary's help and protection.

(v) The quest for ties with Rome. The bishops at first remained aloof from rather than opposed to the independence struggle. They still hoped that royal authority would be reimposed and that the Council of the Indies would nominate new bishops to fill the vacant sees. But once they saw that independence was an accomplished fact, most of them fled to Spain, thereby thoroughly confusing priests, religious and laity. Where a bishop stayed in his diocese, religious life proceeded much as usual, since the debate was political rather than religious.

Where a bishop died or had fled, there were major problems in appointing a new one: the new governments – made up of élites educated in the ideas of the Catholic Enlightenment – considered themselves the natural inheritors of royal patronage and so began to nominate bishops and appeal to Rome for recognition as new republics and above all for recognition of their right to patronage. The sort of approaches they made to Rome varied according to the political philosophy of the leaders of the new republics.

In Mexico, where two priests were the chief architects of a revolution based mainly on scholastic juridical philosophy, it was natural for the government to seek a tie with Rome, and to appoint bishops, as the constitution of Chipancingo clearly claimed the right to do. This declared that the Catholic Religion would be the only one of the state, and denied rights to foreign nationals who were not Catholic, or to its own who might "fall into the crime of heresy or apostasy"; even people passing through were obliged to respect the Catholic religion and not to practise any other form of worship. The Mexicans clearly saw the need for close ties with Rome, not just out of political expediency, probably, but also from religious conviction, and because they could see that the old royal patronage of the Spanish crown did not simply pass to the new state by right, but that in order to exercise it the state would have to obtain a pontifical concession in a future concordat.

In Buenos Aires, where the Council was mbued with Enlightenment ideas, a highly royalist state similar to that designated in the 1812 Cortes of Cadiz was established "*propia et sancta libertatis causa.*" Catholicism was proclaimed the state religion, but the state considered itself the undisputed heir to patronage, and its approach to Rome was therefore essentially political. The 1813 government took on responsibility for all the services normally associated with the Church: hospitals, schools, charitable institutions. It also controlled and regulated tithes, suspended the inquisition and made the religious who were working for their central authorities in "Argentina" independent of them. Though Catholicism was accepted as the official religion, foreigners were not to be harassed, being allowed to "worship God in their homes privately according to their customs." The same Council that officially proclaimed the Catholic religion, since the Argentine people were Catholic above all, also spread the idea of Rousseau's social contract and the philosophy of Voltaire through its schools, and distributed their works in the neighbouring states of Chile, Paraguay and *Banda Oriental* (now Uruguay).

While the liberating armies under San Martín and Belgrano prescribed religious observances for their troops and made them say the rosary, the liberal politicians – whose goal in separating from Spain was to sign a new colonial deal with Britain – set out the new role assigned to the Church in these terms: "[The clergy] being liberated from the oppression of the old regime, should put their eloquence at the service of the new. Those who refuse to do so are unworthy of liberty and will be deprived of it."[11] These threats were real and carried out by deporting most of the bishops and imprisoning the remainder, with the result that by 1812 the episcopate had disappeared from Argentina, with all the consequences that stemmed from this.

(e) The Return of Ferdinand VII and Absolutism

New events were meanwhile convulsing Europe. Napoleon invaded Russia in 1812 and his army was defeated, encouraging European monarchs to form a coalition against him, while he was also defeated in Spain by British troops under Wellington. Faced with all his enemies united, in 1814 Napoleon decided to free Ferdinand VII and the Pope. Ferdinand returned to Spain and tried to turn the clock of history back. He repudiated the monarchical 1812 Constitution, re-established absolute rule and sent a force under the command of Morillo to put down the revolutionary movements in Venezuela and New Granada.

Absolutist sympathizers in America, as in Spain, sought to utilize religion in imposing a complete return to the *ancien régime*. Since the new governments had already sent missions to the Pope, the Pope had at all costs to be made to support the Spanish cause. Spain was informed of the actions of Mexico,

Argentina and Chile, but what most worried it was the mission sent by Bolívar to Paris (while the Pope was still a prisoner there) under Palacio Fajardo to request the nomination of new bishops to Colombia. Spain could not keep out of this process, and from 1814 to 1820 the Spanish ambassador to the Vatican pressed for Spain's nominees to be appointed to the vacant sees. Up to 1814, the Pope's information had been filtered through the nunciature in Madrid, where the nuncio listened to the complaints of the bishops who had been exiled, or who had, in most cases, fled in the face of advancing patriot forces.

In Rome the Spanish ambassador determinedly obstructed any access by republican missions to the Pope, thereby placing the churches in America in a position of complete anomaly. Their contact was limited to the political powers in the new republics, but these could not make contact with the Pope as Spain prevented them from doing so. Furthermore, the situation in America was increasingly chaotic. Morillo had liquidated the intellectuals and revolutionary leaders in the old Viceroyalty; royalist forces had kept control in Peru. Only the River Plate Sates, which had strengthened their ties with Protestant Britain, were still in patriot hands. For his part, Pius VII, who had been a prisoner of Napoleon like Ferdinand VII, viewed absolutist restoration in Europe favourably, and while not openly supporting the Holy Alliance because he would not accept Lutheran Prussia and Orthodox Russia as religious equals, at least welcomed the union of Christian monarchs against Napoleon and liberal France.

This was the background to the Spanish ambassador's success in persuading the Pope to issue the famous encyclical *Etsi longissimo*, addressed to the pastors of Spanish America, on 30 January 1816. This proclaimed the authority of Ferdinand VII and called on them zealously to cooperate in imposing Hispanic order on the rebel colonies. This was obviously not well received by the patriots and undoubtedly served the royalists in attaching the religious authorities to their cause. In territory recaptured by the royalists, the Inquisition was re-established and many clerics were condemned by it, with many more being shot by the Spaniards, who saw the fact that they had placed religion at the service of independence as one of the greatest possible crimes.

In 1816 the current of international politics was running strongly against the revolutionaries. Spain had obtained pontifical approval and was able to utilize the Church in Spanish America in support of its policies; Murillo had taken Cartagena and then Bogotá, and regarded his campaign as one in defence of the poor, who had remained aloof from the struggle, against the "enlightened" of Bogotá society, whom he liquidated with the same ferocity as he had shown in Venezuela. The revolutionary movement in the north of the South American continent seemed to be at an end. Bolívar, already known as the "Liberator," had been forced into exile, going first to Jamaica, confident of receiving support from the Governor of Kingston. But the British would not even pay for his passage to England to enlist support there. He had only one card left: to seek help from Alexander Petión, President of Haiti, the first independent nation of Latin America.

(i) Haiti, the cradle of Latin American independence. On 1 January 1804 the general in command of the ex-slave army of the French colony of Saint Dominique had

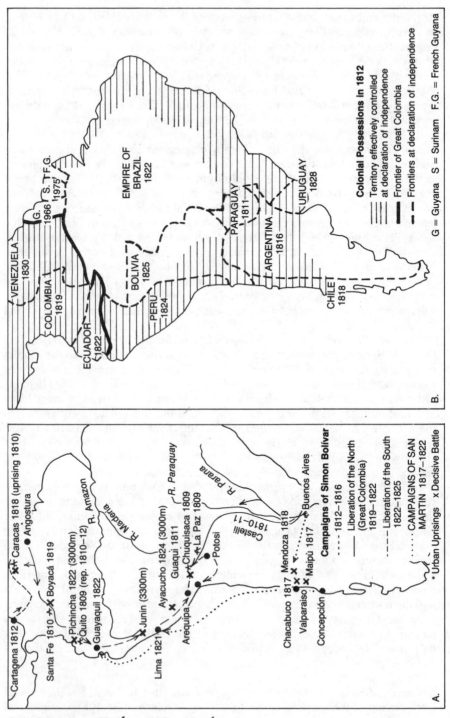

5. A. Campaigns of Bolívar and San Martín
   B. Colonial Possessions in 1812
Source: Zanichelli

declared the independence of Haiti (*haute terre*). Though little remembered, this event was of major significance on several fronts: it was the first achievement of independence by a Latin American country; it was the first successful revolution by slaves in history; it established the first black republic; and above all it provided the place where Simón Bolívar, the great Liberator, obtained unconditional support and training for his revolutionary undertaking.

This unique revolution drew assault and blockade from the armies of France, Britain, Spain and the United States, since all these nations depended on slaves for cheap labour and the Haitian experience set a dangerous precedent for the slaves of the whole region. But armed siege failed, and the imperial forces resorted to a total blockade. Haiti was desperately poor and yet its people managed to raise funds to enable Bolívar to re-enter the struggle. In 1816 he left Los Cayos, only to be defeated on the coast of Venezuela the following year. Once again, Haiti provided support, making just one proviso: that he liberate the slaves wherever his army was victorious.

Bolívar kept to the bargain, promising not only to free slaves but to share out land among the soldiers of the revolution. So after 1816 the war took on a different aspect and became a social revolution. Britain and the United States began to sell him arms and supplies; he rejoined the struggle in the north of the continent, while San Martín prepared his forces to liberate Chile and the Peruvian coast.

Popular mobilization on a scale that could transform the war into one of poor against rich happened only in some places, such as *Banda Oriental* and the plains of Venezuela. But the armies of both sides had to recruit officers from the ruling classes and soldiers from the poor and then, so as to keep the soldiers under control, begin to offer them advancement up the military hierarchy. In this way the *criollo* leaders who were later to be the generals of independent Latin America started to come to the fore. The main victims of the civil wars were the wealthy classes, submitted to a brutal regime of extermination by one side or the other. Bolívar, advised by Petión, saw that a long resistance struggle could only be achieved by a massive uprising of the people, and this was the basis of his eventual triumph.

(b) The International Situation More Favourable to Emancipation

In 1820 a revolt in Riego in Spain imposed a monarchical but liberal constitution, and gave the American revolutionaries the impression that they could reach an agreement with the liberal new Spanish regime. But their hopes were dashed by Spain's need to cling to its colonial empire as its only hope of economic salvation, and five more years of increasingly bloody struggle followed. But the Riego revolt also had major repercussions in the political and religious spheres. Neither wealthy *criollos* nor royalist bishops approved of the new direction taken by the Spanish crown and so transferred their allegiance to the revolutionary movement. Bolívar took advantage of the new situation and secured the support of the bishops of Mérida and Popayán. In Mexico the bishops supported Iturbide rather than swear loyalty to the liberal Spanish constitution. The Vatican also changed tack on receiving information from the bishop of Mérida on the progress and significance of the revolutionary movement; from 1822 Pius VII, while not actually blessing the cause of emancipation, at least declared the Church neutral and concerned only with religious and spiritual affairs – an innovation prejudicial to Ferdinand VII and the royal patronage and therefore very favourable to the cause of independence.

Rome's concern was to make direct contact with and reorganize the churches in Latin America and Pius VII sent a mission to the southern part of the continent in 1823 with this in view. The royalist attitude of the governors of Buenos Aires and Chile conflicted with the Roman proposals, however, and the mission had no effective outcome. Bolívar saw its political importance and took a different view, but the state of war obtaining in Peru made it impossible for the mission to operate there. Bolívar sent repeated delegations to the Holy See from 1819 to 1826 and finally obtained the nomination of bishops. Iturbide in Mexico also recognized the urgent need to approach the Holy See to solve the question of reabsorbing the patronage of the Indies into the new state, but the proclamation and vicissitudes of the Mexican Empire prevented him from nominating an ambassador to the Vatican till 1823, the year Pius VII died, having toward the end of his days seen the advantages of a neutral policy.

Vatican politics, along with those of Europe, turned against the revolutionaries. The Holy Alliance which had intervened in Spain to restore Ferdinand VII planned military intervention in Latin America also. The new Pope Leo XII reversed the Vatican policy of neutrality and, in the encyclical *Etsi iam diu* of 24 September 1824, called on the bishops to extol the merits of Ferdinand VII and deplored the great evils besetting the Church in Latin America. This change of policy was apparently inspired by the ultra-conservative pressure brought by the Spanish ambassador to the Vatican, but also by the activities of masonic lodges and the support given to the republics by the two great Protestant powers, Britain and the United States, which recognized the republics in 1824.

Britain had signalled its opposition to a Holy Alliance expedition to Latin America and in December 1823 President Monroe of the United States had declared his hostility to the idea of a reconquest of Spanish America by the forces of European Restoration. Even if the United States could not intervene directly and immediately, Monroe was anxious to keep Europe as far away from the continent as possible, and also to keep his trade routes to the south open. To commercial interests had to be added the closeness of Mexico and the sympathy the people of the United States felt for Bolívar. The United States recognized Colombia in June 1822, Mexico in December and Argentina in January 1823. Britain saw these recognitions as a threat that could end with the world divided between Americans and Europeans; officially neutral and indifferent to the fate of the recently liberated Spanish colonies, Britain was unofficially selling them arms, finding markets in them for its manufactured goods (it was selling 25 percent more textiles there than on mainland Europe) and frustrating any European machinations to help Spain regain its colonies.

While Britain, the U.S. and the European powers speculated on the outcome of the independence struggle, the battles of Junín on 6 August 1824 and Ayacucho on 9 December effectively put an end to Spanish rule in America, with the exceptions of the islands of Cuba and Puerto Rico, with the *Banda Oriental* under Brazilian control. Britain immediately recognized the new states, demanding protection for its commercial interests in exchange and letting it be known that it would not allow the other European powers to trade in the same goods. Bolívar saw the situation very clearly: "The English and the North Americans are eventual allies and very selfish. The Spaniards are no longer a danger to us, whereas the English are, very much so, as they are all-powerful, and therefore to be feared."[12]

(f) The Independence of Brazil

The 1820 liberal movements in Europe forced the Portuguese king to return to Lisbon, leaving his son Dom Pedro as regent in Brazil. The Portuguese merchant classes who led the liberal movements mooted the urgent need to recolonize Brazil in order to protect Portuguese commercial interests which were threatened by the British presence there. This prompted the formation of the Independence Party or *Partido Brasileiro*, led by José Bonifacio and Joaquím Gonçalvez Ledo, joined by the Prince Regent on 9 January 1822 when he replied "I am staying" (*"eu fico"*) to the Portuguese-dominated Chambers which demanded that he return to Portugal. So, "with a break, without revolution," as the great sugar plantation and slave owners wished, Brazil was born to independent life and kept its national unity through strengthening the central power around the monarchy.

Imperial Brazil inherited basic colonial institutions such as the Church and the army and reinforced its control over the rural Brazil of sugar, cotton and cacao plantations. It kept slavery as the basic labour force, became Britain's biggest commercial and financial customer and continued efforts to rule the *Provincia Cisplatina* (now Uruguay) so as to control the River Plate area.

The Church in independent Brazil continued with the royal patronage and inherited the dependence on the state characteristic of the colonial period. The few bishops hardly amounted to a focus of church unity and most bishops and priests were more state functionaries than pastors, mostly looking after the interests of the great landowners. There were two main currents of thought within the Church: one, led by Fr Antonio Feijó and including the bishop and priests of São Paulo, sought to establish a National Church under a National Council linked to the state; this "enlightened" wing was against clerical celibacy and would have abolished the religious orders. The other, headed by the bishop of Bahía, Antonio de Seixas, proposed a celibate clergy, with closer links to Rome and greater autonomy in relation to the political authorities.

The civil authorities, for their part, regarded the Church as a branch of the absolute power of the state, with the duty of helping to maintain the law and order that was the basic guarantee of national unity. Despite the fact that, unlike Spanish America, relations with Rome became closer and nuncios were appointed, Roman influence on religious life in Brazil was virtually nil, was seen as unnecessary and even suspicious, partly on account of the claims of the patronage system and partly because the nuncios saw themselves as ambassadors rather than pastors, representatives of the Papal States as a political organization, with no interest in becoming involved in Brazilian life.

(g) The Impact of Emancipation on the Religious Life of the People

By the end of the independence process, most sees in Latin America were vacant. The exceptions were Arequipa, Popayán, Maracaibo, Guatemala,

Puebla, Oaxaca and Yucatán. Conventual rules were broken, enormous numbers of priests were laicized, hundreds of small monasteries which attended to the religious needs of scattered rural communities disappeared, seminaries were closed, and lack of communication with Rome foretold the continuation of the institutional crisis of the Church in Latin America.

Besides this, the gap between the "enlightened" piety of élite men and the baroque piety of women and the rest of the people remained. The *criollo* élites of Brazil and Spanish America looked to Europe for their ideological and religious inspiration, seduced by currents of thought stressing the importance of identifying individual will and divine will and casting doubt on the sacramental role of the institutional Church and its ministers, thereby asserting the need for the Church to be dependent on the State. On the other hand, echoing Jansenist criticism of colonial Christendom, they rejected popular piety. European Christendom, itself the result of the symbiosis of Christianity with Greek, Latin, Celtic and Germanic pagan religions, could not accept that the same process could apply to Indian and black religions. So religious marginalization was added to the socio-economic marginalization inflicted on the indigenous populations and blacks since the conquest.

Popular piety survived, however; partly because its observances, though criticized, were tolerated. Religion was the chief expression of social life and every festival was a religious celebration. Baroque Catholicism was festive; it was triumphalist but also nationalist, and this was useful at a time when nation states were being formed. But the main reason for its survival was the nature of colonial religious life. The family was of major importance as a religious expression; prayers and religious observances were learned at the family hearth, while contact between faithful and pastors was often limited to major feast days. Organized religious practice was kept alive not so much by priestly zeal as by confraternities, brotherhoods and third orders. This lay character of the colonial church, together with the central position of mothers as nuclei of families, was what kept religious life going during the tumultuous period of emancipation.

Translated from the Spanish by Paul Burns

NOTES

1. E. Dussel, *Historia General de la Iglesia en América Latina*, vol. I/1, p. 674.

2. Each came into separate contact with the Order of the Company of Mary. This order of nuns dedicated to the education of young ladies had been founded in France at the end of the seventeenth century to give women an overall education. In the spirit of the Council of Trent, the religious order had to be an enclosed one, but the whole convent was seen as a school in which future teachers received their education. The main innovation was to take boarders and day-girls, the latter being educated free apart from the former, but with all being taught to read and write correctly, sew, embroider, count and calculate. See A. M. Bidegain, *Así actuaron los cristianos en la historia de América Latina* (Bogotá, 1985), vol 1, pp. 302ff.

3. In 1780 an indigenous peasant movement broke out in the Viceroyalty of Peru, led by a descendant of the Incas, José Gabriel Condorcanqui, who called himself Tupac Amaru II, as a reaction to land "reforms" which placed extra fiscal burdens on individual peasants and their families, coupled with the demand that they buy goods imported by the crown at far higher prices

than they had previously produced them on the missions before the expulsion of the Jesuits. With clerical support, the movement spread rapidly through Peru and into parts of New Granada and the River Plate. The colonial powers eventually suppressed it brutally by mobilizing militia which they made parish priests raise. Tupac Amaru, his family and other native leaders were slaughtered with frightful tortures, though the movement carried on in "High Peru" (now Bolivia) under the leadership of the Aymara Indian Julian Apaza, "Tupac Catari," till early 1782.

The "Commune" or *Comuneros* movement erupted in New Granada in 1781, triggered by the imposition of a state monopoly on spirits, salt and tobacco, added to a sales tax on cotton, from which spinners suffered badly, as they were forced to buy supplies in the market place. The uprising was started by the women of El Socorro in eastern Colombia, who wove cotton and sold their fabrics in northern and central New Granada. In western Colombia another woman led eight hundred mutineers against the tobacco and spirits tax. Despite a reduction for women and blacks agreed by the Spanish authorities, the mutiny spread, and was supported by elements of the clergy, especially the Dominicans, disaffected on account of the religious reforms. A bloody repression failed to halt it, but it was finally dispersed with false promises of abolition of the taxes made by the archbishop of Bogotá when the rebels were at the gates of the capital. Its leaders were arrested and executed.

4. A. Ariza, OP, *Fray Ciriaco de Archila. Primer prócer de la libertad absoluta en Colombia* (Bogotá, 1971), p. 30.

5. *Instrucciones dadas por el Sr Regente Visitador General*, copied by the scribe of Santa Fé, Dr Nicolás Prieto Dávila. *Fondo de Comuneros* III, Fol. 149–50, in deposit of Rare and Unusual Books, National Library of Colombia, nos. 30 and 16.

6. P. Cárdenas Acosta, *El movimiento comunal de 1781* (Bogotá, 1960), pp. 190–3.

7. Hno. Finestrad, *El vasallo ilustrado* (1786), p. 327. MS in deposit of Rare and Unusual Books, Nat. Lib. of Colombia.

8. Cited in R. Tisnes, *El clero y la independencia en Santa Fé* (Bogotá, 1871).

9. F. de Soto Mayor, "Catecismo o instrucción popular," in F. González, *Partidos políticos y poder eclesiástico* (Bogotá, 1975), pp. 40ff.

10. *Colección de historiadores y de documentos relativos a la Independencia Chilena*, vol. XIX, p. 223.

11. T. Halperin Donghi, *Historia contemporánea de América Latina* (Madrid, 1969), p. 143.

12. Letter from Simón Bolívar to Gen. Santander, 27 Oct. 1825, in *Obras completas*, comp. V. Lecuna, vol. V, p. 293.

SELECT BIBLIOGRAPHY

Aguirre Elorriaga, M. *El abate De Pradt en la emancipación hispanoamericana*. Buenos Aires, 1946.

Ariza, A., OP. *Fray Ciriaco de Archila. Primer prócer de la libertad absoluta en Colombia*. Bogotá, 1971.

Astraín, A. *Historia de la Compañia de Jesús*. Eight vols.: Madrid, 1920–5.

Bidegain, A. M. *Así actuaron los Cristianos en la Historia de América Latina*. Bogotá, 1985.

Beozzo, O. and others. *Historia da Igreja no Brasil no século XIX*. Vol. II/2 of *Historia Geral da Igreja na America Latina*. Petrópolis: Vozes, 1980.

Cárdenas Acosta, P. *El movimiento comunal de 1781*. Bogotá, 1960.

Carro Celada, E. *Curas guerrilleros en España*. Madrid, 1971.

Colmenares, G. *Hacienda de los Jesuitas el el Nuevo Reino de Granada en el siglo XVIII*. Bogotá, 1969.

Dussel, E. *Historia General de la Iglesia en América Latina*. Vol I/1, *Introducción General*. Salamanca: CEHILA, 1983.

—. *History of the Church in Latin America*. Grand Rapids: Eerdmans, 1980.

Halperin Donghi, T. *Reforma y disolución de los imperios ibéricos 1750–1850*. Madrid, 1985.

Hoornaert, E. *Historia da Igreja no Brasil. Epoca colonial*. Vol. II/1 of *Historia Geral da Igreja na America Latina*. Petrópolis: Vozes, 1978.

Fisher, J. L. *Government and Society in Colonial Peru: the Intendant System, 1784–1824*. London, 1970.

Giménez Fernández, M. *Las doctrinas populistas y la independencia de hispanoamerica*. Seville, 1947.

Gutiérrez Isaza, E. *Historia de las mujeres próceres de Colombia*. Medellín, 1970.

Kauffmann, W. *La política británica y la independencia de América Latina, 1804–1828*. Caracas, 1963.

Leite, S. *Historia de la Compania de Jesus no Brasil*. Ten vols., Lisbon-Rio de Janeiro, 1938–50.

Leturia, Fr, SJ. *Relaciones entre la Santa Sede e Hispanoamérica*, Vol II, *Epoca de Bolívar*. Caracas, 1959.

—. *La primera misión pontíficia a Hispanoamérica (1823-1825)* Vatican City, 1963.

Lynch, J. *The Spanish American Revolutions, (1808–1826).* New York, 1973.

Monsalve, J. D. *Mujeres de la Independencia.* Bogotá, n.d.

Phelan, J. L. *The People and the King: the Comunero Revolution in Colombia,* 1781. Madison, 1978.

Romero, J. L. and L. A. Romero, eds. *Pensamiento político de la emancipación.* Caracas, 1977.

Rodríguez Casado, N. "Notas sobre relaciones de la Iglesia y el Estado en Indias en el Reinado de Carlos III." *Revista de Indias*, Jan.–June 1959.

Tisnes, R. *El clero y la independencia en Santa Fé.* Vol IV of church history, vol. XIII of *Historia extensa de Colombia.* Bogotá, 1971.

Gonzalbo, T. L. *Historia de la Iglesia en América Latina. Vol. III, La Iglesia en la crisis de la Independencia.* Madrid, 1963.

Vargas Ugarte. *El episcopado en los tiempos de la emancipación sudamericana.* Buenos Aires, 1932.

Webster, C. K. *Gran Bretaña y la Independencia de América Latina. Documentos escogidos de los Archivos del Foreign Office (1812–1830).* Buenos Aires, 1944.

Whitaker, A. P. *Estados Unidos y la Independencia de América Latina.* Buenos Aires, 1964.

Chapter 6

THE CHURCH AND EMERGENT NATION STATES (1830–80)

Enrique Dussel

The half century 1830–80 covers the period from the end of the wars of independence to the establishment of liberal nation states – processes that took place in Europe from the sixteenth century and in black Africa from the middle of the twentieth. During this period the Church, as the only institution carried over from the Spanish-Portuguese colonial order to the new, politically independent (though still neo-colonial from an economic point of view) phase, was buffeted by a history laden with conflicts that can be seen as a process of establishing the political institutions of the emergent nationalities (often in the hands of élites which exercised a new form of dominion over the people). At the same time, little change took place on the level of the daily life of civil society, which remained frankly traditional.

The Church was largely the victim of the militarism unleashed by the wars of independence themselves, and of emergent nationalism, whose chaotic and ever unfinished gestation led it to lay hands on the wealth it could find (which meant that of the Church, there being no other), while refusing to share its precarious and never quite achieved legitimacy with the Church. Underlying this was a tension that began soon after independence and runs through the whole of Latin American history to the threshold of the twenty-first century: this is the contradiction between affirming an *identity* with the past (Amerindian, colonial, Latin American – the conservative side) and the need for a future *modernity* (as a developed capitalist industrial system – the liberal side). So there is tension between tradition and development, between cultural community and democratic individuality, between respect for what is national and indigenous (the federal viewpoint) and admiration for what is foreign, Anglo-Saxon, technological – and undoubtedly needed – (the unitary viewpoint). The Church in general opted for the first set of values; the founders of the liberal state for the second. A proper solution would have had to take elements of both, but these were times of contradiction and not of synthesis. Furthermore, the poor – made up of Indians, slaves, peasants, migrant workers – sat in the middle of these tensions and were oppressed by both sides for different reasons, though the first, conservative, tendency, including the Church, made somewhat greater efforts to understand their problems.

1. THE ROMAN CHURCH IN THE WORLD SITUATION

Between the end of the Napoleonic wars in 1815 and the revolutions of 1848. Europe went through a period of Restoration that was later to culminate in the expansion of imperialism around 1880. England in the reign of Queen Victoria (1837–1901) reached the height of its world dominance, which in Latin America it had to share partly with the United States since the proclamation of the "Monroe Doctrine" in 1823 (though less so when the United States was weakened by the Civil War of 1861–5). The industrial revolution failed wholly to take root on Latin America, as did imperialism in its later expansion, but still made its effects felt from 1850 onwards. Latin America was too occupied with its chaotic struggle for emergent nation states.

The Holy See, after outspoken criticism of the struggle for national independence in encyclicals of 1816 and 1824, changed its attitude after 1825, thanks to the Muzi mission. The Tejada delegation which Bolívar sent to Rome resulted in the first titular bishops being appointed, on 18 January 1827, after representations made by Cardinal Capelari to Pope Leo XII. Gregory XVI (1831–46) then, at the Consistory of 28 February 1831, nominated six residential bishops to Mexico. The following year, residential bishops were appointed to Buenos Aires, Santiago and Córdoba. On 5 August 1831, Gregory recognized the new republics of Latin America in his encyclical *Sollicitudo Ecclesiarum*.

The most influential pope of the period, though, was undoubtedly Pius IX (1846–78), whose intransigently anti-liberal attitudes served to reinforce the conservative approach of the Catholic Church in Latin America (his *Syllabus of Errors* was promulgated in 1864, and papal infallibility, used to legitimize the romanization of the Church in Latin America, decreed in 1870). This completed the hegemony of ultramontanism, preventing a prudent resolution of the tensions, since Pius' integralism led to violent breaks with governments more inexperienced than anti-Christian, in need of understanding rather than condemnation. The identification of the Latin American hierarchy with the strong papacy of Pio Nono isolated it from the chaos prevailing on the continent, but made it lose a large part of its proper *identity*, forged during more than three centuries of history, and distanced it from popular religiosity, which was far removed from Roman religious expression of the time.

In the whole half century, Rome first appointed one nuncio for the whole of Latin America, in Rio de Janeiro, following this with a second nunciature in Bogotá.

2. THE OVERALL SITUATION OF THE CHURCH IN LATIN AMERICA

The general characteristic of the period is the *crisis of the Christendom of the Indies*, and the transition to a patronal system of concordat, which the emergent nation states tried to effect in the same way that the Spanish and Portuguese monarchies had done in the past. At first, till around 1850, the Church still kept the prerogatives it enjoyed in the colonial period, but it was then – after 1848 in Colombia, 1852 in Argentina, 1857 in Mexico, 1871 in Guatemala, 1889 in Brazil – downright relegated to being one more institution in civil society. The institutions of political society or the state sought to separate the Church from the exercise of political power and from any role in the economic and educational spheres of society. Reduced in this way, the Church nonetheless became strong in civil society and prepared for its return to the political arena with a certain amount of power (though not till after 1930). The liberal states of the mid nineteenth century prepared the "internal" ground for the later, post-1880, "external" expansion of the Anglo-Saxon empires.

The Church could no longer carry out the functions of colonial *Christendom*. It lacked priests: many died in the fighting, others left for Europe, many gave up the priesthood. The religious orders were persecuted by governments, lacked vocations, and declined sharply in numbers. Its churches, seminaries, libraries were destroyed. It lacked revenues for chapters, parishes and chaplaincies, sharing in the generalized poverty brought about by times of war (first the wars of independence and then those for control of the state). It became a poor, disorganized Church.

The general characteristics of the period were defined by the demands of weak, emergent states, nourished by the former wealth of the Church, and struggling to find ideological justifications for a secular society without the Church (a task largely carried out by Freemasonry, with its efficient and secret lay organization). The Church was the only institution that could stand up to the state in the name of *traditional* and historical values. The clash between the two was inevitable, and the Church's very nature forced it to abandon the political field and leave it to the state – though remaining a limitation on its power, which proved the positive aspect of the clash.

3. CHURCH AND CIVIL SOCIETY

One has to bear in mind that the institutional clash between Church and state left one sector out of account: the poor, who found the ultimate meaning of their daily lives in devotions, confraternities, saints and feast days. So, though the conservatives might be convinced Catholics, while the liberals propounded theories way beyond the grasp of the popular imagination, this Christian people was not represented by either camp – nor by the prelates, for whom they might have felt respect, but no cordiality. It was left to a mass of humble parish priests, religious, healers, local holy men and devout women, mothers of families, masters of ceremonies and the like to keep the faith alive among the people during this "transitional" phase from the Christendom of the Indies to the romanized Catholicism of the late nineteenth century.

Furthermore, though the hierarchy of the Cathoic Church constituted an élite, this could never be confused with the political or purely economic oligarchy, since institutional forces themselves compelled it to keep its autonomy. Though the Church was not in the vanguard of society, neither can it be classed as reactionary. It never lost its deep bond with the popular classes – a much closer bond than the liberals ever had, or even than the forces of the left in the twentieth century were to have. It has been criticized for concentrating its influence on women, children, Indians and the poor, but this was in a way rather its glory, since these were the most oppressed sectors of the population. So movements for native or peasant rights always used religious symbolism to define their claims, and the Church often supported them. The Church stayed close to the daily life of the people throughout the wars, persecutions and social upheavals of this tragic period of emergent nationhood; it was the only institution to provide a permanent point of reference.

It is to this period that this popular song belongs – a mixture of monarchism, ultramontanism and moralism with the voice of a people left to drift unguided:

Ya la religión se acaba,
virtudes y devociones;

dan el grito las pasiones,
alza el capricho la espada.
Ya no hay papa santo en Roma;
que nos conceda una gracia.
¡Ay, qué terrible desgracia!
Ya no hay rey, ya no hay corona,
sólo la guerra se entona . . .[1]

(Religion is coming to an end, with its virtues and devotions. Passions cry out, and the sword runs riot. There's no holy pope in Rome to grant us a favour. Oh, what a terrible misfortune! There's no more king, no more crown, only war is intoned . . .)

4. REGIONAL ASPECTS

(a) The Brazilian Empire

While the other regions were struggling to achieve national *unity*, Brazil achieved it thanks to the First Empire of Pedro I. When he abdicated as emperor of Brazil in 1831, Pedro II was six years old and, after a regency lasting six years, was to rule till 1889.[2] In this Second Empire, the Church became more "Roman" (and European) and less "national" (and Portuguese); the growing liberalism made it more "militant," though it was always preponderantly a "white" Church – African slaves and native Indians saw it as something alien, something in which they were second-class citizens. The Church sought its autonomy in relation to the temporal power of the state, continuing the régime of Christendom (which it had had to abandon in Spanish-speaking America).

By the end of the period there were eleven dioceses in Brazil: Rio, Mariana, Diamantina, São Paulo, Rio Grande, Goiás, Mato Grosso, Pernambuco, Ceará, Maranhão and Pará. The bishops were close and united, and supported by Rome in their confrontations with the liberal emperor. The archbishop of Bahía, Romualdo Seixas, and the bishop of Mariana, Antônio Viçoso, were pioneers of church independence; in 1847 the latter challenged the government of Minas Gerais. This led to the "religious debate" between two bishops (Macedo Costa and Dom Vital) and Masonry, in one of the most prototypical conflicts of the century between a romanized Church, reticent with regard to lay autonomy, and the emergent state, anxious to keep its regal trappings out of church control. The losers were the Christian people, oppressed by the twin hegemonies of Church and state. Dom Vital, a pronounced ultramontane, in 1873 suppressed several brotherhoods, confraternities and third orders which refused to expel masons from their membership. The confraternities, which claimed to be mixed civil and religious associations, appealed to the emperor. In 1874, both bishops were imprisoned. The final outcome was in effect greater autonomy for the Church and greater power for the liberal state. The Christian prophet Joaquín Nabuco pointed out that while it was true that the bishops fought against Freemasonry – which was rooted among the people – they did not fight against black slavery.

The Church played a prominent part in legitimizing the war against Paraguay of 1870, proclaiming love of God, love of country and the duty to lay down one's life in the face of the enemy (Paraguay, next to the Empire in the River Plate area, being considered too strong). In the last part of our period, from 1875, however, it was still not capable of raising an unambiguous voice on the subject of the abolition of slavery. In 1817, half the population (1,930,000) had been slaves; by 1874 the proportion was down to 15 percent (1,540,000). The slave population was gradually shifted from sugar to coffee production; their liberation in 1884 was the result of changes in the organization of "agribusiness." The Church put no effort comparable to its evangelization of the Indians into the abolition of slavery. The Franciscans liberated their slaves, and then on certain conditions, only in 1871, the year in which the bishop of Rio, Pedro Maria de Lacerda, issued a pastoral recommending this course. The Benedictines freed all their slaves, without any conditions attached, at the same time; the Carmelites, on the other hand, clung on to their slaves till final abolition was decreed. A few bishops, such as Bentos in São Paulo, became active promoters of abolition, and then welcomed and evangelized freed slaves in the Confraternity of "Our Lady of Remedies," patroness of Brazil.

(b) Mexico

In 1827, Mexico had one archdiocese, nine dioceses, 1,194 parishes and 3,483 secular clergy for a population of eight million – the highest on the whole American continent. From the Casa Mata plan of 1823 to that of Ayutla in 1854, the country was ruled by Santa Ana – the time known as the *Santanismo*, during the first part of which the Church had to defend itself against the reformist laws of Gómez Farias, designed to force bishops into exile, till these laws were annulled by Santa Ana in 1834, bringing him the plaudits of the Church.[3] The process of annexation of the northern states to the United States, from the Texan revolution of 1835 to the treaty of Guadalupe Hidalgo in 1848, removed the states of California (which had been a diocese since 1840), Arizona, New Mexico and Texas from the tutelage of the Mexican Church, to begin their own histories of appalling sufferings.[4]

A second phase, from the fall of Santa Ana in 1854 to the beginning of the "Porfiriate" in 1876, saw the liberal faction unleashing an assault without quarter on the institutional church, so as to set up a secular nation state. The Constitution of 1857, despite beginning "In the name of God and with the authority of the Mexican people," set the tone for the secularization of the state and attempted to impose this on society as a whole, which nevertheless remained profoundly religious and impermeable to the liberal aims. In 1859 Benito Juárez came to power, with a triumphal entry into the capital, after which he expelled the apostolic delegate and the bishops from the country. One of the exiled bishops, Labastida, was later to be archbishop of Mexico City. This time of secularization, of triumphant liberalism, was defined by the Juárez, Lerdo and Churches laws, and the brief *interregnum* of Maximiliano (1864) failed to do much to change relations between Church and state.

(c) Central America

From the time Mexico proclaimed its independence in 1823 to the establishment of the Central American Federal Republic in 1824, the struggle between the conservatives, who sought to unite Central America in one state, and the liberals, who supported the federalization of the region, was continuous.[5] The question of appointing resident bishops to El Salvador and Costa Rica in 1850 was an eminently political one, since each of these nations sought full ecclesiastical power on its own soil, something Guatemala, Honduras and Nicaragua had enjoyed since colonial times. This led to the frustrated schism of El Salvador, led by bishop Matías Delgado.

The later expansion of coffee plantations in the region had its political counterpart in the liberal state, which was also supported by the oligarchy in charge of banana production. The battle with the Church was of a juridical-institutional nature, brought about by the need to legitimize the liberal state, even though the essential conservatism of these groups bound them to the church hierarchy. The matter of the debate was the introduction of civil marriage and divorce, the secularization of civil registers and education, the temporary suppression of some religious orders, the temporary expulsion of some clerical representatives and general adherence to the idea of a lay state.[6] In El Salvador, the conservative regime under Rafael Carrera, Francisco Ferrer and others, lasting from 1839 to 1871, brought about no fundamental change. After 1871, things were different: in Guatemala, under Justo Rufino Barrios, El Salvador under Santiago González and Nicaragua under Zelaya, the Church suffered a sustained liberal onslaught. In Guatemala this liberalism was entrenched in the Constitution of 1879, which opened the way for the influx of foreign capital and the expansion of US interests by the end of the century.

(d) Great Colombia and the Andean Region

In Colombia,[7] the secession of Venezuela and the death of Bolívar in 1830 mark the beginning of this period. In the first phase, beginning with the interregnum of Santander from 1832 to 1848, José Ignacio Márquez challenged the Church, but failed to prevent the conservative Constitution of 1843. From 1848 to 1880, the liberals held power; the militantly anti-church José Hilaro López expelled first the Jesuits and then Archbishop Mosquera, leading to a violent separation of Church and state in 1853. By the end of the period, however, a degree of reconciliation had taken place between conservatives and liberals, Church and state.

In Venezuela, all the bishops, beginning with Archbishop Ramón Ignacio Méndez, were expelled in the early 1830s for refusing allegiance to the Constitution of José Antonio Páez, who was more or less in control of the country from 1829 to 1846. A chaotic, largely conservative-dominated, period came to end with the liberals holding power from 1859 to 1899.

In Ecuador,[8] which was part of Great Colombia till 1830, the governments of Juan José Flores (1829–34) and Rocafuerte proclaimed the "Catholic, Apostolic and Roman Religion" the official religion of the state, to the exclusion of all others. The latter, liberal by conviction, however, encouraged the introduction of Protestantism, as did so many others at the time. The prototypical conservative government of the whole period was that of Gabriel García Moreno (1860–75): a convinced ultramontane, he carried out the aspirations of Pio Nono to the letter. "Under his direction ... Ecuador experienced a progressive dictatotship, based on the most intransigeant Catholicism imaginable."[9] García Moreno sought in Catholicism a way of making his country modern and of integrating Indians, mestizos and whites into the process. Influenced by the teachings of De Maistre, Bonald and Donoso Cortés, he welcomed the *Syllabus* as providential guidance.

In Peru, a self-destructive series of leaders prevented any sort of stability between 1821 and 1845. Independence had left the same landowning oligarchy in power, and their conservatism maintained good relations with the Church at first, with the Constitution of 1823 recognizing Catholicism as the only permitted religion. From 1822 to 1835, José de Goyeneche was the only bishop resident in the whole of Peru. Later bishops were men of personal virtue, from Peru, but all ultramontane. The major figure toward the end of the period was Bartolomé Herrera (1808–64), of humble origin, Rector of the College of San Carlos, a conservative but at the same time committed to defending and educating the Indian population. Overall, however, the Church had lost any deep evangelizing relationship with the Indians.

A second phase, from 1845 to the Chilean invasion of 1880, began with the consolidation brought about by Ramón Castilla (1845–62), and saw the peak of guano and saltpetre exploitation, bringing Manuel Pardo to power. Tithes were abolished only in 1855, and ecclesiastical tax-exemption the following year. The oligarchy of the coast, based on wealth from sugar and cotton plantations, now held the political reins, and though liberal, established a *modus vivendi* with the Church that was to last till the end of the century. The Church failed to resolve the Indian question, but regained much of its former strength and carried out a major internal reform – on the lines of ultramontane Romanization, but nevertheless with a measure of social, popular and national content.

In Bolivia, the Sucre government which came to power in 1825 saw itself, like so many nationalist governments, obliged to reform the Church; it suppressed the smaller convents, unmortgaged ecclesiastical property, regulated parish life, and so on[10] (thereby effectively carrying on colonial policy). Under the government of Andrés de Santa Cruz (1829–39), the episcopate was reorganized – there having been only one bishop, José Mendizabal, in 1827), along with some of the religious orders, such as the Franciscans, of whom ten arrived in 1835. In the political chaos that marked the later part of the period, the church was unable to work out a pastoral policy appropriate to the circumstances.

(e) The Southern Cone

The region that had been poorest during colonial times, for lack of precious metals, tropical products and large native populations, was to be the most favoured under the introduction of capitalism in its free-market phase – as it was in the imperialist expansion post-1880. British influence was generally paramount in national development (with the exception of Paraguay, which dared to pursue its development apart from the British empire, and suffered the genocide of the war of 1870 as a result).

In the United Provinces of the River Plate (later Argentina), the founding Congress of 1816 declared freedom of religion (to allow the presence of English Anglicans) even though many of its members were clerics and religious. In 1822, Bernardino Rivadavia, state minister of Buenos Aires, decreed a church reform law on the lines of the "enlightened Catholicism" of Charles III of Spain: tithes were abolished, as was tax-exemption and the charging of service costs to the state, but the most important provision was freedom of worship, to conciliate English merchants.[11] The hierarchy was reorganized with the appointment of Justo Santa María de Oro as bishop of the province of Cuyo in 1834. Mariano Medrano was appointed bishop of Buenos Aires, and Mariano José de Esclada his auxiliary shortly after, and Benito Lascano was promoted to Córdoba in 1836. These bishops began a slow restoration of church structures, evangelized the Indians, and brought the Jesuits back. In general, the Church and the poor supported the government of Juan Manuel de Rosas, even though in his second administration he became a zealous royalist, ordering the red federal emblem to be displayed in churches, for example. Medrano became a mere puppet of the government, and when the papal envoy Ludovico de Besi arrived, he found a Church completely under the sway of the secular power.

In the 1853 Constitution, though article 2 states that "the federal government upholds Catholic Apostolic Roman worship," article 14 declares that all inhabitants of the country have the right to "profess their religion freely." This was a royalist Constitution, with powers of patronage held by the state.

1859 saw the foundation of the diocese of Paraná, brought about by Juan Bautista Alberdi in Rome and the nuncio Marino Marini in Rio. This time also marked the beginning of a profound change in the daily lives of the people, brought about by the flood of immigration from Europe. In 1869 the population of the country was 1,800,000; by 1914 six million European immigrants had been added, bringing a process of secularization with them. Liberalism, positivism, Freemasonry and the spread of Protestantism all complicated the daily lives of the people of Argentina. New religious orders set up schools to educate the people. One priest who had great influence was Gabriel Brochero, the "*gaucho* priest" who died in 1914; he worked among the poor of Córdoba, founding the "*Tránsito*" house of spiritual exercises in 1879. Under the governments of Mitre, Sarmiento and Avellaneda, the Church made its way into modern Argentina. In 1876, General Julio Argentino Roca, armed with Remington rifles and the electric telegraph, exterminated the Indians of the Pampas. At the same time, Franciscans, followed by Lazarists and Salesians, were beginning their missions to Patagonia.

In Paraguay,[12] the first part of the period was taken up by the "dictatorship" of "Doctor Francia" (José Gaspar Rodríguez), which lasted from 1816 to 1840. He closed convents and held Bishop García de Penés under house arrest. He introduced the royalist catechism of Bishop San Alberto to Paraguay, substituting his own person for that of the king, and held the church in totally unreasonable subjection. When he died in 1840, no Paraguayan priest would pronounce his funeral oration.

Basilio Antonio López, elder brother of the future president, was appointed bishop of Asunción in 1844. In 1862, Francisco Solano López, son of the tyrant, was made President, in which office he called himself "Son of the Most High" and "God on earth." It was not till after the 1870 war, in whch Paraguay was completely destroyed and only forty priests left alive, that the Church could begin a process of reorganization that was to lead, years later in 1894, to the beginning of the modern Church in Paraguay with the appointment of Juan Sinforiano Bogarín as bishop of Asunción, a post he was to hold till 1949. The diocesan seminary reopened in 1880, and it was there that the clergy of the early twentieth century were mostly educated.

Uruguay had no bishopric till 1878, when Jacinto Vera, bishop *in partibus* since 1865, was appointed. Its little Church, with between twelve and fifteen priests from 1830 to 1860, followed the ups and downs of the country's internal struggles and those between Argentina, Brazil and Paraguay. The Constitution of 1830 declared Roman Catholicism the official state religion. In the 1840s, "Protestant" bibles were burned, under the impetus of the Jesuit Ramón Cabré. For the rest of the period, the Church kept a low profile, subject to the watchful eye of liberal powers (in the university) and Freemasonry (in politics). It was not till the appointment of Mgr Mariano Soler as bishop, later archbishop (he died in 1908), that the Uruguayan Church began to grow in a deeply secularized country.

The conservatives took power in Chile in 1830, and the 1833 Constitution recognized Catholicism as the state religion. Under Diego Portales (d. 1837), the state was organized and the conservative Church respected. Santiago became an archdiocese in 1840, with Manuel Vicuña Larraín as its first archbishop. The major figure of the period, however, was Mgr Santiago Rafael Valdivieso, archbishop of Santiago from 1845 to 1878, who reorganized the diocesan curia and the religious orders and was one of the founders of the Pius Latin American College in Rome (1869). The other great personality of the Chilean church in the nineteenth century was Mgr Mariano Casanova, appointed archbishop in 1887. In 1874, in the so-called "theological debate," church tax-exemption was ended, tithes were abolished and the country's doors opened to Protestants, ushering in a liberal period under President Pinto in 1876.

(f) The Caribbean

The history of the Church in the nineteenth century is at its most complex in the Caribbean. Some countries achieved their independence early (Haiti in 1804, followed by Santo Domingo); some had to wait till the end of the century (Cuba and Puerto Rico in 1898), then to fall into the hands of the United States; others, such as the British, French and Dutch colonies, had to wait till the twentieth century to throw off their colonial status. The Catholic Church was the established church in the Spanish Antilles (the larger islands of Cuba, Haiti/Santo Domingo and Puerto Rico, and some other islands), while the other colonies, with the exception of the French, were Protestant.[13]

In Haiti, Toussaint L'Ouverture in 1801 recognized the Catholic Church as the only faith that could be professed in public, while decreeing freedom of private worship. The church of the French whites disappeared for ever from the island. Haiti occupied Santo Domingo from 1822 to 1844, and in 1830 President Boyer expelled the archbishops of Santo Domingo and Port-au-Prince. Various Apostolic Delegates sent by Rome failed to restore relations, till Bishop Joseph Rosati of St Louis signed a concordat with the government in Rome's name. It was not till 1860 that the Church, then made up of an archbishopric and four dioceses, could restore its parishes and missions, bring in religious orders and start schools among the people. Haitian priests were educated at the seminary of St Jacques in Quimper in France.

Santo Domingo,[14] the cradle of Christianity in America, freed itself from Haiti in 1844, proclaiming "God, Country and Freedom!" Mgr Tomás de Portes was appointed archbishop in 1848. Spain occupied the country in 1861, and indigenous priests were replaced by Spaniards in the larger parishes, though not for long, since the occupation came to an end in 1865. In 1880, a priest, Fernando Arturo de Meriño, was elected President, and his is generally recognized as the best government of the nineteenth century. He was later consecrated archbishop of the capital, in 1885, and died in 1906. During this time the Church went through all the crises of the country's history.

In Cuba, a Spanish colony throughout the period, Felix Varela set the tone for the nineteenth century with the opening of the San Carlos seminary, which was to become the conscience of the independence movement. Bishop Espada (d. 1832) wrote a pastoral letter in 1826 declaring slavery unchristian. In 1851, Antonio María Claret, who was later canonized, was appointed bishop of Santiago. Exploitation in the sugar plantations had been brutal since 1792, and mill owners opposed religious teaching for their slaves. But by 1866, rebellions showed them that only a return to Christianity could make their slaves "humble, hard-working and respectful"![15] Nicolás de Azcárate countered this by saying that "if preaching were in conformity with the principles of Jesus Christ, it would be against slavery and would awaken aspirations to freedom."[16] The weight of the Church, however, represented by its hierarchy and élites, was behind slavery. It was a leaderless, manipulated Church.

When the struggle for independence began in Camagüey in 1851, Claret, then bishop, pleaded for the lives of the patriots. When Carlos Manuel de Céspedes rose up in arms in 1868 demanding freedom for Cuba, he also, as a Christian, proclaimed freedom for the slaves. But then those bishops who followed Claret (1859) and Fleix (1865) in the see of Havana tied the church indissolubly and unforgivably to Spain till 1898. Only the Christian freedom fighters of 1895 did something to redeem the honour of Christianity. By the end of the colonial period, the African population was barely evangelized and the few clergy could attend only very inadequately to the white population, whether Spanish or criollo.

The church in nineteenth-century Puerto Rico[17] sided with the conservatives and Spain. The first bishop, Juan Alejo Arizmendi (bishop from 1803 to 1814) left Spain with the impression that bishops more loyal to the colonial power were needed, so his successors (Mariano Rodríguez from 1826 to 1828 and Pedro Gutiérrez from 1828 to 1833) were Spaniards who had fled from the liberated mainland of America. In 1830 the seminary of San Ildefonso – Arizmendi's brainchild, designed to "puertoricanize" the clergy – was founded, but did not last long. In 1851 a Concordat was signed. In 1868 the uprising known as the "Grito de Lares" was supported by many Catholics committed to freedom, and by many priests. When it was put down, Bishop Benigno Carrión pleaded for the captured patriots to be pardoned. The liberals returned to power and declared the Concordat null and void, embarking on outright persecution of the Church. In 1873 the Church's subsidy was cut further and

Church and state were declared separate. In 1876, with Alfonso XII on the throne of Spain, relations became more friendly.

The British Antilles,[18] Barbados, Jamaica and other islands, were evangelized by the Protestant churches, beginning with the Anglican Church, and their story can be found in the chapter on Protestantism in Latin America, with the single comment here that the first Anglican bishop of Barbados, Hart Coleridge (1824–42) taught Christian doctrine to the slaves.

In the Dutch Antilles[19], the need for slave emancipation was accepted early in the nineteenth century. The Catholic Church had established the diocese of Guyana in 1790; it came to Surinam in 1825 and by 1859, four years prior to the abolition of slavery there, there were 9,500 Catholics, slave owners having permitted the evangelization of Africans since 1830. In Curaçao the colonial power allowed Catholic missions after severe struggles.

Translated from the Spanish by Paul Burns

NOTES

1. O. di Lulio, *Cancionero popular de Santiago del Estero* (Buenos Aires, 1940), p. 92.
2. On this, see CEHILA, *Historia General de la Iglesia en América Latina*, Vol. II/2 (Petrópolis, 1980), esp. pp. 143ff.
3. See CEHILA, *Historia General*, Vol V (Salamanca, 1984), pp. 99ff.
4. See CEHILA, *Fronteras: A History of the Latin American Church in the USA since 1513* (San Antonio, 1983), pp. 143ff.
5. See CEHILA, *Historia General*, Vol. VI (Salamanca, 1986), pp. 243ff.
6. R. Cardenal, in *ibid.*, pp 283–4.
7. See CEHILA, *Historia General*, Vol VII (Salamanca, 1989), pp. 299ff.
8. See CEHILA, *Historia General*, Vol. VIII (Salamanca, 1987), pp. 247ff.
9. J. Meyer, *Historia de los Cristianos en América Latina. Siglos XIX y XX* (Mexico City, 1989), p. 128.
10. J. Barnadas, "La Iglesia en la formación del nuevo Estado boliviano," CEHILA, *Historia General*, Vol. VIII, pp. 230ff.
11. See E. Mignone, "El siglo XIX," CEHILA, *Historia General*, Vol. IX (forthcoming, Salamanca, n.d.). This freedom of worship was also included in the "May Letter" from the governor of the province of San Juan.
12. M. Durán, "Historia de la Iglesia en Paraguay," CEHILA, *Historia General*, Vol IX.
13. See CEHILA, *Historia General*, Vol. IV (forthcominmg, Salamanca, n.d.).
14. See W. Wipfler, *Poder, influencia y impotencia. La Iglesia como factor socio-político en República Dominicana* (Santo Domingo, 1980), pp. 54ff.
15. See the mimeographed "Guía para utilizar el *Proyecto de reflexión sobre al Historia de la Evangelización de Cuba*" (Havana, Dec. 1983), p. 36.
16. *Ibid.*
17. S. Silva Gotay, "II. Período de la crisis de la Cristiandad Española en Puerto Rico: 1810–1898," CEHILA, *Historia General*, Vol. IV.
18. K. Hunte, "The Church in the West Indies," *ibid.*
19. J. van Raalte and others, "Historia de la Iglesia en las Antillas holandesas," *ibid.*

CHRONOLOGY

1830 Death of Bolívar
1831 Pope Gregory XVI appoints the first residential bishops

1840 Pedro II Emperor of Brazil
Death of the dictator Francia in Paraguay
1844 Dominican Republic free from occupation by Haiti
1845 Valdivieso appointed bishop of Santiago (Chile) (d. 1875)
1846 Pius IX elected pope (d. 1879)
1848 Liberals come to power in Colombia
Annexation of Texas, Arizona, California and New Mexico to the United States (Treaty of Guadalupe Hidalgo)
1850 Establishment of dioceses of San Salvador and Costa Rica
1851 Antonio María Claret bishop of Santiago (Cuba)
1852 Rosas overthrown in Argentina
1857 Liberals come to power under Juárez in Mexico
1859 Pius Latin American College founded in Rome
1860 Gabriel García Moreno becomes (Catholic) President of Ecuador (assassinated in 1875)
1863 University of Mexico closed
1864 Pius IX issues the *Syllabus of Errors* against liberalism
Beginning of the war of the Triple Alliance against Paraguay (ends in 1870)
Maximiliano President in Mexico (shot in 1867)
1868 The *"Grito de Lares"* uprising in Puerto Rico
Beginning of the first war of independence in Cuba
1869 First Vatican Council opens (closes in 1870)
1871 Liberals in power in Guatemala
1873 Dom Vital bans confraternities in Brazil
1876 Porfirio Díaz President in Mexico
1880 Roca comes to power in Argentina
1889 Brazil declared a republic

SELECT BIBLIOGRAPHY

CEHILA (Commission for the Study of Church History in Latin America). *Historia General de la Iglesia en América Latina.* In Spanish: Salamanca: Sígueme, vol. I/1, 1983; vol. V, 1984; vol. VI, 1986; vol. VII, 1979, vol. VIII, 1987. In Portuguese: Petrópolis: Vozes, vol. II/1, 1987; vol II/2, 1987. In English: *Fronteras. A History of the Latin American Church in the USA since 1513.* San Antonio: MATT, 1983. Vols IV, on the Caribbean, and IX on the Southern Cone, in preparation for Spanish publication.

Dussel, Enrique. *Historia de la Iglesia en América Latina.* Mexico City and Madrid: Mundo Negro, fifth ed., 1984. Eng. trans. *A History of the Church in Latin America.* Grand Rapids: Eerdmans, 1981.

Halperin Donghi, Tulio. *Historia contemporánea de América Latina.* Madrid: Alianza, 1969.

Mecham, Lloyd. *Church and State in Latin America.* Chapel Hill: University of North Carolina, 1966.

Meyer, Jean. *Historia de los Cristianos en América Latina. Siglos XIX y XX.* Mexico City: Vuelta, 1989.

Pape, Carlos. *Katholizismus in Lateinamerika.* Sieburg: Steyler, 1963.

Pape, Richard. *El Catolicismo contemporáneo en Latinoamérica.* Buenos Aires: Fides, 1951.

Pike, Frederick. "La Iglesia en Latinoamérica." *Nueva Historia de la Iglesia.* Madrid: Cristiandad, vol. V, 1977.

Prien, Hans-Jürgen. *Die Geschichte des Christentums in Lateinamerika.* Mainz: Matthias Grünewald, 1987.

Chapter 7

THE CHURCH AND THE LIBERAL STATES (1880–1930)

José Oscar Beozzo

The half-century 1880–1930 incorporated the whole of Latin America and the Caribbean, sometimes silently, but more often violently, into the changing world market. The connections were made through the new transport and communications system, steamships, railways, cars and lorries, telegraph, press and, in the 1920s, radio; through new technology, machines powered by steam and electricity and internal combustion engines; through the region's products, agricultural ones such as cotton, cacao, tobacco, coffee, sisal, wheat, or animal products, especially wool and beef, extractive ones such as guano and rubber or minerals, saltpetre, copper, iron, silver, oil; through its labour relations, in the replacement of slaves or tenant farmers and share-croppers by rural and urban wage-earners; in the diversification of classes, in the make-up of the population, as the import of African slaves was ended and was replaced by "indentured servants" brought from India by the English and from Indonesia by the Dutch, or by colonists and immigrant workers from Europe, the Middle East, China and Japan.

In 1880 Latin America's 21 million or so square kilometres were home to about 50 million people, a number which had become 65 million in 1900 and just short of 100 million in 1930. Some areas underwent spectacular transformations. Argentina had little more than a million inhabitants in 1852. In 1920 it had 10.2 million, and in fifty years the cultivated area had increased sixty times. The population of Brazil rose from 9.9 million in 1872 to 30 million in 1920.

A profound political change was also brought about by the conclusion of a neocolonial pact, in which British hegemony was gradually imposed, in alliance with the new bourgeoisie engaged in the export of agricultural products and minerals and in each country managing the so-called liberal states: there was a pact between these new interests and the new foreign power. In some areas French and especially German capital tried, with greater or lesser success, to compete with British capital and influence, while the United States was able constantly to expand its range of action and influence. The slogan, "America for the Americans" (meaning the United States), coined by Monroe in 1823, became a *fait accompli* in the second half of the nineteenth century in Central America and the Caribbean (the Spanish-American war in 1898 ending in the U.S. occupation of Cuba and Puerto Rico) and in the decade after the first world war in South America. In this period the motor-car displaced the railways, oil ousted coal, and U.S. capital and domination replaced British hegemony in almost the whole continent.

In religious affairs the changes also went deep.

The old Catholic monopoly, buttressed by the union of Church and state under the aegis of the royal patronage enjoyed by the Spanish and Portuguese kings or the successor national states, was legally abolished by the freedom of worship introduced by the liberal constitutions. It was also undermined by the arrival of U.S. Protestant missions and the wholesale arrival of immigrants belonging to different religious traditions: Moslems and Hindus in the Guyanas and British and Dutch Caribbean islands, Confucians, Buddhists and Shintoists among the Chinese "coolies" and Japanese immigrants, Moslems and Maronite and Orthodox Christians among the immigrants from the Ottoman empire, Anglicans, Lutherans and Moravian brethren, Christians of the reformed Churches, Waldensians, Mennonites, Uniate Catholics and Orthodox among the immigrants from Central and Eastern Europe. The Catholicism of the immigrants from Ireland, Germany, France, Spain, Portugal, Poland, and above all Italy, who became the majority in some countries or regions (Argentina, Uruguay, the south of Brazil), clashed with the earlier Spanish and Portuguese Catholicism, now mixed with indigenous and African traditions. In the other countries and regions the arrival of European orders and congregations to replace the native clergy produced the same clash and profound conflict with the popular Catholicism inherited from the colonial period.

The Church itself was challenged and opposed by the rise to power of new, more secularized classes with their vision of a secular and secularizing state and society, nurtured and promoted in liberal clubs, newspapers and parties, in literary societies and above all in the masonic lodges. When the classes propagating the agro-export model took power, they established the corresponding political system, the liberal state, and imposed their ideas in religious affairs: Church and state were separated, ecclesiastical property secularized, schools made secular, civil registers established for births and marriages, cemeteries were secularized and convents and churches became the property of the state. Among the lower classes, the shifts of population in the rural areas, the rise of a working class in the cities, and of secular public schools, eroded the old loyalties and sometimes gave rise to a latent anticlericalism prompted by the Catholic hierarchy's alliances with conservative or even moderate liberal sectors. At the same time, anarchist, left-liberal, and socialist ideas spread. Adherence to the Church was very often replaced by indifference or by contact with and membership of unions and other workers' organizations.

This chapter, then, will examine the impact on the Church, not only of the liberal state, but also of the whole series of changes mentioned above, noting the conflicts and the solutions found in the various regions and countries.

1. ECONOMIC CHANGES AND POLITICAL, SOCIAL AND RELIGIOUS CONFLICTS

The English industrial revolution, reproduced in other European countries, reached Latin America and the Caribbean in a very particular form. In the second half of the nineteenth century a new international division of labour took place, with England as the centre and motor and based on a world market. In this market the role of Latin America and the Caribbean was to be producers of agricultural raw materials and minerals. While no industrial revolution took place on the continent, there was a revolution in the countryside, with the implantation of the agro-export model. At the same time, this situation arrived in the form of transport between the areas of agricultural and mineral production and the ports and urban services of the capitals and great port cities. It also brought with it the ideology of free trade, which identified liberalism with material and scientific progress, travel and the musical leisure of the operas in the theatres visited each year by European opera companies.

With liberalism there came the belief in education and the power of ideas to change the world and human beings. Liberal ideology saw a battle engaged between enlightenment and backwardness and obscurantism, represented by the Catholic religion and the Luso-Hispanic tradition, which would be defeated by the spread of English economic theory, French philosophy and U.S. Protestantism. It was also a struggle of civilization against barbarism (the indigenous, gaucho, African and mixed-race populations), to be won by the elimination or replacement of these populations by European immigrants. Domingo F. Sarmiento, in Argentina, held up as a model the United States, in which European immigration had created an industrious and powerful nation: "Let us not check the United States in its progress, which is essentially what some people advocate. Let us catch up with the United States. Let us be America ... Let us be the United States."[1] Another Argentine champion of modernization through immigration and education, Juan Batista Alberdi, criticizing the hold of the colonial clergy over education, asked, "Will the clergy be able to give our young people the mercantile and industrial instincts which ought to characterize South American man? Will they receive from their hands the fever of activity and enterprise which will make them the Spanish American yankees?"[2] The liberal proposal was to recolonize Luso-Hispanic American America according to this civilizing recipe: "It means regenerating the race, changing minds, the race through massive immigration, the minds through education."[3]

This operation was carried out with success in Uruguay, with a million immigrants in the period we are considering, and Argentina, which received 6.5 million, and with greater difficulty and on a more limited scale in Chile, Costa Rica, and the south of Brazil, where 4.5 million immigrants arrived, either to become small landowners in Rio Grande do Sul, Santa Catarina and Paraná or – 80 percent of them – to be wage-earning settlers on the coffee estates of São Paulo and the south-east of Minas Gerais. The plan proved to be completely unviable, however, for physical and biological reasons in the other parts of Brazil and the Caribbean, because of the economic depression of the sugar-producing areas and the dense population of African origin, and also in countries like Peru, Bolivia, Ecuador, Guatemala and Mexico, because of the weight of their indigenous or *mestizo* world.

At all events the operation was attempted at the cultural, linguistic and religious levels, with all the greater violence where there was fierce resistance to this forced "civilizing" and "Europeanization," which succeeded in penetrating the élites, but ran into stubborn opposition at lower levels of society. The secular press and secular schools were the main weapons of this liberal battle. Within Catholicism, paradoxically, "Romanization" represented a similar "Europeanization," offering the conservative élites Catholic colleges in which they could enjoy, without sending their sons and daughters to the old continent, a European education on a French, Italian or German model, and education which was modern because European, but traditional and "national" because Catholic.

In the connections between capitalism in the rural areas and the world market, three blocs of countries were formed.

The countries of the temperate zone, essentially Uruguay and Argentina, played their part by supplying traditional European products, wheat, wool and meat, basically for the English market, and bringing European immigrants to maintain the expansion of their plantations, pastures and auxiliary services, railways, ports, freezing plants. Immigration supported the urban infrastructure, water, sewerage, gas, electricity, trams and, in Buenos Aires, the largest and richest city on the continent, even an underground railway. All this was basically financed, built and run by the British.

The countries of the tropical zone added new products to the traditional colonial products of sugar and tobacco, rubber from the Amazon forest, bananas, cacao and coffee, which latter spread from Brazil to reach Colombia, Ecuador, Central America, the Caribbean and some areas of Mexico and Venezuela. Since Britain had its colonial regions to supply it with these products, exports went to the U.S. and continental European markets, diversifying dependency.

A third group of countries was linked to the world market by mineral production: Chile by saltpetre and copper, Bolivia by tin, Peru by copper, Venezuela by oil, Mexico by silver and oil.[4]

The visible sign of these economic transformations was the bringing into production of new lands, through steam traffic in the internal river basins (Amazonia, the basin of the River Plate, Paraná, Paraguay, Magdalena in Colombia), on the oceanic coastal trade, the transoceanic routes, and above all on the railways, linking the interiors to the ports.

In every country a capitalist market in land was created, almost always through the nationalization and sale of ecclesiastical wealth, especially the rural and urban properties of the old religious orders, confraternities and Third Orders and, in some countries, of parishes and dioceses.

This occurred in those areas where the Church in colonial times had accumulated very great territorial possessions and had preserved them substantially intact during the revolutionary wars. This was the case in Mexico, New Granada and Guatemala: in large part the opposition to the [religious] orders can be explained here by the greed aroused by their lands, and the expropriation of this land was an irreversible process, as in New Granada, where the restoration of Catholic primacy was accompanied by monetary compensation of the orders, but the new lay owners were not disturbed in the enjoyment of their landed property. However, the hostile attitudes toward the traditional situation of the Church were to be found also where its wealth – relatively small in the colonial period – had been ill defended against the revolutionary whirlwind and no longer offered an attractive booty.[5]

Communal lands and especially indigenous lands were forced into the same market which established the concentration of land in the hands of families and groups, both national and foreign, involved in agro-export businesses. So, in Guatemala, Germans occupied the lands most suitable for coffee, and also controlled both investment and marketing. The United States deprived Mexico of all land west of Louisiana and north of the Rio Grande, occupying Texas (1845) and later Upper California and New Mexico (1848), acquiring in this expansion over two million square kilometres. It also entered Puerto Rico and Cuba, occupying the land suited to sugar-growing and, later, the two islands themselves, in the Spanish-American war (1898).

When gold was discovered in California, the United States tried to occupy Nicaragua, to establish lines of communication between the east coast and west coast of the country via the Río San Juan and Lake Nicaragua, and recognized the U.S. adventurer William Walker as President of the country (1857). In 1903 it intervened militarily in Colombia, to remove from it the province of Panama. It subsequently imposed on Panama the treaty which gave the U.S. the Canal Zone and responsibility for the construction and administration of the canal "in perpetuity." United Fruit and other United States banana companies took over large areas of hot, humid, low-lying lands in Honduras, Guatemala, Nicaragua, Costa Rica and Ecuador, and became accustomed to intervene constantly in the political life of these countries. These interventions were always accompanied by economic demands for the benefit of U.S. capital, and also by religious demands, freedom of worship, meaning in practice permission for the entry of U.S. Protestant missions and for the establishment of schools belonging to these churches.

2 THE CATHOLIC RELIGIOUS WORLD ON THE DEFENSIVE

This reorganization of land and the economy had a number of different religious consequences, which also affected society and the state.

(a) In the countries in which religious orders were expelled and Church assets, especially land, released on to the market – Mexico under Juárez (1856), Colombia under Mosquera (1861), Guatemala under García Granado and Barrios (1872) – the Church emerged weakened by the loss of its personnel and a significant part of its economic base. On the other hand, it was now able – though it did not always achieve this – to free itself from its traditional and uncomfortable position as the natural ally of the large landowners and the exploiters of slaves (Brazil), Indians or landless peasants. The release of church assets in some places provided support to shaky public finances, but never led to a real redistribution of land among those who worked on it. It merely transferred it from large ecclesiastical owners to large agro-exporting liberal owners.

(b) In countries where there was a transfer of territory to the United States, or more or less lengthy occupation, the effects were different. In the territories which had belonged to Mexico, Texas, New Mexico and California, the Catholic population came to suffer severe discrimination, for being indigenous,

Hispanic, mixed-race and finally Catholic in origin, in a country dominated by the WASPS (white, Anglo-Saxon Protestants). Even within the Catholic Church, Mexican Americans were discriminated against through Rome's imposition of a French, and immediately afterwards Irish, hierarchy, which tried rapidly to eliminate the native clergy, creating a communication barrier both linguistic and cultural with the Hispanic-American Catholic population.[6] In Puerto Rico after 1898 the U.S. occupiers imposed English as the official language and encouraged the "Americanization" of the island by bringing Protestant churches and schools, while confiscating convents and other Catholic church properties. Despite the efforts of the local Church, which asked for a bishop drawn from the local clergy, they obtained from Rome the rapid replacement of the Hispanic hierarchy with a bishop of German origin, James Blenk, who came from the United States under the patronage of the U.S. government[7]. In all the other countries the U.S. occupation always opened the way for the entry and consolidation of Protestant missions, as in Haiti (1915–34), Nicaragua (1912–33), and the Dominican Republic (1916–24), even if one of the Protestant churches had a presence in the country going back to the nineteenth century. Alongside this foreign pressure, liberalism and masonry, once in power, always encouraged Protestant churches and schools as a way of weakening the influence of the Catholic Church, as can be seen with the governments of Juárez (1855–64) and Lerdo Tejada (1872–5) in Mexico or during the religious conflict in Brazil (1872–4).[8]

(c) The expansion of the great agro-export estates almost always took place in conflict with indigenous groups and at the expense of their lands. In this process of advance on indigenous lands the economic conflict for possession of the land was generally accompanied by a military and religious process. Many governments tried to associate the Church with their military campaigns against indigenous groups, either to herd them "peacefully" into reductions, leaving their lands free for occupation by large agro-export estates, or to collect into missions the survivors of military expeditions which easily turned into extermination campaigns. The concern of governments was no longer evangelization, but what they called the "civilization" of the savages and their incorporation into the nation as "useful and productive elements."

Within the Church too there was an acceptance of the ideology of the "civilizing" role of the Church and Christianity, in which proclamation of the faith was confused with the imposition of European culture and customs and service of the interests of the new order imposed by the state and of the economic and social domination of the large landowners. While the Church might try to reduce the sufferings and save the lives of the indigenous peoples, it must be recognized that the results were sparse and that little remains of the old missions of this period, and still less of the indigenous peoples they were intended to serve.

In Mexico the rapid expansion of the railways (from 1,073 km in 1880 to 19,280 in 1910, at the end of Porfirio Diaz's rule) which opened land up for logging, mining, cotton and sisal plantations, and cattle pasture, was accompanied by serious conflicts with the indigenous peoples. There was war with the Yaqui in the north, who had been exiled by Porfirio Diaz to the sisal plantations of the Yucatán or sold to the Cuban sugar plantations, the extermination of many groups in the Chiapas region and finally the great peasant revolt of Pancho Villa in the north and of Zapata in the centre of Mexico (1910–17).

In Brazil the rush to exploit rubber in the Amazon forest brought half a million north-easterners to the region between 1870 and 1910, at the same time causing a bloody conflict with the indigenous peoples of the area. The imperial government appealed to the Franciscans of Bolivia, and later of Italy, to group the Indians into villages and avoid clashes with the rubber planters and the tappers. The first Franciscans came in 1870 and opened a total of twenty-two missions. In 1888, however, all the missionaries withdrew to Manaus, after being involved in the whirlwind of violence and greed which set traders, plantation owners, middlemen and even rubber tappers against the Indians.[9] They were unable to protect the Indians, save their lives or catechize them. In the south of the country the government granted European immigrants in Rio Grande do Sul, Santa Catarina and Paraná land in indigenous areas, unleashing bloody conflicts in which the Indians always came off worst, faced with expeditions of professional Indian-hunters hired to exterminate them or put them to flight. The expansion of coffee in the west of São Paulo state advanced through the lands of the Kaingang, Coroados and Ofaye-Xavante, wiping them out implacably. At this moment (1910), after the separation of Church and state (1890), the government itself, faced with an outcry of public opinion and pro-indigenous elements in the army, created the National Indian Protection Service (SPI). While under the direction of General Rondon (1910–30), the SPI succeeded in avoiding large-scale massacres of the indigenous population. Later it became negligent, when not an active accomplice of estate owners, timber and mining companies in the theft of indigenous land.

In Argentina the government decided to eliminate the Araucanos, the Ona and the Fueginos from the lands coveted by the large landowners, cattle-breeders or wheat-growers, and at the same time opened up the humid pampa and the southern plains to the British railway companies. Their expansion was as spectacular, if not more so, as in Mexico, and the railway network grew from 2,500 to 33,000 kilometres between 1880 and 1914.[10]

Avellaneda's first minister of war, Adolfo Alsina, devised a plan for a gradual offensive-defensive advance [on the indigenous territories] which had little success (1874). He was succeeded by General Julio Argentino Roca, who had distinguished himself in the national army in putting down the Jordanist and Mitrist risings and that in Buenos Aires. He produced a plan similar to that of Rosas, worked out in every detail, designed to attack the Indians in their own strongholds and to force them to cross the cordillera or surrender (1876). He enjoyed for this purpose two tactical advantages over his predecessors, the Remington rifle and the telegraph, with which he was able to counter the speed of movement and the weapons of the indigenous. He did not originally intend extermination, but in practice this was the result he achieved.[11] [For the Argentine state] the indigenous problem in the south was solved, and millions of hectares were added to ranching and agricultural land, all appropriated by a few hundred large landowners, friends of the government. Later on, during the presidency of Roca (1880–6), the same method was used in the north-east, and the national territories of Misiones, Chaco and Formosa were organized.[12]

As for the Church's humanitarian and missionary interests, Mignone writes:

> The episcopate of the time and the religious congregations summoned for this purpose (Franciscans, Lazarists and Salesians) were concerned for the evangelization of the Indians, but they conceived of this as a task for after "pacification," consisting in teaching the Indians the rudiments of the faith, administering the sacraments to them and imposing on them the forms of European civilization, without respect for their rights and their moral and cultural values. As a result of the defeat of the indigenous peoples, a large number of tribes were pressed into the army as cannon-fodder: they were herded into settlements, taken by force to other regions and the women were given as servants to families in Buenos Aires. On the basis of this pain and humiliation evangelization was attempted, but achieved few results because the majority of the beneficiaries soon died, worn out by destitution, malnutrition, alcoholism and, above all, tuberculosis, which wreaked havoc. Campaign methods were bloody, and it was common for prisoners and wounded to be executed. There are vivid testimonies in the private papers of the missionaries who accompanied the troops and doubtless made efforts to mitigate the situation. But there was no public, organized, prophetic condemnation which could have moved consciences, offered alternatives and alleviated such huge suffering.[13]

In Chile in the 1870s there was an organized invasion of the lands of the Mapuche, in a violent military expedition which breached the centuries-old frontier of the River Biu-Biu, the northern border of the Mapuche people, established in sixteenth-century treaties. The so-called "pacification of Araucania" was completed in 1881, depriving the Mapuche of 800,000 hectares of agricultural land and 600,000 hectares of jungle. The heart of their lands, Temuco, was given to German immigrants and used for wheat farms and ranching. Jesuit, Salesian and Capuchin missionaries were sent for to minister to the immigrants and to the southern Indians after the military defeat.

(d) The response of the peasant and indigenous world to this violent entry of capitalism into the rural areas took the form of silent resistance, messianic movements, or even of armed risings. A series of uprisings broke out in the Peruvian sierra around Lake Titicaca. "The causes of these rebellions were almost always the same: the abuses by the local administrators, the forced contributions, the salt monopoly, the labour in the mines and other forms of servitude. In 1915 an army sergeant major, Teodomiro Gutiérrez Cuevas, adopted the *nom de guerre* Rumi Maqui ("Stone Hand") and headed a protest movement around Puno. The uprising ended in a massacre of the peasants."[14]

In the Brazil of the early years of the republic peasants driven from their lands by the expansion of the cotton plantations, a process encouraged by the railway between Salvador and Juazeiro and the steamships on the Rio São

Francisco, gathered on an abandoned estate in Vaza-Barris and built the hamlet of Canudos. Under the leadership of Antônio Conselheiro, a lay religious enthusiast, some five thousand mud houses sprang up around the church of Bom Jesus, making this "Clay Troy" the second largest town in the state of Bahia. Occupying the land, restoring peasant subsistence production, and opposing the liberal republic and its acceptance by the church hierarchy, and creating in the starving backlands a refuge for all the abandoned, Canudos attracted more and more people, who saw it as the restoration of the Kingdom of God on earth. The story spread round the backlands that in Canudos the "shanties were made of maize couscous," and that "the dry wilderness would become sea." An Italian Capuchin, Frei João Evangelista, sent by the Archbishop of Bahia and the government to persuade the peasants to disperse and return to their places of origin, where they would find either the centuries-old tyranny of the landowners or the starvation wages of the new agro-export estates, failed in his mission and had to leave the hamlet. This was the green light for police and later military repression, which, after four expeditions, two years of open warfare (1896–7) and a merciless blockade, eventually ground Canudos down with hunger, thirst and artillery which belched fire and iron night and day on to the fragile mud structures. The final assault, with side-arms, taking one house at a time and finally the church, resulted in a pitiless massacre, in which prisoners' throats were cut and which did not spare the women, not even those who were pregnant, whose stomachs were ripped open by bayonets to prevent the birth of more "little gunmen."[15]

In the south of the country, in the region of Contestado, between the states of Santa Catarina and Paraná, another Messianic peasant war broke out. The population which lived in the area of subsistence agriculture and extraction of *mate* from the native forest began to be harassed and expelled by the building of the São Paulo-Rio Grande do Sul railway. The government had given the consortium building the line ten kilometres of land on either side to take wood for the sleepers and the steam locomotives and to divide the land into lots and sell it to settlers, whose production would provide freight for the railway. These lands were occupied, and the peasants, advised by the monks João Maria and José Maria, and after their deaths by the seer Teodora and the virgin Rosa Maria, held out for four years (1912–16) against local troops and later the national army. Once again the signal for military intervention was the inability of the German Franciscan, Frei Rogério Neuhaus, to persuade the peasants to surrender their weapons and submit to the new order.[16]

Already in Mexico the peasant revolution (1910–17) of Pancho Villa and Zapata, especially the former, who came from the more capitalist and modernized north of Mexico, with its large estates, contained an element of anticlerical bitterness, developed in more sophisticated form by more bourgeois leaders such as Carranzas and Calles. According to Johannes Meier:

Under the rule of the liberals (1859–1910) the Catholic Church had carried out a second evangelization, developing the civic and social action movements favoured by Leo XIII. It was thus at the height of its expansion when a revolution intervened, which, for the first three years, favoured it. But the fall of the democratic President, Francisco Madero (February 1913), rekindled the revolution, and the victorious faction, men from the north, white, marked by the U.S. frontier, imbued with the values of Anglo-Saxon protestantism and capitalism, knew nothing of the old mestizo, Indian, Catholic Mexico. To them the Church was the incarnation of evil, "a pagan masquerade which loses no opportunity to make money, making use of the sheerest legends, outraging reason and virtue to achieve its ends."[17]

The 1917 Querétaro constitution embodied in its crudest form the liberal view of religion and of the social position to be assigned to the Catholic Church, which it stripped of any legal status:

> The 1917 Constitution closed the doors of education to the Church, refused to recognize monastic vows and banned religious congregations; it banned worship outside churches, nationalized ecclesiastical property and denied the Church legal recognition. Priests were recognized as a profession and therefore the state had power to control their numbers, their political rights and freedom of speech were restricted, the studies they undertook in seminaries were denied recognition; at the same time denominational political parties were prohibited. It was not a system of separation of Church and state, "but one which firmly established the supremacy of the civil power over religious elements," with a specific goal, to deny the Church any influence within the Mexican society produced by the revolution.[18]

In another sense, the *cristero* revolution (1926–9) in Mexico, represents the dissatisfaction of the Church and vast numbers of small landowners from the Jalisco highlands, and estate labourers, who regarded the implementation by Calles of the religious articles of the 1917 Constitution as intolerable oppression by the state against the faith and its practice.
Among the peasants who took to arms an equally important grievance was the unfulfilled promises of agrarian reform, and there is a thread of discontent running back to remnants of the zapatista guerrillas, now become *cristero* fighters.[19]

In all the peasant and indigenous risings, except the Mexican revolution, the Church hierarchy was always called on to exercise a role of mediation and moderation, in addition to its traditional role of disciplining the rural populations summoned to enter into the new capitalist order, submitting to its values and domination. Even in Mexico, the *cristero* revolt was only ended after the "agreements," sponsored by the United States embassy, between the government and the Catholic hierarchy.[20]

3 THE CHURCH AND POLITICS IN THE LIBERAL ORDER

Most studies of Latin American church history sum up the events of the period under consideration as an unremitting struggle between the Church and the liberal states and their legislation.

The Church is presented as fighting to preserve its status as the religious denomination of the majority of the people and the privileges it inherited from the colonial period, while the liberals make every effort to break its religious, social and political power and reduce its area of activity to the private sphere.

The story is more complex, since within the Church there was a tradition of liberal laity and priests forged in the wars of independence and a small group of political liberals who were sincere Catholics, although they advocated the solution of "a free Church in a free state" which the hierarchy consistently rejected.

The liberal programme was to reduce the power of the Church at all costs. Politically this meant separating it from the state. Economically, it meant secularizing its property, suspending the collection of ecclesiastical tithes and ceasing to pay its ministers and seminary professors or subsidizing its charities, schools and missions. As regards social life, the liberals banned processions and other public displays, and in the ideological sphere they promoted secular and secularizing education in the public schools and an intense anticlerical campaign in the press. At moments of greater conflict the liberal state exiled bishops and priests, expelled religious orders and congregations, banned the entry of new ones and prevented the entry of foreign priests and religious, or even broke off relations with the Holy See. Another general measure was the institution of a civil register for births and deaths, the secularization of cemeteries and legislation for civil marriage and divorce, which deprived the Church of control over the family structure.

The battles over all these points were waged first in the press, then moved to parliament, where the liberal constitutions were produced, or to the presidential palace, where laws and decrees were produced in an authoritarian, dictatorial or revolutionary manner, depending on the regimes which succeeded each other in power.

Another result of these battles was the extreme politicization of religious affairs. While the general attitude of the Church's reforming bishops in the second half of the nineteenth century was to keep the clergy out of political quarrels, in practice a complex and far-reaching alliance formed between the Church and the conservative political forces. The two sides swapped favours, the conservatives supporting the Church's demands and the Church giving them political support and ideological backing. It became common to identify "Catholic" and "conservative" and to assume that liberalism and Catholicism were totally incompatible. In Bolivia José Santos Machicado, a leading spokesman of "the Catholic Union," denounced those who "claim to be Catholics in religion and liberals in politics, weak minds or timeservers, who attempt to produce the impossible amalgam of good and evil, truth and error, [and who] did greater damage to the Church than liberalism itself, like a Trojan Horse in their ranks."[21]

In Chile "the hatred of the conservative Church for President José Manuel Balmaceda was the symbol of necolonial Catholic aggressiveness expressed as the wrath of God. A nephew of the President recalled in this connection his education in the Colegio San Ignacio in Santiago: '[Brother Llanas] ended by telling us that all those who belonged to the Liberal Party were irredeemably condemned to the eternal flames of hell . . . ' ."[22]

This description can be applied generally to the whole continent, as the conflict sharpened, marginalizing on both sides, among Catholics and liberals, those who held more nuanced positions.

If hostility to liberalism was growing within the Catholic Church, and was fanned by the intransigent attitude of Pius IX, who published his *Syllabus of Errors* in 1864, and the First Vatican Council (1869–70), on the other side the liberal position was becoming equally intransigent, all the more since liberalism rarely depended on the mass of the people, who, especially in the countryside, remained faithful to the Catholic tradition. "The Peruvian Mariátegui remarked (1928) that the extreme nineteenth-century development of liberalism led it to postulate Protestantism and the national church as a logical necessity for the modern state. This logic never went beyond speculation in all other countries, but became a reality in Mexico between 1926 and 1934, and after General Cárdenas, at least until 1938, implied the incorporation of the Catholic Church into the state."[23]

By the end of the century and especially after the first world war and the crisis of 1929, these positions were gradually being left behind. The process was encouraged by the growing challenge to liberalism on the left from the popular movement, by the formation of a working class influenced not by liberal ideas of progress, but by the critiques of anarcho-syndicalism, socialism or maximalism, as marxism was labelled at the time.

Liberalism became more and more conservative, being marginalized by the disaster of its agro-export model in the 1929 crisis, by the demand for more democracy from the urban middle classes, and by the rise of various forms of populism, nationalism and authoritarianism on both right and left during the 1930s. The liberal and conservative oligarchies, which at root differed little and were separated merely by the anticlericalism of the one and the clericalism of the other, united against the popular sectors and their political ideas. At the same time Catholic positions became more flexible in politics and more open in the social field and so broke the iron hoop with which the liberal-conservative polarisation had bound them.

According to Pablo Richard, the conversion of the Church during the 1920s and 1930s to the nationalist and developmentalist programme allowed it to break free of a series of contradictions and limits belonging to the previous period (1870–1930):

First, the Church was able to free itself from or abandon the polarization between "liberalism" and "conservativism." This polarization limited, falsified and neutralized the Church's action, since its opposition to liberalism was presented and interpreted wrongly by ideology as opposition to "progress," "science" and "modernity." The Church then moved from the polarization between "conservativism" and "liberalism" to the polarization between "national (or Latin American) liberation" and "foreign domination or dependence," "development" and "underdevelopment." The Church was able, from now on, to oppose positivist liberalism from a nationalist and developmentalist position which it was hard to present as conservative.

Secondly, the nationalist-developmentalist programme forced the Church to change its typically European and Romanized character, which was foreign to life in Latin America. From 1930 onwards, there has been a slow process of nationalization and Latin Americanization of the Church and greater recognition of indigenous Latin American culture and identity.

Thirdly, the Church's option for national and Latin American problems, for social and developmental problems, took it out of the purely devotional, familial and educational world into which it had shut itself during the period before 1930.

Fourthly, the nationalist, populist and developmentalist programme enabled the Church to widen its social base beyond the narrow circle of the oligarchic élites into which it had previously locked itself, and open out to the "middle strata" and the masses. The populist–nationalist–developmentalist programme enabled the Church to widen its social base, not only without breaking with the state and the dominant classes, but by drawing support from them and improving its relations with the state and the dominant classes.[24]

4 LATIN AMERICAN CATHOLICISM IN THE INTERNATIONAL CHURCH CONTEXT

It is impossible to understand Latin American Catholicism in the period 1880–1930 without analysing the crucial role of Rome in the historical developments of this period. More than in any previous period, Rome supplies the key to understanding the changes and expansion of the ecclesiastical apparatus. The particular situation of the royal prerogative, which gave the kings of Spain and Portugal control over church life in their American, African and Oriental possessions, seriously limited the power of Rome and even the implantation of Tridentine Counter-Reformation Catholicism. Nor did independence always bring the end of royal patronage, which became imperial patronage in Brazil (1822–89) or national patronage in the other republics from the beginning of the struggles for emancipation (1810–24). The break was to come only with the advent of liberal governments in the second half of the nineteenth century, beginning with Colombia (1853), Juárez's Mexico (1857), and reaching Brazil only late, with the Republic (1889), which established the separation of Church and state and freedom of worship (7 Jan. 1890). The process reached Chile last of all, in 1925.

The liberals introduced either the separation of Church and state or a renewed intervention by the state in ecclesiastical affairs, as in Mexico with the reform laws (1859) and the revolutionary constitution (1917), in Guatemala (1871), Guzmán Blanco's Venezuela (1870–88), Roca's Argentina (1880), Eloy Alfaro's Ecuador (1895), and so on, country by country.

The results are a paradox. Now that intransigence was the order of the day on both sides, there was no longer any room for those who wanted to be both Catholics and liberals or liberals and Catholics. From the decade 1860–70 the break was complete, and the intellectual and political élites, with rare exceptions, ceased to present themselves publicly as Catholics. The desires for church reform which had inspired some liberal ministers, such as Nabuco in Brazil (1855), were replaced by an attempt to break its backbone by attacking its material base through the nationalization of church property, the end of tithes and financial support for worship and ministers of religion, by eliminating its personnel through the expulsion of the Jesuits and other religious orders, and by reducing its ideological influence through the secularization of public education and the establishment of a civil register of births, civil marriage and public cemeteries.

These measures were never popular outside the narrow circle of the liberal élites, and produced a deep split between the real country, which remained Catholic, and the political leaders, who became militantly anticlerical.

After the wars of independence and the civil wars of the nineteenth century, the state, in its endeavour to build a nation, tried to use the Catholic Church, which retained social and political power. While rarely trying to destroy the Church, the state set out to dominate it in order to dominate and unify civil society. This form of republican regalism lasted until 1960 and longer in some countries. In Mexico the revolutionary state (1914–40) rejected the Church as a social institution and wanted to break it up with the help of masonry, the Protestants and the "reds." It was not a process of secularization, but a process in which one group sought political hegemony over society as a whole. The Church was treated as an obstacle to progress, to science and enlightenment.

Given that positivism and liberalism were toys of the class in power, they were at the same time anticlerical and antipopular, which enabled Mariátegui to write of Peru, "Demos became clerical." This campaign for rationalist education, this "secularization," did not affect popular culture.

The Church reacted to this state of affairs in three ways. With historical continuity, it defended its traditional rights and sought a concordat or alliance with the conservative oligarchs; it put its faith in education and the family, developed educational programmes, the Catholic press, devotional practices. Its aim was to win the élite while keeping the people, in order one day to conquer the state. Finally, it received from Rome, and from the Italian, French, Spanish, German and Belgian churches, support which proved decisive. Personnel, ideas and organizations from these churches transferred to America; the French religious orders and congregations in particular, expelled by anticlericalism, played a decisive part in this Europeanization, this Romanization of the Catholic Church.[25]

The liberal state's offensive had as its immediate and most visible consequence a tightening of links with Rome, as a potential source of help. It also turned the Latin American Church into a deeply ultramontane Church, dependent in everything on Rome. In order to find a space for survival, it tried to redefine its legal status by means of concordats signed between Rome and the state, although the changing political situation had caused concordats signed with conservative governments to be ignored or broken by liberal governments.

Now that the route of public education had been closed by the policies of secularizing education, the local churches tried to create a Catholic school system with religious congregations which reached the continent mainly via Rome. It was these congregations which also brought and promoted the new devotions, made "universal" by the Roman seal of approval. Notable among these were the devotion to the Sacred Heart of Jesus, to which Leo XIII consecrated the world on 1 January 1900, and the cult of Our Lady of Lourdes (1858), closely linked to the dogma of the Immaculate Conception, proclaimed by Pius IX in 1854.

Pius IX was the first pope to have had personal experience of Latin America. He accompanied Mgr Giovanni Muzzi, who was sent by Leo XII in 1823, after the wars of independence, to re-establish episcopal links directly with Rome, without the interference of Spain. He set off at the invitation of Chile's Bernardo O'Higgins. The two travelled the stretch from Buenos Aires to Santiago by land, crossing the desert and the cordillera, in a journey which took nine months from Genoa to Santiago. The journey was essentially a failure, but it gave Mastai Ferretti, the future pope, a stay of almost two years on the continent, which left a deep mark on his life and his relations with Latin America.

It was through the inspiration of Latin American priests (José Idelfonso Peña, a Mexican, in the 1830s, José Villaredo, another Mexican, in 1853, and finally José Ignacio Victor Ezayguirre, a Chilean, who pushed ahead with the idea and founded the college) that Pius IX blessed the foundation in Rome, on 21 November 1859, of the Colegio Pio Latino-Americano, which was to begin preparations for the ultramontane reform of the Church on the continent. The Pio Latino was to be the source of most of the new hierarchy, already with no trace of Gallicanism or ideas of "national" churches and attuned to the directives of the Holy See and reticent, if not openly hostile, toward the religious policies of the national states. The Pio Latino was also to produce the educators of the new clergy, because it provided the professors of dogmatics, moral theology and canon law for almost all the seminaries on the continent. The text books introduced were those of the Colegio Romano (the name at the time of the Gregorian University). The Pio Latino and the Gregorian were both directed by the Jesuits, who in this way left the mark of their educational method, their spirituality and their ideas on the whole of the diocesan clergy of a number of countries.

The Latin American bishops who took part in the Latin American Plenary Council of 1899, which was held on the premises of the Pio Latino, wrote a circular to the other bishops of Latin America, with a pressing appeal "that each should send one student to the College, so that he may learn, in this Eternal City, that spirit, which is truly Roman, of blind faith, perfect obedience and complete dependence on the infallible Chair of Peter, which unites all the churches scattered about the Catholic world with the one true centre of the Church of Jesus Christ, our Redeemer and Eternal King."[26] In the first hundred years of the College's existence 2,283 students passed through it, of whom over a thousand gained doctorates, 482 in theology, 240 in canon law, 436 in philosophy, but only four in church history and two in holy scripture. Almost five hundred more gained licentiates. Of these students 1,504 were ordained priests, 183 became bishops and seven cardinals.[27] These years of study in common, far from their own countries, and living in the same house and attending the same university, created a unique familiarity and camaraderie between these students (future seminary professors and future bishops) from all the countries of Latin America, producing, from Chile to Mexico, a homogeneous corps of clerics imbued with the Roman tradition. Even the continent's linguistic barrier was broken, since Brazilians attended the Pio Latino for almost eighty years, until the foundation of the Colégio Pio Brasileiro in 1934. By this date 423 Brazilians had studied at the Pio Latino.[28]

The revolutions of 1848, the unification of Italy in 1860 under the auspices of Garibaldi and the liberal policies of Cavour, including the military annexation of the Papal States, produced in the Holy See, and Pius IX in particular, an increasingly negative and pessimistic view of modernity and liberal principles. The *Syllabus*, in 1864, is the direct expression of this break, without half measures, with liberal values as a whole, and also ended for Latin America the era of liberal Catholicism and Catholic liberals. The *Syllabus* and its practical application caused an immediate crisis in the confraternities, which had come to include increasing numbers of people of Catholic tradition in religion who were liberals and/or masons in ideology, including priests. It was this period that saw the excommunication of many priests who were masons, and a number of whom, including the famous Padre José Manuel da Conceiçao in Brazil, subsequently joined the new Protestant churches.[29]

Since for these men reconciliation between Catholicism and liberalism had for the moment been made impossible, the only route left for them was to join the Protestant churches arriving from the United States. In these churches dual membership of the church and of the masonic movement was to be a crucial issue in the following decades, drawing the dividing line between more liberal and more fundamentalist protestantism.

At a later stage, with the intensification of Romanization, and the creation of an internationalized version of Catholicism in conflict with local cultural roots, small national Catholic churches were created throughout Latin America, such as the one founded in 1915 in Itapira, in the state of São Paulo, or the Brazilian Catholic church, founded in 1941, in which the nationalist component was the catalyst.

Two other experiences were to stamp the whole continent with the Roman style, the First Vatican Council (1869–70) and the Latin American Plenary Council (1899). After almost four centuries since the arrival of Columbus in America, bishops from the continent now took part for the first time in a conciliar meeting of the whole Church. Although the number of bishops resident in Latin America in the sixteenth century had already reached forty, none took part in the twenty-five sessions of the Council of Trent (1545–63).

At Vatican I the Latin American bishops totalled about forty, ten – the largest group – from Mexico, six from Brazil, five from Chile, two from Ecuador, but only one, the Bishop of Costa Rica, Thiel, for all of Central America.

None of the Latin Americans sided with the conciliar minority, but formed a solid block with the ultramontane or infallibilist party. A Mexican historian comments: "With regard to the burning question of papal infallibility, we may note that their lives of struggle against the theories and abuses of Reform laws, the experience in their own flesh of the discrimination resulting from the regalist and Febronian attitudes of Juárez's and Maximiliano's liberalism, gave them a natural immunity to the temptation (if they ever felt it) of anti-infallibilism."[30]

The dogma of infallibility reinforced papal authority, not only in disciplinary, administrative and pastoral matters, but also in the sphere of doctrine itself, thus providing a harsh response to the erosion of authority brought about by liberalism and modern attitudes, and to the criticism of doctrine rooted in rationalism and philosophical and scientific critique.

The experience of the Council was decisive for the "religious question" (1872–84) in Brazil, which brought two bishops before the courts and to sentences of four years of forced labour for trying to impose Roman canon law which was in conflict with the civil church law of the Empire.[31] Catholic intransigence after Vatican I and the *Syllabus* made Catholicism almost impossible to incorporate into the liberal order, exasperating the holders of power, strong in their political control of the state, but fragile in popular acceptance and consent and almost devoid of broader cultural legitimacy, except among the urban élites. The liberal politician Aquileo Parra, President of Colombia between 1876 and 1878, confessed: "We have to recognize that the only thing that is really widespread and deeply rooted in the mass of our people, and even in almost the whole of the female sex in the educated classes, is Catholic belief."[32]

Even more decisive was the experience of the Latin American Plenary Council, called by Leo XIII to meet in Rome in 1899, though following a suggestion made in 1892 by the Archbishop of Santiago de Chile, Don Mariano Casanova. The Bolivarian dream of uniting the ancient Spanish empire was to be enlarged and realized in religious terms by Rome, which would unite in a common project, not only the bishops of the former Spanish colonies, but also those of the French colony, Haiti, and of the Portuguese, Brazil. In his invitation, Leo XIII expressed himself in these terms: "From the time of the celebration of the fourth centenary of the discovery of America, we began to consider seriously the best way to promote the common interests of the Latin race, to which more than half the New World belongs. What we think most appropriate is that you should meet to discuss among yourselves, with our authority and by our appeal to all the bishops of these Republics" (*Acta*, pp. XXI-XXII). The Council was opened in Rome on 28 May in the Latin American College, with thirteen archbishops and forty bishops from eighteen Latin American republics attending. For the first time, despite much resistance, Brazilian bishops sat with Spanish Americans to plot a future course for the continent.

In reality the Council was prepared entirely in Rome, by a group of Italian, German and Spanish canonists, none of whom had had any contact with Latin America, with the exception of the Spanish Capuchin, Vives y Tuto, for some years a missionary in Ecuador, and the Italians, Angelo di Pietro, for a time apostolic delegate in Paraguay and Brazil, and Vanutelli, who had held the same post in Ecuador, Peru, Colombia and Central America. Moreover, of the eight official consultors with the right to participate in the sessions, none was Latin American. Vives y Tuto, the most influential, who was created cardinal during the Council, had upheld in the Curia since 1864 an "avowed anti-liberalism, derived from the group of Spanish integrists which produced the book *El Liberalismo es pecado* ["Liberalism is sin"]."[33]

The Council's intention was not to get inside the Latin American situation, but to refashion it in accordance with the new model Church entirely centred on Rome. The approved texts run to sixteen chapters and 998 articles, written in Latin, with another volume of appendices. There was an official translation into Spanish, published in 1906, but not into Portuguese. The sources of the Council are essentially Trent, Vatican I and the encyclicals of the latest popes, particularly Pius IX and Leo XIII, but it completely ignores the whole rich conciliar and synodal tradition of Latin America. Thus ended one epoch, and the break with the past and the colonial heritage was complete, at least as regards the Church's clerical corps, who were the object of the bulk of the conciliar prescriptions. At the same time there was a widening of the gulf between the clergy and popular religion, which was fed from other sources and another tradition. The conciliar decrees came into force on 1 January 1900.[34] Some were revoked, but the bulk reinforced, by the promulgation of the Code of Canon Law in 1917, which completed the legal standardization of the Latin Church, and within it of the Latin American Church.

In the period after the Council bishops were urged to meet every three years in their ecclesiastical provinces to apply the norms of the Plenary Council to local circumstances. In Mexico there was a first meeting as early as 1900. In Brazil the southern provinces approved a substantial pastoral manual after fifteen years' work (1901, 1904, 1907, 1911, 1915), which was embodied in the 1915 *Collective Pastoral Guide*, a creative synthesis based on the pastoral realities of southern Brazil and on the conciliar decrees, turned into pastoral rules of a supremely practical kind, intended primarily for parish priests.[35] The northern provinces, which had also been meeting, though with greater difficulties, finally adopted the same manual, from the most modern and Europeanized area of the country, to apply it to regions in profound contrast with the south, by virtue of their indigenous inheritance in the north and the north-eastern scrubland and the Afro-Brazilian tradition of the sugar-growing coast and forest.

The most interesting question, however, is how this movement to Europeanize and Romanize Catholicism's clerical officials reached the popular classes.

The greatest penetration took place, it is true, among the nascent middle classes in the big cities or among the groups of immigrants who were beginning to acquire, through secondary education, new values and standards of behaviour in religion as well as in other spheres. The new Romanized Catholicism was much more individualistic, in the "save your soul" style, less social and more introspective, insisting on doctrinal knowledge and sacramental religious practice: confession, communion and Christian marriage. The great sacrament of the colonial period had been baptism, which effected the transition from pagan to Christian and incorporation into the system of Spanish or Portuguese colonial Christendom. The emphasis now shifted from baptism to the eucharist, preceded by auricular confession, and also from society to the family. The Church, which had tolerated and lived with the almost total absence of the family among African slaves, among whom the illegitimacy rate of children was well over 95 percent, reacted to the institution of civil marriage and its expulsion to the sidelines of the social and political order with a redoubled emphasis on the institution of religious marriage and on the importance of the family for the reproduction of the Catholic faith. Deprived of the state and the public schools, the Church made the family the pivot of the new offensive. The faith, challenged by freedom of worship and by the dissemination of new religious options, especially the Protestant variety, but also of non-religious or anti-religious views, placed the emphasis on the individual, rational and doctrinal appropriation of the faith, accompanied by sacramental practice, and no longer on a diffuse adherence to Catholicism inherited by baptism and the dominant social tradition.

From this point of view, two new measures were to be crucial, the institution of parish catechism classes and the introduction of first communion for children, which was encouraged by Pius X, and the attempt to set up a network of Catholic schools in every country. For this new undertaking, in which the groundwork was done by secular priests, setting up schools or colleges in their parishes, and bishops in establishing diocesan colleges, the decisive factor was the arrival of European religious congregations dedicated to educational work.

The religious were received with affection by the population, with a veiled and sometimes explicit hostility from the liberal press, and from governments they were met with either support, when conservatives were in power, or restrictions going as far as decrees suspending their activities and expelling them from the country. The Jesuits were almost always in the centre of the controversy, and led a tumultuous existence in most countries.

In a country such as Ecuador, under the frankly clerical government of García Moreno (1860–75), it was established by concordat with the Holy See that "the instruction of young people in universities, colleges and schools should be in everything in conformity with the teaching of the Catholic Religion."[36] García Moreno wanted to "civilize" the Indians and mestizos whom he despised. "French religious controlled the school system at every level, and gradually replaced the local clergy, even in church life."[37] The liberal response, under General Veintemilla in 1877, was to secularize education.[38]

Even in Mexico under the Reform Laws (1859) and after the dissolution of the religious orders (1873), religious congregations were to play an extremely important role in the establishment of schools and institutions for the sick, infants and the aged. The Passionists arrived from the United States in 1865, were expelled in 1873 and returned in 1879. The Josephists were established in 1884, the Claretians in 1884, the Salesians in 1889. The Marist fathers came in 1887, the Marist brothers in 1889, the Hospitallars of St John of God in 1901, the Christian Brothers in 1905, the Redemptorists in 1908 and the Sacred Heart Fathers in 1908. Of the women's congregations, the Sisters of Perpetual Adoration came in 1879, the Ladies of the Sacred Heart in 1883, the Sisters of the Word Incarnate in 1885, the Company of St Teresa in 1888, the Salesian sisters in 1893, the Sisters of the Word Incarnate and the Blessed Sacrament in 1894, the De la Salle sisters in 1898 and the sisters of St Joseph of Lyon in 1903. Between 1872 and 1910, twelve other female religious congregations of Mexican origin were founded.[39]

In Peru the arrivals began earlier: Lazarists in 1858, Jesuits in 1871, Redemptorists and Sacred Heart Fathers in 1884, Salesians in 1891, Marists in 1907, Claretians in 1909, and between 1911 and 1920 Carmelites, De La Salle Brothers and Passionists.[40]

In Brazil the Empire, under the influence of liberal cabinets, issued decrees in 1855 banning the entry of Brazilian novices into the existing orders until they were reformed, and placed considerable obstacles in the way of new congregations wishing to enter the country. However, with the establishment of the Republic there was an avalanche of new congregations, both male and female. There was a total of thirty-seven male congregations between 1880 and 1930, twelve from Italy, ten from France, four from Holland and Germany, three from Spain and one each from Belgium, Austria, Uruguay and Ukraine.

The total of female orders, including the period just before 1880, was 109, from France (28), Italy (24), Germany (9), Spain (9), Belgium (5), Portugal (3), Austria (3), one each from Egypt, Colombia, Poland, Uruguay, Russia and Holland and twenty-two native to Brazil. They gave Latin American Catholicism a "modern" face, and revitalized it, working in new fields of the apostolate (press, schools, universities, reception of immigrants, missions among indigenous peoples, the social and relief apostolate) or filling gaps in the parochial ministry.[41]

Many bishops insisted that congregations asking permission to open a college should also take charge of one or more parishes. Even contemplative orders had to do their share of parish work. The other side of the coin was the rapid replacement of the secular clergy by religious and of local clergy by foreign, a feature which continues to be characteristic of the Catholic clergy today, almost a century later. In Peru, for example, on the eve of independence there were three thousand priests for the viceroyalty of Peru, for a population of two million. In 1984 in the same area there were 2,265 priests for eighteen million people. Local clergy, who in 1901 made up 82 percent of the total, had fallen as a proportion in 1973 to 38.8 percent.[42] The greatest novelty was the rapid increase in the active female religious life, including a large number of local foundations, which opened up areas of activity hitherto forbidden to Latin American women, notably in teaching and hospital work. In Brazil the number of women religious recorded in 1872 was 286, and in the 1920 census 2,944, a tenfold increase.[43]

Translated from the Portuguese by Francis McDonagh

NOTES

1. In L. Zea, *Filosofía de la Historia Americana*, (Mexico City, 1987), p. 250.

2. Zea, *Filosofía*, p. 250.

3. Zea, p. 247.

4. Cf C. Furtado, *Formacão econômica da América Latina* (Rio de Janeiro, 1970), pp. 61–5. Eng. trans. *The Economic Formation of Latin America* (London, 2nd ed. 1976).

5. T. Halperin Donghi, *Historia contemporánea de América latina*, (Madrid, 1969), p. 231.

6. Cf Moises Sandoval, *Fronteras – A History of the Latin American Church in the USA since 1513* (San Antonio, 1983), chs. 6–8, pp. 169–222.

7. Steven-Arroyo, "Puerto Rican Migration to the United States," in Sandoval, *Fronteras*, pp. 269–76; S. S. Gotay, *La Iglesia Católica durante los primeros 30 años del dominio colonial de los Estados Unidos en Puerto Rico: 1898–1930*, duplicated, pp. 1–125.

8. Cf D. G. Vieira, *O Protestantismo, a Maçonaria, e a Questão Religiosa no Brasil* (Brasília, 1980); "Protestantes, liberales y francmasones en América Latina – siglo XIX," in *Cristianismo y Sociedad* XXV/2, No 92, with articles by David Gueiros Vieira e Antônio Gouvêa Mendonça (Brazil), Rosa del Carmen Bruno-Jofre (Peru), J. Washington Padilla (Ecuador), Jean Pierre Bastian (Mexico); cf also for a Protestant interpretation of the liberal period in Latin America, H. J. Prien, *La Historia del Cristianismo en América Latina*, (Salamanca and São Leopoldo, 1985), chs. 10–12.

9. Cf J. O. Beozzo, "A Igreja e os Índios 1875–1889," in *História da Igreja no Brasil* II/2 (Petrópolis, 1980), pp. 296–307.

10. Cf Donghi, *Historia contemporánea*, p. 306.

11. E. Mignone, CEHILA, *Historia General de la Iglesia en América Latina*, IX, *Cono sur*, manuscript, p. 51.

12. *Ibid.*

13. *Ibid.*, pp. 51–2.

14. J. Klaiber, CEHILA, *Historia General*, VIII, *Perú, Bolivia y Ecuador* (Salamanca, 1987), p. 280.

15. E. Cunha, *Os Sertões* (São Paulo, 1982, 3rd ed.); D. T. Monteiro, "Um confronto entre Juazeiro, Canudos e Contestado," B. Fausto, *História Geral da Civilização Brasileira* III, Part III (1889–1930), vol. II (São Paulo, 1977), pp. 39–92; M. I. Pereira de Queiroz, *O Messianismo no Brasil e no Mundo* (São Paulo, 1965).

16. Frei A. Stultzer, *A guerra dos fanáticos (1912–1916): a contribuição dos Franciscanos* (Vilha Velha, ES, 1982); D. T. Monteiro, *Os errantes do novo século – Um estudo sobre o surto milenarista do Contestado* (Sã Paulo, 1974); M. V. Queiroz, *Messianismo e conflito social (A guerra sertaneja do Contestado: 1912–1916* (São Paulo, 1977, 2nd ed).

17. J. Meyer, *Historia de los cristianos en América Latina – siglos XIX y XX* (Mexico City, 1989), pp. 321–2.

18. J. M. R. de Solis, "La Iglesia en México," Q. Aldea and E. Cardenas, eds., *Manual de la Historia de la Iglesia* (Barcelona, 1987), pp. 900–01.

19. Cf J. Meyer, *La Cristiada*, vol. 1: *La guerra de los cristeros*; vol. 2: *El conflicto entre la Iglesia y el Estado 1926–1929*; vol. 3: *Los cristeros* (Mexico City, 1973–4).

20. Cf CEHILA, *Historia General* V – (Salamanca and Mexico City, 1984), pp. 332–3.

21. J. Barnadas, CEHILA, *Historia General*, VIII, *Perú, Bolivia y Ecuador* (Salamanca, 1987, p. 311, citing J. S. Machado's speech, *La Unión Católica* (La Paz, 1987), pp. 14–15.

22. In M. Salinas, CEHILA, *Historia General*, IX, *Cono Sur* (manuscript), p. 149.

23. Meyer, *Historia de los cristianos*, p. 238.

24. P. Richard, *Morte das cristandades e nascimento da Igreja* (São Paulo, 1984, 2nd ed.), pp. 97–7. Eng. trans. *Death of Christendom, Birth of the Church* (Maryknoll, N.Y., 1987).

25. Meyer, *Historia de los cristianos*, pp. 205–06.

26. P. Maina, *Memorias del Pontificio Colegio Pio Latino Americano de Roma, desde su fundación hasta nuestros días, 1858–1958* (Rome, 1958), typewritten, quoted by L. M. Ascensio, *Historia del Colegio Pio Latino americano – Roma 1858–1978* (Mexico City, 1978), p. 90.

27. Ascensio, *Historia del Colegio Pio Latino*, p. 339.

28. Ascensio, p. 162.

29. Cf CEHILA, *História Geral da Igreja na América latina*, vol. II/2, *Brasil* (Petrópolis, 1980), pp. 245ff.

30. A. A. Alvarado, CEHILA, *Historia General*, V, *México* (Barcelona and Mexico City, 1984), p. 260.

31. For an interpretation from the point of view of one of the bishops involved in the episode, cf D. Antônio Macedo Costa, *A questão religiosa do Brasil perante a Santa Sé ou a missão especial a Toma em 1983 à luz de documentos públicos e inéditos . . .* (Lisbon, 1886); for an interpretation from a liberal point of view, cf R. S. M. de Barros, "A questão religiosa," S. B. Holanda, *História Geral da Civilização Brasileira*, Part II, vol. 4 (São Paulo, 1971), pp. 338–65.

32. Quoted by Aldea and Cárdenas (eds.), *Manual de Historia de la Iglesia*, p. 491.

33. *Ibid.*, p. 522.

34. Cf "El primer Concilio Plenario de América Latina – 1899," Aldea and Cárdenas, pp. 465–552; *Actas y decretos del Concilio Plenario de América Latina celebrado en Roma el año del Señor de MDCCCXCIX* (Rome, 1906). There is a first Latin edition from the Vatican Polyglot Press, dated 1900.

35. *Pastoral Collectiva dos Senhores Arcebispos e Bispos das Províncias Ecclesiásticas de S. Sebastião do Rio de Janeiro, Marianna, São Paulo, Cuyabá and Porto Alegre, communicado ao clero e aos fieis o resultado das Conferências Episcopães realisadas na cidade de Nova Friburgo de 12 a 17 de janeiro de 1915* (Rio de Janeiro, 1915).

36. J. M. Vargas, CEHILA *Historia General*, VIII, *Perú, Bolivia y Ecuador* (Salamanca, 1987), p. 328.

37. Donghi, *Historia contemporánea*, p. 155.

38. Vargas, *Historia General*, VIII, p. 323.

39. A. A. Alvarado, CEHILA, *Historia General*, V, *México*, pp. 265–8.

40. J. Klaiber, CEHILA *Historia General*, VIII, p. 287.

41. Cf J. A. Beozzo, "Decadência e morte, restauração e multiplicação das ordens e congregações religiosas no Brasil, 1870–1930," R. Azzi (ed.), *A vida religiosa no Brasil. Enfoques históricos* (São Paulo, 1983), pp. 85–129.

42. Cf J. Klaiber, *La Iglesia en el Perú* (Lima, 1988), pp. 59–60.

43. Cf Beozzo, "Decadência e morte," p. 108.

SOUTH AMERICA: TWENTIETH-CENTURY REGIMES

GOMEZ – Military Dictatorship   • Coup d'état bringing change of government
VARGAS – Populist Dictatorship   *Guerrilla movement*

	1900	1910	1920	1930	1940	1950	1960	1970	1980
COLOMBIA	Liberals (from 1895)			SANTOS	LOPEZ	'Bogotazo' LLERAS *'Violencia'* • ROJAS	Liberal/Conservative → *M19 guerrillas*		BARCO
VENEZUELA	GOMEZ →			← LOPEZ	MEDINA • **BETANCOURT**	**JIMENEZ**	BETANCOURT		LUSINCHI
ECUADOR				• VELAZCO	VELAZCO	VELAZCO	VELAZCO		CORDERO
PERU	LEGUIA BENAVIDES	*LEGUIA*		• CERRO BENAVIDES	PRADO	• ODRIA BUSTAMANTE	• BELAUNDE • VELASCO	**MORALES**	BELAUNDE GARCIA FUJIMORO *Sendero luminoso*
PARAGUAY	'Reds' (from 1870)		AYALA		• FRANCO MORINIGO	• STROESSNER			
BRAZIL				*VARGAS*	• DUTRA VARGAS	KUBITSCHEK	GOULART • BRANCO COSTA MEDICI	GEISEL	**FIGUEIREDO** SARNEY C. DE MELLO
BOLIVIA	Liberals		• SAAVDERA	SALAMANCA TORO BUSCH	• VILLARDEL	ESTENSSORO SILES Z.	• BARRIENTOS *'Che' G.*	• BANZER	• GARCIA SILES Z. ESTENSSORO
ARGENTINA	Buenos Aires Oligarchy (from 1860)	YRIGOYEN Radical Union		• JUSTO	*PERON*		• ONGANIA *PERON*	• VIDELA	ALFONSIN MENEM
URUGUAY	'Reds' (from 1868)			• TERRA	• BALDOMIR BATALLE	'Whites' HERRERA	PACHECO	• BORDABERRY *Tupamaros*	SANGUINETTI
CHILE	• Parliamentary democracy (from 1892)		IBAÑEZ ALESSANDRI	ALESSANDRI	Popular front AGUIRRE RIOS	IBAÑEZ ALESSANDRI	FREI	PINOCHET ALLENDE	AYLWIN

6. South America: Twentieth-century Regimes

Chapter 8

THE CHURCH IN POPULIST REGIMES
(1930–59)

Enrique Dussel

This period is clearly set between two major events: the repercussions in Latin America of the economic crisis of 1929, which had immediate effects on the Church there, and the announcement by Pope John XXIII in January 1959 that he was convoking an ecumenical council. The three decades that elapsed between these two events were a time of confrontations, maturation and structural "modernization" for the Church in Latin America, all of which were to bear fruit in the following period.

1. THE CHURCH IN THE WORLD SITUATION

From 1914 to 1945, as a result of two wars for the hegemony of the capitalist world, power passed from Britain to the United States. The "crash" of 1929 came in the middle of this period. The dominance of the "centre" or developed countries over the "periphery" lessened, allowing political and economic space for the rise of the phenomenon of populism,[1] for nations to modernize and key countries (Mexico and those of the Southern Cone in particular) to industrialize. The Russian Revolution of 1917 (and the Mexican one of 1910) raised the spectre of communism in the organs of the Roman Church. Germany, Japan and Italy, with other countries late to undergo the industrial revolution, sought in fascism (centrist populism) the means of developing their industrial and colonial power.

This is the context in which the two pontificates of Pius XI (1922–39) and Pius XII (1939–58) cover the whole of the period under consideration. From the time of Pius XI, who sympathized with "nationalisms" and mistrusted socialism, two key years stand out: first, 1931, when he wrote the encyclicals *Quadragesimo Anno*, criticizing socialism, and *Non abbiamo bisogno*, setting limits to the fascism of Mussolini; second, 1937, when he condemned Hitler's Nazism in *Mit Brennender Sorge*, while setting limits to socialism in *Divini Redemptoris*. Also characteristic of his pontificate was a certain liking for signing "concordats," not forgetting the most ambiguous one with Nazism signed in June 1933.[2]

Pius XII, obsessed with saving the structures of the Church in the midst of a Europe in ruins, saw the German invasion of Russia as a lesser evil, but also appreciated the threat posed by fascist totalitarianism to the institutional Church. He recognized the Franco government in 1937. The installation of the Second Republic in Spain in April 1931, the triumph of the Popular Front in 1936 and the civil war from then till 1939, completely divided opinion among Christians in Latin America. The Mexican "*cristero*" conflict of 1926–9 had done the same.

One fact that needs pointing out is the strange similarity and even intimate relationship between US and Vatican politics in regard to Latin America, from the Cuban, Puerto Rican and Philippine revolutions of 1898, through the solution of the "*cristero*" crisis in 1929, to the politics of the Cold War since 1945.[3]

From 1930 to 1945, a period marked mainly by the presidency of Franklin D. Roosevelt in the United States (1933–45), the Church in Latin America lived with political and economic populism. The more modernized countries, Brazil, Argentina and Chile, set the tone, while Mexico remained atypical owing to the anticlericalism of the 1910 revolution. In Chile, the Church showed the way to the "New Christendom"[4] model, somewhat along the lines laid down by Jacques Maritain in his *L'humanisme intégrale* of 1936, distancing itself from the conservative party and the traditional oligarchy. In other countries, the Church faced up to populism with its own endless series of Congresses or Assemblies. It was recovering the strength it had lost in a century of "persecution" by liberal regimes.

From 1945 to 1959, the Church went through a phase in which, having reorganized many of its basic structures, it was first able to support the populist regimes with an "anti-communism" proper to the Cold War period, and then (since around 1954) begin to distance itself from them, thereby avoiding becoming involved in their downfall. In the time of the Truman and Eisenhower presidencies in the United States and Christian Democracy under De Gasperi and Adenauer in Europe, the countries of the Southern Cone were still those that showed most creative thinking within the Church. By the end of the 1950s the Church had reorganized itself on the national level, and for the first time on the *Latin American* level as a whole, emerging as one of the main protagonists of the following period.

2. THE MAIN CHALLENGES

The Latin American Church found four ways of facing up to the challenges posed by the populist state and of gaining ground against this and the modernization of the dependent capitalism of the continent.

The first was *Catholic Action*. Given the role of the *petit bourgeois* in the fascisms of the centre and the populisms of the periphery in forming the state bureaucracies,[5] the Roman Church (faced with fascism) and the Latin American Church (faced with populist regimes) created a model of lay commitment in world affairs under the direct control of the episcopal hierarchy. Pius XI set up the organization in Italy in 1923, in Poland in 1925, in Yugoslavia and Czechoslovakia in 1927 and Austria in 1928. The project was launched in Buenos Aires around the same time, and gradually spread throughout Latin America. Two young priests, Antonio Caggiano from Argentine (later to become cardinal there) and Miguel Darío Miranda from Mexico studied the Roman model in the late 1920s. In 1938 a central office for World Catholic Action was established in Rome, and the first World Congress of the Lay Apostolate was held in 1951. Earlier, in 1945, the first Inter-American Week of Catholic Action had taken place in Santiago; the second was held in Havana in 1949, and the third in Chimbote in Peru in 1953.

Specialist branches developed: Chardijn founded the JOC (*Jeunesse ouvrière chrétienne*) in Belgium in 1913. It was officially adopted by the Catholic Church in 1925, with some reservations about its class stance. It spread slowly into Latin America, becoming most influential from the late 1950s to the mid 1960s. More important was the JUC (Catholic University Youth), which developed out of JEC (Young Student Catholics) in association with Pax Romana, since it was the forum in which young Christians discovered the need for political commitment, first reformist, and then, after 1959, revolutionary. Jose Comblin's book on "The Failure of Catholic Action," written in Recife in Brazil in 1959, was the first analysis of the end of this period.

The second way was that of the great *mass congresses*, which the Roman Church had tried in Europe since the end of the nineteenth century. The first International Eucharistic Congress of 1881 had "The Reign of Christ in Society" as its theme. In 1922, at the Eucharistic Congress held in Rome in the face of the dawning fascist movement, sixty-nine cardinals requested the celebration of "Christ the King," which was made a feast of the Catholic Church in 1925. In Latin America, National Eucharistic Congresses were held in Mexico City, La Paz and Managua in the 1920s, Congresses of Christ the King in Guayaquil in 1929 and Salvador de Bahia in 1933, and the 1934 International Eucharistic Congress took place in Buenos Aires. These and many other massive demonstrations, bringing hundreds of thousands of believers together, made a considerable impression on populist governments and, deliberately and in effect, gave the Church strength in particular negotiations with the state.

Between 1957 and 1961, another type of happening was organized: the "Great Mission" in a particular city or nation, from Tegucigalpa to Buenos Aires. These had a more spiritual approach and were generally carried out by Spanish priests; their aim was mass "conversion," while the aim in the 1930s had been to achieve political influence. The pilgrimage to the Christ of Esquipulas, which weakened the Arbenz regime in Guatemala in 1953, is perhaps the best example of this type of religious manifestation.

The third way was *social action* in the working-class field above all. The corporatism suggested by *Quadragesimo Anno* in 1931 had opened the way to the "Social Teaching of the Church" (which Pius XII was to give great impetus to), a sort of reformist critique of capitalism. Groups such as Fr Lebret's "Economy and Humanism" of 1942 and the "personalism" of Emmanuel Mounier (who started the review *Esprit* in 1932) were to become influential in Latin America. Such movements were generally "paternalistic": groups of workers without class commitment, anti-communist, often "devotional." Nevertheless, a certain class element did creep in in the 1950s, through the presence of the JOC. Reformist unions became radicalized and began the formation of a Christian working-class consciousness.

The fourth way was that of more or less combative *anti-communism*. Before the Second World War, the Church's anti-communism was linked to its old alliance with conservative parties and traditional oligarchies. After the war, it became much more militant and linked to U.S. Cold War policies, which led it to support the new-style dictatorships – increasingly more authoritarian and less populist – such as those of Trujillo, Somoza, Stroessner and the like. The more militant this anti-communism was (as in Guatemala or Colombia) the closer its ties with the ruling classes became. Where the Church found a democratic or modernizing state, it did not find anti-communism so necessary, as Bishops Sanabria in Costa Rica and Larraín in Chile showed.

3. CHURCH STRUCTURES BROUGHT UP TO DATE

Renewal on the basis of a "New Christendom" model proceeded on three main fronts, slowly in the 1930s and then more quickly between 1945 and 1959.

The first was the *intellectual field*.[6] The anti-positivist drive, begun by the Argentine Friar Mamerto Esquiú (1826–83) and Jacinto Ríos (1842–92), was continued in the modern Thomist re-reading of Martínez Villada (1886–1959), who was connected with Blondel and Maritain. Other influential figures of the period were Jackson de Figueiredo and Tristão de Atayde (Amoroso Lima) in Brazil, José Vasconcelos and Antonio Caso in Mexico, and Victor Andrés Balaunde. Students formed themselves into movements: the first Ibero-American Congress of Catholic Students was held in Rome in 1933, the second in Lima in 1938 and the third in Bogotá in 1944. Catholic universities multiplied: after a long gap since the foundation of the Catholic University of Santiago (Chile) in 1869, came the Xaveriano of Bogotá in 1937, the Catholic University of Lima in 1942, of Medellín in 1945, of Rio de Janeiro and São Paulo in 1947, Porto Alegre in 1950, Campinas and Quito in 1956, Córdoba and Buenos Aires in 1960, Valparaiso and the Central American University of Guatemala in 1961, and more. The first Ibero-American Assembly of Catholic Universities was held in Lima in 1944.

Major philosophical and theological reviews, such as *Sapentia* and *Stromata* published in Buenos Aires, *Revista Eclesiastica Brasileira* in Petrópolis, *Teología y Vida* in Santiago, *Christus* in Mexico, and many others, underpinned the intellectual renewal of the new generation. In 1959, the Jesuit Juan Luis Segundo studied "The Function of the Church in the Conditions of the River Plate Area," published in Montevideo in 1962, marking the start of contemporary Latin American theology, based on observation and analysis of actual conditions.

A second front for renewal was *pastoral practice*. Conditions were analyzed in Institutions of Social and Religious Investigation set up by the Jesuits in nearly every country.[7] The so-called "overall pastoral concept," based on the experiences of Abbé Boulard in France, was gradually brought in. There was a slow liturgical renewal, with modern translations of the Bible and bi-lingual missals. On the catechetical front, renewal led up to the foundation of the Catechetical Institute of Latin America in Santiago in 1961. Spirituality came under the influence of Benedictine monks from Solesmes, established in Las Condes in Chile in 1938, Benedictine nuns in Santa Escolástica in Argentina, the foundation by the Abbey of Einsiedeln of Los Toldos, also in Argentina, in 1947, and the like. These were followed by the spread of the Trappists, and then the Little Brothers and Sisters of Charles de Foucauld. Following Pius XII's encyclical *Mystici corporis Christi*, the Church began to see itself more as a fraternal "community" than a juridical institution, and this in turn led to the renewal of parishes as "missionary communities" – another influence from post-war France.

The third front for renewal was the formation of institutions designed to underpin the "New Christendom" model on both national and continental levels. First came the formation of national conferences of bishops – organs to co-ordinate the work of bishops, who had previously worked in complete isolation, on a national level. These started in 1952, with Helder Camara and Manuel Larraín prominent among the many who helped to bring them into being. Religious of both sexes also formed national bodies in the early 1950s, and then grouped together as CLAR (Latin American Confederation of Religious) on a continent-wide basis in 1958.

More specialized activities also had their "confederations" spanning the continent: seminaries, Catholic Action, JOC, Family Christian Movement, Christian Trade Unions, Christian Education. . . . This whole effort at integration on a Latin American scale bore fruit, in a way, in the first Conference of the Latin American Episcopate, held in Rio de Janeiro in 1955. This conference founded CELAM, the Episcopal Council of Latin America, which was to play such a vital role in the future of the Church in Latin America, and of the continent as a whole. The structures were in place for the next step forward.

4. REGIONAL SURVEY

(a) Brazil

On 2 July 1930, Dom Sebastião Leme was appointed Cardinal Archbishop of Rio, where he was to remain till 1942. In October 1930, Getulio Vargas led a revolution, and the Church was prepared to throw itself into the political arena of populism. João Becker, archbishop of Porto Alegre, where the Vargas uprising began, supported the insurgents from the start. He wrote a pastoral letter on "Russian Communism and Christian Civilization" and appointed Fr Vicente Scherer as military chaplain to the "*gaucho*" forces.[8]

The review *A Ordem*, edited by Jackson de Figueiredo, first appeared in August 1921, strongly nationalistic and "Brazilian Catholic" in tone. The *Dom Vidal* Centre, opened the following year, was equally influential in Catholic restoration.

Immediately after the October 1930 revolution, Cardinal Leme organized huge popular demonstrations in honour of Our Lady *Aparecida* and Christ the Redeemer of Corcovado (the huge statue overlooking Rio), which made the government appreciate the massive power of the Church. The fact that he was also the power behind the Catholic Electoral League in 1932–3, aimed at imposing church claims on the programmes of political parties, shows how far the Church went in political manipulation at the outset of the Vargas regime. The cardinal sent the statute of Brazilian Catholic Action to Rome, and this was approved in 1935. Eucharistic Congresses were held in Salvador in 1933, Belo Horizonte in 1936, Recife in 1939 and São Paulo in 1942, all with massive crowds attending. In 1937, the bishops issued a joint pastoral attacking communism, which marked the end of this phase of church activity. The proclamation of the "New State" in 1939 effectively removed many church prerogatives, and left the first Plenary Brazilian Council of 2–20 July 1939 preparing to defend church unity in the face of a precarious future.

In 1932, Fr Leopoldo Brentano SJ founded the first "Workers' Circle" in Pelotas; three years later it had fourteen thousand members. The movement, inspired by fascist corporatism, spread nationally, and by 1936 the first National Confederation of Catholic Workers was to meet, with 34,000 members, a number that was to grow to 200,000 in the 1950s. While thanks to Maritain's disciple Tristão de Atayde and other intellectuals, the review *A Ordem* abandoned its corporatist line, the conservatism of the Catholic Electoral League, the "Integralist" movement and many others produced a right-wing, fascist-sympathizing sector within Brazilian Catholicism that was to last till the 1980s.

The death of Cardinal Leme in 1942 left the Church leaderless. It was not till 1952 that Fr Helder Camara suggested the formation of the National Conference of Brazilian Bishops. He had revitalized the Electoral League in 1946–50, in order to put pressure on President Gaspar Dutra. Relations with the government remained much the same during Vargas' second period in office from 1951 to 1954. Throughout the period, the Brazilian Church was developing a growing sense of autonomy in relation to Rome, which is why Cardinal Leme had opposed a concordat between the Vatican and Brazil, seeing that it could operate as a dominating force over the Church in Brazil. The present profile of the Brazilian Church was taking shape in this period.

(b) The Southern Cone

In Argentina,[9] Pope Pius X had approved the organization of Catholic Popular Union of Argentina, after it had held numerous congresses since 1883. Pius XI changed the Union into Catholic Action at the request of the hierarchy; this became effective in 1931. In 1934, the Twenty-second International Eucharistic Congress was held in Buenos Aires, with Cardinal Eugenio Pacelli, the future Pope Pius XII, carrying the Cross of Palermo.

The prophetic figure of Mgr Gustavo Franceschi, who founded the rewiew *Criterio* in 1922, and the Courses of Christian Culture, alerted Christian consciousness to the social problems of the country. Despite this, it was nationalist right-wing Catholicism that inspired the military revolution led by José F. Uriburu – known to history as the "decade of infamy." During this, the Church was led by the conservative Cardinal Santiago Copello. Under Perón (1946–55) the Church first maintained an alliance of mutual support, gaining the right to Catholic education in the schools, the appointment of military chaplains and the like, but by 1953 relations had soured and remained so till Perón's downfall. The "developmentist" period that followed brought little comfort to the incipient Christian Democrat movement.

In Chile,[10] the Church separated from the state in 1925, thereby finally doing away with the patronage system inherited from colonial times. This Church on the flanks of the Andes was undoubtedly the one that best read the "signs of the times," providing an example for the rest of Latin America during this period. It resisted the temptation of falling into facile anti-communism, and set up institutions that were to prove valid in the future. It concentrated on two basic approaches: internal strengthening through Catholic Action, and external action in favour of democratic politics and workers' rights.

Catholic Action had been established in 1931, growing out of the 1915 National Association of Catholic Students (which basically changed direction under Fr Oscar Larson in 1928) and the 1921 Feminine Catholic Youth movement. Fr Alberto Hurtado (1901–52) was a major influence on Catholic Action. He also founded the Association of Chilean Trade Unions in 1941, and in the same year wrote *¿Es Chile un país católico?* ("Is Chile a Catholic country?" – anticipating Godin's famous work asking the same question of France); in 1951 he founded the review *Mensaje*. Clotario Blest founded the *"Gérmen"* group in 1928, Fernando Vives SJ organized the Social League in 1931, as well as the Union of Catholic Workers and the Working Youth Vanguard. *Acción Popular* started in 1934, and by 1945 had sixty centres organizing health, legal and financial aid.

The Church's basic stance was its refusal, thanks largely to José María Caro, archbishop of Santiago from 1939 to 1958, made cardinal in 1946, to accept the right-wing Conservative Party as its natural home. His consultations with Rome produced a letter from Cardinal Pacelli, dated 1 April 1934, declaring the Church above party. This led the young people in Catholic Action to found the Falange under the leadership of Eduardo Frei in November 1939, which was to evolve into the future Chilean Christian Democracy. Manuel Larraín, who was appointed bishop of Talco in 1938, and who was, till his death in 1966, the outstanding figure of the Church in Latin America of the twentieth century, responsible for organizing the Chilean Bishops Conference and the First Conference of the Latin American Episcopate in Rio in 1955, upheld the Falange against conservative attacks.

Bishop Caro made a prophetic gesture in accepting the authorities of the Popular Front as legitimate in 1939, paving the way for the First National Eucharistic Congress in 1941. The First Plenary Chilean Council met in 1946, a reminder that it had been a Chilean bishop, Mgr Casanova, who had organized the First Latin American Plenary Council in Rome in 1899. Both events were pointers to the clear leadership of the Chilean Church within Latin America in the period between the Second Vatican Council and Medellín.

(c) The Andean Region

In Peru,[11] President Sánchez Cerro promulgated decrees introducing civil marriage and divorce in October 1930. The bishops reacted with a Pastoral Letter "On problems of religious social order" in November 1931. The departure of the "Aprists" from the government led to improved relations with the Church. In 1935, religious instruction was made compulsory in state schools. Carlos Arenas Loayza founded the Popular Union party in 1931 to defend church interests, supported by the bishop of Cuzco, Pedro Pascual Farfán, who, together with Mariano Holguín, was the leading hierarchical figure of the time. Progressive voices from lay Catholics were those of Víctor Andrés Balaúnde (1883–1966), who published *La realidad nacional* in 1930, and José de la Rivera y Agüero (1885–1944).

The first National Eucharistic Congress, held in 1935, impressed the populist regime, as they did in other countries, but it was the foundation of Catholic Action in the same year that indicated real renewal. In 1941 Fr J. Stiglich organized Catholic Student Youth, and in 1943 the National Union of

Catholic Students made its apperance. Its first chaplain was Fr Juan Landázuri Ricketts, the future cardinal archbishop of Lima. He was followed by Fr Gerardo Alarco, and then Fr Gustavo Gutiérrez. Catholic Action turned its attention to the social sphere in 1953, and this led to the formation of the Popular Action and Christian Democrat parties in 1955 and 1956. All this led up to the first Peruvian Social Week in 1959, which marked the beginning of a new period in the history of the Church in Peru.

Bolivia[12] held its first National Eucharistic Congress in La Paz in 1934, and the second one there in 1939, followed by others in Sucre in 1946 and Santa Cruz in 1964. These and other mass events brought the Church into the public eye. A lack of native clergy led to an influx of foreign missionary priests. Catholic Action got off the ground in 1938, though it had been planned since 1933; it was led by Mgr Gutiérrez, who had been trained in Chile. Politically, despite a series of articles attacking Spanish fascism by R. Estenssoro, support for Franco became the norm. 1957 saw the "Great Mission" preached in towns and throughout the country.

In Ecuador,[13] Carlos María de la Torre, then bishop of Guayaquil (later the first cardinal archbishop of Quito), organized massive celebrations of the Feast of Christ the King, starting in Guayaquil in 1929 and spreading to Quito in 1933. Social organizations of workers began in 1931 and by 1938 the Ecuadorian Confederation of Catholic Workers had sixty thousand members. July 1954 saw the foundation of the Catholic University of Quito, and in 1956 the National Bishops Conference was established. Church-state relations were determined by the *Modus vivendi* signed in July 1937, which has remained in force to the present.

(d) Colombia and Venezuela

In Colombia,[14] Mgr Miguel Angel Builes (1888–1971) orchestrated the Church's opposition to liberals, freemasons and communists in a Pastoral Letter of 1929, endorsed by all the bishops the following year. The ambiguous stance adopted by Mgr Ismael Perdomo, archbishop of Bogotá from 1928 to 1950, contributed to the fall of the conservative government in 1930, but the Church's support for Valencia showed that it never really achieved what the Chilean Church managed: political independence from the conservative oligarchy.

Catholic Action was founded in 1933, and the Union of Workers of Colombia, founded in 1945 with anti-communist, anti-liberal, but "non-political" aims, was influential in social matters, largely through its weekly journal "Social Justice." The National Agrarian Federation, founded the following year, was equally strongly anti-communist. Catholic intellectual life was best represented by the *Revista Xaveriana*, started in 1933.

Church-state relations were affected by the National Congress, which in 1935 challenged the Church's position on education, divorce and other matters, provoking a strong reaction, though in the end the Church agreed to freedom of worship. A new concordat was signed in 1942, which did not prevent the Bishops' Conference from declaring its anti-communism in 1944 and warning against Marxist peril in the university in 1948. Before the death of Jorge Eliécer Gaitán in the same year, the bishops again blamed communists and liberals for attacks on church property, which culminated in the burning of the bishop's palace in Bogotá on 9 April. In September 1958, the bishops were still blaming communism for the "violence" spreading throughout the country.

In Venezuela,[15] the death of Juan Gómez in 1936 changed the position of the Church vis-à-vis the state, allowing Catholic Action to flourish and religion to be taught in private schools. When Democratic Action tried to close the Catholic schools in 1946, it met with a riposte from the bishops that forced it to back down, and led to the formation of Venezuelan Christian Democracy. The Workers' Circle of Caracas was started in 1945 by Fr Manuel Aguirre Elorriaga, and the Church began to modernize itself.

(e) Mexico and Central America

In Mexico,[16] the Church had been a major player on the social scene since the late nineteenth century, organizing social weeks, issuing publications, and even forming a National Catholic Party, lasting from 1911 to 1917, which, after the 1910 revolution, received half a million votes, earning it thirty-one deputies and the majority in four provinces. The 1917 Constitution "outlawed" the Church, forbidding it the most basic rights such as ownership of its places of worship and the legal entitlement to hand on church property from one minister to another. The National Eucharistic Congress held in Mexico City in 1924 was harshly suppressed. Acting in sectarian fashion, the government went on increasing anti-church sanctions. On 25 July 1926, all religious worship was suspended by the bishops in protest, a measure that lasted till 21 June 1929. This produced the "*cristero*" war in the provinces of Jalisco, Colima, Zacatecas, Guanajuato, Michoacán and Durango, around the figure of Mgr Francisco Orozco y Jiménez, taking the form of a peasant uprising against Plutarco Elías Calles and Alvaro Obregón. The Jesuit Miguel Agustín Pro was accused of an attempt on the President's life and shot in the police headquarters. Through the intervention of the US ambassador Dwight Morrow, the Apostolic Delegate and Bishops Pascual Díaza and Leopoldo Ruiz, the "*Cristeros*" laid down their arms; many were later assassinated, and the church remained outlawed. In the early days of the government of Lázaro Cárdenas (1934–40), the situation remained unchanged, but the Church's support for the nationalization of oil in 1938 encouraged a change in the government's posture, leading to a gradually increasing toleration of the Church.

The Mexican Social Secretariat had been founded by the bishops in 1922, and Catholic Action was organized in 1929, under the auspices of the Social Secretariat and its director from 1924 to 1937, Fr Miguel Darío Miranda, future cardinal archbishop of Mexico City. The Secretariat was led from 1946 by Fr Pedro Velásquez, a great organizer of the social apostolate, a militant anti-communist in the 1940s and 1950s, but then one of the instigators of the Medellín Conference.

In Central America, the outstanding figure of the period was Mgr Víctor Sanabria Martínez (1899–1952) of Costa Rica.[17] In a pastoral letter dated 25 April 1938, he wrote: "The *social question*! A word of transcendental value today! What has the Church done to resolve it and what can it do today in this direction?"[18] When the 1940 populist government of Calderón Guardia was under attack from the oligarchy, Mgr Sanabria had him decorated by the Papal

Nuncio. He reached an understanding with the communist party of Costa Rica, which became the "Popular Vanguard," indicating that "those Catholics who wished could join the new group." In this way he preserved the popular government till 1948.

In 1935, Catholic Action had been introduced in a Pastoral Letter by Bishop Rafael Otón Castro. Sanabria reformed it and clarified its objectives between 1942 and 1945, directing its activities mainly toward the workers and peasants, with the "Workers' Spiritual League" as its centre. In 1943, the *Rerum novarum* Union Centre" was founded, and two years later this became independent of the Church. In 1948 it came into conflict with the union centre belonging to the "Popular Vanguard," which led to the civil war and the fall of the government. Fr Benjamín Núñez began a long campaign against the archbishop and played a major part in the anti-government "Liberation Army." Sanabria was succeeded by Mgr Rubén Odio Herrera, archbishop from 1952 to 1959, who supported the post-war anti-communist line of the Figueres government.

In Guatemala, Catholic Action was started in the countryside in 1935, under Archbishop Duroy y Suré. He was succeeded in 1938 by Mariano Rossell y Arellano, who in 1942 organized the first National Catechetical Congress. He was famous for his ceaseless anti-communist campaign. A pastoral letter of October 1945 was entitled "On the Communist Threat," and he returned to the theme two years later, following this with an instruction "On the Excommunication of Communists" in 1949. In 1951 he organized the first National Eucharistic Congress as a show of strength against the elected populist president Jacobo Arbenz Guzmán, attracting a massive attendance of over 200,000.

When Arbenz began his agrarian reform he was opposed by the landed oligarchy, United Fruit (from which he had confiscated 100,000 hectares) and the United States. Mgr Rossell supported Somoza, Trujillo and Carlos Castillo Armas, who wrote in Point 12 of the Tegucigalpa Pact of 24 December 1953: "Its links with the magisterium of the Church have greatly advanced the penetration of communism into Guatemala." On 9 April 1954, a pastoral letter advised that ". . . Obeying the commands of the Church, which orders us to combat and overthrow the efforts of communism, we must once more raise our voice in warning to Catholics. . . . " He was soon to regret the way he had been deceived and speak (10 October 1954) of "other forces lying in wait . . . once again to exercise the ignominious dominion of the past over Guatemala."

When the peasant uprising in El Salvador was bloodily suppressed with thirty thousand dead (including Farabundo Martí), Archbishop Belloso rejoiced that "the evils of the day have been exorcised"; Fr José Alférez said a mass of thanksgiving in the cathedral; Fr Francisco Castro delivered a patriotic oration congratulating the government and the national army on their "struggle against atheism." The Salesian Fr José Miglia launched an anti-communist crusade in the prisons filled with captured peasants, and the national printing press opened its doors to the Church for the first time so that it could print fifty thousand copies of a leaflet on "Christianization and anti-communism." It was only when Luis Chávez González was appointed archbishop of San Salvador in 1938 (where he remained till 1977, being succeeded by Oscar Arnulfo

Romero), that the Church in El Salvador slowly began to change its social outlook.

The Church in Honduras ran a similar course. Archbishop Turcios y Barahona (consecrated in 1947) launched a 1954 pastoral letter declaring communism "intrinsically evil." In 1959 the Great Mission of Tegucigalpa was held, against "the materialist and demoralizing invasion," and the country was dedicated to the Sacred Heart of Jesus. In 1955 the Knights of Christ the King, lay men dedicated to prayer and militancy, were organized, and using the radio station set up by Fr Molina, Fr Domínguez founded various worker and peasant groups.

Archbishop José Antonio Lezcano y Ortega of Managua attributed the Nicaraguan earthquake of 31 March 1931 to public sins against God. A first National Eucharistic Congress had taken place at the end of 1928, and a first Nicaraguan Provincial Council was held in January 1934. When Somoza García took power, the Church showed no unease and mounted no resistance. Its post-war Cold War policies concurred with those of the government. There was church mourning for Anastasio Somoza when he was assassinated in 1957.

(f) The Caribbean

Santo Domingo[19] during this period was completely dominated by Rafael Trujillo, president from 1930 to 1961, who from the start set out to win the Church over to his side. On 20 February 1931, he promised the nuncio, Mgr José Fietta, that the Church would receive "the protection to be offered by the government of which I am President," to enable it to be "a source of comfort, a moral element of strong influence in supporting our progress, our wellbeing."[20] On 6 March he restored the juridical rights of the Church. He eliminated Fr Rafael Castellanos as potential successor to Archbishop Alejandro Noel and managed to install the docile Ricardo Pittini, who rose to unparalleled heights of complicity, even persuading Trujillo to withdraw his renunciation of re-election to the Presidency in 1938.

The 1936 massacre on the frontier with Haiti was hidden even by the Jesuit missionaries. The Church was given three cathedrals; its historic buildings were restored; it was granted schools, rectories, seminaries, convents, retreat centres; the government paid subsidies and salaries for bishops and priests, provided vehicles, audiovisual equipment, liturgical vestments. . . . In 1954 a concordat was signed, with no account taken of the injustices and crimes committed by the tyrant. At the 1956 International Congress on Catholic Culture (attended by no less a figure than Cardinal Spellman of New York), Cardinal de la Torre of Quito praised the *Generalísimo* for being "the faithful interpreter of the wishes of his people." It was not till 25 July 1959 that the Church began to define its responsibilities, when Mgr Hugo Polanco Brito said in a speech: "I personally as bishop of Santiago have no superior other than the pope and God, to whom I have to render an account of my actions."[21]

Puerto Rico, like Cuba and the Philippines, was annexed to the United States in 1898, which left indelible scars on the Church through the process of "Americanization" – which meant anti-Latin American. The outstanding figure here was the fervent and mystical Catholic Pedro Albizu Campos, founder of the Nationalist Party of Puerto Rico, who was later tried and imprisoned till 1948. The regrettable course taken by Mgr Luis Chapelle, archbishop of New Orleans, assisted by Bishop Blenk of San Juan, split the Church into "Americanists" and "Nationalists," a division that exists to this day. There is no doubt that the Vatican saw the US occupation as a positive development and that its nuncios furthered the "Americanization" process – as they did in Cuba and the Philippines.

In Cuba,[22] the central figure of the period is Manuel Arteaga y Betancur (1879–1963), who succeeded Manuel Ruiz y Rodríguez as archbishop of Havana in 1941 and was later made cardinal. Since the 1933 revolution, the Church, under Rome's influence, had been concerned with social questions. The "Catholic University Grouping" had started in 1932, under the Jesuit Felipe Rey de Castro. Catholic Action was introduced in 1938, but began to be effective only in 1942. The JOC opened its first centres in January 1947, while the Catholic University of St Tomás de Villanueva had opened in August 1946. By 1957 Cuba had 209 parishes, six dioceses, 247 religious communities, 162 religious educational establishments with forty thousand students, 667 priests operating in 426 churches and a major seminary, opened in September 1945, where blacks and mulattos were admitted on the express orders of Mgr Arteaga.

From 1955 onward, young Catholics became politicized, despite censure from the bishops. The days of Fulgencio Batista y Zaldívar, who had seized power on 4 September 1933, were drawing to an end.

In Haiti, the United States occupation forces (1914–34) left a "National Guard" in place when they left, as they did in Nicaragua. The Church, whose bishops and higher clergy were almost exclusively French, received a boost from an influx of Canadian missionaries. The upset of 1946 did not lead to a renewal. In 1953 a Haitian, Mgr Rémy Augustin, was appointed auxiliary bishop of Port-au-Prince, but the new archbishop was a Frenchman, Mgr François Poirier. It was not till 1957 that a black, Haitian clergy was encouraged by François Duvalier, but this was simply so that he could make use of the Church in the manner of Trujillo in Santo Domingo. His first two ministers of education were priests – and the Vatican made no protest then, in contrast to its later reaction to the inclusion of priests in the Sandinista government of Nicaragua.[23]

5. TENSIONS IN THE "NEW CHRISTENDOM" MODEL

"Colonial Christendom" (1492–1808) withered in the nineteenth century under attack from the liberals. A new ideal was set in place only around 1930 – and I follow contemporary Latin American sociologists and historians in calling this "New Christendom." The Church, after decades of opposition to, and persecution by, liberal states, could now establish relations of alliance, harmony or at least toleration (with perhaps the sole exception of a fifteen-year period in Mexico) with populist states.

A split between two approaches developed, however. One sought power through strengthening church institutions, and saw a need for alliance with the nascent industrial middle classes in order to preserve the traditional, oligarchic and conservative state of affairs. The other sought to use church strength to turn it in the direction of democracy, modernization and progress, which included an option for social action, though the content of this was still ambiguous. This second course was mapped out by Christian leaders such as Eduardo Frei in Chile and Pedro Albizu Campos in Puerto Rico. The first was charted by movements in sympathy with Franco, "Hispanism" and anti-communist corporatism.

Translated from the Spanish by Paul Burns

NOTES

1. See O. Lanni, *La formación del estado populista en América Latina* (Mexico City, 1975); F. Weffort, *Populismo, marginación y dependencia* (San José, Costa Rica, 1973); G. Germani-Torcuato di Tella, *Populismo y contradicción de clases en América Latina* (Mexico City, 1973); A. Niekerk, *Populism and Political Development in Latin America* (Rotterdam, 1974); E. Dussel, "El estatuto ideológico del discurso populista," *Ideas y valores* 50 (Bogotá, Aug. 1977), 35–69.
2. On the Church in general during this period see H. Jedin (ed.) *History of the Church: Vol VIII, The Church in the Age of Liberalism* (London and New York, 1981).
3. Cf A. Manhattan, *The Vatican in World Politics* (New York, 1949); J. Mitterand, *La politique extérieure du Vatican* (Paris, 1959); R. Graham, *Vatican Diplomacy* (Princeton, 1959). See also S. Silva Gotay, "La Iglesia católica en el proceso político de la americanización de Puerto Rico (1898–1930)," CEHILA, *Historia general de la Iglesia en América Latina*, vol. IV.
4. See E. Dussel, "Introducción General," CEHILA, *Historia general*, vol. I/1, pp. 73–80; P. Richard, *Death of Christendoms, Birth of the Church* (Maryknoll, N.Y., 1984).
5. Cf N. Poulantzas, on the role of the *petit bourgeois*, *Poder político y clases sociales* (Mexico City, 1972); *idem.*, *Las crisis de las dictaduras* (Mexico City, 1976); *Las clases sociales en el capitalismo actual* (Mexico City, 1976); "Las clases medias," A. Solari, R. Franco and J. Jutkowitz, *Teoría, acción social y desarollo en América Latina* (Mexico City, 1976), pp. 301–35; E. De Ipola, *Ideología y discurso populista* (Mexico City, 1982).
6. Cf my *History of the Church in Latin America* (Grand Rapids, 1981), pp. 177ff; also *"Hipótesis para una historia de la teología en América Latina,"* Historia de la teología en América Latina (San José, Costa Rica, 1981), pp. 418ff.
7. Cf I. Alonso, *La Iglesia en América Latina. Estructuras eclesiásticas* (Bogotá, 1964); *idem.*, *La Iglesia en América Central* (Bogotá, 1962); W. J. Gibbons, *Basic Ecclesiastical Statistics for Latin America* (Maryknoll, N.Y., 1960). Alsonso has published sociographic studies of all the Latin American countries: see also "Les statistiques religieuses en Amérique Latine," *Social Compass* XIV (1967), pp. 365–98.
8. J. O. Beozzo, "La Iglesia en Brasil (1930–1939)," CEHILA, *Historia general*, vol. III/1; T. Bruneau, *O catolicismo brasileiro em época de transição* (São Paulo, 1974). See also the chapter by E. Hoornaert in the present volume, pp. 185–200.
9. Cf G. Farrell, *Iglesia y pueblo en Argentina (1860–1974)* (Buenos Aires, 1976); A. Quarracino, "La Iglesia en Argentina en los últimos cincuenta años," *Criterio* 1777 (1977), 724ff; J.C.Zuretti, *Nueva historia eclesiástica argentina* (Buenos Aires, 1972). On Uruguay, see H. J. Prien, *Die Geschichte des Christentums in Lateinamerika* (Göttingen, 1978), pp. 592ff; on Paraguay, ibid., pp. 598ff; A. Methol Ferré, "Las corrientes religiosas," *Nuestra Tierra* 35 (Montevideo, 1969).
10. Cf F. Aliaga, "Historia de la Iglesia en Chile," CEHILA, *Historia general*, vol IX. See also the chapter by M. Salinas in the present volume, pp. 295–310.
11. Cf J. Klaiber, *Religión y revolución en el Perú, 1824–1976* (Lima, 1977); idem. "Historia de la Iglesia en el Perú," CEHILA, *Historia general*, vol IX. See also his chapter in the present volume, pp. 285–294.
12. Cf. J. Barnadas, "Historia de la Iglesia en Bolivia," CEHILA, *Historia general*, vol. VIII.
13. Cf J.-M. Vargas, "Historia de la Iglesia en Ecuador," *ibid.*
14. Cf. R. de Roux, "La iglesia colombiana en el período 1930–1962," CEHILA, *Historia general*, vol VII, pp. 517ff; see also his chapter in the present volume, pp. 271–284.
15. Cf C. Felice Cardot, "La Iglesia venezolana entre 1930–1962," *ibid.*, pp. 552ff; L. Ugalde, pp. 625ff.

16. Cf C. Alvear Acevedo, "La Iglesia en México en el período 1900–1962," CEHILA, *Historia general*, vol. V, pp. 313ff; J. Meyer, *La Cristiandad* (Mexico City, vols. I-III, 1973–4). See also the chapters by M. A. Puente and M. Sandoval in the present volume, pp. 217–230, pp. 231–242.

17. Cf M. Picado, "Historia de la Iglesia en Costa Rica," CEHILA, *Historia general*, vol. VI (1985). See also the chapter by R. Cardenal in the present volume, pp. 243–270.

18. Cited by Picado, *op. cit.*

19. Cf W. Wipfler, *Poder, influencia e impotencia. La Iglesia como factor socio-político en República Dominicana* (Santo Domingo, 1980), pp. 84ff.

20. Z. Castillo de Aza, *Trujillo y otros benefactores de la Iglesia* (Ciudad Trujillo, 1961), p. 216.

21. H. Polanco Brito, *Discursos y Escritos 1934–1965*, vol. 1, ms.

22. R. Gómez Treto, "Historia de la Iglesia en Cuba," CEHILA, *Historia general*, vol. IV; see also his chapter in the present volume, pp. 419–427.

23. On the British and Dutch Caribbean, see E. Williams, *Some Historical Reflections on the Church in the Caribbean* (Port-of-Spain, 1973); R. Buhler, *A History of the Catholic Church in Belize* (Belize, 1976); J. Harricharan, "The Catholic Church and the English-speaking Caribbean," CEHILA, *Historia general*, vol. IV.

SELECT BIBLIOGRAPHY

Berryman, Phillip. *The Religious Roots of Rebellion. Christians in Central American Revolutions.* Maryknoll, N.Y.: Orbis, 1984. Confined to Central America, but very useful.

Bruneau, Thomas. *The Catholic Church and Religion in Latin America.* Developing Area Studies. McGill University, 1984.

Dussel, Enrique. *History and Theology of Liberation.* Maryknoll, N.Y.: Orbis, 1976.

—. *History of the Church in Latin America.* Grand Rapids: Eerdmans, 1981.

—., ed. *Historia General de la Iglesia en América Latina.* Salamanca: Sígueme, 1979ff. See General Bibliography for details

Levine, Daniel. *Churches and Politics in Latin America.* Beverley Hills: Sage, 1980.

—. *Religion and Popular Protest in Latin America.* Notre Dame: Kellogg Institute, 1986.

Mecham, Lloyd. *Church and State in Latin America.* Chapel Hill: Univ. of North Carolina, 1966.

Methol Ferré, A. "La Iglesia latinoamericana de Rio a Puebla (1955–79)," in *Historia de la Iglesia*, ed. Fliche-Martin. Valencia: EDICEP, vol I supp. 1981, pp. 697-725.

Meyer, Jean. *Historia de los Cristianos en América Latina.* Mexico City: Vuelta, 1989, pp. 209ff.

Pape, Carlos. *Katholizismus in Lateinamerika.* Sieburg: Steyler, 1963.

Pape, Richard. *El catolicismo contemporáneo en Latinoamérica.* Buenos Aires: Fides, 1951.

Pike, Frederick. "La Iglesia en Latinoamérica," in *Nueva Historia de la Iglesia.* Madrid: Cristiandad, vol. V, 1977, pp. 316–71.

Prien, Hans-Jürgen. *Die Geschichte des Christentums in Lateinamerika.* Göttingen: Vanderhoek & Ruprecht, 1978.

Zubillaga, Felix. "Die Kirche in Lateinamerika," in *Handbuch der Kirchengeschichte*, ed. H. Jedin. Freiburg: Herder, vol. 7, 1979. Eng. trans. *History of the Church*, ed. H. Jedin and J. Dolan, 10 vols. London and New York: Burns & Oates and Herder and Herder, 1965–81. Vol 7: *The Church between Revolution and Restoration.*

Chapter 9

FROM THE SECOND VATICAN COUNCIL TO THE PRESENT DAY

Enrique Dussel

I. THE CONCILIAR RENEWAL AND MEDELLIN (1959–72)

This period falls between two major events: the convocation of the Council in January 1959 and the fourteenth Assembly of CELAM in Sucre (Bolivia) in 1972, which produced a change in the pastoral outlook of the Latin American Bishops' Conference. Its point of convergence is the Second General Conference of CELAM, held in Medellín in Colombia in 1968, which provided the impulse for the main lines along which the Church was to develop in the following decades.

1. THE CHURCH IN THE DECADE OF DEVELOPMENT AND ITS CRISIS

The election of Pope John XXIII on 28 October 1958 gave no hint that he was to summon a Council the following year. On 1 January 1959, Fidel Castro's revolution triumphed in Cuba. Stalin had died in 1953, and the Twentieth Party Congress of 1956, with Khrushchev in power, buried a whole era in the Soviet Union. This and the election of John F. Kennedy in 1961 ushered in a time of widening horizons. In Latin America the "Alliance for Progress," forged in the middle of the so-called "decade of development" (1955–65), marked the high point of optimism in the system of dependent capitalism. John XXIII issued the encyclicals *Mater et Magistra* (1961) and *Pacem in terris* (1963), which lent wings to the process of renewed political commitment in Latin America. The Pope himself had spoken of a "Church of the poor."[1]

Alongside "developmentism," a revolutionary current was running: Camilo Torres was killed in 1966, and Che Guevara in 1967. In the latter year the next pope, Paul VI (1963–78) issued *Populorum progressio*, in which he spoke of the "international imperialism of money." On 31 July the previous year, seventeen bishops from the poor countries had launched the "Declaration of the Bishops of the Third World," which was to make a lasting impact. Around this time, "dependence theory" was beginning to question "developmentism" and show the need not for reforms, but for a structural *liberation* embracing the whole continent.

1968, with the "May revolution" in Paris, the Berkeley campus revolt against the Vietnam war, and the youth uprising in Mexico, bloodily suppressed in October, was a key year – expressing the 1967 crisis of capitalism. In 1970, Salvador Allende was elected in Chile, and the following year the pope issued *Octogesima adveniens*, legitimizing a democratic socialism.

2. TWO PHASES IN COLLEGIAL DEVELOPMENT

The Church in Latin America went through two phases in an increasing programme of meetings, conferences, assemblies. The first, from 1959 to 1968, was a sort of general renewal in preparation for great events. The Second Vatican Council opened on 11 October 1962. 601 bishops from Latin America took part, 22.23 percent of the total (compared to Europe's 849, 31.6 percent). Cardinal Caggiano of Buenos Aires was one of five presidents of the opening session. CELAM held several annual assemblies in Rome during the Council, under the presidency of Mgr Manuel Larraín. By the time the Council closed in 1965, a deep change had taken place in the Church from Mexico to Argentina.

The change was felt first by several minority but prophetic bodies. The first significant encounter was the Meeting of Latin American Bishops in Baños in Ecuador in June 1966, with those responsible for the commissions on education, the lay apostolate, social policy and general pastoral practice. Then came the Tenth Assembly of CELAM in Mar del Plata on "The role of the Church in development and integration in Latin America," in October the same year – which the dictatorial government of Onganía prevented Helder Camara from attending. There followed the University Pastoral Encounter in Buga in Colombia in 1967, which proposed reform of Catholic universities and opened the way for a major restructuring of important intellectual centres (leading to strikes, sit-ins and student demonstrations in Chile and other countries). Then theological seminaries were reformed after the Vocations Encounter in Lima in 1967; the indigenous question entered the Church's consciousness with the First Pastoral Encounter of Indigenous Missions in 1968; social policy was examined in Brazil in May 1968. All this prepared the ground for the central event in the Latin American Church in the twentieth century: the Second General Conference of the Latin American Episcopate in Medellín, on the theme of "The Church in the Present-day Transformation of Latin America."[2]

This ushered in the second phase (1968–72), beginning the work of renewing the whole Latin American Church through CELAM. The Pastoral Institute of Quito trained more than five hundred pastoral workers – including Fr Rutilio Grande, later to be a Jesuit martyr in El Salvador; Catechetical, Liturgical and Youth Institutes deepened and extended their work; meetings for Episcopal Renewal produced profound changes in many bishops.

On a broader front, Latin American voices had been heard at the Synods of Bishops held in Rome in 1967 and 1969, but at the third (1971) Synod, the Latin American bishops really made their presence felt. They adopted a clear liberationist perspective on the subject "Justice in the World," expressed through the Executive Secretary of CELAM, Mgr Eduardo Pironio. And in Spain still under Franco, at the conference held in the Escorial from 8–15 July 1972 on the theme "Christian Faith and Social Change in Latin America," more than thirty liberation theologians explained to Europe the experience the Church in Latin America was going through during these years.[3]

3. THE MAIN CHALLENGES

There are three areas that can be classified as the main challenges facing the Church during this period. The first is that of the *people* of Latin America, seen as the historical subject of the evolution of society in history, as the social *bloc* whose "memory" goes back beyond the arrival of the Spaniards and Portuguese in Latin America. This involves the whole question of popular culture, of the religion of the people (popular Catholicism), the political protagonism of this people, whom the institutional Church had grown used to "living with," while failing to inspire *from within*. The Church had worked on the people, but not as the Christian people. The "Movement of Priests for the Third World," started in Argentina in 1966, was the first movement to link itself to the *popular* movement (in a non-exclusive class sense, and avoiding populism). The "base church communities" which sprang up in many parts of the continent but above all in north-eastern Brazil, proved the response to the Church's need to organize as "the People of God" (the definition of the Church made in Vatican II's Constitution on the Church, *Lumen Gentium*), increasing in numbers under both "progressive" and "liberation" inspiration from the mid-1970s.

The second was the challenge of whether to opt for reform alone, or also for revolution. The Cuban revolution of 1959 had shown the use of arms to be politically and ethically possible. The "socialist option" was seriously discussed for the first time, with "Christians for Socialism" in Chile beginning the long road of meetings between Christians and Marxists. The "Cold War" had thawed and the anti-Marxism of the 1930s had been left behind, but arguments between progressive, reformist Christians, who hoped for the development of dependent capitalism, and those who struggled for the utopia of the overthrow of this capitalism, continued on all levels. This challenge was to deepen in the following period.

The third concerned the "model" of the Church itself, or the way the Church sees its function in political and civil society. The "Christendom" model, looking to the state to provide facilities for religious education, military chaplains, subsidies for church buildings and the like, was in crisis, being replaced by the concept of the "Church of the poor." This was a matter, in CELAM's thinking from 1963 to 1972, of spreading Christian witness *directly* to the people, to *the poor*. The "poor" became the focus of all options, dicussions and actions. The "theology of liberation" – the reflection of a whole generation of Latin American theologians, the origin of which should not be attributed to individuals – formulated this historic "option for the poor," transforming the Church into the "Church of the poor" and handing over to the people, as the main agents of history, the responsibility for their own evangelization – the "servant Church" of the liberation of the poor people, in the spirit of John XXIII.

4. RENEWAL OF CHURCH STRUCTURES

During this period the bishops ceased to be lone islands and related to one another to the extent of forming real movements. One of the signs of these new times was the attitude they took to the land question, agrarian reform. In Brazil in 1961 Fr Antonio Melo led two thousand peasants in occupying land. Bishop Helder Câmara supported him, as did Cardinal Motta, while Bishop Siguad opposed him and published an "Anti-Communist Catechism" in the vein of the *Fiducia* ("For Tradition, Family and Property") movement. In March 1962 Bishop Manuel Larraín handed over the 342 hectares of "Alto las Cruces" so that the Chilean Institute for Land Reform could settle peasants as new owners of these old church lands. Cardinal Silva Henríquez then gave 1,213 hectares to the peasants in "Las Pataguas." In 1963, the archbishop of Cuzco, Mgr Jurgens Byrne, handed 15,000 hectares of church lands to the peasants. Mgr Leonidas Proaño did the same with 3,000 hectares of the "Tepeyac" ranch in 1969.

These acts of voluntary impoverishment of the Church were followed by concrete actions, not now of aid, but of promotion of the popular movement itself, by Dom Helder Câmara in Brazil, bishops Manuel Larraín in Chile, A. Devoto of Nevares, Enrique Angelelli in Argentina, Sergiò Méndez Arceo of Cuernavaca in Mexico, and others. In Puerto Rico, Mgr Antulio Parrilla Bonilla helped burn military draft cards as a protest action; Mgr Gerardo Valencia of Buenaventura demonstrated in favour of black emancipation; Cardinal Juan Landázuri Ricketts donated the million pesos the governemnt had given him for restoration of his cathedral to repair a prison and build a new hospital. . . .

At the same time, a deep renewal was affecting the structure of the priestly ministry. Movements such as Priests for the Third World in Argentina moved from debating priestly celibacy to opting for the "popular revolution"; similar movements all over the continent showed that priests were no longer just professionals of ritual and worship, but becoming prophets in a real, social, historical sense.

Religious Orders and Congregations were moving along the same lines. CLAR, the Latin American Confederation of Religious, came into being and held its first General Assembly in Lima in 1960. Women's communities, with 140,000 members in total, took the "option for the poor" especially seriously. In August 1968, the Franciscans – with such a long history on the continent – held the First Latin American Franciscan Conference, in the presence of their Superior General, Fr Constantino Koser. In March 1972, the first Course for Latin American Religious Provincials was held in Medellín. There is no doubt that the renewal that took place in the decade 1962–72 was unparalleled in the history of religious orders on the continent.

Lay movements showed a similar and growing vitality. Lay people demanding church reform occupied a church in Buenos Aires in 1966, Santiago cathedral in 1968, the churches of Lima in 1970. Catholic Action was in deep crisis, especially since the demise of Catholic University Youth in Brazil. Christian trade unions became secularized and Christian militants began to "merge" with the mass of other leaders struggling for the working or peasant classes in a strictly classist sense. The encyclical *Humanae vitae* of 1968, on marital morality, in effect gave more scope to the consciences of Christian couples, as embodied in the Family Christian Movement, started in Montevideo in 1961.

At the same time, the reformist political current was finding a channel in Christian Democracy. This spread from Chile to Venezuela in 1947 and the same year saw the foundation of ODCA, the Christian Democrat Organization of America. Christian Democrat parties were founded in Argentina and Bolivia in 1954, in Peru and Guatemala in 1956, El Salvador, Paraguay and Panama in 1960, Santo Domingo in 1961, Uruguay and Brazil in 1962, and Ecuador and Colombia in 1964. When Eduardo Frei came to power in Chile in 1964 and Rafael Caldera in Venezuela in 1968, Christian Democracy began to distance itself from young Christian revolutionaries.

5. THE CHURCH AND SOCIALISM: CUBA AND CHILE

The Church's first reaction to the coming of socialism with Castro's triumph in Cuba on 1 January 1959 was one of "discomfiture" – as Gómez Treto describes in more detail in chapter 24. The bishops' first reaction was a critical letter: "Faced with the shootings . . ."; in February they defended private education; in May they pointed to the socialism inherent in the agrarian reform laws. Finally, in November, they organized a National Catholic Congress, presided over by Mgr Enrique Pérez Santos (who had defended Castro in 1953 during the attack on the Monacada barracks, actually saving his life), at which Castro appeared, to be greeted by shouts of "Christ, Yes; Another, No!" and "Cuba, Yes; Russia, No!" These were still Cold War years. CELAM itself, at its Fourth Assembly held the same month in Colombia, condemned "the traps of communism" and "the incompatibility between Communism and Christianity." On 7 August the following year, the Cuban bishops issued a collective letter stating that "the absolute majority of the Cuban people, who are Catholic, can be led to endorse a communist regime only by deceit." The little wealth the Church possessed was affected by the Urban Reform decreed on 14 September, confiscating property and lowering rents to favour the poor.

The next, "confrontational," phase began in June 1960, with Castro declaring that "Anyone who is anti-communist is anti-revolutionary." Leading Christians of the middle classes joined the opposition *en masse*. The emigration to Miami began and many enrolled in subversive actions against the government. The following June Castro nationalized education, confiscated the cemeteries, banned the procession of the statue of "The Copper Virgin of Charity," and then in September expelled 133 priests, including the future archbishop of Havana, Mgr Francisco Oves Martínez. There were 745 priests in the country in 1960; by 1969 their number had been reduced to 230; the 2225 religious in 1960 were reduced to two hundred by 1970.

The years from 1962 to 1967 were characterized by "flight" – from reality and in many cases from the country – but with signs of a change. New winds were blowing from the Vatican Council; the new Apostolic Delegate was Mgr César Zacchi, who had experience in the socialist countries of Eastern Europe. Fr Guillermo Sardiñas, who had fought with Castro and risen to the rank of Commandant, then returned to his parish of Christ the King in Havana, died in December 1964 and was buried with full military honours. In 1966 a new major seminary was opened; Catholic Action was disbanded and re-organized as FLAC (Formation, Liturgy, Apostolate, Catechesis) to play a part in preparing for Cuban bishops to participate in the 1968 Medellín Conference, though the effects of this were very limited in Cuba.

It was Castro himself who opened a new phase, of "dialogue," saying to the five hundreed delegates to an international "Congress of Intellectuals" in Havana: "These are the paradoxes of history. Such as when we see sectors of the clergy become revolutionary forces shall we resign ourselves to seeing sectors of Marxism becoming ecclesiastical forces?" In April 1969 the bishops issued a *Communiqué* condemning the economic and poitical blockade instigated by the United States. Mgr Oves was consecrated archbishop on 19 July, and in September another *Communiqué* declared: "We should approach atheists in all respect and brotherly love . . . In the undertaking of development, of the advancement of all and of the whole person, there is a vast field of endeavour common to all persons of good will, be they atheists or believers." Castro was in Chile from 5 November to 4 December 1971, where he "dialogued" with the eighty Chilean priests who were to visit Cuba the following February. A Cuban delegation was also to attend the first Latin American Meeting of Christians for Socialism, held in Santiago.

Chile went through a period of "developmentist" renewal between 1959 and 1968, inspired by the Bellarmine Centre. Cardinal Raúl Silva Henríquez became archbishop of Santiago in 1961 and the following year launched the first "Overall Pastoral Plan." On 7 October 1961, five thousand young people went on pilgrimage to Maipú to pray for the success of the Council. The bishops issued a pastoral letter on "The social and political duty of the day." The review *Mensaje* devoted an issue to "Revolutionary reforms in Latin America." The Chilean church could be said to be the most active of all the Latin American churches at the Council: it was well organized, brought its own theologians, and had done preparatory work on the schema "On the Church." In 1963 it organized "social weeks," followed by the Great Mission of Santiago and in 1967 the synods of Santiago, Concepción and Talca; it also played a vital part in preparing for the Medellín Conference.

With the election of Eduardo Frei as President (1964–70), however, its leading role began to decline. His Christian Democrat government suppressed a peasant movement in Puerto Montt in 1967, and splits began to appear in the Church. The bishops issued their last great creative, non-censorial document, "Chile: the will to be," in 1968. Shortly after, the "young church" occupied Santiago cathedral, demanding reforms. At the same time the right-wing group *Fiducia* became more active. The basic crisis that was to affect the whole Church in Latin America surfaced in embryo at the Latin American Institute ILADES: one tendency within it (called "developmentist" by the others) represented by Pierre Bigo SJ and Roger Vekemans SJ, accused another, led by Gonzalo Arroyo SJ (the only Chilean) and Franz Hinkelammert of being "Marxists"; by 1969 the situation had become untenable and ILADES split in two. Vekemans then moved to Venezuela and helped Alfonso López Trujillo on his meteoric rise from priest to auxiliary bishop, then cardinal archbishop of Medellín, while Arroyo went on to found "Christians for Socialism."

In 1969, the Christian Democrats also split, giving rise to the Movement for Popular Unitary Action (MAPU) which formed part of the socialist Popular Unity government which won the elections on 4 September 1970. In April 1971, the "group of eighty" priests met to discuss "Christian participation in building socialism in Chile," leading to a public declaration which said: "As Christians we see no incompatibility between Christianity and socialism." The bishops replied first in a letter addressed to priests and then a pastoral letter in May. In March 1972, the first meeting of "Christians for Socialism" was held. Gonzalo Arroyo said: "Objective analysis of the political reality of Latin America leads to the conclusion that the repeated failure of the Left to draw the masses into a determined struggle against the national and international forces of capitalism, requires the massive incorporation of Christians into the revolutionary process." The conclusions spelt out: "The building of socialism is a creative process alien from any dogmatic schematization and from any uncritical acceptance ... In such conditions religion loses its character of opium of the people ... to become one more inspiring factor in the struggle for peace, freedom and justice." On 11 September 1973, Augusto Pinochet buried this ecclesial experiment under an unparalleled repression. Popular Unity in Chile had provided a new model for democracy, but after its destruction by the military coup, other ways for the future had to be sought.

6. THE CHURCH AND "DEVELOPMENTISM": THE SOUTHERN CONE

In Brazil, Dom Helder Câmara, who had been national assessor of Catholic Action since 1947, founded the National Conference of Brazilian Bishops (CNBB) with the help of the papal nuncio Dom Armando Lombardia and Mgr Montini (later Pope Paul VI), begining a period of charismatic leadership. Forty-three new dioceses, with 109 bishops, were founded; eleven new archdioceses and sixteen prelatures. The progressive young bishops appointed, with a predominance from the poor North-East, were to play a leading role in the CNBB after 1968.

Between 1959 and 1961, the Church tackled the question of education, pressurizing the government through the Association of Catholic Education, with the result that the law on "Basic Directives for National Education" passed on 20 December 1961 incorporated the Church's viewpoint. At the same time, the Church was gradually breaking away from its traditional association with the rural oligarchy. Declarations made in Natal in 1951, in Campina Grande in 1956 and again in Natal in 1959 in support of peasants and rural trade unions opened the way for social change.[4] In July 1962 the Central Committee of the CNBB declared that "no one can ignore the clamour of the masses who are being martyred by hunger."

Based on the experience of Radio Sutetanza in Colombia, a huge movement of radio education took shape across the country, at the same time as the Base Education Movement devised by Paulo Freire was gradually developing in Recife. Catholic Action, meanwhile, particularly its youth branches, was becoming radicalized, largely under the influence of the French Dominican Thomas Cardonell. In 1961 a militant JUC leader, Aldo Arantes, was elected President of the National Union of Students. The Church no longer needed an alliance with the state, as it had under the New Christendom model, to carry out its tasks in civil society; it now had its own institutions to act directly in the world. Its actions, however, were still in the "developmentist" line, through prophetic minorities acting "on" the people.

The military coup of 1964 led to a return to outdated positions. At the 1964 assembly of the CNBB (held in Rome as the bishops were there for the Council), Cardinal Angelo Rossi was elected President and Mgr Brandao Vilela Vice-president. The "Overall Plan," supposed to carry out the 1962 "Emergency Plan," was left in the hands of a Conference – without Helder Câmara – lacking both leadership qualities and determination. Furthermore, members of Catholic Action were being persecuted, MEB was disbanded and popular leaders were being arrested or going into exile. This was the start of the

"National Security" type of regime that was to spread throughout Latin America.

Things changed again, however, when Mgr Aloisio Lorscheider was elected General Secretary of the CNBB in 1968. He immediately showed real organizational ability coupled with a will to change the course of events. This proved to be the gestation period, marked by persecution and martyrdom – such as the assassination after torture of Fr Antonio Herique Pereira Neto, Dom Helder Câmara's secretary, at the age of twenty-eight, on 27 April 1969 – of a Church that was to replace that of Chile in showing a way forward and providing a model of Christian action in Latin America toward the end of the century.

The Church in Argentina during the period 1955–76 (the eighteen years between Perón's second and third governments, marked by "developmentism," and the return of Perón and *Peronismo*) split rapidly into two radically opposite camps: one opting for alliance with the ruling classes (first developmentist under Frondizi and then militarist under Onganía); the other committed to the popular classes, the principal exponents of which were the 850 "Priests for the Third World." Faced with a conservative hierarchy, led by Cardinal Antonio Caggiano, who was also bishop of the armed forces, the younger clergy had to take on themselves the task of renewal during the period of the Council and then from Medellín to the beginning, in 1973, of the most violent repression the Church in Argentina has ever known.

After the fall of Perón in 1955, some sectors placed their hopes in the young Christian Democrat party, but this showed its limitations in the 1957 elections. The student branch of Catholic Action, JUC, enjoyed a revival with a series of national meetings in the early 1960s, moving from university "humanism" and Christian Democracy to more leftist "social Christian" stances; some of these groups took part in the left-wing Peronist movement led by Montoneros. By 1965, Bishop Podestá of Avellaneda, a working-class sector of Buenos Aires, was the spokesperson for a Church committed to the cause of the oppressed.

The military coup led by Onganía in 1966 produced a right-wing pro-military Catholicism opposed by the younger clergy. On 28 June 1965, eighty priests had met with Bishop Podestá and Antonio Quarracino to reflect on the Council. In May 1968 what was to be called the Movement of Priests for the Third World held its first national meeting in Córdoba, with further meetings in the following two years. The "San Miguel Declaration" of April 1969, issued by the bishops after their annual meeting at which they discussed how to apply the principles of Medellín to Argentina, marked the high point of a Church seeking a model of "church of the poor," which was to be violently repressed.

In Paraguay, where Alfredo Stroessner had been in power since 1954, the Church distanced itself from the regime to some extent between 1966 and 1976, beginning an active defence of human rights, with an especially acute confrontation in 1969. Mgr Felipe S. Benítez declared that "the Church cannot remain silent in the face of violation of human rights." The bishop of Villarrica, Mgr Aníbal Mena Porta, supported a group of striking workers; the government accused him of being a communist, and his seventy-five priests supported him.

He also excommunicated the police chief for arresting and torturing suspects. The review *Comunidad* was suspended in October and Fr Francisco de Paula Oliva SJ expelled from the Catholic university. In 1971 Fr Uberfil Monzón was imprisoned and tortured, and the Church definitively distanced itself from the regime.

In Uruguay the export-based populist consensus was running out as a result of U.S. market dominance, producing a deep crisis in the whole society. The Church, persecuted by the liberals in a deeply anti-clerical country, led a quiet life. In 1962 the *Tupamaro* National Liberation Movement was founded, and many young Christians joined it.

The Church was renewed at the time of the Council. In 1968 twenty-seven priests from Tacuarembó and their bishops signed a letter on the "sufferings, anguish and hopes of the people of our zone." Fr Juan Zaffaroni SJ led a protest march of sugar-cane cutters. Mgr Carlos Parteli, in the final document of the socio-pastoral Congress held in Montevideo in December 1968, described the so-called "golden age" of agricultural exports and concluded: "Today we are discovering how far this development of Uruyuan society was a matter of appearances." In 1969 persecution of the Tupamaros began, and with it repression against the Church. On 12 August 1970 the Jesuit provincial interceded for Fr Justo Asiaín and Pastor Emilio Castro (later secretary-general of the World Council of Churches) who had been arrested. In a sermon on 25 August 1972, bishop Partelli spoke of "assassinations, detentions and the ruling terror" in the midst of a wave of imprisonment, torture and killings affecting lay men and women, priests and religious.

7. RENEWAL AND GUERRILLAS: THE ANDEAN REGION

The Church in Peru experienced a profound change in outlook during this period. The first "Social Week" held in Lima in 1959, discussing the subject of "The Social Duties of the Church in Peru," already showed the Church's commitment to social action. The second such week, held in Arequipa in 1961 on the subject of "Property," developed the same course. The bishops issued a pastoral letter on "Catholics and Politics" the same year, following it with one on "Politics: a Christian duty" two years later. Conciliar renewal was led by Cardinal Juan Landázuri Ricketts, consecrated archbishop of Lima in 1962, concentrating at first on liturgy and catechetics.

In 1966 the bishops declared: "We are concerned most particularly with the social and economic situation of the peasant population in the mountain areas." In July 1968, shortly before the Medellín Conference, Fr Gustavo Gutiérrez outlined to a group of priests what was to become the starting point of liberation theology. The military coup led by Velazco Alvarado brought in a populist government, some of whose actions, such as agrarian reform, the Church felt able to support, divesting itself of the lands it still possessed in the diocese of Cuzco. It also approved the nationalization of oil and the industrial law of 1970. In the area of urban reform, though, the Church went further: when a group of dispossessed occupied building sites in Lima, the auxiliary bishop, Mgr Bambarém, celebrated a mass for the "invaders," which produced a confrontation with the government, which was moving steadily to the Right.

At the Synod of Bishops held in Rome in 1871, the bishops of Peru produced perhaps the most forward-looking document presented, entitled "Justice in the World." This analyzed the situation of poverty in Latin America and stated: "That is why many Christians today recognize in socialist currents 'certain aspirations which they hold within themselves in the name of their faith (*Octogesima adveniens*, 31)'."[5]

In Bolivia, as elsewhere, renewal came from "outside" – from the Second Vatican Council. In the 1960s the experiment of an "Aymara church" was made, led by Mgr Adhemar Esquivel, who was appointed auxiliary bishop of La Paz in 1969. Theological renewal began in the seminary of Cochabamba, led by a group of Spanish priests.

"Che" Guevara's experience in the guerrilla force of Nancahuazá (ending with his death in 1967) was continued by the mystical Nestor Paz in Teoponte.[6] ISAL, the organization for Church and Society in Latin America, from 1969 demonstrated its commitment among miners and peasants: its Third National Assembly in February 1971 was a decisive occasion. In the same year Cardinal Maurer himself declared that "we are branding as communists those who are defending legitimate rights." The papal nuncio Mgr Gravelli, however, started exerting pressure in the opposite direction from July 1971, and the military coup led by Hugo Banzer ushered in a period of frontal assault on sectors of the Church committed to the poor.

In Ecuador, an itinerant Pastoral Institute began the renewal of a deeply traditional Church in 1964. This was followed by the formation of a National Pastoral Institute, with a group of priests acting as a "think tank." While Mgr Leonidas Proaño, bishop of Riobamba, was president of CELAM's pastoral department, the Latin American Pastoral Institute (IPAL) was founded in Quito, becoming a central force in renewal throughout Latin America – till it was closed by the new powers in CELAM in 1973. Its director, Fr Rafael Espín, organized a nation-wide movement of trained priests, while the diocese of Riobamba, prototype for many prophetic actions, launched its own "pastoral plan," transforming its parishes into diaconates, in 1969.

In Colombia the Council caused a sensation, but with more attention paid to form – new liturgy, new catechesis, abandoning the soutane . . . – than content. Quite a different line was taken by Fr Camilo Torres Restrepo (1929–66), who came from a wealthy and conservative family, was a well-known sociologist, one of the founders of the "Latin American school of sociology," and had studied at Louvain: "I abandoned the priesthood," he wrote in 1965 "for the same reasons as led me to enter it. I discovered Christianity as a life totally centred on love of one's neighbour . . . I consider myself, however, a priest 'for ever' and understand that my priesthood and its exercise are fulfilled in carrying out the revolution in Colombia, in love of my neighbour and in the struggle for the wellbeing of the majority."

His death as a guerrilla fighter in February 1966 brought a number of consequences. The directors of the review *El Catolicismo* were expelled in September (one of them, Fr Mario Revello, was to return as archbishop of Bogotá in the early 1980s). Then came the XXXIX National Eucharistic Congress in Bogotá in 1968, attended by Pope Paul VI, the first time a reigning pope had set foot in Latin America. The bishops of the Colombian Church, one of the most conservative in Latin America, were basically opposed to the line taken by the Medellín Conference, which therefore had less effect in the country in which it was held than elsewhere. Their December 1973 document on "Justice and Christian duty," so fervently supported by Mgr López Trujillo, was in effect a frontal attack on Medellín.

8. MEXICO, CENTRAL AMERICA AND THE CARIBBEAN

In Mexico the JOC made a late appearance in 1959. In 1961 a coordinating Conference of all the more dynamic lay, clerical and religious institutions in the country came into being under the guidance of Fr Pedro Velásquez, director of the Mexican Social Secretariat from 1946 till his death in 1968. A central figure of this period was Mgr Samuel Ruiz, bishop of Chiapas, involved in the origin of the coordinating Conference, in pastoral strategy for the indigenous peoples, and a major influence at the Medellín conference. A First Conference of Social Secretariats was held in 1962, when they numbered over thirty, though their numbers were to grow to 150 in the 1970s. The more progressive bishops formed themselves into a Union that was to develop into the Pastoral Strategy Commission of the bishops' conference. A Congress on "Development and Integration" was held in May 1964 at the suggestion of the coordinating Conference. Movements concerned with mission to the indigenous peoples and means of communication sprang from the grassroots, and in some cases came into conflict with the bishops. The diocese of Cuernavaca produced two conflicts with Rome: over the use of psychoanalysis in the Benedictine convent founded by Gregoire Lemercier, and the approach developed by Mgr Ivan Illich in his Centre.

In October 1968, thirty-six priests made a public commitment to an option for the poor at Tlatelolco, marking the beginning of a new shift in the Church. The first National Theological Congress on "Faith and Development," held in November 1969, saw the first signs of liberation theology. An *ad hoc* commission produced a document on "Justice in the world" for the 1971 Rome Synod of Bishops that was one of the most advanced of its time, clearly advocating commitment to the poor.

The bishops of Central America issued their first joint pastoral letter from Managua in 1956, in tones of militant anti-communism: "Those who think that its supreme goal is to improve the economic status of workers and peasants know little or nothing of the philosophical basis of atheistic communism." Renewal was to be a slow process.

In Guatemala the bishops' conference was established only in 1959. In 1962 they were still warning of the communist threat in a campaign for "social justice." When Mgr Rossell, bishop of Guatemala City, died in 1964, he was succeeded by Mgr Mario Casariego, whose tenure of such an important see proved one of its darkest periods. In 1966 a huge movement of repression was launched against the Church's popular organizations, marked by assassination and torture on a wide scale.[7] It was not till August 1968, with a meeting of eight hundred pastoral agents, that post-conciliar renewal of the Catholic Church in Guatemala began.

The same process was initiated in Nicaragua early in 1969, with a Pastoral

Meeting organized by Mgr Julián Barni, with 258 delegates – bishops, priests religious and lay people. Fr Noel García SJ declared that the Church in Nicaragua "lacked true spiritual leadership from its pastors," and important contributions were made by Frs Antonio Vega and Florián Ruskamp. Ernesto Cardenal had already founded his contemplative community on the island of Solentiname in Lake Nicaragua, following guidelines laid down by Thomas Merton, and his brother Fernando Cardenal SJ was president of an episcopal commission to organize pastoral care of young people. On 29 June 1971, the bishops issued a pastoral letter on "The duty of witness and Christian action in the political sphere."

In Honduras, the radiophonic schools began broadcasting in 1961. They were extended to the south of the country by Fr Pablo Ghuillet: one parish alone had 160 peasant groups being motivated by its programmes. Their objectives were redefined in Comayagua in 1963, adopting the Brazilian methods developed by Paulo Freire. This led to the formation of "Popular Cultural Action" as a peasant initiative. By 1969 fruits of the renewal stemming from the Council and Medellín were becoming apparent.

In El Salvador, the Italian Fr Lombardini preached at a series of "Updating Meetings" from 1958 to 1962, which prepared the way for renewal. The social secretariat of the archdiocese was responsible for the bishops' letter "On the temporal commitment of lay people" in 1960, but it was not till a decade later that real signs of renewal appeared, at the "First National Pastoral Strategy Week" organized by bishops Chávez and Rivera y Damas. Fr Inocencio Alas was arrested as a result of his contribution to this, and in December the same year Fr Nicolás Rodríguez was assassinated, opening a new era of repression.

In Panama, the arrest and "disappearance" of Fr Héctor Gallegos, organizer of base communities and outspoken opponent of injustice, left its mark on the Church of the isthmus. In their submission to the 1971 Synod, the bishops wrote: "Priests, both Panamanian and foreign, have been subject to personal intimidation, either for their work among the poor, or for having spoken from their pulpits as we have pronounced on the case of Fr Héctor Gallegos."

In the Caribbean, the Church in Santo Domingo was left with no positive role to play after the death of Trujillo in 1961. It accused his popular successor, Juan Bosch, of communism, and an ambiguous sermon by Mgr Polanco Britos probably contributed to his overthrow in 1963. The Church remained silent throughout the U.S. occupation that followed, despite the assassination of Fr Arthur Mackinnon; nor did it raise any objection to the accession of a new dictator, Joaquín Balaguer. In Haiti, on the other hand, the Church suffered severe repression at the hands of François Duvalier, without intervention from the Vatican. He opposed the nomination of Mgr Maurice Choquet as bishop of Cap Haitien in 1959, and in November 1960 even expelled the archbishop of Port-au-Prince, Mgr François Poirier. From then on he expelled foreign priests, and Haitian ones, despite his nationalistic rhetoric, arrested and assassinated lay people and generally carried out a campaign of systematic repression.

SUMMARY: FROM "DEVELOPMENT" TO "LIBERATION"

This period marks the transition from a "New Christendom" model of the

Church (of which Catholic Action and Christian Democracy were the main exponents) to a commitment of the Church to the exploited "people of the poor" (through base church communities, non-confessional, often radical and sometimes even revolutionary political commitment, dialogue with socialism . . .) – to being a "Church of the poor." Juan Luis Segundo was the first to posit this change of model in his "The Future of Christianity in Latin America," in 1963.[8] Writing from my experience with Paul Gauthier in Nazareth, I showed the crisis affecting the previous model in 1964.[9] It was not till 1968, however, with the publication of works by Gustavo Gutiérrez, Richard Schaull and Rubem Alves,[10] that the movement known as liberation theology really began to run its course.

The tension, then, was no longer between a conservative, traditionalist Church and a modernizing one, but between progressives, modernizers or "developmentalists" – supported by the traditionalists, but not yet sufficiently organized into a coherent whole – , on the one hand, and the movements committed to "liberation" on the other. And – one way or another – the Church ceased to be an institution on the sidelines of Latin American history, reacting defensively to external events, and became a historical protagonist acting in the real political, economic, cultural and religious life of the people who make up the exploited poor.

II. THE CHURCH FROM 1972 TO 1992

This final period opens with the Fourteenth Ordinary Assembly of CELAM held in Sucre in Bolivia from 15 to 23 November 1972, and is overshadowed by the military coups that darkened Latin American horizons, the first in Brazil in 1964 and the last in Argentina in 1974. It ends with the "opening to democracy" that began around 1984 and the Fourth General Conference of Latin American Bishops held in Santo Domingo in October 1992. Latin America no longer suffered from military dictatorships, but poverty increased – one of its effects being the cholera epidemic spreading throughout the continent. As Carlos Torres, the Minister of Health in Peru, says: "Peru's problem is not cholera, but poverty. 70 percent of the population live in a state of destitution, and this out of a population of 22,000,000."

1. FOUR PHASES IN A WORLD SETTING

Under the U.S. presidencies of Richard Nixon (1969–74) and Gerald Ford (1974–7), with the State Department in the hands of Henry Kissinger, Latin America underwent a reign of terror.

In the first phase, lasting from 1972 to 1976, during the final years of the pontificate of Paul VI, who died in 1978, the Church in Latin America suffered a repression impossible to imagine in other times. The Synods of Bishops of 1974, 1977 and 1980 failed to make the impact of earlier ones. In December 1975, the Pope issued a great encyclical on the themes of evangelization and liberation: *Evangelii nuntiandi*. The Jesuits had held their Thirty-second Extraordinary Congregation in Rome in 1973, which concluded that: "the Company should be at the service of the Church at this time of rapid change in the world and should respond to the challenge posed by that world." Their option for social justice was a priority laid down at that time.

The second phase dates from the election of Jimmy Carter in 1976. The "Trilateral Commission" set up under pressure of the economic crisis of 1967 (which was to end in the "stagflation" of 1974–5), produced a measure of "openness" and a lessening of support for military dictatorships. The fall of Balaguer and the election of Guzmán in Santo Domingo indicated a change. In Rome, 1978 was the year of three popes, with John Paul I and then John Paul II succeeding Paul VI.

The third phase, from 1979 onwards, opened with two events: the Third General Conference of CELAM, held in Puebla in Mexico in early 1979, and the triumph of the Sandinista revolution in Nicaragua in July of the same year. But at the same time, the accession of Ronald Reagan to the U.S. presidency (1981–9) and the decision to include religious affairs as political problems in the region (with the "Santa Fe Declaration" of 1979 and the "Institute for Religion and Democracy" run by Michael Novak[11]) introduced a renewed tension into the situation. South America was to be the subject of an "opening out," but Central America and the Caribbean were subjected to the traditional "garroting" policy. Pope John Paul II visited Mexico in 1979 and issued the major social encyclical *Laborem exercens* in 1981, but also encouraged a contrary policy on his visit to Nicaragua on 4 March 1983, and above all with the "Instruction on some aspects of Liberation Theology" in September 1984, and the "dialogue" for which Leonardo Boff was summoned to the Holy Office in the same month.

The fourth phase, beginning in 1984, is marked by an "opening" to democracy spreading slowly across the continent. This will drastically change the Church's situation, its pastoral strategy and main commitments. The second "Instruction" on liberation theology of 1986 set minds at rest. The beginnings of *perestroika* around 1985, with Mikhail Gorbachov's bloodless revolution that was to lead to the fall of the Berlin Wall in 1989 and his own resignation and the break-up of the Soviet Union in 1991, together with the Gulf War, marked the end of the Cold War. Also, the end of the Reagan presidency in 1988, and George Bush's term of office, pointed to a "new world order."

2. THE MAIN CHALLENGES

The challenges facing the Church in this period remain much the same as in the earlier one, and the responses to them mark a deepening of the course previously undertaken. The first challenge is to mesh with the *life of the people*, now a suffering people undergoing perhaps the most violent repression known in Latin America since the time of the conquest. But now the people are living in a state of *active resistance*: they know how to celebrate in the midst of their martyrdom. The base church communities have undergone an enormous increase since their inception in 1972. They have held "meetings" on a national scale – five in Brazil, twelve in Mexico, for example. They have also produced real "base" Councils, in the shape of Latin American Encounters of Base Church Communities, the first of which was held in Brazil in 1980. The second, in 1984, with 220 delegates from twelve countries, published its

"Conclusions" in four parts: "The prophetic practice of our communities; the community as alternative form of service; base communities and popular organization; our spirituality as *Church of the poor*."

Their point 28 said: "On our road toward liberation, we meet other brethren who are also organized in seeking *the liberation of the people*, and trying to be an alternative to this system of oppression. It is a reason to thank God, knowing that we have other organizations which, though not born from the light of faith, still seek a new, just and humane society." As can be seen, this is no longer the Church going *out to* the people; this is now a people-church speaking from and for itself. This model of Church makes a clerical or élitist conception of the Church quake, and this is what produces the tensions that exist in Latin America.

The second challenge concerns the defence of *human rights*, ensuring that the blackest side of repression, the torture, death, "disappearing" and exile – there have been thousands of Christians exiled from their countries – are not forgotten and that their victims receive due recognition. Dependent capitalism cannot function without repressing the people: this was recognized in the anti-insurrectional, National Security regime model proposed by Kissinger to Presidents Nixon and Ford. Key dates for the installation of such regimes are: 31 May 1964, *coup d'état* by Castelo Branco in Brazil; 21 August 1971, by Hugo Banzer in Bolivia; 27 June 1973, dissolution of the Congress in Uruguay; 11 September 1973, military coup by Augusto Pinochet in Chile; 28 August 1975, by F. Morales Bermúdez in Peru; 13 January 1976, by G. Rodríguez Lara in Ecuador; 24 March 1976, by Jorge Videla in Argentina. It is worth recording that, on their return from the Second Inter-church Conference of Base Communities in Vitoria (Brazil) on 12 August 1976, seventeen bishops from various Latin American countries (including four "chicanos" from the United States) were imprisoned in Riobamba (Ecuador), causing one of them to exclaim: "If this can happen to us, who are well known, what will happen to peasants, workers or natives when they are arrested?"

So the Church abandoned its earlier narcissistic posture of fighting to defend its own rights (to education, worship, etc.), in order to defend the rights of others, of the poor, the defenceless, those who have no voice. Hundreds upon hundreds of bishops' pastoral letters, declarations by priests, religious, base communities, "Justice and Peace" associations, "Vicariates of Solidarity" and the like show the church "institution" fulfilling its historical mission against National Security regimes. This is a qualitative step forward.

The third challenge, now not from a martyred people but from a people being the protagonist of its own history, is that of revolutionary processes, particularly those in Central America since 1979. This time, the Church did not arrive "late" on the scene to condemn or approve: through its base communities it *played a full part* in the revolutioary processes – not without internal contradictions and violent opposition from its conservative elements. "Christians for Socialism" held their second meeting in Quebec in October 1974, their third in Rome in January 1977 and fourth in Barcelona in 1983, showing that the movement was ongoing and spreading. In effect, however, its most effective course was seen in the daily lives of people in Nicaragua, El Salvador and Guatemala, within the popular movements. So the question of relations with Marxism remained a live one. The General of the Jesuits said as much in his intervention in the Synod of 1977: "Catechesis cannot ignore Marxism, particularly at times when it quite rightly includes the political dimension of Christian life and obligations." The Jesuits, who like other religious orders have produced so many martyrs in Latin America, reaffirmed their stance through their new General, Fr Piet Hans Kolvenbach, in 1983: "For reflection on the Beatitudes to be authentic, it has to be founded on a communion of life and death, as shown by our Lord, with the poor and those who weep, with victims of injustice and those who hunger."[12]

The fourth challenge stems from the ambiguity of the "opening" to democracy, which should give the Church great opportunities of organizing itself on the popular level, but has rather led to its weakening of its base among the people, due to its internal criticism of base church communities and liberation theology. This weakening is leading to an unprecedented growth of Pentecostalism and fundamentalism of all denominations. The end of the Cold War has removed the "bogey" of communism and left the Catholic Right bereft of its traditional enemies, which in fact leaves it in a state of crisis from which it will be difficult to recover.

3. CHURCH GROWTH AND INTERNAL TENSIONS

On the one hand, the church of the poor, whose church model was clearly defined by the bishops of north-eastern Brazil in their 1973 pastoral letter, "I have heard the cry of my people," was growing steadily in all countries of Latin America. Its pastoral policy worked from the religious spirit of the people themselves, not so much utilizing their beliefs as mobilizing them to realize their own interests. It produced its own martyrs in bishops such as Enrique Angelelli in Argentina and Oscar Romero in El Salvador (to name but two, since it is impossible to name all the priests, religious and thousands of Christian lay people martyred during these years). It produced its own theology in the form of reflection on its praxis; it had its own "memory" in the form of a history of the Church that detailed the steps it took.

On the other hand, as the 1977 *Memorandum* of the most representative group of German theologians showed, there was a whole counter-current, opposed to the option for the poor and the theolgy of liberation, mistrustful of the base communities and determined to dismantle (by changing programmes, moving professors and even institutes, etc.) the apparatus built up by CELAM. "The driving force behind this campaign is Fr Roger Vekemans (and) on the part of the Latin American bishops, it is supported principally by the Colombian auxiliary bishops Alfonso López Trujillo and Darío Castrillón."[13] The strength of this campaign was shown at Sucre in 1972 when Mgr López Trujillo was elected General Secretary of CELAM; in 1974 he was elected President and re-elected in 1979 for a second term. When he had to abandon his administrative functions at the Haiti Assembly of 1983, he had been in charge of CELAM for eleven years, and left his *confidants* Darío Castrillón and Antonio Quarracino in place as General Secretary and President respectively. From the heights of this authority, the institutions of CELAM were modified, and campaigns against liberation theologians, the Nicaraguan revolution and the base communities were launched across the continent. The election of churchmen diametrically opposed to this line to the new Commission of the Brazilian National Bishops' Conference in 1983 evened out the situation, but thereby prolonged the constant intra-church tension. The *unity* of the Church was placed under the sign of *contradiction*.

4. THE CHURCH AND NATIONAL SECURITY REGIMES

A frontal assault on the Church in Brazil began with the military coup of 1964, increased by the Constitutional Act No. 5 passed in 1968. Thousands of Christian militants were arrested, tortured and even killed. Tito de Alencar and Frei Betto were imprisoned for four years (the first being tortured to a degree that caused him to commit suicide years later); Frs Rodolfo Lunkenbein and João Bosco Penido Burnier were assassinated, in July and October 1976; in June 1982 Frs Aristide Camio and François Gouriou were condemned to fifteen and ten years imprisonment respectively for their part in supporting the peasants of São Gerlado do Araguaja. Cardinal Paulo Evaristo Arns – defended in August 1984 by three thousand teachers from *state* (not Catholic) schools against attacks by the right-wing Press – led the Church in the spheres of urban industrial relations and universities; Mgr Pedro Casadáliga championed the peasants in the poor and starving *sertão* (drylands) of the North-East; Mgr Tomás Balduino, president of CIMI (the Indigenous Mission Council), led the Church on the indigenous front, where it had become the sole protector of the ethnic minorities. So the Church stood out against the militarist National Security state. Mgr Luiz Fernández coordinated the over 80,000 base church communities which expressed a new way of being church: "A church that is born of the people."

Dom Helder Câmara continued his prophetic denunciation of injustice; Mgr Aloisio Lorscheider became archbishop of Fortaleza after being president of CELAM; Mgr Ivo Lorscheiter led the "new model" Church as president of the CNBB: its basic orientation was defined by the bishops of the North-East in their 1973 document, "I have heard the cry of my people": "Only they, the people of the wildernesses and the cities, in unity and work, in faith and hope, can be that Church of Christ which invites, that Church which works for liberation. And it is only to the degree that we go down into the waters of the gospel that we become Church, *Church-people*, People of God."[14]

In Argentina, on the other hand, bishops carefully chosen for their conservatism (without a Helder Câmara or a nuncio like Armando Lombardi) opposed no resistance to the coup organized by the army and the great landowners. They actually justified repression of guerrilla movements on the grounds of "the common good" in a document issued after their June 1981 assembly, entitled "Church and national community," making a distinction between "legitimate" and "illegitimate" means of repression but offering no justification for the resistance movements.

The killing of a number of young people in Ezeiza in June 1973 marked the beginning of severe repression of popular movements, a process accelerated by the death of Perón in 1974. Fr Carlos Mugica was assassinated at the doorway of his church in a poor *barrio* on 11 May 1974 – one among many. On 4 August 1976, Mgr Enrique Angelelli, bishop of La Rioja, a man deeply committed to his people, on his way back from investigating the murders of two of his diocesan priests, was himself asassinated, by members of the Air Force based at Chamical.

The underlying cause of such widespread martyrdom lies in the country's economic dependence on U.S. capitalism and progressive indebtedness – a policy carried out at its most extreme by Martínez de Hoz. Unfortunately the Church as represented by its bishops failed to oppose the course taken by the military-landowner government, while unreservedly condemning guerrilla opposition. The Church had another face, however, shown in the "Justice and Peace" movement led by Nobel Prize winner Adolfo Pérez Esquivel, and in the "Mothers of the Plaza de Mayo," whose vigils and protests on behalf of the "disappeared" led to the torture and murder of two French nuns on 13 December 1977. But when, after the fall of the military *junta* in 1983, the bishops asked the people to forgive, they no longer had any authority, since justice for torturers and assassins has to be a condition for pardon and reconciliation.

Pinochet's coup of 11 September 1973 brought in a period of repression hitherto unknown in Chile, with a real "theology of massacre" bolstering the military's actions. Just two days after the coup, the bishops condemned Christians for Socialism in a document entitled "Christian faith and political action," by which time most of those implicated had been killed, were being tortured or imprisoned, or were on their way into exile. By condemning the socialist option, though without openly approving the coup, the bishops were leaving the way open for their preferred solution: Christian Democracy. Some bishops openly favoured the *Junta*, others opposed it, while Cardinal Silva Henríquez at first maintained an equidistant stance. Mgr Aristía presided over a "Committee of cooperation for peace," which defended people's rights and when this was suppressed on government orders, the "Vicariate of Solidarity" made its appearance. The Church became the only institution in the country to sustain opposition to the regime, and in doing so discovered new dimensions for its ministry, such as "popular culture" and the indigenous question. With repression continuing, Archbishop Juan F. Fresno Larraín appealed to the government in 1984 to work towards a democratic solution based on national unity.

The Banzer coup of 23 October 1971 in Bolivia was supported by the fascist ECN (Christian Nationalist Army) movement, of which the papal nuncio Gravelli said that "relations between Church and state are cordial." In November 1972 the nuncio welcomed delegates to the sixteenth ordinary assembly of CELAM in Sucre – a meeting that was to change the history of the Church throughout Latin America, largely through its election of Alonso López Trujillo, to the post of general secretary.

Members of Christians for Socialism were expelled from the country, "Radio Pius XII" was closed down, all progressive Christians were persecuted and on 25 January 1974 there was a massacre of peasants in the Valley of Cochabamba, of which a soldier who took part in it said: "We saw heaps of bodies of peasants piled up like firewood." A return to democracy, reversed by another coup on 17

July 1980, failed to ameliorate the sufferings of "all the citizens, but above all the poor, who have been harshly affected by the economic crisis," as the bishops wrote in November 1983.

The bishops of Uruguay opposed the dissolution of parliament on 27 June 1973, but by November were writing of the "effort at reconciliation," a theme often echoed in episcopal pronouncements of the time. On 30 April 1975, Héctor Borrat was arrested and the review *Víspera* closed. In a brave document dated 12 October 1975, the bishops distanced themselves from the repressive, ulta-right-wing government: "The Church does not receive its freedom as a gift of men but as an essential attribute given by God himself. Furthermore, this freedom is recognized by the laws of civilized peoples, Christian or other."[16]

On 1 April 1984, Mgr Carlos Partelli, in a sermon on "the good news of the dignity of man" – the fruit of many years of defending the "Justice and Peace Service" against the actions of the military during more than ten years of repression justified as struggle against the Tupamaros – foreshadowed the democracy promised by forthcoming elections: "Our people stand on the verge of a new historical period, that of the re-establishment of a state in which the rights, duties and safeguards of all will be correctly defined and defended, in an atmosphere of legality in accordance with our national tradition."[17]

The bishops of Paraguay broke with their traditional stance in 1975 by declaring: "The Church, deeply identified with the soul and aspirations of the Paraguayan people, is always seeking the good of the whole country . . . During recent years, through a variety of events that have occurred, a deterioration in the national community has taken place . . . We wish to raise a prayer . . . for the Church to remain faithful to its mission of evangelizing and defending human beings and their dignity."[18]

5. LESS REPRESSIVE SITUATIONS

In Peru, the bishops supported the last reformist acts of the Velazco Alvarado government: "The liberating mission of the Church, which is the effective proclamation of the gospel, means a hope-filled option for all men, as brothers, but especially for those who suffer injustice, for the poor and oppressed . . . It is clear that solidarity with the poor and oppressed also involves acting to change the unjust structures that maintain the situation of oppression," they declared at their forty-second assembly in January 1973.[19]

When poverty increased as a result of the measures introduced by the dictatorship of Morales Bermúdez from August 1975, the Church found more space for its actions with the people, and progressively distanced itself from state. The bishops of the *altiplano* denounced the sufferings of the peasants on 10 July 1977: "Taking up the clamour and aspirations of the poor . . . the suffering of our people . . . the continued rise in the cost of living, the freezing of wages . . . for all these reasons we denounce the violence of the repression."[20]

Shortly before this, in October 1976, faced with criticism from some conservative sectors of the church renewal in process since 1968, the bishops reaffirmed that: "We are renewing this loyalty and fidelity, precisely now that the guidelines laid down at Medellín are in danger of being forgotten."[21] And when in 1983 the Congregation for the Doctrine of the Faith suggested to the Peruvian bishops that they should condemn the theology of liberation, they refrained from doing so. Even though Cardinal Juan Landázuri Ricketts has been accused of being a Marxist, he has abstained from any criticism of Gustavo Gutiérrez. All of which suggests that the Church in Peru is keeping to its traditional autonomy.

In Ecuador, Mgr Leonidas Proaño of Riobamba continued to set an example with his work among the poor indigenous peoples of the mountains, undeterred by a "visit" from Rome prompted by self-interested groups. The bishops as a whole have not broken their traditional ties with conservative agribusiness, but have issued valuable documents, such as the September 1976 exhortation on "The integrity of the Christian message," and the long document on "Social Justice" of August 1977, seemingly produced in preparation for the 1979 Puebla Conference since it tackles questions raised by the Preparatory Document for that Conference, such as the condemnation of Christians for Socialism, of whom there were none in Ecuador.

The Church in Colombia became even more polarized. On one side, Fr Domingo Laín was killed fighting for the guerrilla forces; on the other, the cardinal archbishop of Bogotá received the Antonio Nariño Order from the Colombian army when the State of Siege was declared on 26 June 1975, and was given the rank of general in the Colombian army in June 1976, when he suspended priests and nuns who supported bank employees on strike. The episcopal document "Christian identity in action for justice" of 26 November 1976 condemned a large number of church members, study centres and reviews – all by name. As a memorandum from the Rand Corporation pointed out, it was the most conservative hierarchy in Latin America.

On 10 November 1984 Fr Alvaro Ulcue Chocue, a fully Indian priest, from the Páez tribe, was assassinated by a group of landowners while he was leading his fellow tribesmen in an attempt to occupy land that traditionally belonged to them, following a declaration made by the Indigenous Councils of Cauca. Even the hierarchy expressed their horror: "With this crime the voice of a valiant apostle who preached the gospel by word and witness has been silenced; he exposed himself to the risks inherent in proclaiming salvation according to the words of our Lord: 'Blessed are those who suffer persecution for the sake of justice, for to them belongs the kingdom of heaven' (Matt. 5:10)."[22]

The Mexican bishops issued a pastoral clearly opting for the people, "Christian commitment in the face of social and political choices." Given the lack of worker or peasant movements within the Church, however, this failed to have much effect. In view of continuous church-state conflicts, the hierarchy had in fact been suppressing any movement that might have proved inconvenient to the state. Only on the question of "obligatory texts" to be taught in schools did the bishops stand up to the government (of Luis Echevarría), and the texts were in fact modified. On the other hand, the rapid construction of the new basilica for the Virgin of Guadalupe in 1976, with state and bank funding, showed a certain *rapprochement* in church-state relations.

As in other countries, it was an assassination that pointed to the existence of conflict between power groups and the Church's work among the poor: in this case Fr Adolfo Aguilar, who worked in a poor quarter of Chihuahua, killed on 21 March 1977. The growth of the Church among the poor is evidenced by the spread of the base community movement, with several thousand in existence by 1981, when Bishop Arturo Lona said at their tenth national assembly: "Challenge and suffering on all sides show that this road cannot be travelled without conflicts: repression, torture, denunciation, prison, death . . . There are many thousands of peasants, natives, workers throughout Latin America who have been imprisoned for their involvement in base church communities."[23] At the eleventh assembly of the base communities, held in Concordia in October 1983 with representatives from thirty-eight dioceses, five bishops wrote a heartfelt letter to the other members of the hierarchy. The visit of Pope John Paul II in 1979 at the opening of the Puebla Conference had already mobilized Christian consciousness and proved what an important role the Church plays in Mexico.

6. THE CHURCH AND REVOLUTION: CENTRAL AMERICA AND THE CARIBBEAN

In March 1972 Mgr Obando y Bravo declared in a pastoral letter that "socialism is advancing at great speed in Latin America; socialization should be carried out on all levels and not unilaterally." This was a sort of declaration of independence from the Somoza regime. In the months following the 1972 earthquake a group of young Christians left Fr Uriel Molina's parish of Santa María de los Angeles in a *barrio* of Managua to join the Sandinista Front. He describes seeing them again on 18 July 1979, at the head of the army that had overthrown Somoza: "I was suddenly rooted to the spot. There were Roberto Gutiérrez, Emilio Baltodano, Oswaldo Lacayo and Joaquín Cuadra, marching towards Managua. We embraced. 'We've left death behind in Masaya . . . We've come here to life' . . . It was a great shout of triumph."[24] This euphoric phase lasted till late 1980, and included the Literacy Campaign directed by Fernando Cardenal SJ, using methods based on the pedagogy of Paulo Freire – and the word *iglesia* to demonstrate the syllable *gle* . . .

Tension soon appeared, prompted by pressure from Rome and CELAM for the three priest-ministers – the brothers Cardenal and Miguel D'Escoto – to resign their posts. Reagan had become president in the United States and *Somocista* remnants were beginning their *contra* struggle on the border with Honduras. The hierarchy became increasingly critical of the revolution and the Church more polarized. In June 1982 Pope John Paul II sent a letter pointing out what he saw as the dangers involved in this polarization and asking for obedience to the bishops. This was a change in tone from what he had written in 1980: "I send my best wishes that the beloved people of Nicaragua may live a future of peace, harmony and solidarity, in accordance with their long Christian tradition." In 1980 the Vatican was still advised by the apostolic delegate Pierro Sambi, but later a permanent nuncio was appointed.

Internal tensions increased in the run up to the Pope's visit in March 1983, with the opposition seizing on the "religious field" as the only one in which it could attack the revolution. The Pope's visit, with his demand for unconditional obedience to the bishops and his public rebuking of Ernesto Cardenal, led to a hardening of attitudes. The bishops objected to continuing military service, provoking replies from the Jesuits, Dominicans, base communities and others accusing them of ignoring the real situation in the country. Conflicts such as those over the treatment of the Miskito Indians, the expulsion of Fr Timoteo Merino in 1983 and ten foreign priests the following year showed the Church in Nicaragua within a revolutionary process behaving very differently from the way it had in Cuba: lessons had been learned in twenty years.

In 1985 the Sandinistas won a democratic victory at the polls with 67 percent of the votes cast. U.S. pressure increased. On 4 July 1986 Mgr Pablo Vega supported the grant of twenty million dollars to further the struggle against the Sandinista Front. On 20 December 1989, Fr Uriel Molina, founder of the Antonio Valdivieso Ecumenical Centre, was removed from his parish. On 25 February 1990 the world learned that the Sandinista Front had been defeated in the election by Violeta Chamorro's UNO coalition. It was brought down by the pressure of the *contra* war and economic difficulties, but is still in existence as an opposition party, preparing to return to government after the next elections, due in 1996. 148 priests issued a declaration called "The reason for our hope," saying: "This is the hour for Christians in Latin America. We Christians know that Jesus was faithful to the God of the poor, although all horizons closed in and the Empire crucified him. God and the gospel have not changed. Let us remain faithful. The Kingdom of God is at hand. Let us be converted and believe in the good news (Mark 1:15)."

In El Salvador, massacres of the peasant community had been going on for years. Archbishop Chávez declared that "here coffee devours men" – referring to the exploitation of workers by landowners. The symbolic figure of this period is Fr Rutilio Grande, parish priest of Aguilares, assassinated on 12 March 1977. He was not the only priest to lose his life: Alfonso Navarro was killed on 11 May the same year, Barrera Motto on 28 November 1978 and Octavio Ortiz on 20 January 1979.

Mgr Oscar Arnulfo Romero was appointed archbishop on 22 February 1977 and quickly showed a sympathetic understanding of the situation of the poor and oppressed. On 5 March the bishops declared that "this situation has been categorized as one of collective injustice and institutionalized violence." But the bishops were not united: on the day Rutilio Grande was killed, Archbishop Romero was leading a procession in the parish of Aguilares, facing up to army bayonets, while Mgr Pedro Aparicio supported the government and criticized lay actions at the Roman Synod of 1977. The climax came on 24 March 1980, when professional assassins connected with the army shot Mgr Romero as he was saying mass. On 20 January he had spoken of a programme overshadowing the whole of El Salavdor: "The oligarchic programme seeks to use its immense economic resources to prevent the carrying out of structural reforms which affect its interests but favour the majority of the Salvadorean people."[25]

By 1984, the deaths of over fifty thousand people, including dozens of priests and nuns and the archbishop himself witnessed to a Church that refused to leave the people. The river Sumupul massacre of May 1980, in which more than six hundred men, women and children were killed, will remain forever engraved on the memory of history. The national coordinating committee of the "popular church" (CONIP) worked in the "liberated zones" where Christians could carry on with daily life away from the oppressive ruling system. The new archbishop, Mgr Rivera y Damas, had inherited a situation of fratricidal violence.

On 14 October 1986, Ignacio Ellacuría wrote: "According to CEPAL, by the end of the 1970s 65 percent of the population were living in a state of poverty, with 42 percent in a state of exteme poverty: in overall figures this means thirteen million poor, and eight million extremely poor."[26] It is not surprising that this philosopher-theologian, an acute observer of and militant participant in the Salvadorean struggle, should have been murdered. He died, with five Jesuit companions, their housekeeper and her daughter, on 16 November 1989, seven days after the fall of the Berlin Wall, when everyone in the countries of the "centre" was hailing the advent of democracy and freedom. Finally, in February 1992, a peace treaty was signed between the army and the FMLN. A neutral police force was established and the country began a slow process of "normalization" that will not be easy or without pitfalls. Mgr Rivera y Damas, living in the shadow of Archbishop Romero, is the central figure in the process of building peace.

In Guatemala, the "delegates of the word" movement grew apace. These were militant Christians, mostly from peasant backgrounds, who became leaders of poor communities, mainly in the dioceses of Huehuetenango, Quezaltenango, Verapaces and Izabel. In late 1973 the National Congress of Religious brought 996 sisters and 551 monks and friars together. In June 1976 the bishops' conference, under its president Mgr Juan Gerardi, issued the document "United in hope" – which Cardinal Casariego refused to sign – stating that "for many years Guatemala has lived under the sign of fear and anguish."

There is no space here to detail the horrors to which the Church in Guatemala has been subjected. In June 1980 the bishop, priests and religious fled from the diocese of El Quiché in the face of violent persecution. Mgr Gerardi was himself the subject of an assassination attempt on 19 July 1979. Fr Luis Eduardo Pellecer SJ was violently abducted in front of witnesses on 8 June 1981; on 30 September, after being kept in solitary confinement, tortured and brain-washed, he was forced to appear on television to testify against the Church; he was never seen again. Dozens more priests were killed: among them Augusto Ramírez OFM, parish priest of San Francisco in Guatemala La Antigua, "whose mutilated body was found dumped in a street in Guatemala City" on 7 November 1983.

The repression continued, leading the bishops of Mexico to explain the reason for the fact that a hundred thousand Guatemaltecans were living as refugees in southern Mexico. In 1991 Mgr Julio Cabrera, bishop of El Quiché, spoke out on the situation of the country and asked why the army had grown from 44,000 in 1979 to 176,000 in 1989. The fact is that the military are a class apart, responsible neither to the state nor the people. They are carrying out their own programme of profit and protection. The martyrs go on increasing in numbers and in the horror of the ways in which their blood is spilled.

In Honduras, Mgr Héctor Santos, archbishop of Tegucigalpa since 1962, encouraged the Church's presence in peasant and worker organizations. The "celebrators of the word" movement has grown since 1975, preaching on social reality in the light of the gospel. The landowners saw the threat posed by these base community leaders and organized a campaign to vilify them as Marxists.

On 25 June 1975 Frs Ivan Betancourt and Casimiro Zephyr were killed in Olancho, along with other Christians. Betancourt had founded the Santa Clara Institute for peasant education and knew the threat to his life this posed. On 12 March 1985 Sister Marina Eseverry, who worked in the parish of Tocoa in the province of Colón, was publicly disgraced and expelled from the country, despite the public protests of the bishops.

In Costa Rica, the weekly newspaper *Pueblo*, edited by Xavier Solís, has had a considerable influence. In 1972 the Theological Institute of Central America and the Ecumenical School of the Science of Religion were founded, the only theological institutes operating as part of a national university in Latin America. The DEI (Department of Studies and Investigations), founded by Hugo Assmann in 1974 after he escaped from Chile, with Franz Hinkelammert, Pablo Richard, Guillermo Meléndez and other distinguished figures on its staff, has carried out a major programme of research and publication.

The U.S. invasion of Panama on 20 December 1989 left more than five thousand Panamanians dead, according to *Diálogo Social*.[27] On 3 January 1990 General Noriega gave himself up to the Nunciature in Panama City. The occupying forces, led by General Maxwell Thurman, installed Guillermo Endara as President. The bishops wrote that "dictatorship, the prolonged crisis and the North American invasion have destroyed the structure of the nation," adding: "Panama has claims for restitution for the damage caused by the invasion and the United States has a moral duty to give the aid necessary to rebuild the country."[28]

The confrontational stage between Church and Castro in Cuba had passed, but the Church remained isolated from the renewal taking place elsewhere under the influence of the option for the poor and liberation theology. In March 1974 Mgr Agostini Casaroli visited the island; Mgr César Zacchi was appointed papal nuncio, replaced the following year by Mgr Mario Taglafferi. In December 1975 the First Congress of the Communist Party of Cuba took place, showing some willingness to dialogue but still holding to the "dogmatic" position that "religion and science are irreconcilably opposed." Article 35 of the Socialist Constitution proclaimed that: "The profession of all faiths is free ... the church will be separate from the State, which cannot support any denomination."

Two events – the bishops' condemnation of attacks on the Cuban airline, published in *Granma* in November 1976, and Fidel Castro's dialogue with Christian pastors in Jamiaca in October 1977 – are evidence of growing mutual understanding. At the Eleventh World Youth Festival, held in July 1978, Mgr Oves felt able to say: "The ideal of a society without class conflict on either the social or the economic front is more in accordance with the evangelical requirement of brotherhood in Christ, but I ask myself: how does it help us to encourage Christian commitment to putting this ideal into effect if the Christian faith is presented as something necessarily hostile?"[29] From 26 February to 3 March 1979 a historic meeting of seventy-seven theologians from socialist countries of Asia, Afica and Europe was held in Matanzas, to discuss the possibilities for liberation theology in their respective societies. The Sandinista revolution in July of the same year began to show Cuba a new form of relations between Church and revolution.

In 1986 the Preparatory Document for the "Ecclesial Meeting of Cuba" (ENEC) initiated an unprecedented mass movement. On 25 May that year, the Cuban bishops, referring to ENEC in a "Pastoral Instruction," stated: "Cuba has changed, the Church must change." The ENEC Final Document says: "We live in an age subject to revision and change (GS 5–7). It is not the end of the world, but it is the end of a world. Human thought, social structures and style of life are changing. Cuba has changed greatly in twenty-five years. The Church is one reality within the reality that is changing."[30] Nevertheless, Cuba has been adversely affected by the break-up of the Soviet Union, losing aid and trade; it still has critical times to go through in the political transformation it has to face.

In Haiti the bishops unconditionally supported the regime of Jean-Claude Duvalier till late 1980, but as repression increased, the Haitian Conference of Religious issued a document in October 1980 stating that the Conference "felt it to be its duty to appeal to Christian and patriotic feeling . . . wishing once more to raise our own voices in favour of respect for human rights in our country, of respect for the human rights of our exiled brothers and sisters, of those who have been imprisoned . . . The Church cannot remain silent when life has to be humanized and the people made more aware."[31] The nuncio, Mgr Luigi Conti, spoke out in support of the religious, and the bishops' conference, under the presidency of Archbishop François Wolf Ligondé, did the same in December.

A symposium was held on the occasion of the Marian Eucharistic Congress in December 1982, showing a Church clearly committed to the cause of the poor, the peasants and the blacks who make up the great majority of the population. When the bishops and the conference of religious addressed the people on 27 January 1983 to prepare them for the pope's visit in March, they insisted that the government release Gérard Duclerville, who had been arrested when he was coordinating a meeting of "Church and base church communities." The visit of John Paul II had a completely different effect from that in Nicaragua, and ushered in a period of renewal never previously known in the country. In February 1984 the first National Meeting of Base Communities was held, and the lay leaders wrote in their report: "For the past ten years, some parishes in Haiti have begun to experience something completely new in the Church through what we call Ti Léglis (petite église) or the Fraternities . . . We are convinced that base church communities, in villages and barrios, are an urgent need for us. The base communities are not a passing phase, but the form the Church itself is taking today, similar to that which it had in the times of the Apostles."[32]

7. THE CHURCH AND THE "OPENING TO DEMOCRACY" SINCE 1984

The process of "opening out" to democracy should be seen as starting in 1976, when the Trilateral Commission, under Jimmy Carter, showed the "governability of democracy." In 1978 Luis Guzmán was elected in Santo Domingo; Pereda Asbún was overthrown in Bolivia by a government with pretensions to democracy; Marcos fell in the Philippines, and Duvalier in Haiti. In 1983, Raúl Alfonsín was elected in Argentina, and Tancredo Neves in Brazil in 1985. This opened a stage of "formal democracies" (without social or economic reform), with a "minimal state" programme (inspired by the U.S. thinker Nozik) and a "free market" ideology, neo-liberal in concept (inspired by Hayek and Milton Friedman).

After long compromising with the military,[33] the bishops of Argentina called for reconciliation, without first punishing those reponsible for so many crimes: "We should raise the banner of reconciliation, with humility and faith, with magnanimity and courage."[34] By contrast, on 10 December 1986, CONADEP (the National Commission for Disappeared Persons) published an account of all the actions against human rights carried out during the military dictatorship, in its book *Nunca más* (never again). Mgr de Nevares, bishop of Neuquén, criticizing the "full stop" policy of pardon without punishment for the criminals, exclaimed: "From the start God has shown how to punish the murderer (Cain) who kills another person. At the foot of Sinai, God said: 'Thou shalt not kill!' This is God's full curse, this is a real full stop." The election of Carlos Menem in 1989 did no more than accentuate the suffering of a hitherto unheard-of proportion of the population.

In Brazil the death of Tancredo Neves brought José Sarney, a landowner from Maranhão, to power, heading a formal democracy with no social or economic reforms. Land occupations multiplied, often led by priests and pastors. On 10 May 1986, one such occupation led to the death of Fr Josima Morae Tavares, of the Pastoral Land Commission of the diocese of Emperatriz in Maranhão. A few days earlier, he had written to a friend in Italy: "This is the way of the cross of the people, bathed in the blood of the martyrs I have known and who have left the Church their silent yet eloquent witness: *there is no greater love than to lay down one's life for one's friends.*" His death was followed in October by the killing of Fr Maurizio Maraglio of San Mateus in the diocese of Coraotá, also in Maranhão.

The Brazilian Church that had been the vanguard of great initiatives is coming to the end of its course in 1992. Many of the great bishops who upheld Vatican II and Medellín have either died or are due to retire. The Church is going through a drastic transformation through the appointment of conservative bishops, now the invariable practice of the Congregation for Bishops in Rome. The obsessive persecution of Leonardo Boff shows the way things are moving. Nevertheless, the largest national Catholic Church in the world will go on giving a prophetic witness for many years to come.

In Chile, popular movements since 1983 launched a process that culminated with the election of the Christian Democrat Patricio Aylwin as President in July 1987. The bishops had anticipated this in a Pastoral Letter entitled "Gospel, Ethics and Politics," opening the way for the democracy that had to come. But in 1992 Augusto Pinochet still retains much of his former power.

In Bolivia the election of Jaime Paz Zamora, of the MIR, as President has not succeeded in dragging this impoverished country out of its permanent crisis. Back in 1983, the bishops had declared: "The clamour of the people, especially of the poorest among the people, burdened with great and undeserved sufferings, has reached us, their pastor bishops. All citizens, but above all the poor, have been harshly affected by the economic crisis."

In Uruguay, Julio Maria Sanguinetti was elected to the presidency in November 1984, putting an end to twelve years of dictatorship.

In Paraguay, on 17 March 1987, two thousand people defied the dictatorship and demonstrated against Stroessner. The Catholic radio station *Ñanduti* was closed, and Fr Javier Alarcón expelled from the country. On 20 April, the bishops launched an appeal for "national dialogue." The new government of Andrés Rodríguez, even though he belonged to the old power group, is making moves toward democracy, allowing many exiles to return. Paraguay is thus going through a relatively creative period.

In Peru, the election of Alán García as President in 1985 failed to bring an end to the crisis. The bishops of the Southern Andes region, in their 1987 document "Witness to the Resurrection," declared: "To build the Church as the people of God, according to the vision of Vatican II, is still a challenge to us. The poor of our region have gradually become aware of their being church, people of God." Alberto Fujimori now has the task of managing an increasingly deep economic crisis.

In Ecuador, the death of Mgr Leonidas Proaño, "bishop of the Indians," and one of the saints and great prophetic pastors of the century, in August 1988, was a landmark in the history of the Church. In the second Ecumenical Consultation on Indian Pastoral Strategy, in which fifteen Latin American countries took part, he had concluded that 1492 began the "European invasion" of the continent. In 1990 his spiritual inheritance produced the first "Indian uprising" throughout Ecuador. It was an unprecedented event. Violence and drug trafficking have undermined the foundations of Colombian society. Despite this, a peace process involving the M-19 nationalist guerrillas led to the promulgation of a new constitution in 1991, which gives juridical status to ethnic groups, with the right to work and their own culture.

The Bishops' Conference of Haiti protested against the expulsion of three French priests on 26 July 1985. Jean-Claude Duvalier fled the island the following 7 February, and that June the bishops issued a "Basic document on the transition to a democratric society," one of the clearest declarations of principle to have appeared anywhere in Latin America. On 25 August 1987, a group of *Tontons Macoutes* tried to assassinate the Salesian Fr Jean-Bertrand Aristide. The attempt failed, but was repeated on 11 September 1988, when twelve of his parishioners died. The National Front for Change and Democracy launched "operation *Lavalás*," (landslide) which led to the election of Fr Aristide (known affectionately to the people as "Titide)," as President with a "landslide" 67 percent of votes cast, on 16 December 1990.[35] The president of the Haitian bishops' conference, Mgr Laroche, spoke these words to the new president: "When Moses received from God the mission to guide the people to the promised land, he asked: 'Who am I?' God replied: 'I shall be with you.' Today, your excellency, an important mission has been entrusted to you. It will certainly not be easy, as it was not for Moses: a long pilgrimage through the desert. May the Most High, the almighty God, deign to place in your heart, dear Fr Aristide, the same feelings that inspired His servant Moses." Who would have suspected that the young priest-president, a liberation theologian, was to fall victim to a *coup d'état* in September 1991, less than a year into his presidency? Haiti is back under an unscrupulous military regime, and plunged into even greater poverty than usual by the blockade imposed to help bring the president back to power. But the days of easy *coups d'état* are over, since the United States no longer sees any advantage in them. During the military *interregnum* the Church, especially that wing of it that supports Aristide, has been harshly persecuted.

All these developments mean that the Fourth General Conference of Latin American Bishops, to be held in Santo Domingo in October 1992, to commemorate the fifth centenary of the coming of Christians to these shores, will look forward in the midst of contradictory signs. The preparatory documents have been accused of superficiality – in their history, theology and pastoral strategy. The new authorities of CELAM, elected in 1991, are trying to undo the damage of the past twenty years, but are not finding it easy. The Vatican is nominating the President, Vice-Presidents and Executive Secretary for this Conference, contrary to past practice, when these posts were *ipso facto* occupied by the corresponding authorities of CELAM. In addition, the Commission for Latin America is intervening more and more from Rome. The fact that the Assembly of CLAR (the Latin American Confederation of Religious), held in Mexico in 1991, was suspended, with the religious being refused the right to elect their own officers, in direct contravention of CLAR's statutes, shows how deep the tensions implicit in the present situation run.

CONCLUSION

In these past twenty years of its history, the Church in Latin America has gone through a vast process of growth. It first underwent a long "dark night" of suffering, torture and martyrdom under the miltary dictatorships controlling National Security regimes, when the base church communities proved the means by which the people not only resisted but grew creatively in their faith. From 1979 on, the Sandinista revolution sent waves of hope throughout the continent, although in most contries the increasing burden of external debt forced even greater suffering on the poor. Since the election of Alfonsín in Argentina in 1983 and Sarney in Brazil in 1985 a growing "democratization" has allowed the "people of God" greater freedom, even though still in a desperate economic situation. This political "opening" has created a new situation all over the continent.

The election of Jean-Bertrand Aristide as President of Haiti – and his subsequent overthrow – prove that the "people of the poor," and the base communities, have come to be actors on the political stage. Nevertheless, the Vatican's policy of "restoration" orchestrated by Cardinal Ratzinger, opposed to liberation theology and the pastoral strategy of these base communities, coupled with the nomination of exclusively conservative bishops (recommended by nuncios alone), is paradoxically pushing the people into the arms of the sects, or pentecostalist groups, who are able to fill a void (in expressions of spirituality, community and solidarity) – a void that a Vatican Church determined on institutional rigidity is producing in Latin America.

Great martyrs and saints, thousands of them anonymous members of the people of God, hundreds of them known and recognized, with Bishop Angelelli, Fr Rutilio Grande, Archbishop Romero, and Ignacio Ellacuria, philosopher and theologian of liberation, prominent among them, have marked this period in the history of the Church in Latin America with their blood. So much blood spilt by the people of God and their prophets has made this perhaps the most glorious period of the whole five-hundred-year resistance struggle for liberation.

Translated from the Spanish by Paul Burns

NOTES

1. The expression adopted by Pope John XXIII and the Second Vatican Council.

2. Translations of the final documents of Medellín are in vol. 2 of *The Church in the Present-day Transformation of Latin America* (Washington, D.C., 1970).

3. Cf *Fe cristiana y cambio social en América Latina* (Salamanca, 1972).

4. Cf E. Kadt, *Catholic Radicals in Brazil* (London, 1970).

5. The document is in A.T. Hennelly (ed.), *Liberation Theology: A Documentary History* (Maryknoll, N.Y.,1990), pp. 125–36.

6. Cf H. Assmann, *Teoponte, una experiencia guerrillera* (Oruro, 1971).

7. Cf T. Melville, *Guatemala: The Politics of Land Ownership* (New York, 1971).

8. In Lettre 54 (Paris, 1963), pp. 7–12.

9. Cf the history of theology in Appendix to my *History of the Church in Latin America* (Grand Rapids, 1982); also the recent history in chapter 21 of the present volume.

10. Cf G.Gutiérrez, *La Pastoral de la Iglesia en América Latina* (Lima, 1968); R. Alves, *Religión: ¿opio o instrumento de liberación?* (Montevideo, 1968).

11. Conservative U.S. Catholicism has been highly active. The "Santa Fe Document" is in *DIAL*, D 757 (Paris, 1981). The "Institute for Religion and Democracy" was started in Washington in April 1981: cf *DIAL* 38 (1982), pp. 1ff.

12. Homily given in Rome, Oct. 1983: in *Servir* 28 (1983), p. 1.

13. The complete text is in *Uno más Uno* (Mexico City) 26 Dec. 1977, p. 3.

14. Text in *Brasil ¿Milagro - Engaño?* (Lima, 1973), p. 110.

15. Cf Hennelly, *Liberation Theology*, p. 123.

16. Cf *Signos de lucha y esperanza* (Lima, 1969), p. 199.

17. In *SIAL* VII, 8 (1984), p. 8.

18. Cf *Praxis de los Padres en América Latina* (Bogotá, 1979), pp. 682–3.

19. *Ibid.*, p. 496.

20. *Signos de lucha y esperanza*, pp. 39–40.

21. *Praxis de los Padres*, p. 847.

22. *Servir* 29 (1984), p. 5. See also *DIAL* 173 and 184 (1984).

23. *Servir* 21 (1981), p. 4.

24. U. Molina, "El sendero de una experiencia," *Nicaragua* 5 (Managua, 1981), p. 37.

25. *Servir* 1 (1980), p. 1.

26. *SIAL* 4 (1987), p. 1.

27. The Commission led by U.S. Justice Minister Clark calculated 7000 Panamanian dead, with more than 20,000 rendered homeless. Cf *SIAL* 8 (1991), p. 1.

28. *SIAL* 8 (1991), p. 3.

29. *El Heraldo Cristiano* XXIV, 9–10 (Havana, 1978), pp. 16–18.

30. No. 12. In *SIAL* 21 (1986), p. 2.

31. *Servir* 3 (1981), pp. 10–12.

32. *DIAL* 147 (1984), p. 1.

33. See E. Mignone, *Iglesia y Dictadura. El papel de la Iglesia a la luz de sus relaciones con el régimen militar* (Buenos Aires, 1986). Mignone demonstrates the close relations between Church and military, and the bishops' responsibility for torture and repression and their support for the "dirty war" of 1976–83.

34. *L'Osservatore Romano* 23 May 1985.

35. In Haitian creole *lavalás* means "avalanche" or landslide, preceded by a rush of water down from the mountains, whose first effect is to "cleanse" the dirty streets of poor Haitian towns. So this was a movement of "moral and social cleansing" of the corruption of the black élites of the island, who are continually supported by the U.S. government and other interested parties.

PART TWO

REGIONAL SURVEY

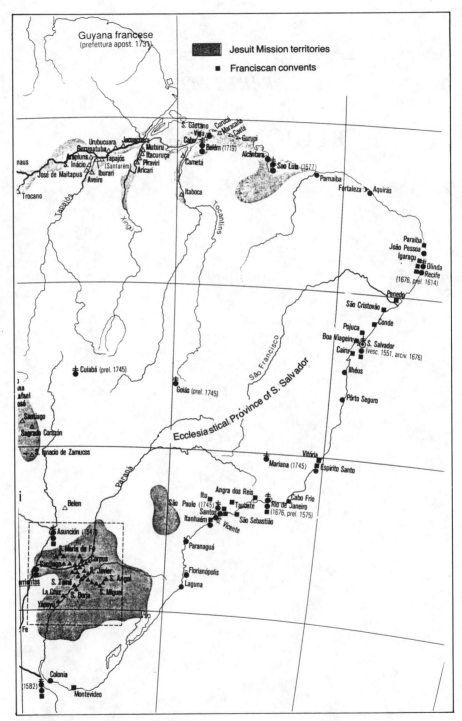

Jesuit Mission territories

■ Franciscan convents

Guyana francese
(prefettura apost. 1731)

S. Gaetano
Curuca
Maracana
Vieja
Caeté
Cabu
Jacuacanga
Gurupi
Belém (1719)
Urubucuara
Muturu
Alcântara
Curupatuba
Itacuruca
Arapiuns
Tapajós
Piraviri
São Luís (1677)
S. Inácio
(Santarém)
Aricari
Cametá
Parnaíba
José de Maitapus
Iburari
Aveiro
Itaboca
Fortaleza
Aquirás
naus
Trocano

Tapajós
Xingu
Tocantins

Paraíba
João Pessoa
Igaraçu
Olinda
Recife
(1676, prel. 1614)

São Francisco

Penedo
São Cristovão
Conde
Pojuca
Boa Viagem
S. Salvador
Cuiabá (prel. 1745)
Cairu
(vesc. 1551, arciv. 1676)
Ilhéus
Goiás (prel. 1745)
Pôrto Seguro

Ecclesiastical Province of S. Salvador

na
afael
osé
Santiago
Sagrado Corazón
Ignacio de Zamucos

Paraná

Vitória
Mariana (1745)
Espírito Santo

i
Belen
Angra dos Reis
Itu
Cabo Frio
São Paulo (1745)
Taubaté
Rio de Janeiro
Santos
(1676, prel. 1575)
Itanhaém
São Sebastião
Vicente
Asunción (1547)
S. Maria de F.
Paranaguá
Santiago
Corpus
S. Javier
Florianópolis
rrientes
S. Tomé
S. Ángel
La Cruz
S. Miguel
Laguna
Yapeyú
S. Berja

Fe

Colonia
(1582)
Montevideo

7. **Brazil: Mission Foundations and Dioceses**
Source: Atlante Universale Storia della Chiesa, Ed. Piemme and Lib. Ed. Vaticana, Casale
Monferrato and Rome, 1991. **(Piemme)**

Chapter 10

THE CHURCH IN BRAZIL

Eduardo Hoornaert

1. LAND, RIVERS, MOUNTAINS

When the first Portuguese landed on the South Atlantic beaches in 1500, they could scarcely imagine the vastness of the lands which would in time come to form their two colonies, Maranhão and Brazil. It was only in 1822, with independence, that these two colonies joined to form Brazil as it is today.

Maranhão covered the Amazon river network, based on the world's longest river, which runs for 6,577km. This network covers 56 percent of Brazil's present area. Brazil itself at this period covered three river systems with their adjacent lands: much of the River Plate basin, consisting of river systems of the Paraná (4,000km long), Paraguay (2,000km) and the Uruguay, the basin of the Rio São Francisco, which covers a large part of the present states of Minas Gerais and Bahia, and was in the colonial period the main area which produced the typical Brazilian of the interior (as opposed to the coast), and finally various less important basins, though still formed by rivers over 1,000 km in length, such as the Mearim and Itapicuru in Maranhão, the Parnaíba in Piauí, the Jaguaribé in Ceará, the Jequitinhonha in Minas Gerais and the Paraíba in Rio de Janeiro. All these rivers were very important because it was along them that the Portuguese invaders succeeded in penetrating the interior.

Control of the River Plate basin was a source of rivalry between Portugal and Spain until 1750, when it was decided by the Treaty of Madrid that Portugal should have the Amazon basin and Spain the basin of the River Plate. Thus was determined the fate of the two great Atlantic estuaries of the South American continent. There were, however, other estuaries, less important geopolitically but still relevant to an understanding of the history of Brazil and therefore of Christianity in Brazil. Along its 5,864km of beaches (9,198km if every detail and inlet is counted), Brazil's coast is generally straight, with little indentation. But there are important openings which have played an important part in history: the Amazonian "gulf", 974km across, the Gulf of Maranhão, 237km across, the bay of Todos os Santos, the future site of the city of Salvador, which was Brazil's capital for the first two hundred years, the bay of Guanabara, on which the city of Rio de Janeiro grew up. Olinda and Recife were not built on a gulf or bay, but behind reefs which protected vessels against the violence of the waves. This description covers the main logistical points of Portuguese settlement along the South Atlantic: Belém do Pará, São Luís do Maranhão, Olinda and Recife, Salvador da Bahia and Rio de Janeiro.

Brazil has no high mountain ranges running across its territory, its relief is modest and 90% of its territory lies under 900 metres above sea level. Even so, the Portuguese did not dare to venture into the vast hinterland except under the pressure of the most urgent necessity. They preferred to cling crablike to some three thousand and more kilometres of coastline and there developed a sugar-cane industry which remained almost unique and the largest until the nineteenth century.

2. THE INDIGENOUS WORLD

Another surprise. During the whole period of their rule over Brazil (1500–1822) the Portuguese certainly never realized the ethnological complexity of the country. They never suspected that Brazil was one of the most complex countries of the world in terms of human culture, with 1,400 distinct peoples belonging to 40 linguistic families, of which only two branches – Tupi and Ge – have been studied to any extent. But there were other language families such as Aruak, Carib, Tucano, apart from isolated and vanished languages, such as Kariri. The "ethno-historical map" produced by Curt Nimuendajú in 1944 revealed this complexity to us, which never appears in any Portuguese text except in heavily disguised form. The Portuguese simply covered everything with the camouflage of the term "Indian": "There's nothing in Brazil, just Indians." This Indian, to the colonizers' way of thinking, was a generic, stereotyped being, a savage and pagan or heathen, in need of civilizing and evangelizing.

In reality the so-called "indigenous world" has confronted Christian civilization with a challenge which remains valid, in that it has proved to be based on the principle of harmony, integration with nature, and not on the "missionary" principle of transforming nature and society. Even today this challenge is not being taken seriously. Through inability or bad faith, the colonizers and their descendants have made little progress in communicating with the cultures they found here. The general attitude has been either to destroy or to reduce to the European colonial plan. There was no lack of signs of vitality and resistance on the part of the subjugated peoples, as shown by the wars and guerrilla struggles which broke out throughout Brazil. There was the Tamoio confederation in the sixteenth century, the Aimoré resistance which lasted until the nineteenth century (in the present state of Espírito Santo), the resistance of the Jesuit-controlled Christian villages against the Bandeirantes in the seventeenth century, the Guaraní war of the 1750s (with Sepé Tiaraju), the confederation of Açu in the second part of the seventeenth century (with Canindé), the revolt of Mandu Ladino in 1710–20 in Piauí and Ceará, the war of the Manao (1724–27), the guerrilla war waged by the Mura on the Rio Madeira for a century, between 1740 and 1840, the Cabanagem revolt in Pará, the greatest popular revolt in the history of Brazil, between 1835 and 1845. As well as these armed conflicts, the so-called Indians have always been very good at waging cultural war, through the resistance of their culture, which in the course of time spread to the mixed race population and the rural population as a whole.

3. AFRICANS IN BRAZIL

The first economic strategy of the new masters of Brazil was the production of sugar-cane for the international market. This required a plentiful supply of labour, and accordingly the idea arose of using the traffic in slaves from Africa, which already existed, on a modest scale, for domestic purposes on the Iberian Peninsula. From 1530 to 1850 an intense slave traffic took place between the Brazilian coast (centred on the four cities of São Luís, Olinda-Recife, Salvador and Rio de Janeiro) and the coasts of West Africa and Mozambique. The number of Africans brought from Africa to Brazil is put at 3,600,000, without counting the illegal traffic, which took place mainly in the nineteenth century.

This flow of African labour made Africa an essential element in the understanding of Brazil. Brazil cannot be understood without looking towards Africa, from which we received life and inspiration, in addition to such a significant labour force that without it nothing gets done in Brazil. The seventeenth-century Jesuit Antônio Vieira could say, "Brazil is sugar and sugar is the black man," and, "Brazil has its body in America and its soul in Africa." The import of black labour firmly established the triangle Europe-America-Africa as a basic pattern for understanding Brazil.

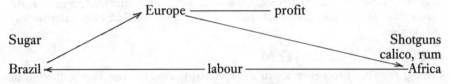

The profit from these connections went to Europe, which retained the capital which made possible investments in labour and the infrastructure to mount new ventures on the international market.

From early on the Africans reacted against the living conditions to which they were subjected in Brazil, whether politically, organizing communities of runaway slaves known as *quilombos*, of which the Quilombo of Palmares (1570–1665) was the most famous, or culturally, preserving the cultural memory of Africa in exile, in Candomblé and other so-called "Afro-Brazilian cults." Political and cultural war was backed up by a not insignificant war of nerves.

4. CHRISTIAN THEORY

A history of Christianity in Brazil cannot avoid facing these two basic phenomena, the indigenous world and the African world. How did Christianity's reaction compare with its basic principles? In order to answer such a question we have to analyze, on the one hand, the basic processes by which first the indigenous and later the Africans were integrated into the European colonial enterprise, and on the other try to define why we mean by a "Christian attitude" or "Christian life." As regards the first point, we shall analyze in turn the village system, the instrument by which the indigenous world was reduced into the European world, and the sugar estate, the setting in which the slaves brought from Africa had gradually to adapt to the new conditions of the "Christian" world. As regards the second point – the definition of the "Christian way of life" – it is a matter for regret that even today, after two thousand years, Christians have not succeeded in producing a "theory of Christianity" which commands consensus. Perhaps it is simply impossible, given the specific nature of the movement started by Jesus and his apostles. Many people avoid this problem by simply identifying Christianity and Western culture. Chroniclers in Brazil have been doing this since the sixteenth century: for them the Christians are the Europeans, and the pagans are the Indians and Africans. In this way matters are apparently resolved: Christianization is confused with Westernization and civilization. The expansion of Catholicism in the sixteenth century coincides simply with the expansion of Christianity and the gospel. We cannot fall into this confusion, but at the same time we regret that Christians start to disagree as soon as they try to find a clear definition of what it is to be a Christian. Does being a Christian mean following the Jesus who said with such force that you cannot serve two masters, God and Money, at the same time, and is it part of being a Christian to make a real option for the marginalized and poor? Faced with the lack of a theory accepted by all, we prefer to follow the precepts of the theology of liberation, which has the merit of being clear: being a Christian means making an option for those whom history leaves on the sidelines and those whom society ignores, not from pure compassion, but from faith that the poor are God's chosen instruments to bring about the transformation of human society as a whole.[1]

5. THE VILLAGE SYSTEM

During the first two centuries of the colonial period (before 1750), though in some regions even until the end of the nineteenth century and even in the twentieth in the shape of the Indian Protection Service (SPI) or National Indian Foundation (FUNAI), the Portuguese, and later Brazilian, colonizers used a particular method for reducing (as it was called) the indigenous populations to submission. This was based on a system of villages or missions ("doctrines" in Spanish America). The secular equivalent today is "Indian post" or "native post".

Many Brazilian cities originated as "missions," indigenous villages or "reductions". Among them are Bragança and Santarém in Pará, Baturité, Crato, Viçosa, and Campina Grande in the North-East, Niterói and Guarulhos in the South-East, and Guarapuava in the South. It is not too much to say that the village system originally organized by the Jesuits, Franciscans, Carmelites, Capuchins, Oratorians and later the Salesians was the way the Brazilian population of indigenous origin was evangelized. It is therefore important to analyze this system before attempting any overall assessment of the history of Christianity in Brazil.

The village system can be described as a way of processing people, a process for producing "new people," with no memory of the past or with a negative memory, rejection, of the past. It meant essentially "converting" the specific Indian – a member of one of the 1,400 peoples already referred to who lived before 1500 in what is now Brazil – into generic Indians known by various derogatory terms, *caboclo*, *tapuio*, *caipira*, *cabra*, etc. with a range of meanings running from "half-caste" to the generic "peasant". Wherever the Portuguese founded colonies, they used this system of missionary villages, so great was their faith in it. In fact, the villages were concentration camps for Indians captured by military force, who came from different peoples, preferably unable to communicate easily with each other, who underwent a process whereby they were stripped of their specific cultures, languages and gods and rapidly introduced to a new religion, language and morality. The best image for the village is that of a cultural mill, which ground and diluted the specificity of the ancestral cultures and so produced a uniform and culturally impoverished mass ready to be launched on to the labour market offered by the capitalist system. Some writers liken it to a brutal process of uprooting in which persons lose the memory of their cultural roots, their own identity and the ability to make plans for the future.

The diagram shows the theoretical model of the village.

	Tribal Indian	Village Indian	Generic Indian (half-caste)
Language	Particular language	General language (Tupi, Nheengatu)	Portuguese
Religion	Particular e.g. Jurupari	Generic e.g. Tupa	Catholic (God of the Portuguese)
Norms	Particular	Generic and impoverished	Westernized

In the village the traditional, specific language of each community was replaced by Tupi, but not the Tupi originally spoken by many Brazilian peoples, but an artificial language created by mainly Jesuit missionaries to enable them to communicate in Brazil. It gradually disappeared after 1750, when the Portuguese government began systematically to impose the use of the Portuguese language throughout Brazil. The specific religion, which, for example, used the name *Jurupari* to identify the indigenous world as opposed to the European, was replaced by a new religion, which was not yet Catholicism but used names like *Tupa* (thunderbolt) to designate a terrifying God who could "strike fear into the Indians" (the phrase is Nóbrega's). This intermediate religion consisted of a repetitive and childish catechesis – still reflected today in parish catechism – made up of mechanical repetition of questions and answers which had to be given correctly on pain of punishment and torture. The rules which governed indigenous society – in relation to education, for example – were replaced by other, impoverished rules of behaviour. The missionaries used to take children away from their parents and introduce them to the behaviour of the Western colonial world.

Among these contradictions it is nevertheless possible to point to two elements of what might be called genuine Christianization in the missionary experiment of the villages:

The first concerns the replacement of the "primary religion" of the indigenous world by the biblical tradition.[2] The encounter was violent, and I do not seek to justify the way in which it was brought about. But at the heart of the question is the uniqueness of the biblical tradition the missionaries brought to Brazil. Unbelievable as it may sound at first, the indigenous were more religious than the missionaries, who had a secularizing effect on the traditions and customs of the ancestral Brazilian societies because they had already "demythified" important sectors of human life, such as politics, social life and, to a degree, morality. The God of the missionaries was different from the "god" of the indigenous in the sense that he was at the same time absolutely transcendent and invisible, involved in human affairs but a respecter of history and freedom. The God of the missionaries did not appear every minute on the stage of events by means of mirages and apparitions, dreams and predictions. This God was more discreet, apparently more distant, but at the same time demanding since he had founded a new morality of commitment to the "neighbour," the "other."

The indigenous religions, in all their complexity, represented the total and unconditional dependence of any human happening on the sacral world, as M. Gauchet has demonstrated.[3] Indigenous religion, in the philosophical sense, was the embodiment of the principle of permanence and immobility. In the end, nothing new happened, everything was repetition through the natural cycles into which human beings were inserted. There was no possibility of a break which would allow change. The missionaries came with violence and broke this covering of immobilism and awakened the cultures to possibilities of change and transformation. I must repeat that this happened among the contradictions of the imposition of the colonial capitalist system which can never be justified. But the two things are different. Evangelization took place in Brazil insofar as the biblical horizon of the exodus, liberation, of movement and transformation, of conversion and change, came to replace the ancient attitude of total dependence on the cycles of nature, on immobilism, on permanence and the rites of the "eternal return" (Mircea Eliade).

A second specifically Christian element in the missionary village experiment was the option for the indigenous as oppressed and marginalized which gradually emerged as part of the missionaries' outlook. The letters and other documents which the missionaries – especially the Jesuits – sent to their superiors in Europe allow us to follow this development in attitudes and practice. The new missionary attitude is most visible in the villages of southern Brazil (the present states of Santa Catarina and Rio Grande do Sul). Here in 1826 two Jesuit missionaries chose to remain in captivity with the indigenous population and endure a forced march for days to imprisonment in São Paulo, after the pioneer leader, Raposo Tavares, attacked the Guairá villages. The attitude of the Jesuits during the Guaraní war is well known, having been dramatized in the film *The Mission*. This, however, was not an isolated case. Throughout Brazil, and especially in the Amazon region, the missionaries gradually realized that their option for the lives of the indigenous implied giving them the military resources to survive the attacks of the pioneer columns and other emissaries of the colonial power[4]. It was this practical support by the Jesuit missionaries for the indigenous population which in 1759 led the Marquês de Pombal, minister plenipotentiary of King José I of Portugal, to decree the expulsion of the Jesuits from all the villages of Maranhão and Brazil.

6. THE SUGAR PLANTATIONS

The sugar plantations were more important than the indigenous villages for the formation of Christianity in Brazil. As was mentioned earlier, until the nineteenth century Brazil was sugar, and sugar meant the Great House, the slave house and the chapel, in Gilberto Freyre's happy phrase.[5] The type of Christianity as it was lived on the sugar plantations for over three centuries – and still exists today in some regions – spread to the whole of Brazil through the simple fact that for the first three centuries the population of the colony remained concentrated in the narrow coastal strip occupied by the sugar plantations and from there spread to the other regions of Brazil. Only southern Brazil, shaped by European immigrants since the first half of the last century, escaped the influence of the type of Christianity formed by the coexistence of masters and slaves on the plantations.

The African slave entered this world with little more ceremony than the slap which Manuel Ribeiro da Rocha, a priest in Bahia in the eighteenth century, ironically called "theological," since its purpose was to indicate forcefully to the recently arrived slave which "God" he would have to obey in future.[6] For him there were no catechisms or primers to teach him the rudiments of the new faith practised in Brazil, and on the day of his arrival he immediately began to accompany the *Nhônhô* (the plantation owner's wife), the slave-women and boys in the daily prayers in the domestic oratory of the Great House. It can be said that the slaves were Christianized, not by catechesis, but by "cultural immersion" in the devotional world of the sugar plantation.

The plantation owner was the absolute master of the little world entrusted to him, the lands, the machines, the animals, the men and women, and especially of the labour brought from Africa, which represented the plantation's main financial investment. The result of the long cohabitation between Europe and Africa on the sugar plantations, masters and servants, whites and blacks, free people and slaves, was a Christianity which was European but also had African features, which was certainly brown-skinned, very different from the model current in Europe, and alarming to the American, English, German and Dutch travellers who came to Brazil in the nineteenth century. It was a Christianity of

> much praying and few priests,
> many saints and few sacraments,
> many feasts and little penance,
> many promises and few masses.[7]

The Christianity of the plantations was a long way from the classical parochial model which came to Brazil from Europe. This is clear from a famous text by Antonil, a Jesuit who in 1711 published the well-known book – today one of the classics of Brazilian historical writing – "Culture and Opulence of Brazil through its Drugs and Mines."[8] In it Antonil describes the function of the priest on a sugar plantation: to say mass in the plantation chapel "with Christian doctrine," "hear its employees in confession," to settle disagreements which might arise in the little world of the plantation, honour God and the Virgin, "by singing the litanies and the rosary to her on Saturdays," not to live in the owner's house, to bless the plantation at the time of the first crushing, the *botada*, to teach the owner's children, and to try to ensure "that all give thanks to

God in the chapel at the end of the harvest." The priest was in fact in the service of the plantation, and not of a parish forming part of a diocese. This is an autonomous Christianity, with no connection with the episcopate and still less with Rome, with interference from no one, except for the sporadic visits of travelling missionaries to give a "mission."[9]

But it was not merely this: it was a Christianity inside out. The "First Constitutions of the Archbishopric of Bahia," of 1707, the first attempt to fit the Christianity of the plantation owners into the forms of canon law, run as follows: "Since the owners . . . are obliged to teach Christian doctrine to . . . servants and slaves, or have it taught" (First Book, Second Title). The owners have to "evangelize" the slaves. But what "good news" could they proclaim to them? The only genuinely "good news" which could be preached to the slaves would be that of their liberation from the power of the owner, and accordingly the owner would be the last to preach what would be the ruin of his own business.

This is an absurd situation, if considered from a specifically Christian point of view. If Christianity means an option for the poor and oppressed, for those who suffer and are deprived of the most elementary liberties, then the Christianity of the plantations is a nonsense. This is what – once more – the Jesuits found as soon as they landed in Salvador da Bahia in 1549. The Society of Jesus was very new in that year, and the seven missionaries who came with Nóbrega were the first to leave Europe for a foreign mission. They showed an excellent Christian sensitivity to the situation they found in slave-owning Brazil, and quickly detected the root evil in the experiment being conducted, the relation between master and servant. Between 1550 and 1580 there was much discussion between them about this issue, with the result that they decided to organize a "strike of the confessionals," refusing sacramental absolution to those who told them in confession that they owned slaves.[10] The strike was organized against the opposition of the secular clergy and the bishop, who stayed on the side of the land- and slave-owners. The stage was set for the first great moral conflict in Brazilian history: was it possible to be a Christian and at the same time a slave-owner? Could a plantation owner be called "Christian"? The situation became intolerable because the Jesuit reasoning went so far as to question the legitimacy of the whole Brazilian undertaking ("without slaves there is no Brazil"), and the first Visitor sent by the Society of Jesus from Europe to Brazil tried to settle the impasse by making the "heads" of the "movement," Fathers Gonçalo Leite and Miguel García, return to the land of their birth.[11]

7. DEVOTIONAL CHRISTIANITY

The previous section briefly mentioned the issue of devotional Christianity, noting that Africans were evangelized through devotion, not through missionary work as such. What does this mean? Is the devotional life, promises to saints, novenas and prayers, processions and pilgrimages, capable of evangelizing? Does this popular religion have evangelical value? Many people say no, regarding the people's religion as purely negative (superstition, religious ignorance, cultural backwardness, fanaticism).

I wish to approach the question historically through an analysis of a book which was a "best-seller" in the eighteenth century in the state of Minas Gerais, going through six (Portuguese) editions between 1728 and 1765, at the peak of the gold cycle, and only lost popularity at the end of the nineteenth century, when romantic novels and poems became the rage. "A Narrative Summary by an American Pilgrim" describes the travels of a pious visitor to Minas Gerais. In the "American Pilgrim" the road to holiness does not involve the reception of the sacraments, but devotion to the saints and the keeping of the commandments.[12] It is a Christianity without specific priestly mediation, even more, a Christianity which seeks to avoid ecclesiastics. The "Pilgrim" says literally:

> Avoid, as far as you can, contact or familiarity with ecclesiastics because, though they are supposedly comparable with angels, it has happened on many occasions that from the path of virtue they have entered on the road of wickedness. It is enough to show them respect from afar, because even on earth it is possible to have devotion to the angels and saints of heaven. Content yourselves with hearing them and seeing them at the altars, in the pulpits and in the confessionals, which are the places in which the priests represent Christ. Remember, the devil is like a thief. A thief steals on the roads, and the devil at any opportunity.[13]

It is as if we are listening to Jesus' denunciation of the priests in Matthew 25 or St Francis' admonitions in his Testament. Where does this tradition of an autonomous Christianity, pious but suspicious of the clergy, come from? How did it develop, this path to holiness which includes the sacraments of the Church only marginally and occasionally, and keeps priests at a distance and views them with a certain suspicion?

We have to go to fourteenth-century Europe to find the roots of the attitude which was current in Minas Gerais in the eighteenth century and continues to exist in Brazil. Around 1370 in Flanders a movement began to take shape – later called the *devotio moderna* – which spread rapidly through Europe, including Portugal, and gave devotion a new status within Christianity. Until then sanctity had been reserved to those who lived in monasteries, separated from the "common people." Only they practised "Christian perfection" through vows: chastity, poverty, obedience. The ordinary run of mortals, on the other hand, remained bound to the laws of imperfection, marriage, the quest for riches or at least subsistence, not surrendering their will to a "superior." The appearance of the *devotio moderna* broke down this conventual cloistering of holiness, this clerical preserve of Christian perfection, and proclaimed that all were called to holiness, without distinction, laity and clergy, married and celibate, hierarchy and faithful. All were equal before God.

In only a few years the *devotio* conquered the Christian people of Europe, without any official support, and as early as 1430 it produced a little book which even today remains the most frequently read text in Christianity after the Bible, the *Imitation of Christ*. We know of three thousand editions of this book, seven hundred manuscripts, translations into ninety-five languages. Today the *Imitation* is criticised for its a-social spirituality, but we have to place it in its period to discover its greatness. It is a text addressed to all Christians without any hierarchical distinction, valid just as much for the pope as for the simplest of the faithful, who does nothing extraordinary but tries to follow Christ in the routine of his or her "ordinary" life. With the *Imitation*, holiness leaves the monasteries and mixes with the people in the streets. It is a fundamental critique of the hierarchical organization of the Church in that it proclaims that those who do not have any particular monastic or theological training can also become perfect in the Christian life. It is also a critique of the sacramental system which produces a separation between clergy and laity, with the clergy dominating the Christian social body.

Through Portugal the *devotio* entered Brazil, especially Minas Gerais in the period of the gold boom (1700–1750), and spread to every corner, especially through the religious enthusiasts. But this was not its only route. We know that Ignatius of Loyola, the founder of the Jesuits, was influenced by the *devotio*, and we see in the correspondence of the first Jesuits in Brazil a deep-seated devotional strand. In the devotion to the crucified Jesus, in the frequency of the invocation "most sweet Jesus," in the rejection of the clergy of St Peter's Habit (the secular clergy) for "not edifying the people" or for "pardoning unjust captures (of natives) and giving sacrilegious communions" or "absolving those who live in concubinage and letting themselves be bought for four *arrobas* (of sugar)," there is a thread of typically devotional attitudes (in the technical sense of the *devotio moderna*) running right through the Jesuit correspondence.[14] Nor was it just the Jesuits who followed devotion. The documents of the colonial period mention priests who kiss images of the saints which the religious enthusiasts carried around, priests enrolled as "brothers" in the confraternities or wearing the habit of the Third Order of St Francis or Carmel. This devotional Christianity created the religious climate typical of colonial Brazil, and, as it were, "absorbed" the cultures which came to Brazil from outside or from the indigenous tradition. Mention has already been made of the way the Africans were evangelized, by cultural immersion rather than by any specifically planned missionary work (catechesis, sermons, doctrine, courses).

The official documents relegate this Christianity to the margins of their considerations, categorizing it as "popular religiosity." This policy corresponds to what happened in Europe in relation to the *devotio moderna*. In Europe, because the influence of the *devotio* proved corrosive of the hierarchical structure of the Church, the authorities invariably regarded it with suspicion, waiting for the right moment to turn the tables, since the influence of the *devotio* was general throughout Europe. The turn came with the appearance of Protestantism in the sixteenth century – it too influenced by the *devotio*, as can be seen from Luther's writings – which paradoxically gave the hierarchy the opportunity to revive the hierarchical programme through the Council of Trent.

In Brazil the harmony between priests and enthusiasts, hierarchy and people, through devotion endured until the Romanization of the second half of the nineteenth century. With the multiplication of seminaries and the imposition of the Roman model on clerical formation, a type of priest began to be produced who was no longer capable of a dialogue with the world of the enthusiasts. The events surrounding Padre Cicero, in Juazeiro in the state of Ceará, say much about this aspect of things.[15] This process broke a vital link between political society and civil society in Brazil, a country sadly lacking in instruments of social communication and articulation.

8. ROMANIZATION

In 1808 Brazil's seaports were authorized to receive non-Portuguese ships. The entry of French, English, American, German and other ships into the ports of Rio de Janeiro, Santos, Salvador, Recife and Belém began a new era, which also affected Catholicism in Brazil. Catholicism ceased to be Portuguese, and received the impacts of Romanization, and also ceased to be the only religion, since Protestantism entered with the first foreign travellers. Brazil began to perceive a world wider than the narrow sphere of Portuguese Catholicism. A new colonial conquest took place, apparently peaceful and liberal, the "bourgeois conquest" of Brazil.

Following the laws of the internationalization of colonialism, Brazil entered at a stroke into the English colonial world. Brazil was practically an English colony during the nineteenth century, disguised under the Portuguese language and the Catholic religion. Brazil was never so colonized as in that century, which produced the instruments for the virtual elimination of the indigenous population (the Lands Law of 1850) and intensified the slave traffic. The *lei aurea* of 1888 – which abolished slavery – only marginalized the powerless black population of the country.

In the nineteenth century the Brazilian Church ceased to be governed by the Board of Conscience and Orders in Lisbon and entered into the orbit of the Vatican in Rome. This Romanization was consecrated at the "Plenary Council" of bishops from the whole of Latin America held in Rome in 1899 during the pontificate of Leo XIII. This Council's decrees constitute the blueprint for Romanization throughout Latin America. Their inspiration had nothing to do with the history of Christianity in the continent, but derived basically from the Council of Trent, held in the sixteenth century but previously largely ignored in Latin America, especially in Brazil. The basic idea was to clericalize church life. In Brazil, however, at the end of the nineteenth century the strength of the Catholic religion lay in the confraternities, at least in the urban centres. In the rural areas, we have already noted that a devotional Christianity predominated, controlled by men and women enthusiasts, which felt no great need for priests. The new clericalization therefore created a situation of conflict, whether between the clergy and the confraternities or between them and the enthusiasts and so-called "religious fanaticism." The "religious question," which originated in a dispute between the Bishop of Pernambuco, Dom Vital, and the confraternities of Recife (1875) is an example of such conflict with urban lay communities, while the tragic case of the war against Canudos (1896–7) shows the incompatibility between the hierarchy and the world of the enthusiasts. Another famous case is that of Juazeiro, centred on Padre Cicero, which was mentioned above (p. 194).

The marked clericalization of church life in Brazil bore no relation to what had emerged and developed in the three previous centuries. The more communitarian principle of the confraternities and the associations of enthusiasts had found a *modus vivendi* with the more hierarchical principle represented by the clergy. There was mutual understanding and the religious movements originating among the ordinary people enjoyed relative autonomy. Now, with Romanization, the whole of church life had to submit to clerical authority, which was within the domain of political society (the area of power).

Behind the conflict over Romanization there developed a discussion about the best way of inserting Christian experience in a society such as Brazil's, whether through alliance with state power (the classical method used by the clergy) or through alliance with the "growth points" of the nation (the method of the communities). What might be called the tendency to state control inherent in any move to Romanize local Christian experiences has to be analyzed in terms of bureaucratic centralization. Roman bureaucracy affected Brazil in every area of church life: liturgy, theology, pastoral work and spirituality.

The great instrument of the Romanization of the Church in Brazil was the seminary. In the seminary the student had to acquire, above all, the "corporate ethos." The underlying thinking was that the "Catholic environment" was, of itself, good for people. However, Catholicism has to be accepted whole because it constitutes – precisely because of its cohesion, which depends on the *esprit de corps* prevailing among the clergy – the best guarantee of salvation for the world in which we live. In short, Catholicism is good simply for what it is, and influences the whole of society through impulses which emanate from the clergy, the repository of all the system's hopes. The most important principle, therefore, is to maintain religious uniformity, which can only be good for everyone.

The thinking underlying Romanization was clearly set out in the famous pastoral letter written by Dom Sebastião Leme, the future Cardinal Archbishop of Rio de Janeiro, in 1916, on taking charge of the diocese of Olinda and Recife. According to Leme, Brazil is the "the biggest Catholic nation in the world", a country which is "essentially" Catholic, but unfortunately this Catholicism is badly publicized, badly understood, and badly assimilated by the people. It is therefore important to evangelize, by every possible means, to spread the Catholic idea among families, schools, universities and the press. Dom Leme's achievements as Cardinal Archbishop of Rio de Janeiro show how he understood pastoral work. A quick list speaks for itself: The Catholic University (PUC, 1921); the Centro Dom Vital, intended to be an instrument for the Christianization of the Brazilian intelligentsia (1922); the journal *A Ordem*, an expression of Catholic thinking (1921); Brazilian Catholic Action (ACB) in 1935; the eucharistic congresses; the Colégio Pio Brasileiro in Rome; the "collective Easters"; the statue of Christ on the summit of Corcovado in Rio; the society for the promotion of priestly vocations; the proclamation of Our Lady Aparecida as patroness of Brazil; the workers' circles movement; the practice of perpetual adoration of the Blessed Sacrament; the Catholic Electoral League (LEC), a sort of super-party to suggest candidates acceptable to Catholics; legislation against divorce and against the establishment of diplomatic relations with Russia.

Dom Leme's thinking was close to the attitudes of Pope Leo XIII (1878–1903), whose frame of reference was, ultimately, the Middles Ages seen as an age in which the whole of society was united in the practice of the faith. Neither Dom Leme nor Leo XIII liked the modern world, which put into people's heads the ideas of liberty, autonomy and scientific research. They thought that modernity would destroy the influence of Catholicism on society through its "liberalism" in tackling questions of life and society from the principle of free enquiry, unimpeded by beliefs or dogmas.

9. REFORM

The death of Dom Leme in 1942 began a new period for Catholicism in Brazil, one characterized by openness to the grave social issues tormenting the country. With a population in majority poor and in a constant process of impoverishment, and above all affected by a rapid urbanization which laid bare for all to see the sore of poverty in the shape of the *favelas* or shanty-towns, Brazil was calling for reform. It was Specialized Catholic Action – of Belgian and French inspiration – which awakened many Catholics to their social and political responsibility. The Young Christian Students (JUC) and Young Christian Workers (JOC) were particularly active, and moved rapidly, as early as the 1950s, from the ideology of development to the idea that poverty in Brazil was not a result of technological or educational backwardness, but basically of foreign domination of the country.[16]

At the same time, Brazil, for the first time in its history, was blessed with an episcopate which presented itself to society as the defender of the rights of the humble and marginalized against the violence of the state, which, after the military coup of 1964, became dictatorial. From 1964 to 1986 Brazil had a prophetic episcopate in the shape of the National Conference of Brazilian Bishops (CNBB). In the years of military repression, the CNBB became the most respected body in Brazilian society, since it took a stand against the serious problems created by the capitalist exploitation of the country.

Under the protection of the CNBB important pastoral work was initiated in the social and political field through organizations such as the Pastoral Land Commission (CPT), Ministry to Workers (PO), and the Ministry to Disdvantaged Youth (PJMP), and the Indigenist Missionary Council (CIMI). These and other dynamic groups brought together a sizable group of pastoral workers, young men and women both talented and inspired by Christian commitment, who began to propagate a more critical and more solidly-based awareness of political and social issues.

At the same time the Church's pastoral work came into contact with the popular movements existing in civil society, which were often engaged in specific campaigns connected with ordinary people's everyday lives: housing, transport, wages, health services, crime, education, and so on, and from this contact there grew up in the 1960s the base church community experiment. The memory of the primitive Christians and their lives among the ordinary people was mentioned many times in the base communities, and this led to the question of the eucharist celebrated in the absence of a priest ("priestless mass"). But since the Vatican firmly resisted any attempt to interfere with the prerogatives of the clergy in sacramental matters, this internal church discussion about ministry was abandoned, and base communities increasingly turned toward issues which did not impinge so directly on the church system.

This whole movement toward the poor and marginalized received strong support from the theology of liberation which grew up throughout Latin America. Its beginning is conventionally dated to the work of Gustavo Gutiérrez in Peru around 1972, but it enjoyed a notable flowering in Brazil in the 1970s through the work of scholars such as Hugo Assmann, Rubem Alves and Leonardo Boff. An important aspect of this theology was its mystical dimension, as it supported the commitment of pastoral workers in situations of poverty. Subsequent writing stressed the political dimension of liberation theology, but it should not be forgotten that in day-to-day pastoral work on the ground it operated primarily as a mystical theology. The God of the Christians was rediscovered as the biblical God who made a covenant with those whom society ignored and excluded.

This is the place to mention the so called "small inserted communities" of religious, especially women religious, in the poor districts of big cities and in poor rural areas.[17] These experiences of insertion are gradually bringing about a reshaping of religious life, especially among women, a rediscovery of the three religious vows in an environment of poverty and solidarity with the poor. The religious women who live in poor districts are still a small minority, but the movement is slowly growing, and will have an influence, in ways which it is too early to predict, on the pastoral ideas of the hierarchy. We are witnessing a popular movement within the larger Church, in the sector which has traditionally been most conformist (or most downtrodden), women.

All this is affecting Brazilian parishes in a new way. There cannot be any Catholic parish in Brazil today which is not being influenced in one way or another by these new currents, whether it be the "committed" ministries (CPT, PO, PJMP, CIMI, etc.) or the small communities of religious men or women, or the base communities, or indirectly the theology of liberation.

10. OPPOSITION

But this transformation of Catholicism is not having things all its own way. Outside opposition is reinforced by internal contradictions. The interests of prevailing capitalism were clearly damaged or at least threatened by what happened within Latin American Catholicism, and especially in Brazil, and this was bound to be reflected eventually on the church level. Today it seems clear that the days (or years) of the prophetic episcopal ministry represented by the CNBB are numbered in the face of the policy of episcopal appointments pursued by the Vatican, which gives unfailing preference to clerics with little social involvement and proven "Roman" loyalty. It remains to be seen how both the base communities and liberation theology will react when they lose the important backing of the CNBB.

But in addition to opposition from outside, the transformation of Catholicism faces internal contradictions. The relationship between the current dynamism evidenced by the base communities and other experiments and the historic dynamism of devotional Christianity described earlier is very confused. Today's pastoral workers are uncertain what attitude to adopt toward the people's devotion, which, in the end, represents the greatest experience of resistance and self-affirmation these people have known in almost five hundred years of domination. The pastoral workers find it difficult to regard this devotional attitude as an authentic Christianity, or at least as authentic as that of the bishops, priests and religious. Successful though pastoral work in Brazil has been in terms of social, political and economic analysis, in cultural terms it is still firmly tied to models imposed by the past and has not shown here the same creativity which it has shown in other areas. Some very specific examples will outline this internal contradiction within the "church of the poor.":

(a) After twenty years or more of work, the base communities have still not succeeded in producing an autonomous popular leadership, as was originally intended. "Pastoral workers" are perpetuating themselves, and not managing to pass on leadership functions to people from the base.

(b) The relationship between the base movement and the money received from abroad remains confused. International organizations support base-level projects in Brazil, something which was necessary at the beginning, but it is unclear how there can be a move to self-financing base-level projects.

(c) The pastoral workers' aims with regard to "conscientization" remain unclear. They do not normally start from the people's historical experience, but bring in elements from outside, with the result that the people at the base have difficulty in knowing what they are dealing with, their ordinary lives or some complicated theory.

(d) There is a latent attempt to convert the base groups into a sort of new "Christendom," that is to say, winning political power seems to be uppermost in people's minds, rather than the specifically Christian dynamic mentioned earlier. The ideology of Christendom has not been totally left behind in the new experiments in the Church.[18]

CONCLUSION

Brazil was evangelized from the top down and from outside in. Both the Christianity of the sugar plantations and that of the Indian villages established by the missionaries were based on an inversion of values which obscured what was specifically Christian. The colonialist was at the altar and the poor man or woman at the door, money opened the doors of the churches and the poor stayed outside, as did anyone who spoke up for them. Financial and economic interests, the interests of foreign groups, always prevailed over the interests of the Brazilian people, even in religious matters.

But there is no need to despair. Brazil had the Jesuits, who before 1759 constituted the main social force opposed to the interests of the sugar-masters, the landowners and the pioneer columns. It had the religious enthusiasts, men and women who led the people along the paths of a devotion which was able to preserve their sense of identity and capacity for cultural resistance. And in this century Brazil has had the prophetic witness of bishops identified with the popular cause, the base communities, liberation theology, and the "small communities" of religious life inserted among the poor.

Above all we have the memory of Jesus and his apostles, the great Judeo-Christian tradition of siding with the excluded and of making a choice between God and the power of money, prestige and violence.

Translated from the Portuguese by Francis McDonagh

NOTES

1. J. Comblin, "Os pobres como sujeito da História", *Revista de Interpretação Bíblica Latino-Americana* 3 (1989), pp. 36–48.
2. M. Gauchet, *Le Désenchantement du Monde (Une Histoire Politique de la Religion* (Paris, 1985).
3. *Ibid.*.

4. B. Prezia and E. Hoornaert, *Esta Terra Tinha Dono* (São Paulo, 1989), pp. 92–93.

5. Gilberto Freyre, *The Masters and the Slaves* (New York, 1946).

6. Manuel Ribeiro da Rocha, *Ethíope Resgatado* (Lisbon, 1758). This important text by a Brazilian abolitionist before his time has never been republished in Brazil.

7. A common summary of so-called "popular religiosity."

8. Antonil, *Cultura e Opulência do Brasil por suas Drogas e Minas* (São Paulo, 1928).

9. *Ibid.*, p. 101.

10. I discuss the importance of this episode in my *História da Igreja no Brasil: Primeira Época* (Petrópolis, 1977), pp. 53, 59, 308. See also Leite, S., *História da Companhia de Jesus no Brasil* (Rio de Janeiro), vol. II, pp. 227, 229.

11. *Ibid.*

12. Nuno Marques Pereira, *Compêndio Narrativo do Peregrino da América*. (Rio de Janeiro, 1939), I, p. 152.

13. *Ibid.*, p. 292.

14. S. Leite, *Monumenta Brasiliae*, (Rome, 1956), vol. I, pp. 114, 115, 372, 420, 421; vol. II, pp. 257, 166, 167, 421.

15. Padre Cicero came into conflict with the heirarchy precisely because he relied on the social support of the religious enthusiasts. See Barros Cavalcanti and O. Luitgarde, *A Terra da Mãe de Deus*. (Rio de Janeiro, 1988).

16. S. Mainwaring, *The Catholic Church and Politics in Brazil, 1916–1985* (Stanford, 1986).

17. M. J. Rosado Nunes, *Vida Religiosa inserida nos Meios populares* (Petrópolis, 1985).

18. C. Perani, "Rumos da Igreja no Brasil," *Cadernos do CEAS*, 100 (1985), pp. 68ff.

Chapter 11

CHRISTIANITY IN THE CARIBBEAN

Armando Lampe

What is wrongly called the "discovery" of America changed the face of history.

Between the early years of the sixteenth century and the abolition of slavery in Cuba in 1886, more than nine million African slaves were forced to populate the New World. At the beginning of the sixteenth century, the Spaniards introduced the cultivation of sugar cane on the plantation system, but there were no longer sufficient natives left to exploit. "The great dying" affected the natives of the islands of the Caribbean first, victims of unjust violence and prey to contagious diseases. Hispaniola, for example, had a million inhabitants in 1492; by 1520 there were only an insignificant number left. As these islands had neither gold nor silver, their contribution to the wealth of Spain and the rest of Western Europe was made in sugar cane, for which cheap manual labour was required. African slaves were originally imported through Spain and Portugal, but then directly from Africa to meet increased demand. It is this institution of slavery that has had most effect on the development of the Caribbean, which includes the archipelago of the greater and lesser Antilles, Belize and the Guyanas.

Despite this predominant factor, the Caribbean presents a very varied historico-social reality. The region that includes the first independent republic of Latin America (Haiti, in 1804) still has French, Dutch and U.S. colonies. In the sixteenth century, the region was Spanish. Since 1625, new European empires have invaded the Caribbean and begun to dismember it. It became the frontier of four great empires: the Spanish, French, British and Dutch. The Spanish retained their hegemony in some islands: Cuba and Puerto Rico were Spanish colonies till 1898, when the two islands began to come under the control of the United States.

The fragmentation of the Caribbean into different colonies also had its effects in religious pluralism. Anglicans, Methodists and Presbyterians were particularly active in the British colonies, the Reformed Church in the Dutch. The Catholic Church did not confine its activities to French and Spanish colonies: today the majority of the population of St Lucia and Dominica, ex-British colonies, is still Catholic. The massive influx of workers from Asia at the end of the nineteenth century further accentuated this religious pluralism. Hinduism and Islam became major religions alongside Christianity in Trinidad, Guyana and Surinam, where there were large concentrations of Asians. Then, of course, African beliefs are widespread throughout the region.

1. THE SPANISH PERIOD

In the Spanish period, the Catholic mission was closely linked to the civil power, using the latter to win over "pagans," while this used the mission to

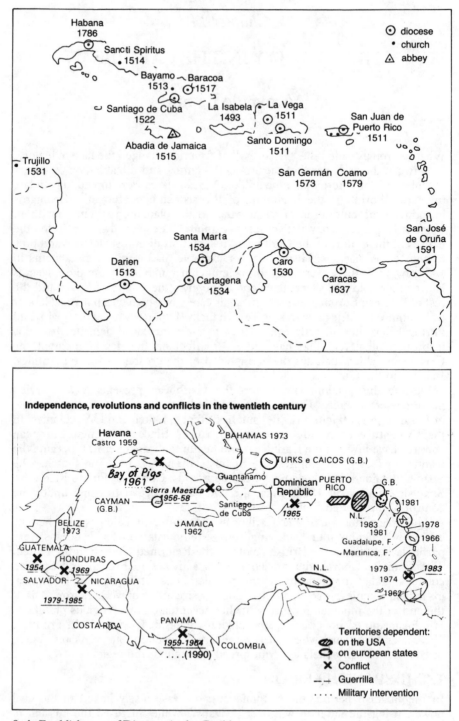

8. A. Establishment of Dioceses in the Caribbean
   B. Independence, Revolutions and Conflicts
Source (B): Zanichelli

control the "savages." Bishoprics were established in 1512 in Concepción de la Vega, in Santo Domingo and in Puerto Rico. The diocese became the culmination of the conquest. Bishops were appointed by the Spanish state. In 1515 the abbacy of Jamaica was founded, in 1531 the diocese of Coro and in 1546 the archdiocese of Santo Domingo.

The first three dioceses were suffragans of the metropolitan see of Seville. This lasted till the province of Santo Domingo was established in 1546, comprising the sees of Puerto Rico, Santiago in Cuba, Coro in Venezuela, Santa Marta in Colombia and Trujillo in Honduras. In the course of the sixteenth century, the diocese of San Juan in Puerto Rico became the most extensive ecclesiastical jurisdiction in America, embracing from 1519 the islands of the lesser Antilles, and from 1588 the provinces of Barcelona, Cumaná, Santo Tomás in Guyana and the islands of Margarita and Trinidad. Jamaica was invaded by the Dutch in 1626 and the English in 1643, and its abbacy came to an end in 1650.

The gospel was preached on the back of force of arms and economic exploitation. The system of Indian tribute and forced labour had been established in 1497 on the island of Hispaniola, and was generally in operation by 1503. When the first bishop arrived, it was already an established fact. And it was in the Caribbean that a joint ecclesiastical and political government was first established; there were bishops who were also governors, and governors who intervened directly in church affairs. Autonomy in church matters was not possible, which produced a very poor level of evangelization among the peoples of the Caribbean.

The first bishop of Puerto Rico showed little interest in protecting the Indians: in fact he helped divide them up among Spanish owners. This Bishop Manso was named Inquisitor General of the Indies in 1519, and collaborated closely with the civil powers. In 1515 an abbot was appointed to Jamaica, but neither he nor his four successors made any attempt at settling on that island. On Hispaniola, the archiepiscopal see remained vacant for a total of nineteen years between 1540 and 1585, leading to a rapid decline in the institutional Church.

This was in some cases worse than the pastoral neglect. In 1511, the King of Spain issued a royal decree authorizing the enslavement of the natives of Trinidad and the other islands, on the supposed grounds that they rejected Christianity, and this persecution was backed up by the Church. Throughout the Caribbean, natives were first enslaved and exploited, then, in most cases, slaughtered. There is no evidence from anywhere in the region of a single pastoral endeavour starting from respect for the indigenous cultures as a pre-condition for evangelization.

In 1510 three Dominicans came to Hispaniola, and with them a new form of evangelization began: pastoral effort on behalf of the voiceless. Antón de Montesinos, representing the Dominicans, said in his famous sermon of 1511: "Tell me, by what right and what justice do you impose such cruel and horrible slavery on these Indians? ... How is it that you keep them so burdened and weakened ... or rather, that you kill them, just for the sake of extracting and acquiring gold every day? Are these not men?" In 1515 Bartolomé de las Casas joined this group of Dominicans. Montesinos and he worked out a new scheme for the reorganization of Hispaniola, based on a new method of evangelization, which created indigenous communities and respected their culture. The plan failed and the prophetic voice was silenced in the Caribbean.

2. SLAVERY

(a) Slavery and the Church

The first slaves from Africa arrived in Hispaniola in 1505. In the French and Spanish colonies, the slaves were incorporated into the Catholic Church through baptism and the other sacraments, and efforts were made to keep them to some degree in touch with the parishes. But the Church had no real interest in evangelizing the blacks, mainly because it was too deeply involved in the slave system. There is a long list of bishops and priests who owned sugar mills and large numbers of slaves in the French and Spanish Caribbean.

Significantly, even the second generation of Dominicans to reach the Caribbean, unlike the first, in which figures such as Antón de Montesinos and Bartolomé de las Casas spoke out so strongly in defence of the rights of the native peoples, became part of the slave system: Dominican convents in Puerto Rico owned sugar mills with large numbers of slaves. In Guyana, the Jesuits, who in early colonial times had protested against the enslavement of the indigenous population, owned mills with large numbers of black slaves. The Jesuits employed very advanced pastoral methods with the indigenous people, after the manner of the reductions in Paraguay, but showed no similar pastoral concern for the blacks.

The Catholic Church played a major role in the semi-feudal organization of the colonies. There was a close link between the Church and the plantations in the French and Spanish Caribbean. Many mills on the larger islands had their own chapels, with chaplains paid by the proprietor. Production needs, however, did not always coincide with those of the Church, which led to numerous conflicts over issues such as working on feast days. But the one could not manage without the other: the mill needed the religious justification for slavery, this being that the main reason for bringing black pagans from Africa was to teach them the way of Christian salvation; the Church had powerful interests in the sugar mills: the seminary of Havana, for example, still drew its revenue from the sugar industry in the nineteenth century. So the dominant factor was the alliance between the Church and the sugar producers, with the former preaching a message of submission to discourage black rebellion.

(b) Slavery from the Seventeenth Century to Emancipation

After the overthrow of Spanish hegemony in the Caribbean, the seventeenth century saw the region split up into different colonies. The slave traffic from Africa reached its apogee in this and the following century. Protestantism also penetrated the English and Dutch colonies during this time, though it was not till the end of the eighteenth century, and more particularly the nineteenth, that it made an impression on the black population. The Anglican and Dutch Reformed Churches, the earliest non-Catholic churches to appear in the region, did not carry out missionary work among the slaves. In 1735 the Moravian Brethren reached Surinam and began a mission to the slaves.

Protestant missions in general practised non-intervention in the political question of slavery, which was tantamount to accomodation to the slave system.

The ruling classes in the English Caribbean and Surinam opposed the christianization of their slaves, which not only meant lost working hours, but might also produce a "dangerous" interpretation of Christianity by the slaves themselves. The only exception was Curaçao, where the vast majority of slaves had been incorporated into the Catholic Church by the seventeenth century. In the other Dutch Protestant colony, Surinam, the permanent presence of the Catholic Church was tolerated only from 1825.

The great change came in the century of emancipation, which took place in 1833 in the English colonies, in 1848 in the French, in 1863 in the Dutch, in 1873 in Puerto Rico and finally in 1886 in Cuba. In 1804, the slaves had themselves abolished slavery and colonialism in Haiti. In this nineteenth century, the ruling classes in many places considered un-christianized slaves much more dangerous than those who professed this religion. Religious instruction then became a means of preparation for emancipation, and most of the Afro-Antilleans in the British and Dutch Caribbean were christianized during this period.

Some slaves interpreted Christianity as favouring their liberation, as appears from the conversation between Tula and Fr Schinck. This, unique of its kind in the Caribbean, took place during the slave uprising in Curaçao in 1795. Tula was the chief leader of this revolt; the Franciscan Schinck had been working in Curaçao since 1778. He visited the rebellious slaves, and brought them official orders to cease their rebellion. Tula replied in these immortal words: "Master Priest, are not all persons descended from Adam and Eve? Did I do wrong in freeing twenty-two of my brothers who were wrongfully imprisoned? . . . I was arrested once, and asked without ceasing for mercy for a poor slave; when they finally set me free, blood was pouring from my mouth; I fell to my knees and cried to God: O Divine Majesty, O most pure Spirit, is it perhaps your will that they should ill-treat us in this way? Master Priest, they treat their animals better . . . We want nothing but our freedom."[1]

This interpretation of the Christian message is also illustrated by the following incident, which took place in a Cuban sugar mill in 1790. The Count of Casa Bayona decided to enact the Last Supper on Maundy Thursday. He, being the master, was going to humble himself before his slaves, washing the feet of twelve of them. This he did, in imitation of Jesus, washing the feet of twelve black slaves, then seating them at his table and serving them a meal. While the lesson the Count read into this may have been that the slaves had to humble themselves in everyday life, the slaves, on the other hand, took the lesson as being proof of their own dignity, and showing that there should be no inequality between master and slave. That same night, after what indeed proved to be their last supper, they rose up and burned down the mill. The rebellion was repressed; the Count ordered them to be beheaded and had their twelve heads mounted on lances.[2]

(d) Cultural Resistance

Generally speaking, the slaves had no weapons of resistance other than their culture: a black protest against the imposition of European values.

Conciousness of this antagonism between African and European culture played an important part in cultural opposition to the planation system. Even in spontaneous revolts, such as that of the Cimarrons, this ethnic challenge was a major factor: the Cimarrons were not only fleeing from the inhuman conditions of slave labour, but seeking an African cultural identity, as opposed to the European one forced on them.

In some cases the slaves considered Christianity part of the white, European world, and so experienced it as antagonistic to their own culture. There is the example of the Cimarrons of Surinam, who have preserved an African form of religion, differentiated from Christianity, to this day. The high level of hostility between Christianity and the slave world makes any triumphalist reading of the history of the role of Christianity in the Caribbean impossible.

This hostility was strengthened by the pastoral approach of the Church. This was dominated by a *tabula rasa* approach: throughout all the islands, without exception, the Church in the slave period adopted a policy of religious persecution of the African slave culture. The Caribbean has no examples to compare with the reductions in Latin America, where pastoral practice was informed by the specific African cultural values of the slaves.

While the Church was hostile to African religious values, the slaves had no alternative but to exercise religious "cimarronage." They emerged from "clandestinity" to make use especially of public Catholic symbols in the service of the survival of their African soul. Despite the fact that the Church upheld a policy of "apartheid" between the Christian and the African traditions, barriers were removed, thanks to the people who presented themselves as "virgin" to the missionaries, while all the time. . . . That is, the slaves gave the impression that they had no African culture in their veins, and the missionaries fell for this pretence that no culture had been brought from Africa. The apartheid approach denied life to both African and Christian traditions; syncretism became the order of the day in Caribbean Christianity, which drew on African as well as Western Christian sources, giving rise to an Afro-Christian religious experience.

(e) Mission and Emancipation

Martin Turner's work *Slaves and Missionaries* has shown that the Baptist mission made a decisive contribution to the slave rebellion in Jamaica in 1831. Contrary to the intentions of the missionaries, the slaves politicized the Christian message in the direction of the cause of their liberation. The Native Baptist Church was founded in 1783 by George Liele, who was born a slave in the United States and was the first black ordained a Baptist pastor and the first black to bring the gospel to the black people of Jamaica. In the so-called Baptist War, as this rebellion has been named, the slaves made particular use of this Native Baptist Church in organizing active resistance against slavery.

The same happened in Guyana. Contrary to the intentions of the missionary John Smith, the slaves took advantage of his Christian preaching, which emphasized equality among people, to spark off their rebellion against slavery. This rebellion too was crushed.

These events served to stiffen the planters' resistance to missionaries, especially the Baptists, in the British colonies. It was then, with this violation of the principle of religious tolerance, that the Baptist missionaries decided that the only course open was the abolition of slavery. This produced the figure of William Knibb, a Baptist pastor operating in Jamaica, who addressed the Annual Meeting of the Baptist Missionary Society in London in 1832 in these words: "God is the defender of the oppressed and will not forget the African . . . I plead for my brethren in Jamaica . . . If I should die without achieving the emancipation of my brothers and sisters in Christ, then . . . I shall kneel before the Eternal One, crying 'Lord, open the eyes of Christians in England that they may see the evil of slavery.'"

The relationship between the emancipation movement, Christianity and society in the Caribbean is a field deserving of further study. The abolition of slavery cannot be explained simply as a result of economic factors, as E. Williams attempted to do in his well-known *Capitalism and Slavery*. This leaves the contribution made to the emancipatory process by popular ideas and movements out of account. S. Jakobsson has remedied this by showing that missionary work in the Caribbean and in England made a major contribution to the process that led to the abolition of slavery in British colonies.

The nineteenth century also brought political independence to the Spanish colonies. This came late in the Spanish Caribbean, despite the fact that the first independent republic of Latin America, Haiti in 1804, was born in the Caribbean, and that in 1816 the Haitian government led by Pétion helped Bolívar with men and arms. But when the despot Boyer seized power in Haiti in 1826, he turned the country into virtually a French colony and ordered the invasion of Santo Domingo. The Dominican Republic did not win back its independence from Haiti till 1844. During the occupation, Haitian policy toward the Catholic Church in Santo Domingo was one of persecution, viewing the Church as part of the Spanish culture it was determined to stamp out. After independence, the Church re-formed in the Dominican Republic on the neo-colonial Christendom model, with Spanish support. In 1879, Fr Arturo Meriño, later Archbishop of Santo Domingo, became President of the Republic and held this post till 1882, consolidating the fragile relationship with the Vatican and strengthening the institutional Church. The neighbouring nation, Haiti, had been the first country of what was to be called the Third World to sign a concordat with the Vatican, in 1860.

3. A NEW ERA: ACCOMMODATION AND REPRESSION

(a) Puerto Rico

The occupation of Puerto Rico by the United States in 1898 opened a new era. The "Americanization" of the island involved the introduction of a large number of Protestant bodies, whose overall tendency in the early years was to lend support to the U.S. occupation. Then the economic crisis of the 1930s brought the pentecostalization of Protestantism, with its main characteristic of indifference to economic, political and social problems. The Pentecostal Church of Puerto Rico is currently the largest indigenous Protestant church on the island. The political crisis of the 1970s produced a multiplication of fundamentalist sects, whose stance is anti-Communist and in support of U.S.

colonial policy. This is the fastest-growing Protestant group, and has resulted in Protestantism accounting for 30 percent of the population of this traditionally Catholic country.

There is another, anti-imperialist, side to Protestantism in Puerto Rico, however, as shown by figures such as the Rev. E. de Mier, and, later, the Methodist pastor J. Hernández Valle, arrested together with the leader of the independence movement, Albizu Campos. Later still, the Rev. Luis Rivera Pagan was imprisoned for protesting against the presence of the U.S. marines.

(b) Dominican Republic and Haiti

The reaction of the Catholic Church, under Archbishop A. A. Nouel, to the military intervention by the United States in the Dominican Republic in 1916, was a critical one. But this same Nouel had been elected President of the Republic in 1912, with U.S. support. After this, the United States opted for supporting "strong men" to defend their interests in the Caribbean, instead of direct military intervention. This accounts for the rise of the dictator Trujillo in the Dominican Republic. Under him, the state gave special privileges to the Catholic Church, to which the official Church responded with silence on human rights violations, a situation that lasted from 1930 to 1960.

Trujillo signed a concordat with Rome in 1954, but only six years later the Bishops' Conference produced its first indirect criticism of his regime, in the form of two Pastoral Letters. Trujillo's response was to persecute certain sectors of the Church, culminating in his order to imprison the bishops, just a few hours before he himself was assassinated. In the constitutionalist revolution of 1965, when the people demanded the return of popular democratic government under the Presidency of Juan Bosch, the official Church took the minority anti-popular side. Once again the Dominican people were victims of military intervention by the United States, this time to prevent "a new Cuba." Unlike in 1916, this time the official Church approved and facilitated this intervention.

In Haiti, the Duvalier regime also sought unconditional legitimation from the Catholic Church. From 1957 to 1966, François Duvalier silenced or expelled religious leaders who were critical of his actions. In 1966 he reached an agreement with the Vatican, which created the conditions for the total integration of the Church into the Duvalierist system. For the next fifteen years the hierarchy gave religious legitimation to the regime. Then in 1980 the Haitian Church of the Poor first irrupted on to the historical scene.

This movement includes the base church communities, which have proliferated throughout the country, and the religious orders, brought together in the Haitian Conference of Religious, which at its first plenary session agreed to work toward a new model of society, church and religious life, one that would do justice to the poor. In 1980 the communities of Verrettes carried out an act of transcendental importance: they sent a letter to all the parishes in Haiti, requesting solidarity with their struggle for life against the Duvalier regime, which produced death. Representatives of the whole Church in Haiti, including the bishops, held a Symposium in December 1982, which denounced the situation of extreme poverty and injustice in which the country found itself. After Pope John Paul II's visit to Haiti in March 1983, the Bishops'Conference broke its era of silence with a declaration that was at least an indirect condemnation of the Duvalierist state.

The regime of Jean Claude Duvalier responded by repressing the Church. In 1985, he expelled three priests, including the director of Radio Soleil, the official broadcasting organ of the Catholic Church. When the Duvalierist dictatorship finally fell in 1986, it was owing to the opposition of the Catholic Church. In the subsequent process of constituting a "Duvalierism without Duvalier," however, the Bishops' Conference broke with the popular movement. In their report to the Twenty-second Meeting of CELAM, held in Curaçao in March 1989, the Haitian bishops denounced the so-called Popular Church as opposed to the teaching of the Catholic Church through reducing the gospel to a message of social liberation, being opposed to the authority of the hierarchy, and preaching class struggle. According to the bishops, the Popular Church was under the supposed leadership of Jean-Bertrand Aristide, a young priest who that same year had been expelled from the Salesian Congregation for being a prophet to the poor. The ruling class also declared the Popular Church public enemy number one, as shown by the massacre carried out in Fr Aristide's church on 11 September 1988.

(c) The English, French and Dutch Caribbean

In the English Caribbean, the Christian churches have given an uncertain and in some cases even a negative response to the movement for political independence of the 1970s. The point of conflict between the nationalist movements and the churches has been the control of the educational system. During the 1970s, some young religious leaders established contacts with the Black Power movement. In recent years, serious conflicts have broken out between the churches and the state, as in Guyana, where a priest was assassinated under the Burnham dictatorship. Today, large sectors of the churches are involved in defending human rights in the social, political and economic fields.

In the French Caribbean, most of the Catholic clergy have come from France, and formation of local clergy has been very much in the French mould. In these colonies, therefore, church life has closely resembled that in the mother country. In general, a policy of understanding and cooperation between church authorities and civil powers has prevailed. The Catholic Church has stood aside from independence movements. But the prophetic voice has not been entirely lacking: in 1985, Chérubin Céleste, a priest from Guadaloupe, went on hunger strike for the liberation of his people in this French *département*.

In the Dutch Caribbean, the decolonization process has evolved on different lines in Surinam and the Antilles. Surinam achieved independence in 1975, with the support of its Council of Churches. In 1979, this Council denounced the fact that since independence, the poor had become poorer while the rich had grown richer. When the Sergeants' Movement produced its *coup d'état* in 1980, the churches showed understanding of the change. But later developments have frustrated expectations: the Bouterse dictatorship came into being, and with it conflicts between state and churches over human rights violations. In the Dutch Antilles, the dominant tendency in the Catholic

Church in recent years has been to place more emphasis on the "religious" dimension, and less on the social.

(d) Cuba and Grenada

In 1959 Cuba freed itself from U.S. imperialism by overthrowing the Batista dictatorship. The poor and believing people carried out the revolution without the institutional church, which adopted a militantly counter-revolutionary stance. This gave rise to a period of conflict between the Catholic Church and the state in the years following the revolution, but since 1968 the Church's position has evolved from anti-communist to detached critical observer, and lately there has been a *rapprochement* from both sides. The Baptist churches, among the most numerous of Protestant churches in Cuba, also took an anti-communist line. The Methodist church was divided into a conservative and a progressive wing, but was predominantly traditional. The Pentecostal churches, with their spirituality of non-intervention in the social sphere, took in those who stood aside from the revolutionary process. The Christian Pentecostal Church and the Reformed Presbyterian Church, however, though few in numbers, generally welcomed the revolution.

In 1979 the people of Grenada attempted to escape the hegemony of the United States and overthrew the dictator Gairy. But this revolution was itself overturned in 1983 when the United States invaded the country. In 1973, the Catholic bishop, Patrick Webster, had protested publicly against the repression under Gairy. Later, Catholic and Protestant leaders representing the Grenadan Conference of Churches, took part in the creation of the "Committee of 22," which became the broadest and most united focus of opposition to the Gairy regime. Then the churches changed their position: Sidney Charles, from Trinidad, was appointed as successor to Bishop Webster, and led the opposition to the revolutionary government of Maurice Bishop, creating the false impression that there was a contradiction between Christianity and revolution, and that the Bishop government was persecuting the churches and religion. When the U.S. invasion took place, the bishop and virtually all sectors of the institutional church supported it as an act of "liberation," claiming that it was necessary to do away with the supposed "Communist invasion." The Grenadan Conference of Churches also adopted this anti-communist stance.

(e) Ecumenical Bodies

The Secretary General of the Caribbean Conference of Churches (CCC), Roy Neehall, gave his support to the revolutionary process in Grenada, in 1981. The CCC is an ecumenical body founded in 1973, representing twelve major Christian traditions in the region, including the Catholic Church. Its foundation was the culmination of a determined process of cooperation among the churches of the region, inspired by a new local leadership capable of taking a more independent line in relation to the "mother churches" in various distant metropolises. The CCC has distinguished itself by its active defence of human dignity and has made a significant contribution to development in the Caribbean. Its review *Caribbean Contact* is the only regional publication, and is distinctly anti-capitalist in tone.

Another notable ecumenical achievement has been the establishment, by eleven Christian churches working together, of the United Theological College of the West Indies in Jamaica, which now trains leaders for all these churches. And there have been other advances in the direction of Christian unity: in 1941 the Jamaican Council of Churches was founded, including the Anglicans, Baptists, Presbyterians, Congregationalists, Methodists, Moravian Brethren, Disciples of Christ, Church of God and Salvation Army. In 1965 the Congregationalists and Presbyterians came together in the United Reformed Church of Jamaica. Many other places have national Councils of Churches, often including the Catholic Church. The Council of Churches of Surinam is at present playing an important role in the country, as it has been officially accepted as mediator between the government and the opposition guerilla forces operating there. Another Caribbean-wide body is the Antillean Bishops' Conference, which embraces sixteen dioceses from all over the Caribbean.

At the local level, the ecumenical movement is lively and active. The potential of Caribbean ecumenism is shown by the fact that the former General Secretary of the World Council of Churches, Phillip Potter, was a Methodist minister from the island of Dominica.

There are also Christian churches of non-Western origin in the Caribbean: the Greek Orthodox Church was first established in the Bahamas, and the Ethiopian Orthodox Church came to Trinidad and Jamaica in 1970. This is just a reflection of the fact that the Caribbean is a melting-pot of different cultures. The indigenous languages, such as Papiamento in the Dutch Antilles, Creole in Haiti and Sranan Tongo in Surinam, reflect the new synthesis that has emerged from a heterogeneous cultural background. The institutional churches – Anglican, Lutheran, Presbyterian and Catholic – however, had long kept their European character. In 1950 the Jamaican Council of Churches brought out a prophetic publication, *Christ for Jamaica*, relating Christ to the experience of the Afro-Caribbean people in search of their identity. The last decade, especially in the Catholic Church, has seen major advances in efforts to adapt to local cultures, most particularly in the fields of liturgy and religious music, as is shown by the massive participation in the School of Liturgy organized every year at Mount St Benedict in Trinidad. The "charismatic churches," such as the Pentecostals and Baptists, have, by their own internal logic, been traditionally more open to accepting contributions from popular culture.

4. THE WIDER ECUMENISM

(a) Christianity and Other Religions

If Christianity, especially since the nineteenth century, has become the most important religious grouping in the Caribbean, it is still not the only one. When the slaves were incorporated into the Christian churches, they did not abandon their African beliefs. As the ruling classes in the seventeenth and eighteenth centuries considered it dangerous to give religious instruction to slaves, the religious domain was effectively left in the slaves' own hands, and this explains the development of Afro-Antillean religiosity. This has evolved into numerous forms, such as Voodoo in Haiti, Santeria in Cuba, Shango in Trinidad, Obeahism in Jamaica, Brua in Curaçao and Winti in Surinam.

In the mid-seventeenth century, a Jewish community established itself in Curaçao, and founded the earliest synagogue still in use in the Americas. Since then, Judaism has had a presence in the Caribbean. After the abolition of slavery, in order to safeguard the plantation economy, a massive wave of Asian immigrants was brought to the region in the nineteenth century. Today their descendants make up between a third and a half of the populations of Trinidad, Surinam and Guyana. These Hindus and Moslems have retained their original religious observance.

Hinduism and Islam have made a considerable impact on these societies. There is a general spirit of tolerance, as shown by the recognition of religious feast days of the different religions as national holidays. But there is still no structure for dialogue between these religions and the Christian churches, though a hopeful sign was the Congress organized in Surinam in 1985, in which Christians, Hindus and Moslems all took part. This decided that there was an urgent need for cooperation between all these religions, and declared that each had a vital contribution to make to the future of the country.

(b) Christianity and New Movements

In recent years a veritable mosaic of new religious movements has taken shape in the Caribbean, some imported and some native. Of the imported ones, the Seventh Day Adventists came from the United States; they were established first in Belize, then in Trinidad, and then spread throughout the region. The Jehovah's Witnesses are also present throughout the Caribbean. The main elements are the Pentecostal churches, which are supported by the United States and have spread everywhere. The charismatic or pentecostal movement has also successfully penetrated the mainstream churches since the 1970s, as well as producing numerous sects. The charismatic movement is at present the strongest tendency within the Catholic Church in the Caribbean, practising healing and trances as manifestations of the Holy Spirit.

All these varied movements have the following points in common: they have spread fastest during the current economic crisis; they involve the poorer classes; most have the neo-conservative characteristic of encouraging accommodation to the ruling system; they represent a renaissance of Afro-Antillean traditions. While some movements are apparently hostile to Afro-Antillean religiosity, overall they are essentially a revitalization of Afro-Antillean identity.

Of native movements, the best known is Rastafarianism, which originated in Jamaica in the early 1930s and has spread throughout the region over the last two decades. It takes its name from that of Emperor Haile Selassie before his coronation: Ras being his title of nobility and Tafari his family name. This movement proclaims that God is black and that the black people are the true people of God, marching toward the new Zion, which is "Ethiopia," where they will no longer be oppressed. In recent years, the Rastas have issued a call for the Africanization of the Caribbean.

The theological and philosophical foundations of Rastafarian thought were laid by Marcus Mosiah Garvey, born in Jamaica in 1887. He was the founder of the "back to Africa" movement: the black people, like the people of Israel before them, are exiles in the land of the whites, and it is God's will that they should be set free. Rather than a matter of geography, this expressed a cultural problem: the Antilleans are in quest of their identity. "Africa" has been present in virtually all social movements in the Caribbean. After five hundred years, the "discovery" has left us with this challenge: the Africanization of Christianity in the Caribbean, because the people of the Antilles are still looking for their God in their history.

Translated from the Spanish by Paul Burns

NOTES

1. A. F. Paula, ed., 1795. *De slavenopstand op Curaçao* (Curaçao: Centraal Historisch Archief, 1974), pp. 268–71. This is a collection of primary sources on the 1795 slave uprising in Curaçao.

2. Account drawn up by Don Diego Miguel de Moya and signed by almost all the mill-owners in the jurisdiction, 19 January 1790. Cited in M. M. Fraginals, *El ingenio*, I (Havana: Ed. de Ciencias Sociales, 1978), p. 117.

APPENDIX I
THE CATHOLIC CHURCH IN THE CARIBBEAN
(Place and date of the first diocese established in the various countries)

Dominican Republic – Santo Domingo, 1512; archdiocese, 1546.

Puerto Rico – San Juan, 1512.

Cuba – Santiago de Cuba, 1522; archdiocese, 1803.

Guadaloupe – Basse Terre and Pointe à Pitre, 1850 (comprising the islands of Guadaloupe, Marie-Garlante, Terre de Bas, Terre du Haut, La Désirade, St Barthélemy and the French part of St Martin).

French Guyana – Cayenne, 1956 (part of the apostolic prefecture of Martinique, 1731; apostolic vicariate, 1933).

Jamaica – Kingston, 1956; archdiocese, 1967 (apostolic vicariate of Jamaica, 1837).

Bahamas – Nassau, 1960 (apostolic vicariate, 1941).

Belize – Belize City and Belmopan, 1956 (part of the apostolic vicariate of Honduras, 1893, apostolic vicariate, 1925).

Bermuda – Hamilton, 1967 (apostolic prefecture, 1953; apostolic vicariate, 1956).

Trinidad – Port of Spain, archdiocese 1850 (formerly apostolic vicariate of the English, Dutch, French and Danish colonies of the West Indies, 1819).

Dutch Antilles – Willemstad, 1958 (comprising the islands of Curaçao, Aruba, Bonaire, Saba, St Eustatius and the Dutch part of St Maarten; apostolic vicariate, 1842).

Barbados – Bridgetown-Kingstown, 1970 (comprising Barbados, St Vincent and the Grenadines; part of the apostolic vicariate of British Guyana, 1837; part of the diocese of St George on Grenada, 1956).

Guyana – Georgetown, 1956 (apostolic vicariate, 1837).

Surinam – Paramaribo, 1958 (apostolic vicariate, 1852).

St Lucia – Castries, 1956; archdiocese, 1974 (part of the apostolic vicariate of the West Indies, 1820; part of the archdiocese of Port of Spain, 1850).

Dominica – Roseau, 1850.
Grenada – St George, 1956 (comprising the islands of Grenada, Carriacou, Petite Martinique, Isle de Hirondelles).
St Kitts and Nevis – part of the Diocese of Roseau, 1850 (comprising Montserrat, Anguilla and the British Virgin Islands).

Sources: Pius Bonifacius Gams, *Series Episcoporum Ecclesiae Catholicae*, 1873; *Caribbean Catholic Directory*, 1985.

APPENDIX II

PROTESTANTISM IN THE CARIBBEAN
(Major churches: source, place and date of first foundation in the Caribbean)

Mainland Europe
Dutch Reformed Church, Curaçao 1650.
Lutheran Church, Virgin Islands 1666.
Moravian Church, Danish Islands 1732.

England
Church of England, Barbados 1626.
Scottish Presbyterian Church, Guyana 1766.
Methodists, Antigua 1760.
Congregationalists, Guyana 1808.
Baptists, Jamaica 1814.
Salvation Army, Jamaica 1887.

United States
Native Baptist Church, Jamaica 1783.
African Episcopalian Methodist Church, Haiti 1823.
Disciples of Christ, Jamaica 1858.
Protestant Epicopalian Church, Haiti 1861.
Fundamental Baptist Church, Barbados 1890.
Lutheran Church in America, Puerto Rico 1899.
Church of God, Trinidad 1906.
Church of the New Testament of God, Barbados 1936.
Conservative Baptists, Haiti 1946.
Holy Unified Church of America, Barbados 1953.
Seventh Day Adventists, Belize (?)
Plus numerous Pentecostal churches established throughout the Caribbean in recent years.

Source: J. E. Braithwaite, ed., *Handbook of Churches in the Caribbean* (Barbados: CADEC, 1973).

SELECT BIBLIOGRAPHY

On the general history of the Caribbean:
Bosch, J. *De Cristobal Colón a Fidel Castro: El Caribe, Frontera imperial*. Barcelona: Alfaguarra, 1970.

Williams. E. *From Columbus to Castro: the History of the Caribbean, 1492–1969*. London: Andre Deutsch, 1978.

Charles, G. P. *El Caribe contemporáneo*. Mexico: Siglo XXI, 1981.

On slavery, see the recent masterly account:

Patterson, O. *Slavery and Social Death. A Comparative Study*. Cambridge, Mass. and London: Harvard U.P., 1982.

On the role of Christianity in slave societies:

Beozzo, J. O., ed. *Escravidão negra e historia da Igreja na America Latina e no Caribe*. Petrópolis: Vozes, 1987.

Bolt, C. and S. Drescher, eds. *Anti-slavery, Religion and Reform: Essays in Honour of Roger Anstey*. London: Dawson & Sons, 1980.

Genovese, E. D. *Roll, Jordan, Roll: the World the Slaves Made*. New York: Pantheon, 1974.

Gisler, A. *L'esclavage aux Antilles françaises (XVIIe - XIXe siècle). Contribution au problème de l'esclavage*. Paris: 1981.

Goodridge, S. S. *Facing the Challenge of Emancipation. A Study of the Ministry of William Hart Coleridge*. Barbados: CEDAR Press, 1981.

Jakobsson, S. *Am I not a Man and a Brother? British Missions and the Abolition of the Slave Trade and Slavery in West Africa and West Indies, 1760–1838*. Uppsala: WCC, 1972.

Turner, M. *Slaves and Missionaries: the Disintegration of Jamaican Slave Society, 1787–1834*. Urbana, Ill.: Univ. of Illinois Press, 1982.

On the twentieth century:

Braithwaite, J., ed. *Handbook of Churches in the Caribbean*. Barbados: CCC, 1973.

Cuthbert, R. W. M. *Ecumenism and Development*. Barbados: CCC, 1986.

Erskine, N. L. *Decolonizing Theology: a Caribbean Perspective*. Maryknoll, N.Y.: Orbis, 1981.

Hamid, I., ed. *Out of the Depths*. Trinidad: St Andrew's Theological College, 1977.

Kirk, J. M. *Between God and the Party. Religion and Politics in Revolutionary Cuba*. Tampa: University of South Florida Press, 1989.

Hurbon, L. *Dieu dans le Vodou haïtien*. Paris: Payot, 1972.

Massé, R. *Les adventistes du septième jour aux Antilles françaises. Antropologie d'une espérance millenariste*. Montreal: Centre de Recherches Caraïbes, 1978.

Osborne, F. J. *History of the Catholic Church in Jamaica*. Chicago: Loyola University Press, 1988.

Owens, J. *Dread. The Rastafarians of Jamaica*. Kingston: Heinemann, 1979.

Simpson, G. E. *The Religious Cults of the Caribbean: Trinidad, Jamaica and Haiti*. San Juan: Institute of Caribbean Studies, 1970.

Thomas-Hope, E., ed. *Afro-Caribbean Religions*. London: 1980.

Various, *Haití, opresión y resistencia. Testimonio de Cristianos*. Lima: CEP, 1983.

Wipfler, W. *Poder, influencia e impotencia. La Iglesia como factor socio-político en República Dominicana*. Santo Domingo: CEPEA, 1980.

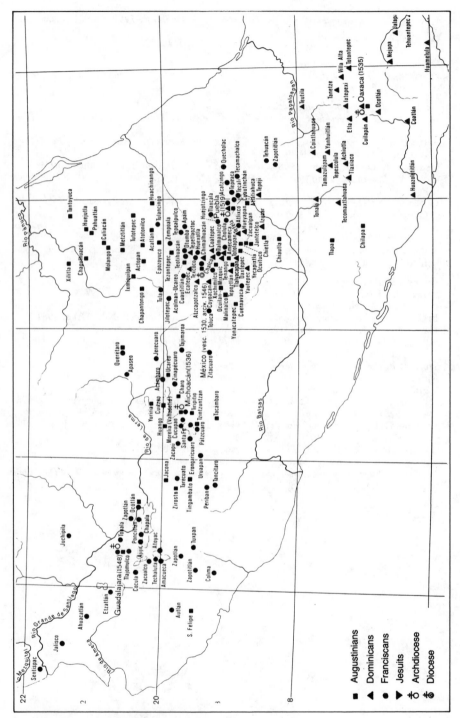

9. Mexico: A. Jesuit Missions up to 1520
          B. Religious Foundations up to 1557
Source: Piemme

Chapter 12

THE CHURCH IN MEXICO

María Alicia Puente

1. THE AUTOCHTHONOUS PEOPLES

In the sixteenth century, the Catholic Church began its work not in a vacuum, but in a multicultural environment peopled by descendants of autochthonous peoples who had produced many and varied cultures: Olmec, Toltec, Teotihuacan, Maya, Zapotec and Mexica among others. Modern archeology has found their traces in sites such as San Lorenzo, Tlatilco, Monte Albán, Teotihuacán, Tula, Chichén Itzá, Mitla, Xochicalco, Tenochtitlán and Tlaltelolco; precious codices allow us to piece together their conceptions of the world, their social structures, their ways of life. There are numberless and varied witnesses to their cultural vitality and achievements.

Their cosmological vision reveals a certain homogeneity: they saw heaven raised above earth, surrounded by a ring of water, the *anáhuac*, with the air, *ehecatl*, being the medium of communication between the two. The gods and humanity have met at a crossroads, where a "fifth direction" is marked, thereby recording a process in which there have been four previous worlds. The axis of their temples made the celebrant face the sun, which they saw as a symbol of divinity.

Politics was a sphere of activity through which the will of Quetzalcóatl, the sun god, could be discerned; this is why exercise of political power was regarded as a religious function. Watching over the way high office was conducted was the *cihuacóatl*, or "serpent-woman" – an adviser or vicar – who could be the same person through several reigns, thereby assuring a degree of continuity of policy. A central feature of all native religious thought was that the human person is the absolute centre of this whole historical process.[1]

By the beginning of the sixteenth century, the dominant empire, made up of a triple alliance of Atzapoyzalco, Tacuba and Tlaltelolco, under Mexica hegemony, had succeeded in subduing most of the other peoples. Two elements in this subjugation are worth noting, however: first, there was no change in social structure or means of production imposed on the subject people; what was a burden was the tribute demanded, together with other political restrictions (need for new appointments to be approved, referral of decisions concerning areas to be irrigated, whether or not to start a war, and so on). The second element that concerns our historical appreciation was that subjection of these peoples to the empire did not impose any change in their religious practices, nor were the religious practices of the conquering people imposed.

Ten years before the Spaniards arrived, eight deadly auguries foretold the destruction of these kingdoms. This also coincided with the year that Quetzalcóatl was expected to arrive from the east.

2. THE CONQUEST

In 1519, Hernán Cortés, with the help of "La Malinche," advanced from the coasts of Veracruz to Tenochtitlán, completing the conquest of this major centre in August 1521, helped by the Tlaxcaltecs and other peoples subjected by the Mexica empire. This marked a new form of subjection: the new conquering group forced a complete break in the cultural process, imposing a new way of explaining existence and ordering society. The conquered peoples were now stripped not only of their lands, but also of their political and economic socio-cultural structures.

This forced change formed the matrix of a different people, mixed in race and various other ways, largely as a result of cultural violation. The territory became known as New Spain, and was ruled by a Viceroy. *Audiencias* (legal administrative units) followed, called New Galicia, New Vizcaya, New León and the like. The transfer of Spanish ways was also evidenced in the names given to the conquered peoples.

(a) Evangelization

Charles V requested Pope Hadrian VI to issue the Bull *Exponi nobis* in May 1522, authorizing the despatch of the first twelve Franciscans, who landed at Veracruz on 13 May 1524. Unlike the three who had disembarked some eight months earlier, among them Fray Pedro de Gante, these twelve had canonical jurisdiction and a specific mission, making their leader, Fray Martín de Valencia, the first ecclesiastical authority in the territory. The Dominicans arrived in 1526 and the Augustinians in 1533. The territory of Mexico was divided among these three mendicant orders. They were followed by two orders of women: the Conceptionists and then the Capucines in 1565. Then came the Jesuits, in 1572, and by the end of the century the Mercedarians, followed by the contemplative Carmelites and Dieguinos.

With the establishment of parishes, colleges, convents and hospitals, the architectural and social scenes both altered. The natives were set to build the towers of the first churches, and religious oversaw the building of roads and hospitals, and organized urbanization and irrigation projects. Outstanding among the latter was the great aqueduct built by Fray Francisco de Tembleque, carrying water to Otumba from a distance of thirty miles.

(b) Establishment of Dioceses, Juntas and Councils

In 1518 Pope Leo X sent a Bull (known as the Caroline Bull) raising the Yucatán region to the status of a diocese, but this did not take effect till Tlaxcala was made a diocese, with Mgr Julián Garcés as its first bishop. A royal letter patent transferred him to the city of Puebla in 1543. Mexico City had been made a diocese in 1530, and Antequera in Oaxaca five years later; Mgr Vasco de Quiroga was proclaimed bishop of Michoacán in 1536, with his see in Patzcuaro. The diocese of Chiapas was founded in 1539, that of Compostela-Guadalajara in 1548 and Yucatán in 1561. In 1546 the first ecclesiastical province was established when Mexico City was raised from diocesan to archdiocesan status. The seventeenth century saw only one new diocese established: Durango (Guadiana) in 1620, and the eighteenth century two more: Linares in 1777 and Sonora in 1779.[2]

Five apostolic and ecclesiastical *juntas* (meetings of clerics and some civil authorities to decide the best way of implanting the Catholic Church) were held. The first was in 1524, with the Franciscans and Hernán Cortés present; the second in 1532, at which were present Sebastián Ramírez de Fuenleal, President of the second High Court, and Fray Juan de Zumárraga, who had been appointed bishop of Mexico City; the third in 1537, with Vasco de Quiroga (who had attended the previous one as a layman) present as bishop of Michoacán. The fourth was held in 1539 in the presence of the recently appointed bishop of Oaxaca. This affirmed the centrality of bishops,[3] prohibited native feasts and dances and made recommendations for the teaching of doctrine and administration of the sacraments. The fifth, in 1544, was held in the presence of a "visitor," Francisco Tello de Sandóval, the Inquisitor of Toledo, entrusted with putting into effect the "new laws" decreed under the influence of Bartolomé de las Casas in 1542.

Three provincial councils were held in the sixteenth century. The first, in 1555, was basically devoted to revising the criteria that had emerged from the ecclesiastical *juntas* and setting out legislation for parish administration and worship, and the way doctrine was to be taught to the Indians and they were to be incorporated into the Catholic Church through reception of the sacraments. The second took place in 1565. Its main task was the application of the decrees of the Council of Trent to the situation of the Church in New Spain. The third, in 1585, besides setting out norms and criteria for the expansion of the Church, was important for the official collective stance it took in favour of justice in the pursuit of the *chichimena* war, thereby recognizing the right of the natives to defend themselves against attacks on their lands and way of life.[4]

These three provincial councils strengthened the ecclesial institution and set out the criteria to be followed in the pursuit of its tasks of evangelization in the conquered territories. A fourth council, held in 1772 at the time of Bourbon rule, reflected the existing intra-ecclesial conflict in relation to the recent expulsion of the Jesuits and the tensions between civil and ecclesiastical authorities. It adopted a strongly "regalist" tone, and was therefore not approved by Rome.

(c) Guadalupe and Mexican Nationalism

Marian devotions are very common in Mexico, with local populations rallying to a particular title of the Virgin. So there is the Virgin of Zapopan in Guadalajara, Our Lady of Health in Pátzcuaro, Our Lady of Light in León, Our Lady of Solitude in Oaxaca, Our Lady of Ocotlán in Tlaxcala, Our Lady of the Lakes in Jalisco . . . to name but a few.

There is one devotion, however, to the Virgin of Guadalupe, that has acquired truly national status. This became a religious symbol that provided a solution to the cultural conflict between Spain and New Spain. It is likewise a symbol of cultural resistance that has become a focus of unity among Mexicans at crucial moments in the country's history. It is also, of course, a symbol that lends itself to manipulation, and has been used in this way. But this does not invalidate the evidence of a liberating and evangelizing message that has always been present in the Guadalupe tradition, preserved and spread in the account known as the *Nican Mopuhua*.[5] Devotion to the Virgin of Guadalupe has been a constituent of the great moments of Mexican history: independence, the Zapata uprising, the *Cristero* conflict . . . and equally of the daily lives of workers in factories, peasants on their smallholdings, women in their villages and families.

3. THE BOURBON CONFLICT AND SECULARIZATION

In the eighteenth century the change of dynasty from Hapsburg to Bourbon merely led to an increase in the absolutism already exercised. Charles III, who reigned from 1759 to 1788, made it his policy increasingly to subordinate the Church as an instrument of the state. In New Spain this policy clearly surfaced in the official visit made by José de Gálvez from 1764 to 1770. Not only did he order the expulsion of the Jesuits in 1767, but he introduced a whole series of measures implying greater control by the metropolis over the colony.

Outward signs of this policy were numerous: military parades alternated with religious processions (the first time the army was given a place in public life); ecclesiastical privileges were diminished; the community life of religious congregations was threatened by various monarchical interventions. The army, by contrast, saw its privileges increase; military authorities took over from mayors and local councils, thereby accentuating more direct control of the implementation of royal decrees concerning education and other matters. Charles III also demanded greater control over ecclesiastical prebends, and imposed restrictions on the number of *criollos* and *mestizos* allowed to take office in clerical ranks, reserving places exclusively for Spanish priests.

These measures, plus the growing spread of Enlightenment ideas, made possible through the growth of learned institutions besides the university, such as the Royal Academy of St Charles (1784), the Botanical Gardens (1788) and the Royal Seminary of Mines (1787), and above all strong economic and political tensions in an increasingly class-divided society, produced a different approach to social questions and the need to act to change society. One interesting figure among many concerned in this question was the Dominican Servando Teresa de Mier (1763–1827), who was suspended from his ministry, imprisoned, persecuted and exiled to London for a speech he made on 12 December 1794, in which he stressesd the indigenous roots of the Guadalupe apparitions. Napoleon's invasion of Spain acted only as a catalyst rather than being the cause of the outbreak of the independence movement.

4. THE NINETEENTH CENTURY

(a) The Church and Emancipation

Some of the clergy were aware of the sufferings of the people most affected by the colonial system, and recognized that the Church was one of the corporate groups most privileged by this system. Among those who supported the independence movement in thought and deed were Servando Teresa de Mier, who supported Hidalgo from his place of exile in London, Miguel Ramos Arizpe (1775–1843), a Deputy in the Cadiz Cortes, and the priests who led the movement: Miguel Hidalgo y Costilla (1753–1811), parish priest of Dolores, José María Morelos y Pavón (1865–1815), parish priest of Carácuaro, and José María Calvillo, parish priest of Colotlán.[6]

Some four hundred parish priests of small towns and villages showed their awareness of the needs of the majority of the population by witnessing that the Catholic faith could be a suitable starting-point for opting for the cause of the oppressed and for national autonomy in the political sphere. Other Catholics, including priests and the bishops, opted for the royalist cause. Bishop Abad y Quiepo of Michoacán issued a document in 1811 excommunicating Hidalgo and depriving the other priests most involved in the movement of their canonical status. In view of the fact that Hidalgo had carried the standard of the Virgin of Guadalupe, the bishop declared: "The Mother of God cannot protect crimes," and decreed that the parish priest of Dolores had committed two sacrileges, in insulting religion and insulting Our Lady.

The independence struggle in fact, however, merely substituted one form of dependence for another. What is known as the "consummation" of independence by Agustín de Iturbide on 21 September 1821 should rather be called a betrayal of independence, since it left the social aspirations of the people unfulfilled. The effect of the declaration on the Church was to leave it headless, virtually without bishops for a decade and a half. It was not till 1831 that Gregory XVI appointed six bishops to Mexico – and then as to a mission territory, since he refused to recognize its independence.

Throughout the nineteenth century, relations between religious and civil authorities were marked by tension between the quest for church autonomy on one hand and maintenance of control over the Church by civil government as an extension of the royal patronage of colonial times. Efforts were made from 1823 to establish a juridical framework on royalist lines: before the fall of Iturbide in 1822, the Interim Constituent Congress (which preceded the First Federal Republic) sent Fray José María Marchena to Rome to canvas support for this model. Don Guadalupe Victoria, the first President of Mexico, asked Canon Francisco Pablo Vázquez of Puebla to go to Europe in order to make the arrangements with Pope Leo XII, who around the same time issued *Etsi iam diu*, in which he declared his admiration for the outstanding qualities of Ferdinand VII and all his works. ... The 1824 Constitution recognized the Catholic religion as that of the state; other forms of worship were tolerated and religious freedom decreed in the Constitution of 1857.

(b) Rupture and Conciliation

There was, then, a constant tension between the church hierarchy and the civil government throughout the nineteenth century. This tension reflected the struggle going on throughout the first half of the century between centralist groups and those favouring a federal system, the latter backed by the increasing power of the Masonic lodges originating in Scotland and York, of which the dominant figure was Joel R. Poinsetti from the United States. This was the time when Mexico suffered radically from the expansionist aims of the United States, losing at one time and another more than two million square kilometres, over half its territory: Texas was lost in 1836, and further "frontier adjustments" made in 1848 through the Treaty of Guadalupe Hidalgo, and in 1853 through that of Mesilla (see map, p. 216).

One of the first ruptures occurred in 1833 when Valentín Gómez Farías tried to introduce a *first reform* suppressing the religious orders, secularizing the missions in Upper and Lower California, excluding the clergy from teaching in favour of state education, suppressing the Royal and Pontifical University of Mexico, abolishing the payment of tithes, and so on. After a series of advances and setbacks in the search for a form of religious tolerance that would facilitate immigration from various European countries, the Reform Laws promulgated by Benito Juárez from Veracruz in 1859 and 1860 legislated on freedom of worship, separation of Church and state (replacing what had really been the subservience of Church to state), nationalization of church property, establishment of a civil register, secularization of cemeteries, and other related matters.

The highest points of tension, causing complete breaks at times, came after the liberals took power, when in 1857 all public employees were required to swear an oath of loyalty to the Constitution. The bishops reacted by excommunicating all those who observed this government ruling. The most combative bishops included Mgr Clemente de Jesús Munguía (1810–69), bishop of Michoacán, and Mgr Lázaro de la Garza y Ballesteros (1785–1862), archbishop of Mexico City, who were both expelled from the country with other bishops and the Apostolic Delegate, Mgr Luigi Clementi, by the Juárez government. It was not till the government of Lerdo de Tejada (1873–6), however, that the Reform Laws were incorporated in the Constitution and more strongly enforced. In this period, even the Sisters of Charity, who had generally been respected till then, were expelled from the country.

Relations with the Holy See varied in tone. Pontifical representatives in Mexico were allowed differing ranks according the the government and constitution in power at the time: Nuncio, Apostolic Delegate, Chargé d'Affaires, Apostolic Visitor, Ambassador Extraordinary. ... The first Apostolic Delegate named was Luigi Clemente (1851–61); the only Papal Nuncio Mexico has had lasted a mere six months, from December 1864 to June 1865, during the reign of Maximilian of Hapsburg (1863–7).

During the next thirty years of liberal ascendancy the government did not accept any papal representatives. It was not till near the end of the century, during the dictatorship of Porfirio Díaz, that Nicola Averardi arrived in Mexico as Apostolic Visitor. His chief work was to encourage new provincial councils in 1896 and 1897 in preparation for the Plenary Latin American Council held in Rome in 1899.

5. THE TWENTIETH CENTURY

After the triumph of the revolution in 1920, only three Apostolic Delegates were admitted to the country: Ernesto Filippi in 1921, Serafín Cimino OFM in 1925 and Giuseppe Caruana in 1926. The last of these was expelled in the period preceding full scale religious persecution (1926–9).

After the acute phase of religious conflict, the Mexican government allowed only a Mexican to be appointed Apostolic Delegate. The person appointed was the archbishop of Morelia, Mgr Leopoldo Ruiz y Flores, one of the two participants in the talks that formally ended the *Cristero* movement. The archbishop of Mexico City, Mgr Luis María Martínez, acted as Chargé d'Affaires for eleven years from 1937 to 1948, when an Italian Apostolic Visitor, Mgr Guillermo Piani, arrived, staying in the post till 1951 and establishing a new *modus vivendi*. He was followed by other Italians acting as Apostolic Delegate: Luigi Raimondi from 1957 to 1967, Guido de Mestri from 1967 to 1970, Carlo Martini from 1970 to 1973, Mario Pio Gaspari from 1973 to 1977 and Geronimo Prigione from 1978 to the present. In recent years, he has been functioning practically as Apostolic Nuncio, in view of the increasing influence allowed him by the government.

At the beginning of the century, the Church moved from conciliation and recuperation to seige. The Mexican revolution was preceded by over thirty years of the dictatorship of Porfirio Díaz (1976–1910). Thanks to his policy of conciliation, under which the Reform Laws were applied somewhat sketchily, the Catholic Church was able to use his dictatorship to strengthen its public presence, its organization, educative mission and the activities of the religious orders. In 1895, the coronation of the Virgin of Guadalupe was solemnly enacted, in the presence of ecclesiastical dignitaries from all parts of the world. This was followed by coronations of other Virgins, which both encouraged and demonstrated the strength of religious feeling in the country.

These were years of increasing recuperation: the religious orders returned, new ones were founded, seminaries were opened, new dioceses established, and the Pontifical University reopened in 1896. The first provincial council was held in Antequera in the diocese of Oaxaca in 1892, followed by others in Durango, Guadalajara, Michoacán and Mexico City (the fifth) in 1896 and 1897. Social Catholicism showed its strength at this time, with various congresses being organized: in Tulancingo and Puebla in 1903, Morelia in 1904, Guadalajara in 1908 and Oaxaca in 1909. "Social weeks" alternated with congresses, encouraging study of the various problems affecting society.

Generally speaking, the bishops and the President were both looking for accommodations that would favour their own projects. The government sought the support of the Church through its religious orders, so that they would spread their missionary endeavours in zones of uprising and perform other services, while the government did not object to the Church's growing numbers. Outstanding among the bishops of the time were Eulogio Gillow Arz of Oaxaca (1841–1922), intellectually head and shoulders above his fellow hierarchs and the President himself, Crescencio Carrilo y Ancona of Yucatán, Archbishop Pelagio Antonio de Labastida y Dávalos of Mexico City and Ignacio Montes de Oca of San Luis Potosí, who, returning from the Plenary Latin American Council, spread to Europe the message that despite the laws, the Church in Mexico was alive and well "thanks to the wisdom and superior mentality of its ruler."

The triumph of the Mexican revolution brought with it an anti-ecclesiastical tone explained as much by the posture of the hierarchy during the dictatorship as by the support they gave to Victoriano Huerta, who seized power and assassinated President-elect and acting President Madero, the instigator of the revolution with his cry of "effective suffrage not re-election." So the Church went from recuperation to seige and then persecution.

(a) The "Cristero" Movement

When the constitutionalist faction led by Venustiano Carranza triumphed, he convoked a Constituent Congress in Querétaro in 1917 at which a new

Constitution was approved. In this new "Magna Carta," articles 3, 5, 24, 27 and 130 legislated on education, freedom of profession of faith and of religious observance, church property, the civil and political rights of clergy and a number of other restrictions. Plutarco Elías Calles held the Presidency from 1924 to 1928 and early in 1926 promulgated the Reglamentary Law of Article 130, which put it into effect. The reactions of Catholics and their organization against it, together with the way the law was applied, unleashed a decade of religious persecution on the part of many civil authorities and suspension of public worship by the bishops (in their Pastoral Letter of July 1926). Catholic peasants from various parts of the country rose up in arms to the shout of "Long live Christ the King and the Virgin of Guadalupe." Old men, women and children joined the movement. Various groups adhered to it and formed the League for the Defence of Religious Freedom in March 1926. This body organized publicity overseas, giving its version of the reasons for the struggle and the circumstances that had led to it. The armed struggle lasted for three years (in nineteen states of the republic), during which the federal army with all its resources was unable to subdue the *Cristeros*. The movement, it is important to note, was complex in composition, with land, oil and religious interests all playing their part.

In June 1929 two bishops negotiated with the interim President Emilio Portes Gil and reached an agreement that was supposed to produce peace. Most of the *Cristeros* agreed to lay down their arms out of obedience to the bishops, but many did not and the struggle continued for another decade in seven states of the Republic. The agreement involved no change in the law which had occasioned the conflict in the first place, but only an offer not to apply it rigorously. Pope Pius XI issued three encyclicals on the movement, in 1926, 1932 and 1937, in the last two of which he explained that the agreement had been accepted as a lesser evil, and exhorted special efforts in the establishment of Catholic Action and priestly formation.

(b) Various Approaches: Increased Priestly and Lay Participation

During the six years of Lázaro Cárdenas' presidency, the *Cristero* conflict was still a burning issue. Towards the end of this period, motivated by the nationalization of oil, the bishops urged Catholics to support the President. From 1940 the post-revolutionary governments adopted a new stance and an effective period of *modus vivendi* between Church and state was ushered in. An indication of governmental compliance with ecclesiastical decisions was the regime's acceptance of the nomination of the first Mexican cardinal, José Garibi Ribera, in 1958, in contrast to the reaction when Bishop Gillow was proposed for a cardinal's hat during the Díaz dictatorship, when, for political reasons and faced with the objections of the liberal clubs, the government refused to accept his nomination.

Following their experiences in the *Cristero* conflict, a significant nucleus of lay people (and priests) managed to make an important mental clarification in their religious life: the bishops are one thing and their faith is another. They can at one and the same time follow different paths along the road, and even cross over from one to another.

The social involvement of Catholicism during the second decade of the century showed significant advances. Workers' circles were encouraged with such force that they came together to form the Catholic Confederation of Labour, as an alternative to the CROM (Workers' Mexican Regional Confederation) founded in 1918. Initiatives grew under the new Catholic Action founded in 1929 (replacing that founded in 1913 by Fr Bernardo Bergoend), which was to be strengthened in the 1950s and 1960s.

In the early 1960s Bishop Sergio Méndez Arceo of Cuernavaca welcomed various initiatives, including the controversial experiments in community carried out by Ivan Illich and Grégoire Lemercier. New organizations dealing with family matters, and the "Cursillo" movement, had a major influence on lay formation (though not in a social direction) at the time of the Second Vatican Council. A Mexican couple, José and Luz María Alvarez Icaza, attended this as observers and contributed to the modification of Schema XIII by collecting and presenting the experience of married people in Latin America.

At the same time, a more socially-oriented pastoral approach was being developed by Fr Pedro Velázquez (1913–68), the director of the Mexican Social Secretariat, who promoted the formation of a network of workers' savings banks, co-operatives for those engaged in agriculture, husbandry and craftwork, schools for social workers, and the like. Concern for the native peoples and for a stake in social communications led to the creation of CENAMI (the National Centre for Indian Pastoral Work) and CENCOS (National Centre of Social Communication). Both centres have evolved in the way they conceive of and perform their function. The first has moved from a "charitable" view of services for the Indians to working from them and with them; the second from producing and spreading information to the public along known lines to giving out information withheld by official sources. Both forms of evolving their services have led to these bodies seeking greater independence from the church hierarchy.

Under the influence of the 1968 CELAM Conference in Medellín, base church communities have spread in Mexico, while groups trained in universities and social institutes have shown various forms of commitment to popular causes. Numerous initiatives aimed at broadening the basis of priestly formation and the religious life were successful for a number of years, but in the last decade church repression has made its appearance in the suppression of some educational centres of this nature. To mention but two: the ITES (Theological Institute for Church Studies) was closed in 1985; in the most recent incident, the Regional Seminary of Tehuacán, which brought seminarists from seven dioceses in the South Pacific region together for a biblical, theological, social and pastoral training, was closed in November 1990.

To sum up this survey of the Church in Mexico, one can say that it has always faced tensions as an institution in that some of its officials have sought accommodation with the political authorities, while others have taken the side of the disadvantaged: Bartolomé de las Casas, Vasco de Quiroga and Julián Garcés in the sixteenth century; Hidalgo, Morelos and Mora in the nineteenth; Bartolomé Carrasco, Samuel Ruiz, Arturo Lona, José Laguno and Méndez Arceo in the twentieth. Also, to the extent that lay people have become conscious of their autonomous mission, co-responsible with the hierarchy and not dependent on them, so the possibilities for services and initiatives have multiplied. These have often been mediated through recognizable experiences, ranging from Confraternities, church societies, the Catholic Press, social congresses (in the nineteenth century), and the National Catholic Party to social and university-based pastoral groups, the base communities, the organization known as Christians Committed to the Peoples' Struggle and the proliferation of groups committed to human rights, now so much under attack in this period of selective repression. All these are reasons for keeping hope, the basic ingredient in the Church's mission, alive today.

Translated from the Spanish by Paul Burns

NOTES

1. See C. Siller, "La religión indígena," *Hacia una Historia mínima de la Iglesia en México* (Mexico City, 1990).
2. See J. Bravo Ugarte, *Diócesis y Obispos de la Iglesia en México* (Mexico City, 1965).
3. See J. Aparecido Gómez Moreira, *Don Vasco de Quiroga: pensamiento indigenista, jurídico y teológico* (Master's thesis, Mexico City, 1989).
4. See J. A. Llaguno, *La personalidad jurídica del indio y el III Concilio Provincial Mexicano* (Mexico City, 1965).
5. This account is one of the precious productions stemming from the work of the privileged Indian students admitted to the College of Santa Cruz of Tlatelolco. The *Nican Mopohua* is attributed to one Antonio Valeriano, a native of Atzcapozalco.
6. See J. Gutiérrez Casillas, *Historia de la Iglesia en México* (Mexico City, 1984), pp. 227–63.

CHRONOLOGICAL TABLE

1325 The Mexicas settle and found Tenochtitlán
1430 The Mexicas conquer the Tecpanecs of Atzcapotzalco
1519 Cortés' expedition reaches Mexico
   "Caroline" Bull founding the first diocese
1521 Fall of Tenochtitlán
1524 Arrival of first twelve Franciscans
1526 Foundation of first bishopric: Tlaxcala, later transferred to Puebla
1531 Apparitions of the Virgin of Guadalupe
1536 Foundation of the College of Santa Cruz de Tlaltelolco
1537 Letter from Bishop Julián Garcés of Tlaxcala to Pope Paul III soliciting recognition of the Indians
1524–45 First apostolic *juntas*
1545 Large-scale Indian deaths from the *cocoliztli* epidemic
1555 First Council of Mexico
1565 Second Council of Mexico
1571 First tribunal of the Inquisition in Mexico
1585 Third Council of Mexico
1647 Conflict between Bishop Palafox and the Jesuits
1695 Uprisings in Mexico over food shortages
1725 Widespread deaths from three-year epidemic
1736 Enormous edifice constructed for the Inquisition
1737 The Virgin of Guadalupe declared principal patron of Mexico
1767 Expulsion of the Jesuits
1772 Fourth Provincial Council of Mexico
1810 The priest Miguel Hidalgo initiates the independence movement
1821 Iturbide "consummates" a different independence from that sought

1857, 1867 Reform Laws, separation of Church from State, nationalization of church property
1876–1910 Dictatorship of Porfirio Díaz. Conciliation with the Church; regrowth of seminaries, congregations; foundation of new colleges; new provincial councils; Catholic social congresses
...
1924 National Eucharistic Congress
1926–9 Religious persecution; the *Cristero* movement
1940–68 *Modus vivendi* between hierarchy and government
1979 Third General Conference of CELAM held in Puebla. John Paul II visits Mexico for the first time
1988 The new President of Mexico invites (for the first time since the revolution) church dignitaries to his inauguration
1990 Second visit of John Paul II. Accentuation of conflicts and polarization within the Church; stronger emergence of groups committed to the popular struggle.

DIOCESAN AND ARCHDIOCESAN FOUNDATIONS

		Diocese	Archdiocese
Colonial Times	Tlaxcala*-Puebla	1525	1904
	Mexico City	1530	1546
	Oaxaca	1535	1891
	Michoacán	1536	1863
	Chiapas	1539	
	Guadalajara	1548	1863
	Yucatán*	1561	1906
	Durango	1620	1891
	Linares	1777	1891
	Sonora	1779	
Nineteenth Century	San Luis Potosí	1854	
	Baja California	1855	
	Tamaulipas	1861	
	Querétaro	1862	
	Chilapa	1862	
	León	1862	
	Tulancingo	1862	
	Veracruz	1862	
	Zacatecas	1862	
	Zamora	1864	
	Tamaulipas	1870	
	Tabasco	1880	
	Colima	1881	
	Sinaloa	1883	
	Cuernavaca	1891	
	Chihuahua	1891	1958
	Saltillo	1891	
	Tehuantepec	1891	
	Tepic	1891	
	Campeche	1895	
	Aguascalientes	1899	
Twentieth Century	Huajuapan	1902	
	Toluca	1950	
	Jalapa	1950	1951
	Chihuahua	1950	1953
	Ciudad Juárez	1950	
	Tapachula	1957	
	Torreón	1957	

Acapulco	1957	
Matamoros	1958	
Mazatlán	1958	
Hermosillo	1958	1959
Ciudad Obregón	1958	
Culiacán	1959	
San Andrés Tuxtla	1959	
Ciudad Valles	1959	
Texoco	1960	
Autlán	1960	
Tula	1961	
Apatzingan	1961	
Linares	1961	
Tehuacán	1962	
Tuxpan	1962	
Veracruz	1962	
Tijuana	1963	
Ciudad Altamirano	1963	
Ciudad Victoria	1963	
Tlalnepantla	1964	1990
Tuxtla Gutiérrez	1964	
Mexicali	1965	
Ciudad Guzmán	1965	
S Juan de los Lagos	1972	
Celaya	1972	
Cuautitlán	1972	
Tuxtepec	1979	
Cd. Nezahualcóyotl	1979	
Cuautitlán	1979	
Coatzacoalcos	1984	
Atlacomulco	1984	
Lázaro Cárdenas	1985	
Nuevo Laredo	1990	

There are at present fifty-three dioceses and fourteen archdioceses.
There are also seven prelatures: Ciudad Madera, Chetumal, Casas Grandes, El Salto, Huautla, Jesus María, Mixes; and one Apostolic Vicariate: Tarahumara.

* The Caroline Bull (1519) was destined to Yucatán as first diocese, but was not put into effect till 1525, when it was applied to Tlaxcala, from where the diocesan see was transferred to Puebla in 1543.

SELECT BIBLIOGRAPHY

Autochthonous Cultures
Casas, B. de las. *Apologética historia sumaria*. 2 vols. Mexico City: UNAM, 1967.
Garibay, A. M. *Teogonía e Historia de los mexicanos*. Mexico City: Porrúa, 1965 and 1986.
Lafaye, J. *Quetzalcóatl y Guadalupe*. Mexico City: Fondo de Cultura Económica, 1985.
León Portilla, M. *Visión de los Vencidos: relaciones indígenas de la conquista*. Mexico City: UNAM, 1984.
—. *Toltecayotl*. Mexico City: Fondo de Cultura Económica, 1980.
López Austin, A. *Hombre-dios. Religión y política en el mundo náhuatl*. Mexico City: UNAM, 1973.
Sahagún, B. de. *Historia general de las cosas de la Nueva España*. Mexico City: Porrúa, 1956.

The Church in Mexico: Colonial Era
Andrade, V., de P. *Ensayo bibliográfico mexicano del siglo XVII*. Mexico City, 1972.
García Icazbalceta, J. *Bibliografía mexicana del siglo XVI*. Mexico City: A. Millares Carlo, 1954.

Gallegos Rocafull, J. M. *El pensamiento mexicano en los siglos XVI y XVII*. Mexico City: FCE, 1951.
Gonzalbo Aizpuru, P. *Las mujeres de la Nueva España*. Mexico College, 1987.
Martínez, E. *Repertorio de los tiempos e historia natural de esta Nueva España*. Mexico City, 1606.
Ricard, R. *La conquista espiritual de México. Ensayo sobre los métodos misioneros de las órdenes mendicantes en la Nueva España, 1523–1572*. Mexico City: Porrúa, 1947.
Rojas Garcidueñas, J. *El teatro en la Nueva España en el siglo XVI*. Mexico City, 1973.

Nineteenth and Twentieth Centuries
Adame Goddard, J. *El pensamiento político y social de los católicos mexicanos 1867–1914*. Mexico City: UNAM, 1981.
Alcalá Alvarado, A. *Una pugna diplomática ante la Santa Sede. El restablecimiento del Episcopado en México*. Mexico City: Porrúa, 1967.
Carrillo y Ancona, C. *El Obispado de Yucatán del siglo XVI al XIX*. Mérida, 1883.
Cuevas, M. *Album Histórico Guadalupano del IV Centenario*. Mexico City, 1930.
Esparza, M. *Gillow durante el porfiriato y la revolución en Oaxaca (1887–1922)*. Tlaxcala, 1985.
González Ramírez, M. *Aspectos estructurales de la Iglesia católica mexicana*. Mexico City: ESAC, 1972.
Guzmán García, L. *Tendencias eclesiásticas y crisis en los años ochentas*. Mexico City: CIESAS, 1990.
López Gallo, P. *Relaciones diplomáticas entre México y la Santa Sede*. Mexico City: El Caballito, 1990.
Medina Ascensio, L. *México y el Vaticano*. Vol 1. *La Santa Sede y la Emancipación Mexicana*. Mexico City: Jus, 1965.
Ramírez Cabañas, J. *Las relaciones entre México y el Vaticano*. (Compliation of documents) Mexico City: Secretariat for Foreign Affairs, 1928.
Staples, A. *La Iglesia en la Primera República Federal Mexicana (1824–1835)*. Mexico City: SepSetentas, 1976.
Valverde Téllez, E. *Bio-Bibliografía eclesiástica mexicana (1821–1943)*. Mexico City: Jus, 1949.

General works
Alvear Acevedo, C. *La Iglesia en la Historia de México*. Mexico City: Jus, 1975.
Bravo Ugarte, J. *Diócesis y Obispos de la Iglesia Mexicana*. Mexico City, 1941.
Cuevas, M. *Historia de la Iglesia en México*. El Paso, 1928.
Dussel, E. *Historia General de la Iglesia en América Latina*. Vol 5. Salamanca and Mexico City: CEHILA, Sígueme, Paulinas, 1984.
Gutiérrez Casillas, J. *Historia de la Iglesia en México*. Mexico City: Porrúa, 1974, 1984.
Olmedo, D. *Historia de la Iglesia Católica*. Vol 3. *La Iglesia Católica en la Edad Moderna*. Mexico City, 1963: Porrúa, 1978.
Puente Lutteroth, M. A.. (ed.) *Hacia una historia mínima de la Iglesia en México*. Mexico City: Paradigma, 1990.
Quirarte, M. *El problema religioso en México*. Mexico City: Talleres gráficos de la Nación, 1927.

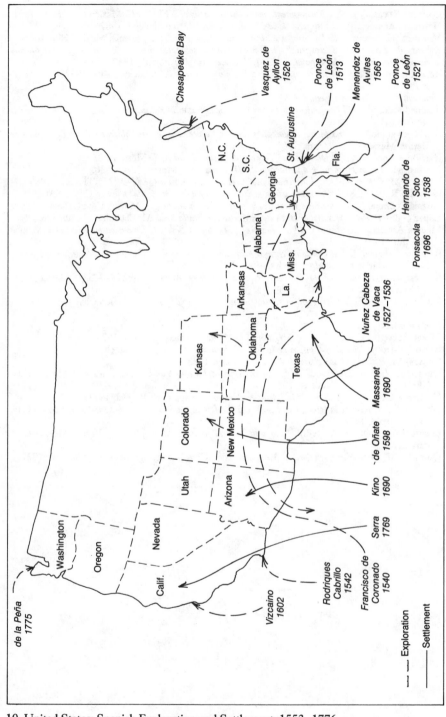

10. United States: Spanish Exploration and Settlement: 1553–1776

Chapter 13

THE CHURCH AMONG THE HISPANICS IN THE UNITED STATES

Moises Sandoval

An Hispanic Church first appeared on lands currently part of the United States in 1513. On 2 April of that year, the explorer Juan Ponce de León came ashore briefly on the eastern coast of Florida near the present site of St Augustine. Because it was the Easter season, he named the new land *La Gran Pascua Florida*, the Spanish name for that feast. Since missionaries always travelled with such expeditions, that is the first time that the Church touched those lands. From there it would eventually extend across what is now southern United States and up the West Coast to the Olympic Peninsula in what is now the state of Washington, the northernmost outpost of the Church throughout its long history in this part of the world.

Finding the Florida Indians hostile, the Spaniards reboarded their ships and sailed down the coast and up the other side of the peninsula where they also landed briefly before returning to Puerto Rico. Other pursuits would keep Ponce de León from returning until 1521 when he was fatally wounded trying to establish a colony near present-day Tampa. Almost half a century passed before a colony was established. But the expeditions that failed led to the exploration of lands now known as the Southeast and Southwest of the U.S.

In 1527, an expedition led by Pánfilo de Narvaez was driven off course and shipwrecked on Galveston island. Of the survivors, who were enslaved by the Indians, four escaped to make an epic eight-year trek across the Southwest. Alvar Nuñez Cabeza de Vaca and his three companions arrived in Culiacan, Mexico, in 1536 with a report that there were seven cities with great riches in a region called Cibola. Between 1540 and 1542, Francisco Vasquez de Coronado explored Arizona, New Mexico, Oklahoma and Colorado looking in vain for the seven cities of Cibola. Three priests and a Brother remained among the Indians to evangelize them, but all but the Brother were killed.

In 1538, Hernando de Soto explored the Carolinas, Georgia, Alabama and Louisiana. He died and was buried on the banks of the Mississippi. From there his men went on to explore Arkansas, Texas and Oklahoma. In 1542, Juan Rodríguez Cabrillo discovered the bay of San Diego in California; Sebastián Vizcaíno, the Bay of Monterey in 1602.

The people the Spaniards found in the lands they explored were on the periphery of indigenous civilization in the Americas. They were primitive in comparison to the advanced civilization of the Aztecs, Mayas and Incas. The most advanced among them had reached the level of planters and some still led a semi-nomadic existence of hunter-gatherers. The Pueblos, whose ancestors had appeared in the Southwest around 8,000 BCE, had passed their zenith between 1,300 and 900 BCE. Furthermore, some of the plains tribes in particular would regress to a nomadic stage once they acquired horses, which the Spaniards brought with them.

Though these people came from a few major cultural groups, they were divided into hundreds of tribes with as many languages. Life was an elemental struggle for food and security. Warfare among various groups was constant. They did not have the skills, knowledge, riches, complex political and social systems of, say, the Aztecs. One or more chiefs led each tribe. There were associations of various kinds: warriors, leaders of religious rituals and cults. Lifestyle was communal, with the monogamous family the basic unit of society, though some tribes practised polygamy. Their world view was a cosmic dualism, for some the spring struggling against winter, the sun against the moon; for others, the sky representing the masculine principle, the earth the feminine. For the most part, however, their broad sense of social morality – on such questions as murder or adultery, for example – was the same as that of their conquerors.

Settlement (and evangelization) proceeded slowly once the Spaniards ascertained that there were no rich kingdoms. Political concerns, rather than evangelistic zeal, led to colonization. In Florida the goal was to protect the sea lanes for the galleons carrying the treasures of Mexico to Spain; in Texas, to keep the French out; in California, to prevent the Russians, who were working their way down from Alaska, from claiming what is now the West Coast of the United States. Pedro Menéndez de Aviles finally established St Augustine in 1565, the first permanent Catholic mission in the United States. The second colony was not established until 1696, in Peñascola. In all, the Spaniards built about a dozen settlements in Florida, their name for all of the territories now in southeastern U.S.

In 1598, Juan de Oñate began colonizing New Mexico. With 400 settlers, 138 of them women, he took possession of the territory near present-day El Paso, Texas, on the feast of the Ascension. Eight Franciscans and three Mexican Indians who had not taken their final vows were part of the expedition. Oñate established Santa Fe, which in time became the centre of Spain's largest colony in the United States. Alonso de León and Fray Damian Massanet established the first mission in East Texas, San Francisco de Los Tejas, in 1690. Others followed but Indian attacks and other difficulties forced the Spaniards to abandon the region three years later. But efforts continued and, in 1718, they founded San Antonio de Valero, a mission that endured. The first mission in California was established by Fray Junipero Serra in San Diego in 1769. In rapid succession, the Spaniards built a chain of twenty-one missions up the coast of California. By 1776, the mission at San Francisco was being built. In 1775, a colony was established on the Olympic Peninsula of what is now Washington State and mass was celebrated for the first time in that region.[1]

The process of implanting the faith began with conquest, characterized by violence and intimidation designed to enable the conquistadors, who were few, to rule over the many. One of Coronado's lieutenants executed several hundred Tewa warriors when the tribe refused to provide food for the expedition. Oñate and Diego de Vargas, who reconquered New Mexico after the Pueblo revolt of 1680, used the same tactic. Evangelization was carried out in an atmosphere of terror. Alonso de Benavides, custodian of the New Mexico missions, wrote in 1634: "So great is the fear which God has instilled in them of these few Spaniards that they do not come near where we are."[2]

The main structure of evangelization in many areas was the reduction, consisting of church, shops, village and surrounding cultivated or grazing areas where the Indians lived and worked, voluntarily or under coercion. In the Southwest, however, the missionaries usually located the mission compound within or just outside existing *pueblos* or villages. In some areas, the Indians had to work in *encomiendas*, private holdings usually owned by military officers who received the work of the Indians in lieu of pay. Though some of the Indians came voluntarily, many, especially those who were nomadic, were held against their will. The Indians toiled at various tasks, from building the churches to caring for livestock to cultivating the soil and raising the crops. Corporal punishment was not uncommon, including prolonged kneeling and flogging.

Demanding that the Indians give up their religious beliefs, the Spaniards confiscated instruments of worship such as masks, prayer sticks, and totems and destroyed or closed prayer houses such as the *kivas* of the Pueblos.

While teaching Catholic dogma, the missionaries also taught Spanish and respect for Spanish law and authority. They preached the values of sedentary life, urged the Indians to accept the Spanish political system, social customs and dress codes. Indian women had to convert to Catholicism and have a legitimate marriage to a Spaniard. Taken together, the programme of the missionaries demanded that the Indians abandon both their religion and culture.

By the Spaniards' own accounts many of their missions were a great success. By 1634, thirty-four Franciscans ministered to forty thousand Indians in Florida; in 1655, seventy friars worked in thirty-eight missions from St Augustine north to Georgia and west to present-day Tallahassee. In 1674, Bishop Gabriel de Calderon, who spent eight months visiting the missions, confirmed 13,152 persons.

The reports from New Mexico were even more impressive. By the end of 1625, twenty-six missionaries worked there. The colony was divided into seven missionary districts. Churches and chapels had been built in many *pueblos*. In the larger ones, there were workshops to teach weaving, leatherwork, blacksmithing and other skills. In 1630, Benavides wrote that sixty thousand Pueblo Indians in ninety villages had been converted to the Catholic faith. "All the Indians are now converted, baptized and well ministered to, with thirty-three convents and churches in the principal pueblos and more than 150 churches throughout the other pueblos." he reported. "Here where scarcely thirty years ago all was idolatry and worship of the devil, without any vestige of civilization, today they worship our true God and Lord. The whole land is dotted with churches and convents and crosses along the road."[3] In California, where the missions were in operation for sixty-five years, the Franciscans claimed to have converted 54,000 Indians.

Half a century after Benavides' glowing report, in 1680, the Pueblo Indians revolted. They killed 380 settlers and twenty-one missionaries and and forced the survivors to retreat south to El Paso. The suppression of Indian beliefs was one of the causes. In 1675, Pope, the leader of the uprising, and forty-five other Indian leaders had been whipped publicly for not giving up their religious practices. In Georgia, the Indians revolted because they were not allowed to practise polygamy. There was a similar revolt in California at a later time.

Whether or not large numbers were converted, disease and forced labour decimated the Indian population. In New Mexico, only sixteen thousand Indians remained in 1680, out of an estimated forty thousand when the Spaniards came. In Florida the Indian population was decimated not just by the Spaniards but by the United States after it took possession in 1821. Out of 72,000 Indians in California in 1769, only fifteen thousand remained in 1836. While some tribes, e.g. the Tewas and the Papagos of the Southwest, converted to Catholicism, many others complied with their Christian duties only under compulsion or out of love for ritual and ceremony. But eventually many returned to their old beliefs. After two hundred years the Pueblo Indians, the most susceptible to evangelization because they were sedentary, conformed to Christianity only superficially.

Conflict between Spain and other nations ended many of the missions. Between 1702 and 1704 the British and their Indian allies destroyed virtually all of the Florida missions. By 1708, only St Augustine remained.[4] The French and Comanches forced the Spaniards to abandon East Texas and the Indians overran many of the missions. Furthermore, the missionaries were decimated on four occasions. In 1767, the Jesuits were expelled from the Spanish empire. Secularization, which occurred between 1793 and 1830, left many missions without clergy. Then when Mexico won its independence from Spain in 1821, many of the missionaries, being Spanish nationals, returned home. Finally, in 1827, because of the influence of the freemasons, the Mexican government ordered the expulsion of Franciscans from New Mexico and Arizona.

Though the evangelization of indigenous peoples was hardly a great success, the Spaniards nonetheless planted the faith firmly in many of the lands they colonized. They did this by creating a hardy new people – the mestizos – who nurtured and lived their faith during trying times. By 1800 in New Mexico, for example, the missions served an Indian population of only ten thousand but the settlements of colonists had increased to 102, with a population several times as large. Though not necessarily at the same time, the mestizo settlers in other areas eventually became more numerous than the Indians who had accepted the Catholic faith.

To them, these hardly literate peasants, the faith owes its existence in the Southwest. Often without their own indigenous priests, they developed a self-reliant religion. When the missionaries were removed or died out, they were sustained by beliefs, rituals and practices that one day would be disparaged as superstition by those bishops and clergy unable to recognize their true value. In New Mexico, the piety of the mestizos was dominated by the "spiritual and material images of their crucified Nazarene and the queenly virgin."[5] They had a strong penitential spirit, a legacy from the first settlers; Oñate, for example, scourged himself, a practice later followed by a group called the *Fraternidad Piadosa de Nuestro Padre Jesús Nazareno*, commonly known as the *Penitentes*.

In the absence of priests, *Penitentes* frequently led the people in remote villages in religious observances. For Lent and Holy Week they had elaborate penitential rituals, re-enacting the crucifixion and leading the congregation in the rosary and the stations of the cross. The *Penitentes* also taught Christian doctrine to the young, led burial services, provided material assistance to those in need and mediated disputes among families. "It would not be an exaggeration to say that these *Penitentes* assured the survival of the Catholic faith in New Mexico during the Mexican period and beyond," wrote the chaplain of the *Penitentes* in 1988.[6]

There were few priests because the missionaries, never numerous, did not recruit local vocations. Dioceses were not established during the colonial period even though requested several times. In New Mexico and Texas, dioceses were formed only after those territories had been seized by the United States during the Mexican War (1846–8). In upper and lower California, a diocese came into being in the early 1840s but was not properly organized before the United States seized upper California. Though these territories were part of Mexican dioceses, the bishops seldom visited. During one period in New Mexico, seventy years passed between episcopal visits.

More than a hundred years elapsed after Juan de Oñate established the first mission in New Mexico before the area could claim its first priest. Santiago de Roybal, ordained about 1728 by the bishop of Durango, was the first native secular priest in the Southwest.[7] Parishes led by secular priests did not exist in New Mexico until 1798. In Texas, two parishes were founded during the eighteenth century. As late as 1840, California had no secular priests and Texas had only two. Even after that, there were few indigenous priests. It was a different story in New Mexico, thanks to the efforts of Padre Antonio José Martínez. In 1833, Martínez received permission from the bishop of Durango, Antonio José Laureano de Zubiria, to establish a preparatory school for seminarians. Of the thirty young men who studied there, about sixteen were eventually ordained to the priesthood, most of them by Bishop Zubiria and four by the French Bishop Jean Lamy, the first prelate of the diocese of New Mexico. Conquest of the region by the United States in 1846 effectively halted the development of a local clergy.

Dioceses were rapidly established following the signing of the Treaty of Guadalupe Hidalgo ending the Mexican War in 1848. Even before, after Texas had won its independence from Mexico in 1836, the process to establish one there had begun, with the creation of a vicariate. By 1847, the diocese of Galveston, encompassing all of Texas, was established. The diocese of New Mexico, which also took in Arizona, and the diocese of San Francisco were created in 1853; Sacramento (then called Grass Valley), in 1868; San Antonio, in 1874; Denver, in 1887; Dallas, in 1890, and Tucson, in 1897.

The rapid growth of an institutional Church was due, at least in part, to tremendous population growth. The discovery of gold in California late in 1848 brought a flood of settlers, swelling the population to 380,000 by 1850, of whom only 15 percent were Hispanics. In Texas, which had thirty thousand people in 1836 (only five thousand of whom were Hispanics), the population increased to 140,000 by 1846, with little of that increase consisting of Hispanic people.[8] As a result, Hispanics became a tiny minority in the Southwest, except in New Mexico, where they numbered sixty thousand in 1848. They remained the majority of the population well into the twentieth century.

Though the Hispanics residing in the lands seized from Mexico were guaranteed full rights of citizenship, they were categorically rejected by U.S. society. In a few years, they were dispossessed of their lands, deprived of a political voice, displaced from all but the most menial jobs and, sometimes, forced to emigrate to Mexico by violence whose toll will never be known. The bishops of the new dioceses of the Southwest – Frenchmen in Texas and New Mexico, Spaniards and then Irishmen in California – did not defend their Hispanic members. It was a time when the Church, the target of much religious bias, was trying to gain acceptance in American society. As a result, it was silent or cautious about criticizing the actions of the majority.

In much the same way that civil society had purged Hispanic political leadership, the new bishops rejected indigenous church leadership. What happened in New Mexico occurred in other areas as well. When Bishop Jean Lamy arrived in 1850, there were sixteen indigenous priests, but seven were old and sickly. Lamy removed five of those remaining, including Antonio José Martínez, who had done much to develop a local clergy. Lamy also tried but failed to neutralize the organized lay leadership of the *Penitentes*. Furthermore, though the early bishops founded many institutions, seminaries were not among them. They were content to bring in clergy and nuns from Europe. As a result, apart from the lay leadership of the *Penitentes* and other lay groups, Hispanics had no opportunities for ministry. This led some to join Protestant denominations.

The North American Church provided only a limited ministry to Hispanics in the latter half of the nineteenth century. As religious orders and congregations came from Europe, they established themselves first among non-Hispanic Catholics, who had the resources to support them. Though some also tried to start institutions or services for the Hispanics, these often failed for lack of support. Instead of advocating the rights of the Hispanics, as they often did for other groups, such as the Irish or Germans, the bishops and clergy pleaded that the work of the Church was not of this world, that its role was to prepare people for life after death.

During that period, two Churches were, in effect, established in the Southwest, one for people of Hispanic heritage and one for Anglos.[9] Hispanics usually worshipped in separate churches because they lived in separate neighbourhoods or *colonias*, settlements outside the towns, or in isolated rural communities. Where both groups lived together, there were separate churches in the same parish. When that was not possible, Hispanics were assigned seats in the back of the church or were welcomed only at specified times.

But in another sense, Hispanics were not a church at all because they did not have their own ministers. They were a community that was the object of ministry by outsiders. The bishops and their European clergy judged the faith of the people to be too weak or inferior to develop vocations. Not until the 1920s would the bishops begin to revive the tradition of priesthood just beginning when the Southwest was taken away from Mexico. Seminarians, however, frequently encountered prejudice and many were forced to abandon their studies.

The Hispanic population began to grow after 1882 after decades of stagnation and even decline in some areas. That year Congress passed the Chinese Exclusion Act halting immigration from that country. Early in the twentieth century limits placed on the entry of Japanese and Eastern Europeans also helped provide a limited place for Hispanic labourers in agriculture, the mines, a few industries and the railroads. Soon Mexicans began to appear in areas where they had not been seen before.

The Mexican Revolution, which began in 1910 and brought turmoil that lasted for two decades, caused a million Mexicans to emigrate to the United States. At the same time the Hispanics of the Southwest, drawn by work opportunities caused by labour shortages during World War I, began to move to the cities of the West Coast and Midwest. Migrant farm labourers, who worked north every summer, ending the harvest in the upper Midwest and Northwest, gradually began to settle in small towns near their summer work.

Meanwhile, Puerto Ricans began moving to the mainland in search of work, establishing themselves principally in the cities of the Northeast, although the exodus would not come until after World War II. Cubans, Central and South Americans, driven by tyranny or want, soon began to establish their own enclaves. Periodic massive deportations – during the depression of the 1930s for example – failed to halt growth.

In 1944, the Church began to establish special structures to serve the Hispanics. That year Archbishop Robert E. Lucey of San Antonio sponsored a seminar attended by fifty delegates from western and south-western dioceses. They established a Bishops' Committee for the Spanish-speaking. With funds from the American Board of Catholic Missions, the committee's staff began a programme of social and spiritual aid in four episcopal provinces. It provided for clinics, settlement houses, community and catechetical centres, maternal and child care for migrant workers and other services. Eventually, Hispanics in other parts of the country began to receive some special attention, too. In New York's Lower East Side, Jesuits at Nativity Mission Center provided special educational help to poor children. Some parishes in large and small cities became in effect national parishes for Hispanics at a time when, in its efforts to gain acceptance in American society, the Church was phasing out that kind of parish.

The committee's regional office for the Spanish-speaking, located in Texas, eventually became a national office and was moved to Washington in the 1960s. Regional offices were created in the Midwest and West Coast and some dioceses established offices for the Hispanic apostolate.

While the work of the bishops' committee and its offices was largely palliative, some priests, Anglos as well as Hispanics, made a deeper commitment. For example, four priests, one of them Hispanic, established a mission band in 1949 in California that devoted itself to meeting the social and spiritual needs and teaching the workers their rights. For twelve years they went up and down the valleys of California, until the growers forced the bishops to end the committee's work. Others followed the example of the members of the mission band, some working with farmworkers and others in inner-city apostolates across the country. As a general rule, those who made such special commitments were eventually forced by their superiors to give up those apostolates.

In the 1960s and 1970s, the farmworkers in California, who finally succeeded in organizing after decades of failure, demanded that the church walk alongside them in their struggle. Pressured by the example of Jews and Protestants, the bishops eventually came to their support and the farmworkers union was able to win many contracts. But that kind of corporate commitment by the bishops did not last long and, by the 1980s, the farmworkers had lost many of the gains they made in the 1960s and 1970s.

Almost a century after the first black bishop was ordained in the United States, the Church finally named its first Hispanic: Patricio Flores, appointed auxiliary of San Antonio in 1970. Flores, who spent his youth as a migrant worker, did not shrink from speaking out for farm workers, immigrants and other poor people. In the next two decades, twenty more Hispanic bishops were named. A few of them also made a special option for Hispanics, though none matched the stand of Flores. A few Anglo bishops also made a special commitment, temporary or permanent, to Hispanics. While he headed the Diocese of Stockton, California, Bishop Roger Mahony (later elevated to archbishop of Los Angeles) fought hard for the rights of the poor, especially the farmworkers and undocumented immigrants. Bishop Sidney M. Metzger of El Paso gave strong support to Hispanic workers in their successful struggle to organize a union in clothing plants along the border in the 1970s. Bishop John Fitzpatrick of Brownsville, Texas, became the strongest episcopal defender of the refugees from Central America who came to the United States by the hundreds of thousands in the 1980s.

Many Hispanic priests, nuns and Brothers previously assigned to posts where they were not able to serve their own people, won reassignment to Hispanic ministry. Mexican American priests organized PADRES, an acronym for priests united for religious, educational and social rights. They played a leading role in the quest for Hispanic bishops. In general, they demanded a more effective ministry, addressing not only spiritual and social concerns but also seeking to liberate the people from the oppression they had suffered as a despised minority. Hispanic religious women organized *Hermanas*, whose goals in part paralleled those of PADRES. They also lobbied for the rights of Mexican nuns who work in U.S. religious institutions as domestics. These groups helped to establish the Mexican American Cultural Center, a pastoral institute in San Antonio, Texas, that became a model for others founded later in other regions.

At the same time, lay leaders arose among Hispanics who began to make an impact on the Church. One of these was Pablo Sedillo, who became the head of the national office for Hispanics, first as a division in a department of the United States Catholic Conference and then as a secretariat in the Bishops' Conference. Another was César Chavez, who persuaded the Church to support the farmworkers in their struggle to organize. Ernie Cortez, an activist trained by the Industrial Areas Foundation using the methods of the late Saul Alinsky, organized the *barrios* of San Antonio and Los Angeles into powerful community organizations. Willie Velasquez, who headed the Southwest Voter Education Project, won the vote for many Hispanics thoughout the Southwest.

Under pressure from the civil rights movement, which reached its zenith in the 1960s, token Hispanics were named to Church boards, chanceries and national offices.

Following the pattern begun in the 1940s, the bishops continued to permit or encourage special structures for Hispanics. Most of the dioceses eventually set up an apostolate office for them in their chanceries. Regional offices were put in place in all parts of the country. In 1972, Hispanic leaders from throughout the nation met in Washington for the first National Encuentro. They passed dozens of resolutions asking the bishops to take action in many areas, many of which were ignored. A second National Encuentro was held in 1977. In 1983, the bishops promulgated a pastoral calling the Hispanics a "blessing from God" and calling for a third National Encuentro, held in 1985. In the past, they had considered them a problem. Out of those meetings came the outlines of a national plan for Hispanic ministry enacted by the bishops in 1987.[10]

The Campaign for Human Development, the Church's anti-poverty programme, established in 1970, contributed to many self-help projects or causes: leadership development, voting rights for disenfranchised Mexican Americans and grass-roots organizations such as Communities Organized for Public Service (COPS), organized by Ernie Cortez. A federation of Catholic parishes in the *barrios* of San Antonio, Texas, COPS brought political power and many civic improvements. It was duplicated in Los Angeles, Houston, the lower Rio Grande Valley and other areas.

The Cursillo movement, a one-time weekend experience of spiritual renewal founded in Spain in 1947, was brought to the United States in 1957 by two airmen who came to train in Texas. They introduced it to Father Gabriel Fernandez, of Waco. In time the Cursillo spread throughout the nation, revitalizing the faith of hundreds of thousands of Anglos and Hispanics. It played an important role in the lives of César Chavez, leader of the farmworkers, and Patricio Flores, who became the first Hispanic bishop. Also of Spanish origin, the marriage encounter movement followed later and also achieved dramatic results. Latin America later contributed liberation theology and the base church communities. Hispanics in the United States also developed their own liturgy and charismatic movement.

In the meantime, the Hispanics continued to increase. In 1950, the Census estimated the Hispanic population at four million; in 1960, 6.9 million; in 1970, 10.5 million and in 1980, 14.6 million. Between then and 1984, it went up another 20 percent.[11] By the end of the decade, demographers were projecting that by the year 2000 or 2010, Hispanics would be the majority of Catholics in the United States.

Between 1950 and 1960, the Puerto Rican population living on the mainland increased from 300,000 to 887,000 and by 1989 it was 2.2 million. Following the Cuban Revolution in 1959, a total of 875,000 Cubans left the island to settle in the U.S.. By 1989, that group added up to one million. Those of Mexican origin numbered 11.7 million; Central and South Americans, 1.1 million, and another group classified simply as "other Hispanics" totalled 1.5 million.

The bishops, however, could no longer assume that they would maintain their traditional loyalty to the Church. In the 1980s, about sixty thousand were leaving each year to join Protestants, mainline as well as evangelical and pentecostal groups. As of 1990, an estimated four million out of twenty million Hispanics in the United States were members of Protestant denominations.[12] Failure of the Church to minister adequately was one cause of the defections.

The Catholic Church, increasingly middle-class in its Anglo membership, found it difficult to minister to a population in which 30 percent were poor. In 1988, six out of ten Hispanic families were among the two-fifths of the poorest families in the nation. For the most part, effective Hispanic ministry represented the commitment of individuals – a few bishops, clergy, religious men and women who could make that special option for the poor. But the U.S. Church as a whole – dioceses, religious orders and congregations – had not made the corporate commitment necessary to serve that growing population adequately. As a result, there was what the social scientists called "a social distance" between Hispanics and their Church.

At least in part, the alienation was a product of the history Hispanics had lived in the United States. Many still exhibited the marks of a conquered people: apathy, aggression, lack of goals and distrust. Many, especially Mexcian Americans, were anticlerical, in part because of *machismo*, which sees the practice of religion as unmanly, something only for the women and children.

Regular church attendance lagged behind that of other groups, some surveys showing it as low as 30 percent. In terms of Church leadership, Hispanics were still deprived. In 1990, they did not have even a tenth of the nation's four hundred bishops or of the 53,000 priests. Fewer than two hundred Hispanic priests were native-born; with the immigrants, they added up to less than two thousand. The same disparities applied to nuns and Brothers.

Socially, Hispanics were an uprooted people. Some had moved to the cities from rural areas, in which the majority of long-time inhabitants had lived until World War II. Others had immigrated from other Latin nations. That exodus had ruptured traditional societies. There was a great need to unite families and reconstruct cohesive communities.

The Hispanic Church, like its people, therefore faced an uncertain future in the United States. What was clear, though, was that these people and their values and lifestyle would continue to challenge those of the main Church. Optimists said that Hispanics would one day redeem it.

NOTES

1. M. de J. Ybarra, "Los Hispanos en el Noroeste: Primera Migración, 1774–1820," an unpublished paper citing research by E. Gamboa and T. J. St Hilaire, SJ.

2. F. W. Hodge, G. P. Hammond, and A. Rey, eds., *Fray Alonso de Benavides' Revised Memorial of 1634* .Albuquerque, 1945), p. 68.

3. Ibid., p. 80.

4. J. P. Dolan, *The American Catholic Experience: A History from Colonial Times to the Present* (New York, 1985), p. 30.

5. A. Chavez, *My Penitente Land, Reflections on Spanish New Mexico* (Albuquerque, 1966), p. 111.

6. J. Martínez y Alire, "The Influence of the Roman Catholic Church in New Mexico during Mexican Administration 1821–1848," an unpublished paper presented at the CEHILA symposium in Las Cruces, New Mexico, in 1988.

7. J. Romero and M. Sandoval, *Reluctant Dawn: Historia del Padre A. J. Martinez, Cura de Taos* (San Antonio, 1976), p. 11.

8 D. J. Weber, *Foreigners in Their Native Land: Historical Roots of the Mexican Americans* (Albuquerque, 1973), p. 145.

9. This term refers not only to people who were products of the Anglo-Saxon culture that established itself in New England but to people from other European cultures who assimilated into that society.

10. The value of the plan eventually came into question because no funds were allocated for implementation. By late 1989, Archbishop John May of St Louis, the president of the National Conference of Catholic Bishops, said that the funds would have to come from individual dioceses. With many dioceses in financial crisis, having to close parishes and other institutions, the plan had little chance of full implementation.

11. Population Reference Bureau, "The Hispanic Population: Current Demographic Trends," a document prepared by Wendy Patriquin for a briefing of the U.S. Catholic Conference, 5 Feb., 1988.

12. M. Sandoval, *On the Move: A History of the Hispanic Church in the United States* (Maryknoll, N.Y., 1990), p. 118.

CHRONOLOGICAL TABLE

1513 An Hispanic Church first sets foot on lands now in the United States when Ponce de Léon comes ashore near present-day St Augustine, Florida.

1565 Pedro Menéndez de Aviles establishes the first permanent Hispanic colony: St Augustine, Florida.

1536 Alvar Nuñez Cabeza de Vaca arrives in Culiacan, Mexico, after an epic journey across the Southwest.

1540 Francisco Vásquez de Coronado begins a two-year exploration of Arizona, New Mexico, Oklahoma and Colorado, leaving three missionaries to evangelize the Indians.

1598 Juan de Oñate begins the colonization of New Mexico.

1680 The Pueblo Indians expel the Indians from New Mexico, only to be reconquered in 1693.

1690 The first missions are established in Texas.

1767 The Jesuits are expelled from the Spanish empire.

1769 Construction of the California missions begins.

1775 A colony is established on the Olympic Peninsula, territory now in the State of Washington.

1793 Secularization of the missions begins.

1821 Mexico wins its independence; many missionaries return to Spain.

1846 The United States invades the Southwest, seizing half of Mexico's territory.

1847 The Diocese of Galveston is created, the first of many others created in the Southwest.

1882 Hispanics gain a limited place with the passage of the law excluding Chinese immigrants.

1898 The United States invades Puerto Rico, annexing the island.

1910 The Mexican Revolution breaks, causing a million Mexicans to emigrate to the United States.

1944 The Bishops' Committee for the Spanish-speaking is created, setting a pattern of special ministries for Hispanics.

1945 A mass migration of Puerto Ricans to the mainland begins, eventually bringing 1.4 million people.

1959 The Cuban exodus begins, a migration that eventually brings 875,000 people to the United States.

1965 The Hispanic civil rights movement reaches its peak.

1970 The first Hispanic bishop, Patricio Flores, is ordained.

1972 Hispanics hold their first National Encuentro.

1977 The second National Encuentro.

1985 The third National Encuentro approves the outlines of a national pastoral plan for Hispanic ministry.

1987 The bishops approve the national pastoral plan for Hispanic ministry.

1989 The Hispanic population in the United States reaches twenty million.

SELECT BIBLIOGRAPHY

Acuña, Rodolfo. *Occupied America: A History of Chicanos* (2nd ed.). New York: Harper and Row, 1981.

Chavez, Fray Angelico. *My Penitente Land: Reflections on Spanish New Mexico*. Albuquerque: University of New Mexico Press, 1974.

—. *The Old Faith and Old Glory: the Story of the Church in New Mexico since the American Occupation (1843–1946).* Santa Fe, N. M.: Santa Fe Press, 1946.

Clark, Juan. *Why? The Cuban Exodus: Background, Evolution and Impact in U.S.A.* Miami: Union of Cubans in Exile, 1977.

Deck, Allan Figueroa. *The Second Wave: Hispanic Ministry and the Evangelization of Cultures.* New York: Paulist Press, 1989.

Dolan, Jay P. (ed.) *The American Catholic Parish: A History from 1850 to the Present,* 2 vols. New York: Paulist Press, 1987.

—. *The American Catholic Experience: A History from Colonial Times to the Present.* Garden City, N.Y.: Doubleday, 1985.

Dunne, John Gregory. *Delano: The Story of the California Grape Strike.* New York: Farrar, Strauss & Giroux, 1967.

Dussel, Enrique. *Historia General de La Iglesia en America Latina,* Vol. I/1, *Introducción General.* Salamanca: Sígueme, 1983.

Gamio, Manuel. *Mexican American Immigration to the United States, A Study of Human Migration and Adjustment.* New York: Dover Publications, 1971.

Gomez, David F. *Somos Chicanos: Strangers in Our Own Land.* Boston: Beacon Press, 1973.

Grebler, Leo, Joan W. Moore, Ralph C. Guzman. *The Mexican American People, the Nation's Second-Largest Minority.* New York: The Free Press, 1970.

Hennesey, James. *American Catholics: A History of the Roman Catholic Community in the United States.* New York: Oxford University Press, 1981.

Holland, Clifton L. *The Religious Dimension in Hispanic Los Angeles, a Protestant Case Study.* South Pasadena, CA: William Carey Library, 1974.

Hurtado, Juan. *Social Distance Between the Mexican American and the Church.* San Antonio: Mexican American Cultural Center, 1975.

McMurtrey, Martin. *Mariachi Bishop: The Life Story of Patrick Flores.* San Antonio: Corona Publishing Co., 1987.

Meier, Matt S. and Feliciano Rivera. *The Chicanos: A History of Mexican Americans.* New York: Hill and Wang, 1972.

Meyer, Jean A. *The Cristero Rebellion: The Mexican People Between Church and State 1926–1929.* London: Cambridge University Press, 1976.

Mosqueda, Lawrence J. *Chicanos, Catholicism and Political Ideology.* New York: University Press of America, 1986.

Perez, Arturo. *Popular Catholicism: A Hispanic Perspective.* Washington, D.C.: The Pastoral Press, 1988.

Puerto Ricans in the Continental United States: An Uncertain Future, a report of the U.S. Commission on Civil Rights, October 1976.

Romero, Juan, with Moises Sandoval. *Reluctant Dawn: Historia del Padre A. J. Martinez, Cura de Taos.* San Antonio: Mexican American Cultural Center, 1976.

Sandoval, Moises (ed.) *Fronteras: A History of the Latin American Church in the USA since 1513.* San Antonio, Texas: The Mexican American Cultural Center, 1983.

Stevens Arroyo, Antonio M. *Prophets Denied Honor, An Anthology on the Hispanic Church in the United States.* Maryknoll, N.Y.: Orbis, 1980.

Swadesh, Frances Leon. *Los Primeros Pobladores: Hispanic Americans of the Ute Frontier.* South Bend, Ind.: University of Notre Dame Press, 1974.

The Hispanic Community, the Church and the Northeast Center for Hispanics, a report by the Northeast Pastoral Center for Hispanics, New York, N.Y., 1982.

Weber, David J. (ed.) *Foreigners in Their Native Land: Historical Roots of the Mexican Americans.* Albuquerque: University of New Mexico Press.

Weigle, Marta. *The Penitentes of the Southwest.* Santa Fe, N.M.: Ancient City Press, 1970.

Chapter 14

THE CHURCH IN CENTRAL AMERICA

Rodolfo Cardenal

1. THE COLONIAL CHURCH

(a) The First Missions

The presence of the Church in Central America began with the conquest of the area and was dependent on the spread of colonization. The conquest of Central America was carried out from Mexico in the north and Darien (Panama) in the south, the former by Pedro de Alvarado beginning in 1523, the latter under Pedrarias Dávila, beginning in 1522. The military phase of the conquest was prolonged to 1540 on account of squabbles among the conquistadors themselves. After this date they set about organizing the territories and their conquered peoples into so-called Indian townships. Throughout the whole of the colonial period, however, they had to put down continual uprisings by the inhabitants of these townships.

So the presence and activity of the clergy was different before and after 1540 – with the exception of Costa Rica, which was not penetrated till 1542. The first priests, almost all secular, came with the conquistadors and devoted themselves to administering the sacraments to them and baptizing the natives *en masse*. They built the first churches in the first white settlements, persecuted the priests of the pre-hispanic native religions and burned their codices. They were paid a salary by the early town administrations, but also took advantage of the booty produced by the conquest.

Then the first Dominicans and Franciscans arrived, and began to denounce the abuses they saw. The secular clergy regarded these religious as intruders and enemies, since they were not interested in benefitting from the conquest, but only in preaching the faith to the natives and defending their rights.

The Dominicans were firmest in their opposition to the enslavement of the natives and the *encomienda* system, and firmest among them was Bartolomé de las Casas. Thanks to his denunciations and diplomatic representations, they succeeded temporarily in calling a halt to the activities of the conquistadors and early settlers. In 1542 they obtained the passage of the "New Laws" condemning slavery and *encomienda* and allowing the establishment of Indian townships, whose inhabitants were to be considered as subjects of the crown and therefore not obliged to work for the colonists. Their work was to be free. Within a decade, through the efforts of the Franciscans and Dominicans, eight hundred townships had been established throughout Central America. The process was a violent one owing to the determined opposition of the *encomenderos*. In it, the bishop of León, Fray Antonio de Valdivieso, lost his life, assassinated by the richest *encomenderos* on 26 February 1550. In the end, the colonists won, and succeeded in forcing the natives to work on their plantations

243

and construction projects, in their mines and mills. From then on the townships became redoubts of oppression, whose inhabitants lived in terror. When oppression overstepped the limits of tolerability and they managed to overcome their terror, they mutinied.

The end of the military phase and the New Laws opened up a new stage. The Franciscans and Dominicans founded convents in the more important white settlements, and from there extended their activities to the Indian townships, establishing distinct zones of influence for each order. The Franciscans founded convents in León (Nicaragua) in 1530, in Guatemala in 1539 and San Salvador in 1574. The Dominicans established their convent in Guatemala in 1529, one in San Salvador in 1551, and also had one in León. In 1535, reinforcements arrived from Nicaragua to missionize Verapaz, among them Bartolomé de las Casas. The Mercedarians arrived in 1537, and they and the Franciscans missionized Honduras; they set up the first convents there, in Comayagua, Tegucigalpa, Gracias, Tencoa and Choluteca toward the end of the sixteenth century. The Jesuits reached Guatemala in 1582, the Augustinians in 1610, the Brothers of St John of God in 1636 and the Oratorians in 1664.

Convents for women, all enclosed, were numerous in Guatemala, large and rich in property. The biggest was that of the Immaculate Conception, founded in 1578, where the richest nuns were to be found. In 1606, a group of nuns left there to found the convent of St Catherine Martyr, also in Guatemala. The Discalced Carmelites arrived in 1667 and the Poor Clares in 1700. Poor whites, *mestizas* and *mulattas* had their own special convents, known as *beaterios*, which depended on the donations of wealthy families for their upkeep. Nearly all these convents had magnificent buildings and churches, and vied with one another in splendour.

(b) Missions to "reduce" the Natives

Despite the time the conquest took, El Petén (the central mountainous region of Honduras), the Atlantic Coast of Honduras and Nicaragua, and Talamanca (Costa Rica) were not subdued. Many attempts were made in colonial times to conquer these mountainous, forested regions with their adverse climates, with missionaries in the forefront of these endeavours. The same procedure was followed everywhere: the missionaries went first, with armed guards to protect them; they made some conversions and settled their converts around little hermitages. Then the unconverted attacked the converts, spurred on by their traditional religious leaders, while the armed colonists provoked the natives. Eventually, all the natives allied themselves against the intruders, destroyed the settlement and killed anyone they found there. The colonists reacted by organizing a punitive expedition, capturing natives under the pretext that they had revolted. And so the cycle was closed until another group of missionaries decided to try again. . . .

The Franciscans in Honduras made special efforts to penetrate Taguzgalpa and the Mosquito Coast, though with little success. The human resources for these expeditions came from Guatemala. One of the missionaries recorded in Taguzgalpa was Esteban Verdelete, who undertook three expeditions and was thrice deceived by the natives, he and his twenty-eight companions finally being

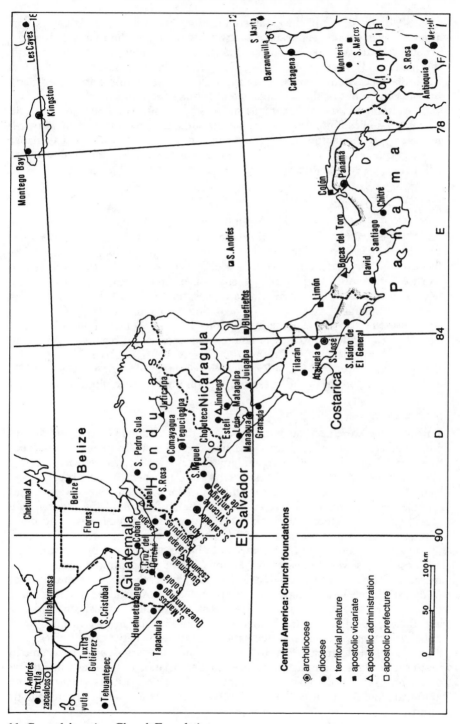

11. Central America: Church Foundations
Source: Piemme

ambushed and killed. In the eighteenth century, missions to the Atlantic Coast assumed even greater importance as a way of holding up the English advance – again with little success. Missionary failure was associated with failure to settle the natives. Between 1857 and 1864, the Claretian missionary Manuel Subirana succeeded in converting the Xicaque people of the Yoro department, bringing them out of the mountains and settling them in townships.

The Atlantic Coast of Nicaragua was neither conquered nor colonized, and so not missionized intensely either, despite some unsuccefsul attempts. English influence predominated in the region in the eighteenth century. Talamanca proved equally difficult mission territory, and as late as 1815 missionaries were still being driven out with sticks by the settlers.

(c) Church Organization

Cortés and Alvarado obtained the Bull establishing the diocese of Guatemala on 18 December 1534, covering the territories of Guatemala, Chiapas, Honduras and El Salvador, with Francisco Marroquín as its first bishop. The diocese was dependent first on the archdiocese of Seville, then on that of Mexico City from 1547. In 1538, Chiapas was dismembered when Cuidad Real became a diocese. Verapaz became a diocese in 1559, with Bartolomé de las Casas as bishop, but was once again taken into Guatemala in 1607. Guatemala was elevated to an archdiocese by Benedict XIV on 16 December 1742, with the dioceses of Ciudad Real, Comayagua and León as suffragans. León was in fact the oldest diocese, established by Clement VIII on 26 February 1531, taking in Nicaragua and Costa Rica, which was annexed to it on 9 March 1545, and dependent on the archdiocese of Lima till it was annexed into Guatemala.

(d) Preaching and Catechesis

Both activities were very much influenced by the situation in Europe. Preachers and catechists insisted on truths that had to be known in order to be saved; these were learned by endless repetition, till they were known by heart; this was enough to ensure salvation. These truths were reduced to basic prayers (the sign of the cross, the Our Father and Hail Mary, Creed, Salve Regina and Gloria), the ten commandments and the commandments of the Church, the sacraments, the virtues, the works of mercy and the capital sins. The more advanced were taught the meaning of the basic tenets of the Creed and sacred history. These and lives of the saints were much appreciated by the natives.

These truths were repeated in sermons, which concentrated more on the moralizing aspects, and in catechetical classes, in which they were memorized, using catechisms in question and answer form. Missioners and catechists made full use of the natives' creativity and imagination and their enthusiasm for dance and theatre. So they set the truths of faith and sacred history to music and dramatized them, often in free adaptations made by the natives themselves. The missionaries made great efforts to learn the native languages, so as to be able to teach the truths in them, facing up to serious translation difficulties when trying to convey Western theological concepts for which no vocabulary existed. The grammars and dictionaries they produced are still useful – a real tribute to their efforts.

A major part of these efforts was the establishment by the bishops and religious orders of centres of learning for teaching the sons of the remnant of pre-Hispanic nobility, particularly in Guatemala, Nicaragua and Honduras, followed by schools for the rest of the native population. Most attention, however, was concentrated on educating the sons of the colonists, the clergy and the members of the religious orders themselves. Girls were taught in the convents and *beaterios*. The Jesuits, Dominicans and Franciscans embarked on secondary education in their convents, and seminaries were opened in Guatemala and León. In 1676 the Pontifical University of San Carlos was opened, and the religious there taught native languages as well as theology.

The pastoral consequences of the Council of Trent and the "enlightened" reformism of the Bourbons made themselves felt in tendencies to "castilianize" the natives and hand parishes over to the secular clergy in the late eighteenth century. Learning of native languages was abandoned and the catechism taught in Spanish. The religious orders were pressurized into handing over their parishes, but they clung to the richer ones, while the secular clergy refused to take over the poorer ones. The net result was a decline in standards of preaching and catechesis, with the secular clergy showing little enthusiasm for building on the achievements of their predecessors. They scarcely moved from their parish centres, did not learn native languages and hardly even administered the sacraments. In the meanwhile, the religious retired to their huge convents in the cities.

(e) Final Results

By the end of the colonial era, the more clear-sighted bishops realized that evangelization had been virtually nil and at best superficial. One of the most important testimonies is that of Pedro Cortés y Larraz, bishop of Guatemala from 1768 to 1770, who left a clear description of the situation in his *Descripción Geográfico-moral de la Diócesis de Goathemala*. The natives who attended catechism classes only knew by rote "a brief formulation of the mysteries of the Trinity, Incarnation and eucharist, but nothing of faith, hope and charity." As a result, the bishop concluded that they were receiving the sacraments in "sacriligeous" conditions, since they knew nothing of what they were doing and were doing it only because they were forced to by bailiffs, town mayors and parish priests. "I can produce no other witnesses," he wrote "than my chaplains, who all or nearly all . . . show clearly and prove by examples and reasons that the Indians generally keep their old idolatries; that their Christianity is no more than appearance and hypocrisy; that the sacraments are adminstered to them because everyone does so, but in the knowledge that the prudent bases for persuading them to adminster and receive them worthily are lacking, that the Indians believe in nothing spiritual, nor in any life other than the present; that their confessions are no more than telling or denying what they please, without any disposition; that they receive communion absolved or without absolution. . . ."

Nevertheless, the native peoples had a great devotion to the saints. Churches were always well kept and provided with everything necessary for the liturgy, furnishings and adornments. But Bishop Cortés mistrusted these appearances, considering them "excessive outward worship," and concluding that "these wretches have no religion, because the Christian religion was established without regard to the laws of the gospel, baptizing first and then teaching, when it should have been the other way round . . . It was implanted contrary to the laws of the gospel, so no fruit can be expected of it." Parish priests told him how they found the natives burning resin in the hills and using the parish ornaments in their pagan rites: "It was certain that soothsayers, healers and witches existed." Those who dared to investigate or prevent these customs placed their lives in danger; the bishop had met several priests whose lives had been threatened in this way. Cortés was probably close to the truth when he wrote: "Among the Indians there is no church other than what suits their whims," a situation that parish priests accepted out of fear of the people. He saw the root of the problem elsewhere, however, not just in misconceived evangelization: "(The Indians) see the Spaniards and Spanish-speaking Indians as foreigners and usurpers of these lands, for which reason they regard them with implacable hatred and insofar as they obey them do so out of pure fear and servility. They want nothing from the Spaniards, neither religion, nor teaching, nor customs."

2. CLERICAL CONTRIBUTION TO NATIONHOOD

In the first half of the nineteenth century, the most important question for the life of the Church was the participation of the clergy in struggles for independence and their contribution to the setting up of nation states. Neither process could have come about without the clergy. Yet the second half of the century was taken up with conflicts between Church and state, since the latter could not tolerate the presence of a colonial Church. For the Church itself, this conflict was of less importance than its consequences.

(a) Clerical Participation in the Independence Movement

Many of the leaders of the independence movement were *criollo* priests. Curiously enough, the legitimacy of their participation in politics in this way was never questioned; furthermore, Central American states today ignore the fact that the clergy were basically largely responsible for their establishment as nations. The clergy took an active part in the Cortes of Cadiz in 1812, in conspiracies and uprisings, in ideological struggles, in university debate and in the political process that led to the emergence of nation states.

Two priests from Central America took part in the Cortes of Cadiz: the Guatemalan canon Antonio Larrázabal and Florencio del Castillo from Costa Rica. Both priests, but especially the former, acted as spokesmen for the complaints and claims of the *criollos*. Larrázabal asked, among other things, for the return of the Jesuits to engage in teaching, since the *criollos* were not satisfied with the current levels of education in Guatemala and wanted their children taught by the Jesuits. The Spaniards refused to accede to his request.

Later, priests took part in the four major conspiracies and uprisings preceding independence proper. The first of these took place in San Salvador in 1811–12. On 5 November 1811, the *criollos* of the city rebelled and succeeded in uprooting the colonial authorities and replacing them with *criollo* ones. Among the leaders of the uprising were the priests José Matías, Miguel Delgado and Nicolás, Manuel and Vicente Aguilar. There were also uprisings in other *criollo* cities, directed from San Salvador. In San Vicente, San Miguel and Sonsonate, however, the parish priests took a belligerent stance and attacked the uprising from their pulpits, demanding fidelity to Spain. The natives did not take part in these movements, often remaining on the sidelines deliberately. The movement did not succeed because those directing it from San Salvador feared that independence would slip out of their control. Archbishop Casaus y Torres sent missionaries to the province to preach against the insurgents and in favour of fidelity to the king. The second movement also took place in San Salvador, in 1814. Once again, its leaders took fright and opted for parleys to restore calm.

The third uprising took place in the province of Nicaragua. In December 1811, the *criollos* of León took to the streets and succeeded in replacing the city authorities. The friars Antonio Moñino and Tomás Ruiz, who had been conspiring in El Viejo since 1805, took part in this uprising. The bishop of León, Nicolás García Jerez, intervened with other priests to mediate and restore calm. Besides replacing the city authorities, the mutineers demanded a reduction of taxes and an end to the monopolies on tobacco and spirits, to which the bishop agreed. But as disorder in the streets continued, with demands for this agreement to be implemented, the bishop put together a *junta* of priests to replace the provincial authorities and proclaimed himself governor of the province.

On 22 December 1811, the *criollos* of Granada (Nicaragua) also demanded the replacement of their colonial authorities. Fr Benito Soto took part in the new *criollo* government. As their demands were not met, the inhabitants of Granada rebelled, and the governor-bishop of León sent troops to put down the rebellion. On 23 December, a similar uprising took place in Rivas. The parish priest of the town, whom the leaders of the movement recognized as their chief, agreed to all the petitions presented to him. These uprisings were put down by military force, and their leaders imprisoned, tried and sent to Guatemala.

The last major conspiracy of this time was in Belén, based on the Dominican convent of that name in Guatemala City, in 1813. The prior of the convent, Juan Nepomuneco de la Concepción, together with other brothers and priests, took part in the conspiracy, which did not last long, since it was betrayed in advance to the colonial authorities. Apparently, the conspirators planned to seize the authorities, including the archbishop, set the prisoners sent from Granada free, and capture money and arms.

Throughout this period, some members of the clergy took an active part in the debates surrounding the subject of independence. Canon José María Castilla debated the appropriateness of declaring independence and the characteristics of the nation state. He and the Dominican Matías de Córdova, together with Fr Fernando Antonio Dávila and Dean Antonio García Redondo from Colombia, put forward proposals for freeing the native peoples from the miserable state they were in through economic development and defended their rights as free citizens. Specifically, they proposed an end to all ethnic discrimination, recognizing that the Indians were the only ones who worked, while all the others were parasites. Later, they denounced *criollo* calumnies and prejudices against the Indians. They had all been parish priests among the Indians of the *altiplano*, and therefore spoke from personal experience.

In the university, another group of religious allowed the sons of the *criollos* to familiarize themselves with the ideas of the European Enlightenment, which then became an ideological basis for their aspirations and ambitions. Among this group, outstanding figures were the Franciscan José Antonio Liendo y Goicoechea and Francisco de Paula García Peláez, later (in 1844) archbishop of Guatemala, who defended Adam Smith's thesis in 1814 and wrote an interesting treatise on political economy, *Memorias para la historia del Antiguo Reyno de Guatemala*.

Criollo clergy were an active majority in the two provincial delegations (from Granada and León) set up to allow *criollos* to take part in the administration of the provinces. The delegation from Guatemala was almost entirely made up of priests, the only exception being the deputy from Sacatepéquez.

In the session that proclaimed the independence of Central America on 15 September 1821, the clergy played a decisive role, which is not surprising in view of their presence and activity in the events of the preceding years. Of the forty-nine notables invited to the session that was to decide what to do faced with a seemingly inevitable independence, seventeen were churchmen – an archbishop, a rector, a dean, canons, priests, religious. ... The Captain-General outlined the situation and asked what should be done. A first intervention proposed consulting the provinces; Archbishop Casaus immediately rose and declared his implacable opposition to independence. His intervention raised tempers and was followed by a series of speeches demanding immediate proclamation of independence, with clerical voices inevitably among these. As a result, it is not surprising to find clergy taking part in the process of constituting nation states. At first there were clergy delegates in the various federal and national assemblies which gave juridical form to the federal state and the five national states.

3. CHURCH-STATE CONFLICTS

After the failure of the plan to annex Central America to Mexico (1822–3) and with the formation of the Central American Federation in 1824 (which lasted till 1840), the national élites who held power began to modernize their states in accordance with the most advanced theories of the time. This required secularization of the state and its official separation from the Church. This process took place in two stages, the first taking place early and not lasting long, the second later and more lasting.

(a) The First Crisis

The first series of measures was begun in 1824, with the state deciding that bishops' pastoral letters would be subject to prior censorship, parish priests would be appointed by the Head of State and a poll tax imposed on the clergy. In 1826, the state decreed that illegitimate children had the right to inherit even if not included in a will, including the children of priests and nuns, reduced tithes by half, set a lower age limit on entry into convents, and forbade local religious superiors to communicate with their respective superior generals based in Spain.

When General Francisco Morazán seized Guatemala City in 1829, the second series of measures was introduced. Morazán pressured the ecclesiastical authorities into agreeing to withdraw parish priests hostile to his views and government. In June 1829, his government forced the archbishop to appoint José Antonio Alcayaga, a known adherent of Voltaire, a confirmed regalist and personal friend of the General, as vicar general. The following month, the government expelled the archbishop, the Franciscans, the Dominicans, the Recollects and some secular priests: 176 persons in all. Their properties were declared state property. The government also suppressed some religious feast days and banned professions in convents. All monasteries were suppressed, though the Bethlemites were allowed to remain as seculars. In December, the former convent churches were constituted parishes. During this period, a large quantity of money, furnishings and plate went missing from churches.

On 7 September 1830, the archbishop was declared a traitor and the existence of religious orders forbidden. In August the government expropriated all chaplaincies, seized all benefice funds and forbade the promulgation of papal bulls. In May 1832 the federal assembly, while recognizing Catholicism as the majority religion, decreed freedom of worship, gave the executive power to appoint officers to the metropolitan council and suppressed tithes. In February 1834 it instructed the civil authorites not to keep nuns who wanted to leave in their convents. In 1836 it authorized civil marriage and introduced divorce.

Surprisingly, some notable local clerics took part in this secularization process, some of them adopting even more radical positions than the lay politicians. The Honduran Francisco Antonio Márquez, for example, in the first constituent assembly of Central America (which produced the federal constitution), proposed the total secularization of the state, and later, as president of the national assembly of Honduras, defended the right of priests to civil marriage and the legitimacy of their children. Besides being president of the assembly, he was treasurer and vicar general of the Church in Honduras; he owned a mine, a mill and several houses, as well as having a number of children. Under his presidency, the assembly (which contained a number of other priests) approved civil marriage for priests in 1830, though the measure was repealed a year later. In 1834, children of priests were equated with natural children. These measures confused the parish clergy and were not accepted by the population at large, nor were funds available to enforce them, so the state was obliged to withdraw on various points.

In El Salvador the situation was rather different; once the *criollos* held state power they declared themselves the heirs of the royal patronage and used their privileges to nationalist ends. The politicians, with several priests among their number, established the diocese of El Salvador without canonical sanction and appointed its first bishop in 1822, not wanting to be dependent on Guatemala in ecclesiastical matters when they were independent of it politically. The assembly in fact thought of seeking papal approval, but the bishop nominated, José Matías Delgado, never one to lose an opportunity for self-advancement, took possession of the see immediately.

The archbishop of Guatemala reported the matter to Rome in October 1824. In December 1826, Pope Leo XII wrote to Delgado refusing to confirm his nomination. Delgado responded by sacking more than fifty parish priests who would not recognize him as legitimate bishop. Leaflets and pamphlets attacking his actions in terms laden with biblical and patristic insults circulated among the clergy; the faithful did not accept him, and his position became untenable. The federal government did not support the government of El Salvador in the matter, fearing that Costa Rica and Honduras would follow its example, and taking the stand that it did not interfere in the religion of the people. In July 1825, however, it agreed to ask for canonical approval of the diocese, but this was never done owing to bureaucratic intrigues and the outbreak of war. After Morazán had seized Guatemala and expelled its archbishop, Delgado continued to administer the ecclesiastical province of El Salvador, but in his capacity as parish priest and vicar general. The schism died of inanition.

The assembly of Costa Rica did in fact set up its own diocese in 1825, but this had no similar consequences, since it could not find a priest willing to act as its bishop. Twenty-five years later, Pius IX canonically established the diocese of Costa Rica and appointed Anselmo Llorente y Fuente as its first bishop.

(b) Consequences

This first conflict affected the internal organization of the Church, causing the local churches to share in the instability affecting the region at the time. Rome, caught up in its European commitments and very distant, could not intervene. Normality was restored when officially Catholic governments came to power and signed concordats with the Holy See guaranteeing the status of the Church.

Since the expulsion of Archbishop Casaus, the metropolitan see of Guatemala remained vacant till the diplomatic envoy of Guatemala, El Salvador and Honduras persuaded the Holy See to nominate Francisco de Paula García Peláez archbishop in 1842. Relations with the state were normalized with the new government disposed to recognize Catholicism as the official religion. The Jesuits returned to take charge of the seminary; Paulist fathers came to do educational work, and the Franciscans, Dominicans, Recollects, Capuchins and Oratorians also returned, together with various contemplative orders of nuns and the Daughters of Charity. This process culminated on 7 October 1852, when the state signed a concordat with the Holy See.

In Honduras and El Salvador, the situation was rather more complicated. The Honduran see of Comayagua had been vacant since the late eighteenth century. When bishop Cardinaños died, his successor Navas delayed five years before presenting himself, dying shortly after taking possession; his successor Rodríguez del Barranco waited for seven years for his bull of appointment to reach Guatemala and also died shortly after taking possession, and the next bishop never even reached the see. This was the situation when further events led to the outlawing of the vicar general José Nicolás Irías: annoyed by the secularizing tendencies of the state, he denounced the gatherings held in Tegucigalpa as freemasonic and against religion, while his brother called the legitimacy of the state into question and demanded new elections. With both brothers trying to prevent the establishment of a nation state as being contrary to their views, the ecclesiastical authority was in turn accused of conspiring against the state; Irías excommunicated the Head of State, who responded by outlawing him. He then placed himself at the head of an armed uprising, which went in his favour till Morazán intervened and forced him out of Honduras; he went on claiming his rights from exile for a number of years, during which the see remained vacant and parish priests acquired more power. Finally, Francisco de Paula Campoy y Pérez was appointed bishop of Comayagua.

The canonical establishment of the diocese of El Salvador and the appointment of its first bishop did not suffice to quell fresh ecclesial crises. It was in fact the government of El Salvador that initiated the canonical process; in April 1841, Fr Jorge Viteri y Ungo was appointed envoy to the Holy See; Gregory XVI signed the bull establishing the diocese in September 1842 and Viteri was selected as its first bishop in February 1843. He, however, proved a bad solution, as his intrigues and conspiracies obliged him to leave the diocese very shortly. At the end of 1843 he publicly sued the government over some measures that had displeaed him, organized street protests and conspired with General Malespín to depose the Head of State. Malespín took his place and the bishop manipulated his government at will, until it declared itself officially Catholic. But the alliance did not last long: in February 1845, the bishop excommunicated Malespín for killing one priest and humiliating another in León, where he was trying to gain control. The bishop prevented the general from returning to the country, and in July 1846 tried to depose him, but this time his manipulations were exposed and he was forced to abandon his see. Exiled, he sought Malespín's help in defeating the government forces; the general died in the attempt, and Viteri remained in León, and was nominated to the see in November 1849, after it had been vacant for twenty years. He died on 25 July 1853, probably poisoned by his political enemies.

His successor in El Salvador, Tomás Pineda y Zaldaña (1853–75) was also exiled, expelled by the government of General Gerardo Barrios. The bishop had protested against certain public attacks on religion, to which Barrios responded by forcing the clergy to swear an oath of allegiance to the state; the bishop refused them permission to do this, and was exiled in November 1861, along with a number of priests who also refused to swear. The situation was resolved with the signing of a concordat in April 1862, which authorized the oath subject to amendments to its text which safeguarded the freedom of the Church.

Concordats seemed a good solution at the time in Guatemala and El Salvador. Nicaragua, where Morazán's decrees had scattered the clergy and produced the long vacancy in León, signed a concordat (which was to remain in force for thirty years) on 2 November 1861. Costa Rica, where reforms had been carried out by Braulio Carrillo between 1838 and 1842, had signed its concordat on 7 October 1852. In these concordats, the governments recognized Catholicism as the official religion of the state and gave the bishops the right to oversee education and impose censorship. The state, for its part, undertook to protect religion, to recognize the rights of the Church, and to support the bishop, his diocesan curia, the seminary and parish priests economically. In exchange, the Church granted the state the right to present candidates for bishoprics and curial posts, and agreed to act in common accord with the state in setting up new dioceses and parishes. Furthermore, the Church renounced its claim to church property that had been nationalized or confiscated by the state.

The see of Costa Rica fell vacant in 1858, eight years after its establishment, when bishop Llorente was expelled. In 1852, taking advantage of a rise in the price of coffee, he had tried to reinstitute tithes, suppressed some years earlier, for which the Church had been indemnified. The government refused. In 1853, he imprudently tried to attach the title "pontifical" to the University of St Thomas. Finally, the government expelled him in December 1858, but he was back in August 1859, recalled by a new government which included relations of his. On his death in 1871, the president tried to use his right to present a successor, but his nomination was not accepted by the Holy See. The president then blocked the papal nominee, and the see remained vacant till 1880, when Bernardo Augusto Thiel was agreed as bishop.

(c) The Great Liberal Crisis

In the 1870s the new coffee barons violently seized control of the state and determined to modernize it by total secularization: freedom of worship, civil marriage, divorce, secular civil registers, cemeteries and education, freedom of the Press, suppression of all religious orders, including contemplatives, and abolition of church privileges. These changes were very radical in Guatemala, less so in Honduras and El Salvador, and much gentler in Costa Rica and Nicaragua, though preceded by an aggressive anti-clerical campaign in all countries.

In Guatemala, Justo Rufino Barrios began by expelling the Jesuits, first from Quezaltenango and then from Guatemala City, in September 1871, expelling seventy-six of them in all. In October he expelled Archbishop Bernardo Piñol y Aycinena and his auxiliary bishop; in December he suppressed tithes. In 1872 the government forbade the return of the Jesuits in perpetuity and nationalized their property, prohibited the wearing of clerical dress, suppressed all the religious communities and confiscated their goods. The wealth thus acquired formed the funds of the new national bank.

In February 1874, all religious communities in Guatemala were reduced to one in the convent of Santa Catalina, new religious professions were forbidden and nuns were offered "escape" from their orders. The government tolerated only the Daughters of Charity, since their hospital work was irreplaceable. It prohibited religious worship outside churches, suppressed religious education in state schools, cancelled all religious privileges, prevented the clergy from inheriting, discounted religious vows and secularized the university of San Carlos. The Constitution of 1879, which remained in force to 1944, included and regularized all these measures.

When the archbishop died in Havana, without formally annulling the concordat of 1852, the government and the Holy See signed a new agreement, by which the Church accepted the reforms, while the state accorded it freedom of action and an annual sum of thirty thousand dollars for its maintenance. The Church was still obliged to consult it over the appointment of bishops and chapter officials. Barrios' successor, General Manuel Lisandro Barilla, broke this agreement by forbidding the clergy entry into the country in 1887, obliging priests to perform military service and imposing censorship on the church hierarchy. Archbishop Ricardo Casanova y Estrada was expelled from the country for protesting in 1886, but returned under a general amnesty in 1897.

After that there were no more conflicts till 1919. In December of that year,

Archbishop José Piñol y Batres became the mouthpiece for the opposition to the dictatorship of Estrada Cabrera (1898–1920) through a series of sermons he preached in the church of St Francis in the capital, for which he was imprisoned and then exiled. The sermons, however, had lit the spark that led to the dictator's overthrow. His successor, General José María Orellana, renewed the anti-clerical campaigns and once again exiled the archbishop in September 1921. He died in exile in 1927.

In El Salvador, the coffee barons took control of the state in April 1871. The constituent assembly that year still included six priests as deputies, including the bishop-elect. These lost their first battle when the assembly refused to accept the Jesuits expelled from Guatemala into the country. In October they lost the next, over the constitution that enshrined various reforms typical of the time. Successive constitutions further defined the juridical status of the clergy and the Church, culminating in that of 1886, which remained in force to 1944. The church authorities tried to defend themselves through the Press, but in vain. In 1872, on the pretext of an internal uprising, the government expelled the few remaining Jesuits and Bishop Ortiz Urruela, followed by three parish priests and the eighteen Capuchins left in the Convent of Santa Tecla.

After another uprising, in San Miguel, early in 1875, the government expelled Bishop Cárcamo, and the treasurer and vicar general and a canon in June, followed by the ecclesiatical governor, another canon and three parish priests later in the year. On the death of Bishop Zaldaña in August, the see remained vacant. To put pressure on the government, Bishop Cárcamo tried to govern the diocese from Chinandega in Nicaragua, finally succeeding in nominating a vicar general and returning to the country in 1876 at the invitation of the government. His invitation was due to the need to unite the country in the face of imminent war with Guatemala. The bishop and the clergy immediately fell to the task of promoting national unity and supported the government in its military campaign. This led to an understanding which lasted almost into the 1960s.

In Nicaragua, changes were late and superficial. The Jesuits who had come into the country after being expelled from Guatemala in 1871 were expelled from Nicaragua too in 1881, falsely accused of taking part in the popular uprising in Matagalpa. During the decade they spent in the country, they concentrated on training their own personnel and preaching missions among the people. The 1893 constitution brought about separation of Church and state, annulling the concordat of 1862, and introduced other reforms characteristic of such liberal documents. Verbal protests from the clergy led to the expulsion of Bishop Simeón Pereira y Castellón and some religious congregations in 1904. In 1909 a change of government brought about better relations, though the reforms were enshrined in the constitution of 1911.

In Honduras, changes were introduced by Marco Aurelio Soto, Ramón Rosas and Fr Antonio Vallejo. Liberal reforms were codified in the constitution of 1880. One of the stipulations was that foreigners could not hold church office, but the archbishop (Agustín Hombach) was of German extraction. Relations with the state improved when Manuel Francisco Vélez, a friend and companion of Rosas, was elected bishop in 1888.

Under pressure from Guatemala, the Jesuits and Bishop Thiel were expelled from Costa Rica in 1882. Liberal reforms were promulgated in 1884 and the concordat of 1852 annulled. Nevertheless, the state continued to support the Church financially. Bishop Thiel found himself isolated in his struggles against the reforms, since the clergy were indifferent to them and failed to support him. This strange attitude was apparently brought about by deep divisions produced during the years the see had remained vacant, and the fact that many clerics did not recognize the new bishop. He was allowed back in 1886 and immediately plunged into polemics over education.

The importance of these end-of-century crises should not be exaggerated: often referred to as persecutions, they affected only the church institution, not its basic Christian mission, and their decisive outcome was the later understanding reached between Church and state. The Church was attacked for defending its institutional character and its privileges, not for preaching the faith directly, let alone for working for justice. The Church kept a complete silence in the face of the social and economic reforms introduced by the coffee barons, which directly affected the peasants and the natives. The Church saw its traditional institutional character as basic to its mission, while the state, concerned with its process of modernization, could not tolerate the Church's traditional position. The Church clung to the idea that official recognition and protection were essential, lacking the imagination to redefine its mission independently from the state. This was what brought the crisis about; its main outcome was to leave the Church compromised with the established order for decades to come.

In a vain effort to recover its old position, the Church offered itself to the state as the most effective agent for controlling the rural population. The state, for its part, needed the Church to confer the legitimacy it sought. For these reasons, the separation between Church and state was more one of form than content. It meant that the state gained control over the Church, which then became its ally in upholding the established social order. Conservative by temperament and anxious to recover its former influence and privileges, the Church fell into temptation and became, together with the military, one of the major props of the oligarchic social order imposed by the coffee barons, a state of affairs that lasted till the mid twentieth century.

4. A NEW ELEMENT IN THE CHURCH

The churches of Central America have now introduced a new element, relative in scale, but nonetheless authentic and sealed with persecution and martyrdom. This new element is the introduction of the notion of salvation in history into evangelization. It has preached the Kingdom of God for the poor and the closeness of God as Father to the hearts of the poor and oppressed. Major consequences have stemmed from this concept: first, evangelization has been extended to cover all that makes the goodness of God present in words and deeds to the poor; second, evangelizing means denouncing social as well as personal sin; third, this proclamation requires specific credibility on the part of the evangelizers.

This "preferential option for the poor," as Mgr Oscar Romero said, consists in defending the minimum which is God's maximum: life itself. It has made the Church exert a positive influence on society: that is, the Church has introduced the Christian leaven into struggles for justice and peace. This in itself has made this new element conflictual, by changing the signals that came from its traditional role. Differences in society and the Church come not from theoretical questions, but from the attitude to be taken toward the poor and the right to life. Each of the churches in Central America has made this option in the course of the present century, each in its own way, so for the sake of clarity the historical journey taken by each needs to be examined separately.

(a) Costa Rica: on the Fringe of Church Renewal

In terms of church building, mass attendance and formalistic morality, the people of Costa Rica are very religious. The Church's mission has been seen in anti-communist terms, as was proved in the banana strikes of the first two decades of the century.

The most notable initiative taken by the Church was in the 1940s, when Archbishop Víctor Sanabria collaborated with President Rafael Calderón in building the welfare state that has characterized social life in Costa Rica. Calderón needed the support of the Church and of the communist party to carry his reforms through. Such a consensus was possible because all parties were agreed on the need to improve the lot of the workers. The right-wing was quick to react against the archbishop; not even his archdiocesan clergy supported him. The liberals were those who made the loudest protests. According to the archbishop, they had never sought a dialogue with the Church and had simply used its anti-communist stance to further their own interests. The archbishop's support for the government was rewarded in 1942 with the suppression of the liberal decrees of 1884.

In support of the presidential reforms and as part of the Church's mission, the archbishop set up a Catholic trade union movement to parallel the communist party one. When the "labour code" was promulgated in September 1943, he inaugurated the "Rerum Novarum Union Centre," which grew rapidly, till it had 102 unions under its umbrella by the end of the year. But lack of direction caused the experiment to wither fast, and rivalry between the Catholic and communist movements sharpened between 1945 and 1948. In the civil war of 1948, the Catholic union centre sided with the traditional oligarchy and liberal reformism against the government, social Christian movements and the communists. The oligarchy saw their objective as overthrowing a supposedly communist government that had arbitrarily annulled elections which it had lost. When "National Liberation" triumphed in July 1948 it suppressed the communist party and its union centre. The new government kept up social reforms and consolidated the welfare state, but the Catholic union movement died of inanition.

When Mgr Sanabria died in 1952, the archdiocese lost its renewal impetus and fell back on a triumphalist pastoral stance of "neo-Christendom." Priests most sympathetic to reform were removed from the capital and emphasis was placed on developing Catholic movements focussed on internal church affairs, such as Catholic Action. Interest was concentrated once more on the subjects of Protestantism, communism and education. The Church installed itself cosily alongside middle class interests without playing a part in changing society.

Except for a few isolated personal examples, the Church in Costa Rica remained on the fringes of the ecclesial renewal undertaken at Vatican II and the Medellín Conference. It was generally agreed that all the Council meant was the altar facing the people and saying mass in Spanish. The explanation of this remarkable interpretation lies in the authoritarian and conservative approach of Archbishop Carlos Rodríguez and the secular clergy, whose training and spiritual formation prevented them from seeing any farther. The clergy, mostly native Costa Ricans and relatively numerous for the population, have been distinguished by their lack of intellectual vigour. They have also suffered a deep process of "bourgeoisification," favoured by the inclusion of religious instruction in state education curricula. Classes in religious education became their main source of recruits, and the education of the adult laity in parishes was relegated to a secondary concern. Some priests became expert mediators between parish needs and the welfare state, which on a higher level meant close collaboration between state and Church, with the benefits flowing from the former reaching the people. Religious orders, whose numbers have grown since 1950, have not changed the picture, concentrating almost entirely on educating the urban children of fee-paying parents.

All later attempts at renewal have failed, with most of the clergy accepting the myth that there are no social problems in the country. The few priests and movements concerned with social questions have generally been isolated and silenced. By the end of the 1970s, only a small group working in the banana plantations and among the so-called "precarious" understood the faith as commitment in solidarity with the poorest.

Set in a context that kept the country outside the conflicts typical of other Central American countries in the 1980s, the Church in Costa Rica has not undergone significant experiences of renewal. With the exception of Mgr Coto Mongo, notable for his support for base church communities and his denunciation of the social injustices brought about by international banana companies, the Bishops' Conference has remained substantially allied to the social democrat governments, supporting their "welfare state" policies and giving charitable aid to alleviate the effects of economic crises. With the accession of President Calderón in 1990, the bishops began to distance themselves more from the executive, criticizing his neo-liberal policies.

(b) Honduras: to the Brink of Persecution

Up to 1916, Honduras, with rather more than 112,000 square kilometres, was a single diocese. After 1921, it suffered from vacant sees, and when they were occupied, from unsuitable occupants. This was caused by a mixture of state interference, interventions by nuncios and lack of good candidates. In 1921 it proved difficult to find a successor to Mgr Martínez Cabañas, who had been bishop of Tegucigalpa and Comayagua since 1902; the same was true of a successor to Mgr Agustín Hombach, bishop from 1923 to 1933, since the dictator Carías tried to have a friend of his appointed. In 1943, Rome nominated José de la Cruz Turcios, who had to wait until Carías died in 1946 to occupy the see (by then an archdiocese), and then showed no interest in church leadership or administration. To fill this *de facto* vacancy, Mgr Evelio Domínguez was appointed auxiliary bishop in 1957, but he retired to a rural parish four years later. In 1962, the nuncio forced the archbishop to retire and appointed Mgr Héctor Santos in his place. The diocese of Santa Rosa de Copán has experienced similar problems.

Another feature of the Church in Honduras has been the lack of native secular clergy. The few there were worked disjointedly during the long crises of leadership at diocesan level. The lack was partly made up by an influx of religious from overseas: Franciscans and Jesuits from the United States, Passionists from Spain and missionaries from French Canada. In two decades, the number of priests doubled, and the foreign religious orders supplied money, too, which was used to address the two great problems facing the Catholic Church: the expansion of Protestantism and communism, the latter in particular in the wake of the great banana strike of 1954.

During nine months of 1959, a group of twenty-five missionaries, integrated into a team known as the Holy Mission, preached and adminstered the sacraments throughout the country. In the South, they made a tremendous impact, and revitalized old religious organizations. The religious revival was cemented in 1965 in the movement of "delegates of the Word" in the department of Choluteca; the scheme later spread to Nicaragua and El Salvador.

Alongside the delegates movement, a Catholic radio station opened in 1959 in order to transmit a programme of religious education borrowed from Radio Sutatenza in Colombia. The results were rapid and surprising: in 1962, it had 343 "schools" with 7,250 students; by 1964 the numbers had jumped to 754 schools with 14,624 students. This success was due in large part to the fact that the schools were inserted into traditional religious organization based on the parish. The delegates of the word and the radio schools moved out into the field of rural development, committing the Church to work to overcome underdevelopment.

The need for greater financial and technical resources led the Church to make a public and formal commitment, in the creation of Popular Cultural Action of Honduras, which was managed by professionals from 1960. Local movements sprang up in the countryside, sometimes embracing whole communities, and rural workers experienced a new type of Christianity concerned with social relationships, whose strength made community development projects possible.

The radio station soon abandoned the Colombian material in favour of more radical programmes based on Brazilian examples. "Popular advancement" created a network of organizations to facilitate the participation of the rural poor in political processes. Starting with committees for community development, it moved on to set up savings and loan cooperatives and even consumption and production cooperatives, which came to take the place of schools and religious activities. More than ninety of these were organized into the Federation of Savings and Loan Cooperatives of Honduras between 1964 and 1968. In 1967, the bishops reorganized Caritas as a developmental organization; by 1971 its most important programme, the "housewives club," had more than seven hundred branches. Parish priests felt able to take part in such development programmes, which were financed largely by overseas agencies, one of which, AID, forced the programmes to become independent of the hierarchy. The latter had no alternative but to accept this, having no other funds of its own. By the end of the 1970s, the umbrella organization, the Social Christian movement, had grown to a point where neither the hierarchy nor the clergy formed part of the decision-making process.

The movement became radicalized with the land disputes which began in the south of the country in 1969, when the rural unions seized land for the workers. The social Christian infrastructure lent its support to the organized peasants, drawing the opposition of the landlords. The bishop of Cholutega at first defended the right of the peasants to seize land belonging to the government, and to agrarian reform, but when pressure increased, the clergy of the diocese dissociated themselves from the popular movement they had helped to mould. In the diocese of Olancho, events were later and more violent, with the landowners forewarned of the intentions of the peasant movements. Threats were made against the bishop, and in June 1975 two foreign priests were assassinated along with some twenty peasants. The army occupied churches and threw pastoral workers, including the bishop, out of the diocese.

The hierarchy distanced itself publicly from the peasant organizations, denounced violence as a solution and refused to support land seizures. The clergy and bishops then concentrated on the urban middle classes, who enthusiastically welcomed back a repentant church frightened by its recent adventure, and ready to find a comfortable refuge in an a-political and neutral stance in relation to social conflict. The bishops orderd the clergy not to support rural development programmes, and in 1974 closed down Caritas, the radiophonic schools and the development centres.

Assimilation of Medellín was seen at its best in the "Celebrants of the Word" movement and the promotion of peasant organizations, halted in 1975 by the massacre at Los Horcones, in which fifteen persons died, including two religious. In the 1980s the Church denounced human rights abuses with increasing vigour; in many parishes, organs of "juridical aid" made their appearance, while many parish priests in rural areas were threatened by the armed forces. Since the signing of Esquipulas II Agreement for peace in the region, the bishops have criticized the presence of U.S. military bases and anti-Sandinista *contra* forces in the country, and in 1989 they declared their opposition to the free market policies of President Callejas.

(c) Guatemala: between Terror and Hope

After the liberal reforms of the 1850s, Church and clergy remained under liberal control for seventy-five years, with the clergy reduced to 119 priests, most of them concentrated in the capital. Popular and indigenous religiosity was forced more and more back on "custom," which combined Catholic practices with pre-Hispanic survivals and colonial traditions, while the Spanish-speakers lost interest in organized religion. Some small changes took place under the dictatorship of Jorge Ubico, such as the return of the Jesuits to take charge of the national seminary in 1936, followed by the Marist, Salesian and Maryknoll Fathers. Ubico allowed the religious orders to open schools for the urban upper classes, mostly in the capital. More foreign religious and secular priests arrived over the next two decades.

The foreign clergy, mostly pre-conciliar in outlook, soon outnumbered the native. Some of them took over native parishes abandoned for decades, and on seeing the reality of the villages and townships realized that they had to help in their development. Foremost among these were priests from the United States and Europe, who obtained financial support from their dioceses and congregations back home, above all from German bishops and their agencies. The U.S. priests clandestinely channelled money from government agencies, with AID regarding them as suitable agents of development and the CIA using them as sources of information. The growth in numbers of the clergy allowed new dioceses to be created, thereby diminishing the immense power of the archbishop. It also created a division between foreign and native clergy, forcing nationalism and conservatism to rear their heads; by 1975, the government, with the connivance of the bishops, was expelling priests devoted to promoting the development of the indigenous communities.

Catholic Action was especially promoted in native parishes, and unlike in other Central American countries, became a means of renewal through its catechists. This brought the young, formed by the catechists, up against the adults, faithful to "custom." Besides Catholic Action, US priests in Huehuetenango and Sololá established a network of radiophonic workshops, as did the Belgian priests in Chiquimula; working with nuns, both groups also set up savings and credit cooperatives in their parishes. After Vatican II and Medellín, major pastoral initiatives were launched, with the "delegates of the Word" movement and "indigenist" pastoral strategy, which, without any very clear objectives, succeeded in politicizing the native communities.

In the cities, most effort was concentrated on the upper classes, to hold off the liberals. Sections of Catholic Action were influential among students, professional and married people, but Opus Dei has been gaining most ground among these since 1953. There is less interest here in questions of economic development and social reform than in the country parishes, and most parishes are happy to administer the sacraments and promote pious associations, though many run their own school and health centre.

Politically, the Catholic Church in Guatemala has been reactionary. During the 1944 revolution, the hierarchy aligned itself with the opposition to the reforming government of the time and actively collaborated with the counter-revolutionary forces, contributing anti-communist propaganda. In 1956, after the triumph of the National Liberation Movement, the Church regained some of the privileges it had lost in liberal times. At the end of the 1960s, the hierarchy kept quiet while the army, backed by the United States, flattened towns and villages in a counter-insurgency campaign. A group of university students, led by Maryknoll missionaries, however, questioned the hierarchy's attitude and in late 1966 decided to form a Christian-inspired guerrilla movement. The Maryknoll fathers were expelled and the students fled to Mexico. In 1971, various Christian groups, including some priests and even bishops, publicly demanded the return to a legal state; the foreigners were expelled and the nationals threatened, with the bishop of Verapaz being forced to leave the country temporarily. Under the counter-insurgency scheme, all those who supported community development were considered communists and enemies of society. The government called the bishops to account for the activities of their priests. Most of the priests assassinated since 1975 had spent long years working in the field of community development.

The earthquake of 1976 showed up the lack of clarity in the Church: most church people saw aid to the victims as an act of charity, while some made it a way of acting in solidarity with the poorest. These dissidents organized themselves into the so-called Christian Committee. After the earthquake, the workers demanded the right to organize into unions, and higher wages; the peasants demanded land, organization and better working conditions, especially for those who had migrated from the high plateau to the southern coast. Priests and religious took part in all these struggles; indeed many of them were made possible through their social and community development projects.

Persecution and martyrdom were soon part of the repression carried out against popular movements. In November 1976 the Maryknoll missionary William Woods, who had worked in the jungle region of Huehuetenango for seven years, was assassinated. In June 1978 the parish priest of San José Pinula was machine-gunned to death. In May 1980 the Filipino parish priest of Tiquisate was kidnapped, never to reappear. A Belgian religious was killed in the same month, and in June a Spanish missionary was shot in the back in El Quiché, where many catechists had been taken out of their homes and shot; he was followed by another Spanish religious who had been a parish priest in El Quiché for fifteen years. At the same time the government was using the media to attack the Jesuits for their protests against this repression and persecution. The peaceful occupants of the Spanish embassy were killed in late July 1980. Yet another Spanish religious was killed in February 1981; the parish priest of Tecpán was shot in his sacristy in May, and in July, September and the following February, three United States missionaries, Stanley Rother, John Troyer and James Miller were all killed. The bishops were divided in the face of this persecution, with most of them remaining silent.

In the 1980s the Church experienced at first hand the repression unleashed on the population as a whole. Hundreds of pastoral agents and some ten priests fell victim to the "death squads" and the army. The Church's actions have been distinguished by defence of human rights, a quest for deep social change and efforts to achieve peace. Particularly significant were the bishops' 1988 pastoral letter "The Clamour for Land," which underscored the urgency of land reform, and Mgr Quezada Toruño's mediation in negotiations between the government and the guerrillas. Meanwhile, the spread of the sects led to the election of Latin America's first evangelical president, Jorge Serrano, in 1990.

(d) El Salvador: Witness to Faith and Justice

The Church emerged from its alliance with the state traditional in outlook and lacking in leadership or any defined pastoral strategy (with the continued exception of the archdiocese of San Salvador). These characteristics made it a negative social influence, supporting the status quo. This traditional Church, which still persists in the majority of the country's dioceses, has been more concerned with Protestantism and communism than with the actual state of affairs. Its pastoral approach has been limited to administering the sacraments, with the exception of a few timid attempts at *aggiornamento* under charismatic influence. Nevertheless, there have always been groups of priests and religious ready to follow the way mapped out by Vatican II and Medellín. Such groups have had to come together and work without the support of the hierarchy, and often in open opposition to them. In general, the Church has been marked by its failure to respond the the renewal currents of the 1960s.

The archdiocese of San Salvador, however, has been definitively stamped by the long rule of Mgr Luis Chávez, archbishop from 1939 to 1977, who was close to the people in his pastoral work, open-minded and not fearful of new ideas, initiating a number of projects to bring the archdiocese up to date. At first he promoted Catholic Action, but later encouraged cooperatives and a social secretariat. He supported the development of communications media and looked after the educational needs of the poorest through a network of parish schools. He had been accused of being a communist as early as 1937; at the end of his life the accusations and threats multiplied, particularly when he placed the institutional weight of the Church on the side of justice and the poor. He gave the Church a presence in all the crises affecting the country since 1939.

Vatican II went unnoticed till Medellín. But the options taken at Medellín shook Salvadorean society, forcing people to look back to the Council for foundations for the new directions. Centres for peasant advancement were started at each end of the country, with the pastoral experiments carried out in the parishes of Suchtoto, Tecoluca and Aguilares influencing the archdiocese, and being translated to the suburbs of the capital. A mobile pastoral team broke the traditional sacramentalist pattern, and celebration of the word took the place of parish mass, with the result that mass attendance and reception of the sacraments declined markedly, to the considerable disquiet of the clergy, supported by other bishops, who saw the breakdown of traditional patterns as a major crisis.

From 1970 on, the archdiocese made a great effort to work out a consistent pastoral approach. After the failure of the first national "pastoral week" owing to its blockade and condemnation by the other bishops, the archdiocese organized its own week in 1976. Here the new pastoral experiments were examined and the conclusion drawn that evangelization had to be intensified, paying special attention to adapting popular religiosity to the requirements of liberation, through empowering local communities, training their pastoral agents and promoting the integral liberation of all Salvadoreans.

This line, backed by the personal prestige, first of Mgr Chávez and then of Mgr Romero, united the clergy, sometimes in most impressive ways. The archdiocesan clergy became a major social force; the people identified with them and felt that this church was their own. A new way of being church and priest made itself felt. Nuns abandoned their fee-paying convents and took charge of rural and suburban parishes without priests, where they set up base communities and trained pastoral agents. This brought them into direct contact with the real state of affairs in the country: communicating this back to their congregations brought about a new understanding of their mission. Among male religious congregations, change has been more patchy, with the exception of the Jesuits and others devoted to parish work, where it has been rapid. Since 1980, all religious, particularly women, have done brave and irreplaceable work in humanizing the war and looking after refugees.

Celebration of the word took root unstoppably in the rural communities, awakening community consciousness among the peasants. Mass attendance rose, as did reception of the sacraments. Increasing numbers of short courses gave the peasants a theoretical framework for understanding the social structure of poverty and oppression. Preaching and the "delegates of the word" movement produced a structural, demythified and even rigorous understanding of social reality and the possibility of seeing the dynamic of history in terms of class struggle. Religious and social categories, such as exploitation and violence, became interchangeable, till there was open talk of the class struggle, a decisive step in accepting the analyses made.

Peasant organizations spread rapidly between 1972 and 1975, and then joined up with urban groups; the two together occupied city streets. The ruling oligarchy rushed to magic away the danger through military deployment, enlarging spy networks, imprisonment, kidnappings, torture and assassinations. This repression only had the effect of strengthening the popular movement. Pastoral work prepared the way for peasant organization; once established, this used parish structures to spread and consolidate, which meant that it became difficult to see where the church ended and the organization began. Despite this, the archdiocese did its best to see that repression did not fall on the organized peasants.

The leaders of the organization were clearly influenced by the gospel, which gave them a desire to give their lives for others. Peasant organization originally had a basically Christian mystique: this became Christian-revolutionary, and then revolutionary-Christian, each stage bringing about a crisis of development in both the parishes and in the organization, which had to cope with its own autonomy. Gospel and mystique led to organizational growth; organizational euphoria and mystique grew as the organization made its power felt against the ruling classes. Peasants went through a sort of political conversion process as they moved out of parish structures and into organizational ones.

Mgr Romero took on the mantle of Mgr Chávez in 1977 amidst general uncertainty, since he was known as a bishop of the traditional Church, but his spiritual uprightness and the harshening of the persecution at the time he took office proved more powerful than his traditional patterns of thought. Unexpectedly, he reinforced Mgr Chávez's approach, and during his three years of office became the Christian conscience of the nation, criticizing the injustice and violence produced by the ruling structures and giving hope and strength to the poor masses. His actions went far beyond normal church boundaries and he became a powerful social influence, with his Sunday homilies attracting more listeners than any other radio programme. Without wishing to, he became the centre of the country's life, appealed to by all socially-minded groups during the most critical times of those three years.

In pastoral matters he developed the lines laid down by Vatican II and Medellín, that is, an approach rooted in evangelization and the preferential option for the poor, which pointed up the desperate problems of the country. This led him to lay great stress on the formation of base communities and the training of pastoral agents on one hand, and to a general defence of the people's right to life on the other. He made the Church a presence in the popular struggle, born under the Church's umbrella and encouraged by it, but with due respect for its autonomy. He had serious reservations about the use of violence by politico-military groups, but was always ready to act as good Samaritan. He considered himself the pastor of the organized groups, giving them humanitarian aid and at the same time criticizing them strongly. All this made him a conflictive figure and the focus of attacks. Some traditional sectors of the Church regarded him as the cause of all the country's ills, but to the people he was simply their pastor. He had major quarrels within the bishops' conference and with the papal nuncio. Rome neither approved of nor understood him. Finally, he was assassinated while saying mass on 24 March 1980.

When the persecution began in 1977, the bishops were united against it, but a repressive law for the maintenance of public order brought division. The nuncios failed to reconcile the bishops of the archdiocese with those of the rest of the country. Ten priests, beginning with the Jesuit Rutilio Grande, a deacon and five nuns were assassinated in the first wave of persecution that culminated in Mgr Romero's death. Forty priests were seriously threatened, tortured or expelled; all the Jesuits were threatened with death between 1977 and 1980. Many Christians from the base communities were threatened, arrested, harassed, tortured and assassinated for their activities as Christians. Liturgical celebrations were broken up and there was a constant stream of attack from the media. Church buildings and Catholic colleges were attacked; the archdiocesan radio station was bombed several times and systematically jammed; presbyteries and convents were bombed and machine-gunned, as were the homes of their lay collaborators. The army occupied churches, profaning the host and the sacred vessels. The way the clergy stood firm against this wave of persecution made a deep impression on the nation and gave the Church great credibility in the eyes of the people.

In the 1980s, the persecution continued, but now in a war context, with catechists, delegates of the word and pastoral agents being the main targets of this second wave. Again, persecution was concentrated on the archdiocese, whose socially committed evangelization programmes aroused the suspicions of the armed forces. Arrests, calumnies and searches of buildings belonging to the archdiocese have been constant. The army has reviled and attacked the archdiocesan bishops for their denunciations of the massive infringements of human rights, the injustice of the war and the social situation in general, and for requesting a negotiated settlement of the conflict.

This second wave of persecution came to a head on 16 November 1989, when the army murdered the Jesuit community that ran the Simeón Cañas University of Central America, together with their housekeeper and her adolescent daughter. This massacre horrified the international community with its brutality and on account of the impunity with which the Salvadorean army was able to act in such a manner. The Rector, Fr Ignacio Ellacuría, and his companions were killed for their academic commitment to the cause of the poor, because they always thought and worked as university personnel in the interests of the masses, because they were constantly asking for a negotiated settlement to the civil war and because they always spoke the truth in a society dominated by cover-ups and lies. In 1991–2 the first fruits of this struggle and sacrifice began to appear, when a "cease-fire" agreement was finally signed in New York and a process of pacification and national reconstruction was undertaken.

(e) Nicaragua: the Challenge of Revolution

The Church in Nicaragua has been sleepy and uncreative. With rare exceptions, the hierarchy has accepted each new development, while the people have stuck to traditional religiosity, with little connection with social change. The bishops kept silent during the U.S. invasion earlier this century, and adapted easily to the Somoza dictatorship that followed, giving it their benediction in several ways.

First signs of dissatisfaction with the dictatorship were timid, appearing in pastoral letters in the 1970s. Only in the last two years of *Somocismo* did the bishops take a stronger tone on the illegality of the regime. They lacked both unity and clarity of purpose, and their lack of unity goes a long way to explain the attitude they took after the triumph of the Sandinista revolution in July 1979.

The revolution shook the Church and the most painful and obvious consequences of this can be seen in its subsequent crises of unity and identity. Since 1980 the Church in general and the archdiocese of Managua in particular have taken a confrontatory stance against the revolutionary government and the so-called "popular church." On the Atlantic coast, however, the Church has followed its own dynamic, as a result of its historical links with the Moravian Church there, the ethnic components of any dispute, and because the region is a sensitive one militarily.

The bishops refused to accept the triumph of the Sandinista revolution from the outset. The bishop of Juigalpa, for example, published leaflets on his own account in which he criticized the new revolutionary government. They were incapable of seeing what was new in the revolution and were therefore unable to appreciate the novelty of the FSLN's communiqué on religion published on 7 October 1980, the central thesis of which was that experience had shown that it was possible to be a Christian first and a revolutionary second, and that there was no irreconcilable contradiction between the two positions. The bishops replied by denouncing the participation of priests in the revolutionary government, a point that was to become a constant refrain. They also reiterated polemical phrases such as "humiliating interventionism," "atheistic proselytizing" and "classist materialism."

These declarations led to the divisions in the Church becoming open, with communiqués from organized Christian groups whose faith led them to question the political stance of the bishops, particularly their objection to compulsory military service, introduced to counter the growing *contra* threat in August 1984. For its part, the government replied in ever harsher tones, but at the same time sought support and legitimation from those Christian sectors most committed to the revolutionary process. The conflict over the presence of four priests in the government (Fernando and Ernesto Cardenal, Miguel D'Escoto and Edgard Parrales) involved the highest levels of the Vatican at one extreme and the people themselves at the other. Military service and the U.S.-backed *contra* aggression saw the bishops taking a clearly pro-U.S. line. Both causes of conflict were exacerbated by the confused and polemical communications media. The confrontation between the Church and the revolutionary government has been caused mainly by the former's desire to restore a Christendom-model Church and its inherent fears of the state attacking religion.

The bishops not only mistrusted the state, but also mistrusted their own clergy, pastoral agents and base communities, seeing them all as drawing people into the revolutioary process. Generalized mistrust has been compounded by the bishops' refusal to dialogue. Since July 1981, the archbishop of Managua and the bishop of Juigalpa have been removing priests sympathetic to the revolution from their parishes. At the same time, the bishops as a whole have unconditionally supported charismatic and pentecostalist movements.

The government reacted to episcopal provocations. In June 1981 they suspended the televising of Sunday mass after some intemperate declarations by the archbishop. In June 1982 they censored a letter from the Pope to the bishops, and in August expelled the first Spanish priest, followed by another the following May. When, also in May 1983, the archbishop declared that he had no knowledge of any U.S. aggression, he was furiously attacked in the media. That October, popular organizations controlled by the government physically blocked protest processions against compulsory military service, and the government expelled two foreign Salesians. In June 1984, the government accused a parish priest in Managua of being involved in counter-revolutionary activities, including drug trafficking and dealing in explosives. The archbishop refused to take the evidence provided seriously and organized a protest demonstration, which led the government to cancel the residency permits of ten foreign priests. The priest in question was acquitted of the charges in November. These government reprisals have been labelled persecution, and the priests and institutions of the "popular church" accused of taking part in it, with the spokesmen of the traditional church claiming that the government wants only the popular church in the country.

This "popular church" grew out of the various renewal movements of the 1960s, which spread from rural areas to the towns, sometimes inspired by parish priests, sometimes by delegates of the word. Peasant delegates became religious leaders of their communities, thereby making up for the lack of priests. These communities produced the leaders of peasant organizations and of the revolutionary government's land reform projects. On the Atlantic coast, the Capuchins trained hundreds of Miskito-speaking evangelizers; base community experiments were organized in some parishes in the capital; the cursillo movement contributed greatly to the education of the middle and upper classes, and produced many of those Christians who held Sandinista government posts, though the movement itself later turned against the revolution. An outstanding example was the peasant community of Solentiname, founded by Ernesto Cardenal in 1965. The art, theological reflection and poetry it produced were collected in books that became best-sellers in many parts of the world and for years projected the dominant image of the Church in Nicaragua. Despite this, none of these experiments changed the structure of the Church, which stayed fundamentally traditional.

The first steps taken by the popular church were characterized by emphasis on religious change. People gradually became conscious of their human and Christian dignity and then took charge of the religious movement with missionary zeal. The determining factor was the Bible, which they read in community and commented on from the standpoint of their community needs. The first dimension rediscovered was that of vice and virtue; then they took an active part in the liturgy, and from moral concerns went on to analyze their social situation on the basis of the Bible. Then oppression, social injustice and the sinful make-up of the dictatorship became part of their religious discourse, reinforced by the repression they suffered from Somoza's National Guard, who first attacked the outstanding pastoral agents and then rural communities in general, as young men joined the FSLN. After the 1972 earthquake, political protest began in the parishes, then spread nationally, with open letters, declarations, church occupations, hunger strikes and vigils. When the National Guard prevented people from taking to the streets they stayed in the churches and prayed, reflected and protested.

Young people played an especially prominent part in the base communities, and their Christian commitment led them toward political struggle: by 1977–8, most young people were linked in some way to the FSLN. A major influence was the student community of the Riguero *barrio* of Managua, which brought its Christian education and thorough knowledge of Marxism to the FSLN, helping it to abandon the dogmatism that had characterized it and unite its various factions.

The majority of the clergy stayed stuck in its fears and anxieties, outside this process, first of renewal and then of revolution. The religious orders showed most enthusiasm, and after the triumph of the revolution, the committed clergy were reinforced by the arrival of religious and pastoral agents from outside the country. The aim was to develop a new pastoral strategy in a new and original setting, resolving the differences between Marxism and Christianity in a new experience. But these pastoral agents came from more advanced parts of Latin America, and soon found that they had to slow down and rethink the process, particularly as the bishops failed to see what was new in the pastoral opportunity presented to them. When a decade of revolutionary experience was brought to an end in February 1990, the Church was still mainly traditional and opposed to the new initiatives the revolution had brought. Its task now is to help make the proclaimed "reconciliation" process in the country a reality.

The election victory by UNO, a coalition of anti-Sandinista forces, in February 1990, has brought about a new equilibrium between Church and state: polemic and collision have vanished, but with them have gone the fruitful pastoral initiatives of the previous decade: calm of a traditional nature reigns.

The failure of the economic improvements promised by UNO in their election campaign to materialize have left the country in a deep and widespread crisis. Furthermore, the traditionalism of the bishops and most of the clergy and other leaders of the Catholic Church means that they can neither offer new ideas nor act as a stimulus in facing up to the difficult period through which the country is going, in the social, political, economic, but also religious spheres.

Translated from the Spanish by Paul Burns

CHRONOLOGICAL TABLE

1522 Beginning of conquest from the south, led by Pedrarias Dávila
1523 Beginning of conquest from the north, led by Pedro de Alvarado
1531 Foundation of the diocese of León (Nicaragua) comprising present day Nicaragua and Costa Rica

1534 18 December: bull establishing the diocese of Guatemala

1535 Bartolomé de las Casas reaches Guatemala

1540 End of military conquest

1547 Diocese of Guatemala made dependent on archdiocese of New Spain

1550 Assassination of Bishop Antonio Valdivieso

1559 Foundation of diocese of Verapaz (Guatemala); included in Guatemala diocese again in 1607

1676 Foundation of the Pontifical University of San Carlos (Guatemala)

1742 16 December: establishment of archdiocese of Guatemala, with suffragan dioceses of Ciudad Real (Chiapas), Camayagua (Honduras) and León

1811 *Criollo* uprising in León, with bishop and clergy taking part

1812 Active participation by Central American clergy in the Cortes of Cadiz

1813 Conspiracy of Belén (Guatemala) with several religious involved

1814 *Criollo* uprising in San Salvador

1821 15 September: Central America declared independent, with active clerical participation

1822–3 Central America annexed to the Mexican Empire

1822 Non-canonical establishment of the diocese of El Salvador and appointment of its first bishop

1824–40 Central America becomes a federation

1825 Non-canonical establishment of the diocese of Costa Rica, but without a bishop

1824 First series of anti-clerical measures

1829 Morazán seizes power in Guatemala and imposes the second series of anti-clerical measures. Expulsion of Bishop Casaus

1839 Repeal of anti-clerical laws and return to the situation of 1829

1842 Vacancy of see of Guatemala ended. Canonical establishment of diocese of San Salvador

1843 Crisis caused by Bishop Viteri y Ungo of San Salvador, exiled in 1846

1850 Canonical establishment of the diocese of Costa Rica

1852 Concordats signed between Holy See and Guatemala and Costa Rica

1858 Expulsion of bishop of San José (Costa Rica), who returns the following year

1862 Concordat signed between Holy See and El Salvador

1870 Secularization of the state and anti-clerical measures in Guatemala and then the rest of Central America

1871 Jesuits expelled from Guatemala

1872 Various church personnel, including the Jesuits, expelled from El Salvador

1875 Temporary expulsion of bishop of San Salvador and other clerics

1879 Constitution of Guatemala embodying liberal reforms, lasting to 1944

1871–80 See of San José vacant

1880 Liberal constitution in Honduras

1881 Jesuits expelled from Nicaragua

1882 Bishop Thiel and Jesuits expelled from Costa Rica, the bishop returning in 1886

1884 Agreement between Church and state in Guatemala, broken in 1887. Costa Rica reneges on its concordat

1886 Archbishop of Guatemala expelled, leaving see vacant to 1897. Liberal constitution in El Salvador, lasting to 1944

1893 Nicaragua annuls its concordat

1904 Bishop Simeón Pereira and several religious congregations expelled from Nicaragua

1911 Constitution embodying liberal reforms in Nicaragua

1919 Archbishop Piñol of Guatemala imprisoned and then expelled, dying in exile in 1927

1921 Successive vacancies of sees in Guatemala

1940 Sanabria elected archbishop of San José; supports a series of social reforms

1946 Vacancies ended in Honduras with appointment of José de la Cruz as archbishop in Tegucigalpa

1954 Widespread banana strike in Honduras

1959 Mission in Honduras leading to establishment of delegates of the word and Catholic radio station

1960 Foundation of Popular Cultural Action in Honduras

1964–71 Community development programmes in Honduras

1965 Community of Solentiname founded in Nicaragua

1971 Development Coordinating Council founded in Honduras

1972 Honduran army kills eight peasant leaders. Beginning of religious persecution in El Salvador

1975 Honduran army and landowners assassinate priests Iván Betancur and Miguel Cipher with eighteen peasants; bishop of Olancho forced to flee his diocese and the country
1976 Earthquake in Guatemala. Priests and catechists first assassinated
1977 Oscar Romero elected archbishop of El Salvador. Jesuit Rutilio Grande assassinated with two peasants in March, first of a long list of priests, religious and delegates of the word killed
1979 Triumph of Sandinista revolution in Nicaragua. Reformist coup d'état in El Salvador
1980 State terror in El Salvador, lasting to the end of the decade
1989 Massacre of Jesuits and helpers at the Central University in El Salvador
1990 Sandinistas lose elections in Nicaragua
1992 Peace agreement signed in El Salvador

SELECT BIBLIOGRAPHY

Adams, Richard. *Crucifixion by Power. Essays on Guatemalan National Structure,* 1944–1946. Austin: Univ. of Texas, 1970.

Calder, Bruce J. *Crecimiento y cambio de la Iglesia católica guatemalteca 1944–1966.* Guatemala: Seminar on Social Integration, 1970.

Campos, Tomás R. "La Iglesia y las organizaciones populares en El Salvador." *Estudios Centroamericanos* 359, 1978, p. 692.

Cardenal, Rodolfo. *Acontecimientos sobresalientes de la Iglesia de Honduras, 1900–1962.* Tegucigalpa, 1974.

—. *Historia de una esperanza. Vida de Rutilio Grande.* San Salvador: UCA, 1986.

—. "En fidelidad al evangelio y al pueblo salvadoreño. El diario pastoral de Mons. Romero." *Revista Latinoamericana de Teología,* 1985, 4 and 1986, 8.

—. "La crisis de la teología nicaragüense." *Revista Latinoamericana de Teología,* 1986, 8.

—. *Manual de historia de Centroamérica.* San Salvador, in preparation.

CEHILA. *Historia General de la Iglesia en América Latina.* Vol. VI, *América Central.* Salamanca: Sígueme, 1985.

Holleran, Mary. *Church and State in Guatemala.* New York: Columbia Univ. Press, 1949.

Jérez, César. "Fe, esperanza y amor en una Iglesia que sufre. La Iglesia de Centroamérica después de Puebla." *Diakonía* 15, 1980, p. 59.

La fe de un pueblo. Historia de una comunidad cristiana en El Salvador (1970–1980). San Salvador: UCA, 1983.

Lernoux, Penny. *Cry of the People. The Struggle for Human Rights in Latin America. The Catholic Church in Conflict with U.S. Policy.* New York: Penguin, 1980, 1982.

López Vígil, José María. *Muerte y vida en Morazán. Testimonio de un sacerdote.* San Salvador: UCA, 1987.

Martínez, Avelino and Rosa María Pochet. *Nicaragua. Iglesia: ¿ manipulación o profecía?* San José: DEI, 1987.

Mecham, J. Lloyd. *Church and State in Latin America.* Chapel Hill: Univ. of North Carolina, 1934, 1966.

Paredes, Iván. "La situación de la Iglesia Católica en El Salvador y su influjo social." *Estudios Centroamericanos* 369, 1979, p. 370.

Picado, Miguel. "¿Desintegración de la neocristiandad costarricense?" *Senderos* 7, 1980, p. 34.

—. "Para una historia de la Iglesia en Costa Rica." *Senderos* 3, 4, 5, 6, pp. 4, 109, 227, 330; 9, 1980, p. 165.

Schlesinger, Stephen and Stephen Kinzer. *Fruta amarga. La CIA en Guatemala.* Mexico City: Siglo XXI, 1982.

Chapter 15

THE CHURCH IN COLOMBIA AND VENEZUELA

Rodolfo de Roux

1. THE COLONIAL CHURCH

When the Spanish conquistadors arrived, they did not find major population groups and civilizations as in Mexico and Peru, but a bewildering multiplicity of small tribes dispersed over a wide area. The most important native group in numbers and cultural development, was the *chibcha* or *muisca* tribe, who occupied a large part of the Andean region of Colombia; it is estimated that at the beginning of the sixteenth century they numbered around one million. The total number of native inhabitants of what is now Colombia is estimated at between two and three million, with some 300,000 in Venezuela, grouped mainly in the coastal region and the mountains. The huge regions of the Plains and the Orinoco and Amazon basins were sparsely populated, by small tribes living as gatherers, fishers and hunters.

Some native groups, such as the *guajiros* of the Atlantic coast, kept a relative degree of independence throughout the time of Spanish rule and proved resistant to conversion to Christianity. In other regions, such as the Plains and the southern Orinoco basin, Christianity made little headway till after the seventeenth century. The tribes of the vast Amazon forests effectively remained beyond the reach of the colonial-evangelizing endeavours until the twentieth century.

The gospel came in with the sword. The first churchmen to explore the territory did so in the capacity of chaplains to the conquistadors, since the Spanish crown required the captains to take at least two priests on all expeditions.

Spanish colonization began on the Atlantic coast in the early sixteenth century, and in Colombia advanced rapidly into the lands of the *chibcha*, impelled onwards by the lust for gold engendered by fabulous and mythical accounts of *El Dorado*. It took longer, however, to bring this territory under control, owing to native resistance and the geographical obstacles. Colonial settlements were confined to places along the coast and in the mountain valleys of the Andes; here the Spaniards managed to keep more or less effective control of stretches of territory adjoining a few main settlements.

Church structures, as elsewhere in America, were established at the same time as civil ones. The towns of Santa Marta and Cartagena, founded in 1526 and 1533 respectively, became episcopal sees in 1534. The diocese of Popayán was established in 1546, nine years after the founding of the city. Santa Fé de Bogotá, founded in 1538, was elevated to an archdiocese in 1564. In Venezuela, Coro, founded in 1527, was given a bishopric in 1531. The civil capital was moved from there to Caracas in 1577, but the bishopric followed only in 1615.

These dioceses – which remained the only ones throughout the colonial period – covered virtually the whole of present-day Colombia and Venezuela. With such vast areas involved, the few occasions on which a prelate set out to visit the whole of his diocese passed into history as heroic feats. This applies to Hernando Arias de Ugarte, bishop of Bogotá, who took five years to visit his diocese, starting in 1619, and to Mariano Martí, bishop of Caracas, over a century later, who took over twelve years to visit his, from 1771 to 1784. Covering such extents as they did, diocesan hierarchies could naturally exercise very little pastoral and disciplinary control over their clergy. Furthermore, the religious orders were strong, independent of the hierarchy, and of one another.

During the sixteenth century, the great majority of the bishops were Franciscans or Dominicans. Their reports emphasize a number of recurrent aspects: the lack of respect shown for the lives and dignity of the natives; the difficulty of evangelizing these; the shortage of clergy and, in the case of Venezuela, the poverty of the land, which obliged this jurisdiction to depend on the Royal Coffers of the New Kingdom of Granada (Colombia) to supplement its meagre income from tithes, and produced a counter-current of immigrants, clerical and lay, moving from there to New Spain (Mexico), Peru and the New Kingdom.

Indians living on the perimeters of the "towns of Spaniards" were gathered into "doctrines" (places in which doctrine was taught). Once a doctrine reached an appropriate size, it became a "parish of Indians" and the doctrine teacher became the parish priest.[1] The Indians in the doctrines were, with few exceptions, those who became subject to the *encomienda* system.

In the early days most of the doctrines were entrusted to members of religious orders, who were later progressively replaced (despite their resistance) by members of the growing diocesan clergy. The scale of this change and the increase in diocesan clergy is evidenced from an official report dated 1663, showing that in the archdiocese of Bogotá the diocesan clergy had ninety-six doctrines, the Franciscans twenty-eight, the Dominicans twenty-seven and the Augustinians twelve.

There was not much the "protectors and defenders of Indians," as the *doctrineros* set out to be, could do to improve the sad lot of a native population rapidly decimated by war, forced labour and newly imported diseases, such as smallpox, which cut swathes through the New Kingdom in 1566 and again in 1588. They continually admitted as much in their reports. Friar Alonso de Zamora, for example, said that one of the reasons that impelled the future St Luis Beltrán, who had come out to the New Kingdom as a missionary in 1562, to return to Spain was his feeling of impotence to remedy the harsh treatment meted out to the natives.[2]

Bishops and religious in fact kept addressing a stream of denunciations of the affronts against the natives to the Spanish crown throughout the sixteenth century.[3] The restraints placed on such struggles on behalf of the natives by the colonial powers are well known, but it is only just to point out that outstanding voices were raised in their defence in the name of the gospel by such as Juan del Valle, first bishop of Popayán and a disciple of Las Casas[4] and his successor, the friar Agustín de la Coruña.

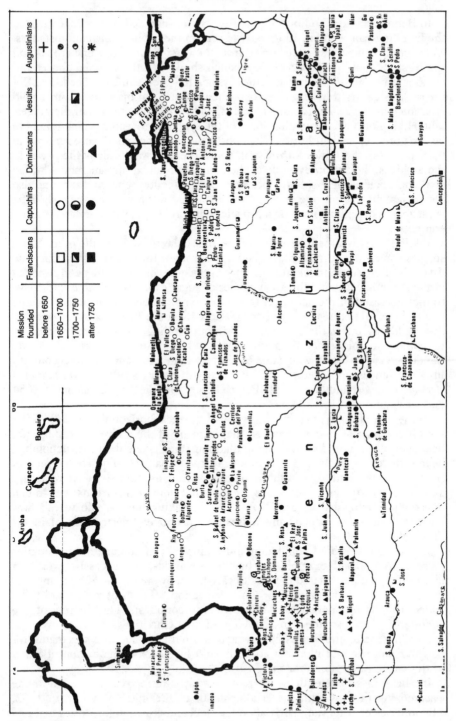

12. Colombia and Venezuela: Mission Foundations up to 1817
Source: Piemme

In Bogotá, the first archbishop, the Franciscan Juan de los Barrios, convoked the first diocesan synod in 1556 to try to reform the habits of the conquistadors. Many of its dispositions were copied from the First Council of Lima (1551) and the First Council of Mexico (1555), which shows that the colonial church did try to apply consistent criteria; future synods followed similar procedures. But the archbishop tried in vain to enforce the provisions of his synod against solid resistance by the *encomenderos*, who managed to enlist the support of the judges. The High Court also overruled some of the synodal provisions which it held to be disruptive of civil authority. The constitutions of the synod were referred to the Council of the Indies for revision, and there they were quietly filed away in the archives. This is an example of the complex colonial bureaucracy in which civil and ecclesiastical spheres not only complemented one another, but also kept a jealous eye on one another and intrigued against each other, showing great zeal in defending their own jurisdictional privileges, which led to repeated conflicts.

While the natives had their defenders, black slavery was, on the other hand, seen as something normal. Slaves had been brought from West Africa since the first half of the sixteenth century to work in the gold mines, in the pearl fisheries of the Atlantic coast and the great estates of sugar cane, cacao and cattle. Slave traffic increased in the seventeenth century, and Cartagena de Indias became one of its main centres in Spanish America. Even the religious used slaves on their holdings and in their convents. Two outstanding Jesuits were honourable exceptions to this generalized unconcern for the fate of blacks: Alonso de Sandoval (1576–1652), who came to Cartagena in 1605 and left an account of his experiences and methods in an important work entitled *De instauranda Aethiopum salute*, and his disciple Peter Claver, who died in Cartagena in 1654 and was canonized in 1888.

At the end of the sixteenth century the evangelical horizon was dark. In 1583 the High Court of Bogotá declared that in many of the natives "there has not been, and is not found more religion than in name," since their instruction had been reduced to teaching them a few prayers in Spanish.[5] The 1606 Synod of Santa Fé recognized that "in this kingdom, its Indians, after sixty-five years, are as full of idolatry as at the outset, a fact that should inspire us with much questioning and discomfort."[6] A "new breaking-out of idolatries" was diagnosed and denounced, and a fresh campaign of "destruction of idols" undertaken.

Besides the scattered population and multiplicity of languages, missionaries pointed to the bad example set by the Spaniards, the excessive workload imposed on the natives and the lack of care taken by the *encomenderos* to instruct them, as obstacles in the way of Christianization.[7] To all of which had to be added the hatred engendered by a violent conquest. This hatred of the conquerors was extended to the God of the Christians, "and to work at persuading them otherwise is like trying to drain the sea and provides matter for laughter and jest and mocking at Christ and his law," as the bishop of Santa Marta wrote to the emperor in 1540.[8]

In the mid-seventeenth century, a new dynamism was injected into the evangelizing process with the establishment of the mission system in 1652. Missionaries became vanguards of both gospel and crown in territories that had hardly been explored till then. In 1662, a "missions council" met in Bogotá and divided the territory of the eastern Plains among Franciscans, Augustinians, Dominicans and Jesuits. The Franciscans also set up missions on the Pacific coast, and the Capuchins and Augustinians on the Atlantic coast. In Venezuela mission work spread out from three nuclei: the central coastal region, the Andean region (a dependency of the viceroyalty of the New Kingdom) and, most importantly, the eastern region spreading from Cumaná along the Orinoco river. Here too the missions were staffed by Franciscans, Dominicans, Capuchins and Jesuits.

Mission technique consisted basically of "reducing" the native population into townships, which could then be organized and their inhabitants catechized. This "reduction" of the natives was carried out either by the method known as "apostolic," using peaceful approaches, or, if this failed, by approaching with armed escorts.[9] Great founders of towns, the missioners contributed in this way to the control of territory and inhabitants: in Venezuela the Capuchins alone were responsible for founding 201 towns.[10]

Despite some efforts to learn native languages,[11] the solution of teaching the indigenous population in Spanish was generally adopted (by the beginning of the eighteenth century, most of the *chibcha* were already speaking Spanish). Language has always gone with empire, but it must be said that the babel of Amerindian languages was enough to discourage even the greatest enthusiasts. To take just one example: on the Plains of Caracas there were more than thirty native peoples, each with its own language, none of them written down.

By the early part of the seventeenth century, the Church was well established institutionally and had developed into the ideological cement holding colonial society together. In 1610 a tribunal of the Inquisition was established in Cartagena.[12] Every city, even those of lesser importance, has its one or more convents of religious, who collaborated with the diocesan clergy in administering the parishes. Alongside these, lay "third orders" of St Francis and St Dominic, together with "confraternities" of Our Lady of the Rosary (Dominican), and the Immaculate Conception (Franciscan), together with the Congregations of Mary (Jesuit) played a major part in the life of the Church. Nuns, on the other hand, played little part in the colonial church; their convents, numbering only five in the New Kingdom with another five in Venezuela, were mainly places of refuge for young "society" ladies who for lack of dowry or other reasons had failed to find a husband.

The Catholic Church controlled behaviour, dictated discourse on the meaning of life, accompanied the faithful from cradle to grave; it paced daily life to the sound of church bells, gave shape to the week with Sunday observance and to the year with the numerous feast days and the "strong" liturgical seasons such as Christmas and Holy Week. In Colombia the numbers of clergy, diocesan and religious, both mainly *criollo* (with the exception of the Jesuits), had grown sufficiently in the seventeenth century to ensure that this pervading church presence was especially marked. When the Provincial of the Dominicans asked for twenty-two more friars to be sent out from Spain in 1630, the three judges and auditor of the High Court in Bogotá adjudicated that they were not needed, since the number of religious was already adequate.[13]

The Catholic Church also had control of education and public charity in its hands. The Brothers of St John of God, for example, were in charge of the hospitals of Cartagena (established in 1613), Bogotá (1635), Tunja, Villa de Leiva, Pamplona and Santa Marta (1746), Cali (1759), Medellín and Cúcuta. The Jesuits owned a dozen schools in the New Kingdom; in Venezuela they were less involved in education, which probably accounts for the fact that the Dominicans and Franciscans ran more schools there than normal.

Two universities were founded in Bogotá in the seventeenth century: the Jesuit Javeriana (1623) and the Dominican Santo Tomás (1639), both of which continue to educate hundreds of students to this day. The Dominicans also ran what was the important College of Our Lady of the Rosary, founded in Bogotá in 1653 and now another university. In 1727, the seminary of Caracas, founded in 1673, was raised to university status.

With the coming of the Bourbons to the Spanish throne in 1700, Spanish regalism took on a more lay and anti-Roman aspect. The royal patronage lost its original sense of privilege granted by the pope and ended by being seen as a right inherent in regal power. As a result, efforts were made to subordinate the Church more effectively to the interests of the state. Nevertheless, the Church kept the strong control it exercised over society, since it held in its hands not only the eternal destiny of the faithful but a good part of their temporal lives as well: it legitimated the authority of the civil powers, controlled education, public charity and civil status (all were required to marry according to church law). To all of which must be added the large measure of economic autonomy it enjoyed, thanks to the considerable wealth it had accumulated. The secrecy in which the financial affairs of the Church had been wrapped was broken with the expulsion of the Jesuits in 1767, since their archives came into the public domain.[14] Apart from this, all the indications are that collective poverty was not a virtue of the religious orders as a whole in the colonial church. The liberal governments of the nineteenth century were to try to break this economic power and use it for their own ends.

The union between throne and altar, never entirely conflict-free, also became a troublesome inheritance which the Church was made to pay for in the republican period. A sign of this risky alliance is that the first two archbishops of Bogotá in the eighteenth century gathered both civil and ecclesiastical power into their hands, since both in turn were Presidents of the Royal High Court. Toward the end of the century there was also an archbishop-viceroy, Antonio Caballero y Góngora (1723–96), famous for his decisive and Machiavellian contribution to the "pacification" of the *Comunero* revolt of 1781, a major rebellion in advance of independence and contemporary with the uprising led by Tupac Amaru II in Peru.

2. THE CHURCH IN THE INDEPENDENCE STRUGGLE AND UNDER THE REPUBLICS

The whirlwind of the wars of independence (1810–21) shook the Catholic Church violently, causing it to divide openly. Most of the bishops remained loyal to the king, to whom they owed not only fidelity but their appointment. Any sign of indecision, such as Bishop Coll i Prat of Caracas showed, was sufficient grounds for suspicion of siding with the rebels, and earned recall to Spain.

Among the *criollo* clergy, however, there was a strong group on the "patriotic" side. These clergymen had become increasingly resentful of the virtual monopoly over high ecclesiastical office held by the "peninsular" clergy: there was, for example, only one Venezuelan bishop among the twenty-seven bishops who ruled the diocese of "Caracas and Venezuela" during the whole colonial period. Furthermore, under Bourbon regalism, many clerical privileges had been threatened, particularly the "ecclesiastical exemption (*fuero*)" which granted them immunity from the civil authorities. The crown also threatened, in a decree dated 26 December 1804, to appropriate land and capital belonging to religious foundations and chaplaincies, the revenue from which the "lower clergy" depended on to augment their meagre salaries. When the moment came, the Colombian Act of Independence of 1810 had sixteen clerical out of fifty-three signatories; five priests signed the Venezuelan Act the following year.

There was also a large group of royalist priests, particularly those belonging to religious orders, where the proportion of Spaniards was higher. Priests fought for the king on one side, the country on the other, and God on both. Opponents shared the same faith in what the "God of hosts" and the Virgin Mary could bring them by way of help. Harangues, sermons, excommunications flew from one side to the other, and both developed pious practices, such as patriotic novenas "in honour of the Virgin of Dolours," or royalist ones "in honour of glorious St Isidore, patron of Madrid."

Religious legitimation of politics was widespread – not surprising in view of the Church's involvement in all aspects of society at the time. A notable example is the *Catechism* compiled in 1814 by Juan Fernández de Sotomayor (1777–1849), parish priest of Mompós and a Freemason (as many clergy were at the time).[15] His Catechism was designed to show why Spanish rule had no foundation in justice and how the war of independence was "holy and just" (while the same was done the other way round from the opposing ranks). The Inquisition tribunal condemned this booklet for its anti-monarchical ideas, excommunicated its author in his absence and declared him "guilty of high treason and lèse-majesté to the sovereign Ferdinand VII." Once the patriots were victorious, Fernández de Sotomayor was eventually appointed bishop of Cartagena (in 1834).

The church institution was deeply affected by the struggle. Several dioceses remained without bishops for years, such as Caracas from 1817 to 1827 and Bogotá from 1818 to 1827. Church property was subject to frequent sackings by one side or the other. Clergy numbers dropped markedly as seminaries closed, ordinations dried up, religious were expelled from their convents, priests were killed fighting and royalist ones returned to Spain. The figures from the diocese of Caracas give an idea of the scale of this: it had 547 clergy in 1810; only 110 in 1819.[16]

Between 1819 and 1830, Venezuela and Ecuador formed part of the Republic of Colombia (Great Colombia). The Church had been weakened, but clerical participation on the side of the emancipation cause earned it a prominent position in the new society under construction: in 1823, for example, a third of the members of the Colombian Chamber of Representatives were priests.[17]

Conflicts, however, soon appeared. The governors of the young republic saw themselves as legitimate heirs of the royal patronage system. In 1824 they voted a "Republican Patronage" by which they tried to set limits to the social influence of the Church while at the same time claiming religious legitimation of their civil powers. A time of tensions between Church and state was beginning.

The definitive clash in Colombia came in the middle of the nineteenth century, when the "radical liberals" in power took a series of anti-clerical measures: suppressing the ecclesiastical exemption, abolishing tithes, expelling the Jesuits (1850) and several bishops.[18] They decreed the separation of Church and state in 1853, promulgated a law on religious freedom, made civil marriage obligatory and divorce legal in 1855. They expropriated church property ("unmortgaging mortmain goods") and claimed the ("tutelary") right to inspect religious services in 1861.

In its struggle against the liberals, the Church could count on the support of the Conservative Party. The religious ingredient was a constant in the numerous civil wars that afflicted the country, from which conservatism eventually emerged victorious. After the Constitution of 1886 and the signing of a Concordat with the Vatican in the following year, the dominant regime was one of "republican Christendom."

The Concordat of 1887 (re-negotiated in 1973) declared that "the Catholic, Apostolic, Roman religion is that of Colombia; the public authorities recognize it as an essential element of the social order, and are obliged to protect it and make it respected." So they did, and with a vengeance. After fifty years of "conservative republic" (1880–1930), the Catholic Church had consolidated its position and exercised considerable influence in the life of the nation.

After an interregnum of "liberal republic" from 1930 to 1946, the conservatives returned to power and enjoyed firm support from the Church in their bloody conflict with the liberals (known simply and significantly as "The Violence"), a civil war that left 160,000 dead in the space of less than a decade (1948–56), ending in a pact between liberals and conservatives to form a "National Front" in 1957.[19] There was then a plebiscite that approved a constitutional reform whose preamble endorsed "the recognition given by the political parties that the catholic, apostolic and roman religion is that of the nation and that as such the public authorities will protect it and make it be respected as an essential element of the social structure."

After the Second Vatican Council and the General Assembly of CELAM in Medellín in 1968, a significant degree of protest arose within the Church against the social conservatism of institutional Catholicism. A precursor of this movement was the "guerrillero" priest Camilo Torres Restrepo, who was killed in 1966. After his death, the leftist clerical movement Golconda arose, lasting from 1968 to 1972, followed by SAL ("Sacerdotes para América Latina") from 1972 to 1980, and a varied series of "Christians for socialism" groups down to the present, generally following the lines of liberation theology.

The challenge facing the Catholic Church today does not come from outside (the Freemasons are a thing of the past, the liberals have become allies, the Protestants are now "separated brethren" and the Marxists are in deep crisis), but precisely from its deep-seated involvement in the power structures and institutional life of a nation going through a period of deep crisis. This crisis is caused by unjust economic and social structures and a quasi-endemic situation of violence (military, para-military, guerrilla and common criminal), to which the past decade has added the degradation of the social fabric and the extra violence perpetrated by the mafia of the drugs trade.

The "Catholic nation" over which the bishops claim to preside and which the President of the Republic has consecrated to the Sacred Heart of Jesus every year since 1903 is a country rapidly shaking off its agrarian and pastoral past. At the beginning of this century, 80 percent of the population lived in the countryside and 20 percent in the cities; now the proportions have been reversed. This marked process of urbanization and industrialization has been accompanied by a tremendous demographic explosion: there were four million inhabitants in 1900; thirty million in 1990. So those over forty years of age in Colombia know two things: what a "Catholic society" means, and how quickly it can become secularized – not to say, in some aspects, fall apart.

The Catholic Church's confrontation with the liberals was even harsher in Venezuela, where there was no conservative party to support it. In 1833 the Republican Patronage was ratified; tithes were suppressed and the clergy became dependent on the national exchequer. The following year freedom of worship was decreed; in 1848 male convents were abolished and Jesuits were forbidden to enter the country. The state took over education, setting up public schools in the dioceses, financed by the income from the old enclosed convents. In 1870 Archbishop Guevara y Lira was exiled. In 1872 the seminaries of Caracas, Mérida, Guayana, Maracaibo and Barquisimeto were suspended, and the following year the clergy were forbidden to accept "first fruits" – voluntary donations from the faithful to make up for the abolition of tithes; civil marriage was introduced and the bishop of Mérida exiled. In 1874 all female convents were dissolved and their goods impounded.

The climax of this process of confrontation was reached during the rule of the liberal Antonio Guzmán Blanco (1870–88), by the end of which the Church was left exhausted. While there had been 547 priests in the archdiocese of Caracas in 1810, by 1881 there were only 393 in the whole of Venezuela.[20] Guzmán Blanco was succeeded by a series of unstable governments and dictatorships which began to re-open the doors to religious orders so that they could take care of hospitals, schools and missions. Under the twenty-seven year dictatorship of Juan Vicente Gómez (1908–35), party leaders and public freedoms were abolished . . . and persecution of the Church came to an end. Gómez, though, applied the Patronage law rigorously and kept strict control of the clergy.

He allowed several religious orders into the country, mainly to devote themselves to education: Christian Brothers, Jesuits, Carmelites, Benedictines, Redemptorists, Marist Brothers, Brothers of St John of God, Paulists and others. Their arrival strengthened the Catholic Church in Venezuela and gave it features that still prevail today: predominance of regular clergy over secular, of foreign priests over native-born ones, and a relatively high concentration on educational work.[21]

In the 1930s, like Colombia, Venezuela changed from an agrarian society into an urban, industrialized one, based largely on oil. The Church came into this new age poor (thanks to the elimination of tithes and the sequestration of its property), economically dependent on the state (which forced it to reduce its social and prophetic commitment) and facing a generalized atmosphere of anti-clericalism, all of which made a clerical vocation a somewhat unattractive proposition.

Gradually, however, the Church began to reap the fruits of its educational policy for the élites and to regain a position of respect from the ruling powers. The signing of a treaty between the Venezuelan government and the Vatican in 1964 put Church-state relations on a regular footing. When the Social-Christian Party, COPEI, came to power in 1968, this was felt in some quarters to be a triumph for the Church: long years of work with Catholic Action groups and university students, workers and peasants in the 1950s and 1960s, largely led by the Jesuit Manuel Aguirre Elorriaga, had certainly prepared the ground for this result.

Paradoxically, the changes of outlook produced by the Second Vatican Council and the Medellín Conference came at a time when the Catholic Church in Venezuela appeared to be in better health than at any stage in the 150-year history of the republic. This meant that new ways were adopted more in principle than in practice: "heard but not carried out" was a general attitude to the new "orders." Parts of the Church, however, have taken to heart the message that the Church's mission is not to legitimize the existing social order; they have questioned the educational policies being carried out and set up structures to work with the poorest sectors of society. There still remains the longstanding structural problem of an overall lack of clergy, coupled with the fact that 80 percent of them are of foreign origin, coming from over twenty different countries. In the meantime, the population has grown dramatically, from two million in 1900 to over eighteen million in 1990.

* * *

Protestantism in Colombia and Venezuela was virtually non-existent under Spanish colonial rule. The first groups of Protestants to settle were soldiers who came with the "British Legion" during the wars of independence. Traders, diplomats and Bible *colporteurs* followed in the first three decades of the nineteenth century. In 1826, a Bible Society was established in Bogotá and another in Caracas.

The various liberal governments of the nineteenth century gradually allowed Protestantism to spread as a reaction against and form of opposition to the dominant Catholicism. The liberals regarded Protestants as bearers of economic and political modernity, and of ethical principles capable of superseding the "black darkness of the Middle Ages" and "theocratic yoke" of the Catholic Church.

In 1834 an Anglican church was built in Caracas; the same year, 374 German Protestants came as immigrants and settled in the north of the State of Aragua. In 1858 Pastor Henry B. Pratt of the Presbyterian Church arrived in Santa Marta, followed by several other missionaries in the next few years. In the second half of the century, "American colleges" were founded in Bogotá (1869), Barranquilla (1890) and Caracas (1896).

According to the record of the First Latin American Evangelical Congress, held in Panama in 1916, there were then 326 "communicating members" of all evangelical churches in Colombia, with 558 attending Sunday school, eighteen foreign missionaries and forty-three Colombian "workers." In Venezuela, there were 139 "communicating members," 719 Sunday school pupils, twenty-seven foreign missionaries and eleven local "workers." Fifty years later there were an estimated 200,000 Protestants in Colombia and a similar number in Venezuela;[22] this was a notable increase, though it still represented only 1 and 1.5 percent of the respective populations. The highest growth rates were recorded among the poor and the urban middle classes.

Besides the United States Presbyterian Church, no other denomination with roots in the sixteenth-century Reformation offered missionaries to Colombia at the 1916 Panama Congress. But other "non-traditional" missions were established: the Gospel Missionary Union in 1901, the Scandinavian Missionary Alliance in 1918, the Christian and Mission Alliance in 1923 and the Interamerican Mission in 1945. By 1945 there were five Protestant denominations in Venezuela besides the Presbyterians: the "Scandinavians" (Free Evangelical Church and Scandinavian Mission), the Orinoco River Mission, the Plymouth Brethren (known as "The Church of Right Doctrine"), the Pentecostalists and the Assemblies of God.

When the conservatives returned to power in Colombia in 1946, they and the Catholic Church instigated a campaign of harassing Protestantism on the grounds that it was a divisive and anti-patriotic movement damaging the religious unity of the country and opening the way for the propagation of alien systems that would eventually destroy the nation. According to the Evangelical Confederation of Colombia, in the ten years from 1949 to 1959, 116 persons were assassinated for being Protestants, 270 schools were closed on government orders or through violence, and sixty churches destroyed.[23]

With Vatican II ecumenism arrived – timidly and suspiciously, but it did. The danger to the religious hegemony of the Catholic Church was no longer posed by the "historic Protestant churches," even though they still projected an image of foreign religious sub-culture, alien to the history of the nation and characterized by "social disengagement" (instead of commitment to tackling social problems) and the ideals of the conservative U.S. middle classes. The threat is rather – and it is a threat to the Protestant churches too – from the numerous sects and pentecostal groups that have been "*criollized*" and multiplied exponentially among the poorest sectors of the population. These sects are estimated now to account for the majority, perhaps 75 percent, of the Protestant population, but statistical studies of them have yet to be made. This type of Protestantism – detached from the historical roots and the purpose of intellectual and moral reform associated with nineteenth-century liberal Protestantism – seems to be turning into an illiterate milleniarism for the marginalized and oppressed.

Translated from the Spanish by Paul Burns

NOTES

1. Many of the regulations governing the "doctrines" can be found in J. M. Pacheco, "El Catecismo del Illmo. Señor D. Luis Zapata de Cárdenas," *Ecclesiastica Xaveriana* 8–9 (Bogotá, 1958–9). pp. 166–72.

2. A. de Zamora, OP, *Historia de la Provincia de San Antonio del Nuevo Reino de Granada* (Caracas, 1930), p. 209.

3. Cf for eleven cases of denunciation, CEHILA, *Historia general de la Iglesia en América Latina*, Vol. VII *Colombia-Venezuela* (Salamanca, 1981), p. 30.

4. J. Friede, *Vida y luchas de Don Juan del Valle, primer obispo de Popayán y protector de indios* (Popayán, 1961).

5. E. Ortega Ricuarte, *Libro de acuerdo de la audiencia real del Nuevo Reino de Granada*, vol. 2 (Bogotá, 1949), pp. 254–6.

6. "Constituciones sinodales," ch. 2, *Ecclesiastica Xaveriana* 5 (Bogotá, 1955), p. 157.

7. Cf "Proemio" to *Recopilación historial de Fary Pedro de Aguado*.

8. Letter from the bishop of Santa Marta, Fernández de Angulo, to the Emperor Charles V, 20 May 1540, in J. Friede, *Documentos inéditos para la historia de Colombia*, vol. 5 (Bogotá, 1957), p. 331.

9. On these approaches with armed escorts see B. de Carrocera, "La cristianización en Venezuela durante el período hispánico," *Memoria del II Congreso venezolano de historia eclesiástica* (Caracas, 1975), pp. 190–6.

10. See the detailed account in CEHILA, *Historia general*, VII, pp. 82–7.

11. The first grammar of the *chibcha* language, by the Dominican Bernardo de Lugo, was published in Madrid in 1619.

12. Cf J.T. Medina, *Historia del tribunal del Santo Oficio de la Inquisición de Cartagena de Indias* (Bogotá, 2nd ed., 1952).

13. In 1625 the archdiocese of Santa Fé had 216 parishes, of which 130 were staffed by diocesan priests. The Franciscan province of Santa Fé had 286 religious in 1698; there were 172 Augustinian priests in 1674, and 142 Jesuits in 1696. Cf CEHILA, *Historia general*, VII, p. 190.

14. Cf G. Colmenares, *Haciendas de los jesuitas en el Nuevo Reino de Granada, siglo XVIII* (Bogotá, 1969).

15. Cf A. Carnicelli, *Historia de la masonería colombiana*, vol. 1 (Bogotá, 1975). For the years 1810–26, he lists nearly forty mason priests, diocesan and regular.

16. CEHILA, *Historia general*, VII, p. 613.

17. D. Bushnell, *El régimen de Santander en Colombia* (Bogotá, 1966). p. 227.

18. Between 1850 and 1877 the archbishop of Bogotá was expelled from the country three times, the bishops of Cartagena and Pamplona twice each, and those of Popayán, Pasto and Medellín once each. Cf CEHILA, *Historia general*, VII, pp. 361–2.

19. See P. Oquist, *Violencia, Conflicto y Política en Colombia* (Bogotá, n.d.) for chronological statistics of numbers of dead.

20. CEHILA, *Historia general*, VII, p. 619.

21. In 1970 there were 2007 priests, of whom 1158 (57.7%) were religious; 40 percent taught in schools. Out of the 2007, only 369 (18.4%) were natives of Venezuela.

22. Cf CEHILA, *Historia general*, VII, pp. 591, 593.

23. Cf J. Goff, *The Persecution of Protestant Christians in Colombia: 1948–1958* (Cuernavaca, 1968). Goff's work is the official account of what happened, written for the Evangelical Confederation of Colombia. The main spokesman for the Catholic side was E. Ospina, SJ, *Las sectas protestantes en Colombia* (Bogotá, 1955).

SELECT BIBLIOGRAPHY

Abel, Christopher. *Política, Iglesia y Partidos en Colombia: 1866–1953*. Bogotá, 1987.
Aguirre, Manuel, SJ. *La Compañia de Jesús en Venezuela* (Bogotá, 1971).
Arcila Robledo, G., OFM. *Las misiones franciscanas en Colombia: estudio documental*. Bogotá, 1950.
Ariza, Alberto, OP. *Los dominicos en Venezuela*. Bogotá, 1971.
Cadavid, Iván. *Los fueros de la Iglesia ante el liberalismo y el conservatismo en Colombia*. Medellín, 1955.

CEHILA. *Historia general de la Iglesia en América Latina*. Vol. VII, Colombia y Venezuela. Salamanca: Sígueme, 1981.

Del Rey Fajardo, José, SJ. *Documentos jesuíticos relativos a la historia de la Compañia de Jesús en Venezuela*. Caracas, 1974.

De Roux, Rodolfo. *Una Iglesia en estado de alerta. Funciones sociales y funcionamiento del catolicismo colombiano: 1930–1980*. Bogotá, 1983.

Gómez Canedo, Lino, OFM. "La provincia franciscana de Santa Cruz de Caracas." *Fuentes para la historia colonial de Venezuela*. 3 vols. Caracas, 1974.

Groot, José Manuel. *Historia eclesiástica y civil de Nueva Granada*. 5 vols. Bogotá, 3rd ed., 1953.

Haddox, Benjamin E. *Sociedad y religión en Colombia*. Bogotá, 1965.

Levine, Daniel H. *Religion and Politics in Latin America: The Catholic Church in Venezuela and Colombia*. Princeton, 1981.

Mutchler, David. *The Church as a Political Factor in Latin America with Particular Reference to Colombia and Chile*. New York, 1973.

Navarro, N. E. *Anales eclesiásticos venezolanos*. Caracas, 2nd ed., 1951.

Ocando Yamarte, Gustavo. *Historia político-eclesiástica de Venezuela (1830–1847)*. 2 vols. Caracas, 1975.

Ordóñez, Francisco. *Historia del cristianismo evangélico en Colombia*. Cali, 1956.

Pacheco, Juan Manuel, SJ. *Los jesuitas en Colombia*. 2 vols. Bogotá, 1959–62.

Phillips, C. Arthur. *A History of the Presbyterian Church in Venezuela*. Caracas, 1958.

Restrepo, Juan Pablo. *La Iglesia y el Estado en Colombia*. London, 1885.

Restrepo Posada, José, ed. *Iglesia y Estado en Colombia - sus relaciones desde la colonia hasta nuestros días*. Medellín, 1969.

Rodríguez Iturbe, J. *Iglesia y Estado en Venezuela*. Caracas, 1968.

Suria, Jaime. *Iglesia y Estado (1810–1821)*. Caracas, 1967.

Tisnes, Roberto. *El clero y la independencia en Santafé*. Vol. XIII/4 of *Historia Extensa de Colombia*. Bogotá, 1971.

Watters, M. *Historia de la Iglesia católica en Venezuela: 1810–1930*. Caracas, 1951.

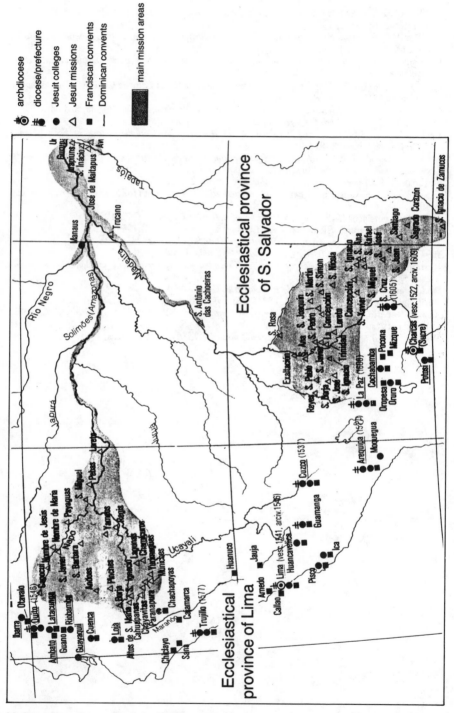

13. Peru, Ecuador and Bolivia: Mission Foundations
Source: Piemme

Chapter 16

THE CHURCH IN PERU, ECUADOR AND BOLIVIA

Jeffrey Klaiber SJ

The greater part of the Andes mountain range is located in the three adjoining republics of Peru, Bolivia and Ecuador. Peru was the centre of the Inca empire, and under Spanish rule the Viceroyalty of Peru included all of South America except Portuguese Brazil. The Incas, who spread out of the Cuzco valley in southern Peru in the thirteenth century, carved out a vast empire that extended from northern Ecuador to the middle of Chile. The empire absorbed a multitude of different cultures and languages, many of which survive to this day. The Incas imposed their own Quechua language upon the conquered subjects, thus conferring a linguistic unity upon that region of South America. Under Spanish rule Bolivia, known then as "Charcas" or "Upper Peru", and Ecuador were both *Audiencias*, or regional jurisdictions under the viceroy in Lima. Charcas was torn away from Peru in 1776 to become part of the Viceroyalty of La Plata (Argentina and surrounding countries), and in 1825 it became an independent nation named after Simon Bolívar, the Liberator. When Peru won its independence in 1821 Ecuador was incorporated into Great Colombia, but won its own independence in 1830. Given these common historical, ethnic and geographical ties these three republics form a natural unit.

Peru, with 1,285,215 square kilometres, had a population of 20,727,000 in 1987. Close to 40 percent of the population is Quechua-speaking, while the majority of the rest are Spanish-speaking whites or *mestizos*. There is also an appreciable black and Asiatic population. Ecuador to the north is much smaller, with a territory of 283,561 square kilometres and a population (1986) of 9,647,000. At the time of the Inca conquest there were only small, scattered indigenous groups in that northern region of the Inca empire. Ecuador's capital, Quito, was founded by the Spanish in 1534. Bolivia, linked to Peru by a great, austere plateau called the *altiplano*, and sharing a border in the middle of Lake Titicaca, was the ancestral home of the Aymara-speaking Indians, who to this day inhabit the region around the lake in both countries. Bolivia, which was also the centre of a pre-Inca empire, Tiahuanaco, has an area of 1,098,581 kilometres and a population (1987) of 6,547,000

Francisco Pizarro toppled the Inca empire in 1532 and soon afterwards the Spanish superimposed a European culture on their Andean subjects. The biological impact of the conquest was devastating: within a century after the arrival of the Europeans, the Indian population of the former Inca empire had dropped from around seven to eight million to 600,000. Under the system of the *encomenderos* (land grantees) the Indians were forced to work in the rich gold and silver mines of Peru and Upper Peru. When Viceroy Francisco Toledo arrived in 1569 the Indians were relocated in reductions, or Indian towns, in order to protect them from further indiscriminate exploitation and to speed up the process of evangelization.

1. EVANGELIZATION

The first stage of evangelization was rather unsystematic. The conquerors and *encomenderos* ordered the Indians to be baptized, but with little prior instruction. The first missionaries, Franciscans, Dominicans, Augustinians and Mercedarians all resorted to mass conversions. In 1537 Cuzco was erected as the first diocese in all South America. In 1541 Lima was made the metropolitan archdiocese upon which all other dioceses of Spanish South America depended. The first archbishop was Jerónimo de Loayza, a Dominican. Quito was named a diocese in 1545 and in 1552 so was La Plata (Chuquisaca, or present day Sucre, in Bolivia). By the end of colonial times Peru had one archdiocese (Lima) and five dioceses; Charcas, one archdiocese (La Plata) and two dioceses; and Ecuador, two dioceses (Quito and Cuenca). In every settlement of any significance the religious orders founded universities, seminaries, hospitals and grade schools.

The coming of Toledo and the Jesuits (1568) signalled the beginning of a second stage of evangelization. The Jesuits founded model missions in Juli by Lake Titicaca and the Jesuit provincial, José de Acosta, called for a deeper study of the Indian cultures and languages. But the great organizer of the church was Toribio de Mogrovejo, of the secular clergy, who arrived in 1581 as the second archbishop of Lima. Toribio convoked the Third Lima Council (1582–1583) which laid down norms for evangelizing the Indians in ways which were more sensitive to their cultures. Priests in the *doctrinas*, or Indian parishes, were obliged to learn the Indian languages. A century later, Alonso de la Peña y Montenegro, the bishop of Quito, published a famous work, *Itinerario para Párrocos de Indios* ("Vademecum for Pastors of Indians") which reinforced the missionary advice of Toribio (who because of his extensive travels throughout Peru to baptize and confirm the Indians was canonized in 1726).

The inquisition was formally established in Lima in 1569, but the Indians were exempted from its jurisdiction. As a result of this limitation, and given the absence of Jews and Protestants, the Lima Inquisition devoted its energies largely to matters of public morality. Toward the end of colonial rule it turned its attention to *criollos*, priests and laymen, accused of disloyalty to the Crown. The Jesuits were the principal order in charge of overseeing the orthodoxy of the Indians. In the many anti-idolatry campaigns that were conducted thousands of idols and mummies were destroyed.

Within the *doctrinas*, however, the new faith took hold. Sunday mass became central to the lives of the Indians, who learned by memory the catechism which the Third Lima Council published in Spanish, Quechua and Aymara. Also, many of the truths of Christianity were conveyed by morality and biblical plays which the Indians acted out. The Indians also assumed a variety of roles as cantors, sacristans, catechists and deputies of the priest. But the Lima councils forbade them to become priests (a prohibition which was lifted in later colonial times).

Although formal education was restricted to the Spanish and *criollo* population, there were some notable exceptions. The Flemish Franciscan,

Jodoco Ricke, founded a short-lived school for Indians in Quito, and the Jesuits founded schools for the sons of Indians *caciques* (chieftains) in Lima and Cuzco. Tupac Amaru, who led the great Indian revolution of 1780, was the most famous graduate of the Cuzco school. The sixteenth-century Indian chronicler, Felipe Huamán Poma de Ayala, who worked as a catechist, wrote at length criticizing the harsh treatment which some of the "doctrine" priests meted out to the neophytes. He also proposed ways to evangelize with more humane methods and often cited the example of the Jesuits.

By the middle of the seventeenth century the process of evangelization was formally completed. The anti-idolatry campaigns ended and the Indians everywhere practised Catholicism. Nevertheless, they did so by assimilating Spanish Catholicism in a way which most responded to their felt needs. Andean Catholicism blended communitarian festivity with stoic resignation, reverence for the *Pachamama* (Mother Earth) with deep devotion to the Virgin Mary, Christ and the saints, ritual (and collective) drinking at funerals with deep and prayerful participation in the liturgy. Whatever its defects, religion pervaded the daily life of the Andean dwellers. Among the most important manifestations of this Andean popular Catholicism are the pilgrimages to great regional shrines, such as Our Lady of Copacabana, by Lake Titicaca. In 1583 an Indian, Francisco Tito Yupanqui, fashioned the statue which became the centre of this devotion.

The black slaves, who were imported to work on the coastal sugar plantations, gave rise to their own blend of "*criollo*" (a reference to the culture of the American-born Spanish) and African religiosity. In 1641 an anonymous slave painted an image of the crucified Christ on a wall in the black district of Lima. The wall survived a devastating earthquake and soon afterwards an image of the original was taken out in procession. The "Lord of Miracles," as it was known, soon became the principal devotion of the blacks and finally of all social groups in Lima. In the late twentieth century it has come to be the most popular devotion of all Peru.

2. THE BAROQUE AGE

By the seventeenth century, which corresponded roughly to the "Baroque Age," Peru had become a highly stratified society. At the apex were the Spanish, then the *criollos*, followed by the *mestizos*, Indians and blacks. A key instrument of evangelization were the confraternities. Almost everyone belonged to these lay associations according to their rank, class and race. Saints abounded. The most famous in Peru were Rose of Lima (1586–1617), daughter of Spanish parents, and Martin of Porres (1579–1639), a *mulatto*, who endeared himself to Lima by his acts of charity. In the jungles on the other side of the Andes the Jesuits in the northern Amazon region called "Mainas", and the Franciscans to the south set up missions among the many Indian cultures that exist there to this day. These two orders also worked among the Indians of eastern Bolivia.

3. TUPAC AMARU AND INDEPENDENCE

Bourbon absolutism reached its zenith in Peru under the Viceroy Amat y Junient (1759–1788). Amat carried out the order to expel the Jesuits (1767), who numbered about 503. Long before that crisis, however, the Crown had been facing mounting resistance to its plans to reform the religious orders. In 1680, for example, Spain imposed the "alternative" on the Franciscans in Lima to stem rising *criollo* influence in the Church. By this measure the successor of a *criollo* superior in each religious order necessarily has to be a Spaniard. The orders, which exhibited many of the deficiencies of the medieval European church – a surfeit of unfit members, large land holdings, scandalous conduct – certainly needed to be reformed. But the Crown's aggressive policies only served to exacerbate tensions between Spaniards and *criollos*.

The eighteenth century witnessed a series of *criollo* and Indian rebellions provoked in part by the Bourbon reforms. In 1742 a *mestizo* by the name of Juan Santos Atahualpa inflamed the Indian tribes of the eastern jungle region around Tarma into open rebellion. In this classic messianic movement Christian and pagan symbols were mixed together. Juan Santos used the cross as a symbol of resistance and called for the creation of an Indian clergy. His movement was successfully put down by 1756. Tupac Amaru's revolution in 1780 represented a far greater threat to Spanish power. José Gabriel Condorcanqui was an Indian of Inca nobility who studied at the Jesuit school for the sons of *caciques* in Cuzco. His well-planned movement, which engulfed the entire area south of Cuzco, called for the creation of a Christian Inca state. José Gabriel assumed the title, "Tupac Amaru II", in honour of Tupac Amaru, the last Inca, who was beheaded by Viceroy Toledo in 1572. By May of 1781 the revolution had been bloodily repressed by an army sent from Spain. Tupac Amaru revealed his biblical formation by comparing his uprising with the flight of the children of Israel and with David pitted against Goliath. His wife, Miacaela Bastidas, was also a practising Christian and frequently sought the counsel of priests.

This revolution signalled the eclipse of Spanish power in Peru. Although the bishop of Cuzco, Juan Manuel Moscoso, excommunicated Tupac Amaru, it was known that many *criollo* priests were sympathetic to the Indian rebel. When Napoleon invaded Spain, Peru like the rest of Spanish America proclaimed its loyalty to Ferdinand VIII during his captivity. But this initial loyalty soon gave way to outright rebellion in favour of independence. Churchmen played a prominent role throughout the entire movement. In general, with a few notable exceptions, the hierarchy condemned the rebellion while the *criollo* clergy, who made up the majority of the lower clergy, vigorously supported the cause. In 1812 Bishop José Curero y Caicedo of Quito was elected, somewhat reluctantly, president of a *Junta* which called for separation from Spain. in 1814 José Pérez Armedáriz, a *criollo*, lent support to an independence movement that swept through southern Peru. When the army from Cuzco reached Arequipa a *criollo* clergyman, Mariano José de Arce, called for a complete break with Spain, while another priest, Ildefonso Muñuecas led an army toward "Upper Peru". When General José de San Martín proclaimed the independence of Peru in July, 1821, the *criollo* clergy, and some Spanish, hailed the news. Many priests were elected to Peru's first constitutional assembly, 1822–3.

The Venezuelan patriot, Simon Bolívar, defeated the last Spanish armies in South America on the plains of Ayacucho in December, 1824, and although the "liberator" attempted to hold the five republics (Venezuela, Colombia,

Ecuador, Peru and Bolivia) together in a single confederation, each region chose separate nationhood: Peru in 1821, Bolivia in 1825, and Ecuador in 1830.

4. NINETEENTH CENTURY CRISES

The Church survived the wars of independence relatively intact. The new republics proclaimed the Catholic Church as the official Church and excluded all other religions. Nevertheless, the liberals who assumed control sought to control the Church and to curtail its privileges. The governments of Peru and Bolivia decreed the closing of many monasteries of the men's religious orders, and in 1856 the Peruvian congress declared the end of state support to the Church, with the exception of bishop's salaries. In Bolivia, the liberal high tide occurred in the first years of the twentieth century when freedom of religion was granted to all (1901) and church property was confiscated. Ecuador provided a classic case of the liberal-Catholic struggle in the contrast between García Moreno and Eloy Alfaro. Gabriel García Moreno, president of Ecuador between 1860 and 1875, attempted to create a near theocratic Catholic state, which culminated in the consecration of the nation to the Sacred Heart in 1874. Although he also promoted public development projects, he was assassinated in 1875 by an anticlerical liberal. In 1895 General Eloy Alfaro brought about a full liberal revolution and sought to undo every measure that García Moreno had decreed, including a ceremony to "unconsecrate" Ecuador to the Sacred Heart. Many priests were expelled and education was laicized. In 1937 Church and state in Ecuador finally normalized their relations. Peru avoided most of these tensions, although the liberal tradition lived on well into the middle of the twentieth century especially in the Aprista party.

The Church faced the liberal attack in a number of ways: greater reliance on the papacy, inviting new religious orders over from Europe to found schools or to do mission work in the jungle, and open support of conservative groups. As in the rest of Latin America the Churches in these Andean republics acquired a distinctive Roman identity, but at the expense of their own Latin American identity. The new bishops appointed by Rome tended to place great importance on European issues, such as the dangers of freemasonry and liberalism, but neglected the Indian realities of their own countries. The European religious who arrived, such as the Jesuits, the Sacred Heart fathers and sisters, the De La Salle Brothers, etc., founded schools which were esteemed by the middle and upper classes.

The Church, however, failed to resolve a greater crisis: the increasing shortage of priests, a phenomenon most noticeable in areas with a large Indian population. With state support cut off, a church career became much less attractive for many young men who were attracted by the new possibilities that came with the entrance of Latin America into the world capitalist markets especially after 1850. Furthermore, in its battles with the liberals, the Church increasingly acquired a conservative image. Finally, the Indians lacked the educational tools to enter the westernized (and romanized) seminaries of Latin America. By the late 1880's about 60 percent of the clergy in Peru and Bolivia were foreign-born missionaires, and 30 percent in Ecuador.

In spite of these setbacks for the official Church, however, popular Catholicism, largely untouched by liberalism, continued to thrive. In the numerous peasant rebellions throughout the nineteenth century, for example, Indian leaders displayed no animosity toward religion or the Church. In 1885 in Huaraz, a city in the northern Peruvian Andes, a peasant leader by the name of Pedro Pablo Atusparia led one of the more significant of these revolts against the abuses of landlords and government authorities. He celebrated his initial victory with a mass of thanksgiving and had a priest act as his spokesman before government troops. Atusparia was defeated but later pardoned by the central government.

5. POPULISM AND REVOLUTION

In 1924 Víctor Raúl Haýa de la Torre founded the Aprista party which became a major force for years in Peruvian politics. The party, which was the first mass party of workers and the middle class in Peru's history, was proscribed and persecuted during most of the 1930s, 1940s and 1950s. Many young Peruvians, in the absence of a socially sensitive Church, transferred their religious sentiments to the Aprista movement and the charismatic Haya de la Torre. The cry of an Aprista militant who was shot in 1932, "May God save my soul, and APRA alone will save Peru!", revealed the explosive potential of mixing politics and religion in the new context of the political awakening of the popular classes. The other founder of the Peruvian left was José Carlos Mariátegui whose work, *Seven Interpretative Essays on Peruvian Reality* (1928) became a classic in Latin American Marxist thought. But Mariátegui was not a classical Marxist: he openly admired the religious instinct in man and dreamed of a Latin American socialism that would flow out of the deep religious faith of the workers and peasants. The only Andean populist movement which came to power and effected a social revolution, however, was the Nationalist Revolutionary Movement of Victor Paz Estenssoro in Bolivia in 1952.

The Church's principal response to these movements was the creation of Catholic Action, which took as its model Catholic Action of Italy. Catholic Action forged a new militant lay consciousness and created an awareness of the Church's social teachings. Many forerunners of the post-Vatican II Church were formed in these years. Bishop José Dammert of Cajamarca (1962–) was an adviser in the 1940s to a Catholic group headed by Gustavo Gutiérrez, a student of medicine at San Marcos state university in Lima. Also, many of the founders of the Christian Democratic parties came out of Catholic Action. Other Catholic leaders of the 1930s and 1940s, however, sought to create a new Christendom modelled on the medieval corporative state. The two leading Catholic intellectuals in the 1930s in Peru were Víctor Andrés Belaunde, who favoured a "Christian Democracy", and José de la Riva-Agüero, who favoured an authoritarian state based on Hispanic values. The Catholic University of Peru, founded in 1917, became a centre of the Catholic revival.

6. THE CHURCH OF THE POOR

Within a relatively short period of time the conservative and somewhat lethargic Churches of Peru, Ecuador and Bolivia became transformed into models of a socially progressive Church pastorally attuned to the deepest felt needs of the lower classes. Under Cardinal Juan Landázuri Ricketts, archbishop of Lima from 1955 to 1990, the Peruvian Church led the way. The presence of religious personnel from the western democracies, and especially the United States, helped to accelerate the process of transformation. The populist government of Fernando Belaúnde (1963–8) promised to be a showcase for the developmentalist policies of the Alliance for Progress. But Belaúnde's reformist plans failed and the military under General Juan Velasco Alvarado seized power (1968–75) and set in motion many sweeping social changes. This revolution of "rising expectations" made its impact on the Church as well. The bishops' conference at Medellín in 1968 gave further impetus to the desire for change.

The most significant manifestation of change was the emergence of liberation theology and a grassroots popular movement within the church. Gustavo Gutiérrez (1928–), a priest of the secular clergy born in Lima, is the national adviser to Catholic students and he served as an adviser to the bishops at Medellín. His book *A Theology of Liberation*, first published in 1971, had a worldwide impact. In 1974 Fr Gutiérrez founded the Bartolomé de Las Casas Centre in Lima to promote change within the popular church. The Catholic University organizes a biblical course each year which attracts between two and three thousand participants, the majority of whom are students, peasants and workers of both sexes. Fr Gutiérrez and other theologians analyze biblical themes in the light of contemporary social problems. For a while the priests' organization known as "ONIS" (National Office of Social Information) played a prominent role in calling for social reform. Certain bishops were especially influential in shaping the new church: José Dammert in Cajamarca, Luis Bambarén, first in Lima and later in Chimbote, Germán Schmitz, an auxiliary bishop of Lima, and Cardinal Landázuri. The big parishes in the "Young Towns" (the term used for the massive squatter settlements ringing the cities) became centres for promoting development.

The so-called "Southern Andean Church" in Cuzco and Puno distinguished itself especially for its commitment to land reform and improving conditions for the peasants. The Las Casas Centre in Cuzco, run by the Dominicans, and the Andean Pastoral Institute in Sicuani, founded by the bishops, have decisively influenced the growth of this popular church. Even though the foreign clergy is still highly visible, this fact is offset by an increase in Peruvian vocations and most of all by the emergence of a lay church. In every progressive diocese (Peru now has fifty-two dioceses) these are numerous catechists, "animators" or community leaders who assume roles as coordinators of religious activities.

Bolivia has followed much the same lines as Peru. Archbishop Jorge Manrique of La Paz (1967–87) and Julio Terrazas, bishop of Oruro and president of the Bolivian Episcopal Conference (1988–), among others, helped turn the Bolivian Church into one of the most socially progressive in Latin America. On numerous occasions the Church has mediated between the government and the miners (a major segment of the working force) although it usually acts as spokesman of the latter. The American Dominicans founded the Bolivian Institute for Social Action (IBEAS) in 1964 to promote research for social change. A programme to form a lay diaconate among the Aymara peasants has been very successful. In all three republics the *Fe y Alegría* ("Faith and Joy") schools for the poor run by the Jesuits (in Bolivia alone there are over 120) have become an important part of national education.

In Ecuador Bishop Leonidas Proaño (1954–85) turned the rural mountain diocese of Riobamba into a model of the Vatican II Church. Proaño attracted world attention in 1976 when he and seventeen other bishops and invited guests were arrested by the military government on charges of "subversion". Both he and Cardinal Pablo Muñoz Vega (Quito) supported the agrarian reform.

The papal visits, first to Ecuador and Peru in 1985 and then to Bolivia in 1988, produced the greatest public rallies in Andean history, a clear sign that the renovated Church enjoys wide acceptance among the poor. Nevertheless, although the vast majority (between 90 and 98 percent) of people in the three countries claim to be Catholics, only a minority attend church on a regular basis. Most practise what is called "popular Catholicism," which includes some of the sacraments, processions, devotions to particular saints, etc. Although the Church in this region has not faced systematic government persecution in recent times as in other Latin American countries, it has suffered from right and left-wing terrorist violence. In 1980 the Jesuit Luis Espinal was murdered in La Paz for his criticism of the military. In Peru the "Shining Path" has systematically destroyed all social projects of the Church and killed two priests.

7. PROTESTANTISM

Statistics on the number of Protestants in the three Andean republics vary anywhere from 5 to 8 percent of the total population. The first Protestants belonged to the small groups of foreigners, mostly English, that engaged in commerce after independence. Diego Thomson, sent by the British & Foreign Biblical Society, distributed bibles and promoted the Lancasterian system of education in Peru and Ecuador in the 1820s. In 1877 the first Methodist missionaries from the United States arrived but it was not until the coming of Francisco Penzotti in 1888, that Protestants preached openly in public. Penzotti, an Italian-Uruguayan, was imprisoned but released under pressure from the liberals. The first group to work among the Indians were the North American Adventists, who arrived in 1898. They founded numerous clinics and schools and won the general admiration of liberals and pro-Indian advocates. The first missionaries to Bolivia (1898) were Canadian Baptists. The Eloy Alfaro regime in Ecuador (1895–1911) welcomed Protestant missionaires, who came mostly from the United States.

In Peru Dr John MacKay, a Scottish Presbyterian minister, founded the Anglo-Peruvian school in Lima and befriended Haya de la Torre. In 1931 the "Voice of the Andes", destined to become one of the most powerful radio transmitters in South America, with programmes in Quechua and other Indian languages, was founded in Quito. Protestantism did not make notable progress, however, until after World War II. The Wycliffe Bible Translators began working with jungle tribes in Peru in 1945, in Ecuador in 1953 and in Bolivia in 1955. Also, in 1953 the Mennonites began work in the Chaco region of Bolivia.

In the 1960s three phenomena occurring simultaneously significantly influenced Andean Protestantism: the emergence of national leaders, the ecumenical movement and the sudden growth of the fundamentalist sects and other new religions. For years the Seventh Day Adventists were the largest

Protestant denomination in all three countries. By the 1990s however, the greatest proportion of non-Catholics belong to the Pentecostals and other fundamentalist groups. The historical churches, Lutherans, Methodists, Presbyterians and others sought closer ecumenical ties among themselves. In 1968 the Evangelical Christian Union of Bolivia joined with the Evangelical Church of Peru to form a confederation. At the same time these churches became noticeably more inculturated. In Bolivia the Methodists and Quakers have quite successfully promoted the creation of an Aymara church. Finally, the historical churches have all established permanent ecumenical ties, flowing out of a common concern for human rights and social development, with the Catholic Church.

CHRONOLOGICAL TABLE

1532 Pizarro conquers Peru.
1537 Cuzco is erected as the first diocese of South America.
1568 The first Jesuits arrive.
1569 Vicery Toledo begins relocation of the Indians in reductions.
1582–1583 Toribio de Mogrovejo presides over the Third Lima Council.
1609 The Anti-idolatry campaigns begin.
1651 A black slave paints the image of Our Lord of Miracles.
1742 Juan Santos Atahualpa leads a rebellion in the jungle.
1767 The Jesuits are expelled.
1780 Tupac Amaru II sets off a social revolution.
1821 General San Martín declares the independence of Peru.
1825 Bolivia declares its independence.
1830 Ecuador secedes from Gran Colombia.
1890 Francisco Penzotti is imprisoned for proselytizing.
1895 General Eloy Alfaro establishes a liberal regime in Ecuador.
1935 The first National Eucharistic Congreee is held in Peru.
1952 The Bolivian National Revolution.
1954 Leonidas Proaño is named bishop of Riobamba.
1955 Juan Landázuri Ricketts is named archbishop of Lima.
1968 Gustavo Gutiérrez calls for a "theology of liberation".
1968 General Juan Velasco Alvarado initiates major reforms in Peru.
1980 Jesuit priest Luis Espinal is assassinated in La Paz.
1985 Pope John Paul II visits Ecuador and Peru.
1988 The Pope visits Bolivia.

SELECT BIBLIOGRAPHY

Bruno-Jofré, Rosa del Carmen. *Methodist Education in Peru: Social Gospel, Politics and American Ideological and Economic Penetration, 1888–1930.* Waterloo, Ontario: Wilfred Laurier University, 1988.

Crahan, Margaret. "Church-State Conflict in Colonial Peru: Bourbon Regalism under the Last of the Hapsburgs". *The Catholic Historical Review.* LVII (April, 1976): 224–44.

Cushner, Nicholas. *Lords of the Land. Sugar, Wine and Jesuit Estates of Coastal Peru, 1600–1767.* Albany, New York: State University of New York Press, 1980.

Dussel, Enrique (ed.) *Historia general de la Iglesia en America Latina,* Vol. VIII: *Perú, Bolivia y Ecuador.* Salamanca: Sígueme, 1987.

Gutiérrez, Gustavo. *A Theology of Liberation: History, Politics and Salvation.* 2nd ed. Maryknoll, N.Y.: Orbis, 1988.

Judd, Stephan. "The Emergent Andean Church: Inculturation and Liberation in Southern Peru, 1968–1986". Doctoral Dissertation. Berkeley, California: Graduate Theological Union, 1987.

Kessler, J. B. A. *A Study of the Older Protestant Missions and Churches in Peru and Chile*. Oosterbaan & Le Cointre N.V.: Goes, 1967.

Klaiber, Jeffrey. *La Iglesia en el Perú: su historia social desde la Independencia*. 2nd ed. Lima: Pontificia Universidad Católica, 1988.

—. "The Posthumous Christianization of the Inca Empire in Colonial Peru". *Journal of the History of Ideas* XXXVII (July–September, 1976): 507–20.

—. *Religion and Revolution in Peru, 1824–1978*. Notre Dame, Indiana: University of Notre Dame Press, 1977.

Mackay, John. *The Other Spanish Christ*. London: SCM Press, 1932.

Malloy, James, and Eduardo Gamarra. *Revolution and reaction: Bolivia, 1964–1985*. New Brunswick, N.J.: Transaction, Inc., 1988.

Maloney, Thomas J. "The Catholic Church and the Peruvian Revolution: Resource Exchange in an Authoritarian Setting". Doctoral Dissertation. Austin: University of Texas, 1978.

Mariátegui, José Carlos. *Seven Interpretative Essays on Peruvian Reality*. Austin: University of Texas Press, 1971.

Martin, Luis. *The Intellectual Conquest of Peru: The Jesuit College of San Pablo, 1568–1767*. New York: Fordham University Press, 1968.

Marzal, Manuel. *Los caminos religiosos de los inmigrantes en la Gran Lima*. Lima: Pontificia Universidad Católica, 1988.

—. *La Transformación religiosa peruana*. 2nd ed. Lima: Pontificia Universidad Católica, 1988.

Meiklejohn, Norman. *La Iglesia y los Lupaqas durante la Colonia*. Cuzco: Centro Las Casas, 1988.

Padilla, Washington. *La Iglesia y los Dioses Modernos: Historia del Protestantismo en el Ecuador*. Corporación Editora Nacional Veintemilla y 12 de Octubre, 1985.

Stern, Steve (ed.) *Resistance, Rebellion, and Consciousness in the Andean Peasant World. 18th to 20th centuries*. Madison: The University of Wisconsin Press, 1987.

Tibesar, Antonine. *Franciscan Beginnings in Colonial Peru*. Washington, D.C.: Academy of Franciscan History, 1953.

—. "The Peruvian Church at the Time of Independence in the Light of Vatican II". *The Americas* XXVI (April, 1970): 349–75.

Vargas, José María. *Historia de la Iglesia en el Ecuador durante el Patronato español*. Quito, 1957.

Vargas, Rubén. *Historia de la Iglesia en el Perú*. Burgos, 1953–1962. 5 vols.

Werlich, David P. *Peru, A Short History*. Carbondale, Illinois: Southern Illinois University Press, 1978.

Chapter 17

THE CHURCH IN THE SOUTHERN CONE: CHILE, ARGENTINA, PARAGUAY AND URUGUAY

Maximiliano Salinas

1. THE COURSE OF THE IMPERIAL CHURCH FROM IMPOSITION TO ECLIPSE

(a) The Imperial Church, Official Religion of the Spanish Crown

The official form in which Catholicism was established and organized was through an imperial Church controlled and financed by the Spanish crown. In the Southern Cone this Church was imposed through six bishoprics originally dependent on the archbishopric of Lima. These, with their foundation dates, were: Asunción in 1547, Santiago de Chile in 1559, La Imperial or Concepción in Chile in 1561, Córdoba del Tucumán in 1570, Buenos Aires in 1620 and Salta in Argentina in 1806.

The imperial Church had to make its evangelizing task coalesce with maintaining the legal and administrative system of the overseas empire; this made it the most powerful instrument for controlling both the ethics and the politics of the whole population. Such an undertaking, as arduous as it was contradictory, produced a Church whose characteristic features were a strange mix between the interests of God and those of Caesar: the absolute state and the absolute of God.

The Southern Cone produced a number of prominent bishops, who favoured one set of interests at the expense of the other according to their inclination. So Francisco de Vitoria OP, first bishop of Tucumán from 1582 to 1590, pioneered commerce between the River Plate area and Brazil and was a staunch practitioner of the Inquisition, while Manuel Abad Illana, who succeeded to the see in 1768, distinguished himself by defending the Indians and telling the rich *encomenderos* who forgot their duties to the crown that they were damned. The disastrous consequences the Spanish invasion brought on the native population – hunger, disease and forced labour – tested to the ultimate the Church's double allegiance to God and Caesar, which it practised with anguish and guilt. The Franciscan Diego de Humanozoro, bishop of Santiago from 1662 to 1676, was so affected by the oppression of the Mapuche Indians, and by his own political and religious responsibility for it, that he ended up proclaiming God's adverse judgment on the whole Spanish empire in the Indies. But for church leaders to show such a degree of conscience was the exception. More characteristic, up till the end of the wars of independence in the nineteenth century, was an alliance of interests between God and Caesar, seen at perhaps its most excessive in the "Royal Catechism" produced by José Antonio de San Alberto, bishop of Tucumán, in 1786.

(b) The Organization and Typical Piety of the Imperial Church

The imposition of Catholicism as the official religion of the Southern Cone started from the supposition that Christian salvation had to mean that the native peoples accepted, and subjected themselves to, European civilization and its representatives, taken at face value as images of a superior religion or culture. This conviction was enshrined in miraculous "apparitions" of the Virgin or Spanish saints routing the natives, as St Blaise was made to do to the Guaranís, or the Virgin and St James (known as *matamoros*, Moor-slayer, in Spain) to the Mapuches. It was upheld by the Jesuit theologian José de Acosta at the Third Council of Lima, and in his *De procurando indorum salute* of 1576.

The imperial Church, displaying an ethnocentricity that was as ingenuous as it was eloquent, tried to convince the natives that they had to submit to God and Caesar at the same time. This was the message preached by, for example, the Franciscan Pedro Angel de Espiñeira (1727–78), bishop of Concepción, on his mission to the Pehuenche Indians of the southern Andes in Chile.

What sort of response did this proposition by the imperial Church arouse in the Southern Cone? Basically, there were two contradictory responses, which determined whether the institution worked well or badly in relation to the native population. The Guaranís of Paraguay and Uruguay accepted protection from the Spanish Church, and thereby acknowledged its supremacy; the Mapuches of southern Chile resisted and prevented the imperial Church from taking root.

Among the Guaranís, the imperial Church operated through the Jesuit reductions, begun in 1609 and continuing with the support of the Spanish crown till 1750. In their most flourishing period (1656–1750), the reductions were the repository of the hope of harmonizing the interests of God and Caesar, by defending both the empire and the Indians. This balance was upset in the eighteenth century when the interests of Caesar became more overbearing, resulting in the expulsion of the Jesuits in 1768, despite the fact that the Guaranís, anxious to keep their "Jesuit protection," themselves promised to increase their tributes to the crown.[1]

With the Mapuches, the imperial Church never made headway: they simply could not understand the alliance between God and Caesar. The Jesuit plan to "reduce" them to population centres provoked the uprising of 1766. Some missionaries, such as Antonio María Fanelli SJ, writing in 1699, declared the Mapuches incapable of ever belonging to the Church. Others, including one of the most outstanding Spanish missioners to the country, Luis de Valdivia SJ (1561–1642), tried to link evangelization to ending the offensive war against the Mapuches, but to no avail.

Whether the imperial Church operated successfully or not, there is no doubt that it elaborated a style of piety suitable to its basic imagery of the harmonization of the interests of God with those of the empire. This emerged in the baroque style, austere, solemn and triumphalist, which travelled from Europe to the southernmost confines of the New World.[2]

An evangelization process tied to the civilizing (or barbarizing) outreach of the Spanish state could not but do violence to the native religions and cultures. The missionaries brought the practice of flogging to the Guaranís and as late as 1744 the Fourth Synod of Concepción in Chile decreed that any Indians who failed to attend catechesis should be flogged. The post-tridentine ethos was

14. The Southern Cone: Jesuit Foundations in the Eighteenth Century
Source: Guillermo Furlong, SJ, *Los Jesuitas y la cultura rioplatense*. Montevideo, 1993.
(Furlong)

present in all its force. The Kingdom of God could be visualized even as clad in the military uniforms of the Spanish armed forces. This was caricatured in verses collected in Jujuy in Argentina at the beginning of this century:

Cristo va de coronel
marchando con gran primor
y de sargento major
el Patriarca San José ...
El Santo Tomás de Aquino
va como primer soldado ...
Marchan al son del tambor
con cajas y con clarines. ...

(Christ goes dressed as a colonel/ marching in great splendour/ and the Patriarch St Joseph/ goes dressed as a sergeant-major ... / St Thomas Aquinas/ is dressed as a first soldier ... / They march to the sound of the drum/ with side drums and trumpets. ...)

In the Southern Cone the imperial Church developed not only a piety but a whole style of life – a baroque culture following European models. In the intellectual sphere, for example, it founded the university of Córdoba, granted its charter by the crown and the Holy See in 1622, and the Jesuit College of Santa Fe, responsible for the education of most of the colonial élite of the River Plate. In economic terms, the imperial Church was a vast enterprise, owning esates, ranches, herds and slaves. In 1767, for example, the Society of Jesus in Chile possessed goods to the value of two million pesos, by far the greatest accumulation of wealth in this poor Captaincy General.

(c) Decline

The overthrow of Spanish dominion in the Southern Cone in the early nineteenth century plunged the imperial Church into institutional and theological crisis. The local churches were left leaderless: the bishops of the six dioceses of the region were deposed and even exiled for their political stance of loyalty to the crown – imposed on them by ordinance of the Holy See. Bishops Orellana of Córdoba, Videla del Pino of Salta and Rodríguez Zorrilla of Santiago, amongst others, were exiled, along with a large number of priests, such as the Franciscans in Paraguay in 1810 and the last Franciscan missionaries in Chillán in Chile in 1817. The new liberal governments set about reforming the Church in such a way as to leave whole regions virtually without regular clergy. This was the case, for example, in Argentina with the reforms carried out by President Bernadino Rivadavia in 1826.

The revolutions that brought about independence revealed the limits of the established Church, since there was no lack of clergy, let alone lay people, who adopted revolutionary ideals. So of the twenty-nine signatories to the Act of Independence of Tucumán in 1816, sixteen were clergy. A number of liberal or enlightened priests, such as Juan Ignacio Gorriti (1767–1842) in Argentina and Camilo Henríquez (1769–1825) in Chile, challenged the ethical and political convictions of the imperial Church by criticizing the Inquisition or religious intolerance. In the River Plate, the existence of a revolutionary body of clergy was shown by Franciscan participation in the *gaucho* movement led by José Gervasio Artigas (1764–1850).

Catholics who sided with independence questioned the basic error of the imperial Church: the alliance between God and Caesar which had for centuries been proclaimed immutable. This made the revolution into a sort of diabolical confabulation in monarchist eyes, but for those disenchanted with the imperial Church it was a liberating experience: God distancing himself from the empire to raise up the American peoples and cast down the Spanish crown for its part in colonial oppression.[3]

2. THE ADVENT AND DEVELOPMENT OF POPULAR CHRISTIANITIES

Whatever its intentions and conscience, the imperial Church became a colossal centralized and bureaucratic apparatus that never managed to take the character and culture of the masses of the people seriously. These, in their multi-coloured mass of natives, poor Spaniards, blacks, mestizos and so forth, were above all an object to be assisted and repressed by a paternalistic Church. In the face of this religious domination the oppressed majorities refused to be objects of the Church's pastoral endeavours, and used their own cultural matrices to develop their own style of popular Christianities, which turned out to be profound expressions of the evangelization of the poor.

(a) Native and Black Resistance to the Imperial Church

In 1579, a native called Oberá, who had been educated by a Catholic priest, led a movement within the context of Guaraní resistance. He called himself the liberator of his people and incited his followers to subversive dances that would bring about the downfall of the Western system. In the following century, the movement led by the *cacique* Yaguacaporo in Paraguay between 1635 and 1637 "ordained" native bishops and priests with a view to forging a Guaraní confederacy against the Jesuits. (Guaraní folklore produced the figure of Perurimá, a native who symbolized protest against the missionary tutelage of the reductions).

Mapuche resistance to the imperial Church was overwhelming. Their rebellions against the white invaders resounded with protests against the Church. During the uprising of 1598 the natives "profaned" more than fifty churches or chapels and renounced their Christian names. Mapuche peasant materialism was a wall of contention raised against Catholic eschatology: the former owners of the land of Chile did not accept the doctrine of hell and imagined a heaven full of earthly delights.[4]

Black resistance to the imperial Church and its teachings was also deep and widespread. Some of the missionaries who tried to evangelize the blacks of the Southern Cone, such as Alonso de Ovalle SJ in the seventeenth century, left accounts of their frustrations, and the records of the Inquisition in the sixteenth century show evidence of black rejection of the European God and his representatives.

(b) The Influence of Popular Spanish Christianity

The rise of popular Christianities in the Southern Cone should be seen as influenced by the Christianity of the poor who escaped from Spain to the New

World, fleeing from the hunger, misery and exploitation they suffered in their homeland. Popular Latin American Christianity has its roots in the religiosity of this mass of outcasts and petty criminals or *"pícaros,"* the anti-heroes of the empire, who spread their culture and faith into the evangelization of America.

Often in conflict with the norms and values of the state and the official Church – the canons of the Counter-Reformation saw the *pícaro* as a type of sinner – popular hispanic religion transposed a lay, festive, jongleuristic and anticlerical Christianity to the Indies. In Spain its expression can be found in literature from Juan Ruiz's *Libro del Buen Amor* of the fourteenth century to Alfonso de Rojas' famous picaresque novel *Lazarillo de Tormes* of the sixteenth.

This Christianity soon took deep root among the poor of the colonies; it was not a religion of power, of the empire and its sacrality, but of the basic needs of men and women, of the desires felt by the poor. Sixteenth-century Chile provides expressions of this religion that were condemned by the imperial Church: Marcos Rodríguez, a silversmith of Santiago, complained that God did not do things properly; Gonzalo Hernández, a tailor from Concepción, was not afraid to say that he believed in Jesus but not in St Paul.

This was the piety of the ordinary run of the people, the *pícaros* who populated the Southern Cone, resentful and mocking toward a Church that for all its dignity and theology failed to rise to the level of human dignity. The Spanish folklore that has survived in Chile and Argentina expresses its own convictions:

> *Si el Santo Papa de Roma*
> *me dijera que no amara*
> *yo le diría que no*
> *aunque me recondenara.*

(If the Holy Pope of Rome/ were to tell me not to love/ I would say "No way"/ however much he condemned me.)

(c) A Religion of the Oppressed and Marginalized

Popular Christianities – native, Afro-American, mestizo and the like – were woven into an amazing tapestry on the back of the imperial Church. Lay by definition, they freely generated expressions suited to the poor and their cultures: festivals, devotions, prayers, poems, legends and behaviour proper to exploited outcasts who discovered God, Mary and the saints as liberators of the poor.

Romances (ballads) found in the Salta region of Argentina, many of Spanish origin, show the miserable condition of the poor, and Christ's solidarity with them. Such are *Si un pobre llega a una casa* (If a poor man comes to a house), *El rico no piensa en Dios* (The rich don't think about God), *Señora yo he visto un niño* (Lady, I have seen a child), *Salió un pobre una mañana* (A poor man walked out one morning). . . . In them, the rich are shown as hostile to the Jesus of the poor, while the poor are welcomed by God for their spontaneous solidarity; this is the message of the legend of Caá Yarí, or of the Yerba Mate, widely current in Paraguay and Argentina, which shows God taking the side of the oppressed.

In the Southern Cone, the imperial Church with its power and wealth loomed before the poor as an irritant, turning its clerics into superhuman (or inhuman?) beings. This typically picaresque criticism of the baroque Church enjoyed wide currency in Argentina and Chile:

> El cura no sabe arar,
> ni menos uncir un buey,
> pero por su justa ley,
> él cosecha sin sembrar . . .
> De la Trinidad del cielo
> él es la cuarta persona . . .
> Gana plata, gana bienes,
> para el cura no hay mal año. . . .

(The priest can't handle a plough/ let alone yoke an ox,/ but because his law is just/ he reaps without having to sow . . . / He is the fourth person/ of the Trinity in heaven . . . / He earns money, he gets goods,/ the priest never has a bad year.)

The poor also knew how to turn features or personalities of the imperial Church to their own ends. This happened in the case of St Francisco Solano, in real life a Franciscan missionary not especially concerned with the social condition of the Indians. A popular legend has him attending a dinner with rich people, and squeezing a piece of bread which wept blood, while he spoke these prophetic words: "I cannot eat at a table where bread kneaded with the blood of the oppressed is served."

Popular Christianities tended to have their major manifestations of devotion in places remote from the centres of influence of the established Church. There, closer to nature, devotion to Mary, Mother of God and daily protector of the poor, emerged with special force. Pilgrimage centres developed, such as Andacollo in Chile from 1584, Caacupé in Paraguay from 1602, or Luján in Argentina from 1630, all on the fringes of official imperial religion and culture, and probably more concerned with reappropriating the native goddesses of land and water.

3. THE CONSERVATIVE CHURCH AND ITS DECLINE UNDER NEO-COLONIALISM

(a) The Conservative Church, the Neo-colonial State and the Role of the See of Rome

The overwhelming expansion of capitalism in the West from the second half of the eighteenth century led to the inexorable financial and political crisis of the Spanish Empire and eventually to the loss of its colonies. The old imperial Church likewise succumbed to the constitutions of the new states, and to the influence of liberal clergy and laity.

Under these conditions, as a way of "preserving" Catholic order in the region, the See of Rome, at first under Gregory XVI, financed a vast project of church restoration. The first papal legate in Latin America, Archbishop Giovanni Muzi (1772–1849), came to the Southern Cone after emancipation. His visit led to lively debates: expelled from Buenos Aires, he nevertheless succeeded in establishing an Apostolic Vicariate in Montevideo in 1832. Politically, he made no secret of his monarchist sympathies and his unease at the "patriotic" and liberal tendencies manifested in the new republics of the Southern Cone.

The conservative Church developed through a process of discipline and hierarchization imposed by Rome: archbishoprics were established in the four republican capitals – Santiago in 1840, Buenos Aires in 1865, Montevideo in 1897 and Asunción in 1929 – and the number of bishoprics was greatly increased. Pius XI alone created seven dioceses in Chile in 1925, and thirteen in Argentina in 1934.

The new ecclesiastical authorities were notable for the energy with which they rejected all "modern" ideological and cultural tendencies emerging in neo-colonial society: liberalism, laicism, socialism. Mariano Medrano (1767–1851), who was bishop of Buenos Aires in 1832, was an outright opponent of the reform of the Church undertaken by President Rivadavia, the republican leader influenced by De Pradt and H. Grégoire; Rafael V. Validivieso (1804–78), the second archbishop of Santiago, criticized and censured Francisco Bilbao, who was introducing the ideas of Lammenais into the country. At the beginning of the twentieth century, two of the thirteen archbishops who had attended the Latin American Plenary Council in Rome in 1899, Mariano Soler of Montevideo (1846–1908) and Mariano Casanova of Santiago (1833–1908), were determined champions of fidelity to Rome and Western Christian civilization in the Southern Cone.

Certain prelates whose vigilance for the established social order far exceeded their concern for the ever more precarious cause of social justice in the region showed just how far the conservative Church could go. In 1863, Gregorio Ubieta, bishop of Paraguay, approved the re-publication of José Antonio de San Alberto's eighteenth-century "Royal Catechism," which gave religious legitimation to the dictatorships of his country. In 1919 Mariano Espinosa, archbishop of Buenos Aires from 1900 to 1923, dissolved the Christian Democratic League, founded in 1902 by the Redemptorist Friedrich Grote, thereby paralyzing any Catholic participation in trade unions.

One of the most prominent bishops of this conservative Church in the Southern Cone was Juan Sinforiano Bogarín (1863–1949), first archbishop of Asunción. He had taken part in the Rome Council of 1899, and was a declared enemy of laicism, Protestantism and communism. Disturbed by social unrest, he founded Catholic Action of Paraguay in 1932. On his death the Holy See praised him as the finest fruit of the four hundred years of the diocese of Paraguay!

(b) Conservative Devotion

The conservative Church grew out of the crisis of the imperial Church and of colonial Catholic social order, which it saw as a grave threat to world order. In the Southern Cone this awareness of crisis can be seen in verses collected from the oral tradition in Santiago del Estero in Argentina:

> Ya la religión se acaba
> virtudes y devociones;
> dan el grito las pasiones . . .
> Ay, que terrible desgracia!

Ya no hay rey, ya no hay corona . . .
Ya no hay obispos, no hay curas . . .
Ya la religión se acaba. . . .

(Religion is coming to an end/ with its virtues and devotions;/ passions are in full cry . . . / Oh, what a terrible disaster!/ There's no more king, there's no more crown . . . / There are no more bishops, no more priests . . . / Religion is coming to an end. . . .)

The profound and generally unjust economic and social changes produced by the advance of neo-colonial capitalism led the Catholic Church to a sort of piety of desolation. The liberal struggle to take over the power accumulated by the Church during the period of Spanish rule served further to exacerbate this sort of piety, which was embodied in devotion to the person of Jesus Christ and his afflicted Sacred Heart. "In these calamitous times," declared the Plenary Council of 1899, "[Jesus' Sacred Heart] is afflicted every day, not only by neglect, but also by still more criminal injuries and assaults."

While the new states in the Southern Cone at first recognized Catholicism as the official religion of their republics, as in the constitutions of Uruguay in 1830, Chile in 1833 and Argentina in 1853, new historical developments eventually modified the colonial legacy, leading to the separations of Church and state in Uruguay in 1917 and Chile in 1925, and the ending of the systems of church prerogative in Argentina and Paraguay in the last third of this century.

The conservative Church tried to hold back the advance of neo-colonial culture through a generally indiscriminate policy of subjection to the See of Rome and propagation of the tenets of Spanish and French traditionalism. In the Southern Cone this process was led by a hierarchical élite made up of Mamberto Esquiú (1826–83), bishop of Córdoba in Argentina, whose beatification process was begun in 1952, José Manuel Estrada (1842–97), also from Argentina, opponent of the liberalism of President Roca, Francisco Bauzá (1851–99) and Juan Zorrilla de San Martín (1855–1931) in Uruguay, and José Ignacio Víctor Eyzaguirre (1817–75), known as the "Balmes of Chile," who founded the Pius College of Latin America (known as the "Pio Latino") in Rome in 1858 for the education of clergy from the continent.

Although the poorer classes affected by neo-colonial economic developments found space and specific answers in the conservative Church, its religion was organized by members of the ruling classes. In nineteenth-century Uruguay, the conservative "Whites," in their struggles against the liberal "Reds," defended the clergy alongside the ranch owners. The Civic Union which opposed the separation of Church and state in 1917 was closely linked to prominent businessmen. In Chile the conservative party which took the Church's part defended the interests of landowners along with those of the Catholic middle classes from 1880 to 1930.

The conservative Church, like the imperial Church before it, continued to be a church of the powerful and of power in its social and visual expression. It may have been in decline, but it was determined to rise again in glory. To this end it took over aspects of European triumphalist devotion such as the feast of Christ the King, Eucharistic Congresses and the like. Its monumental style of architecture bore witness to its aims: the basilica of Luján in Argentina, built between 1887 and 1935, had towers nearly 350 feet high and a mass of chapels, altars, stained-glass windows and bells brought from Europe, all of which hardly suited its humble little image of the Virgin, which in the seventeenth century had been looked after by one black man.

(c) Decline

Despite the aggressive stance it maintained up to the time of the Second Vatican Council, the conservative Church was in fact all the time being eroded by the historical development of neo-colonial society. New social, cultural and religious developments – liberalism, socialism, evangelical churches (Methodist and Presbyterian in the nineteenth century, Pentecostal in the twentieth) – weakened the Catholic restoration project. Perhaps one of the most painful means of support this found was to lean on the neo-colonial system itself, even in its fascist manifestations. This happened when the conservative Church backed regimes of national security in the latter part of this century, notably in Argentina, which had a strong integralist tradition.

Other sectors of the Catholic Church adopted a different stance showing greater understanding of the new historical conditions that were leading to democratic changes in the region. This was the position taken by prelates of conservative provenance such as Crescente Errázuriz (1839–1931), who was archbishop of Santiago at the time of the Chilean Church-state separation in 1925, and his cousin Manuel Larraín Errázuriz (1900–66), bishop of Talca, who founded the Latin American Bishops' Conference, CELAM.

The growing decline of the conservative Church accelerated after the Second Vatican Council of 1962–5, which brought a radical reversal of its position. Many of its adherents found that their aspirations went unheard – the archbishop of Concepción and rector of the Catholic University of Chile, Alfredo Silva Santiago (1894–1975), for example, vainly pleaded for the Council to make a solemn condemnation of communism.

In the Southern Cone, as on the rest of the continent, there arose a movement of clergy and lay people devoted to bringing in "conciliar renewal," which involved a radical questioning of the historical identity of the conservative Church. This led to conflict between a group of priests from Mendoza in Argentina and Archbishop Buteler in 1965, and to conflict between Catholic students and the papal nuncio Forni in Uruguay. The "young church" movement in Chile came into being with the occupation of Santiago Cathedral in 1968; this sought to link the Catholic Church with popular movements. 1968 also saw the first national gathering of "Priests for the Third World" in Córdoba in Argentina; this group was soon to find itself in conflict with the bishops and the military government.[5]

One of the most decisive signs of the decline of the conservative Church was the appearance of church leaders who, following the spirit of Vatican II and the CELAM Conferences of Medellín in 1968 and Puebla in 1979, bore personal witness to the signs of a reformed Church: a servant Church incarnate in the struggles of the oppressed. Their lives themselves signified (or presaged) the end of the conservative Church. Among these were two bishops apppointed by Pope John XXIII: Enrique Angelelli (1923–76), bishop of Córdoba and La

Rioja in Argentina from 1961 till he was assassinated in La Rioja on 4 August 1976, and Enrique Alvear (1916–82), bishop of Talca, San Felipe and then Santiago from 1963 to 1982. Both had the foresight and judgment to attack the neo-colonial capitalist order from the standpoint of the liberation of the oppressed, and to delineate the new "church of the poor" ushered in by the Council.

4. THE CHALLENGE OF POPULAR CHRISTIANITIES

(a) Religious Criticism of the Conservative Church by the Poor

The revolutions that brought independence from the Spanish empire in the early nineteenth century forced official (and clerical) Catholicism back in on itself. This led to widespread criticism of the official Church of the empire from popular quarters. In 1814 the monarchist bishop of Concepción, Diego Antonio Navarro (1759–1827) complained that the people were using the institutional crisis of the Church to attack the clergy. A somewhat "heretical" climate made itself felt in the closed society of the extreme South of Latin America.

The countryside, and the towns more so, resounded to sustained criticism of the actions of the conservative Church. This had its roots partly in the picaresque traditions dating from colonial times, and partly in the new secularizing influences. While there were cases of the oppressed people introjecting the canons of the conservative churches, those who did so were also subjected to mockery by less respectful elements, who called them "priest-sucklings" in Chile. Folklore pillorying the conservative clerical order spread from the countryside and the mines to the poor districts of the cities of the Southern Cone. Priests and religious were established as figures of evil omen, sinister beings who had to be neutralized by magical rites.[6]

The conservative clergy were shown as a privileged caste, charging parish levies and "stole fees" for administering the sacraments to the common people, and living lives unrelated to those of the working classes. An expression of this comes from Salta and Jujuy in Argentina:

Cásate, me dice el cura,
yo no me quiero casar
si el cura quiere mi plata
que se ponga a trabajar.

Cásate, me dijo el cura,
yo le dije: no, vicario,
si quiere que yo me case,
que se case el comisario.

(Get married, the priest says to me,/ I don't want to marry/ if the priest wants my money/ let him set to work./ Get married, the priest said to me,/ I said to him: No, vicar,/ if you want me to get married,/ make the Commissar marry first.)

Another verse popular in Argentina and Chile reveals the hidden complicity between the conservative clergy and the rich:

En las novenas que corren
los padres de San Francisco
el pobre paga las velas
y el milagro es para el rico.

(In the novenas run by/ the Fathers of St Francis/ the poor buy the the candles/ and the rich get the miracle.)

As well as attacking the clergy, symbol of official religion, the poor of the Southern Cone embarked on a carnivalesque process of dissolution (and desacralization) of the beliefs and obligations of the Catholic Church. They used the traditional forms of comic popular verse, with its inversions, parodies and exaggerations:

Antinoche tuve un sueño
que me parecía de risa,
soñé que me levantaba
al alba para ir a misa.

Estuve en el purgatorio
y vide todas las penas,
y vide que por querer
ningún alma se condena.

Cuando Cristo vino al mundo,
de sur a norte a poniente,
dejó para bien del hombre,
vino, chicha y aguardiente.

Y Dios en su omnipotencia,
y su corazón tan noble,
al rico lo tiene rico,
y al pobre lo tiene pobre.

(Last night I had a dream/that struck me as absurd,/ I dreamt I rose at dawn/ just to go to mass./ I found myself in purgatory/ seeing the sinners suffer,/ and I saw that for loving,/ no one was condemned./ When Christ came into the world,/ from North to South to West,/ for our good he left us/ wine, *chicha*[7] and fire-water./ And God who's so almighty/ and has such a noble heart,/ keeps the rich man in his castle/ and the poor man at his gate.)

(b) Festivals and a Changed World

The popular Christianities of the Southern Cone grew out of a festive tradition of changing the world in favour of the least and forgotten – the victims of first colonial and then neo-colonial oppression. While it is questionable how far the poor actually identified with a sort of festive and carnivalesque Christianity that dreamed of changing the world on their behalf, there is no doubt that Carnival itself – disapproved of by the Church – was an event with which they could identify and where they could show their own religious fervour (which was probably related to the pre-Columbian cosmic religions, worship of Pachamama and the like).

Many popular Catholic festivals, such as those dedicated to the Virgin of Carmel, the birth of Christ, the saints, Holy Week, the May Cross and the like, lent themselves to being turned into carnivals or placed in the setting of a changed world favouring the least of the world and their culture. This is why "archaic" popular rites signifying a changed world, such as "burning Judas," can be set in contexts of social criticism.

Popular Christianities of the Southern Cone have in a way created a parallel eschatology to that of official religions, with a heavenly world peopled by the mass of hero-victims of the poor in their history: simple women and men canonized by the tradition of the oppressed. Examples are: *La difunta Correa* and *La Telesita* in Argentina, or *La Marinita* in Chile, or social bandits such as "The Gaucho Bairoletto", who lived from 1894 to 1941 and "The Gaucho José Dolores" (1805–58) in Argentina. Nor were messianic movements of the oppressed lacking in the region. One such, in Argentina in the last century, was led by Jerónimo Solané, a healer and preacher known as *El Tata Dios* ("Daddy God"). Persecuted by the freemasons, he spoke with St Francis, made rain fall, proclaimed freedom for captives in 1872, and rode through the skies on his horse "Holy Spirit."

(c) The Challenges

What has become of popular Christianities today, in the face of growing neo-colonial domination through capitalist social structures and bourgeois culture? The basic fact is that they have not gone away, and their influence is just as strong. Particularly those influenced by Protestantism, however, are tending to drift away from the social struggles against oppression.[8] In those that have stayed in the Catholic tradition, historical expressions are still growing stronger and they give spiritual support to the struggles of the workers. The twentieth-century workers' movement has itself produced mystical figures inspired by a Christ who identified with the poor and their cause. The outstanding example is Clotario Blest from Chile (1899–1990), who founded the "Workers' Single Centre" in 1953.

The decline (and fall?) of the conservative Church in the Southern Cone has released pastoral agents to work in the popular quarters, where they can encourage new liberative religious and social practices among the poor. In Paraguay, between 1960 and 1976, for example, the "Christian Agrarian Leagues" demonstrated the power of a social movement of the poor prepared to face up to the landowners and the Catholic hierarchy itself. And finally, the Christian base communities have begun to open up a space in which the little ones of this world can find room to feed their hopes, struggles and popular traditions in the name of Jesus Christ.

Translated from the Spanish by Paul Burns

NOTES

1. "Memorial del pueblo guaraní de San Luis al gobernador Bucareli" (of Buenos Aires), 1768.

2. The Spanish Counter-Reformation work *De la diferencia entre lo temporal y eterno*, by J. E. Nieremberg SJ was translated into Guaraní in 1703.

3. "Carta de Mons. José Ignacio Cienfuegos al dirigente republicano Bernardo O'Higgins," Valparaiso, 1822.

4. Reports by the missionary F. J. Wolfwisen, 1742, and Bishop Espiñeira, 1769.

5. On critique of the conservative Church by these "conciliar renewal" movements, see R. Muñoz, *Nueva conciencia de la Iglesia en América Latina* (Salamanca, 1974).

6. See J. Vicuña Cifuentes, *Mitos y supesticiones recogidos de la tradición oral chilena* (Santiago, 1915).

7. *Chicha* is an alchoholic drink made from maize, sacred to the Andean peoples.

8. See C. Lalive d'Epinay, *El refugio de las masas. Estudios sociológicos del protestantismo chileno* (Santiago, 1968).

CHRONOLOGICAL TABLE

(A) The Imperial Church and Popular Christianities: Colonial Period

1547 Asunción (Paraguay) diocese founded
1561 Santiago (Chile) diocese founded
1579 Oberá movement in Paraguay
1584 Beginning of native devotion to the Virgin of Andacollo in Chile
1597 First Synod of Tucumán (Argentina)
1603 Beginning of Guaraní devotion to the Virgin of Caacupé in Paraguay
1609 First Jesuit reductions in Paraguay
1619 Failure of Luis de Valdivia's mission to establish peace with the Mapuches
1622 Establishment of the University of Córdoba (Argentina)
1635–7 Yaguaraporo movement: Guaraní Christian creeds
1656–1750 Jesuit reductions flourish in Paraguay
1744 Popular Christian festivals in Concepción (Chile) censured by Bishop Pedro F. de Azúa
1754 Franciscans of Chillán (Chile) found Propaganda Fide College.
1766 Mapuche uprising in Chile against the empire and the Jesuits
1786 The "Royal Catechism" of Bishop San Alberto of Tucumán: enlightened despotism
1818 Battle of Maipú: end of Spanish dominion; Bishop Orellana of Tucumán returns to Spain

(B) The Conservative Church and Popular Christianities: Neo-colonial Period

1824 Rome sends G. Muzi on Apostolic Mission; Bishop Rodríguez Zorrilla expelled from Chile
1840–50 Death and miracle of "La difunta Correa": popular cult to her
1850 Archbishop Valdivieso of Santiago attacks the social romantic intellectual Bilbao
1865 Buenos Aires raised to archdiocese
1870–80 "Tata Dios," Jerónimo Solané, healer and preacher, active in Argentina
1910 Laval's collection of popular songs *Oraciones, ensalmos y conjuros del pueblo chileno* published in Chile
1917 Church-state separation in Uruguay
1919 Archbishop Espinosa of Buenos Aires dissolves the Christian Democratic League
1934 J. A. Carrizo's *Cancionero popular de Jujuy* published in Argentina
1951 Popular devotion to "La Telesita" in Argentina banned by government and Church
1960–76 Struggle of the Christian Agrarian Leagues in Paraguay
1965 Renato Poblet SJ publishes *Crisis sacerdotal* (one priest for 2,783 faithful in Chile)
1968 The sociologist Aldo Buntig shows the chasm between church and "faithful"; first National Meeting of "Third World Priests" in Argentina; occupation of Santiago cathedral and "young church" movement in Chile
1976 Bishop Angelelli of La Rioja assassinated in Argentina
1990 Death of Clotario Blest, workers' leader and mystic, in Chile

SELECT BIBLIOGRAPHY

1. The Imperial Church from Imposition to Eclipse

Carbia, R. *Historia eclesiástica del Río de la Plata 1536-1810*. Buenos Aires, 1924.
Furlong, G. *Los Jesuitas y la cultura rioplatense*. Montevideo, 1933.

Martínez Paz, E. *El Deán Funes: un apóstol de la libertad.* Córdoba, 1950.
Medina, J. T. *Historia del tribunal de la Inquisición en Chile.* Santiago, 1952.
Melia, B. *El guaraní conquistado y reducido.* Asunción, 1986.
Morner, M. *Actividades políticas y económicas de los Jesuitas en el Río de la Plata.* Buenos Aires, 1968.
Pinto, J. *Misioneros en la Araucanía.* Temuco, 1988.

2. Advent and Development of Popular Christianities

Carambula, R. *Negro y tambor. Poemas, pregones, danzas y leyendas sobre motivos del folklore afro-rioplatense.* Buenos Aires, 1952.
Carrizo, J. A. *Antecedentes hispano-medievales de la poesía tradicional argentina.* Buenos Aires, 1945.
Dussel, E. and M. Esandi, *El catolicismo popular en la Argentina.* Buenos Aires, 1970.
Pereira de Quieroz, M. I. *Historia y etnología de los movimientos mesiánicos.* Mexico, 1969.
Tormo, L. "Los pícaros en los comienzos de la evangelización de América." *Actas del I Congreso Internacional sobre la Picaresca.* Madrid, 1979, pp. 975–94.
Vargas, R. *Historia del culto a María en Iberoamérica y de sus imágenes y santuarios más celebrados.* Madrid, 1956.

3. The Conservative Church and its Decline under Neo-colonialism

Anon. *Enrique Angelelli, obisop y mártir.* Córdoba, 1984.
Hurtado, A. *¿Es Chile un país católico?* Santiago, 1941.
Irala, J. "La evangelización durante el episcopado de Juan Sinforiano Bogarín." *La evangelización en el Paraguay.* Asunción, 1979.
Mignone, E. *Iglesia y dictadura.* Buenos Aires, 1986.
Millimaci, F. *El catolicismo integral en la Argentina 1930-1946.* Buenos Aires, 1988.
Salinas, M. "Teología católica y pensamiento burgués en Chile 1880–1920." *Raíces de la teología latinoamericana.* San José, 1985.

4. The Challenges of Popular Christianities

Carrizo, J. A. *Cancionero popular de Salta.* Buenos Aires, 1933.
Coluccio, F. *Cultos y canonizaciones populares de Argentina.* Buenos Aires, 1986.
Hoyos, N. de. "Folklore de Hispanoamérica. La quema de Judas." *Revista de Indias* 41, 1950, pp. 561–87.
Laval, R. *Oraciones, ensalmos y conjuros del pueblo chileno.* Santiago, 1910.
Parker, C. *Anticlericalismo y religión popular en la génesis del movimiento obrero en Chile 1900–1920.* Santiago, 1986.
Salinas, M. *Clotario Blest, profeta de Dios contra el capitalismo.* Santiago, 1987.
Spadaccino, A. *Comunidades de base. Uruguay 1982–1988.* Montevideo, 1988.
Various. *En busca de la tierra sin mal. Movimientos campesinos en el Paraguay 1960–1980.* Bogotá, 1982.

PART THREE

SOME SPECIAL SUBJECTS

Chapter 18

PROTESTANTISM IN LATIN AMERICA

Jean-Pierre Bastian

Latin-American historiography has shown scarcely any interest in Protestant-ism as a religious phenomenon. The predominant tendency has been to write hagiographical and apologetical accounts of actors on the sectarian stage. These efforts derive from exclusively Protestant sources and stem from the specific viewpoint of Protestant groups as such. For the most part, therefore, they are not attempts at scholarly interpretation but testimonies to and documents about forms of Protestantism in themselves.

Many theses and much research emanating from Protestant theological institutions do not escape the vicious circle of subjective and apologetical analysis. Recently, however, some courageous scholars have tried to assess Latin-American Protestantism from the angle of social and political history, and in so doing to stress appropriately the actual part which Protestants played in specific political and social events. My contribution is along these lines.

I think that Protestantism should be approached as a social fact, and assessed on the basis of a social history which locates heterodox religion within the framework of its links with society as a whole. Accordingly it is important to discover new sources beyond those peculiar to Protestantism itself. Such new sources would be related to protagonists of the civil societies and of the states with which Protestantism may have interacted. Accordingly I have come to see the Protestant presence in Latin America not only as that of a religious organization but primarily as a social phenomenon involved in the relations between Latin-American societies and modern thought and the modern world, ranging over the period from the Portuguese and Spanish colonizations to the present day.

The reconstitution of Protestant history as a long-term development has enabled me to see how distant contemporary Protestant movements are from their past, and thus to detect changes more proficiently. In other words, Protestantism exists as a question and as a problem within a social and political order which has always treated it as an exotic growth, in spite of the syncretic products of the Protestant sects themselves. Protestantism is a religious heterodoxy, but one which is in the minority and on the periphery of the Latin-American arena and consciousness. Its analysis and study, however, are a challenge and an incitement to elicit the major Latin American problems. The minority religious culture is an ever-present suasion to consider the overall phenomenon, and vice versa. Consequently, in my particular account of Protestant history I do not seek to delineate a seamless, self-sufficient Protestantism, but to describe a religious actuality that is necessarily also a political reality in a continent where the secularization of civil society has scarcely any significance. All the way from the colonial forms of Protestantism

313

to the new tendencies within contemporary Protestantism there has been a close connection between heterodox religion and politics.

1. COLONIAL PROTESTANTISM, 1492–1808

The Protestant Reformation in Europe and the colonial expansion of Spain and Portugal in Latin America were contemporary events. In this respect, though the development of Protestantism in Latin America was indeed a phenomenon associated with the processes of nineteenth-century liberal secularization, the history of Protestantism in the continent began with the Portuguese-Spanish conquests. This was so because Protestantism interrogated and challenged Catholicism exactly where and when the particular configuration of the colonial geo-political map originated. Spain, on the one hand, was the symbol of the Counter-Reformation in Europe, and heterodox ideas were systematically eradicated throughout the American colonial area. The struggle for maritime and commercial supremacy in the Atlantic, on the other hand, had a religious connotation inasmuch as on the seas the Catholic nations (Spain and Portugal) confronted Protestant nations (the Netherlands and England, principally). Within the Portuguese-Spanish colonial territories, therefore, Protestantism was conceived of as a heresy threatening the ideological and political integrity of a composite socio-political totality which had been established with Christianity as a model. The threat of Protestant heterodoxy was apparent on two levels. First, it was feared inside the colonial area, for it might be adopted by possible opponents of colonial rule and was thus potentially subversive. Second, it was also effective beyond the confines of the colonial territories, for it was the religion of the maritime enemy. The history of Protestantism in Latin America began against the background of a "Protestant question" with two aspects: first, at the periphery of the Portuguese-Spanish colonial empires; second, in the margins of colonial awareness.

(a) Peripheral Forms of Colonial Protestantism

The presence of the colonial enterprises of European countries in which Protestantism had prevailed was very soon felt on the American continent. As early as 1528 German miners from the Augsburg area, which had recently become Lutheran, took part in the venture promoted by the Welsers, bankers to the Emperor Charles V, on the territory of present-day Venezuela. Nevertheless the first Protestant colony was the short-lived French Huguenot enterprise of Admiral Nicolas Durand de Villegaignon, who in 1555 took possession of Guanabara island opposite what is now Rio de Janeiro, and named it "Fort Coligny" after the great Huguenot admiral and politician. The Huguenot colony was potentially at the disposal of an eventual French expansion in the New World and received Calvin's support. Among those whom the reformer sent to the colony was the Genevan pastor Jean de Léry. His "Account of a Voyage to the Land of Brazil," published in 1578, is a valuable testimony to a venture which came to an end in 1560, when the Portuguese succeeded in expelling the French, who took to their boats. During the five years of Huguenot presence, regular services and other religious acts were celebrated in accordance with Calvinist norms. Nevertheless, as Michel de Certeau has confirmed, the "French island" was not so much a missionary centre as an exotic means of refuge, and it was not long before European religious polemics held sway over national solidarity there, at the edge of the New World. Léry offered a first ethnological approach to the Americas when he recorded his admiration for the indigenous Topinamba society which he was able to study during his visits to "terra firma".

Apart from this transient Brazilian initiative, all early French attempts at implantation in the New World failed. The presence of French Huguenots in Florida in 1564–5 was the result of inaccurate direction-finding; a long-lasting settlement was not possible until one was made at the Gulf of St Lawrence from the seventeenth century.

At this point in the sixteenth century, however, after the defeat of the invincible Spanish Armada (1588), Dutch and English mariners began to dominate the seas. Thereafter they extended the commercial relations of the new Republic of the United Provinces of the Netherlands, which adopted Calvinism as a state religion at the Synod of Dordrecht (1619).

The West Indies Company founded in 1621 to promote Dutch commercial interests on the Atlantic organized various expeditions aimed at the north-eastern coast of Brazil, which seemed easy to take from the Portuguese. After a first uncertain attempt at Bahia in 1624, the Dutch succeeded in taking Recife in 1630, and shortly afterwards Olinda. This enabled them to ensure control of the Pernambuco for twenty-four years, and by 1641 to hold sway over some fourteen Portuguese captaincies in north-eastern Brazil. There was an emphatic religious aspect to Dutch colonization and Calvinism became the religion of Dutch Brazil, but in a context of broad religious tolerance of Judaism and Catholicism, along the lines of that practised in the metropolitan Netherlands. The political structures of the colony were consolidated with the arrival in 1537 of Prince Jan Maurizius of Nassau-Siegen. A convinced Calvinist, he supported the creation of a Calvinist religious structure on the metropolitan model. During twenty-four years of Dutch colonization, twenty-two churches and congregations were organized; the most important were those at Recife and Olinda. Over the same period some fifty pastors built up a Reformed Church with a consistory as its administrative body and nineteen presbytery meetings and four synods were held between 1636 and 1648, all in the town of Recife, the political centre of the colony.

The Dutch colony of Pernambuco is one of the significant instances for any comparison of Catholic and Protestant evangelization in Latin America. The religious tolerance which the Dutch ensured was in marked contrast to the constitutive intolerance of the Portuguese and Spanish colonies, where the tribunal of the Inquisition was the chosen instrument. Nevertheless, Protestants and Catholics shared the same attitude to slavery. Admittedly, the Dutch when they arrived were imbued with the Calvinist ethic, which celebrated the dignity of labour and the sacredness of vocation; accordingly they tried to replace the production relations proper to serfdom with free labour. However, since the Dutch population was concentrated in the towns, they were subject to "the pressure of economic interests stronger than the morality of John Calvin" and, because of the lack of an adequate work-force in the sugar cane fields, were forced to recapture runaway slaves. Roger Bastide puts it well: "Above a reality which wholly refuted it, the Calvinist ethic drifted like an image devoid of creative impetus."

A similar process occurred in the context of the other Protestant colonies in the Caribbean, which began to develop gradually after 1655, when a Cromwellian expedition seized Jamaica. The Dutch on the island of Curaçao, the Danes in the Virgin Islands (1666), and the English in the lesser Antilles established a sugar-cane plantation economy dependent on the exploitation through slavery of a work-force of African origin. The Anglican Church tended to legitimize colonial interests, and the Protestant sects, especially the Methodists and Baptists, adopted anti-slavery ideas only after some delay. Although the Slave Code in Jamaica (1696) obliged colonists to make provision for their slaves' evangelization, this proved a somewhat fitful process and was favoured more by the Nonconformist sects than by the Church of England. As Eric Williams observes, the Anglicans shared in the rewards of slavery and the clergy themselves owned slaves. Similarly the Puritan and analogous sects were not opposed to slavery. In 1680, for instance, the sixty-five Quaker planters of the island of Barbados owned 3307 acres of land and 1631 slaves.

It was only at the end of the eighteenth century that the Methodists, and a little later the Baptists, began to develop their own efforts at evangelization with a strong anti-slavery content, and these very soon led to their persecution by the planters. On Trinity Island the governor forced the Methodists to close their mission, and on Barbados, on 26 October 1823, the planters destroyed the Methodist chapel which they claimed was used to promote that "wretched African society" (for the abolition of slavery). In Jamaica, at the end of the 1820s, the Reverend William Knibb was a symbol of this resolute evangelical anti-slavery tendency. It was evident most emphatically in August 1833 when the British parliament passed the Emancipation Act. This came into effect gradually from August 1834.

The anti-slavery feeling of the Nonconformist sects became apparent when the plantation economy of the British colonies in the West Indies went into decline and British interests shifted first to the New England colonies and then to India, and after the loss of the former much more to the latter. At the end of the eighteenth century the great pietistic revival aroused Christian consciences and inspired the anti-slavery struggle of humanists and Christian philanthropists. In 1792 the French revolutionaries proclaimed the rights of man and of the citizen. At the same time, the revolutionary slave movement in Haiti led to a black republic in 1804, with Dessalines and Toussaint l'Ouverture at its head. In the British, Dutch and Danish "Protestant" colonies slave emancipation was slower but less violent. It was not so much the spirit of Wesley as the fight for freedom of the Haitian slaves which awakened the consciousness of Protestant blacks in the West Indies.

(b) Lutheran Heresy on the Periphery of the Portuguese and Spanish Colonial Identity

The Portuguese-Spanish colonies were evangelized with the plain conviction that the Christianity under reconstruction in the New World would avoid the ruptures of the Old World. One of the chroniclers of the conquest of New Spain was quite sure of this when he described the work of Fray Martín of

Valencia, one of the twelve Franciscan apostle-evangelists of New Spain: "The cloak of Christ which Martin the heretic rent in two was restored by another holy and Catholic Martin" who brought into the bosom of the Church even more faithful than it had just lost. The first evangelization of the Spanish colonies was essentially the work of the religious orders following their particular interest. The Franciscans and Dominicans, intent on purifying Catholic religious practice in the spirit of Erasmian humanism, soon came into conflict with the secular clergy.

This struggle for influence resulted in the bishops' triumph over the regular clergy and in that of the Catholic Counter-Reformation spirit over the ethos of Erasmian humanism. From the second half of the sixteenth century, the establishment of the apparatus of the Spanish Inquisition throughout the colonial territory (Cartagena, 1568; Mexico, 1571; Lima, 1610) marked the emergence of a Catholic Counter-Reformation Christianity dependent on Jesuit shock-troops. The model of Catholic Christianity, inspired by an Aristotelian-Thomist philosophy, was applied to the Portuguese-Spanish colonial territories. The colonial order became a corporative and patrimonial, hierarchical and vertical structure. At its core Catholicism reinforced the perception of the social order as something approximating to the natural order. Its castes were distinguished by racial characteristics, and were conceived as a hierarchy descending from white to Indian or black, with all sorts of admixtures *en route*.

In this context, from the second half of the sixteenth century, Protestantism was seen as a threat to ongoing colonial development. It was evident on two levels.

Ad extra, it was a question of disabling the maritime enemy and of condemning as heretics the English, Dutch and French Huguenot corsairs and pirates. Of course they had never shown any inclination to evangelize, but their mere presence and the anti-Spanish and anti-Catholic mentalities which they represented were a danger associated with possible territorial conquest. Their systematic condemnation during the last third of the sixteenth century had another consequence. Spectacular *autos-da-fé* promoted an anti-Protestant and anti-foreign attitude in the colonial population so that Protestant and foreigner became synonymous in the collective unconscious. Of 224 pirates and corsairs tried by the Spanish Inquisition in the Americas during the second half of the sixteenth century a mere eighteen were sentenced to death. Nevertheless the *autos-da-fé* and the trials had a psychological effect. It can still be traced in suspicion, and in the equation of "Protestant" with "heretical", so that Protestants are virtually prime agents of alien penetration. Paraphrasing Serge Gruzinski, we may say that the Protestant virtually joined the "company of deviants, spooks and obsessions that haunt the imagination of Iberian societies along with Jews, sodomites and sorcerers."[1]

Ad intra, from the seventeenth century, it was the domestic political enemy who was accused and sentenced on account of Protestant heresy. This was the case both with Guillen de Lampart who was accused of wishing to make New Spain an independent kingdom (1649), and with the priests Miguel Hidalgo and José María Morelos, fathers of Mexican independence, who were sentenced in 1810. The last-named were condemned not only as Lutheran heretics but equally as materialists and atheists. In addition to the Protestant varieties which already packed the heresy list there were now the heresies of the Enlightenment and especially those of "tolerationism."

Compared with the Catholic colonial identity, the various forms of Protestantism were certainly thought of as conveying a liberal modernism that was anathema to the colonial order. They were seen as endangering the "natural" order and forms of racial as well as economic and political domination. In fact, there were scarcely any more Protestant heretics than at the start, but once Protestant ideas were associated with modernity they represented a much greater threat to the established order. The persecution of books and of clandestine readers increased rapidly even in the context of Bourbon reforms (from 1701) in New Spain, or of Pombal's reforms in Brazil, which meant a relative degree of opening up of colonial territories. Of course this exposure occurred within the framework of a quest for a Catholic modernity *sui generis*, and of one which claimed to dispense with Protestant ideas and their republican and modern democratic political manifestations. It was more for these reasons, and not so much because of the marginal presence of heretics, that the Protestant question shifted from the periphery of the collective unconscious. Now it appeared as something to be resolved at the heart of the whole problem of the relations betweeen the ethos of the colonial Catholic world and liberal modern thought and culture. This challenge persisted through three centuries of Portuguese and Spanish colonization. It re-emerged intact with the independent nations which issued from the revolutions at the beginning of the nineteenth century, and proved so resilient that a conciliation between Catholicism and the liberal modern world proved difficult if not impossible.

2. PROTESTANT SOCIETIES AND THE LIBERAL MODERN WORLD, 1808–1959

The independence revolutions (1808–26) aroused the Latin-American continent and prompted the formation of nation states which adopted republican constitutions. A sizeable exception was Brazil, which was transformed into an empire under the aegis of the Portuguese monarchy in exile. In fact, from 1822 Emperor Don Pedro I introduced a constitutional monarchy which would last until the declaration of a republic in 1899. Mexico experienced a short monarchical interlude under the Holy Emperor Agustín de Iturbide (1821–4), before becoming a republic like the other nation states which emerged from the former Spanish empire. The new constitutions relied less on French or U.S. precedents than, fundamentally, on the liberal Spanish constitution of Cadiz (1812). Now, one of the main problems for the liberal élites in power was how to build a liberal modern society while managing to reconcile Catholicism with republicanism.

Republicanism was one of the conditions of entry to the British world economy and for the opening of nascent nation states to the benefits of economic progress. Catholicism, however, was seen as the only ideology capable of forging national identities and of cementing fragile nationalities threatened by the centrifugal forces of regional interests and the latent or apparent rebellions of indigenous "nations".

The *criollo* and white élites as against the mestizo and indigenous or black masses saw Catholicism and the Church as a necessary and useful social force for the defence of their interests. But they required the Church to agree to some kind of reform and especially to adapt to the new republican form of "prerogative". Accordingly the liberal Spanish constitution of Cadix was extremely attractive to the Latin-American *criollo* élites, for it retained Catholicism as a state religion but defended the principles of a form of liberal democracy. The national Catholic Churches' resistance to moderate republican "prerogative", their constant support for conservative interests, and the emergence of an ultramontane Catholicism which swept away liberal Catholicism and straightforwardly attacked liberal modernism, sounded the death-knell of the moderate liberal project. Accordingly, from the middle of the nineteenth century, when faced with the impossibility of any reconciliation between Catholicism and liberalism, second-generation liberals were forced to turn radical. They imposed a form of secularization by means of new constitutions (in Colombia in 1853; in Argentina in 1854; and in Mexico in 1857) which broke with the Catholic religious monopoly, and at best led to a separation of Church and state. The restructuring of relations between the Catholic Church and the oligarchical state in order to conciliate interests, and the subsequent triumph of neo-corporative forms of populism together with their confrontations with the Catholic Church or their co-opting of Catholicism, all influenced the emergence and development of Protestantism, which was intimately linked with radical liberal modernism.

(a) Reformation of Catholicism, Religious Toleration and Immigration

One of the dilemmas which first-generation liberals tried to resolve was how to ensure the "political march of progress", the symbols of which were first Britain, then the United States, without having to "Protestantize" the Latin-American nations. In other words, they asked how, faced with a different reality moulded by centuries of forms of colonial Catholicism, they could elicit moral and religious values like those which seemed to accompany the development of Anglo-Saxon liberalism. That first generation of liberals considered the appropriate course to be not the adoption of Protestantism but a reform of Catholicism leading to modernization. Consequently they welcomed the initiatives of the first bible colporteurs sent by the recently-founded British and North American Protestant bible societies.

One who may stand for ten others is the Scottish Baptist minister James Thomson (1788–1854). He was the first to distribute bibles in the Catholic version, from 1818, when he disembarked at Buenos Aires. He was sent by the British and Foreign Bible Society, which also charged him with propagation of the Lancasterian system of instruction in literacy.

Thomson was received in Argentina with the support of President Bernardino Rivadavia. He made a tour of the continent which took him successively to Chile (1821), Peru (1822), Ecuador (1824), Colombia (1825), Mexico (1827) and the Caribbean (1833 and 1837). Everywhere he received the enthusiastic support of moderate liberals. His activities accorded with the aims of the Catholic reform favoured by the moderate liberal élites, which included many clergymen, such as the Mexican José María Luís Mora (1794–1850).

In the context of progressive political and economic reform, moderate liberals expected such efforts to yield an enlightened Catholicism. They hoped that it would help to reorientate ideas and beliefs and reinforce nascent nationalities. In its attitude to religion, this initial form of liberalism was an extension of the enlightened reformism of the Bourbons or of Pombal's reforms. This continuity was reflected especially in the exclusive status which the new constitutions gave to Catholicism, apart from such transient exceptions as the Fundamental Law of the province of San Juan in July 1825 (Río de la Plata), and the decree of the Guatemalan Congress presided over by Mariano Gálves, of 2 May 1832, which guaranteed religious liberty. During the first half of the century, the problem of religious tolerance and the much more radical question of freedom of worship were subjects of numerous debates throughout the countries of the continent. The liberal Ecuadorian Vicente Rocafuente (1773–1847) in particular wrote an exemplary treatise defending the principle of general religious tolerance (in 1833) as the necessary condition for political and economic modernism. Neither the moderate liberals nor (even less) the conservatives who alternated in power during this first half of the nineteenth century approved of the principle of religious tolerance for their own citizens. Such tolerance was acceptable only after external pressure and exclusively for Protestants who were foreign nationals resident in Latin America. This dual pressure was exerted by commercial treaties and immigration policies.

The trade agreements between Latin American countries and Britain, Prussia and the United States included, often after bitter and long-lasting negotiations, a clause authorizing Protestant religious practices for resident foreign nationals. Thus the Anglo-Portuguese treaty of 1810 was one of the first to allow British subjects to build churches, and a chapel was erected at Río de Janeiro and a cemetery established there in 1819 for British Protestants. The same procedure was followed between Britain and the United Provinces of Rio de la Plata and, in the Rivadavia Constitution of 1826, resulted in a clause providing for toleration of their own form of worship for British subjects. In Mexico, the first version of the Anglo-Mexican Treaty of 1825 did not include religious tolerance for British subjects, since President Guadalupe Victoria felt that "the requirement of religious tolerance did not accord with the Mexican Constitution, and that a resolution of this kind would be unacceptable to the Mexican people." In the definitive 1826 version of the treaty, the question of free exercise of religious worship was resolved only in an oblique manner, by restricting actual Protestant worship to the private confines of British residences in Mexico. Mexicans in Britain, however, were allowed to attend their own religious services in existing Catholic churches.

Under the guarantees of international treaties, foreign residents' churches were built in the main ports and commercial centres of the continent. For example, at Buenos Aires, a first Anglican church was inaugurated in 1831, a Scottish Presbyterian church in 1833, and a U.S. Methodist church in 1843. Nevertheless, even though a non-Catholic foreigner was legally entitled to enjoy the benefits of the protection of his religious rights, in civil life he suffered fierce ostracism and onerous social pressures because of Catholic mentalities moulded by three centuries of the colonial Inquisition. Above all, if there was a possibility of marriage with a Catholic, as a general rule the foreign national had to yield to family and social pressure and become a Catholic himself.

These minorities consisting of foreign merchants and residents deserve more proficient study. As William Glade emphasizes, they certainly had a decisive effect on the development of Latin-American economies throughout the nineteenth century. In-depth research is needed to reconstruct these religious communities and to try to understand their defence of freedom of worship as an integral part of the modern world which they wanted to promote. Nevertheless, the problem of tolerance and freedom of worship was just as much linked to something other than commercial policies: to the need to attract immigrant populations to the empty areas of the continent.

In fact one of the main precoccupations of the governments of the young independent nations was to encourage European immigration, for it was seen as an essential factor for stimulation of economic modernization. This policy did not meet with the same success wherever it was promoted. Of course it was influenced by various factors, such as the quality of the land proposed for settlement and its cost, the commitment of the companies commissioned to recruit and transport Europeans to the shores of the continent, and, naturally, prevailing political conditions. One of the decisive factors was also the existence or not of religious tolerance, and in this respect it is interesting to compare the policies of Brazil and of Mexico on immigration and religious tolerance.

In Mexico, as Bernecker has shown (1989), in spite of many attempts by German diplomats to negotiate religious tolerance as a condition for German immigration, it was always refused between 1830 and 1854. This discouraged the immigration of German colonists who preferred to go to the United States. In Brazil, on the other hand, the Imperial Constitution of 25 March 1824 protected the freedom of religious expression, while maintaining Catholicism as the state religion, which was not satisfactory for non-Catholics. From 1824 onwards this moderate religious policy favoured the immigration of German colonists to the States of Rio Grande do Sul, Santa Catarina and Paraná, all in the south of the country. Among the 300,000 German immigrants calculated as arriving up to 1871, little over half were Protestant and the remainder were Catholic. Hence, in the region of Porto Alegre and São Leopoldo, Rio Grande do Sul, among the 5393 colonists registered in 1847, 3365 were Lutherans and had eight chapels, whereas the others, who were Catholics, had four churches. A comparison of the results of policies on migration to Mexico and Brazil yields interesting results. Brazil obtained an immediate geopolitical advantage by populating a frontier region which was almost wholly uninhabited and coveted by Argentina. As Dreher (1984) notes, this strategic factor was additional to the desire to "render the race white," to confront the natives, to exploit the land and to raise an inexpensive labour force. In Mexico during the same period the frontier regions of the north were also uninhabited. Non-acceptance of religious tolerance would seem to have acted as a decisive brake on immigration there, and these territories coveted by the United States soon came under its control. It is interesting to learn that the independence of Texas had scarcely been proclaimed in 1837 than the principle of freedom of worship was adopted; this favoured immigration, which also undoubtedly accorded with U.S. expansionist interests. The same was true of the transient republic of Yucatán (1843–4), which hoped to be able to reinforce its autonomy vis-à-vis Mexico by adopting freedom of worship and trusting that this would help to open up the Yucatán to European immigration.

In Peru, an intolerant policy similar to that of Mexico closed the country to immigration; Argentina, on the other hand, on the fall of Rosas' conservative government (1829–52), adopted a liberal constitution (1853) protecting tolerance of worship and freedom of expression, which reinforced an especially dynamic immigration policy. The founding of the colonies of Esperanza (Santa Fé) in 1856 and of San José (Entre Ríos) in 1857 occurred with the participation of Swiss and German Protestant colonists who soon adopted Methodism as their denomination. In several other colonies which populated the states of Chubut, Buenos Aires, Entre Ríos and Santa Fé, Protestant congregations founded by immigrants came into being. Nevertheless, the 1895 census revealed the limits, for scarcely 2 percent of the population of these provinces were Protestants, and less than 1 percent of the population of the country as a whole. From the other side of the Río de la Plata, Italian colonists from the Vaudois valleys of Piedmont settled in Uruguay from 1856, to live there in accordance with the Protestant religious traditions of the Val d'Aosta.

In the same way as other transplanted churches, the religious societies established by Protestant immigrants reinforced ethnic identity and served to distinguish the Protestant group from the rest of a civil society, where withdrawal into one's own group was preferred to integration. This proved a very slow process given the minority status of Protestant bodies within societies moulded by Catholicism and where, apart from the south of Brazil, the immigration was predominantly Italian, Spanish and Polish Catholic.

For the Argentine liberals Domingo F. Sarmiento (1811–88) and Juan Bautista Alberdi (1810–84), European colonization would surely impose new styles of country life associated with the development of the small estate and put an end to rural "barbarism." In the same way, as far as they were concerned, religious tolerance and the presence of Protestant colonists must favour the spread of the values of Protestantism, a religion of progress, which would perhaps eventually, or so they hoped, replace Hispanic Catholicism, which they saw as embodying values that restrained the advance of modern thought. In Brazil, the liberal Aureliano C. Tavares Basto also thought that the economic progress of the country depended to some extent on Anglo-Saxon and Germanic immigration, and on the correlated spread of Protestantism. Nevertheless, with the exception of the south of Brazil, the presence of Protestant immigrants was very limited.

Moreover, it was not so much policies regarding migration as the anti-Catholicism of the radical liberal minorities, exacerbated by the Roman ultramontanism of the pontificate of Pius IX (1846–78), which favoured the implantation of Protestantism, supplying it with endogenous roots that would allow it to circumvent its reduction to the level of mere foreign enclaves.

(b) Free-thought Societies, Anti-Catholicism and Radical Liberalism

From the end of the first half of the nineteenth century, a new generation of liberals tried to bring an end to conservative and authoritarian republican regimes answering to corporatist interests and with the Catholic Church as their main support. Moderate liberal initiatives had been unable to eradicate corporatist interests associated with the big landowners, or to destroy military and religious structures of colonial origin. Accordingly, the liberals made their policies more radical in order to get rid of the conservative coalition. This new generation fought to ensure that the instruments of liberal and capitalist modern thought would prevail within societies deeply marked by traditional corporatist mentalities, behaviour-patterns and values. In contradistinction to the corporatist tendencies, they freed property in mortmain from the big landowners, the Church and indigenous communities. Consequently they also liberated a work-force which until then had been in a state of semi-servitude, and set out to form a migrant labour force to serve the industries coming into being and gradually constitute an embryonic working class. They also imposed secular education in order to provide the foundations of a middle-class democracy.

Similarly, they tried to force the Church to submit to the state and, at best, to separate the two. This process of modernization associated with the expansion of an international capitalism anxious to invest excess income in a continent rich in raw materials came to rely on a process of political reform symbolized by the period named, indeed, "the Reform" in Mexico (1855–60) under the leadership of Bénito Juárez (1806–72), a radical liberal lawyer of native origin. Because of the Church's opposition to the laws regarding the liberation of property subject to mortmain, and to a constitution (1857) that was liberal, though still quite moderate in respect of church-state relations, the Mexican liberals became more radical. This radicalism took a violently anti-Catholic direction. Forthwith, from 1859, they promulgated a series of reform laws during a state of full civil war. They separated Church from state, laicized the civil register and cemeteries as well as education, proclaimed freedom of worship (1860) and broke off diplomatic relations with the Holy See. This anti-Catholic radicalization of liberal politics was echoed in Colombia in 1853 on the initiative of President Thomas Cipriano de Mosquera, and also in Argentina, though in a much more moderate form, during the liberal governments of the "National Organization" (1852–80). In Ecuador, on the other hand, liberalism was banished by the Catholic theocracy of Gabriel García Moreno. He was in power from 1859 to 1875 and tried to create a model form of Catholic modernism, uniting the nation "in an integrative system which was archaic in terms of its clerical roots and modern in that it suppressed the religious orders and intermediary bodies," while signing a concordat with the Vatican.

Hence the Latin America of the mid-nineteenth century veered between two extremes: violent liberal secularization of the Mexican type on the one hand, and the authoritarian Catholic republicanism of a García Moreno in Ecuador on the other hand. Between these two extremes several intermediary political and religious positions corresponded to the actual power relations between state and Church.

This conflict was constitutive of modern society in Latin America. It is within its framework, therefore, that we must study and assess the emergence of Protestant religious associations and their involvements. Far from being the first results of U.S. missionary expansion, these associations had their roots in the political culture of Latin American radical liberalism, and in the associative ferment and enthusiasm which those same liberals tried to encourage in civil society in order to give themselves a power-base. Latin American historiography has hardly begun to show interest in the new associations, which embodied a liberal and democratic political culture. They took the shape of reform clubs in Mexico and Brazil, of egalitarian societies in Chile around 1850, and of democratic societies in Colombia between 1850 and 1854.

Among these new types of association some, we must remember, were in a state of change, such as the freemasons' lodges which, in the context of Roman ultramontanism, lost the participation of the liberal clergy and were gradually inspired by a burgeoning anti-Catholicism.

This anti-Catholicism persuaded these new associations to instigate Catholic schisms and dissident religious activities which very soon took the course of Protestantism, but also, from the 1860s onwards, of spiritualism and theosophy. In fact, in a continent where, as in Europe, liberal Catholicism was on the wane, the liberals had lost all hope of reconciling Catholicism with liberal republican modern thought. They believed the establishment of new non-Roman Catholic religious societies would offer a possibility of extending, reinforcing and consolidating a new ultra-minority, radical liberal nation which had emerged from the centre of the void opened up by the free-thought societies. To the extent that the Catholic schisms failed, the Protestant societies as well as the spiritualist circles and even the positivist churches, as was the case in Brazil, seemed a potential religious alternative.

Recent essays by Gueiros Viera (1980) on Brazil in the period of the "religious problem" (1872–5), and by Bastian (1989) on Mexico in the Reform period (1855–76) and under Porfirio Díaz (1876–1911), allow us to hypothesize a close connection and continuity of activity between Latin American liberal societies and burgeoning Protestant associations.

In Brazil, it was the networks of Grand Orient freemasons' lodges of the Valley of the Benedictines, under the chairmanship of the liberal Joaquin Saldanha Marino, and those of the liberal Catholic congregations under the influence of the former priest and freemason José Manuel da Conceição (1822–73), which preceded and served as a basis for Presbyterian and Methodist expansion after 1863. Da Conceição in particular became a Presbyterian in 1863 and integrated the network of Catholic congregations under his control in the state of São Paulo into the nascent Presbyterian Church. Similarly, one of the first Brazilian Presbyterian leaders was Pastor Miguel Vieira Ferreira (1837–95), a signatory to the Republican Manifesto of 3 December 1870, a forerunner of the anti-monarchical struggle, and a supporter of the liberal republic. In Mexico too it was the bases of the Mexican Church of Jesus, a Catholic schismatic body started unsuccessfully on two occasions, in 1861 and 1867, as well as the "Catholic evangelical" networks modelled on freemasons' lodges and run by former officers in liberal armies, especially in the rural areas of conflict between *hacienda* and small village landowners, which acted as an encouragement and as a basis for future Presbyterian, Methodist and Congregationalist Churches. Simultaneously, as it were, close ties developed between the Protestant congregations under formation and the mutual societies recently established in working-class textile and mining areas, where a form of Christian anarchism was to be found, represented by such figures as Poltino C. Rhodakanati, founder of mutual societies and Professor of Greek and philosophy at the seminary of the Mexican Church of Jesus, the forerunner of the present Protestant Episcopalian Church.

In Cuba, too, during the thirty years before independence (1868–98), Protestant congregations established on an exclusive basis by liberals and Cuban soldiers served as networks for liberal ideas. Their leaders and those of the lodges were persecuted by the Spanish authorities. Similar affinities between liberals who had recently come to power and the development of Protestant societies occurred both in the Colombia of Mosquera (1861) and in the Guatemala of Justo Rufino Barrios (1885). The few respectable studies of the existence of free-thought societies, which preceded the Protestant societies by a few years, in Mexico and in Brazil, support a preliminary major judgment in our interpretation of the origins of Protestantism as a Latin American phenomenon. The emergence of Protestant congregations and societies during the period of confrontation between Church and state is not evidence of a penetration, an invasion or a supposed conspiracy, as the Catholic conservative press claimed, but corresponds to the urgent demands of ultra-minority radical-liberal circles seeking to expand their bases.

I find that this demand existed on three levels at least: first, and above all, among the radical liberal associations of a religious bent which were already in existence; second, among the liberal leaders in power who hoped by this means to reinforce their struggle against the Roman Catholic Church and against conservative political circles; and, third, among the remnants of a liberal Catholic clergy who, finding no possibility of developing a liberal Catholicism by means of fruitless schisms, saw Protestantism as a potential means of continuing their reformist activity. It is absolutely essential to understand this organic connection between nascent Protestant associations, radical liberalism and free-thought societies which promoted democratic and secularizing political models, if we are to distinguish the indigenous from the imported aspects of Latin American Protestantism in subsequent years.

While awaiting the results of other research, it is permissible at least to suppose that when missionaries belonging to U.S. Protestant societies began their proselytizing activities, they did not meet with desert and infertile soil. On the contrary, the fertile foundations of a Latin American Protestantism had been laid by the radical liberal minorities. It was this ground that the U.S. Protestant missionaries were able to penetrate with their equally liberal values and their associative models, which offered a major chance of cohesion to various pre-existing and heterogeneous religious dissident movements. Rapidly deploying their primary and secondary schools, they accorded with a specific thrust toward education in those social sectors which supported Protestantism. In this perspective, it is easy to understand how certain negotiations took place when the missionaries arrived. The Latin American Protestant leaders who had emerged from circles associated with free-thought societies and were soaked in a radical liberal form of culture, put at the disposal of the missionaries the networks and contacts which they had established beforehand. These were promptly rebaptized in the names of various Protestant denominations. For their part, the missionaries offered the liberals the financial means to carry on their work, together with schools and a militant press. Consequently Latin American Protestantism came to life in the shape of a liberal religious syncretism. More effectively than Luther, Calvin or Wesley, from the start the heroes of the anti-conservative liberal struggles, such as Hidalgo, Juarez and Ocampo for Mexico, Tiradentes for Brazil, Sarmiento in Argentina and Martí in Cuba, helped to nourish their civic thought and involvements and to constitute them in societies dedicated to unfettered thought.

(c) The Distribution of Protestant Liberal Associations

The Latin American Protestant societies took root at the time of the anti-Catholic and anti-corporatist radicalization peculiar to the liberal "reform" movements. Their development and expansion, however, occurred in the context of liberal oligarchical and neo-corporatist governments which succeeded the former and reinforced themselves by relying on the Catholic Church to assure their long-term power. During the 1880s, the liberal oligarchical régimes attempted to introduce an authoritarian form of economic development, connected with the interests of international capitalist companies prepared to invest capital in high-return transport, industry, mines and agriculture. The face of the continent changed rapidly during the last two decades of the nineteenth century, with accelerated urbanization, the appearance of middle sectors of the population associated with services, and constant migrations by a nascent working class towards the poles of economic development. Positivism, with its slogan of "order and progress," was the privileged ideology of power-holding minorities, which did not hesitate to enlist the support of the Catholic Church to maintain consensus and peace when social inequalities and differences became more obvious.

For its part, thanks to the tacit or explicit support of the oligarchical state, the Catholic Church went through a period of expansion and restructuring. After the Catholicism of the situation obtaining in 1850 and 1860, which was on the defensive, as indicated by the encyclical *Quanta Cura* and the *Syllabus of Errors* of 1864, a renewed Catholicism came into being. It was now on the offensive, and found its main lines of expression in the encyclical *Rerum Novarum* (1891) and the pontificate of Leo XIII. It was no longer a matter of openly condemning liberal modernism, but rather of accepting it or, better still, of remoulding it in order to recover the Church's influence, which had been lost as a result of liberal secularization. In this sense, as Emile Poulat puts it, a Catholicism of movement, organization and association was to lead to the active participation of Catholics in political and social change. Of course this always occurred in a Thomist perspective, that is, with the claim of christianizing the social order and proffering a model of Christian society in contradistinction to secularizing socialist and capitalist models. The religious orders burgeoned and were key elements in the reconquest of civil society; new dioceses were founded; Catholic educational systems as well as seminaries and priests multiplied; and even a form of social Catholicism appeared and established Catholic workers' societies.

It is in this kind of authoritarian oligarchical political context, and in one of Catholic recovery, that one must locate the development and expansion of the

Protestant societies at the end of the nineteenth century and during the first two decades of the twentieth century. In fact, the interest in Latin America of the U.S. Protestant missionary societies (which were almost the only ones actually in Latin America, for European forms of Protestantism thought of the American continent as already Christian) became established firmly only after the civil war which raged in the United States from 1862 to 1865. It was only from the 1870s that the systematic arrival of missionaries commenced, and only after the 1880s that most of the Protestant schools and cultural efforts in Latin America came into being. As I have stressed, these missionaries (ministers, teachers, doctors, nurses and so on) did not encounter a reality devoid of "Protestant" societies. Almost everywhere there were pre-existing schismatic religious movements influenced by liberal Catholicism or by the masonic lodges, whose leaders served as primary recruits for constitution of the Protestant Churches, which owed their formation to the combined action of both elements. In other words, the foreign Protestant missionary societies reinforced a heterodox Latin-American "Protestant" movement anchored in the radical liberal political culture of the 1850s and 1860s. Moreover, the spread of Protestant associations during the years that followed occurred in a precisely defined area corresponding to what one might term a Protestant liberal geography.

The Protestant societies which were expanding within the liberal minorities recruited their members from social sectors in a state of transition. Neither the oligarchy nor the bourgeoisie nor the traditional middle classes, neither the natives nor the peons and rural workers on the haciendas, were interested or could have been interested in Protestantism. It was mainly the mine-workers, textile workers and railwaymen who joined the new religious societies. Moreover these societies recruited among the small landed proprietors (*rancheros, aparceros, medieros, arrendatarios* and *inquilinos*) and the wage-earning agricultural workers on modern plantations, who were constantly migrating. Finally, the urban social sectors associated with services (education, banks, commercial clerks and so on) were also receptive, especially when they were members of a second generation of "urbanized" Protestants deriving especially from the above-mentioned rural sectors. For each country one would have to reconstruct the networks of congregations in order more proficiently to gauge their elective affinity with these transitory social sectors, nourished by a firm desire for progress and influenced at the same time by an economic uncertainty resulting from their specific position in a production structure that was especially sensitive to recurrent economic crises. In the case of Mexico, a systematic study of this kind has revealed a precisely defined topography for these Protestant minorities.

It is true that the Protestant congregations were established in modern urban centres close to mines and textile industries as well as railways. However, a systematic examination of the whole network of congregations discloses a pattern of concentration in a number of rural areas, all situated on the periphery of regional power centres, in political districts with a liberal tradition, where Indians had confronted Spaniards, and the small property predominated, alongside a modern agro-export economy (coffee, bananas, lemons, rubber, cotton and so on). These rural districts, with histories of pre-existing antagonisms to the traditional centres of political, economic and religious power, were interested in a Protestant religious practice and ideology which, in addition to reinforcing radical liberalism and their religious autonomy in respect of control by an authoritarian liberal centralism and by the Catholic Church, offered the good quality educational services which they sorely lacked. It is scarcely surprising, given its reinforcement of an anti-oligarchical and anti-conciliatory radical liberalism, to find the same Protestant liberal distribution at the basis of the Mexican revolutionary movements of 1910, after forty years of inculcating democratic principles and values within these minorities.

In addition, a rare regional study on the spread of Protestantism in the state of São Paulo in Brazil during the 1870s and 1880s has revealed a chain of Presbyterian congregations along the entire coffee production frontier, among a population of small proprietors or *inquilinos* (*sitiantes*) of coffee *fazendas* as well as among waged and migrant agricultural workers. The Presbyterian congregations proliferated in a triangle on the frontiers of the states of São Paulo and Minas Gerais, within a rural population inspired by a radical, republican and anti-monarchical (later, from 1889, anti-oligarchical) liberal-ism; as in Mexico, it included many soldiers from the lower ranks of the republican forces.

In Colombia it was also in the coffee-growing expansion regions that the Protestant congregations were to be found and a radical liberal distribution developed. It was there, almost a century later, from 1948, that the anti-liberal violence, persecution and executions especially focussed on Protestants, freemasons and spiritualists suddenly increased.

Admittedly, in absolute terms the Latin American forms of Protestantism were numerically insignificant and hardly progressed, since the Protestant populations never rose above 1 percent of the Latin American populations before the 1940s and 1950s. On the other hand, if one compares the associative networks formed by these societies with other similar systems, such as those of masonic lodges, spiritualist circles, mutual societies and even Catholic social associations, the Protestant networks were of the same size, though often better structured and above all more independent of governmental influence.

Within these Protestant associations, as otherwise within free-thinking societies, a new kind of membership developed; these people were different from those in Catholic and corporatist groups. They were ultra-minority, and came to the fore because of the inculcation of religious, democratic but also political values and practices. We may say, in fact, that associative life acted as a veritable experimental laboratory within a general authoritarian and anti-democratic political context. Indeed, with their regime of assembly, synod and convention, the Protestant societies, whose modern form of organization certainly derived from U.S. models, instilled practices and principles disapproved of by the Roman Catholic Church and by the conservative, anti-democratic and neo-corporatist form of liberal oligarchical state.

(d) Protestant Liberal Instruction

One major contribution which the Protestant associations made to Latin American life was that of the educational systems which these societies established. This educative activity did not consist solely of the transmission and development of modern educational methods; the Protestant enterprise as a whole was an educational project.

On the one hand, the chapel and the primary school were always connected and the minister was also a schoolteacher. This educational function of the Protestant pastor also operated through the Sunday schools, whose importance for the formation of a popular culture Laqueur has stressed in regard to the English working class of the first half of the nineteenth century (1976).[1] On the other hand, the Protestant educational agenda was always considered to be a means and an end at one and the same time. It was a means of obtaining acceptance more smoothly in the moderate sectors of the population which sympathized with Protestant intentions, quite apart from acceptance by governments and by liberal local authorities that saw the Protestant societies obtaining a certain degree of legitimacy. It was an end inasmuch as the aim of the educational process was to hand on Protestant and liberal but also democratic values, and to see them extend beyond the chapels and Protestant circles of association.

In transitional social sectors membership of the Protestant Church was seen as a privileged means of access to the educational services associated with them. Especially in the rural areas devoid of state and any good educational resources, the Protestant primary schools were the main educational locations. These systems of primary schools established by the Presbyterians, Methodists, Baptists and Congregationalists, above all, were very restricted in comparison with the means which states had at their disposal to promote public education. Their budget was limited and two-thirds of it depended on generous contributions from U.S. missionary societies. Nevertheless these systems were undoubtedly significant when compared with similar networks which other ideological associations tried to establish, and even in comparison with the Catholic school systems. Thus, in Mexico in 1910 Protestant schools represented 1.7 percent of all schools surveyed and Catholic schools 4.8 percent; but the former were the only primary schools which were able to compete with the latter. In most cases Protestant primary schools bore the name of some liberal hero, which showed that they belonged to that particular political culture, such as Juárez, Hidalgo and Ocampo in Mexico, Sarmiento and Alberdi in Argentina, and Martí in Cuba. In the case of girls' schools they became the "daughters of Juárez" or "of Hidalgo," as against the "Daughters of Mary" of their Catholic opponents.

The major importance of the Protestant educational system is evident when one takes into account the higher, secondary, preparatory, vocational, commercial, industrial and theological schools comprising a high-level urban educational network which usually surpassed the level of similar Catholic systems and was at the same level as the public educational system. The entire Latin American continent was served by Protestant higher schools by 1920, the effort having begun in 1880. Cuba, Mexico and Brazil especially had between thirty and fifty of these schools, which to a great extent were devoted to the education of girls, neglected by the oligarchical states. Most of these colleges were founded by U.S. schoolteachers and profited from the help of the best liberal teachers of the day, such as Médardo Vitier in Cuba, Ignacio M.

Altamirano in Mexico, and Luis Alberto Sánchez and Raul Porras Barrenechea in Peru. Moreover, these schools produced generations of superb Protestant educators, among whom were such figures as Erasmo Braga and Julio Ribeiro in Brazil or Andrés Osuna and Moisés Sáenz in Mexico. The last-named in particular was the father of indigenism and one of the proponents of active instruction in the Dewey tradition; in fact he had been a student of Dewey's at Columbia University, New York. It would take too much space to show the pioneer role of these Protestant educators in Argentina, Uruguay, Bolivia, Peru, Mexico and Cuba, among others. The influence of the Protestant colleges has yet to be researched; for the moment it is important to emphasize the specific contribution of the Protestant education project in propagating an anti-oligarchical form of modern thought.

In the context of the oligarchies, the educational method of the Protestant schools is to be distinguished as much from that of the Catholic schools as from the public schools under the influence of positivism. From the start they rejected the world view rooted in the Thomist tradition which saw the social order as a natural order, with a corporative, integrationist and vertical structure. In regard to the positivist schools, the Protestant educators criticized the "scientistic" view of the world from which atheists on principle supposed they could exclude questions of ethics, using it to establish modern thought and culture not on the basis of the moral individual, but by the unifying dynamism of a science which would make economic and social progress the road to democracy in the Latin America of the future. In fact, positivism reinforced the authoritarianism and corporativism inherent in a culture moulded by centuries of colonial Catholicism. The positivists relegated democratic ways to some future time, when the masses would be able to read and write. Contrary to this liberal oligarchical approach, the Protestants promoted a form of education whose roots were in the experience of the liberal old guard of the reform movement period of the first half of the nineteenth century. Additional influences were Anglo-Saxon, or came from the liberal Spaniard Emilio Castelar, and from Spanish Krausism, which thought it was possible to construct economic and social progress on the basis of the ethically regenerated individual. This approach was condemned as "metaphysical" by positivist educators who, following Comte's law of three states, believed that the metaphysical state would be definitively surpassed by rational positivist thought, which was the unique and necessary condition of progress. For Protestant educators, the way of progress was also laid open by capitalist economic and social change. However, economic progress must be grounded in democracy and democracy itself in the individual citizen, who was the subject of a sovereignty established and confirmed by suffrage. The emphasis which Protestant education placed on the individual came together with the Anglo-Saxon educational principles of the Dewey school and the major ideas of radical liberalism, especially freedom of conscience and liberty of thought.

This amalgam entered Protestant teaching through an instructional method which stressed individual effort, character and will, and which was grounded in the concept of a conscience that was both moral and religious. The various types of primary school promoted this educational approach as much as the secondary schools and other forms of instruction, which encouraged both intellectual and manual labour and recommended sport as a means of educating the will and inculcating competitiveness. The democratic political project was closely associated with this educational effort, which explains the unflagging contributions of individual Protestants, above all the products of Protestant higher education, to the anti-oligarchical democratic struggles of the 1880s. Democratic practices were thought through didactic exercises known as "educational communes or republics" and literary and civic associations which acted as laboratories and test-benches for associative and democratic life.

At the same time a radical liberal form of civic spirit developed which was certainly one of the endogenous elements of an eminently civic religion. It defended the anti-Catholic and democratic liberal tradition and in Mexico took the exaggerated form of a liberal liturgical calendar. This was observed both in schools and in chapels and in the Protestant press: with 5 February (Constitution of 1857), 5 May (Battle of Puebla against the invading French forces), 18 July (death of Juárez), and 16 September (Independence from Spain) among many other dates of a local or regional significance. This elevated form of civics was opposed to the "weak" civics of official oligarchic liberalism. It embodied a veritable political culture of opposition to the régime of Porfirio Díaz (1876–1911) and explained the considerable part played by Protestant base groups in the revolutionary movement of 1910. A similar phenomenon, though perhaps less extreme because of the different political context, was to be found in Brazil, above all after the triumph of the Republic (1889), which had fallen into the hands of positivists and oligarchists, and where the Protestant schools celebrated not only the anniversary of the proclamation of the Republic, but Tiradentes, the hero of the anti-Portuguese struggle during the colonial period, as well as the day on which slavery was abolished. In Cuba too the Protestant schools celebrated the abolition of slavery as well as the anniversary of José Martí's death. As Pereira Ramalho (1976) has stressed in the case of Brazil, it was a question of "preparing the children to practise an effective form of citizenship (in accordance with liberal ideas), though that happened only in the schools, for society as a whole offered no such preparation, being dominated by an élite opposed to the principles of such colleges".[2]

Even though these Protestant colleges used U.S. educational models, they were scarcely the only ones to do so, for the governments themselves employed U.S. educators, as Sarmiento did in Argentina, to establish educational systems, or sent their schoolteachers to be trained in the United States just as Díaz but also Carranza did in Mexico. Nevertheless, in the Protestant colleges the content of education was nationalist, given the sheer weight of the radical liberal political culture of the Protestant base organization, the schoolteachers and ministers, as well as syllabuses which included radical liberal history, civics courses and the study of liberal constitutions according to the country. For this reason the Protestant schools were important means of developing an anti-authoritarian and democratic culture grounded in the notion of individual conversion as a means of simultaneously acquiring religious, moral and civic responsibility. The principle of free thought was allied to an anti-Catholicism which was not anti-clerical (in the sense of being anti-religious), and to an anti-positivism which did not deny the value of science and reason for the march of progress. This dual opposition resulted from the rejection of an authoritarian culture moulded by the Catholicism with which behaviour and consciences were imbued. It also resulted from the rejection of any reconciliation with an oligarchical liberalism which, denying its own principles, had joined forces with the Catholic Church to ensure order and progress and a social peace established on inequality.

Confronted with corporatist interests, the Protestant minority and its radical liberal sympathizers formed a liberal population consisting of a simultaneously religious and political avant-garde within the Protestant associations. One of its main features was the ability of Protestantism to establish close relations with its liberal political culture, and to carry on a dynamic relationship with its national culture. Its leaders could conceive of a social and political alternative such as that adumbrated by Moisés Sáenz in his *México Integro* (1936), Alberto Rembao in his regional writings, *Chihuahua de mis amores* (1920) or his continental work, *Discurso a la Nación evangélica* (1949), and even the missionary and Hispanic scholar John A. Mackay in his *El otro español* (1932). This close relationship of a dissident religion with the national and liberal culture was the fruit of Protestant educational systems and of the liberal origin of leading lights of Latin American Protestant societies. From the 1940s the disappearance of the liberal tradition, the loss of the nationalized Protestant schools, and the appearance of a Pentecostal and illiterate Protestantism, transformed Latin American Protestant organizations into a lower-level anomic religious culture devoid of intellectuals.

(e) Protestantism and Anti-oligarchical Struggles

Around 1910 Protestantism was firmly established throughout the Latin American continent, within the confines described in the foregoing: those of a radical liberal, ultra-minority collection of sectors undergoing social transformation. This religious minority gradually organized itself and, under the influence of missionary models, developed a style of administration by structures ranging from the meeting through the synod to the conference and convention, in accordance with Presbyterian, Congregationalist, Lutheran, Methodist or Baptist traditions, among others. These organizational structures resulted in Protestant societies and were leading settings for instruction in democratic practices and values. At the same time, unifying tendencies developed and the various societies came together annually at a national level. This soon produced a similar movement at a continental level, and the first congress of Protestant societies in Latin America was celebrated in the city of Panama in February 1916.

One of the paradoxes of the movement was that the Protestant societies which emerged from Latin American radical liberal interests could not escape from continual economic dependence on U.S. missionary societies in particular. This economic dependence was never an exclusive feature of Latin American Protestantism but rather a structural economic phenomenon influenced by international monetary conditions. During the decade after the end of the first World War U.S. capital exceeded British and European investments, which had been dominant until then. This increasing U.S. economic presence was closely linked to a policy of control of Latin American political régimes through military intervention. At the same time the world economic crisis of 1929 resulted in a Latin American reorientation of economic policy toward the substitution of imports. It also fired an increasing nationalism which took the form of neo-corporatist populist régimes, and these gradually replaced the liberal oligarchies in power.

The Protestant societies were directly involved in the overall political changes on the continent. First, they actively supported the democratic movements. Second, they also promoted a form of nationalism inherited from the radical liberalism of their time of origin, and one which persuaded them to declare the boundary lines between their own and U.S. missionary interests. But this nationalism was not sufficiently aligned with populist neo-corporatist interests, and economic dependence on the U.S. missionary societies soon transformed them into special targets for attacks from Catholic circles and from a populist Left to some extent bemused by Stalinism.

Protestant political activity was especially significant in four countries. In Peru the Anglo-Peruvian College established by the Scottish missionary John A. Mackay (1889–1983) was one of the main centres of promotion and practice of the ideas of Victor Raúl Haya de la Torre (1895–1978), founder of the American Popular Revolutionary Alliance (APRA) after his Mexican exile in 1924. The links between Mackay and Haya de la Torre were close in 1916 when they were contemporaries at the University of San Marcos in Lima. Haya was also a teacher at the Anglo-Peruvian College and other well-known "Aprists" taught there. Mackay's house was a place of refuge for Haya de la Torre when in flight after a worker-student demonstration against the 1923 attempt to consecrate Peru to the Sacred Heart of Jesus, which was supported by the oligarchical government of Augusto Leguía (1919–30). As Mackay himself stressed, Puritan ministers and lay people were very enthusiastic supporters of APRA, which for them as for Mackay stood for an anti-conservative, anti-imperialist and anti-authoritarian politics, while attempting to establish a programme for a democratic society on the basis of a strong ethical imperative. Moreover, when Haya de la Torre returned to Peru in July 1931 only to lose the presidential elections before being imprisoned by the winner, Colonel Sánchez Cerro (May 1937), the Protestants who had supported him also became victims of political persecution.

This alliance of Protestants and democrats had its counterpart in Brazil, where the "tenentist" military movements of 1922, 1924 and 1930 and the Paulist constitutionalist revolution of 1932 counted on the active support of Protestant lieutenants (*tenentes*), and in 1932 more than three hundred former students of Mackenzie Presbyterian College lost their lives. The *Estado Novo* of Getulio Vargas (1930–45) put an end to the reign of the positivist oligarchy and established a populist neo-corporatism on the basis of a coalition of interests which admittedly included a Protestant party. This, however, did not respond to the Protestants' radical democratic demands; therefore some of them later supported the Brazilian Workers' Party (PTB).

In Cuba, in the same way, there was a considerable Protestant presence in the struggles against the authoritarian régime of General Gerardo Machado Morales (1925–33). As Marcos A. Ramos has shown (1986), Protestants fought in the oppositional political movements which resulted in the democratic revolution of 1933. A precarious government emerged from this revolution during the summer of 1933. After re-establishing the liberal constitution of 1901 the liberal government was overthrown by the coup d'état of Sergeant Fulgencio Batista Zaldivar, who retained power until his fall in 1959, when another democratic revolution removed his regime.

Mexico above all was the country where there were obvious signs of links between the anti-oligarchical democratic political process and Protestantism. Tens of ministers and hundreds of members of Protestant congregations carried arms when they took part in the anti-Porfirist revolutionary movements led by Francisco I. Madero between November 1910 and June 1911. The fall of the Díaz dictatorship was provoked by the slow development of a dissident political culture through the pre-political networks established by the free-thought societies, and by Protestants, among others. The main revolutionary centres erupted in November and December 1910, precisely in those rural areas where the Protestant congregations were concentrated.

The main regional revolutionary leaders themselves, such as Pascual Orozco and his lieutenants in the village of San Isidro, Chihuahua, or the merchant Ignacio Gutiérrez Gómez in Chontalpa, Tabasco, belonged to Protestant networks. Whereas the former came from the founding family of the Protestant congregation in his village, the latter was a local Presbyterian preacher. The revolution had failed in the urban centres, where the Díaz police had easily arrested suspects during the days before 20 November 1910 (the date set aside for the general uprising); but it flourished and consolidated its base in places where for forty years the associative work of the free-thought societies had reinforced a radical liberal political culture and a pre-political organizational network.

In February 1913, when Madero was assassinated and a military régime supported by the Catholic Church came to power, the Protestants re-mobilized in the armies of the constitutionalist revolutionary movement led by General Venustiano Carranza, the former governor of the state of Coahuila. Significantly, after the triumph of Carranza in August 1914, many ministers and teachers in Protestant schools served as lower rank officials in the revolutionary apparatus. The schoolmaster and former Methodist pastor Andrés Osuna became minister of education from 1916 to 1918 and was succeeded in 1919 by the Presbyterian Eliseo García when Osuna became governor of Tamaulipas. Moreover in 1914 the Presbyterian minister Gregorio A. Velásquez became head of the constitutionalist propaganda and information office which he founded. In 1918 he was in charge of the official daily of the regime, El Pueblo, which he transformed into one of the main ideological props of Carrancism. Most Mexican Protestants suppported the formation of a civil government to succeed Carranza, as the latter wished. That is why, when a militarist revolutionary faction was victorious after a coup d'état and General Alvaro Obrégón placed himself at its head, Protestants were temporarily marginalized by his administration (1920–24), which established a neo-corporatist form of populism.

Even though it is clear that to some extent throughout Latin America Protestants supported democratic movements in the period 1910 to 1940, at the same time there was an intensification of the Catholic campaign which accused them and denounced them eventually as "agents of American imperialism," especially in the books of the Jesuits Régis Planchet (1928) and Augusto Crivelli (1932). During the 1920s and 1930s the same Catholic propaganda defended the Hispanic legitimacy of the continent against heterodox religious societies and against secularizing populist régimes such as that of Calles (1924–32) in Mexico.

Admittedly the ambiguous connections which the Latin American Protestant societies maintained with their U.S. co-religionists, on whom they depended economically, invited such attacks. Moreover, the U.S. Protestant missionary societies and the Committee of Cooperation in Latin America which they had organized from 1914 under the direction of Samuel Guy Inman, supported a moderate U.S. policy in the area. Against the invasions by marines and the big stick politics promoted by the economic interests of the cartels, Inman wrote several books defending pan-Americanism and the policy of "good neighbour-liness" which tried to improve relations between the north and the south of the continent. The vast majority of missionaries supported this viewpoint, even trying sometimes to represent Latin American interests in their own country by testifying in favour of the self-determination of Latin American peoples as against the lobbies.

For the Latin American Protestant leaders, the overheated nationalism of their respective countries, under the influence of various forms of populism, caused them to defend similar viewpoints against the U.S. missionaries. The congress of Latin American Protestant Churches which took place at Havana, Cuba, in 1929, reflected this search for a Latin American Protestant identity in the face of Catholic criticisms and suspicions of a pro-imperialist allegiance. Under the guidance of a young Mexican journalist and revolutionary, the Methodist Gonzalo Báez Camargo, and with a strong Mexican presence, the Havana congress analyzed ecclesiastical relations with the U.S. societies and the theme of U.S. imperialism in the area. It especially condemned the tax on sugar planned by the U.S. government, which imperilled the economy of the island. Above all, with an exclusively Latin American management and leadership this congress expressed a Latin American Protestantism which affirmed itself as just that. This search for a Latin American Protestant identity appropriate to an "evangelical nation" would become more emphatic during coming years with the creation of Churches that were administratively autonomous in regard to the U.S. missionaries.

(f) Latin American Protestant Churches between Persecutiuon and Revolution

The Protestant nationalism of the 1930s and 1940s was grounded in a Christian humanism embodying a representative and participative form of bourgeois democracy. The "address to the evangelical nation" of the Mexican Alberto Rembao in 1949 synthesized what had been the basis of Protestant and radical liberal ideology since the beginnings of these societies in Latin America in the middle of the nineteenth century. It was a matter of transforming a deep, corporative and vertical society, and of democratizing it by creating a new type of man and woman, morally regenerate as well as active and disciplined economic agents, creators of socially redistributed wealth, and political subjects of a sovereignty yet to come. This kind of discourse, which was typical of most Latin American Protestant writing since the second half of the nineteenth century, was opposed to the entire Hispanic culture and heritage of a deep-rooted society whose social agents were collectives and a social, corporatist, organic order. It was for this reason that Protestantism, in the 1920s and 1930s, did not progress numerically, even though its minorities had been very active politically, educationally and socially.

Moreover, the narrow path which the Protestant societies had followed had to veer between the persecution they suffered from the traditional agents of the deep-rooted society and active participation in bourgeois democratic revolutions, if they wished to experience an eventual overall transformation of behaviour and mentalities.

The persecution of Protestant bodies lasted throughout the 1940s and 1950s and was just as much religious as political. Colombia was the main though not the exclusive arena of this dual persecution of forms of Protestantism which, since they were linked to the liberal political culture, were inexorably involved in the fate of liberal forces. After the popular uprising known as the "*bogotazo*", which was led on 9 April 1948 by the populist working-class militant Jorge Eliecer Gaitan in the city of Bogotá, a bloody political persecution developed, together with a repression of the popular and liberal sectors by the armed forces and the conservative regime of Laureano Gómez. Thereupon the country entered into a veritable civil war which up to 1958 produced some 85,000 dead on the liberal side. 126 victims in the Protestant ranks seems a somewhat insignificant figure, but it probably does not reflect the real nature of a liberal front in which Protestants, freemasons, freethinkers, spiritualists and leaders of mutual societies were integrated, and among whom the Protestant sympathizers were more numerous than the strict statistical number of communicant members. To these figures must be added the closure of 270 Protestant schools by order of the government and the violent action of the conservatives, and the destruction of sixty chapels, without taking into account the pressure and coercion in everyday life which included anti-Protestant hymns and sermons from the clergy, threats, insults, house searches, confiscations of property, interference in religious practices, and other violations of the rights of man, meticulously recorded by James E. Goff (1968).

This situation recurred elsewhere in Latin America, especially in Mexico, but in a less extreme way, after 1940 when the government of Avila Camacho made peace with the Catholic Church. In the 1940s and 1950s this forced the Protestants to participate, against Catholic and conservative interests, in democratic movements. In Guatemala, the revolutionary movement of General Juan José Arevalo (1945–51), and above all that of his successor General Jacobo Arbenz (1951–4), received the support of Protestants who were especially keen to promote agrarian reform. It was in Cuba that their support for a democratic revolution was most obvious when a young lawyer and student leader called Fidel Castro became leader of the Movement of 26 July 1953, which some years later, in January 1959, ended in the triumphal entry of revolutionary troops into Havana. Several Protestants such as the Presbyterian doctor Faustino Pérez were in the guerrilla forces of the Sierra Maestra. The most remarkable of them was certainly a young primary school teacher and son of a Baptist pastor, who came from Santiago de Cuba, Frank Isaac País García (1934–57). Frank País organized the revolutionary action movement in the eastern part of the island; he was thought of as the revolutionary second in command of the 26 July Movement, before he was murdered by the existing powers on 30 July 1957 and was buried with the rank of colonel, the highest rank among the rebel forces. On the entry of the rebel forces into Havana on 8 January 1959, "a considerable number of Protestant pastors" were on the rostrum from which Fidel Castro addressed the crowd and several Protestants were appointed to political posts in the new democratic government, three of them with the rank of minister and two others as deputy-ministers. During the same year 1959 the pastors of the capital met in a Havana park to celebrate a civic-religious ceremony of support for the revolution, and shortly afterwards entertained Commandant Raúl Castro when he visited Candler Methodist College. Cuban Protestants supported the agrarian reform programme which was under way, the literacy programmes, and the struggle against administrative corruption, always within a liberal democratic framework.

On the other hand, when Prime Minister Fidel Castro made a sharp turn and proclaimed the Cuban revolution to be Marxist-Leninist, 80 percent of the pastors and members of Protestant congregations went into exile between 1961 and 1965. They did so as a result of the stress caused by the closure of Protestant schools, the suspension of religious broadcasting on the radio, a strict control of consignments of bibles and religious literature, the closing of rural chapels abandoned because of the emigration of worshippers, and the despatch of recalcitrant pastors for forced labour to which homosexuals and common criminals were also sentenced. These measures were directed in the first place against the Catholic Church which continued as the main force of opposition to the revolution. They resulted from the Cold War context as well as the anti-clericalism of certain sectors of the revolution. Nevertheless Cuban Protestants, moulded by the liberal political culture of the independence struggles at the end of the nineteenth century, were not prepared to understand the direction and challenges of a socialist democracy. Only a minority who shared the goals of the revolution tried to keep what remained of the Protestant heritage within a revolution which opened up new perspectives for blacks, mestizos and poor whites, and also made firm ethical demands, at least in its initial stages.

The radicalized Cuban Revolution uncovered the limits of the Protestant political and social agenda which, having emerged from the radical liberalism of the nineteenth century, proved incapable of forming a democratic alternative apart from a rejection of authoritarianisms of the right and of the left. But at the same time this liberal Protestantism was threatened from within the religious field by a new Protestant religious manifestation. This had taken root on the continent at the start of the twentieth century and seemed destined to grow at an unexpected rate within the area laid open by the destruction of traditional relations of rural production in dependent capitalist societies.

In fact, at the beginning of the twentieth century an exceptional phenomenon anticipated and interrupted the uniform liberal patterns of Latin American Protestantism. This was the surprising onset between 1902 and 1910 of a new religious mentality within the Methodist congregation at Valparaiso in Chile. As

Lalive d'Epinay has remarked (1968), this new Protestant religious attitude was condemned by the annual Conference of the Chilean Methodist Church at its session of 10 February 1910, as "anti-Methodist, contrary to Scripture and irrational." In an article of 3 November 1909, *El Mercurio*, the liberal Santiago paper, had also denounced these new religious manifestations, considering them to be signs "of a sick fanaticism," whereas another daily in the capital termed them "Indian ceremonies."

This dual condemnation by the Methodist Church and by a liberal paper revealed from the first appearance of these new Pentecostal religious phenomena the existence of a tension, indeed of a conflict, between two forms of expression of Latin American Protestantism that is still with us. It is a question of two antagonistic attitudes: the first, which came into being as a kind of subsidiary manifestation of free-thought societies and of radical liberalism, considered Protestantism to be an instrument of social regeneration through education; its purpose was to create democratic, religious and political vanguards which in the long run would contribute to the transformation and "regeneration" of the Latin American nations. In this sense, this "historical" Protestantism conceived itself as a religious, intellectual and moral reform movement in accordance with the norms of the great European Reformation of the sixteenth century and its later religious variations. Therefore it tried to contribute actively to the creation of a simultaneously democratic, liberal and Protestant culture in a continent dominated by the authoritarian culture of an intransigent Catholicism. Its activity developed within a religious and cultural front of generous proportions and influence though minority status, alongside other societies for free thought. Even though this Protestant movement was initially associated with transitional social sectors, its proponents did not rule out an eventual penetration of élite groups and the development of its capability to train them in Protestant schools.

But the new form of Protestantism which made its mark for the first time in Chile, and which was to spread at an unprecedented rate thereafter, was not in the least interested in propagating a democratic culture. It appeared much more as a popular religion of the oppressed and the marginalized, ignored by the élites and by liberal and Protestant ideological avant-gardes. In this context it was shrewd of the secular Chilean newspaper to remark the association with popular indigenous religion.

Pentecostalism developed more as a religious syncretism than as a manifestation of Protestantism. It evolved as a religious movement that was independent of, and even antagonistic to, Protestant political and religious culture. It also developed as a denunciation and as a judgment of the inability of Protestantism to emerge from radical liberal ultra-minority networks.

Pentecostalism, which had been ignored and denigrated by historical Protestantism until just before the 1960s, began from the 1920s a process of spread and expansion which by now has completely upset the Latin American religious spectrum, for it has even succeeded in establishing a relationship of some power vis-à-vis the Catholic Church.

At the start of the 1960s, therefore, liberal Protestantism was involved in a project embodying a religious and social form of modern thought for minorities whose restricted geographical spread indicated the limits of its possible influence. On the other hand a popular, ebullient form of Protestantism with an oral tradition was becoming ever more prominent. It seemed to be developing gradually towards the point where it might attract the marginalized masses that were permanently liable to migration and to anomie produced by accelerating economic change.

3. THE DOMESTICATION OF PROTESTANT BODIES, 1959–89

One of the noteworthy social phenomena in Latin American and Caribbean societies in the last thirty years which indicates the nature of their development is the increasingly rapid transformation of the religious spectrum.

The Roman Catholic Church remains predominant at the national level in most countries, but in many regions it is on the way to representing less than half of all existing religious forces. According to Johnstone's statistics, quoted by Stoll (1990), in 1986 Protestants were wavering between 5 and 10 percent of the population in Argentina, Honduras, Nicaragua, Bolivia, Costa Rica, the Dominican Republic and French Guiana; between 10 and 20 percent in Brazil, Salvador, Haiti, Panama and Surinam; between 20 and 30 percent in Belize, Chile, Guatemala, Guiana and Puerto Rico; and at more than 30 percent in the English-speaking Caribbean (Bahamas, Barbados and Jamaica). On the other hand, the Andean region (Venezuela, Ecuador and Peru), Paraguay and Uruguay together with Cuba and Mexico have rates lower than 5 percent. These wholly approximate figures serve only to indicate a trend, and one which has been observable since the beginning of the 1960s, towards an exponential atomization of the religious spectrum and a correlative differentiation which mean that today the various forms of Protestantism scarcely represent all secondary religious movements and bodies. Though it is true that forms of Pentecostalism probably still constitute the dominant part of the secondary religious spectrum, numerous non-Protestant (Mormons, Jehovah's Witnesses), syncretic (*La Luz del Mundo*), thaumaturgical (Umbanda), and milleniarist Catholic bodies, proliferate in a religious universe which is still in the process of expansion. To the foregoing we must now add religious movements of eastern origin and the older (spiritualism) and new (The Great Fraternity) forms of esotericism.

One of the prime methodological consequences of this development of the religious field is the impossibility of studying forms of Protestantism in and for themselves, and in isolation. We have still less chance of adequately explaining the changes in the present-day Latin American religious field if we restrict our inquiry to forms of Protestantism. We must have recourse to comparative studies like those of Rodrigues Brandão (1986 and 1987) in Brazil, prescinding from a theory of the religious spectrum itself, if we are to avoid the dangers of reductionism.

Nevertheless, we cannot even begin to analyze contemporary Protestantism without some initial acquaintance with the fundamental and hitherto unsurpassed efforts of Lalive d'Epinay (1968 and 1975). Lalive and Willems (1967) were the first to observe, on the basis of Protestant evidence, the accelerated transformation of the field of Latin American religion in the 1960s. The limits of Lalive d'Epinay's work are apparent today, resulting as they do

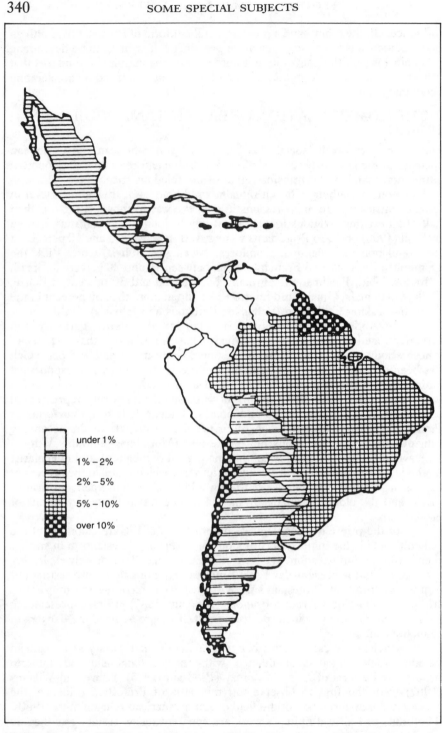

15. Protestants as a Percentage of Population (1961). (For updated figures, see section 4 of this chapter) *Source*: Piemme

from the limitations of the region surveyed, which consists essentially of Argentina and Chile, atypical in regard to the vestiges of an indigenous, black and mestizo continent, and also because the subject-matter is restricted to Protestant bodies. Nevertheless this author has posed the fundamental questions. On the one hand he has developed a still valid typology by trying to classify the broad spectrum of Protestant religious movements on the continuum of Church–sects–forms of worship. On the other hand he was the first, *pace* Willems, to discern the process of acculturation of forms of Protestantism and to define it in terms of the values of popular religion and culture.

Within the framework of a theory of economic and social crisis, and of the corresponding anomie derived from it, d'Epinay has proffered an interpretation of sectarian-type Protestant societies as counter-societies within which a reconstruction has occurred of the "hacienda model" (his term). Within the dissident religious society, the pastor plays the role of a proprietor, establishing client relations with his parishioners, in accordance with an authoritarian and non-democratic model of religious administration. Since the 1960s the majority of Protestant societies have taken sectarian forms, and d'Epinay has proficiently revealed the trend of acculturation to corporatism, but he has neither located the break which that implies with previous Protestant models, nor has he questioned the use of the term Protestantism to describe basically syncretic religious movements. Nevertheless he does address the question of sectarian Protestantisms in regard to the continuity and redevelopment of a popular religious culture, and asks whether these forms of Protestantism "should not be interpreted as a reform of popular Catholicism as much as a type of renewal within Protestantism itself." Further in his analysis he locates these sectarian forms of Protestantism within the "panorama of popular religions, alongside animisms, spiritisms, Afro-American religions, messianic religions, popular forms of Catholicism which have grown up around shrines, and so on . . .".[3] Whereas Willems explained the growth of forms of Protestantism in terms of urbanization and rationalization, Lalive d'Epinay, confirming the rural as much as urban implantation of sectarian forms of Protestantism, has located them within a strategy of adaptation to popular religious mentalities. Accordingly, the appropriate form of analysis for their relation to politics is defined by the author as that of a "conformist disengagement" which he qualifies as a "passive modality of the function of bearing witness."[4]

All the questions posed by Lalive d'Epinay and the conclusions to which he comes are fundamental and relevant to the discussion of the role of forms of Protestantism in present-day Latin America and the Caribbean.

Nevertheless, from my viewpoint, the expansion of Pentecostalist societies corresponds neither to a reform of popular Catholicism nor to a renewal of Protestantism. It is a question rather of a renewal of popular religion in the form of a readjustment and an acculturation of forms of Protestantism to the values and practices of popular Catholic culture. During the 1970s, when the theme of popular religion was fashionable, several scholars stressed the autonomy of popular Catholic religious practices vis-à-vis hierarchical controls. They remarked on juxtaposition of practices which are articulated but not integrated.

It is probable that both the centralizing and vertical development of Catholicism towards Romanization, and the destruction of traditional relations of production in indigenous areas, as well as correlated migrations, favoured attempts at symbolic redevelopment by secondary sectors of Latin American societies. In this perspective, a hypothesis put forward by Pierre Chaunu in 1965 may be relevant. According to this, popular forms of Protestantism would be more correctly conceived as substitute forms of Catholicism which have filled a vacuum; as he says: "Surely this radical Protestantism, without dogmatic demands, entirely centred on inspiration, wholly subject to the divine presence, is ultimately closer to the priestless Catholicism of a section of the masses?"[5]

A number of recent studies devoted to the study of Pentecostalism in an indigenous setting indicate how cogent the thesis is. Thus, among the Toba Indians of the Argentine Chaco, both Miller (1979), Wright (1984 and 1988) and Santamaría (1990) have confirmed the continuity of Pentecostalist practices with shamanic rites, giving rise to a veritable syncretic religiosity. According to Wright, the creation of the United Toba Evangelical Church in 1961, administered by an indigenous religious hierarchy in accordance with the traditional norms of symbolic and political power, represented an attempt to legitimize certain aspects of their ancestral culture by appropriating the language and location of a religious entity recognized and accepted by the overall society which has adopted the indigenous codes of communication.

For Santamaría it is a question of an adaptation strategy which redefines ethnicity in terms of a new form of worship; this, like the overall society, is Christian in origin but by recourse to its own particular religious practices invokes its own ancestral ethos. Samandu (1988) records a similar continuity in Central America when he remarks the fact that "Pentecostalist beliefs make possible the free expression of the popular religious world inhabited by demons, spirits, and divine revelations and cures... so that believers acknowledge Pentecostalism as 'their' religion with deep roots in a popular culture long deprecated as supersition by the educated classes."[6]

This kind of acculturation is not specific to forms of Pentecostalism. Most historical Churches, with the exception of the transplanted Churches of the southern cone, have a pentecostalized form of practice with which they have ensured their numerical growth and the possession of an indigenous rural base; an example is the Mexican national Presbyterian Church. But we cannot understand the acculturation process unless we locate the various current expressions of Protestantism in the actual religious spectrum, where, as in the case of the Brazilian village of Santa Rita, "no candidate religion has succeeded in imposing its hegemony, and instead religious mobility and a plurality of beliefs" often characterize the religious practices of the population. In other words, popular forms of Protestantism participate in a syncretic religious culture where "transitions from one Church to another are frequent; and members of the Assembly of God often go to the Umbanda *terreiro*, and less often the Catholic church."

In 1973 Roger Bastide aptly described this persistence of traces of popular religious and social culture when he wrote of Protestantism in Puerto Rico: "What I as an anthropologist find most striking is the process of acculturation of Protestantism to the Catholic culture of the masses. The Protestant seminarists wear chains with crosses or even holy medals; the men and women separate into two opposed groups in the chapels; feast-days (on the pretext of collecting funds) play a more important part than biblical studies; Hispanic 'caudillism' survives the conflicts of various Churches, but is reinterpreted in the form of dogmas or liturgical variations; and institutional indifference affects the younger generations so that many individuals are now at one and the same time Catholic and Protestant, or Protestant and spiritist; or abandon the life of the Churches in which they were baptized."[7]

The assimilation of forms of Protestantism by milleniarist and messianic religious and political culture enables us to see them as a continuity more than in terms of a breakdown of the Latin American cultural and religious universe. Accordingly we must ask whether it is relevant still to talk of forms of Protestantism, and whether it is not rather a matter of new syncretic religious movements within the strategy of a symbolically effective resistance and survival of secondary sectors of the population dependent on syncretic religiosity.

For twenty years most researchers have noted the exponential growth of forms of Pentecostalism within rural societies with violent political conflicts of agrarian origin. Several case-studies have shown an increasing cacique-type control by traditional indigenous or mestizo élites which, through popular Catholicism and by controlling religious affairs, maintain power and a monopoly over land and trade as well as the political structures of rural society. In the face of the monolithism of political control structures, the new religious movements have become the only means of breaking symbolic power, and the prelude to an eventual rupture of political power.

Garma (1987), in his pioneering study of the forms of Protestantism of the northern sierra of the State of Puebla in Mexico, has shown that the mestizo élites which controlled the commercialization of coffee were Catholics, whereas in the 1960s the indigenous natives opted for Pentecostalist religious practices. They hoped in that way to disrupt the mestizo commercial and political hegemony, for a dissident religion would allow them a certain degree of autonomy. It is probable that in the rural environment heterodox religious leaders represent themselves as a means of renewing the politico-religious leadership, for they call in question the power of the traditional rural élites.

In the case of the Paez and Guambianos, indigenous to the south of Colombia, Rappaport (1984) also noted that syncretic Protestantism reinforced ethnic identity by allowing worship to take place without non-indigenous intermediaries, and by "integrating their new beliefs with traditional systems of thought and especially those aspects which legitimize and structure their political activity, which is oriented to self-determination."[8] This is true in the context of a historical neglect of Catholicism as the instrument of political violence in previous years.

It seems permissible to speak of an active resistance linked to a creative symbolism allowing of a restructuring of the identity of the dominated group by modification of symbolic and political power relations, in the hope of obtaining a short-term advantage. Undoubtedly these forms of Pentecostalism are to be assigned to the typology of messianisms and millenarisms proposed by Pereira de Queiroz (1969), who made a distinction between restorative, reformist and subversive movements. Within this framework of analysis an apparently dominant passive conformism represents an aspect of the resistance strategy of these secondary sectors.

This "passive" resistance may operate, as Hurbon remarked (1987), in the Caribbean "by the mysterious operation of a system of symbols and images, with the aim of producing a Caribbean culture irreducible to the level of western culture."[9] By a process of "legitimation or of rejection of symbolical nuclei and traditional images, the convert commits himself or herself to a process of distancing from dominant values," according to Hurbon. Perhaps the main expression of the resistance and passive conformism remarked by Lalive d'Epinay is to be found in the protection which the religious society offers to the individual by enclosing him or her in a counter-society and in a relatively autonomous secondary religious culture. However, I think that we shall understand more of the purpose of the passive conformism of popular forms of Protestantism by examining its connections with the dominant political and religious culture transformed by means of a corporative, authoritarian and anti-democratic symbolism to be found both in Pentecostalist societies and in new religious movements.

The studies carried out into Pentecostalist societies have scarcely ever explicitly taken up the points made by Lalive d'Epinay regarding the religious organization model transposed from that of the hacienda and the correlative function of the pastor-*patrón*. Though Lalive d'Epinay has tried to refine the model's application by emphasizing a novel aspect of it inasmuch as, contrary to the practice of a hacienda, anyone may now become a *patrón*, he has not sufficiently stressed the points of continuity with the traditional values and practices of the corporative political and religious culture. Today most Pentecostalist religious societies are run by virtual bosses, proprietors, *caciques* and *caudillos* of the movement which they have founded and handed down from father to son in accordance with a corporative model within which parent relations play a decisive role. Hence the big Pentecostalist Church *Brazil para Cristo* operates under the rule of its founder. *La Luz del Mundo* in Mexico was founded by a *bracero* (migrant agricultural worker) transformed into a messiah, who on his death handed on to his son the control of an international religious empire. The boss of the Pentecostalist society known as "The Israelites" in Peru was gradually messianized and called himself "Compilador bíblico, Gran y unico misionero general, Guía espiritual, Profeta de Dios, Maestro de Maestros, Espiritu Santo y Cristo de Occidente."[10] This messianism is typical of all the big Pentecostalist societies, is to be found at all levels and begins locally, where the pastor not only owns the land and the chapel of his religious enterprise but is its absolute master. As Wright notes, among the Toba Pentecostalists, "the religious leaders are recognized by their elevation above the other members, a superiority which is based on powers of supernatural origin, and on social and economic prestige."[11] There is a need to examine with greater exactitude the networks of reciprocities and redistributions which emanate from Pentecostalist leaders, and to see clearly the continuity with the corporative political culture, and the uniform opposition to the political culture of Latin American Protestantism of the nineteenth century.

This phenomenon is not exclusive to Pentecostalism. It also affects historical forms of Protestantism, which have not only been pentecostalized by the adoption of demonstrative religious practices, but have also assimilated the models of a corporative political culture after abandoning the very missionary and radical liberal models which had given birth to them. A recent thesis adumbrated by Carrasco (1988) has elegantly described this process of "episcopalization of leading Latin American Baptist officials." He concludes that "the Baptist evangelical Churches are administered by an élite of oligarchical tendency which capitalizes on a symbolic power and a traditional authority in terms of an ongoing institutional visibility."[12] This acculturation of a historical Protestant society, one of the most radical in terms of its original Congregationalist model, betokens a reality affecting most historical Protestant societies, with the exception of the transplanted Protestants of the Southern Cone. On the other hand, the same authoritarian model, centred upon a founding individual and proprietor, appears in numerous ecumenical studies which have proliferated since the 1960s, under the aegis of the World Council of Churches.

As Carrasco has stated, this process of verticalization and episcopalization puts the leaders in a position of social importance and, I should add, does so in accordance with the norms of the dominant, corporatist culture. In this context, I made a comparative study of the relations of the popular Protestant bodies of Guatemala and Nicaragua to the political domain of the antagonistic régimes, and discovered that, ultimately, they were governed by the same corporatist logic. In each case the urban Protestant officials entered into relations proper to privileged religious clients with their state bosses in a situation in which Catholic Church-state tensions were intensified.

Passive conformism, far from proving a kind of self-reflection of the religious counter-society, is in fact a major characteristic of the corporatist dynamics of contemporary forms of Protestantism in Latin Amertica. For this reason over the last twenty years the Pentecostalist leadership in certain countries has become a political leadership in the traditional sense of corporatist mediation. We must remember, of course, as in Guatemala in 1984 ((Jorge Elías Serrano), and in Peru in 1990 (the leader of the Israelites), that the actual Protestant leaders are no longer diffident, on the basis of their religious clientele, about offering themselves as candidates for the presidency of their country.

In overall terms, it is therefore permissible to offer the hypothesis that present-day Latin American forms of Protestantism no longer transmit a democratic religious and political culture but, on the contrary, have assimilated, or have allowed themselves to be assimilated by, religious culture and authoritarian politics, and that they now develop in accordance with the logic of corporative negotiation.

CONCLUSION

On examining the overall development of Latin-American forms of Protestantism from the second half of the nineteenth century until today, it becomes clear that they they have undergone a most remarkable transformation since the 1960s. In general, we may say that whereas the Protestantisms of the nineteenth century emerged from a political culture of democratic radical liberalism which was adjusted to an education system focussed on the individual will, contemporary forms of popular Protestantism derive rather from a popular, corporative and authoritarian Catholic religious culture.

Whereas the former represented a religion of the written word, and one which was civic and rational, the latter comprise a religion of orality, illiteracy and excitement. Whereas the former were bearers of practices which served to inculcate democratic behaviour, the latter convey *cacique* and *caudillo* models of religious and social control. The strength of popular forms of Protestantism as a model of expansion means that now for the most part the historical forms of Protestantism have broken with their liberal heritage, have become assimilated to corporatist values and have joined in authoritarian political programmes. Accordingly, they have to be studied from the viewpoint of a sociology of religious change such as that proposed by Bastide.

In general, we may say that Latin American forms of Protestantism, with the exception of transplanted Churches in the south of the continent and a few ecclesiastical growths on the bodies of historical Churches, are syncretistic. Therefore they do not differ very much from other new religious movements, and can be analyzed only in a comparative perspective. It is appropriate to ask if the popular Protestantisms which feature millenarianism and ebullient messianism "in a very different situation might not in some way represent an historical redefinition of the messianic movements of the nineteenth and early twentieth century which have ceased to be viable."[13]

On the other hand, it is appropriate to inquire into the relation of popular Protestantisms to modern democratic thought in Latin America. As I have remarked, historical forms of Protestantism were bearers of a liberal and democratic modernism as against the traditional social agents of the corporative culture, and consequently became involved in social struggle and democratic politics. On the other hand, popular forms of Protestantism today would seem to have assimilated the political culture of repression, as Alves has shown (1985). It is in the context of this relation to traditional political culture that we must view the overall transformation of Latin-American Protestantisms over the last thirty years, together with their support for authoritarian, right-wing, or left-wing politics, and as they promote religious versions of client relations in situations of conflict between the Catholic Church and the state.

Fundamentally, the Protestant bodies have moved from a state of protest to a state of witness. Their elective affinity with a corporatist and authoritarian political culture prompts us to ask if we are still dealing with forms of Protestantism: with, that is, a movement of intellectual, religious and moral reform, or rather with a new version of popular Latin American religious culture in the sense of an adaptation to, and a reinforcement of, traditional mechanisms of social control.

In so far as Protestant principles no longer inhabit these popular forms of Protestantism, we have to deal not so much with a Protestant religious phenomenon as with a collection of new non-Roman Catholic religious movements. Their situation is something like that of a relatively autonomous popular Catholic religion set over against the Church. Instead of following Stoll's hypothesis (1990), according to which Latin America is in a condition in which it could become Protestant, I think rather that Protestant bodies have been Latin Americanized to the point of assimilating a corporatist religious culture.

Finally, one may ask if the differentiation of the Latin American religious spectrum and its atomization will reinforce the autonomy of social agents and assist the development of a strong civil society, which are conditions for the formation of independent public opinion and consequently of democratic practice. As the French sociologist Alain Touraine says: "There can be no representative institutions if there are no representative social agents up ahead. Democratization cannot be defined as the passage from chaos to freedom, or from the masses to government. It presupposes an existing organization of social demands and the autonomous action of associations, syndicates and other interest-groups. It also supposes the formation of a debate, and of one located in public opinion, before that which takes place in political institutions. If that previous process of discussion is dominated by a confrontation of parties, then democracy is without a basis."[14] But the Protestantisms of the nineteenth century, as free-thought societies, were indeed settings in which public opinion was adjusted by the affirmation of a religious freedom of choice and by the affirmation of debate.

The present-day vertical and authoritarian forms of Protestantism are rather relay-stations of the vertical social-control apparatus of a society which has found its way of development toward liberal and democratic modern thought and practice blocked. Now the democratic transformation of Latin American societies, which is a condition of economic democracy, seems to have faltered. As Touraine also observes, during the 1960s and 1970s the military regimes triumphed; the 1980s and 1990s would seem to have proclaimed the return of forms of populism rather than a democratic transformation.

In this context, popular and millenarian forms of Protestantism would seem to have acted as bearers of a social and political restoration programme rather than one of reform. As Touraine also reminds us, Latin American societies "continue to be irremediably dualist. On the one hand there is the world of language: of, that is, a participation which is the privilege not only of the rich but of the middle class, and one which affects a considerable section of the working class. On the other hand, there is the world of blood, which is the world of poverty and of repression."

In this dual universe, popular forms of Protestantism emerge from the world of blood and represent no more than a vast effort to move into the world of discourse. But such an exercise is necessarily confined, for it must proceed in accordance with the logic of the world of discourse: of, that is, the world of models of corporative control of both social and religious dimensions, and those models are fixed in the long tenure of a Catholic culture and mentality.

Translated from the French by John Cumming

NOTES

1. T. H. Laqueur, *Religion and Respectability, Sunday Schools and English Working Class Culture, 1780–1850* (New Haven & London, 1976).
2. J. Pereira Ramalho, *Práctica educativa e sociedade, um estudo de sociologia de la educação* (Rio de Janeiro, 1976).
3. C. Lalive d'Epinay, *Dynamique sociale, religion et dépendance. Les mouvements protestants en Argentine et au Chili* (Paris, 1975), pp. 178–9.

4. Lalive d'Epinay, *op. cit.*, p. 279.
5. P. Chaunu, "Pour une sociologie du protestantisme latino-américaine," *Cahiers de Sociologie Economique* (Le Havre, May 1965), No. 12, 5–18.
6. L. Samandu, "El pentecostalismo en Nicaragua y sus raíces religiosas populares," *Pasos* (San José, Costa Rica), May-June 1988, No. 17, 1–10.
7. R. Bastide, "Contributions à une sociologie des religions en Amérique Latine," *Archives des sciences Sociales des Religions* (35, 1978) , 139–50.
8. J. Rappaport. "Las misiones protestantes y la resistencia indígena en el sur de la Colombia," *América Indígena* (Mexico City), XLIV/1 (1984), 111–27.
9. L. Hurbon, "Nuevos movimientos religiosos en el Caribe," *Cristianismo y Sociedad*, XXV/3, No. 93, 37–64.
10. M. J. Granados, "Los Israelitas," *Socialismo y participación* (Lima, March 1988), No. 41, 95–105.
11. P. G. Wright, "Quelques formes du chamanisme Toba," *Bulletin de la Société Suisse des Américanistes* (Geneva, 1984. No. 48, 29–35.
12. P. E. Carrasco, *Les cadres dirigeants baptistes latino-américains entre le croire et le pouvoir* (Doctoral thesis, University of Strasbourg. December 1988).
13. R. Reyes Novaes, *Os escolhidos de Deus, pentecostais, trabalhadores e cidadania. (Cadernos do ISER*, No. 19) (Rio de Janeiro, 1985).
14. A. Touraine, *La parole et le sang: politique et société en Amérique Latine* (Paris: 1988).

SELECT BIBLIOGRAPHY

Alberro, Solange, *Inquisition et société au Mexique, 1571–1700*. Mexico City: Centre d'Etudes Mexicaines et Centroaméricaines, 1988.
Alves, Rubem. *Protestantism and Repression: A Brazilian Case Study*. Maryknoll, N.Y.: Orbis, 1985.
Bastian, Jean-Pierre. *Historia del protestantismo en América Latina*. Mexico City: Casa Unida de Publicaciones, 1986 and 1990.
—. "Dissidence religieuse protestante dans le milieu rural méxicain." *Social Compass*, XXXII/2–3, 1985, 245–60.
—. "Protestantismo popular y política en Guatemala y Nicaragua." *Revista Mexicana de Sociología*, XLVIII/3, 1986, 181–99.
—. *Los disidentes, sociedades protestantes y revolucíon en México, 1872–1911*. Mexico City: Fondo de Cultura Económica, 1989.
—. (ed.) *Protestantes, liberales y francmasones, sociedades de ideas y modernidad en América Latina, Siglo XIX*. Mexico City: Fondo de Cultura Económica-CEHILA, 1990.
Bastide, Roger. "Contributions à une sociologie des religions en Amérique Latine." *Archives des Sciences Sociales des Religions*, 35, 1978, 139–50.
Bernecker, Walther L. "Intolerancia religiosa e inmigración en México, Siglo XIX." *Cristianismo y Sociedad*, XXVII/1, 1989, No. 9, 7–24.
Bruno-Jofre, Rosa del Carmen. *Methodist Education in Peru, Social Gospel, Politics, and American Ideological and Economic Penetration 1888–1930*. Waterloo, Ontario: Wilfrid Laurier University Press, 1988.
Carrasco, Pedro Enrique. "Les cadres dirigeants baptistes latino-américains entre le croire et le pouvoir; étude sociologique d'un processus d'épiscopalisation dans une société religieuse congrégationaliste en Amérique Latine." Doctoral Thesis Strasbourg University, December 1988.
Cepeda, Rafael. "Un congreso en La Habana, 1929." *Taller de Teología*. Mexico City, 1981, No. 9, 61–74.
Chaunu, Pierre. "Pour une sociologie du protestantisme latino-américain." *Cahiers de Scoiologie Economique*. Le Havre, May 1965, No, 12, 5–18.
Crivelli, Camilo. *Los protestantes y la América Latina; conferencias, acusaciones, respuestas*. Rome: Isola de Liri, 1931.
Dreher, Martin N. *Igreja e germanidade, estudo crítico da historia da Igreja Evangelica de Confissao Luterana no Brasil*. São Leopoldo: Editora Sinodal, 1984.
Dussel, Enrique. *Introducción general a la historia de la Iglesia en América Latina. Historia general de la Iglesia en América Latina*. Salamanca: Sígueme, 1983. Vol. I/1.

Garma Navarro, Carlos. *El protestantismo en la Sierra norte de Puebla.* Mexico City: Instituto Nacional Indigenista, 1987.

—. "Liderazgo, mensaje religioso y contexto social." *Cristianismo y Sociedad,* XXVI/1, 1988, No. 95, 89–100.

Glade, William P. *The Latin American Economies.* New York, 1969.

Goff, James E. *The Persecution of Protestant Christians in Colombia, 1948–1958. Sondeos No. 23.* Cuernavaca, Mexico: CIDOC, 1968.

Gouvea Mendonça, Antonio. *O Celeste Porvenir, a inserção do protestantismo no Brasil.* São Paulo: Paulinas, 1984.

Granados, Manuel Jesús. "Los Israelitas." *Socialismo y participación.* Lima, March 1988, No. 41, 95–105.

Gueiros Vieira, David. *O Protestantismo, a Maçonaria e a questão religiosa no Brasil.* Brasilia: Universidade de Brasilia, 1980.

García Jordán, Pilar. "Progreso, inmigración y libertad de cultos en Perú a mediados del siglo XIX," *Cristianismo y Sociedad,* XXVII/1, 1989, No, 99, 25–44.

Gruzinski, Serge and Carmen Bernand. *De l'idolâtrie, une archéologie des sciences religieuses.* Paris: Seuil, 1988.

Halperin Donghi, Tulio. *Reforma y disolución de los imperios ibéricos, 1750–1850.* Barcelona: Alianza, 1985.

Hurbon, Laënnec. "Nuevos movimientos religiosos en el Caribe." *Cristianismo y Sociedad,* XXV/3, 1987, No. 93, 37–64.

Lalive d'Epinay, Christian. *Haven of the Masses.* London: Lutterworth, 1969.

—. *Dynamique sociale, religion et dépendance, Les mouvements protestants en Argentine et au Chili.* Paris: Mouton, 1975.

Laqueur, Thomas Walter. *Religion and respectability, Sunday Schools and English Working Class Culture, 1780–1850.* New Haven and London: Yale University Press, 1976.

Linch, John. *Las revoluciones latinoamericanas.* Barcelona: Seix Barral, 1976.

Mansilla, H. C. F. "La herencia ibérica y la persistencia del autoritarismo en América Latina." *Cristianismo y Sociedad,* XXVII/2. 1989, No, 100, 81–94.

Monti, Daniel P. *Presencia del protestantismo en al Río de la Plata durante el Siglo XIX.* Buenos Aires: La Aurora, 1969.

Miller, Elmer S. *Los Tobas argentinos, armonía y disonencia en una sociedad.* Mexico City: Siglo XXI, 1979.

Pereira de Queiroz, María Isaura. *Historia y etnología de los movimientos mesiánicos.* Mexico City: Siglo XXI, 1968.

Pereira Ramalho, Jether. *Práctica educativa e sociedade, un estudo de sociologia de la educação.* Rio de Janeiro: Zahar, 1976.

Pietschmann, Horst. *Staat und Staatliche am Beginn der Spanischen Kolonisation Amerikas.* Münster: Aschendorf, 1980.

Pike, Frederick B. *The Politics of the Miraculous in Peru, Haya de la Torre and the Spiritualist Tradition.* Lincoln and London: University of Nebraska Press, 1986.

Planchet, Régis. *La intervención protestante en México y Sudamérica.* El Paso, Texas, 1928.

Poulat, Emile. *Eglise contre bourgeoisie, introduction au devenir du catholicisme actuel.* Paris: Casterman, 1977.

Prien, Hans Jürgen. *Die Geschichte des Christentums in Latein Amerika.* Tübingen: Van de Hoek und Ruprecht, 1978.

Ramos, Marcos Antonio. *Panorama del protestantismo en Cuba.* Miami: Caribe, 1987.

Rappaport, Joanne. "Las misiones protestantes y la resistencia indígena en el sur de la Colombia." *América Indígena.* Mexico City, XLIV/1, 1984, 111–27.

Reyes Novaes, Regina. *Os escolhidos de Deus, pentecostais, trabalhadores e cidadânia. Cadernos do ISER,* No. 19. Rio de Janeiro, 1985.

Rodrigues Brandão, Carlos. *Os deuses do povo, um estudo sobre a religião popular.* São Paulo: Brasiliense, 1986.

—. "Creencia e identidad; campo religioso y camb cultural." *Cristianismo y Sociedad,* XXV/3, 1987, No. 93, 65–106.

Rodríguez, Jaime E. *El nacimiento de Hispanoamérica, Vicente Rocafuerte y el hispanoamericanismo, 1808–1832.* Mexico City: Fondo de Cultura Económica, 1980.

Rolim, Francisco C. *Pentecostais no Brasil, uma interpretaçao socio-religiosa.* Petropolis: Vozes, 1985.

Saint Martin, Monique de. "Quelques questions à propos du pentecôtisme au Brésil." *Actes de la Recherche en Sciences Sociales.* Paris, Nos. 52–53, June 1984, 111–14.

Samandu, Luis. "El pentecostalismo en Nicaragua y sus raíces religiosas populares." *Pasos.* San José, Costa Rica, May–June 1988, No. 17, 1–10.

Schalkwijk, Frans Leonard. *Igreja e estado no Brasil Holandés, 1630–1659.* Recife: Fundarpe, 1986.

Santamaría, Daniel J. "Pentecostalismo e identidad étnica." *Cristianismo y Sociedad*, XXVIII, 1990, No. 105.

Stoll, David. *Fishers of Men or Founders of Empire? The Wycliffe Bible Translators in Latin America.* London: Zed Press, 1982.

—. *Is Latin America Turning Protestant? The Politics of Evangelical Growth.* Berkeley: University of California Press, 1990.

Touraine, Alain. *La parole et le sang, politique et société en Amérique Latine.* Paris: Odile Jacob, 1988.

Willems, Emile. *Followers of the New Faith.* Nashville: Vanderbilt University Press, 1967.

Wright, Pablo G. "Quelques formes du chamanisme Toba." *Bulletin de la Société Suisse des Américanistes.* Geneva, 1984, No. 48, 29–35.

Wright, Pablo G. "Tradición y aculturación en una organización socio-religiosa toba contempóranea." *Cristianismo y Sociedad*, XXVI/1, 1988, No. 95, 71–88.

Zea, Leopoldo. *El positivismo en México, nacimiento, apogeo y decadencia.* Mexico City: Fondo de Cultura Económica, 1968.

Chapter 19

THE REDUCTIONS

Margarita Durán Estragó

1. FIRST ATTEMPTS (1503–80)

The Europeans who came to America viewed its inhabitants as *identical* to themselves: that is, they could be assimilated to their way of life and should, therefore, speak like them, dress like them and live in accordance with the cultural patterns of the West. But besides being identical, they were also *different*, since they went naked and lived scattered lives in the forest, drank themselves stupid and danced till they dropped, ate human flesh and worshipped false gods.

What the Spaniards did not see in the native inhabitants of America were beings *equal* to themselves; they saw *inferior* subjects whom they had to "humanize." Their nakedness, the paints and feathers with which they adorned their bodies, their long hair, their polygamy, witchcraft, cohabitation and drunkenness and other vices all formed strong barriers against the entry of "civilization" into America.

The fact that the natives lived in scattered groups made it impossible for them to be "reduced" to *political* and *human life*, the first requirement if they were to be converted to *Christian faith and life*. The need to gather them into settlements made the Spanish crown, at the beginning of the sixteenth century, issue the first legal ordinances designed to establish "reductions" or settlements. The first royal instructions sent to the governors and officials of Spanish America relating to the concentration of natives in settlements are in fact dated 20 and 29 March 1503, decrees signed in Alcalá de Henares eleven years after the first conquistadors landed in America. These orders were renewed in March 1509, sent this time to Diego Colón, son and heir of Admiral Christopher Columbus.

The famous Burgos Laws of 1512, written under the influence of the Dominican friar Antón de Montesinos from Hispaniola (Dominican Republic), established reductions as a basic method of colonizing. The instructions handed to the Jeronymite friars in 1516 again adverted to the need to gather the natives into villages or settlements in order to achieve their "civilization" and christianization.

Fray Bartolomé de las Casas, an *encomendero* Dominican from Cuba, realized the injustice of his attitude to "his Indians" and changed his way of life, dedicating his priesthood to obtaining justice and liberation for the native peoples of America. Las Casas left Cuba in 1514 and returned to Spain, where he presented a Memorandum defending the Indians. In 1519 he obtained royal consent to his project of establishing "settlements of free Indians" with the cooperation of Spanish and Indian landowners. His first attempt at a settlement was made on the coast of Paria, in the Cumaná region of Venezuela, in 1520.

351

The experiment lasted only two years, owing to the interests of the *encomenderos* of Santo Domingo, the fact that Las Casas was occupied with a thousand other things, and finally, the revolt of the Indians themselves, who ended by attacking the settlement in 1522.[1]

The Dominican Juan de Zumárraga, bishop of Mexico, facilitated the foundation of a school for children of *caciques* at Tlatelolco in 1536. This foundation failed to prosper owing to pressures from the Spanish inhabitants who prevented the priests "of the place" from going out to carry the mission to the natives. Zumárraga insisted on the need to concentrate the natives into settlements and so prevent them from scattering into the forests where they lived without anyone caring for either their bodies or their souls, since under such conditions, he said: "faith and good order will never reach them unless they are brought together."[2] Zumárraga's sermon brought about the promulgation of decrees founding cities, such as Michoacán in 1534. This was the first order of any importance issued for concentrating the natives in settlements in Mexico.

A major influence there was Bishop Vasco de Quiroga, who had first expressed his views in favour of reductions in a letter to the Council of the Indies in 1531. In this, he put forward the "reduction" of the natives as a means of protecting orphans and poor people, and maintaining the faith of those new Christians who were being taught by the friars in their convents.[3] As first bishop of Michoacán, Quiroga founded the "hostel-villages of Santa Fe" as a complement to religious education. In these, Indians were taught basic reading and some rudiments of agriculture. Quiroga's pedagogical method was based on understanding of and respect for those being taught. He tried to suppress the bloody side of the "conquest" so as to attract the Indians through "good works."

Quiroga devoted his life to the native population of Michoacán, but his educational endeavours turned out to be a utopian adventure that remained in the realm of "good will."[4] Here too, the *encomenderos* and other Spanish settlers opposed the bishop's evangelizing actions and threatened to take over the communal properties of the hostel-villages of Santa Fe. Quiroga's first aim had been to shelter those Indians who came to the settlements, as well as pilgrims who stayed in the hostels on their travels and and adopted the good habits and virtues practised by the inhabitants during their stay.

After various unsuccessful experiments, the first successful attempt at free and peaceful evangelization of Indians was carried out in Guatemala from 1537–9, under the inspiration of Bartolomé de las Casas. This was the Verapaz mission, an event which inspired the promulgation of the "New Laws" of 1542, thanks to the success of Las Casas' thesis expressed in his "Of the only way to attract all peoples to the true religion," and led to the land known as Tetzulutlán, "land of war," being re-named Verapaz, "land of true peace." This mission was situated in the forest region of north-east Guatemala, where Maya groups lived, still free from conquest by Spaniards. The Dominicans reached them through Indian messengers, whom they sent playing melodic music, whose verses, translated into Quiché, spoke of the creation of the world, of paradise, of the need for redemption, the passion and death of Jesus Christ and his second coming. These converted Indians came to the chief *cacique* and entertained him by their singing. Their success was dramatic. The Mayas listened to this new teaching in song with great interest, and the *cacique* invited the messengers to bring those religious – described by the singers as Spaniards who dressed in white and had very different customs from the other Spaniards.

The Dominicans who founded the Verapaz mission knew the Indian language, which made communication and the transmission of the gospel message much easier. The beginnings of the settlement date from 1537, but it was not finally established till 1544, when Las Casas, by then bishop of Chiapas in Mexico, came back from Spain with more than a dozen royal letters patent approving his requests and supporting the Guatemala mission. One of these letters extended by a further five years the prohibition on Spaniards from entering these lands to make war, "to ambush, to scandalize, or to disturb the Indians, either by way of trading or by any other means, under pain of perpetual exile from the Indies and loss of half the goods of anyone who should do so."[5] These royal decrees produced a very tense atmosphere in Guatemala. The ban on entering the territory and the suppression of the *encomienda* led many Spaniards to revolt and tested those who were defending the rights of the Indians.

Facing trials, persecutions and martyrdom, the missionaries in Guatemala carried on extending the boundaries of territory brought under pastoral care. They established new centres of Indian settlement till Verapaz had been brought within the area of official church control. In recognition of the merits of Fray Pedro de Angulo, the distinguished missionary of Tutzulután, Pope Pius IV appointed him first bishop of Verapaz in 1561.

The project of "reducing" the Guaraní Indians of the southern Atlantic coast region dates from 1538. Bernardo de Armenta and Alonso Lebrón, Franciscan missionary friars who reached the island of Santa Catalina off Brazil with Alonso Cabrera's expedition, made contact with the local Guaranís. Some months after their arrival, Armenta wrote to the Council of the Indies about the need to send agricultural workers and tradesmen of all sorts, who, he said, would be more useful "than soldiers, in view of the fact that it is easier to attract these savages through gentleness than through force."[6] Some Portuguese Franciscans, who were evangelizing the Tupís of present-day Brazil, were, according to Manuel de Nóbrega, writing in 1549, killed through the fault of the "Christians" themselves.[7] When the Jesuits reached Brazil in this same year, they opened a school for Portuguese and Indian children. They took part in founding cities, learned the Tupí language, wrote its grammar and began to collect the natives in settlements. Towards 1566 they extended their activities into La Florida, then into Peru, Mexico, New Granada (Colombia and Venezuela) and finally Paraguay.

The Viceroy of Peru, Francisco de Toledo, in 1570 developed a policy based on all these efforts at gathering the natives into settlements. This "reductionist" policy was envisaged as meeting the requirements of evangelization, and aimed at slowing the drastic decline in native populations.

The Peruvian chronicler Juan de Matienzo produced a work on "The Government of Peru" in 1567, in which he laid down a set of rules for applying the system of reductions to the whole territory. Basing the need for applying such a plan on the serious difficulties posed by the dispersion of the native population in the countryside, he suggested that the territories they occupied should be explored, and a census made of the *caciques* and their people. He suggested that villages be established with a population of five hundred Indians, each of which should have a water supply, firewood and good agricultural land. He even drew up a standard plan for these settlements, which were to be in blocks around a central square. One of the blocks would contain the church and missioner's house, with some guest rooms, and beyond these, the Spanish magistrate's house and the prison, with stocks and cells. Another block would contain the Chapter or Council House, as well as the residence of the chief *cacique*. Other central blocks would house those married Spaniards who wished to live among the Indians. Farther out would be houses for the Indians, each with a parcel of land, or two if the family was numerous or had the title of *cacique*.[8]

Viceroy Toldeo put his reductionist plan into effect with the foundation of Santiago (now Lima) in 1570. This was generally known as *El Cercado* ("The Enclosed"), on account of the walls built to surround it in order to control the Indians and prevent them from escaping. Toledo's policy consisted in bringing the Indians into towns to provide an abundant labour force, and to ease the problem of collecting the tribute that they were obliged to pay to the Spaniards. The "reduction" of *El Cercado* was divided into thirty-five "fractions," each of which was further sub-divided into *encomiendas*, the number depending on the number of Indians who could be brought to Lima and put under the control of their *encomendero*. The whole reduction was governed by a Spanish magistrate, with its spiritual direction entrusted to the Jesuits. There was an Indian Council made up of magistrates, mayors, a chief constable, a treasurer and guardians of the hospital and the town, and a secretary. The *caciques* were charged with fulfilling the terms of the *encomienda* and arranging regular payment of the tribute. Fugitives, idolators and fetishists, thieves and murderers, were punished by flogging and other means. On the evangelical side, the missioners were obliged to teach Christian doctrine and administer the sacraments. The church was looked after by a sacristan and cantors, who were exempt from paying tribute, as were *caciques* and members of the Council. All male Indians over the age of eighteen were forced into the *mita*: work in the mines or plantations owned by their *encomenderos*. This obligation lasted till the age of fifty, though the Spaniards often forced those still physically capable of work to go on beyond this age.

Between 1570 and 1575, the population of the Viceroyalty of Peru decreased considerably. The policy of forcibly "reducing" the Indians was carried out with such harshness and cruelty that those charged with putting the plan into effect snatched Indians from their lands, burned their farms and drove them in herds to the new settlements near work places, where they could better be exploited and kept under control. Epidemics also played their part in lowering the native populations of the settlements, and, one way or another, Viceroy Toledo's reductions had the opposite effect to that intended by those who devised it.

The reductions of *El Cercado* and the other centres established in Peru were short-lived. The Indians were constantly escaping, fleeing from forced labour in the silver and mercury mines, from the varied sufferings imposed on them, to get back to their homelands and their own religious rites and ceremonies. What Toledo's reductions did achieve, by dragging the Indians away from their birthplaces and forcing them to live so differently from their traditional ways, was the destruction of the socio-economic system of the Inca regime.

2. NEW FORMS OF REDUCTION, 1606–1800

Lasting and systematic evangelization of the Guaranís began with the arrival of the Franciscans Luis Bolaños and Alonso de San Buenaventura in Paraguay in 1575. Bolaños learned their language and translated the Lima catechism, approved at the Third Council of Lima in 1583, into Guaraní.

Once the language barrier had been overcome, Bolaños and his companion began gathering the Indians scattered in the countryside into reductions, beginning the process of "reducing" the Guaranís in 1580. Although Spain had for some time recommended the establishment of reductions and some experiments had been made, what was new in Paraguay was the basic role played by the missionaries and the weight given to economic and social institutions, which distinguished them from the reductions or nuclear townships of Guatemala and Peru. The new type of organization begun with the first Franciscan missionaries to Paraguay emerged as the system of "peripheral reductions," which Bolaños was the first to employ.

When these first Franciscans arrived in Paraguay, the whole province was in a state of war. The *encomienda* system imposed by the governor, Domingo Martínez de Irala, in 1556, had roused the Indian population, abused and ill-treated by the *encomenderos*, to revolt. The religious took stock of this situation and set out to pacify the natives by "reducing" them to settlements. Although this pacification process involved defending the Indians, it also had the effect of bringing them into the *encomienda*. Before the end of the sixteenth century, the reductions of Altos, Itá, Yaguarón, Guarambaré, Tobatí and many others had brought about what force of arms had failed to do: pacify and subject the Guaranís, thereby not only allowing them to be evangelized, but also subjecting them to *encomienda*.[9]

These sixteenth-century Guaraní reductions, however, still had no permanent missionary presence. The small number of religious operating among the Indians forced Bolaños and his companions to divide their time among a number of tasks: itinerant preacher, social worker, teacher. . . . Government of these reductions was left mainly in the hands of settlers or overseers, and to a lesser extent to the chief caciques of the people. The Spanish overseers taught the Indians how to handle a plough on the smallholdings, supervised the spinning activities of the women, organized and enforced the personal service due to *encomenderos*. The Synod held in Asunción in 1603 accused the settlers of "scandalizing" the Indians, of "living like demons," of making the Indians work on feast days, whipping them for no reason and sexually abusing their women.

In these early Guaraní reductions, the economy still depended on hunting, fishing and gathering wild fruits and honey, though oxen and ploughing were introduced toward the end of the sixteenth century, when the first carpentry workshops and a foundry also appeared, in the Itá reduction. The burden of the

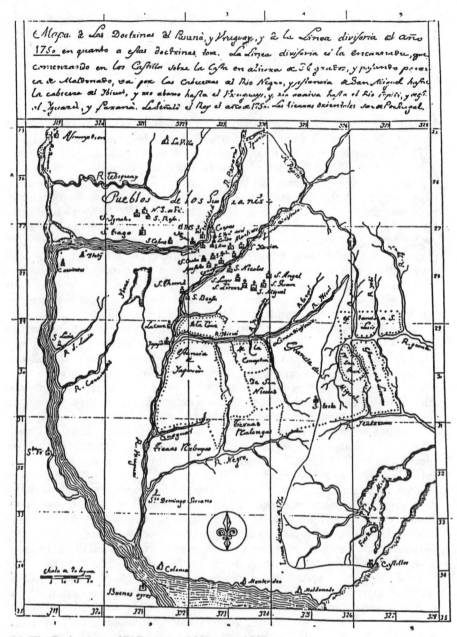

16. The Reductions of El Paraná and Uruguay, 1750
Source: Furlong

encomienda and the lack of permanent missionary presence had led to their decline by the end of the century.

Seeing the defects of these early efforts, Bolaños and his companions, with the help of the governor, Hernando Arias de Saavedra (known as Hernandarias), devised a new scheme of reduction. From 1606, when Caazapá was established, missionaries replaced *encomenderos* and personal service was abolished for the first ten years the Indians spent in reductions.

This change of policy was made possible by the increase in the number of priests available to missionize the Indians, the diocesan synod of 1603 and the orders that Hernandarias laid down on that occasion. In these, he made the establishment of reductions obligatory, and set out a series of measures for the protection of the Indians in them, as well as obliging the *encomenderos* to give financial assistance to the priest-in-charge.

Another major event that helped to consolidate the authority of the religious priests-in-charge in relation to the *encomenderos* was the application of the Ordinances of Francisco de Alfaro, Judge of Charcas, in 1611. These laws gave great importance to reductions, not only as instruments of "humanization" and control of the Indians, but also as centres where they could be protected against abuses by the *ecomenderos*: "for them not be harmed depends on their being reduced into settlements. . . ."[10] Apart from this aspect, these laws increased the power and influence of the priests-in-charge by entrusting them with not only the spiritual care of the Indians, but also the temporal administration of the goods produced by the community and supervision of elections to the native Council.

The establishment of Caazapá brought about the pacification of the Paraná sub-group of the Guaranís and consolidated the power of the priests-in-charge. From then on, in both Franciscan and Jesuit reductions, begun in 1611 with the foundation of San Ignacio Guazú, the native inhabitants were exempt from *encomienda* for the term of ten years. After this period, the Jesuits managed to prolong the term till "their" Indians were completely freed from the colonial regime, in all their reductions except three, Santa María de Fe, San Ignacio Guazú and Santiago, which they did not for a long time suceed in withdrawing from *encomienda* service. The Franciscan reductions, on the other hand, with the exception of Itapé, are known to have been subject to *encomienda*, at least from 1618 onward.[11]

The Guaraní reductions started by the Franciscans reached the height of their splendour under the Jesuits, with their famous thirty townships situated mainly on both banks of the Paraná and Uruguay rivers. The basic difference between both forms stemmed from the fact that the Franciscans collaborated with the colonial system. They accepted *encomienda* service for the Indians living in their reductions, while at the same time struggling to apply laws designed to protect the native peoples, which often brought them into conflict with provincial governors.[12] The Jesuits, on the other hand, isolated the Indians in their reductions so as to free them from *encomienda*, though they were subject to other obligations which did not apply in other reductions, such as military service, work in quarries, hauling and cutting stone for the building of churches, schools and workshops.

Although some reductions were founded by secular clergy, or handed over to them, the vast majority were run by Franciscans or Jesuits, not only in the River Plate area, but throughout America. In the second half of the eighteenth century, after the expulsion of the Jesuits in 1767, other religious orders, such as the Dominicans and Mercedarians, took over the spiritual care of the ex-Jesuit reductions.

Indian reductions lasted till about the middle of the nineteenth century, when they were turned into towns and parishes. Other settlers moved in and the races began to intermarry.

3. THE URBAN STRUCTURE OF THE REDUCTIONS

Franciscan and Jesuit reductions, as well as those founded by secular clergy and other orders, kept in general terms to the rules laid down by Viceroy Toledo between 1570 and 1580 and the plans of 1573. All had the same basic arrangement of elements such as church, school or priests' house, workshops and dwellings.

There were, however, some significant differences between Franciscan and Jesuit reductions. The former had the church in the middle of the square, separating it from school, workshops, stores and other services. In Paraguay and other areas along the River Plate, this pattern was maintained for centuries and still gives country towns their characteristic appearance. Jesuit reductions had a central square with the church built into one side of it, with school and workshops next to it. The native dwellings were in long "stretches" of streets surrounding the square, arranged in "island blocks" that were very characteristic of Jesuit missions.

In both, the houses had covered walkways running the length of the building, protecting their inhabitants from heat, rain and cold. All houses were built to the same dimensions, with the door giving on to the square, which allowed the Indians to be watched and prevented from escaping. In the centre of the single room was a fire which the wife tended for cooking, lighting and warmth. They slept in hammocks, which they hung up at night and "put away during the day."[13]

The church was the centre of the external aspects of religious worship, and its construction, decoration and conservation were the responsibility of the Indians, who were "most diligent that all pomp and riches should shine in their churches ..."[14] The altarpieces, statues and other furnishings, as well as a variety of musical instruments, were made in the reduction workshops. The school or priests' house generally had two courtyards; it contained the rooms of the priest or priests, the refectory and storerooms for the community goods.

On one side of the square was the Council House, with the royal arms on the door. This building had two stories and included the jail with its stocks and cells. Justice was completed by the "*rollo*," a large standing stone or tree trunk usually set up in the square. It was not like the gallows found in Spanish towns, since the death penalty was not employed, but Indians were tied to it to be flogged in punishment of crimes that carried a public sentence.

Either next to the Council House or in the school house, elementary classes were given, where the sons of *caciques* learned to read and write in Spanish, by royal decree: "Let the Indians be instructed ... in Spanish ... since this is proper to the Monarchs and ... so that ... they may come to love the conquering nation. . . ."[15] They also learned to read Latin, so that they could serve mass and chant the psalms of Matins and Lauds. But reading and writing in their native language were not neglected either: this is attested by several petitions sent by Councils to Spain or handed to the local authorities. In each reduction there was also a music school, in which the Indian cantors showed great ability and talent.

Workshops produced a great variety of products: master craftsmen taught wood-carving, polychroming and gilding; they made carts and waggons, clothes, furniture, vases, cloth and good musical instruments. There were potteries to make bricks and tiles, bakeries and beehives. One of the *caciques* was in charge of the inn or hostelry, where merchants or others coming to visit the reduction could spend the night.

The hospital and cemetery completed the urban structure of the settlements. Outside them were smallholdings and ranches worked as common land, with all kinds of herds, especially of cattle. Jesuit reductions also had a house set apart for widows, old women, orphans and women shut away for crimes.

4. WORK ORGANIZATION

Work was obligatory in the reductions. All Indians of suitable age and physique had to give service to the community. In reductions subject to the colonial regime, they had to fulfil their service to the *encomenderos* and then work to support the community and their families.

Local governors also arrogated the right to use native labour for their own use or to work for Spanish settlements. They periodically asked the priest to send natives to guard block-houses, paddle rafts, work in Spanish sugar factories, repair the streets, rebuild churches, and so on. Not even children were exempt from the governor's "commandments." They were taken from their homes to work as domestic servants in Spanish houses. Women were taken to wet-nurse Spanish babies, forced to neglect feeding their own. The *encomenderos'* abuse of the natives in their service caused great damage to families and to the economy of the reductions.

Women's work was to look after the house and to spin a weekly batch of cotton. They also fetched firewood and water, and helped on the land at sowing and harvest times.

Both Jesuit and Franciscan settlements ran two economic sectors, one for the natives and one for the community. The former assured family subsistence, and the size of each plot of land assigned for this purpose was related to the number of children in each family. The harvest belonged to the native family, but not the oxen and ploughs, which belonged to the community. They could keep animals such as hens and pigs, for domestic consumption, in their houses. The private sector scarcely functioned in reductions subject to *encomienda*, where Indian men were kept by their masters and when they returned from the towns, had to work for the community. In these cases, women took over their private sector tasks so as to be able to feed their families.

The communal sector comprised the lands devoted to crops and livestock which were sold in order to support the community, pay for church worship and, in reductions exempt from *encomienda* service, pay the annual tribute to the crown. Work in the workshops, and their products, also belonged to the community sector, as did the spinning and weaving destined to produce clothes for the inhabitants.

The smallholdings, grazing grounds and ranches were provided with chapels and shelters for the Indian overseers and peons who worked in them, since distances were too great for them to return home each evening. Large numbers of natives were employed in the production of tobacco, cotton, *yerba mate*, coffee, sugar cane and other crops, though not all reductions produced such a variety of produce. They traded with the outside world for their other needs, generally importing gold and silver for gilding, oil, linen and silk, salt, iron and metal tools, wax and wine, for which they traded agricultural produce and cotton goods.

5. DAILY LIFE

Daily life in the reduction generally started at dawn. Drums summoned the Indians to the priest's house, where they chanted the *Benedictus*, and thence to the church to hear mass.

The children were given breakfast all together in the atrium of the church, after a period of religious instruction. Then they carried out communal tasks, such as tidying the square and cleaning the streets. In the afternoon they came back to the school for elementary education and further religious instruction, after which they had lunch together.

The able-bodied women were given cotton to spin on Mondays, and handed in the spun thread on Saturdays, after it had been weighed in front of the treasurer and the clerk who kept a ledger detailing the amount weighed. If any of them refused to work or handed in less than her quota, she received "twenty-five strokes of the whip on the move."[16] In Jesuit reductions, women were whipped on the back, while men were whipped on the buttocks and "in the middle of the square when it was convenient to make an example of them."[17]

The priest handed out communal goods, food and clothing, since the whole settlement "is made up of minors, whose tutor and guardian is the priest."[18]

The men worked in the workshops, in the fields, on the ranches or plantations, producing maté, coffee or sugar cane in accordance with the production policy of the reduction. Besides this, they had to work for their *encomendero*, or carry out military service in Jesuit reductions in frontier zones.

On feast days, all went to church to hear mass. After this, they engaged in hunting, fishing, or competitive games on horseback such as spearing a ring, ritual dancing and other recreational activities. Weddings were celebrated in front of the whole community, and people were usually married at fourteen to sixteen years of age in order to compensate for population decline through early deaths.

CONCLUSION

Indian reductions were a pattern of evangelization used by religious orders, mainly the Jesuits and Franciscans, but were at the same time a means of pacifying and subjecting the native peoples to Spanish domination. The reductions put an end to Indian uprisings by removing the hostility the Indians showed to priests and governors. They did not, however, remove the passive resistance the Indians continued to show to imposed Western religion and culture. Louis Nécker maintains that idleness, drunkenness, theft, slovenliness, escaping and adherence to their old values were passive symptoms of Indian resistance.

The regime of the reductions succeeded in transforming many intermediate Indian cultures from hunter-gatherers to settledd agricultural peoples. Despite escapes, epidemics and ill-treatment, the reductions did succeed in stabilizing and maintaining the level of native populations, which did not prove possible in places where religious orders did not employ this type of organization. In short, Indian reductions or "doctrines" were a lesser evil within the ruling oppressive colonial system.

Translated from the Spanish by Paul Burns

NOTES

1. E. Dussel, "Coloniaje y Liberación 1492–1983," *Historia de la Iglesia en América Latina* (Madrid, 1983), p. 92.

2. P. Borges, *Métodos misionales en la cristianización de América, siglo XVI* (Madrid, 1960); "Vasco de Quiroga en el ambiente misionero de la Nueva España," Missionalia Hispánica, año XXIII 69 (Madrid, 1966), p. 323.

3. Borges, "Vasco de Quiroga," p. 373.

4. A. G. Matabuena, "Origen y exigencias históricas de la obra misional de Verapaz." Offprint from *Ciencia Tomista*, vol. CVII, 350, (Salamanca, Jan-April 1980), p. 95.

5. Idem., p. 107.

6. L. Cano, "Las órdenes religiosas en los Treinta Pueblos Guaraníes después de la expulsión de los jesuits. Los franciscanos." Offprint from Third Congress of Argentine and Regional History, held at Santa Fe-Paraná, July 1975 (Buenos Aires, 1877), p. 123.

7. M. Pereira, "Actividad evangelizadora y cultural de los Franciscanos Portugueses en Brasil durante el siglo XVI." Offprint from Second International Congress of Franciscans in the New World, 16th Century (La Rábida, 1987), p. 908.

8. L. Hurtado Galván, "As Reduções de Toledo no Planalto Peruano (1570–1580)," *Das reduções Latino-Americanas as Lutas Indígenas Atuais*, Ninth Latin-American Symposium of CEHILA, July-Aug. 1981 (São Paulo, 1982), p. 27.

9. L. Nécker, *Indiens Guaraní et Chamanes Franciscains: les Premières Réductions du Paraguay* (1580–1800) (Paris, 1979), p. 81.

10. E. de Gandía, *Francisco de Alfaro y la condición social de los indios* (Buenos Aires, 1939). Contains transcript of art. 3 of "Ordenanzas de buen gobierno" by Hernandarias de Saavedra, 1603.

11. "Información de servicios de 1618," A. Millé, *Crónica de la Orden Fanciscana en la Conquista del Perú, Paraguay y el Tucumán y su convento del antiguo Buenos Aires, 1612–1800* (Buenos Aires, 1981), pp. 407ff.

12. Letter from the superior of the Franciscan doctrines in Paraguay, 1704, in National Archive of Asunción, vol. 8 SH; sermon preached by Fray Manuel de Espinosa on the feast of the Assumption 1677, considered by the Council of Asunción in Paraguay as an "infamous libel against the *encomenderos* of the city," NAA, vol 11, p. 673.

13. P. F.-X. Charlevoix, *Historia del Paraguay* (Madrid, 1912–13), vol. II, p. 62.

14. P. J. de Parras, *Diario y derrotero de sus viajes, 1749–1753* (Buenos Aires, 1943). p. 170.

15. Royal Decree of 10 May 1770 outlawing from the Kingdoms of the Indies "the various languages spoken in those Dominions and that Spanish alone is to be spoken," NAA, vol.62 SH.

16. Parras, *Diario*, p. 171.

17. D. Muriel, *Historia del Paraguay* (Madrid, 1918), p. 542.

18. Parras, *Diario*, p. 170.

SELECT BIBLIOGRAPHY

Albó, Xavier. "Jesuitas y culturas indígenas. Perú 1568-1606. Su actitud. Métodos y criterios de aculturación." *América Indígena*, XXVI. Mexico. 1966.

Balbas, Antonio. *Recopilación de las Leyes de Indias*. 2nd ed. Madrid, 1756.

Borges, Pedro. *Métodos misionales en la cristianización de América, siglo XVI*. Madrid, 1960.

——. "Vasco Quiroga en el ambiente misionero de la Nueva España." *Missionalia Hispánica, año XXIII*. No. 69. Madrid, 1966.

Carvalho, João Renor F. de. "Presença e Permanência da Orden do Carmo no Solimoes e no Rio Negro no Século XVIII." Various. *Das Reduçoes Latino-Americanas as Lutas Indígenas Atuais*. São Paulo: Paulinas, 1981.

Charlevoix, Pierre F.-X. *Historia del Paraguay*. Trans. Pedro Hernández. Vol. II. Madrid, 1912–13.

Durán Estragó, Margarita. *Presencia Franciscana en Paraguay, 1583–1824*. Biblioteca de estudios Paraguayos, vol. XIX. Asunción: Universidad Católica, 1987.

Fragoso, Hugo. "Os Aldeamentos Franciscanos do Grão-Porá." *Das Reduções*. op. cit., pp. 119–60.

Gandía, Enrique de. *Francisco de Alfaro y la condición social de los Indios*. Buenos Aires: El Ateneo, 1939.

Hernández, Pablo. *Organización social de las doctrinas guaraníes de la Compañía de Jesús*. 2 vols. Barcelona, 1913.

Hoornaert, Eduardo. "As missões Carmelitanas na Amazônia. 1693–1755." *Das Reduções*. op. cit.,pp. 161–74.

Las Casas, Bartolomé de. *Del único modo de atraer todos los pueblos a la verdadera religión*. Mexico, 1975.

Levillier, Roberto. *Correspondencia de la Ciudad de Buenos Aires con los Reyes de España* (1588–1615). Madrid, 1953.

——. "Ordenanzas del Virrey Toledo." *Gobernantes del Perú*. vol. VII. Lima: Sucesores de Rivadeneira, 1921.

Lozano, Pedro. *Historia de la Compañía de Jesús de la Provincia del Paraguay*. 2 vols. Madrid, 1754–5.

Marzal, Manuel M. "As Reduçoes indígenas na Amazônia do Vice-reinado Peruano." *Das Reduções*. op. cit., pp. 77-118.

Matabuena, Antonio G. "Origen y exigencias históricas de la obra misional de Verapaz." Offprint of *Ciencia Tomista*, vol. CVII, no. 350. Salamanca, 1980.

Menacho, Antonio. "As missões as Mojos." *Das Reduções*. op. cit., pp. 191–204.

Melia, Bartomeu. "El Guaraní conquistado y reducido." *Ensayos de Etnohistoria*, vol. 5. Asunción: Universidad Católica, 1986.

Miranda, Francisco. "As Reduções Quiroguianas de Santa Fe. Uma experiência utópica na Nova Espanha do Século XVI." *Das reduções*. op. cit., pp. 50–63.

Muriel, Domingo. *Historia del Paraguay*. Trans. Pablo Hernández. Madrid, 1918.

Nécker, Louis. *Indiens Guaraní et Chamanes Franciscains: Les Premières Réductions du Paraguay (1580–1800)*. Paris: Anthros, 1979.

Porto, Aurelio. *Historia das Missões orientais do Uruguai*. Rio de Janeiro, 1943.

Solorzano y Pereyra, Juan de. *Política Indiana*. Madrid: BAC, 1972.

Zavala, Silvio. *El servicio personal de los Indios en el Perú*. Mexico: TI, 1978.

Chapter 20

3. THE CHURCH AND AFRO-AMERICAN SLAVERY

Laënnec Hurbon

The history of relations between the Church and slavery in the New World is obviously calamitous. As a general rule the clergy owned slaves and served to legitimize slave-owning on behalf of the administration.

Though rigorously proved by virtually every historian, these facts are nevertheless open to varied interpretations, quite apart from theological discussion about the nature of the Church's role in the world. The Church, it is often said, claims to work solicitously on human minds in order to bring about gradual change in social structures. Therefore its approach was not to assail people directly but to adopt an educational stance that would lead eventually to the abolition of slavery. This strategy accords with the very nature of Christianity, which has an essentially spiritual outlook. In general terms, for example, the Church's role in the Roman Empire in regard to the practice of slavery may be seen as positive. From one angle, the egalitarian teaching of Christianity enunciated by St Paul – "There is no longer Jew, Greek, master or slave . . ." – if adopted by the slaves, would have sufficed to point them toward their collective emancipation. From another angle, perhaps, since the dignity of every human being was paramount, slavery would necessarily become obsolete wherever Christianity took root. Whichever view one accepts, I find it difficult to see the history of the Church's association with slavery in the modern era in a neutral perspective. In any case, it seems appropriate to revive the debate, which is both historical and theological in nature. It is timely, in so far as the point at issue has considerable bearing on the course of liberation theology, which says that it is necessary to maintain a permanent association between the spiritual and the political activity of the Church. It is also appropriate in so far as it relates to the future of black communities in the United States, Latin America and the Caribbean, for sooner or later they must come to terms with the past history of slavery, which the views of the western missionary Church have tended unduly to represent in trite formulas.

In this essay, I intend to show that the Church was a vital structural element in the legal and ideological apparatus of slavery in the New World. I shall also examine the courageous attempts of certain members of the clergy to oppose the institution of slavery as such. Finally, I shall try to indicate the origins of the ambiguities and vacillations in theological approaches to the problem of slavery in modern times.

1. THE CHURCH'S INVOLVEMENT IN THE INSTITUTION OF SLAVERY IN THE NEW WORLD

When the New World was discovered, slavery was not an institution in the sense that there could have been any dispute about its principle. It was still

practised in fifteenth-century Europe, especially in Sicily and Italy. In 1434 a
bull of Pope Nicholas V gave King Alfonso of Portugal the right to enslave
heathen peoples. In 1495, therefore, the possibility of subjecting the Indians to
slavery allowed an appeal to the natural right to preach to and convert the
heathen. Consequently, slavery as such entered public opinion in Europe. It
could be a practice associated with the just war which made slaves of the
defeated instead of sentencing them to death. It could be a penitential interlude
which the "wicked" were granted to ensure their conversion. The Indians of
the Caribbean, whom Columbus and the first conquistadors considered to be
cannibals and resistant to evangelization, were therefore proposed for slavery.
Queen Isabella, to be sure, did summon theologians and lawyers to offer their
opinions on the legality of enslaving Indians.[1] A year and a half later, however,
she accepted the principle of slavery for all those who rejected conversion. This
opinion was so widespread that when Las Casas argued for the freedom of the
Indians, he had repeatedly to expound his belief that they were neither
barbarians, nor heathen, nor enemies of Christianity, and therefore did not
deserve the fate of slavery. We know that Las Casas' pleas fell on deaf ears; the
Indians did not survive forced labour in the gold-mines of Hispaniola and were
decimated.

It was decided therefore that they should be replaced with a work-force
better suited to slavery, and the black slave-trade began. Blacks had already
been present as slaves in Hispaniola since 1503. By means of the "asiento", a
monopoly which Portugal granted companies for the purpose of trafficking in
African slaves, the institution of slavery spread in the three Americas and did
not decline until three centuries had passed.

Few voices were raised against slavery after Las Casas' death. During the
entire sixteenth century slavery, legally sanctioned and justified by the Church,
was the main mode of production in the Canary Islands.[2] The bishops,
admittedly, criticized the acquisition of slaves by such illicit methods as unjust
wars. But for the Church the purpose of slavery was the conversion of black
African heathens. Slavery was good for their souls. Thus slavery came to seem
respectable, so that in the Canaries bishops, canons, cantors, priests and monks
alone owned 21 percent of slaves.

Nevertheless, to understand how the Church was a leading player in the long
drama of slavery in the New World (for almost four centuries), we have to
consult not only the testimonies of missionaries but the ordinances, regulations
and laws originating in the administration which sought to define the Church's
part in the slavery system. The essential aspects of this part of church history
are to be found in Gisler's magisterial and, in my opinion, unsurpassed work
Slavery in the French Antilles (17th-19th centuries).[3] Gisler's theses are merely
confirmed by Maxwell's more recent *Slavery and the Catholic Church* (London,
1975).

The fundamental argument which Louis XIII used to authorize the
slave-trade and slavery in French colonies in the seventeenth century was the
very same one put forward by Pope Nicholas V to justify the conversion of
Africans. To lead them to true religion and to save them from idolatry was the
purpose of slavery. For three centuries this argument was to be repeated in
almost all royal ordinances and disciplinary regulations. From the papal

viewpoint, as from that of royal authority, the Church does not just come along after the event and put down roots in a slave-owning society, to humanize it or even merely to place itself at the service of masters and slaves. Instead, the Church should direct all its activities to the service of the colonial slave-owning structure: that is, in subservience to the interests of the masters, the administration and royal authority. More precisely, to establish parishes and to strengthen the foundations of slave-owning society were one and the same thing. After Portugal and the Netherlands, France duly entered the black slave-trade by founding the notorious West Indies Company in 1664, to which it entrusted the task of conveying churchmen to the islands "to preach the Holy Gospel there and teach these peoples to believe in the Catholic, Apostolic and Roman religion, to build churches, and to install priests and rectors there to celebrate divine service".[4] The colonists were therefore obliged, under penalty, to take their slaves to catechism classes and to mass. Furthermore, as a general rule, slaves were baptized before embarking on slave-ships. Under royal pressure, the Portuguese never risked taking unbaptized slaves to Brazil. It was claimed that the fundamental aim of deporting Africans was to encourage their conversion.

It has often been observed that although the first missionaries in the Spanish, French and Portuguese colonies were few in number, they were all dedicated to their task of conversion. In reality they carried out their work in a spirit of subordination to the royal will, and the monarch took charge of the recruitment and maintenance of priests. Very soon they were paid with slaves and had their own dwelling-places. As they founded parishes they consolidated the slave system. They, far more than the administrators and comptrollers, were the pillars of the system. It was within the churches that masters and slaves learned the rules of their correct social relationship. A theology of the responsibilities of state and calling[5] inspired preaching and made the Church the breeding-ground of the institution of slavery.

2. THE TESTIMONY OF MISSIONARIES

I shall briefly consider the testimony of the seventeenth century, for instance Father Dutertre's account of life in the French colonies. For Dutertre there was no distinction between religious and social life in the colonies. But this was not primarily because religion was the deep preoccupation "of an age when the tone of life was regulated by prayer and religious observance".[6] It was much more that in the slave colonies the ordered slave system would have broken down if the missionaries (Capuchins, Carmelites, Jacobins, Dominicans and Jesuits) who accompanied the colonizers had decided to pronounce the slave his master's equal, even spiritually. In this respect, I suggest the Catholic Church had regressed in comparison with its position under the Roman Empire.

There is no question that in the seventeenth century it gradually lost all its autonomy *vis-à-vis* the power of the throne, but it still had an opportunity to apply to some advantage its fifteen long centuries of experience, yet did not. No one can dismiss the evidence that its status as a slaveowner was a major handicap for the clergy in their task of evangelization. Yet it is disquieting to note that in the seventeenth century no voice was raised in the Church, either in the colonies or at home, to challenge even the principle of enslavement of the blacks.

Father Dutertre (1654) is considered to have shown the greatest sympathy for black slaves, yet never at any moment did be betray any doubt that the institution of slavery was justified. The slave, he said, worked from morning till evening, and even at night. He was badly clothed, badly housed and even in death he was wretched: ". . . out of fifty who die, not even two are wrapped in a shroud: they are interred in their vile rags . . . ." Dutertre admitted that he had "often deplored the appalling misery of their lot," but he believed that the missionary's task was to comfort "the poor negro,"[7] since in the colony profit was the supreme factor: that is, the desire to amass riches as quickly as possible by extracting "from the negroes as much toil as they could."[8] In a context where the master's cruelty knew no curb and the slave was as nothing, the missionary had only a spiritual role. To be sure, there was often evidence of an obsessive interest in not allowing a slave to die without a priest's visit, and thus in saving souls, but what was really important was persuading master and slave to enact their respective roles more proficiently. The fact that the slave's misery was so pitiful and that it was even necessary to persuade the master to show more humanity only helped the slave system to operate more smoothly. In one sense the Church was more perceptive than the colonists and understood its evangelizing duty as a social and political task of correction of the masters' errors and excesses in their treatment of the slaves. It was with this attitude that the missionary sought to make slaves pray each evening under the overseer's direction, organized catechism classes every Sunday, and, finally, framed the slave's entire life so that he adjusted to his condition, or rather so that he could make his very predicament his means of salvation.

The masters, however, were ill-disposed toward the religious instruction of slaves. But, Dutertre believed, the slaves would perform their duties better if their conversion to Christianity was the more sincere. Similarly, the more one sanctioned the marriage of slaves, the more opportunities there would be to multiply the work-force. "Our Frenchmen see to it that the slaves marry as soon as possible in order to have children who will eventually replace their father, do the same work, and bring them the same benefits."[9] On the subject of runaway slaves, Dutertre described his notion of slavery more precisely. In fact he discounted the desire for freedom as the main cause of revolt by citing the harsh suffering of black Africans: "They feel much happier as our slaves, when they are tolerably nourished and treated amenably, than they would be as free men in their own countries where they die of hunger."[10] We must remember that during the seventeenth century the "white-biblical" myth of the curse of Ham was used by the missionaries to justify the enslavement of blacks. It was part of the execution of the mysterious divine plan for the blacks, which allowed Dutertre to write: "Their bondage is the basis of their happiness; their predicament is the cause of their salvation."[11]

Another witness to the Church's attitude to slavery is the Jesuit Alonso de Sandoval, who in 1627 published at Seville his *De instauranda Aethiopum Salute. El mundo de la esclavitud negra en América*. The Jesuits were indeed pioneers in the Church with their promotion of a less improvised evangelization of black slaves. Sandoval wished to encourage the Society to undertake this task, and summoned all the resources of theology to his assistance. Once again, however, it is extraordinary to find he had no qualms about accepting the principle of slavery. At most, Sandoval managed to discuss the justification for the black slave-trade. For him, in accordance with the opinion common among theologians and canon lawyers, there was no need for scruples when buying "negroes" who were already captives. Religious in Brazil, he was sure, had never considered this trafficking to be illicit and had themselves bought slaves.[12] On the other hand, in regard to the slave system, he cited the need to evangelize the blacks, for the same reason as for Indians. The blacks, he said, served our temporal needs; it was only right to show concern for their spiritual salvation.[13] At the same time, however, religion taught them more effectively that their vocation was to obey their masters faithfully, even when the latter were guilty of excesses.[14] The theology of duty according with one's state in life, which appealed especially to Pauline texts, was used here to reassure masters, and no less the missionary clergy, that it was justifiable to own slaves.

In the French Antilles, towards the end of the seventeenth century, the Dominican Father Labat was unusually zealous in catechizing slaves and introducing them to the practice of confession.[15] He represented his efforts as humanity and compassion, but also understood his dedication as that of a slaveowner for whom conversion to Christianity was a trustworthy means of persuading a slave inwardly to accept his state in life, and thus of dissuading him from rebellion. Labat also described in generous detail the methods of torture he used to train his own slaves in total submission to their lot. He even, so it seems, proffered as a model for others his indifference to the slaves' suffering, because he felt that without the use of intimidation the black would either run away (even rebel), or attack his master. In this context, the religious instruction of slaves was a syllogism already available for use as the essential element in a system of terror. This is even more clearly evident on perusal of the disciplinary regulations and codes of laws in which the royal power and the administration set out for the Church its plan of action in a slave-owning society.

3. LAWS, CODES AND REGULATIONS

In this section I shall restrict my remarks to the articles of the French *Black Code* (of 1685), which are pertinent to the foregoing. The relevant works of Peytraud (1897)[16], Gisler (1964) and, more recently, Sala-Molins[17] suffice to spare me a detailed commentary.

The *Black Code*, in respect of its detailed provisions, long validity (lasting until abolition in 1848) and authoritative status, was in fact the most important legal enactment regarding slavery. Almost everywhere in the Americas where slavery was practised the laws promulgated by the administration ascribed a central role to religion. In the Spanish and Portuguese as in the French colonies the Catholic Church was the locus for conforming slaves to a submissive attitude. The royal powers could not take effect without the consent of the Holy See and of religious superiors and metropolitan theologians. The preamble to the *Black Code* opens with a statement of the Throne's intention to use its authority to "uphold the discipline of the Catholic, Apostolic and Roman Church." At that time the Church tended to rely on the secular power in its struggle against Protestantism. The repeal of the Edict of Nantes was part of the background to the formulation and promulgation of the *Black Code*. Little by little, the absolutist state was securing its hold and intended to control and subordinate religion to its own ends.

To be sure, long before that, from the beginning of the sixteenth century, the Church was an integral part of the apparatus of colonial conquest of the known New World, with a view to extending (European) Christianity, and thus already possessed on its own account a theology which justified slavery. This theology was quite simply put into effect by the royal power in France as in Spain and Portugal.

Article 1 of the Black Code proposed that the administration should pursue Protestants and Jews present in any numbers in the islands, arguing that they were "enemies of the very name Christian." The intention was thus to ensure the complete hegemony of Catholicism and to defend the notion that slavery would remain in tune with the plan to evangelize the blacks. Attention was focussed here on religion, as if it were the main and self-sufficient concern. Article 2 stated that "All slaves in our islands will be baptized and instructed in the Catholic religion." But articles 3 to 11 were careful to maintain a clear distinction between slaves and royal subjects, even in the case of religious practices such as marriage and burial. For the slaves, in fact, this meant that the task of scrupulously ensuring their spiritual edification devolved on the masters, with the overseers as their intermediaries. As in Roman law, priests were forbidden to bless a marriage between slaves without the master's consent (art. 10–11). Ultimately, the main aim of the legislator would seem to have been to weld the Church to the power of the master. The latter did not have to rationalize or ensure his relation to the slave, which was a burden the state wished to remove from him by means of the Code, which paradoxically stated the sole right of the master and the slave's lack of rights. But this required a preliminary justification of that absence of rights in the irreproachable sphere of religion.

What Dutertre called the mysterious divine plan for the blacks was thereby fulfilled in equity. An osmosis of Church and administrative activity was a basic requirement for an unassailable system of slavery. Yet there was an obvious contradiction in the Black Code. The concept of the slave as object, a chattel without rights, did not accord with that of the slave as a man with a spiritual destiny like that of his master, a human being who by virtue of his soul could be redeemed for heaven. In theory, of course, religious practice should have enabled a slave to acquire the civil status of a royal subject. This contradiction, however, was resolved by a promise which ran through the entire Code: the promise of a slave's humanization. But that would occur only on a so to speak eschatological level at the end of the purgatory which was slavery. The black slave was seriously disadvantaged: he did not possess the parameters of cultural life which defined the human being. It was necessary to have recourse, through the Code, to the racial divide. The black slave suffered from biological defects and his conversion to Christianity did not automatically confer on him the dignity of a human being whole and entire.

4. THE CHURCH AND THE SLAVES' STRUGGLE FOR EMANCIPATION

On examining the practices developed by the Church after the promulgation of the Black Code, it is evident that until the eve of abolition (1834 in British, 1848 in French colonies), the Church was always under strict surveillance.[18] The least departure from the norm was punished by the administration,[19] and meticulously revoked in every instance, whereas even more severe new regulations governing the religious aspect were imposed from time to time in order to reinforce the Code. We must remember that the slave trade reached its height during the course of the eighteenth century. For example, Britain alone deported about 2,130,000 slaves to the West Indies, at an average rate of 20,000 a year. Brazil alone had received 2,000,000 by the end of the eighteenth century. In 1774 the south of the United States reached a total of 500,000 blacks.

Since the number of slaves increased at such a rate, the risks of rebellion grew accordingly. In each instance, however, clergy were were asked to obey governors and administrators more scrupulously. The Jesuits, for example, who were in charge of most of the blacks in Santo Domingo (a French colony which towards the end of the eighteenth century held more than 400,000 slaves as against a population of 30,000 whites), were expelled in 1763. They were suspected of trying to catechize the slaves in creole, their own language, and even of some sympathy with runaways. In the same period it proved necessary to found a seminary in France for the colonies, with papal consent, to train clergy capable of serving the slave system to the letter. In 1777, a document entitled *Disciplinary Regulations for Negroes addressed to Priests of the French Islands in the Americas*, originating from the Prefect Apostolic of the Capuchin missions to the Windward Islands, Father Charles-François de Contances, not only equated "public interest, the masters' interest and the salvation of souls" with the major tenets of the slaves' catechetical instruction, but suggested that the Church was the right place for runaway slaves to carry out their disciplinary penance. In fact, on Sunday and feast-days for three to six months, a slave denounced by his master had to kneel at the threshold of the church porch. On Easter Day the priest pronounced the following words over the runaway: "Disloyal and wicked servant, since you have failed in the service of your master ... in such a way as to risk the loss of your salvation and of your life, we sentence you by the authority of our ministry to do penance. ..." Over poisoners he said: "Infamous villain, hateful to God, unworthy of being counted among men, more cruel than wild beasts... the vile nature of your crime deserves death and all possible torments. ...."[20]

As rebellion (by escaping, poisoning or abortion) recurred, urgent demands were made for the Church to use its ideological resources more efficiently to restrain such revolts. It is hardly relevant here to go into details of the mediocre nature of the clergy, their immorality or their lack of discipline. In general they usually did quite effectively what the system expected of them. Before the French Revolution at any rate, but more certainly before the major slave rebellion of 1791 in Santo Domingo, we have no accounts of priests opposing the slave system as such on the colonies' actual territory. The administration had no reason to think that the religious instruction laid down for the slaves harboured anything dangerously suspect. On 11 April 1764 the Governor of Martinique opined that the safety of the whites required that slaves should be kept "in a state of profound ignorance," but that the monastic orders more than the secular priests were possible sources of "a revolution instigated in the colonies by the negroes."[21] Later indeed, in 1781, to some extent almost everywhere in the colonies, and on Bourbon Island, in Guiana or on Martinique, and in Guadeloupe, measures were taken to check the directives of ecclesiastical superiors. But once the slave uprising had begun in Santo Domingo, on 22 August 1791, cases (rare to be sure) were noted of priests and religious siding with the rebels. Fr Cachetan, for example, priest at Petite Anse, after hearing the evidence of a colonist who had been held prisoner in a rebel camp, preached the holy and legitimate nature of the insurrection. Similarly, Fr Philémon, priest at Limbé, offered his presbytery as a place of refuge for the rebels. There were also accounts at this time of the nuns of Notre Dame du Cap who decided to follow the slave bands that had rebelled in Santo Domingo. Priests sometimes even participated in negotiations between slaves and masters. Nevertheless it is difficult to find convincing evidence that the clergy were divided into two camps when the slaves revolted in Santo Domingo. In the special event of slaves freeing themselves by their own efforts, the Church, as a body allied and associated with the white colonists, necessarily just disappeared. Of course there were echoes in the slave colonies of the ideas of emancipation which began to spread on the eve of the French Revolution, especially in Britain, then in France. But news of the 1791 uprising had first to reach Europe and the United States, for the slaves' determination to undermine the slave system finally to be taken into account. The French Revolution had indeed proclaimed the grand universal principles of equality and freedom, but ideas of gradual emancipation prevailed among the most active proponents of abolition. On the church side, the voice heard in favour of abolition was that of Fr Grégoire, who very soon perceived the need to send Toussaint l'Ouverture twelve priests, who had accepted the civil constitution of the clergy, to support the policy of emancipation. But Rome had condemned the French Revolution, and declared that the clergy who had arrived in Santo Domingo with Grégoire's assistance were schismatics.

We may say, therefore, that was was some evidence of church solidarity with the anti-slavery rebellion which was spreading throughout the slave plantations of the New World. On the other hand, there was an observable tendency to denounce the immorality of the priests, their neglect of the slaves' education, and their complicity with the colonists.[22] Freed from slavery from 1791 and an independent State in 1804 under the name Haiti, Santo Domingo was isolated from the rest of the world in order to prevent ideas about abolition contaminating the other French, Spanish and British colonies, as well as the southern United States and Brazil, where slavery was not to disappear until forty years and more had passed.

Ultimately, abolitionism grounded in human rights as promulgated by the French Revolution was unsuccessful among the committed priests in the slave-owning societies of the New World. Instead the concept persisted of a reform of the slave-owning system, or at most that of a gradual emancipation. In the Church, however, not everything was negative from the slaves' viewpoint. To assist their liberation the slaves made some use of management by the clergy and of religious ceremonies (especially baptism and funerals, marriages being unusual), as well as religious instruction, in spite of the intentions of clergy, masters and administration. The blacks had to find in themselves, within their own culture and their own religious system, the resources for a recovery of human dignity. They were able to reinterpret several elements of Catholicism (calendar, symbols, images, doctrine, cult of the saints) and to organize their integration within new cultural creations. Among these Voodoo (in Haiti and the Dominican Republic), Santeria (in Cuba), Obeayism (in Jamaica) and Candomblé and Macumba in Brazil, are still alive to this day. These creations were African practices and beliefs, reworked into a coherent system of myth and ritual. In spite of the extremely disparate ethnic mixture in plantations and workshops, they acted as a means of assembly, as a cohesive context for the slaves, and as a force of inspiration for revolt and the struggle for freedom.

5. THE CHURCH'S UNDERSTANDING OF THE BLACKS

Far from having supported the slaves in this cultural strategy, the Church was the first barrier between them and the recovery of their actual dignity. The conception of the African black shared by all the clergy in Europe as in the overseas territories, from the beginning of the sixteenth to the end of the nineteenth century, was entirely racist. It is undoubtedly the best key to understanding the Church's pastoral policy towards the slaves. The curse of Ham which was said to mark the African blacks, entirely because of their colour, was the key paradigmatic image for the colonial clergy in the Americas. In the sixteenth and seventeenth centuries, the reports of missionaries (such as Dutertre, Labat and Sandoval) depict blacks as brutalized beings uninterested in freedom and even indifferent to suffering and death. Father Labat went so far as to maintain that masters should "exceed the limits of moderation in punishing slaves."[23] The curse of Ham was accompanied by the additional defects of idolatry and sorcery. Every negro was held to be a sorcerer and showed an inherent tendency to practise sorcery, even if all the signs of conversion to Catholicsm were present. The 1685 Black Code for the French colonies and the regulations governing the Spanish colonies provided that clergy must systematically prevent the slaves from indulging in dances and cults which allowed them to invoke demons. The slaves' own medical practices were also interpreted as acts of sorcery. In 1686 the Jesuit Father Moreau, at St Christophe, described the "black sorcerers" who used drugs "with the cooperation of the demon who acts in secret as the result of a pact. . . ."[24] From time to time in the eighteenth century administrators, but just as often ecclesiastical authorities, noted instances of poisoning associated with crimes of witchcraft which frightened the whites as much as the slaves. The taste for blood, human sacrifices and cannibalism were associated, especially in Santo Domingo, with Voodoo, which was evidently of central importance in the 1791 uprising. The sorcerers were marked out as rebel leaders: Don Pedre, Makandal and Boukman were the most infamous names in voodoo "witchcraft". In the Catholic Church this diabolization of African-type cults,[25] restored to high esteem by the slaves with an admixture of several Catholic elements such as the cult of the saints, persisted until the twentieth century. In the clergy's opinion only ignorance and savagery could explain the slaves' reluctance to embrace Catholicism pure and simple. Black Africa was thought of as largely fated to brutalize blacks, much more than slavery, which at that time was considered to be a lesser evil and a means of access to civilization.

The above-mentioned *Disciplinary Regulations for Negroes addressed to Priests of the French Islands* referred to concepts which were current in European public opinion of the period, such as that of a "coarse race," "low intelligence," or "absence of religion, laws and morals." We may say that the dualism barbaric/civilized was a paradigm governing the preaching and activity of the clergy to such a degree that the Church must have seemed to the slaves the very place where the racism applied in the slave system was most forcibly exercised.

The sources of this racism must be sought primarily in the process by which the Church was subordinated to the state in the seventeenth century. Bossuet, for example, justified slavery on the basis of his understanding of the imperial state as a providential device for the realization of universal salvation, and by transferring the idea of barbarism to non-Catholics. On this foundation the debate about natural law reopened by Las Casas in the sixteenth century entered another phase.

Even those seventeenth-century theories (Grotius, Bodin or Pufendorf) which grounded the concept of the just state, but also, later, the works of Montesquieu, Rousseau and Kant which all opposed the notion that slavery was an institution amenable to the *ius gentium*, or was based on nature, won no support in theological circles. For the most part the Church still acknowledged the theses of St Augustine, St Thomas and Suarez on slavery, which held that it accorded not with man's primary but with his second nature, his social role. When the slave's fate was not due to the curse of Ham, it was the result of sin, or at least of a brutalized nature, in short of a barbaric state from which the civil power could gradually free him.[26] Nevertheless it was necessary to submit to it, as if to a decree of providence, as St Paul recommended: "Slaves, obey your masters."

After the French Revolution and in the flurry of debates about abolition, some historians tried to reassess the Church's attitudes to slavery, and to support the idea of the Church's positive role in alleviating the slave's lot, and even in introducing the principle of equality into social morality. Thus Henri Wallon argued that Christianity was incompatible with slavery.[27] But one can search in vain through the interventions of the Holy See – those of Pius V, Urban VIII and Benedict XIV – for any condemnation of the actual principle of slavery.[28] As far as the popes were concerned, the Thomist theses on slavery were still valid. Indians and blacks should be conceived of as human beings whole and entire, but just wars yielding captives could make slavery legitimate, and all that was open to criticism was the improper recruitment of slaves.

6. THE CHURCH AND HUMAN RIGHTS

Remedial slavery, penitential slavery or slavery as a discipline for guiding the slave towards a human state; these comprised the theology of the colonial clergy. Moreover they could always deprecate the masters' excesses without ever disputing the right to own slaves. They could also weep with compassion at the slaves' lot and request favours for them while denying them the right to freedom and revolt.

On the other hand, paradoxically, the slave never ceased to resort to the Church and, against the will of clergy and masters, to make it a place of struggle and for expression of his human rights. Admittedly he did so more effectively in Protestant Churches, as Genovese has clearly shown in regard to the Christianity of black Americans[29]. There too, however, masters very often opposed the conversion of their slaves. Protestantism, however, allowed the believer easier access to the Bible. Hearing a message of salvation and spiritual redemption for all must surely have led the slave to criticize his earthly state. Nevertheless, both masters and slaves were parties to a conflict about the interpretation of Christianity in terms of their respective interests. Now, perhaps, liberation theology has renewed the debate about recognition of human dignity as the inviolable right for all human beings, irrespective of culture or religion. Perhaps it has also sanctioned a conflict of interpretations at the very heart of the Church, which no longer necessarily aligns itself with the dominant political powers, or equates itself with European culture.

Translated from the French by John Cumming

NOTES

1. On the hesitations and uncertainties of the Church about defending the Indians, see E. Dussel, *El episcopado latino-americano y la liberación de los pobres 1504–1620* (Mexico, 1979), pp. 28–56; H. Méchoulan, *Le sang de l'autre ou l'honneur de Dieu, Indiens, Juifs et morisques au Siècle d'or* (Paris, 1979).

2. Cf M. Lobo Cabrera's "El clero y la trata en los siglos XV y XVII: el ejemplo de Canarias," S. Dageet (ed.), *De la traite à l'esclavage* (Paris, 1988), pp. 481–96.

3. I have used the new revised and corrected edition: A. Gisler, *L'esclavage aux Antilles françaises XVII-XIXème siècle* (Paris, 2/1981).

4. Cf. J.-B. Dutertre, *Histoire générale des Antilles habitées par les français*, vol. III (Paris, 1666), p. 47.

5. For more details of this direction of the Church's activities in regard to slavery in the 17th century, see my "A Igreja católica nas Antilhas francescas no seculo XVII," CEHILA (ed.), *Escravidão negra e história da Igreja na America Latina e no Caribe* (Petrópolis, 1987) pp. 84–103.

6. G. Debien, *Les esclaves aux Antilles françaises XVII-XVIIIème siècles* (Basse Terre, 1974), p. 252.

7. J. B. Dutertre, *op. cit*, vol. II, p. 538.

8. *Ibid.*, p. 523.

9. *Ibid.*, p. 469.

10. *Ibid.*, p. 535.

11. *Ibid.*, p. 502.

12. A. de Sandoval, *De instauranda Aethiopum Salute* [Seville, 1627] (Bogota, 2/1956), p. 98.

13. *Ibid.*, pp. 584–5.

14. *Ibid.*, p. 202.

15. Père Labat, *Voyage aux Iles d'Amérique*, 1693–1705, vol. II (Paris, n.d.), pp. 54–5, where he tells how he had to beat a "black sorcerer to death."

16. L. Peytraud, *L'esclavage aux Antilles françaises avant 1789* (Paris, 1897).

17. L. Sala-Molins, *Le code noir ou la calvaire de Canaan* (Paris, 1986). For an analysis of the Spanish ordinances on slavery of the *Código negro* of 1784, see C. Esteban Deive, *La esclavitud del negro* en Santo Domingo 1492–1844, 2 vols. (Santo Domingo, Dominican Republic, 1980), esp. vol. II, pp. 377–99: "Los negros y la Iglesia Catolica." For Jamaica and the British West Indies see O. Patterson, *Sociology of Slavery* (London, 1967).

18. Cf. the provisions in the 19th century regarding Bourbon Island, Martinique, Guadeloupe and Guiana for censuring ecclesiastics in A. Gisler, *op. cit.*, pp. 174–5, n. 2.

19. G. Debien, *op. cit.*, p. 288.

20. A. Gisler, *op. cit.*, pp. 185–6.

21. *Ibid.*, pp. 172 & 175.

22. See H. Wallon, *Histoire de l'esclavage dans l'antiquité* (Paris [1879], 2/1988), pp. 37–9.

23. Labat, *op. cit.*, vol. II, pp. 134–5.

24. L. Peytraud, *op. cit.*, pp. 187–8.

25. On the diabolization of African cults see my most recent work: *Le barbare imaginaire* (Paris, 1988).

26. Cf. also my articles "Etat et Religion au XVIIème siècle face à l'esclavage au Nouveau Monde," *Peuples méditerranéens* (Paris, 1984), Nos 27–28, 39–56; "Esclavage moderne et Etat de droit," *Chemins critiques* (Port-au-Prince & Montréal, August 1989), vol. I, No. 2, 37–57.; and my *Comprendre Haïti* (Paris, 1987), pp. 75–87.

27. H. Wallon, *op. cit.*, p. 864.

28. Cf again A. Gisler, *op. cit.*, pp. 155–6, n. 2.

29. E. Genovese, *Roll, Jordan, Roll: The World the Slaves Made* (New York, 1972. For a discussion of interpretations of the Pauline teaching see O. Patterson, *Slavery and Social Death: A Comparative Study* (Harvard, 1982), pp. 66–76.

Chapter 21

THE RELIGIOUS ORDERS IN LATIN AMERICA: A HISTORICAL SURVEY

Johannes Meier

The religious orders have decisively influenced the shape of Christianity in Latin America for five centuries. They have played their part in the history of the Church in the western hemisphere almost from its first appearance there.

Christopher Colombus entered the Caribbean for the second time in November 1493. With him were seventeen vessels and a company of some 1500 men, including a number of religious. The latter were led by Bernal Boyl, whom Pope Alexander VI in his bull *Piis fidelium* of 25 June 1493 had appointed vicar apostolic of the newly discovered territories. Boyl was a Montserrat Benedictine. In 1492 he had joined the Order of Minims (*Minimi*), founded by St Francis of Paola.[1] We know the names of eight other members of the group. Four were Franciscans. They were Fray Rodrigo Pérez, a priest, and three lay brothers: Juan Deledeule, Juan Tisin and Juan Pérez. There were also two Mercedarians, Juan de los Infantes and Juan de Solórzano, and Fray Jorge from the Santiago Order of Knights and the Jeronymite Ramon Pané, a lay brother.

The chronicler Peter Martyr of Anghiera tells us that on 6 January 1494 Columbus founded the first Spanish town in the New World, on the northern coast of Haiti. He named it "La Isabella" after the Castilian Queen: ". . . On the day on which we celebrate the feast of the Three Holy Kings a holy mass was said in accordance with our use, at which thirteen priests celebrated so to speak in another world, far from all civilization and religion."[2]

Contrary to their commission, Padre Boyl and most of the clerics with him avoided any missionary endeavours among the population of Haiti. They were much more concerned to join in the plots and disputes of their fellow-Europeans, who were devoting their energies to the colonial venture. Some of the clergy returned to Spain as early as 1494; others in 1495. A foretaste of the history of Latin American Catholicism, in which lay and popular piety became – as it still is – so important, may be found in the fact that only three lay brothers remained on the spot, persisted until the end of the 1490s, and developed a missionary interest in the natives, and in their culture and religion. They were the Jeronymite Ramón Pané and the two Franciscans Juan Deledeule and Juan Tisin. In 1498 Ramón Pané, who called himself a "pobre ermitano," a poor hermit, wrote a short account of his experiences among the Indians of Haiti, the Tainos, and also described his very basic attempts at evangelization.[3] All we know of the other two, Juan Deledeule and Juan Tisin, is that they went to Spain in 1499 and asked Archbishop Francisco Jiménez de Cisneros of Toledo to send some Franciscans to Haiti to increase their numbers. In 1500 three Franciscans were duly despatched to the New World in the delegation of Governor Francisco de Bobadilla. Another seventeen arrived in the West Indies in the delegation of Governor Nicolás de Ovando in 1502;

Fray Alonso de Espinal was the superior of this group.[4] At Santo Domingo, which had been established in the meantime as the Spanish capital on Haiti, they prepared "a meeting-house, and also began to say masses and preach in the same, and also reserved the most holy Sacrament in it. This cabin was the first church of all the churches in these Indies."[5]

1. THE COLONIAL PERIOD

With the despatch of the group accompanying Alonso de Espinal, the Spanish Crown began its major commitment to the overseas mission. The Crown expressly allowed members of the mendicant orders to travel to America, and later to the Philippines and intentionally excluded the contemplative orders of Benedictines and Cistercians, which were so closely associated with the agrarian structures of feudalism. The monarchy also excluded the orders of Knights Hospitaller, responsible for the *Reconquista*, or total expulsion of the Moors from the Iberian peninsula. After the Franciscans it was the Dominicans who in 1509 were permitted to enter the American mission, then the Mercedarians (1514), the Augustinians (1533), later the Jesuits (1565), and finally the Capuchins (1657). Without previous examination and approval by the Council for the Indies, the central authority founded in 1524 for the Spanish overseas possessions, no member of a religious order could reach America.[6] Strict criteria were applied in such cases. Religious enthusiasm and exemplary conduct were requisite, as well as the agreement of superiors.[7] The number of *frayles* who made the journey was also decided by the Council for the Indies, which based its decision in part on petitions which reached it from ecclesiastical or even secular authorities in America through local governors or the presidents of *Audiencias* and viceroys. The religious communities themselves appointed a commissioner who assembled the number of brothers agreed by the Council from the monasteries of Spain.[8] When a group of this kind had been formed and had been granted the *despacho* of the Council, it applied to the *Casa de la Contratación* at Seville, which paid for the equipment needed – clothing, vestments, sacred utensils, books and provisions – and also made arrangements with the shipowners for the costs of the voyage for passengers and for freight. Each traveller also received a form of pocket money – the *entretenimiento* – for intermediate stopovers.[9] Whereas the secular clergy usually made their own arrangements for the voyage to America, the Crown had to allocate large sums annually for the missionaries provided by the religious orders.[10]

The royal right of patronage was not only the basis for choosing religious and for the means and details of transport to America; it also determined essential aspects of the life of communities once they arrived there. The governors, presidents of *Audiencias* and viceroys had to keep up-to-date with details of the monasteries and their inmates within their localities.[11] Every three years these officials had to report to the Crown about such religious, and the Crown reserved the right to arrange visitations from time to time.[12] The state representative had access to the provincial chapters of the orders; the provincials elected by the chapters required royal permission to assume their office.[13] At the same time the Crown empowered its officials in America to support in every respect those religious who were engaged in the conversion and instruction ("conversión y doctrina") of the natives "y animen á que prosigan, y hagan lo mismo y más, si fuere posible, como de sus personas y bondad esperamos".[14]

The membership of the religious communities active in Spanish America increased continuously. According to entries in the *Casa de la Contratación*, by the end of 1518 altogether 124 religious had set out for the West Indies. Of these eighty-nine were Franciscans and thirty-two Dominicans; one was a Mercedarian, and the affiliation of two of them is unknown.[15] This total increased to some 16,000 over the next 300 years, until the end of the colonial period (c. 1820). Of the religious sent by the official method to the New World 15,097 are identified[16]; the following table gives a detailed break-down of the orders:[17]

	15 c.	16 c.	17 c.	18 c.	19 c.	Total	in %
Franciscans	5	2782	2207	2736	711	8441	55.91
Jesuits	–	351	1148	1690	–	3189	21.12
Dominicans	–	1579	138	116	4	1837	12.16
Capuchins	–	–	205	571	26	802	5.31
Mercedarians	3	312	73	–	–	388	2.57
Augustinians	–	348	31	1	–	380	2.51
Carmelites	–	28	12	–	–	40	0.26
Various	2	18	–	–	–	20	0.13
	10	5418	3814	5114	741	15097	100.00

At first the religious communities in America remained dependent on their mother provinces in Spain. If, however, a sufficient number of monasteries was established they were separated from Spain and elevated to the status of a province. When Juan López de Velasco compiled the *Geografía y descripción universal de las Indias* around 1570, he listed eight provinces of the Franciscan order in America with 127 friaries, only two Dominican provinces with altogether 126 friaries, two Augustinian provinces with seventy monasteries, four Mercedarian provinces with twenty-six monasteries, and two Jesuit houses.[18] By 1600, the number of Franciscan provinces had reached ten, whereas the Dominicans had seven, the Augustinians four, the Mercedarians had four and even the Jesuits three.[19] The increase continued in the seventeenth century, by the end of which Latin America possessed seventeen Franciscan, nine Dominican, eight Mercedarian, seven Augustinian and seven Jesuit provinces.[20]

From the very start the religious orders in America enjoyed far-reaching privileges which ensured them liberty of operation and favourable conditions. Pope Hadrian VI's bull *Omnimoda* of 9 March 1522 was most significant.[21] In the interests of the christianization of America, the Pope conferred on the religious orders "omnimodam auctoritatem nostram in utroque foro": which meant in practice that, beyond a distance of two days' travel to the next diocesan centre, the orders were accorded complete freedom of religious activity, including the celebration of sacraments otherwise reserved to the bishop.[22]

In various briefs Pope Paul III confirmed and extended the permission granted by his predecessor in the 1530s and 1540s.[23] These exemptions often hindered the episcopal extension of diocesan organization. Accordingly, after the Council of Trent, which reassessed the role of bishops, disputes arose regarding jurisdiction, and these lasted for many years.[24] In such instances the religious orders defended themselves from any curtailment of their rights and precedence by reference to their services in the evangelization of the American terrritories. At first they were successful in this, for Pope Pius V with the brief *Exponi nobis* of 24 March 1567 once again ensured that they could exercise the cure of souls in the missionary areas without the express permission of the local ordinaries.[25] This provision, which deviated from general canon law and contradicted the intentions of the Council of Trent, was nullified by Gregory XIII on 1 March 1573 with his brief *In tanta rerum.*[26] But the orders continued for a long time to try to retain their traditional privileges. In this context the Franciscan Juan de Focher first deployed the notion of the vicariate of the Spanish monarchy. Since the Crown had sent the religious to the American missions at the direct behest of Pope Alexander VI, the same religious – so Focher explained – required no special jurisdiction from the local bishops.[27]

The Franciscans exerted themselves to escape stricter control by the ordinaries, and therefore sought to attach themselves even more closely to the Crown. In 1572 they established the office of a general commissioner for the West Indies. The general of the order bestowed on him almost all possible powers as a deputy controller of the Spanish American monasteries. This development accorded with the mind of Philip II, who, as was apparent from the "Junta Magna" of 1568, was primarily interested in the greatest possible extension of the royal rights of patronage over the Spanish American Church. Since the Dominicans, Augustinians and Mercedarians refused to create a similar office, by their device the Franciscans assured themselves numerous advantages in the Council for the Indies over and above the other religious orders.[28]

The disputes between bishops and secular spirituality, on the one hand, and the religious communities on the other hand, which resulted from the reforming decrees of the Council of Trent, lasted for some considerable time in the Spanish American Church. The contradictory nature of this development is partly explained by the fact that most of the bishops at that time were themselves members of religious orders. Thus Bishop Diego de Salamanca of Puerto Rico, a member of the Augustinian order, made it very clear to the King in his letter of 3 January 1578 that he thought it was for the best "que las iglesias de por aca fuesen regulares reduziendolas a la antigua ynstitución, en que persevera oy la de Pamplona." In other words, after unfortunate experiences with the secular clergy, especially those who were not born in Puerto Rico, he thought he would exercise his responsibilities more effectively if he employed only members of religious orders for pastoral work.[29]

Pope Gregory XIV's brief *Quantum animarum cura* of 16 September 1591 once again acknowledged the achievements of the orders, confirmed their exemption from episcopal inspection in their hereditary pastoral territories, and exempted them from financial contributions to the new seminaries for the priesthood.[30] On the other hand, more and more highly discontented complainants discerned a lack of religious enthusiasm and a growing absence of discipline in the religious orders; they attributed these inadequacies to the extraordinary increase in their membership,[31] to the useless fragmentation caused by establishing a number of smaller houses,[32] but principally to the growing wealth of the monasteries.[33] Against this background, with the brief *Inescrutabili Dei providentia* of 5 February 1622, Pope Gregory XV definitively revoked all existing exemptions of the religious orders which contradicted the Tridentine decrees. In so doing he invoked two ordinances of 1614–15 of his predecessor Paul V; these said that priests active in the missionary territories ("doctrinas") must always be examined and approved by the bishop responsible, and that in the process precedence should be given to the secular clergy.[34]

As these provisions were applied, in the course of the seventeenth century the orders lost something of their earlier significance. They were weakened too by internal tensions between *criollos* and those born in Spain.[35] In the centres of Spanish America the secular clergy increasingly decided the outward image and pattern of the Church, but in certain areas religious could claim leading positions, for instance as preachers, teachers and scholars.[36] They were still essential in the peripheral country areas, where pioneer evangelization among the Indians remained a prime need. In addition to the orders who had been responsible for it in the past, the Society of Jesus began to play a special role in this work. The Jesuits were also the only order in the colonial period that was able to send considerable numbers of foreigners to Spanish America – among them about a thousand Middle Europeans.[37]

The Jesuit missionaries were indeed typical "frontiersmen" of the Spanish colonial empire in America, but not without certain reservations on the part of the political and military powers. In principle the Jesuit fathers always used peaceful means as they travelled in twos among the Indians, "who according to their ancient usage lived in forests, mountains and valleys, on remote streams, in three, four or six individual huts, two, three or more miles from one another." The Jesuits tried "attentively and solicitously ... to bring them together in larger settlements and to persuade them to live a civil and human life."[38]

In these "reductions" the Indians were carefully introduced to European civilization and versed in the practice of the Catholic faith. At the same time, however, they were subjects of the Spanish crown. The Jesuits exquisitely exploited the legally established possibilities of separate development, and succeeded in forming an alternative society within the colonial system. It was one in which Indian culture and Christendom coexisted until, with the expulsion of the religious orders, the reductions were opened up to colonial exploitation before they were completely destroyed in the independence struggle and the subsequent wars.[39] In the years 1768–69, 2617 Jesuits were expelled from the order's provinces in Paraguay, Chile, Peru, Quito, New Granada, Mexico and the Philippines.

A similar drama had been played out a decade before in Brazil and the other Portuguese colonies.[40] The first Jesuits reached Brazil in 1549, much earlier than Spanish America. Until the repression by the Marquês de Pombal, their influence and their prestige in Portuguese America were certainly much greater than in the Spanish colonial empire, though the union of the two Iberian crowns between 1580 and 1640 resulted in various adjustments in religious and church politics. Born in Lisbon and raised in Brazil, Antônio Vieira especially embodied the particular role of the Portuguese Jesuit. He was court preacher to João IV, and worked in Maranhão as a courageous missionary. He laboured no less passionately for the existential and human rights of the Indians in the Amazonian forests than for the fame and precedence of Portugal before all nations of the globe.[41]

The women's orders of Poor Clares, Dominicans, Carmelites and others also made a firm impression on the image of American colonial towns. The unmarried daughters of the aristocracy and of the bourgeoisie could enter their convents. As a rule they brought with them one or more Indian or black girls as servants or slaves. At the end of the seventeenth century Mexico City possessed twenty-two women's convents, and Puebla ten. At that time Sister Juana Inés de la Cruz fell victim to an epidemic while looking after her fellow-nuns. She was one of the most unconventional women of the early modern age.[42]

For the most part women's convents undertook educational tasks, such as the schooling of the daughters of Spanish and *criollo* families and the care of orphan children. Often widows entered such convents and often rich widows founded them. Many pious and charitably active women also assembled in religious communities without canonical recognition; in Brazil such *beatas* constituted a pillar of traditional popular Catholicism.[43]

The expulsion of the Jesuits was a kind of premonition of changes and fissures that would soon grievously affect the other orders, the Church as a whole and – in spite of numerous political reforms – colonial rule altogether. Of course rebellions such as those of José Gabriel Tupac Amaru in the Peruvian Andes (1780–81), and of Joaquim José da Silva Xavier (*Tiradentes*) in Minas Gerais (1789–91), were fiercely repressed by the colonial powers. But repressive politics could not stop the pressure of liberal ideas. This progress was nourished by enlightened reforms in the Spanish American universities and at the University of Coimbra; it was even apparent among the clergy, though more obviously among the *criollo* diocesan clergy than in the religious orders.

Alexander von Humboldt, who as a scientist and explorer made his way through Venezuela, New Granada, Ecuador, Peru, Mexico, Cuba and the already independent United States from 1799 to 1804, may be taken as an unimpeachable and especially trustworthy eye-witness of conditions at the time. Humboldt came into contact with many missionaries, for during his expedition he constantly made use of the ecclesiastical infrastructure.[44] On the one hand he emphatically acknowledged the lasting cultural achievements of the missionaries. When assessing the work of the Aragonese and Catalan Capuchins in eastern Venezuela, he said that "in a space of more than 120,000 square miles ... without money or physical resources, but with Herculean will-power and traditional Christian enthusiasm of an enduring cast, they have established among several thousand Indians the basis of communal ties. They have induced people to live together, and have taught them to build stronger and more comfortable dwelling-places, make fabrics for clothing, and grow useful plants."[45]

On the other hand, Humboldt readily and straightforwardly criticized many inadequacies which he constantly found in the missions in the course of his journey. He found especially damaging the "compulsion and lamentable monotony of the missionary régime." The dismal, closed attitude of the Indians in many missions betrayed "how unwillingly they have sacrificed freedom for placidity. The monastic discipline . . . transplanted to the wildernesses of the New World, applied to all aspects of civil life . . . represses intellectual development from race to race; it inhibits intercourse among peoples; it is inimical to everything which elevates the soul and extends the field of comprehension":[46] "Because the Indians from the forests are treated in most missions as serfs inasmuch as they do not enjoy the fruits of their labour, the Christian dependencies on the Orinoco are running to waste."[47]

2. THE NINETEENTH AND TWENTIETH CENTURIES

On 3 September 1804 Alexander von Humboldt landed at Bordeaux and once again set foot in the Old World. In Paris in the following year he met Simón Bolívar, the future liberator of northern South America. Soon after the Napoleonic troops occupied Portugal and Spain in 1807–8, revolutions started in many regions of Spanish America; Chile, Uruguay, Paraguay, New Granada and Venezuela declared their independence.

In Brazil the process was somewhat different. The Portuguese Court moved to Rio de Janeiro in 1808. The papal nuncio was among the accompanying diplomats. For the first time in church history a papal ambassador had arrived in a Latin American country. But his influence was relatively slight. In those years it was much more a matter of the liberal clergy managing to strengthen their position, in order to extend the national-Brazilian character of the Catholic Church. Instead of returning to liberated Portugal in 1814, King João VI elevated Brazil to the level of a kingdom with equal entitlement. Only in 1821, on account of a rebellion, did he decide to return to Lisbon. He made his son Pedro Regent of Brazil. In 1822 Brazil separated from Portugal without loss of life and was proclaimed an empire.

The revolutions in Spanish American countries were the work of *criollos* who found themselves politically, economically, socially, culturally and even ecclesiastically disadvantaged when compared with Spaniards. The attitude of the Church to the independence movements was divided. Whereas the lower clergy sympathized with the revolution or even took an active part in it, the vast majority of the bishops remained loyal to the Spanish throne. Many of them were expelled by the new régimes or made their own decisions to return to Spain. On 9 December 1824, when Bolívar's Chief of General Staff, José de Sucre, forced the last Spanish army in South America to capitulate at Ayacucho in the Andean highlands and took the Viceroy José de la Serna prisoner, most of the forty-four Spanish American dioceses were deserted. Of their own free choice or under compulsion, a large number of the Spanish clergy had left the continent. The constant stream of religious from Spain to the overseas territories for more than three hundred years had dried up.

In Mexico the number of religious dropped from 3112 in 1810 to 1726 in 1831; the number of monasteries from 208 to 155. The number of nuns dropped after 1810 by 187 to 1911. In Peru the number of 1891 religious in

1792 had dropped considerably by 1820. In the Franciscan province of Lima between 1770 and 1800 an annual average of 6.9 religious made their professions, in 1810–20 only 2.3, and in 1821–37 none.[48] The Holy See saw the nationalist movement in America as an aberration akin to the French Revolution. In the brief *Etsi longissimo* (1816) Pius VII, and similarly in *Etsi iam diu* (1824) Leo XII, required clergy to submit to the Spanish throne. Both popes refused to recognize regimes which owed their existence to revolutions. Only when pastoral problems came to a head and there was the additional question of the legitimacy of the new regimes in Belgium and France after the July Revolution of 1830, did a realistic attitude prevail in the Roman Curia. This was evident in the bull *Sollicitudo Ecclesiarum* (1831) of Gregory XVI.

Accordingly, one after the other, resident bishops were appointed for Greater Colombia (Venezuela, New Granada, Ecuador), Mexico, Argentina, Chile, Peru and other countries. In 1836 an internuncio with responsibility for the entire Spanish-speaking area of Latin America was despatched to Bogotá. From 1829 there was already a nunciature in Rio de Janeiro. Accordingly Rome recognized the transfer of the right of prerogative from the Portuguese monarch to the Brazilian Emperor. The Curia did not accord this succession to the republics, but later on, to a considerable extent – when concordats were concluded – awarded them privileges along the lines of the earlier form of patronage.[49]

In the nineteenth century the Latin American clergy, for much longer than the European priests, tended to enlightenment, patriotism and a secular Church. This was especially noticeable in Brazil during the minority of Pedro II (1831–40), when the liberal priest Diego Antônio Feijó was regent for a time. The keynotes of his regalist ecclesiastical policy included the cancellation of canonical penalties for married priests and reform-minded interventions in the life of the religious orders; individual monasteries which remained almost empty were confiscated. Although Pedro II, after succeeding to the throne in 1840, trimmed the political influence of the liberal clergy, state pressure on the orders traditionally represented in Brazil (Franciscans, Benedictines, Carmelites, Mercedarians) was retained. In 1855 the minister of justice, Jose Tomás Nabuco, forbade these orders to accept novices until their reform was regulated by a concordat. It is noteworthy that this measure was approved by the Archbishop of Bahia, Romualdo Antônio de Seixas, and by the Bishop of Mariana, Antonio Ferreira Vicoso. Ferreira Vicoso, appointed in 1844, energetically pursued the policy of recruitment from other orders not yet in Brazil, which therefore had to send religious from Europe. It is interesting that this bishop was a member of the Lazarists of St Vincent de Paul's Congregation of the Mission, who reached Brazil only in 1820, first with a few Portuguese fathers, then later with some French Vincentians; the priests' seminary of the diocese of Mariana was also assigned to them. In 1840 Italian Capuchins were permitted to join the Indian mission in Brazil. In 1854 Bishop Antônio Joaquim de Melo entrusted French Capuchins from Savoy with the training of the São Paulo clergy.[50]

These measures were signs of the great transformation of the Catholic Church in Brazil since the middle of the nineteenth century – its so-called Romanization. Step by step, a new ecclesiological concept focussed on the papacy came to prevail and was instilled in the seminaries of the subsequent generation of clergy. Ultramontanism was imported to Brazil along with the foreign religious. The catechism, the sacraments and the authority of the clergy moved to the centre of religious practice and displaced the traditional popular piety with its emphasis on feasts of Christ, Mary and the saints.

Things in most Latin American countries went the same way as in Brazil. In 1858 Pope Pius IX founded the "Pio Latino" college in Rome where the élite clergy acquired moral superiority, an apostolic thrust, and distance from the world. In the same period the Holy See signed concordats with a number of countries: Bolivia (1851), Guatemala (1852), Costa Rica (1852), Honduras (1861), Nicaragua (1861), El Salvador (1861), Venezuela (1862), and Ecuador (1862). This ensured the recognition of the Catholic faith as the state religion and significant privileges for the Church in education and so on.

President Gabriel García Moreno of Ecuador, a rabid Ultramontane, tried between 1861 and his assassination in 1875 to make the country an exemplary Catholic state. He orientated the legal code in accordance with the encyclicals of Pius IX and the "Syllabus of Errors"; assigned all school and higher education to the Church; and to help realize his policy invited numerous European religious orders to Ecuador. His religious enthusiasm was so far-reaching that he dedicated the country to the Sacred Heart of Jesus and deprived all non-Catholics of civil rights.[51]

From the middle of the nineteenth to the first third of the twentieth century Latin American Catholicism suffered a change of identity. In the case of Brazil it is especially clear how far this transformation coincided with the increasing influence of the religious orders in the national Church. When Brazil became a republic in 1889, and in the following year state and Church separated legally without major hostilities, this process was still accelerating. Franciscans, Benedictines and Carmelites, who for decades had been forbidden to accept novices, were now revitalized by the influx of German and Dutch members of their orders.[52] The Brazilian Church opened its doors to a vast number of orders and congregations which streamed into the country from Europe, especially from Italy, the homeland of so many immigrants, and from France, where a phase of anti-ecclesiastical politics began after the turn of the century. The following is the breakdown of the male communities in terms of countries of origin and point of establishment in Brazil:[53]

	Braz.	Spain	It.	Fr.	Holl.	Germ.	Belg.	Austria	Urug.	Ukr.	Total
1800–1879	–	–	–	1	–	–	–	–	–	–	1
1880–1889	–	1	1	2	–	1	–	–	1	–	6
1890–1899	–	2	–	1	2	1	–	–	–	1	8
1900–1909	–	–	1	4	–	1	–	–	–	–	6
1910–1919	–	–	6	1	1	1	1	–	–	–	9
1920–1930	1	–	4	1	1	–	–	1	–	–	8
Total	1	3	12	10	4	4	1	1	1	1	38

The equivalent table for the women's orders is as follows:[54]

	Sp	Aus	It	Fr	Por	Br	Egy	Col	Bel	Pol	Ukr	Ru	Hl	Ger	Total
Until 1880	2	–	3	2	–	3	–	–	–	–	–	–	–	1	11
1881–1890	–	1	2	2	–	–	–	–	–	–	–	–	–	1	6
1891–1900	–	–	4	4	–	4	–	–	2	–	–	–	–	2	16
1901–1910	–	–	4	12	–	3	1	–	1	–	–	1	1	1	24
1911–1920	4	1	3	4	3	4	–	1	1	–	1	–	–	–	22
1921–1930	3	1	8	4	–	8	–	–	1	1	–	–	–	4	30
Total	9	3	24	28	3	22	1	1	5	1	1	1	1	9	109

The 1872 census registered 2256 secular priests in Brazil, and another 107 male and 286 female members of religious orders.[55] The 1920 census is not quite comparable, since it did not distinguish diocesan clergy from members of religious orders, but only gender and nationality. 6059 male clergy were registered, of whom 3218 were Brazilian and 2838 foreigners, with three whose nationality was not given.[56] Fifteen years later (in 1935) the total number of clergy had still risen slightly to 6269; here the proportion of secular priests (2466) and male members of religious orders is known (3803).[57] If these figures are compared with those for 1872, then in 63 years the secular clergy had increased by a mere 9.3 percent, whereas the number of male religious had increased thirty-five times. The number of female religious increased more than fourteen times between 1972 and 1920, from 286 to 2944, of whom 1761 were Brazilian, 1181 foreigners and two of unknown nationality. It is especially remarkable that their number increased threefold in the fifteen years to 1935, from 2944 to 8826 sisters. Here we have a reflection of the heavily increased presence of the Church in education, in the care of the sick, and in social work, a rate of growth which had been made possible since the beginning of the twenties by the crisis of liberalism.[58]

To assess the overall development since the nineteenth century correctly, we have to take the historical context into account. In 1872 there were only 9,930,478 inhabitants in Brazil, whereas in 1920 there were 30,642,041. In addition to the natural growth of the population, in this period the country had also accepted some five million immigrants, mainly from Italy, Spain, Germany, Poland, the Middle East and Japan. In the Federal State of São Paulo alone some 1.7 million immigrants settled between 1877 and 1914, half of them Italians (845,816). The identity of the Catholic Church in Brazil did change, but the transformation coincided with an alteration of the ethnic composition of the Brazilian people.[59]

Brazil may be a spectacular instance of change but it is by no means exceptional. In its confrontation with liberalism the Church recruited ever new forces to its ranks; for example, in Bolivia Jesuits (1881), Salesians (1896), Lazarists (1905), Redemptorists (1910), Mercedarians (1912), Poor Clares (1919), De La Salle Brothers (1920), Passionists and Cistercians (1928), Carmelites (1929) and Augustinians (1932). A similarly long list is available for the women's orders.[60] In the late nineteenth and early twentieth centuries, these orders helped to establish many connections between Germany and Latin America. To quote only two examples: in 1873, during the "Kulturkampf", the Vincentians were expelled from Germany; after a detour through the Ecuador of President García Moreno they arrived in Costa Rica in 1875, with Fr Bernhard August Thiel among them, who as early as 1880 was appointed the second bishop of San José and served the country exemplarily in his office, in the social field, until 1901. In 1848 Thiel's father had been one of the first companions of Adolph Kolping in Elberfeld.[61] In 1895 the Bavarian Capuchins became responsible for the cure of souls in Araucania, the territory of the Mapuche people in southern Chile; in the best tradition of the missionaries of the colonial period many of them, above all Frs Felix Joseph Augusta and Ernst Wilhelm Mosebach, studied the language and myths, customs and practices of the Mapuche. Fr Sebastian Englert from Dillingen also deserves mention in this respect; for three decades he was parish priest on Easter Island, a zealous student of the island's culture, and for much more than that alone highly esteemed by the Norwegian ethnologist Thor Heyerdahl.[62]

The points of contention between the Catholic Church and the liberal state in Mexico escalated from 1910 within the context of a social revolution. The state confiscated ecclesiastical lands, secularized education, prohibited the Catholic press and forbade all religious activity outside church associations. In the 1920s a law was introduced to suspend all ecclesiastical events and instances in which priests might participate. As a result the *Cristiada* broke out, the resistance movement of the faithful masses. Some twenty thousand *Cristeros*, mostly young peasants, workers and students, took up arms. Thousands of them died fighting the army.[63] In the period of persecution (1926–9) seventy-eight priests and religious were murdered, including the young Jesuit priest Miguel Agustín Pro, whose execution at the express order of President Plutarco Elías Calles aroused Catholics all over the world.[64] A standstill agreement was made under the next President, Emilio Portes Gil, but state-Church tensions continued in Mexico during the 1930s.

The events in Mexico seem atypical in comparison with the rest of Latin America at the same time. In the large countries to the south (Argentina, Brazil and Chile) in this period the Church played an increasing part in politics, culture and social life. An important instrument in this process was "Catholic Action," which stressed the Christian apostolate of the laity in the modern world. In 1928 Catholic Action was established in Argentina, in 1931 in Chile, and in 1935 in Brazil. Christian élites, it was hoped, would become active in various sectors of society, among the proletariat, peasants, artisans, employers, and intellectuals.[65] At the same time a spiritual renewal was expected from the new dependencies of the old contemplative orders, such as the Cistercians from Himmerod in Itaporanga, Brazil (1936), the Benedictines of Solesmes in Las Condes, Chile (1938), and of Einsiedeln in Los Toldos, Argentina (1948).

In the same period the Church in Chile succeeded best in according with the signs of the times. The Jesuit priest Alberto Hurtado wrote his book "Is Chile a Catholic Country?" in 1941 – two years before Abbé Henri posed the same question about France in his own work.[66] Soaked in Catholic social teaching – even as a student he had taken up the cause of the many unemployed who after the collapse of the nitrate industry in the north of the country had flocked to

Santiago – Hurtado criticized the egotism of the well-to-do. In 1941 he founded the trade union association "Asociación Sindical Chilena" and established a training course for trade union leaders. He founded homes for the homeless, poor and orphans under the title "Hogar de Cristo". The Chilean Jesuit paper *Mensaje*, which Hurtado issued for the first time in 1951, a year before his death, is a testimony to his intellectual and spiritual inspiration. In the year of Hurtado's death the Little Brothers of Jesus moved into a poor quarter of Santiago. As early as the 1950s, the challenge of poverty and of the poor became an increasingly urgent matter of concern for the Church.[67]

In 1958 CLAR – the Latin American Confederation of Religious – was founded. It held its first plenary assembly in Lima in 1960. The statistics for that year are 185,050,000 Catholics in Latin America, with 18,647 secular priests and 19,464 priests in religious orders[68]; the number of women religious was about 113,000.[69] Between the Lima meeting and the next one in Rio de Janeiro in 1963, the Second Vatican Council had opened. CLAR offered several points of attention for the Council, but above all, after the Council, CLAR accepted its invitation to undertake an up-to-date renewal of religious life, welcoming it with great commitment and courage. Traditional tasks were examined critically and new priorities were acknowledged in the light of the gospel, especially in the world of the impoverished. Male religious, but even more female religious, contributed to the birth of base communities, in which the ecclesiology of the Council took shape: ". . . in the poor and suffering the Church recognizes the image of Him who founded it, and who was himself poor and suffering. It seeks to reduce their need and tries to serve Christ in them".[70] It is scarcely surprising, in view of its dimensions and significance, that this process should not have developed, or continue to develop, without controversy, both in the orders themselves and between the orders and the hierarchy.[71] Yet the same process is already sealed with the blood of a number of sisters and brothers – a process which increases year by year: the blood of those who have discovered in Christ and the poor something "which is worth living for, perhaps even something which you can die for."[72]

Translated from the German by John Cumming

NOTES

1. F. Fita, "Fray Bernal Buyl y Cristobal Colón. Nueva colección de cartas reales, enriquecida con algunas inéditas," *Boletín de la Real Academia de la Historia* 19 (Madrid, 1891), 173–233; B. Biermann, "Die ersten Missionen Amerikas," *Festschrift 50 Jahre Katholische Missionswissenschaft in Münster 1911–1961* (Münster, 1961), pp. 115–30, esp. 120.

2. Peter Martyr of Anghiera, *Eight Decades of the New World*, first decade II, 11.

3. R. Pané, *Relación acerca de las antiguedades de los indios.* New version by J. J. Arrom: *Colección América Nuestra* 5 (Mexico City, 5/1984). The report was published in Venice in 1571 for the first time in Ferdinand Columbus's biographical description of his father Christopher. Peter Martyr had already noticed the account and reproduced some extracts in his *Decades* (first decade IX, 49–54).

4. A. Tibesar, "The Franciscan Province of the Holy Cross of Española, 1505–1559," in *The Americas* 13 (1956–7), 377–89, esp. 379–81; L. G. Canedo, "Evangelización y conquista. Experiencia franciscana en Hispanoamérica," *Biblioteca Porrúa* 65 (Mexico City, 1977), pp. 4–6.

5. V. Fricius, *Indianischer Religionstandt der gantzen newen Welt beider Indien gegen Auff und Niedergang der Sonnen* (Ingolstadt, 1588), p. 160.

6. *Recopilación de leyes de los Reynos de las Indias.* Prólogo por R. Menéndez y Pidal, estudio preliminar de J. M. Manzano. Vols I-IV (Madrid, 1973; facs. of ed. of 1681), lib. I, tit. xiv, ley 5 (I, f.60v).

7. *Recopilación* (n. 6), lib. I, tit. xiv, leyes 13 & 15 (I, f.62r).

8. *Recop.*, I, xiv, 3 & 4 (I, f. 60r/v).

9. *Recop.*, I, xiv, 6 (I, f. 60v-61r).

10. H. Jedin, "Weltmission und Kolonialismus," *Saeculum* 9 (1958), 393–404, esp. 395.

11. *Recop.*, I, xiv, 1 (I, f. 59v).

12. *Recop.*, I, xiv, 42 & 43 (I, f. 66v).

13. *Recop.*, I, xiv, 60 & 64 (I, f. 69v & 70r).

14. *Recop.*, I, xiv, 65 (I, f. 70v).

15. L. Tormo, *Historia de la iglesia en América Latina*, Vol. I: *La evangelización de la América Latina.* Estudios Socio-Religiosos Latino-Americanos 8 (Freiburg & Bogotá, 1962), p. 78.

16. I would cite here the devoted researches of the Mercedarian J. Castro Seoane, continued since his death in 1971 by his confrère R. Sanlés Martínez. For more than three decades the results have appeared in a series of articles in the *Missionalia Hispanica*. Based on the sources of the "Archivo General de Indias", this research work offers an extremely detailed survey of all expeditions by missionaries to Spanish America during the 16th century, collected according to the particular order.

17. Cf P. Borges Morán, *El envío de misiones a América durante la época española:* Bibliotheca Salmanticensis, Estudios 118 (Salamanca, 1977), p. 537.

18. J. López de Velasco, *Geografía y descripción universal de las Indias*, ed. M. Jiménez de la Espada: Biblioteca de Autores Españoles 248 (Madrid, 1971), p. 2. For the Franciscans, López de Velasco mentions another charge in addition to the eight provinces; his list of the Dominican provinces is incorrect for there were already five in 1570: cf. B. Biermann, "Die 'Geografía y descripción universal de las Indias' des Juan López de Velasco als Quelle für die Missionsgeschichte (1570)," *Neue Zeitschrift für Missionswissenschaft* 17 (1961), 291–302, esp. 293, n. 3.

19. H. Pietschmann, "Die Kirche in Hispanoamerika," W. Henkel, *Die Konzilien in Lateinamerika*, Pt I: *Mexico 1555–1897* (Paderborn, 1984), pp. 1–48, esp. pp 27f; P. Castaneda Delgado, *Die Kirche in Spanisch-Amerika: Gold und Macht. Spanien in der Neuen Welt. Eine Ausstellung anlässlich des 500. Jahrestages der Entdeckung Amerikas* (Vienna, 1986), pp. 125–32, esp. p. 127. By an error of translation the Mercedarians have been confused with the Merciful Brethren.

20. A. M. Heinrichs, *La cooperación del poder civil en la evangelización de Hispanoamerica y de las islas Filipinas*, diss., Laval University (Laval, 1971), pp 136f.

21. B. de Tobar, *Compendio Bulario Indico*, Vols. I-II, ed. M. Gutiérrez de Arce, Publicaciones de la Escuela de Estudios Hispano-Americanos de Sevilla 82 & 167 (Seville , 1954 & 1965), esp. I, pp. 90–2 (anomalously dated to 10 May 1522); F. J. Hernaez, *Colección de Bulas, Breves y otros documentos relativos a la Iglesia de América y Filipinas*, Vols. I-II (Brussels, 1879), esp. I, pp. 382–4.

22. P. Torres, "Vicisitudes de la 'Omnimoda' de Adriano VI en el aspecto de sus insignes privilegios en la labor misional de Indias," *Missionalia Hispanica* 3 (1946), 7–52, esp. 7f; R. C. Padden, "The Ordenanza de Patronazgo 1574. An interpretative essay", in *The Americas* 12 (1956), 333–54, esp. 337; A. Ennis, "The Conflict between the Regular and the Secular Clergy," R. E. Greenleaf (ed.), *The Roman Catholic Church in Colonial Latin America* (Tempe, 1977), pp. 63–72, esp. 66f.

23. Bull *Alias felicis* of 15 February 1535: B. de Tobar, *Compendio Bulario Indico*, I, p. 124f; F. J. Hernaez, *Colección*, I, pp. 390 f; brief *Exponi nobis* of 13 October 1539: B. de Tobar, Comp., I, pp. 239f; brief *Ex debito* of 9 January 1544: *ib.*, pp. 256f; F. J. Hernaez, *Colección*, I, pp. 392f.

24. C. R. Boxer, "À Igreja e a Expansâo Iberica (1440–1770)," *Lugar da Historia* 11 (Lisbon, 2/1989), 86f.

25. Tobar, *Compendio*, I, pp. 351f; Hernaez, *Colección*, I, pp. 397f. (dated to 23 March 1567); Torres, "Vicisitudes," pp. 31f.; A. Ennis, "The Conflict", p. 70.

26. Tobar, *Compendio*, I, p. 398; Hernaez, *Colección*, I, p.. 477 (wrongly dated 1 March 1572).

27. A. de Egaña, "La teoría del Regio Vicariato Español en Indias," *Analecta Gregoriana* 95, Series Facultatis Historiae Ecclesiasticae, Sectio B, No.. 17 (Rome, 1958), pp. 60–76; P. Leturia, *Relaciones entre la Santa Sede e Hispanoamérica 1493–1835*. Vol. I: *Epoca del Real Patronato 1493–1800*, ed. A. de Egaña (Rome & Caracas, 1959), pp. 107–22; B. Biermann, "Das spanisch-portugiesische Patronat als Laienhilfe für die Mission", in J. Specker & W. Bühlmann (eds), *Das Laienapostolat in den Missionen. Festschrift Prof. Dr J. Beckmann SMB: Neue Zeitschrift für Missionswissenschaft*, Supplementa X (Schöneck-Beckenried, 1961), pp. 161–79. esp. p. 175.

388 SOME SPECIAL SUBJECTS

28. E. Schäfer, *El Consejo Real y Supremo de las Indias. Su historia, organización y labor administrativa hasta la terminación de la asa de Austria.* Vols. I-II (Seville, 1935 & 1947), esp.. II, pp. 229–32; P. Borges Morán, "La Santa Sede y América en el siglo XVI," *Estudios Americanos* 21 (1961), 141-688, esp. 145f.

29. Seville, Archivo General de Indias (=AGI), Santo Domingo 172, No. 49. Diego de Salamanca is alluding to the fact that the Bishop of Pamplona was traditionally from Leyre monastery.

30. Tobar, *Compendio*, I, p. 483; Hernaez, *Colección*, I, p. 408.

31. Letter from Governor F. Carreño of Cuba to Philip II of 20 June 1577, quoted from I. Teste, *Historia eclesiástica de Cuba*, Vols. I-V (Burgos & Barcelona, 1969–75), esp. I, p. 93; L. Marrero, *Cuba: Economía y sociedad*, Vols. I-II (Rio Piedras & Barcelona, 1972 & 1974), esp. II, p. 153.

32. Report by the Bishop of Santiago de Cuba, Juan de la Cabezas Altamirano, to the King of 24 June 1606 (AGI, Santo Domingo, 150, No. 34, f.7r).

33. In the course of time many monasteries like other ecclesiastical institutions became major landowners and accumulated vast properties. They also took on the functions of banks and provided credit, so that in some instances more than half of the existing real estate was controlled by the Church directly or through mortgages, which will have contributed in no small way to the anticlericalism that was so widespread in middle-class circles in Latin America. Cf. B. R . Hammett, "Church Wealth in Peru. Estates and Loans in the Archdiocese of Lima in the Seventeenth Century," *Jahrbuch für Geschichte von Staat, Wirtschaft und Gesellschaft Lateinamerikas*, 10 (1973), pp. 113–32; P. Castañeda Delgado & J. Marchena, "Las órdenes religiosas en América. Propiedades, diezmos, exenciones y privilegios," *Anuario de Estudios Americanos* 35 (1978), pp 125–58, esp. pp. 131–6; N. Cushner, *Lords of the Land: Sugar, Wine and Jesuit Estates of Coastal Peru 1600–1767* (Albany, 1980).

34. Tobar, *Compendio*, II, p. 85; Hernaez, *Colección*, I, pp. 481–6.

35. A. Tibesar, "Social Tensions among the Friars," R. E. Greenleaf (ed.), *The Roman Catholic Church*, pp. 98–107; the criollos were already in a majority in the 17th century, and in the 18th century represented more than three-quarters of the membership of the individual orders: P. Borges Morán, "Características sociólogicas de las órdenes misioneras americanas," *Evangelización y Telogia en América (Siglo XVI). X Simposio Internacional de Teología de la Universidad de Navarra*, Vol. I (Pamplona, 1990), pp. 619–25, esp. 621.

36. R. Gomez Hoyos, *La iglesia de América en las leyes de Indias* (Madrid, 1961), p. 194.

37. Borges Morán, "Características . . .", p. 621.

38. A. Ruiz de Montoya, *Conquista espiritual feita pelos Religiosos da Companhia de Jesus nas Provincias do Paraguai, Paraná, Uruguai e Tape*, ed. A. Rabuske (Porto Alegre, 1985), p. 34.

39. J. Meier, *Die Missionen der Jesuiten bei den Guarani-Völkern in Paraguay – eine unterdrückte Alternative im Kolonialsystem: Wem gehört Lateinamerika? Die Antwort der Opfer* (Munich & Zürich, 1990), pp. 59–79 (lit.).

40. The Portuguese membership of the Society of Jesus amounted in the year of expulsion, 1759, to 1698 men, of whom 909 were overseas, and another 453 in Brazil: L. von Pastor, *Geschichte der Papste seit dem Ausgang des Mittelalters*, Vol. XVI/1: *Benedict XIV und Klemens XIII, 1740–69* (Freiburg, 1931), pp. 574ff, n. 1.

41. The following is recommended as an introduction to Vieira's personality: A. Vieira, *Die Predigt des heiligen Antonius an die Fische* (intro. by H. Loetscher) (Zürich, 1966).

42. K. Vossler, *Die "zehnte Muse von Mexico": Sor Juana Inés de la Cruz. Sitzungsberichte der Bayerischen Akademie der Wissenschaften*, Phil.-Hist. Abt., 1934, 1 (Munich, 1934); L. Pfandl, *Die 10. Muse von Mexiko: Juana Inés de la Cruz* (Munich, n.d.= 1943); N.M. Scott, "Sor Juana Inés de la Cruz", *Orientierung* 54 (1990), 213–6; O. Paz, *Sor Juana Inés de la Cruz* (Ger. tr., Frankfurt, 1991).

43. R. Azzi, M. V. V. Rezende, "À vida religosa femina no Brasil colonial," R. Azzi (ed.), *A vida religiosa no Brasil. Enfoques Historicos* (São Paulo, 1983), pp. 24–60; D. E. Zegarra Lopez, *Monasterio de Santa Catalina de Sena de Arequipa y Da. Ana de Monteagudo, Priora* (Arequipa, 1985).

44. ". . . I saw with my own eyes and with no hatred of the monks, who have never done anything to distress me personally, and among whom I encountered a number of very worthy individuals . . . I was well received in the missions, I was received there neither out of kindness nor by stealth, but at the King's direct command. A historian has no duty other than that of veracity, and it must be all the more sacred to him when the misfortune of vast territories depends on it". Quoted from A. von Humboldt, *Lateinamerika am Vorabend der Unabhängigkeitsrevolution*. M. Faak (ed.) (Berlin, 1982), p. 145.

45. Humboldt, *Lateinamerika*, p. 157.

46. Humboldt, *Die Reise nach Südamerika. Von Orinoko zum Amazonas*, J. Starbatty (ed.) (Bornheim-Merten, 1985), p. 69.

47. Humboldt, *Die Reise . . .*, p. 225.

48. Statistics from: H.-J. Prien, *Die Geschichte des Christentums in Latein-Amerika* (Göttingen, 1978), p. 396, n. 74. Prien relies on P. Murray, *The Catholic Church in Mexico. Historical Essays for the General Reader. I: 1519–1910* (Mexico, 1965), pp. 115ff; D. Olmedo, "Modern Mexico," *New Catholic Encyclopedia* (NY, 1967), IX, pp. 775–83, esp. p. 777; A. Tibesar, "The Peruvian Church at the Time of Independence in the Light of Vatican II," *The Americas* 26 (1970), 349–75, esp. 356f.

49. K. M. Schmitt, "The Clergy and the Independence of New Spain," *Hispanic American Historical Review* 34 (1954), 289–312; C. H. Hillekamps, *Statt und Kirche in den unabhängigen Staaten Lateinamerikas: Religion, Kirche und Staat in Lateinamerika* (Munich, 1966), pp. 119–38; J. F. Schwaller, "The Episcopal Succession in Spanish America 1800–50," *The Americas* 24 (1968), 207–71; G. Vilar de Carvalho, *A liderança do clero nas revoluções republicanas 1817–24* (Petropólis, 1980); H.-J. König, "Auf dem Wege zur Nation. Nationalismus im Prozess der Staats-und Nationbildung Neu-Granadas 1750 bis 1856," *Beiträge zur Kolonial-und Überseegeschichte* 37 (Wiesbaden , 1988).

50. J. O. Beozzo, "Decadência e morte, restauração e multiplicação das ordens e congregações religiosas no Brasil 1870–1930," R. Azzi (ed.), *À vida religiosa no Brasil*, pp. 85–129, esp. pp. 87–92 & 99–101.

51. L. R. Dávila, *García Moreno: Orígenes del Ecuador de hoy*, Vol. IV (Puebla, Cajica, 1968)); for the situation at the same time in the other countries of Latin America see the account in C. Pape, "Katholizismus in Lateinamerika," *Veröffentlichungen des Missionspriesterseminars St Augustin, Siegburg*, No. 11 (Steyl, 1963), 92–113.

52. For the northern Franciscan province (St Antony): cf. V. Willeke, "Die Neubelebung der nordbrasilianischen Franziskanerprovinz," *Zeitschrift für Missionswissenschaft und Religionswissenschaft* 52 (1968), 277–88; on the southern province (the Immaculate Conception): cf. A. Stulzer, "Da Restauração da Provincia da Imaculada Conceição," *Vida Franciscana. Provincia Franciscana da Imaculada Conceição*, LV, No. 52 (June 1978), 5–15; on the Benedictines, cf. M. E. Scherer, "Domingos Machado, der Restaurator," *Studien und Mitteilungen zur Geschichte des Benediktinerordens und seiner Zweige*. New series 74 (1964), 7–162; Id., Ein grosser Benediktiner: Abt Michael Kruse von São Paulo (1964–1929), *Studien und Mitteilungen zur Geschichte des Benediktinerordens*, supplementary issue 17 (Munich, 1963).

53. Beozzo, *Decadencia . . .*, 120.

54. *Ibid.*, 126.

55. *Ibid.*, 97.

56. *Ibid.*, 105.

57. *Ibid.,*, 108.

58. *Ibid.*, 105 & 110.

59. *Ibid.*, 97 & 105–7.

60. J. M. Barnadas, "La reorganización de la iglesia ante el estado liberal en Bolivia," E. Dussel & J. Klaiber (eds), *Historia general de la iglesia en América Latina*, Vol. VIII: *Peru, Bolivia y Ecuador* (Salamanca, 1987), pp. 308–24, esp. 314.

61. V. M. Sanabria Martínez, *Bernardo Augusto Thiel. Segundo Obispo de Costa Rica. Apuntamientos historicos* (San José, 1941).

62. A. O. Nogler, "Vierhundert Jahre Araukanermission. 75 Jahre Missionsarbeit der bayerischen Kapuziner," *Neue Zeitschrift für Missionswissenschaft*, Supplement XX (Immensee, 1973).

63. R. E. Quirk, *The Mexican Revolution and the Catholic Church 1910–29* (Bloomington, 1963); J. Meyer, *La Cristiada. I: La guerra de los cristeros. II: El conflicto entre la iglesia y el estado en Mexico. III: Los cristeros. Sociedad e ideología* (Mexico City & Madrid, 1973–4).

64. W. M. Havers, *Christliche Befreiung in Mexico. Lebenszeugnisse aus fünf Jahrhunderten* (St Augustin, 1986), pp. 93–168; M. Sievernich, "Märtyrer im mexikanischen Kirchenkampf. Zur Seligsprechung von Pater Miguel Agustin Pro SJ (1891–1927)," *Geist und Leben* 61 (1988), 285–302.

65. On Catholic Action see: L. Gera, "La iglesia frente a la situación de dependencia," A. J. Büntig, O. Catena & L. Gera, *Teología, pastoral y dependencia: Dependencia* 10 (Buenos Aires, 1974), 102–4.

66. H. Goudin, *La France, pays de mission?* (Paris, 1943).

67. E. Dussel, *Die Geschichte der Kirche in Lateinamerika* (Mainz, 1988), pp. 178f.

68. Pape, *Katholizismus* . . ., p. 154.

69. Dussel, *Die Geschichte* . . ., 332. Neither Dussel nor Pape gives the number of male religious who were not priests. They must have numbered between 15,000 and 118,000. The number of foreigners among the religious was always very high. In 1967, of the then 23,029 priests in religious orders 110,908 were Latin American nationals and 12,121 foreigners: Dussel, *Die Geschichte* . . ., 330. At the end of 1959 there were 7352 Spanish priests (to mention only one nationality) in Latin America, and up to 352 diocesan priests were all members of religious orders. Moreover, at the time there were also 1342 religious brothers from Spain and 10,491 sisters from the same country. From Germany there were 1480 priests, 513 brothers, 2464 sisters and three lay missionaries (figures for 1957); with the exception of 16 diocesan priests all others belonged to religious communities. The strongest contingents were provided by the Franciscans (350)), the Steyler Missionaries (310), the Pallottine Fathers (127), and the Missionaries of the Holy Family (101): cf. C. Pape, *Katholizismus* . . ., p. 259, n. 35 & 260, n. 37. In regard to the very high number of Spanish religious who were priests in 1959, it should be noted that not a few of them later acquired a Latin American nationality.

70. Vatican II: *Dogmatic Constitution on the Church: Lumen gentium*, 8.

71. Dussel, *Die Geschichte* . . ., pp. 332–7 (lit.); for the eleventh plenary assembly of CLAR in Cuautitlán, Mexico, in February 1991, see N. Klein, "Unerwünschte Propheten?" in *Orientierung* 55 (1991), 137–9.

72. From a letter of 2 December 1980 from the Maryknoll sister Ita Ford, murdered in El Salvador, to her 16-year-old niece Jennifer on her birthday in August 1980.

Chapter 22

RECENT LATIN AMERICAN THEOLOGY

Enrique Dussel

This chapter concentrates on the last thirty years, rather than trying to give an overall view of theological development in Latin America, on which a number of studies exist.[1] So, effectively, it recounts the rise and development of liberation theology, which I have divided into five periods.

1. PREPARATION (1959–68)

Since 1959, the year of the announcement of the second Vatican Council, the failure of Catholic Action has gone hand in hand with the collapse of populism. Several basic lines developed during this period. The first is the renewal of the Church under the impetus of the Council (1962–5), which was to have a powerful effect on the future theologians of liberation. The first generation of Catholic liberation theologians had gone to France or Belgium by preference to study, the Protestants to the United States. The Methodist José Míguez Bonino (b. 1924) studied in the U.S. during the 1950s; the Catholic Juan Luis Segundo (b. 1925) studied at Louvain in the second half of that decade, Gustavo Gutiérrez (b. 1928) at Louvain and Lyon, José Porfirio Miranda (b. 1924) in Frankfurt and Rome; Hugo Assmann (b. 1933) studied in Brazil and then taught at Münster from 1967; the writer (b. 1934) studied theology in Paris and Münster, going to Spain in 1957 and on to Paris in 1961 in connection with the *Mission de France*, and most of that generation made similar odysseys. It was, inevitably, a time of theological dependency.

If one were to point to a first text that marked the appearance of a properly Latin American theological reflection, still using functionalist sociology, this would have to be the little book published by Juan Luis Segundo in 1962 on what the Church should stand for in contemporary conditions in the River Plate area,[2] based on a course of lectures on "Christian fulfillment" given in Montevideo in 1961. In it he writes: "To pose our question better and more concretely, let us begin with an observation of a *sociological nature*. We shall try to discover something deeper about what the church means for the Catholics of the River Plate area. For our research, let us take that category of Christians . . . who possess what is generally called the apostolic spirit . . ., but as a more indirect apostolate carried out through the community, their profession, political action, etc."[3] Theologically, the political commitments made by young Christians in organizations such as JUC and JOC, should not be forgotten. But these approaches – including the "theology of revolution"[4] – cannot yet be considered an expression of an "autochthonous" Latin American theology. They belong more to the critical, modernizing and even revolutionary current of European theology. The basic step was still to be made.

The ground was prepared by two factors. First, there was a deep aspiration to "poverty" in the Church, shown in the individual "poverty" of bishops, priests and committed lay people, produced by the conversion brought about by the Council.[5] Secondly, there was the "class" experience originating in the "specialist" branches of Catholic Action: the Young Catholic Workers (JOC) who began to take on proletarian consciousness, Catholic University (JUC) or Student Youth (JEC). Among Protestants, the equivalent body was the Student Christian Movement (FUMEC). It was from these groups of militants, working-class or *petit bourgeois* (not only is the latter not a pejorative term here: this class showed itself an essential component in the revolutionary process throughout Latin America, as the Sandinista Front was to show) in origin, that the church as a whole learned a new type of understanding of what Christian life meant in general, and Christian political life in particular. It was from both the practice and theory of these groups that the most important theological break in Latin American history was to emerge.

In 1967 my "Hypothesis for a History of the Church in Latin America" was published, in the full consciousness that a new era was dawning.[6]

2. THE FORMULATION OF LIBERATION THEOLOGY (1968–72)

1968 was a foundational year, and the Protestant contribution should not be forgotten. Rubem Alves, a Presbyterian from Brazil, presented his theology thesis in Princeton that year, though it was written the previous year. Its title was "Towards a Theology of Liberation"; though when it was published in English the following year,[7] the title was changed to *Theology of Hope* (perhaps on the assumption that the term "liberation" would not be understood?); in Spanish it appeared as "Religion: opium or instrument of liberation?".[8] Its first criticism was levelled at purely technological or economic solutions to human problems in general. It used the diagnosis made by Marcuse, particularly in *One-dimensional Man*, and through him the Frankfurt school, but also other contemporary thinkers such as Paulo Freire, A. Vieira Pinto, Franz Fanon, with references back to Feuerbach, Marx, Buber, Bloch, Kierkegaard, Heidegger and Nietzsche; its theology was in sympathy with theologians such as Harvey Cox, John Robinson, Gerhard Ebeling and Dietrich Bonhoeffer, critical toward Bultmann, Barth and Moltmann. In the same line, Richard Schaull enquired into the link between eschatological hope and "human liberation".[9] Hugo Assmann warned of the limitations of a theology of development, thereby hastening its replacement.[10] In March 1968, I gave a course at Villa Devoto in Buenos Aires, on "Church history and culture," pointing to the importance of pre-hispanic, colonial and popular culture.[11]

When the Second General Conference of Latin American Bishops was held in Medellín in August 1968, a new theology could be seen in germ in some of its documents. In the first, on Justice, it said: "There are in existence many studies of the state of the Latin American people. The misery that besets large masses of human beings . . . is described in all these studies. . . . Thus, for our authentic liberation, all of us need a profound conversion."[12] In the Peace document, for which Gustavo Gutiérrez was one of the advisers, it said: "We refer here, particularly, to the implications for our countries of dependence on a centre of economic power, around which they gravitate."[13] In the same year Gutiérrez published a work on pastoral strategy that did not yet show the basic lines that were emerging.[14] In some of his notes made for a lecture given in Chimbote in 1964, the "theology of liberation" appeared as a subject, though the talk was not published till 1969.[15] He returned to the subject in November 1969, at a meeting held in Cartigny in France, to which he contributed "Notes toward a theology of liberation,"[16] along the lines adopted in sociology – where the Protestant Fals Borda had just written on the "sociology of liberation" in Bogotá – and philosophy, – where Augusto Salazar Bondy had published his work on the "culture of domination" in Lima in 1968.

Also late in 1969, first in pamphlet form and then as a small book, Hugo Assmann produced a "prospective evaluation" of a theology of liberation, its first "demarcation" in regard to other theologies, its first clear epistemological definition.[17] He added to the dawning theology of liberation a demarcation with respect to German theology, whereas before it had been seen rather in relation to French. It is true that Alves had referred to Moltmann, but not to Metz. When Assmann "demarcates" the new theology of liberation from German political theology or theology of hope, he is not seeing them as being at the origins of liberation theology, but simply as different theologies. Liberation theology springs from the reality of Latin America: its ecclesial, political, revolutionary and "scientific" (the "social sciences") reality of the continent. The theoretical horizon of French theology was of little help to a strongly marked theology tied to political and revolutionary processes. Assmann used his first-hand knowledge to relate the whole of current German theology to it at one go.

During this time, a whole series of meetings, assemblies, symposia and courses on liberation theology were being held. The Mexican Theological Society held a Congress on "Faith and Development" from 24 to 28 November 1969, and published the proceedings in two volumes.[18] More than eight hundred people took part, including distinguished figures such as Luis de Valle, and the conclusion was that the main theme was really liberation theology. An international meeting on the subject "Liberation: option for the Church in the 1970s" was held on 6 and 7 March 1970, again publishing its proceedings in two volumes.[19] From 3 to 6 August, ISAL brought twenty theologians together in Buenos Aires, publishing their contributions in *Fichas del ISAL* 26 and *Cristianismo y Sociedad* 23–4. A second symposium on liberation theology was held in Bogotá in July 1970, and its conclusions published in a review entitled *Teología de la liberación*, edited by Gustavo Pérez, in Bogotá later that year. A Seminary on Liberation Theology was held in the city of Juárez in Mexico from 16 to 18 October; its proceedings were circulated only in photocopy.[20] A pastoral course on liberation theology took place on Oruro in Bolivia from 2 to 19 December. In Buenos Aires, from 14 to 17 August 1971, a number of theologians, including Oscar Ardiles, Hugo Assmann, J. C. Scannone and myself, met to discuss the relationship between theology and philosophy of liberation.[21]

These examples are given to show that liberation theology is a "church movement," the fruit of a point reached by the church as a whole, and by a whole generation of theologians. It differs from the situation in Europe or the United States, as Rosino Gibellini wrote, looking at the three thousand students attending a course on liberation theology which I organized in Mexico City in 1975: "Europeans who read a liberation theology text can conceptually understand the setting for liberation theology, but they cannot realize that it is a church movement."[22] Equally important was the meeting of biblical scholars in Buenos Aires in July 1970, discussing the subject "Exodus and liberation."[23] In the Autumn of the same year, the Secretary-general of CELAM, Mgr Eduardo Pironio, himself contributed a paper on "The theology of liberation" for the annual meeting of the Argentine Department of Education.[24]

All this meant that when Gustavo Gutiérrez published his *Teología de la Liberación* in Lima in 1971 (written, from internal evidence, in late 1970 and early 1971), it came as the conclusion of the development period of the new Latin American theology.[25] In it he shows that this theology is not the work of some individuals, but the fruit of reflection on "an option made by the Latin American church"[26]: it is the theology of an ecclesial experience (especially so since 1968) on a continent-wide scale, unlike theological schools with a particular founder.

In the meantime, Juan Luis Segundo continued writing. His massive five-volume work *Theology for an Open Church* was the first full-scale overall vision produced by the new theology – though it still stems from the renewed and progressive theology of the post-conciliar period rather than from liberation theology as such. His "From theology to society," published in 1970, however, shows the beginnings of a theology of the vision that was to occupy him much more in the future.[27]

This period, in my view, culminated in the Escorial Meeting, held at the site of Philip II's famous palace in Spain in July 1972. It planned the issue of the international review of theology, *Concilium*, which appeared in June 1974 under the title *Liberation and Faith*, with contributions from Segundo Galilea, myself, Gustavo Gutiérrez, Leonardo Boff, Jose Comblin, Juan Luis Segundo, Raúl Vidales, Ronaldo Muñoz and José Míguez Bonino.

3. CAPTIVITY AND EXILE (1972–9)

During this period, beginning with the CELAM Assembly held at Sucre in Bolivia in 1972, the first criticisms of liberation theology began to make their appearance. These were expressed at gatherings held in Bogotá in November 1973, at which Boaventura Kloppenburg in particular outlined all the current arguments against liberation theology,[28] and Toledo in 1974, attended by Jiménez Urresti, Yves Congar and López Trujillo among others, which spoke of "as many theologies as there are authors," but failed to define the conflictuality inherent in a situation of sin: domination of one nation or class over another, etc., seeking a "universalism" that would hide all contradictions.[29] A further critical meeting was held in Lima in September 1975, from which all liberation theologians were excluded.[30] At about the same time, Roger Vekemans published a critical study of "Liberation theology and Christians for socialism,"[31] using the same sort of arguments as were to be brandished by the

Congregation for the Doctrine of the Faith in its 1984 "Instruction on Certain Aspects of the Theology of Liberation."

During this period too, some theologians were forced into exile: Jose Comblin and Hugo Assmann were forced out of Brazil by the military regime, and both subsequently ejected from Chile, along with Gustavo Arroyo, Franz Hinkelammert and many others; I was exiled from Argentina. . . . the military regimes frequently acting with the complicity of some church officials. New theological figures came on the scene: Ignacio Ellacuría and Jon Sobrino in El Salvador,[32] Luis de Valle in Mexico,[33] Virgil Elizondo among the chicanos of the United States,[34] Raúl Vidales, a Mexican, but working originally in Lima,[35] Alejandro Cassiánovich in Peru,[36] Rafael Avila in Colombia,[37] and Ronaldo Muñoz in Chile.[38]

At the same time, martyrs were sealing with their blood what theology later made patent in theory. Antonio Pereira Neto was assassinated in Brazil in 1969, Héctor Gallegos "disappeared" in Panama in 1972, Carlos Mujica shot in Argentina in 1974, Ivan Betancourt killed in Honduras in 1975, the Jesuit Rutilio Grande killed in El Salvador the same year, inspiring Mgr Romero's "conversion" that was to lead to his own assassination in 1980, making them both symbols of an age of martyrs.[39]

Latin American theology opened out to the rest of the Third World, and began a process of direct dialogue with its other parts, without intermediaries from the "centre." The first meeting took place in Dar-es-Salaam in Tanzania from 5 to 12 August 1976. Twenty-two theologians from Asia, Africa, Latin America and the minorities in the United States, set a Third World theological dialogue under way. This was followed by a second meeting in Accra in Ghana from 17 to 23 September 1977, and a third in Wennappuwa in Sri Lanka in January 1979.[40] These meetings certainly opened up new channels of reflection, spread world-wide a theology reflecting from the actual situation of Christians oppressed in the present-day world, and brought about a mutual enrichment of Asian, African, Latin American and U.S. minority theologies.

There were major advances in the field of christology: "The prospect for the near future in Latin America," wrote Assmann "makes one foresee that there will go on being *Christs* on both sides: the side of the revolutionaries and that of the reactionaries."[41] Leonardo Boff's *Jesus Cristo liberador* was the first full-length work on the subject.[42] Jon Sobrino's *Cristología desde América Latina* tackles not the "first Enlightenment" theme of "Christ-reason," but the "second Enlightenment = Marxism" one of "Christ-transformative praxis," so a christology of liberation.[43] Going forward a little in time, Juan Luis Segundo's five-volume work, *Jesus of Nazareth Yesterday and Today*, written in Spain during the long exile back to his native country imposed by the military government of Uruguay, is the most complete treatment of the subject,[44] despite his disclaimer that: "My objective here can be defined rather as *anti-christology* than one more christology. I would not even define it as the christology corresponding to Latin American liberation theology." He does in fact take issue with a number of other Latin American christologies.[45]

Liberation was also to take its own special line on the subject of ecclesiology: it is not "ecclesiocentric." Writing from experience with the "base church communities," Leonardo Boff[46] was to have enormous influence with a series of books, especially *Church: Charism and Power*, whose chapter on "Roman Catholicism: Structure, Health, Pathologies" in particular was to draw down the wrath of the Roman authorities on his head.[47]

The contemplative movement generated by the liberation process emerged as a new "spirituality." Arturo Paoli was one of the first in the field here with a series of books starting with a collection of "liberation dialogues" dating from his arrival in Latin America back in 1959.[48] Ernesto Cardenal had been a Trappist with Thomas Merton for a number of years, then created a completely new form of community life in Solentiname; he expressed his revolutionary commitment in *Psalms* ("Blessed is the man that heeds not the dictates of the Party,/nor attends any of its meetings;/nor sits down at table with the gangsters/nor yet with Generals in courts-martial. . . . "), and in "The holiness of the revolution" ("I believe it is important that there should also be persons who remind humanity that the revolution also lives on beyond death . . . But the revolution exists so that humanity can mature and then celebrate a wedding feast with God.")[49] – "holiness" belonging not only to Christians but to all those who lay down their lives for their brothers and sisters. Since the death of Pablo Neruda, he can be considered Latin America's greatest living poet, and his *Cántico cósmico* (1990) is unique in its genre in Latin American literature. Between 1969 and 1971, Frei Betto wrote his "Out of the Catacombs: letters from prison," in Brazil under the miliatry dictatorship.[50] Jon Sobrino reflected on Christian prayer – personal and community – from the agonizing situation in El Salvador.[51] Gustavo Gutiérrez himself expounded the spirituality of a people filled with hope in the midst of suffering in two major works.[52] The anthology compiled by Eduardo Bonnin, and the study by Robert McAffee Brown both show the riches of Latin American spirituality of liberation.[53]

4. THE CENTRAL AMERICAN REVOLUTION AND THE BRAZILIAN MODEL (1979-)

The Third General Conference of the Latin American bishops held at Puebla in Mexico in February 1979 and the triumph of the Sandinista revolution in July the same year mark the beginning of a new period, producing two basic currents that diverged from one another over the following years. One was made up of those church people who became more closely linked with the ruling groups – military juntas, local bourgeoisie or transnational companies – taking their line from the U.S. State Department; the other of those who, following another tradition, carried on the commitment to the poor that had developed since the Council.

One needs to go back to 1976 to see the emergence of a joint approach in various parts of Latin America and Europe. This was the year Roger Vekemans published his work on "liberation theology and Christians for socialism," the most comprehensive critical presentation to date of liberation theology. In Germany, under the auspices of "Adveniat," a "Study Group on Church and Liberation" met from 2 to 7 March 1976 in Rome, attended by López Trujillo, Vekemans, Mgr Hengsbach (bishop to "Adveniat" and later to the German Army) and others, to discuss the subject of "Christian hope and social praxis." Hans Urs von Baltasar wrote: "In reality, situations can be unjust, but in themselves they are not sinful; the sinners are those who are responsible for such situations and consent to them when they could eliminate or improve them," which shows an individualistic and ingenuous sense of sin as a matter for personal conscience, failing to capture the meaning of "institutional sin." Boaventura Kloppenburg went so far as to say that "the popular church is a new sect". Similar views appeared in articles in reviews such as *Medellín, Tierra Nueva* and the like.[54] In October 1976 the International Theological Commission pronounced on liberation theology (the first forerunner of what was to become the 1984 "Instruction"). This text is measured and in fact does not condemn either liberation theology or any of the great Latin American theologians by name; the warnings it does give had actually already been made earlier by liberation theologians themselves.

Particularly relevant to the time was Franz Hinkelammert's *The Ideological Arms of Death* on account of the connection it drew between the persecution in Chile under Pinochet and the Sandinista revolution under way in Nicaragua. In another book which appeared a few months earlier, he reflected on the experience of repression in Chile, initiating reflection on the relationship between economics and theology: "Valuation of life as it is has always been the starting point for the ideologies of the oppressed, as opposed to the absolutization of values by the dominant classes."[55] On 17 November 1979 the bishops of Nicaragua declared: "If . . . socialism means that the interests of the majority of Nicaraguans are paramount . . . , a social program that guarantees that the country's wealth and resources will be used for the common good . . . , if socialism means the injustice . . . will be progressively reduced, then there is nothing in Christianity that is at odds with this process."[56] The Church was then in support of the revolution. On 8 May 1980, however, a seminar of Central American bishops was organized under the auspices of CELAM, and from then on everything changed.

The encyclical *Laborem exercens*, written in 1981 to mark the ninetieth anniversary of *Rerum novarum*, gave rise to a number of theological reflections. A little book published first in Central America and then in Peru showed how the encyclical used a new conceptual framework: concepts such as "class" (LE no. 3), "work in the objective sense" (no. 5) and "in the subjective sense" (no. 6), "the priority of labour over capital," "capacity for work" (no. 12) and the like, showed the influence of Marxist thought.[57] In this context, Otto Maduro's study of religion and social conflicts made a considerable impact.[58]

In the meantime, progress was being made on a number of fronts. First, the question of the theology of *women*: women as historical and theological agents. At the seminary on "Latin American women and the praxis and theology of liberation," held in Tepeyac in Mexico from 1 to 5 October 1979, Elsa Tamez showed herself a pioneer in this field with her paper on "Women as the subject of theological production."[59] Another question tackled was racism, especially as applied to the Afro-American population. The first seminar on this subject was held in Kingston, Jamaica, in December 1979. Through the work of – in particular – Laënnec Hurbon and Jose Oscar Beozzo, the subject has provided a flourishing chapter of liberation theology in the Caribbean and Brazil. The Ecumenical Association of Third World Theologians (EATWOT) held a meeting on the subject "Black culture and theology in Latin America," at which

Armando Lampe, of Aruba, said: "Afro-Antillean liberation theology will draw on the following sources: the Bible, Christian tradition, the present process of oppression-liberation and Afro-American and non-Western religious traditions (such as Hinduism). This last is what differentiates Caribbean from Latin American liberation theology."[60] Another new central theme was the *indigenous* question. Ethnicity, the ancestral Amerindian people, was the subject of a meeting held in Chiapas in September 1979: "The indigenous movement and liberation theology." With indigenous participants from a dozen countries, the theological capabilities of the autochthonous inhabitants of the continent were amply demonstrated.[61]

In Nicaragua, the revolutionary process required a theological clarification of the meaning of faith, since Sandinista ideology was not simply a repetition of earlier ideologies. The change of heart by the hierarchy, influenced by certain figures in Rome and CELAM, led to a lack of dialogue between the bishops and the revolutionary leaders. In September 1979, two months after the triumph of the revolution, a seminar was held on the subject of "Christian Faith and the Sandinista Revolution," at which the situation was first defined in theological terms, by, among others: Jaime Wheelock, Raúl Gómez Treto and Sergio Arce from Cuba, and Pablo Richard from Costa Rica. An important collective work was *Nicaragua, trinchera teológica* ("Nicaragua, theological trench"), with contributions from Pedro Casaldáliga, Miguel D'Escoto, Fernando Cardenal, Uriel Molina, José María López Vígil, Giulio Girardi, Juan Gorostaiga, Franz Hinkelammert, José Argüello, Ernesto Cardenal and others. To my mind, the basic book on the subject is Giulio Girardi's work on "Sandinismo, Marxism and Christianity in the new Nicaragua," published in 1986.[62]

5. SINCE THE 1984 "INSTRUCTION"

The "Instruction on Certain Aspects of the Theology of Liberation," signed on 6 August 1984 and issued on 3 September,[63] had the undesired effect of bringing Latin American theology into the limelight worldwide. The editorial board of *Concilium* (with Yves Congar abstaining) had rallied to its defence in June (in response to an article surprisingly published in March by Cardinal Ratzinger) and produced a "Statement of Solidarity with Liberation Theologians";[64] it now pronounced on the inopportuneness of the document, this time including Congar among the signatories. In March, Karl Rahner had written to the Cardinal archbishop of Lima: "Liberation theology ... is thoroughly orthodox, and is aware of its limits within the whole context of Catholic theology. Moreover, it is deeply convinced (correctly, in my opinion) that the voice of the poor must be listened to by theology in the context of the Latin American church."[65]

A few days after the "Instruction" appeared, Leonardo Boff was summoned to Rome to answer criticisms of his book *Church: Charism and Power*. For the first time, the world's press was taking an interest in the question of liberation theology. The Holy Office found itself up against "public opinion," and lost the battle. The "Instruction," paradoxically, was found too weak in its argumentation. Juan Luis Segundo, the only person who had the patience to study the question in detail, concluded: "In my view, and after the most careful analysis I am capable of, the document emanating from it (the Congregation for the Doctrine of the Faith) has not yet presented proof that liberation theology, in its basic and universally known features, is a 'grave deviation from Christian faith', still less that it is 'a negation in practice' of that faith."[66]

The new "Instruction on Christian Freedom and Liberation" of March 1986 and Pope John Paul II's letter to the Brazilian bishops of 9 April that year, in which he wrote that liberation theology was "not only opportune but useful and necessary," were much more positive in tone and ushered in a new phase in Christian theology linked to popular practice.[67] Around this time, a group of leading liberation theologians formed an editorial committee to plan and publish a major series of some fifty titles under the general heading "Theology and Liberation," designed to present all the major topics of liberation theology in a systematic and accessible form. The project was initially supported by a "Sponsorship Committee" with the names of 129 bishops, mainly from Brazil. It was this aspect above all that drew the renewed attention of the Congregation for the Doctrine of the Faith, and difficulties multiplied to the point where the names of this Committee were omitted after the first few volumes. The series is originally published in Portuguese and Spanish, with German, French, Italian and English translations following. The French, Spanish and Italian publishers, all dependent on religious orders, have likewise encountered difficulties with "Rome," leading to delays in publication. The English edition continues slowly, with a selection only of the volumes being translated. Further pressures are being put on the Brazilian publisher, Vozes, owned by the Franciscans, to discontinue the series.

Since September 1989, a new challenge has appeared: the collapse of "real socialism" in the Eastern bloc and the Soviet Union itself. Some theologians, such as Jan Tischner in Poland, have viewed this collapse of socialism, and of Marxism as a theoretical tool, as spelling the demise of liberation theology. But liberation theology – as the coming decades will show – is not in fact dependent on Marxism as a major source of inspiration. If its purpose of liberating the poor and oppressed of the Latin American continent requires a revitalized form of Marxism, it will be able to produce this; if not, it will not need it.[68]

Finally, faced with the massive scale of the progressive "impoverishment" of Latin America under the recessive peripheral capitalist system imposed by the World Bank and the IMF, theology must remain true to its ability to express the "cry of the oppressed." There is no escape from this; it is its responsibility before history. In November 1989 a liberation theologian, Ignacio Ellacuría, was martyred in El Salvador; in February 1991 another liberation theologian, leader of base communities and Salesian priest, Jean-Bertrand Aristide, was elected President of Haiti – to be forced into exile by a coup in September 1991: signs of the times!

Translated from the Spanish by Paul Burns

NOTES

1. For a historical sketch of theology in Latin America, see E. Dussel, *Hipótesis para una historia de la teología en América Latina* (Bogotá, 1986). Also CEHILA, *Historia de la teología en América*

Latina (San José, 1981); P. Richard, ed., *Raíces de la teología Latinoamericana* (San José, 1985). For the recent period, see S. Silva Gotay, *El pensamiento cristiano revolucionario en América Latina* (Salamanca, 1981); R. Oliveros Maqueo, *Liberación y teología: Génesis y crecimiento de una reflexión (1966–76)* (Mexico City, 1977); J. Comblin, "Kurze Geschichte der Theologie der Befreiung," J. Prien, ed., *Lateinamerika: Gesellschaft, Kirche, Theologie* (Göttingen, 1981); J. Prien, *La Historia del Cristianismo en América Latina* (Salamanca, 1985), pp. 1072ff; D. W. Ferm, *Profiles in Liberation. Thirty-six Portraits of Third World Theologians* (Mystic, Conn., 1988), pp. 114–93; idem. *Third World Theologies: An Introductory Survey* (Maryknoll, N.Y., 1986), pp. 3–58; A. T. Hennelly, ed., *Liberation Theology: A Documentary History* (Maryknoll, N.Y., 1990). For general introductions, see P. Berryman, *Liberation Theology* (New York, 1987); L. and C. Boff, *An Introduction to Liberation Theology* (Maryknoll, N.Y. and Tunbridge Wells, 1988).

2. J. L. Segundo, *Función de la Iglesia en la realidad Rioplatense* (Montevideo, 1962).

3. *Ibid.*, p. 6.

4. In the Protestant field, more closely involved in Africa and Asia, which had known liberation struggles since 1948, a "theology of revolution" became associated with the World Council of Churches in Geneva, but this was really an "application" of European theology to the field of revolutionary politics. Its first exponent in Latin America was Sergio Arce of Cuba.

5. I came to know the demands of poverty during my stay in Nazareth with Paul Gauthier (1957–9). He later wrote the prophetic *Jésus, l'Eglise et les pauvres* (Tournai, 1963), in which he posed the question of who "the poor" are. Gauthier's work inspired Pope John XXIII to speak of "the church of the poor" to various bishops at the end of the Council. Its scriptural basis is in the text from Isaiah that Jesus read in Nazareth: "*Ruaj Adonai Alai* . . . The Spirit of the Lord is upon me. He has anointed me to bring good news to the poor . . . " (Luke 4:18).

6. Dussel, *Hipótesis para una historia.*

7. R. Alves, *Theology of Hope* (Cleveland, 1969).

8. Alves, *Religión: Opio o instrumento de liberación* (Montevideo, 1970).

9. See "Theological Considerations on Human Liberation," *IDOC* 43 (1968); "La liberación humana desde una perspectiva teológica," *Mensaje* 168 (1968), pp. 175–9.

10. H. Assmann, "Tareas e limitaçoes de uma teologia do desenvolvimento," *Vozes* 62 (1968), pp. 13–21.

11. *Cultura latinoamericana e historia de la Iglesia* (Buenos Aires, 1968); R. Melgarejo and L. Gera, "Apuntes para una interpretación de la Iglesia argentina," *Víspera* 15 (1970), pp. 59–88.

12. "Justice," in Hennelly, *Liberation Theology* (see note 1), pp. 97–105, here p. 97.

13. Hennelly, pp. 106–14, here p. 107.

14. G. Gutiérrez, *La Pastoral de la Iglesia en América Latina* (Montevideo, 1969); idem., "De la Iglesia colonial a Medellín," *Víspera* 10 (1970), pp. 3–8.

15. Pamphlet *Hacia una teología de la liberación* (Montevideo, 1969).

16. *Inter alia*, as "Notes pour une théologie de la libération," *IDOC* 30 (1970), pp. 54–78.

17. H. Assmann, *Teología de la liberación: una evaluación prospectiva* (Montevideo, 1970); a first draft, in shorter form, is included in his *Teología desde la praxis de la liberación. Ensayo teológico desde la América dependiente* (Salamanca, 1973); Eng. trans. *Practical Theology of Liberation* (London and Maryknoll, N. Y., 1975), pp. 43–108. [The author later objected to the translation of the title, saying he did not know what a "practical theology" could be! – Trans].

18. *Memoria del primer Congreso Nacional de teología: Fe y desarollo* (Mexico City, 2 vols., 1970).

19. J. Hernández and others, *Liberación: opción de la Iglesia de la década del 70* (Bogotá, 1970).

20. They can be consulted at the IDOC centre in Rome.

21. See "Dialéctica de la liberación latinoamericana," *Strómata* 1–2 (Buenos Aires, 1971); later published as *Hacia una Filosofía de la liberación latinoamericana* (Buenos Aires, 1973).

22. In *Christus* 479 (Mexico City, 1975), p. 9.

23. The 1970 volume of the *Revista Bíblica* was devoted to this. See also H. Bojorge, "Exodo y liberación," *Víspera* 19–20 (1970), pp. 33–7; P. Negre, "Biblia y liberación," *Cristianismo y Sociedad* 24–5 (1970), pp. 24–5; J. M. Bonino, "Teología y liberación," *Actualidad Pastoral* 3 (Buenos Aires, 1970), pp. 83ff; J. de Santa Ana, "Notas para una ética de liberación," *Cristianismo y Sociedad* 23–4 (1970), pp. 43–60.

24. E. Pironio, "Teología de la liberación," *Teología* 8 (Buenos Aires, 1970), pp. 7–28; idem., "Teología de la liberación," *Criterio* (Buenos Aires, 1970), pp. 1607–8. See also H. Borrat, "Para una teología de la vanguardia," *Víspera* 17 (1970), pp. 26–31.

25. G. Gutiérrez, *Teología de la liberación, Perspectivas* (Lima, 1971); Eng. trans, *A Theology of*

Liberation (Maryknoll, N.Y. and London, 1973; revised edition with new Introduction, 1988).
26. Part 3, "The Option Before the Latin American Church," pp. 49–78.
27. J. L. Segundo, *Teología abierta para el laico adulto*, 5 vols. (Buenos Aires, 1969–71); Eng. trans. *Theology for an Open Church* (Maryknoll, N.Y.,); *De la Sociedad a la teología* (Buenos Aires, 1973).
28. Conclusions published in *Liberación: Diálogos en el CELAM* (Bogotá, 1974); see in particular the article by B. Kloppenburg, "Las tentaciones de la teología de la liberación,", pp. 401–515; Eng. trans *Temptations for the Theology of Liberation* (Chicago, 1975); see also Kloppenburg, *The Practical Church* (Chicago, 1976), and an attack on Gutiérrez's thesis of theology as "reflection on praxis" in J. Gutiérrez González, *The New Libertarian Gospel* (Chicago, 1977).
29. *Teología de la liberación. Conversaciones en Toledo* (Burgos, 1974).
30. *Conflicto social en América Latina y compromiso cristiano* (Bogotá, 1975). On the new outlook of CELAM, see F. Houtart, "Le Conseil Episcopal d'Amérique Latine accentue son changement," *Informations Catholiques Internationales* 481 (1975), pp. 10–24.
31. R. Vekemans, *Teología de la liberación y cristianos para el socialismo* (Bogotá, 1976).
32. I. Ellacuría, "Posibilidad, necesidad y sentido de una teología latinoamericana," *Christus* 471 (1975), pp. 12–16, 472 (1975), pp. 17–23; *Freedom Made Flesh* (Maryknoll, N.Y., 1976).
33. L. de Valle, various articles in *Christus*, theologian of the "priests for the people" (later "church in solidarity") movement; see "Hacia una teología prospectiva a partir de acontecimientos," *Liberación y Cautiverio*, pp. 103–27.
34. V. Elizondo, *Galilean Journey. The Mexican-American Promise* (Maryknoll, N.Y., 1983). Elizondo was for many years director of the Mexican American Cultural Center in San Antonio, Texas, and the theological animator of Spanish-speakers of the U.S.A.. See also A. Guerrero, *A Chicano Theology* (Maryknoll, N.Y., 1987).
35. R.Vidales, *La Iglesia latinoamericana y la política después de Medellín* (doctoral thesis, Quito, 1972); *idem.*, "Evangelización y liberación popular," *Liberación y cautiverio*, pp. 209–34.
36. A. Cassiánovich, *Nos ha liberado* (Salamanca, 1973): a work directed to base communities, teaching liberation theology by the "see-judge-act" technique of JOC; also, *Desde los pobres de la tierra* (Salamanca, 1977).
37. R. Avila, *Biblia y liberación* (Bogotá, 1973); *Implicaciones socio-políticas de la Eucaristía* (Bogotá, 1977). Avila is a lay theologian from Colombia, specializing in catechesis and the Eucharist, who has contributed very creative intuitions.
38. R.Muñoz, *Nueva Conciencia de la Iglesia en América Latina* (Santiago, 1973). A classic work of ecclesiology.
39. A "martyrology" was published in *Scarboro Missions* (Ontario, June 1975). J. Marins, *El martirio en América Latina* (Mexico City, 1982), pointed out the need for a pastoral strategy to support those tortured and imprisoned, and the families of the "disappeared," as was done in the early church, in another time of persecution and martyrdom.
40. Resultant publications: *The Emergent Gospel* (1976), *African Theology in Route* (1979), *Asia's Struggle for Full Humanity* (1980), and from the fourth meeting in São Paulo, *The Challenge of Basic Christian Communities* (1981), all published by Orbis Books (Maryknoll, N.Y.). There is a good bibliography in J. Ramos Regidor, *Gesù e il Risveglio degli Oppressi* (Milan, 1981).
41. See H. Assmann, "La actuación histórica del poder de Cristo. Notas sobre el discernimiento de las contradicciones cristológicas," R. Gibellini, *La nueva frontera de la teología en América Latina* (Salamanca, 1977), p. 135.
42. L. Boff, *Jesus Cristo liberador* (Petrópolis, 1972); Eng. trans. *Jesus Christ Liberator* (Maryknoll, N.Y., 1973). Also *A resurreiçao de Cristo* (Petrópolis, 1972); "Salvation in Jesus Christ and the Process of Liberation," *Concilium* 6, 10 (June 1974), pp. 78–91; "Pasión de Cristo y sufrimiento humano," *Jesucristo y la liberación del hombre* (Madrid, 1981), pp. 283–443.
43. J. Sobrino, *La cristología desde América Latina* (Mexico City, 1976; 2nd revised ed. 1977); Eng. Trans. *Christology at the Crossroads* (Maryknoll, N.Y., 1977).
44. J. L. Segundo, *Jesus of Nazareth, Yesterday and Today* 5 vols. (Maryknoll, N.Y., 1983-). Vol. 1, *Faith and Ideologies*, is in fact a separate work, dialoguing with Marx via Lukacs and Althusser, but always from a Latin American perspective.
45. Segundo, vol. 2, *The Historical Jesus of the Synoptics*, p. 29 (Spanish). See also J. Comblin, *Jesus de Nazareth (Petrópolis, 1971); I. Ellacuría, "The political character of Jesus' Mission," Freedom Made Flesh* (Maryknoll, N.Y., 1976), pp. 23–86.
46. L. Boff, *Ecclesiogênese* (Petrópolis, 1977); Eng. trans, *Ecclesiogenesis* (Maryknoll, N.Y., 1978); with C. Boff, *Comunidade eclesial, comunidade política* (Petrópolis, 1978). See also my "Base

Communities," *Concilium* 7, 10 (June 1975).

47. Boff, *Church: Charism and Power* (New York and London, 1985), pp. 65–88.

48. A. Paoli, *Diálogo de la liberación* (Buenos Aires, 1970); *La Iglesia que nace entre nosotros* (Bogotá, 1970); *El evangelio político de San Lucas* (Buenos Aires, 1973); *Pan y vino, Tierra (del exilio a la comunión)* (Bilbao, 1980).

49. E. Cardenal, *Salmos* (Buenos Aires, 1969); *La santidad de la revolución* (Salamanca, 1976).

50. Frei Betto, *Das catacumbas. Cartas da prisão* (Rio de Janeiro, 1978).

51. J. Sobrino, *La oración de Jesús y del cristiano* (Bogotá, 1979); see also his *Spirituality of Liberation* (Maryknoll, N.Y., 1985).

52. Gutiérrez's *The Power of the Poor in History* (1980) is his first treatment of the subject, developed in *We Drink from Our Own Wells* (1984) and *On Job: God-talk and the Suffering of the Innocent* (1987, all Maryknoll, N.Y.).

53. E. Bonnin, ed., *Espiritualidad y liberación en América Latina* (San José, 1982); see also Various, *A cruz, teologia e espiritualidade* (São Paulo, 1983). R. McAffee Brown, *Spirituality and Liberation* (Philadelphia, 1988).

54. Group "Studienkreis Kirche und Befreiung," *Kirche und Befreiung* (Ascheffenburg, 1975); idem., *Kirche in Chile* (1976); idem., *Utopie der Befreiung* (1976); idem., *Christlicher Glaube und gesellschfticke Praxis* (1978). More academic is, K. Lehman, *Theologie der Befreiung* (Einsiedlen, 1977). See my *Ethics and Community* (Maryknoll, N.Y. and Tunbridge Wells, 1988), pp. 27–34.

55. F. Hinkelammert, *The Ideological Weapons of Death* (Maryknoll, N.Y., 1979); *Ideología del sometimiento* (San José, 1977).

56. In Hennelly, *Liberation Theology*, pp. 282–91, here p. 286. See also below, chapter 24, 2.

57. DEI team, *Sobre el trabajo humano* (San José and Lima, 1982). My only reference to Marxism in *Ethics and Community* is in relation to the encyclical.

58. O. Maduro, *Religion and Social Conflicts* (Maryknoll, N.Y.,1982).

59. E. Tamez, La mujer latinoamericana, la praxis y la teología de la liberación," *Mujer Latinoamericana, Iglesia y Teología* (Mexico City, 1980); idem., "La fuerza del desnudo," *El rostro femenino de la teología* (San José, 1986). See also Various, *Teólogos de la liberación hablan sobre la mujer* (San José, 1986); L. Boff, *The Maternal Face of God* (Maryknoll, N.Y., 1981); E. Dussel, *La erótica latinoamericana* (Bogotá, 1980).

60. See *¿Cómo enfrentar el racismo en la Década del 80?* (Lima-Geneva, 1980); see also my "Racismo, América Latina negra y teología de la liberación," *Servir* 86 (1980), pp. 163–210. Also the conclusions of the Trinidad & Tobago meeting of CEHILA in *La esclavitud negra y la historia de la Iglesia en América Latina* (São Paulo, 1987); see also L. Hurbon, A. Lampe, J.O. Beozzo and others, *Cultura negra y teología* (San José, 1986).

61. A paradigmatic example is A. Wagua, "Erfahrungen im Dialog zwischen dem Christentum und der einheimischen Religion der Kuna," J. B. Metz and P. Rottländer, eds., *Lateinamerika und Europa. Dialog der Theologen* (Munich-Mainz, 1988), pp. 135–45. This volume contains the papers given at a theological seminar held in Münster in November 1987, and contains pieces by L. Boff, G. Gutiérrez, J. C. Scannone, E. Dussel, R. de Almeida Cunha and others.

62. See D. C. Hodges, *Intellectual Foundations of the Nicaraguan Revolution* (Austin, 1986); also A. M. Ezcurra, *Agresión ideológica contra la revolución sandinista* (Mexico City, 1983); J. Wheelock, P. Richard and others, *Fe cristiana y revolución sandinista en Nicaragua* (Managua, 1980); P. Casaldáliga and others, *La trinchera teológica* (Managua, 1987); G.Girardi, *Sandinismo, marxismo, cristianismo en la nueva Nicaragua* (Mexico City-Managua, 1986).

63. Hennelly, *Liberation Theology*, pp. 393–414.

64. Hennelly, pp. 390–2.

65. Karl Rahner's letter to Cardinal Juan Landízuri Ricketts, ibid., pp. 351–2, here p. 351.

66. J. L. Segundo, *Teología de la liberación. Respuesta al Cardenal Ratzinger* (Madrid, 1985), p. 95. He concludes that the theology underlying the "Instruction" contradicts that of Vatican II, in that: "There is no visible continuity between different expressions of the ordinary magisterium." A brave and vital book.

67. "Instruction" in Hennelly, *Liberation Theology*, pp. 461–97; letter pp. 498–506.

68. The writer has completed a third volume on the mature work of Marx, *El último Marx (1863–1882)*, which paves the way for a complete reinterpretation of his work.

Chapter 23

BASE CHURCH COMMUNITIES IN BRAZIL

Faustino Luiz Couto Teixeira

In Brazil today base church communities are one of the most important factors in the shaping of a new vision of the Church. They play a key part in realizing the goal of creating a Church of the poor. They display not only "the Church's preferential love for the common people" (Puebla 643), but also help the Church "to discover the evangelizing potential of the poor" (Puebla 1147).

Base communities are a community experience which enables the poor to assert their civil rights as active participants in society and Church. The internal dynamic of the base communities generates a phenomenon of enormous importance, the inbreaking of the word or, better, the discovery of a voice. It is, without any doubt, a cell-by-cell process of breaking down isolation which makes it possible for the poor to assert their civil rights. The experience of community enables the poor to become conscious of their dignity and worth as active participants in society. It is an experience which is felt as a personal enrichment, "an intensification of one's position as a subject".[1]

As well as asserting their dignity, the poor in the base communities are discovering the community dimension. The community is beginning to be recognized as the space in which the human and social fabric which is wearing thin can be repaired. The community produces an atmosphere of exchange (sharing), affectivity, recognition, tolerance, sociability and solidarity. It is this atmosphere which creates the group identity and is the fundamental basis for the emergence of a critical sense. The poor in community find that the problems which afflict them are common, that everyone has the same worth and deserves the same respect (an experience of equality in common deprivation). Out of this combined perception of the dignity of the individual and of collective need comes effective action to change society.

In the base communities the poor experience a dynamic process which makes them citizens in the full sense; in all this the faith dimension is a fundamental element which cannot be overlooked. Faith is the source from which flow all the strength and hope of the poor in community. It is generally considered an essential dimension "in the formation of the motivational system."[2]

The base communities not only stimulate the growth of a new consciousness and a new activity in the public sphere; they also promote the affirmation of the baptismal dignity of the poor, that is, the recognition of the poor as bearers of ecclesiological values, as having rights in the Church.

1. FACTORS IN THE EMERGENCE OF BASE COMMUNITIES

Understanding the importance of the base community experience implies a consideration of their origins: "The history of the problem is the problem of the history."[3] I start from the premise that in order to gain a better understanding of any partial structure we must place it in the context of the structure which immediately includes it. The explanation for the emergence of base communities is to be found within the broad context of social, political and cultural phenomena, and it is within this that we must look for a proper understanding of their meaning and of the interaction of faith and life which takes place within them.[4]

To understand the process of the emergence of the base communities in Brazil we have to look along two main axes. The first has to do with the Brazilian socio-cultural and ecclesial context, and the second with the broader ecclesial context.

(a) The Brazilian Socio-cultural and Ecclesial Context

As a more distant factor we can point to the lay tradition of popular Catholicism and the energy present in the way the Church was organized before the process of romanization.[5] Catholicism in Brazil, down to the middle of the nineteenth century, had taken on a predominantly lay appearance. This peculiarity was encouraged by the precariousness of the control exercised by the church structure on the centres of religious life of the period. The key institution of the royal prerogative, which delegated to the kings of Portugal the task of evangelization and religious administration, reinforced this state of affairs, as did the paucity of dioceses, the long vacancies of sees, the lack of administrators to cover the huge territory and the limited application in Brazil of the regulations of the Council of Trent.

As a result of the royal prerogative the clergy occupied a secondary position. The priest played the role of a public official, paid by the royal Treasury to exercise the liturgical functions of the colonial society's official religion. In practice it was lay people who developed religious initiatives, in the introduction of certain devotions, in the construction of oratories and hermitages for the cult of venerated images, in the organization of confraternities and pious associations, in the organization and management of devotional activities. The principal feature of popular Catholicism in this period was devotion to the saints; this was the base on which the whole of religious life was built.

The link between laity and clergy was effected through the so-called "ministry of visits," that is, by means of the annual "dispensations" (visits the priest made at least once a year to the chapels in his parish to celebrate the sacraments) and popular missions (visits by missionaries to preach and renew the faith). Such occasions were the basis of the contact between official Catholicism and popular Catholicism. These contacts were sporadic, but sufficed to guarantee and maintain the religious unity of the social body at the level of signifiers. They were the channels of the "religious consensus" between the different social groups who recognized each other as part of the same Catholic group.

This whole religious system was to be severely shaken by the process of romanization of Brazilian Catholicism after the middle of the nineteenth century. A series of processes was set in train in order to produce a radical change in the physiognomy of Catholicism as it had hitherto existed. This so-called "romanization" is connected with the process of Catholic restoration in Europe, with its emphasis on centralization round the religious power of the Holy See. In the Brazilian context it meant the restructuring of the Brazilian "ecclesiastical apparatus," notably through the actions of the reforming bishops of the second half of the nineteenth century to assert greater control over the laity and their associations. This control was designed to implant a universalist model which would subordinate Brazilian Catholicism to the centralizing directives of Rome.

The romanizing process had a disruptive effect on popular Catholicism. It was effective in its action on its public manifestations, which came under clerical control. Popular Catholicism came to be restricted to domestic practice: it went private.

In this way lay people gradually came to be passive in the religious sphere. The bases of lay activity increasingly came to be controlled through a complex network of intermediate institutions (associations, parishes, dioceses), which set up a truly molecular system. This system did not begin to be questioned until after the Second Vatican Council (1962–5). Despite the vigour with which romanization was carried out in Brazil, it is important to stress that the devotional current continued to have a strong presence (a primary presence in the sociological sense), whereas clericalization took place at the level of secondary socialization. This conflict goes some way to explain why a popular initiative which had been long maturing suddenly exploded to produce the base communities.

It is difficult to prove a real, organic, link between "lay colonial Catholicism" and the Catholicism of the base communities. Nevertheless it is undeniable that there are some familiar features which create a resemblance between the two. The base communities have made possible the re-emergence of a lay-based Catholicism. They have brought back, on a new basis, the "ethos" which marked the life of traditional popular Catholicism, the practice and freedom of organizing the Church. The forms now are new, and meet different needs. The base communities have brought back an experience of Catholicism in which lay people can take an active part in the religious community, can be initiators, producers of religious values. In the base communities figures from the past – the prayer leader, the master of ceremonies, the religious enthusiast – reappear in the figure of the animator of the base groups. The animator's qualification for religious activity comes, as in traditional Catholicism, from recognition by the community of his or her competence and authority in the exercise of his or her religious function. The base group animator is recognized as a bearer of ecclesiality and an agent of evangelization.

With the arrival of the base communities this situation which existed before romanization has been recovered and enriched by a new factor, the people's access to the gospel.

It is important to realize the extent to which the birth of the base communities was also encouraged by the crisis of the church institution (the crisis of the parish, the lack of ordained ministers to meet pastoral needs, etc.). The need to renew the whole of the Church's pastoral activity was a key factor in many of the initiatives and movements which developed in Brazil in the 1950s and the beginning of the 1960s. In all of these pastors were driven to give greater responsibilities to the laity. In other words, in addition to the more distant factor described above, we must point to specific factors in the Brazilian Church in more recent years which prepared the ground and sowed the seed of the base communities.

One group of such factors springs from concern with basic education and community evangelization: the experiment with popular catechesis in Barra do Piraí, the Natal Movement, the Nízia Floresta pastoral experiment, and the Basic Education Movement.

The *experiment with popular catechesis in Barra do Piraí*, in the state of Rio de Janeiro, arose out of the need felt by Dom Agnello Rossi, the bishop of the diocese, in 1956 to devise a system of evangelization which could cover the whole extent of his large diocese, and counter the spread of Protestantism which was worrying the Catholics of the region. Since the number of priests and religious was insufficient to cover the whole area, it was decided to use lay people as popular catechists. To fill this role, it was enough that the candidates were taught to read. The basic task of the catechists was to read in each village the material prepared by the diocese. In other words, the whole operation took place strictly within the limits of the existing ecclesiastical system. The clergy controlled the activity of the catechists. Nevertheless it is important to stress that the popular activity stimulated by the Barra do Piraí experiment did not always remain confined within the limits set by those who started the experiment. Work with the poor has its own dynamic. Although the experiment had conservative aims, popular catechesis gradually awakened the people's consciousness, and they in turn developed it. The popular catechists gathered the people together for the reading of the catechetical lesson, daily prayer, the organization of the singing, spiritual reading, the spiritual accompaniment of the mass celebrated in the cathedral, the organization of novenas, litanies, etc.

While the limits inherent in this experiment cannot be ignored, it represented a first step in the recognition of lay ability. The laity began to take into their own hands what previously were, and were regarded as, exclusively clerical functions.

The *Natal Movement* may be defined as the set of social and religious activities undertaken by the diocese of Natal, in the state of Rio Grande do Norte, in the north-east of Brazil, beginning in 1948. Characterized by sensitivity to the serious problem of underdevelopment in the region, the Movement directed its projects to three main ends, basic education, change in political, social and economic structures, and religious education. One of the methods used to attain the goals was education by radio. This initiative began in 1958, with the encouragement of Dom Eugênio Sales, then bishop and apostolic administrator of the Archdiocese of Natal. This was the first Brazilian experiment in the use of radio schools for basic education, and it followed a similar model already being tried out in Colombia (Sutatenza). The Brazilian experiment, however, was original in introducing social, community and religious elements, and political conscientization, into its broadcasts. Its aim was not merely literacy, but basic education. The results were impressive, and after three years' operation the experiment was adopted by the National Conference of Brazilian Bishops (CNBB) and extended to large areas of Brazil. By about 1963 there were about 1410 radio schools in Natal alone, with a range including about fifty municipalities and involving 24,000 students.

The Natal Movement did not limit its activities to basic education, but was also active in the field of rural trade union organization. Here too the movement was a pioneer. The diocese's decision to encourage the formation of agricultural trade unions was intended to counter the penetration of the peasant leagues promoted by Francisco Juliao. In other words, the underlying aim of the trade union work was to contain the socialist threat.

Even though it did not call in question the fundamental structure of society, and maintained from the beginning a "centrist" position, subject to permanent hierarchical control, the Natal Movement created a space for a liberation perspective on education and evangelization which considered human beings in their totality. In this respect it sowed the seed of something which was later to be fundamental in the experience of the base communities, the connection between religion and life.

There was a close connection between the Natal Movement experiment and the *Nízia Floresta pastoral experiment*. This experiment was prompted by the need to solve the problem of the lack of priests for the work of evangelization. The idea emerged around 1962 and was further elaborated in 1963. The project, a missionary experiment in parishes without priests, took shape in the small town of Nízia Floresta, some twenty-five miles from the state capital of Rio Grande do Norte, Natal. Four missionary sisters from the Congregation of Jesus Crucified were invited to manage the experiment, with responsibility for all aspects of evangelization. The sisters devoted particular attention to stimulating community life, with a particular sensitivity to the mass of the people. They stressed that faith and Christian life had to be sustained in community, emphasized the role of the laity, the training of leaders and liturgical life. There was great concern to harmonize the community work with the instructions contained in the CNBB Emergency Plan of 1962.

Though limited in this way, the Nízia Floresta pastoral experiment was the beginning of a questioning of an image of the Church as exclusively clerical, with no room for lay participation. It was an example of how the Church could be active in evangelization even where priests could not be present to advise. As regards the specific case of base communities, this experiment is unique in helping to show the importance of religious, men and women, in opening up new spaces for community participation in the Church. Countless base community experiments in Brazil grew out of the presence of religious women and men in grassroots pastoral work, carrying out their mission of encouraging communities of life and prayer. The influence of the Nízia Floresta experiment on the base communities was very indirect, but it contributed to creating a climate of participation in which lay people emerged and grassroots work was de-clericalized.

Among the movements which prepared the ground for the emergence of base communities, one of the most important was undoubtedly the Basic Education Movement (MEB). This was one of the largest in scale of all the Church's initiatives in grassroots education in Brazil. The Movement began in March 1961, when the CNBB proposed extending the successful experiment in radio education begun by the diocese of Natal. In association with the Federal Government, the CNBB threw itself into this project with high hopes, and designated as priority areas the north-east, the north and the centre-west.

The personnel of MEB was made up of organizers, in local, state and federal teams, and trainers. The organizers were professional people, teachers or university students. Many of these organizers were drawn from Specialized Catholic Action, especially from the Young Catholic Students (JUC). The trainers were from rural backgrounds (peasants, small farmers, agricultural labourers), and their activity was to organize, sustain and supervise the communities. They were natural leaders in their areas, and constituted the link between the Movement and the communities. The role of the trainers was central to the whole process of basic education and grassroots organization. The radio schools were based in their houses, and they were also responsible for encouraging and guiding the students in their educational activities. They were in permanent contact with the local organizing teams.

It is interesting to see how MEB in practice outgrew the conservative mould from which it came. Created as an alternative to the Peasant Leagues, and so with a markedly anti-communist stamp, it steadily developed in the direction of conscientization and grassroots training. This development was encouraged by a series of events, notably the movement's initial method of popular education, which combined theory and practice, the hopes aroused by the summoning of the Second Vatican Council, the atmosphere generated by the publication in Brazil of John XXIII's encyclical *Mater et Magistra* (May 1961), and also the climate of political openness which obtained in the north-east. The convergence of these and other factors gave the Movement in practice a much more radical style than had originally been envisaged by its founders.

The Basic Education Movement operated in various fields: basic education, grassroots organization, and the formation of rural trade unions. One of its main objectives was conscientization. This is a word which was to become common currency in all popular organization work in the next few years. Conscientization was regarded as essential to basic education. It meant giving students not only the information they needed to live a dignified life, but also the motivation to take part in action for social change. The educational method used in MEB sought to maintain a profound respect for the freedom of the students. There was great flexibility, so as to incorporate students' initiatives at any point of the process. There was a firm rejection of anything that smacked of levelling down or authoritarianism. There was a consensus that the ordinary people had to be the makers of their own history.

One of the most fruitful experiments carried out by MEB was known as Popular Animation (ANPO). This grew out of the need for a greater integration between school and community. ANPO stimulated genuine work for community development. It created unprecedented channels of communication between the workers and the local populations, which fostered creativity and new initiatives and made possible an encounter with and development of popular culture. Contact with the world of the poor through work in ANPO radically changed the worldview of the animators: they discovered the creative capacity of their students, their culture and their knowledge.

MEB produced an undeniable advance in popular education. The practical link with social conditions brought an undoubted enrichment, both in theoretical description and in educational creativity, as compared with earlier experiments. MEB did crucial groundwork in the redefinition of critical activity by Christians both within the Church and in Brazilian society. It represented a stimulus to lay participation in the Church, a dialectical interaction between pastoral practice and political practice, and a commitment to the poor. It identified key questions which, in one sense, foreshadowed and anticipated the issues which were to emerge later in the theology of liberation and the reflections of the base church communities.

Another important factor which played an essential part in the origin of the base communities has to do with the assertion of the rights of the laity through the unique experience of Specialized Catholic Action in Brazil, and in particular the two Catholic student movements, JUC for universities and JEC for high schools, and the Young Catholic Workers (JOC). Brazilian Catholic Action is one of the movements which created a climate of great ecclesial openness in Brazil, and made a decisive contribution to preparing lay people for a critical role, and to a new interaction between faith and the social situation.

Officially established in Brazil in 1935 on the Italian model, which was more centralized and conservative, the Catholic Action Movement in fact gained importance mainly after its reorganization in 1950. In this period the traditional Italian model gave way to the Belgian, French and Canadian model of Specialized Catholic Action, organized into sectors targeting particular fields of activity. JUC and JEC in particular had already begun to show great vitality as early as the late 1950s. JOC's critical influence was to be felt during the second half of the 1960s, when it adopted a commitment to radical social change as an element of Christian faith.

The development of awareness and action among members of the university student movement is a model of the transformations which took place in Catholic Action. If we accept the periodization suggested by Luíz Alberto Gómez de Souza, we can distinguish three stages in the evolution of the movement. The first (1950–8) is marked by a gradual insertion into the university world and student politics. The second stage (1959–64) represents a shift from involvement in universities to political activity which became increasingly intense and radical. The third stage (1964–7/8) shows a rethinking of political activity and involvement in universities as a result of the new political situation created in the country by the 1964 coup.[6]

The congress which marked the tenth anniversary of JUC, held in Rio de Janeiro in 1960, marked a new transformation in the world of the *jucists*, in comparison with the previous National Councils. Now the level of awareness among activists reached a keen sense of reality. The forms of social action in which they were involved enabled them to break with the old culturalist position and encouraged a greater political involvement.

There was a widespread longing among activists for Christian solutions for the problem of development, and ways forward towards a common line of action to fight injustice. Inspired by the thinking of Fr Lebret and Emmanuel Mounier, the *jucists* set out firmly on the road of political involvement, with an explicit critique and rejection of the attractions of capitalism and a growing option for socialism.

These choices on the part of JUC did not fail to generate crises and conflicts with certain sectors of the Catholic Church. Disagreements with the hierarchy sharpened steadily, in direct proportion to the critical involvement of the activists on the national stage. As the deadlocks and disagreements continued, especially after 1961, when a very tense National Council meeting took place in the city of Natal, it was suggested that a broader channel for political participation should be created in which the *jucists* could organize independently. This was how Açao Popular (AP) was born in 1962, on the initiative of a group of *jucists* and some Christian professionals. The *jucists* believed that this vehicle would bring them a final solution to the problems of their relations with the hierarchy. Despite having large numbers of Christians in its ranks, AP did not present itself as a denominational movement. It sought to be a vanguard movement, with the aim of preparing for revolution by means of a process of general mobilization. During the period of its legal existence (1962–64), AP grew significantly. It rapidly became one of the three main left-wing organizations in Brazilian politics. It was a national organization, with branches in the main cities of the country, and had significant influence in the university movement, the other student movements and among other social class segments. During this period the AP did not advocate a rigid ideology. The movement had a flexibility, an openness and sensitivity to the real movement of events, and an experimental approach which distinguished it from other ideological groups active at the time. "AP's humanism, its emphasis on freedom and participation, and its criticisms of stifling bureaucratic socialism constitute a significant link to the popular Church of the 1970s."[7] On going underground after the 1964 coup, the AP was to undergo a rapid political and ideological radicalization until, in 1966, it proclaimed its adherence to Marxism-Leninism. The direct consequence of this evolution was that it lost its social base, which was progressive Christians. From then on it was to be characterized by an aggressive anticlericalism.

Brazilian Catholic Action was undoubtedly important in preparing the ground from which the base communities were later to spring. Its main task was to create a new space for social and political involvement by Christians. The activity of Catholic Action (and especially JUC, JEC and JOC) made acceptable the idea that Christians should be active in social and political affairs. Indeed, it put into practice the "see-judge-act" method, giving it new force as an instrument of social critique and transformation. This method was later to underlie the whole experience of base communities. It was the thinking and activity of JUC, JEC and AP activists which established the relationship between faith and politics as a fundamental datum for Christian reflection and action.

The steps taken by the Brazilian Bishops' Conference (CNBB) to develop national planning are a further important element in the origin of the base communities. The plans were preceded by a period of intense discussion throughout the country about the need for pastoral renewal and coordination of evangelization. The *Better World Movement* (MMM), which operated through courses given by bishops, priests, religious and lay people, is very typical of this preparatory phase. It played a unique role in renewing the Brazilian clergy and streamlining pastoral activity, breaking down barriers and preparing the clergy and Christians in general for a vision of the Church subsequently endorsed by Vatican II. Brazil was perhaps one of the countries most open to this movement, which was highly valued by Pius XII (who gave it its name). 1960 was the high point of its implantation in Brazil, at the Seventh National Eucharistic Congress held in Curitiba, though even before this the movement had organized a number of courses.

Out of this atmosphere of opening up and renewal of church life came the CNBB's pastoral plans, which concentrated attention on pastoral planning. The first expression of this was the Emergency Plan of 1962. This initiated renewal in parishes, the ministry, education and the presence of the Church in social and economic life. It played a historic pioneering role in initiating important changes in the CNBB, creating a favourable climate for the wide-ranging reforms of Vatican II and awakening the Brazilian Church to the need for thoroughgoing renewal. It took the first moves to bring the bases and the growth points of the Church into contact in a framework of co-responsibility and communion. Among the significant features of the Emergency Plan were the stress on the need to modernize the parish, renew dioceses, and give greater importance to the particular church, the stress on episcopal collegiality and the pastoral insertion of religious, and the recognition of the role of the laity and their charismatic and ministerial activity in the Church. Although there was as yet no mention of base communities, the Emergency Plan implied a recognition of the natural communities already present within the larger community of the parish. Such communities, it was felt, offered greater possibilities of community life than the parishes, which were large in area and in population.

The results and experiences of the Emergency Plan were drawn on three years later in the *Comprehensive Pastoral Plan* (1965), which was discussed and approved at the seventh assembly of the CNBB in Rome. This plan sought to "be a first, firm application to the Brazilian Church of the main lines and decisions of the Council".[8] Accordingly, the plan attempted to promote the institutional renewal of the Church and the process of organic pastoral planning within a framework of communion and co-responsibility. It encouraged the involvement of lay people both in diocesan action plans and in church structures, stimulating them to missionary witness and secular concern. The plan also reinforced the questioning of the parish and argued for decentralization, promoting the creation and fostering of small base communities. For the first time at the level of the national bishops' conference there was talk of base communities as a force for church renewal and a stimulus to community life and cohesion, places where Christians could feel welcome and responsible. The Comprehensive Pastoral Plan identified the base communities as privileged spaces for the lay apostolate, for lay missionary witness in secular life, for the promotion of the proclamation of the word, deepening and energizing faith, and a means of increasing liturgical participation.

The Comprehensive Pastoral Plan created a new space for pastoral activity in Brazil, stimulating a broader sense of the Church. It was a practical attempt to implement the idea of the Church as the people of God. In the most sympathetic dioceses the plan helped to consolidate experiments in renewal or stimulated the growth of new grassroots experiments, and so contributed to the renewal of the Church's pastoral activity.

In addition to the movements already discussed, the *realignment of grassroots pastoral work and the pressure of the political situation* were also important factors in creating a climate favourable to the emergence of the base communities. We must not overlook the growth of grassroots movements and social forces, which, mainly from the 1960s onwards, began to be active in efforts for social change. There can be no doubt that the Church was affected by this whole popular movement. In the beginning the Church's contact with the lower classes was limited to isolated movements, but gradually significant sectors of the Church moved to a position much closer to the movements representing the lower classes. This shift was encouraged by various factors, most notably the events which followed the 1964 military coup, the increasing poverty of the mass of the people, disregard for human rights, the restrictions on political activity, repression against the popular movements and against the Church itself. After the 1964 coup all the sectors which had offered opposition were the objects of violent repression. Even church sectors (MEB, Catholic Action, etc.) were affected by the growing wave of violence: denunciations (true or false), trials, summonses, censorship, bans, expulsions, arrests, torture and killing. The experience of repression unified the Church and made it more cohesive. The situation had the opposite effect to what might have been expected, and led further sectors of the Church to move to an explicit position of defending human rights. Especially after Institutional Act No 5 (AI5) of 1968, which revived the repression, even sectors of the Church considered centrist or even conservative were angered by the situation. The effect of *esprit de corps* in the Church should not be underestimated, especially when members of the episcopate experienced the effects of the repression. Not a few bishops had their attitudes changed by the repressive methods and the subhuman situation imposed on peasants and workers: this was the case of, among others, Dom Paulo Evaristo Arns, Dom Moacyr Grecchi, Dom Adriano Hypólito and Dom José Hanrahan. At this time the Church became almost the only space in which the popular movement could meet, express itself, work out its ideas and reorganize. The Church, converted by the popular sectors, became little by little the "voice" of this base, committed to its cause. The base communities were to emerge within this committed space.

It will be apparent from the preceding discussion that there was a series of complementary factors in the emergence of the base communities, and that they operated at different levels. Some movements created spaces within the Church for pastoral renewal, lay involvement as a vital force within the Church, and promoted community activity, etc. Other movements – notably MEB and Specialized Catholic Action – initiated lines of critical reflection, theological analysis and political commitment, in other words, developed the fundamental intuitions which took on popular features in the base communities. They were factors "which found a major resonance in the base communities in the development of a new kind of theological thinking, in a common critique of the dominant social system, and in the hope shared, though at different historical moments, by the emerging popular movement, some as an aspiration, in the case of the base communities as a form of action already under way".[9]

(b) The Wider Context of Theological and Pastoral Renewal

The socio-cultural and ecclesial context in Brazil, while fundamental, does not provide a sufficient explanation for the complex process of the emergence of base communities.

We must also take account of the wider ecclesial context of the initiatives for theological and pastoral renewal begun in the early twentieth century, assimilated and endorsed by the Second Vatican Council and reinforced by the Medellín and Puebla Conferences (1968 and 1979).

Included in this dynamic process were the various *renewal movements*, biblical, liturgical, and ecclesiological, the religious evaluation of poverty and the efforts to implement the Church's social teaching. This renewal contributed to the creation of a climate of dialogue and participation, an emphasis on community, promotion of the laity, openness to the world, simpler worship, a pastoral attitude and social awareness. The biblical movement in particular increased the access of the faithful to the scriptures. This great evangelical ferment, present in the Church especially since the 1930s, was to swell the great Spirit-event of the Second Vatican Council (1962–5). It was characteristic of this Council that it encouraged the Church to move in new directions, and created space for new and original ecclesial experiments. One of its roles was to legitimize, consolidate and accelerate theological, liturgical and pastoral innovations already taking place throughout the Church. In Latin America in particular, Vatican II accelerated developments in the Church at an unprecedented rate, opening the Church to social conditions, awakening it to a new ecclesial identity, giving it space for creative and original experiments. It is impossible to have a correct understanding of the origin of base communities apart from the context of this powerful prophetic and libertarian current which swelled to a flood with the Council. The embryonic base communities were nurtured in this environment.

The *Medellín Conference* (1968) took place in the wake of the Second Vatican Council. Medellín not only confirmed the mood of renewal created by the Council, but also developed it in the area of the Church's involvement with social issues, bravely adopting the option for the poor and for integral liberation. This bishops' assembly was of fundamental importance in encouraging base church communities. In continuity with Medellín, the *Puebla Conference* (1979) confirmed all the decisions taken previously by the bishops, especially the option for the poor and for the base communities.

Despite this enumeration of factors which created the conditions for the emergence of the base communities both in Brazil and elsewhere, it is important to stress that this does not mean that the communities were no more than a continuation of the earlier movements; this would be mere mechanistic determinism. The truth is that the base communities were not simply a product of these factors, but present original characteristics of their own. To this extent they are a break with previous experiments, and gave a new rhythm to pastoral activity. They gave it a characteristic "popular" stamp, resulting from their abandonment of the clericalism, élitism, defensiveness and apologetic outlook still present in many of the experiments regarded as their precursors.

2. THE DEVELOPMENT OF THE BASE COMMUNITIES

The preceding section of this chapter has attempted to identify some of the factors in the emergence of base church communities in Brazil. Two main sets of factors were suggested which combined to create the necessary conditions, the first connected with the socio-cultural and ecclesial context in Brazil and the second with the wider ecclesial context. On the one hand we have the popular ferment in the country followed by the dark night of repression after the military coup of 1964, and on the other the Church in a rapid process of renewal.

Both sets of factors have to do with prior conditions which contributed to the emergence of the base communities. They situate the communities in the broad historical context. They still leave open, however, the question of the origin of the base communities themselves, their initial form. The base community experiment was not simply a natural consequence of the factors which preceded them, but introduced original elements which were a break with the past. Information on the origin of the base communities is still (at least in Brazil) very fragmented. There is important information scattered in articles or studies of the phenomenon, but no rigorous historical study.

It is difficult to specify precisely the first experiments which gave rise to base communities in Brazil. The very definition of a base church community is subject to different interpretations, which makes the task of locating their origin even more complicated. Some studies tend to place the origin of the experiment as early as about 1960, while other studies suggest that the first experiments began around 1964. However we can safely say that the experiment was recognized in the wake of the Second Vatican Council and in the context of the broad popular movement which was shaking Brazil in the 1960s. If we take into consideration the reports produced as a result of the various Inter-Ecclesial Meetings of Base Communities, we can say that the vigorous spread of the small communities came in the wake of the religious renewal fostered by Vatican II and subsequently reinforced by Medellín.

We find that as a rule base communities started for both religious and social reasons. They could start, on the one hand, as a result of the need for liberationist pastoral activity, from the suggestion, by a priest, religious or lay person, that small groups should be formed for discussion, for bible study or for the celebration of the word. They might also start as the result of the transfer of a priest, whose work was then continued by lay people, as the result of a leadership training course, from a casual, informal meeting with local people, from the example of other active communities, etc. On the other hand the group could be sparked off by local problems: the formation of a group to discuss neighbourhood problems, to resist persecution, etc., to demand the right to housing, to avert the danger of a land invasion. Facts like these made the groups aware of the importance of meeting as a community, in the light of the word of God, to reflect, pray, sing and look for solutions to the agonizing problems of daily life.

The base communities did not come into being as the result of prior planning, although various reports from the Inter-Ecclesial Meetings stress the importance of the moves for pastoral renewal (sometimes even diocesan decisions) inspired by Vatican II and Medellín.

At the root of the experiments we find the active presence of pastoral workers encouraging the formation of the small communities. In general the initiative for the formation of base groups comes from priests, religious or lay people. In some cases the presence of the bishop was also important. Inspired by deeply held gospel ideals, these people had chosen practical involvement with the poorest sectors of the community. In many cases it is evident that a whole process takes place, going from the pastoral worker's slow settling into the local community to the gradual formation of groups. For the worker the process is one of learning, living alongside the poor, coming to understand the problems of the people, etc.

The process by which the communities organize and mobilize to form an alternative structure can take place at different speeds and is determined by both internal factors (connected with the internal workings of the community) and external factors (connected with the historical moment and the immediate situation). Normally communities begin their struggles with basic needs, connected with their immediate and pressing problems (water, light, housing, health, education, etc.). In time, as the communities discuss their problems and their practical responses in terms of self-help and mutual help, they develop a broader understanding of the situation of oppression which underlies the local situation of poverty, and this leads to the need for new forms of collective participation and organization to combat this situation. The ecclesial aspect is stressed in the permanent contact with the word of God, which constitutes the essential element in the whole community dynamic, and in the celebrations of the sacraments and the communities' own liturgies.

Even if it is impossible to reach a single comprehensive definition of a developing phenomenon, some characteristic features can be identified: a local base (the members come from the same area), the presence of the word of God and regular worship, the participatory style and the ministerial services, the mutual commitment and the energizing contact made between faith and life.

3. THE BASE COMMUNITIES AS A RENEWAL OF EVANGELIZATION

Since they started to come into being, mainly in the late 1960s, the base church communities took on a very important role both in the redefinition of pastoral activity and in the articulation of the popular movements. On the one hand it is natural that the whole internal dynamic of the communities should produce a decentralization of pastoral life and a greater popular presence in the life and building up of the Church. The fact that the poor found their voice in the base communities meant an increasing desire on the part of the communities to be involved in pastoral decisions. This popular participation can also be seen as a move to a more political form of activity, involvement of members of the communities in neighbourhood associations, trade unions, parties and other popular movements. All this ferment took place particularly in the 1970s and early 1980s. This was a period of rapid growth for the communities. It was now that the Inter-Ecclesial Meetings began, as a means of encouraging greater contact between the communities. The first was held in Vitória, in the state of Espírito Santo, in 1975.

The present moment might be labelled as one of "pastoral transition." Today pastoral work among the popular classes, and especially the base communities, faces a very diverse situation. The present political situation is extremely serious, a crisis affecting all dimensions of society. The general climate is one of great scepticism, confusion, and increasing distrust among the mass of the people, reinforced by the daily revelations of scandals and corruption involving the élites and members of the ruling classes. In the broad ecclesial perspective we find a clear neo-conservative restoration (many people talk of a winter in the Church), which does not encourage the creative energies of the base communities.

While we should not ignore the impact (and paralyzing effect) of this restoration in the Church on the present situation of the base communities, it would be a mistake to reduce the unique moment through which this experiment is passing to a byproduct of the ecclesiastical situation of the moment. It is a phenomenon with much more complex roots.

Many dioceses which were cradles of the base community experiments in Brazil have in recent years been undertaking a pastoral evaluation: these include Vitória, in the state of Espírito Santo, Goiás Velho, in Goiás, Sao Félix do Araguaia in Mato Grosso, Crateús in Ceará. This is very important as an expression of a new stage in the journey of the base communities, marked by a "lessening of certainties" and an "increase of questioning." There is a growing sense of the base communities as something that is alive and in process of permanent creation and recreation, attentive and open to the new signs of the times, discovering new directions and resistant to manicheistic and simplistic temptations. Today there is a clear conviction that the history of the base communities is an open history and not a defining one. There is no longer any room for idealist reification. It is time for a new sensitivity to the movements of the real world.

This new perspective reveals the present challenges facing the base communities. Among them are the inculturation of the faith and dialogue with popular religion, the challenge of the spirituality and religious identity of the base communities, the challenge to develop the missionary dimension of the communities in the world of the most impoverished, the challenge of internal pluralism and of finding means of participation, the challenge of the emergence of subjectivities, of gratuitousness and symbol, the challenges of ecology and the quality of life, the challenge of the relationship with the non-poor, intermediate sectors of society and opinion-formers. These are fundamental challenges, and ones which are already engaging the attention of the communities, even if the process is still at an early stage. They are issues which will develop, but they do not negate or reduce the importance of the fundamental issue present from the beginning of the community process, the affirmation of life and the gospel option for the poor. The commitment to the cause of life and to social involvement has certainly not been abandoned. The aim today is to put it into practice within a new synthesis, in which the new challenges are given equal attention.

Translated from the Portuguese by Francis McDonagh

NOTES

1. E. R. Durham, "Movimentos sociais: a construção da cidadania," *Novos Estudos CEBRAP*, 10 (1984), p. 28.

2. H. Assmann, "Quando a vivência da fé remexe o senso comum dos pobres," *Revista Eclesiástica Brasileira* 46, 183 (1986), p. 565.
3. Cf L. Goldmann, *Cultural Creation in Modern Society* (Oxford, 1977).
4. An essential reference for this whole historical section is my book *A gênese das CEBs no Brasil* (São Paulo, 1988).
5. For a more systematic account of the romanization of Catholicism in Brasil, cf P. Assis de Ribeiro, *Religião e dominação de classe: gênese, estrutura e funçao do catolicismo romanizado no Brasil* (Vozes, 1985).
6. L. A. Gómez de Souza, *A JUC: os estudantes católicos e a política* (Petrópolis, 1984), pp. 103–4.
7. S. Mainwaring, *The Catholic Church and Politics in Brazil, 1916–1985* (Stanford, Ca., 1986), p. 65.
8. CNBB, "Balanço do Plano de Pastoral de Conjunto, janeiro a junho de 1986", G. F. de Queiroga, *CNBB: comunhão e coresponsabilidade* (São Paulo, 1977., p. 374, n. 2.
9. L. A. Gómez de Souza, Preface to Teixeira, *A gênese das CEBs no Brasil*, op. cit., p. 11.

SELECT BIBLIOGRAPHY

Azevedo, M. *Comunidades eclesiais de base e inculturação da fé.* São Paulo: Loyola, 1986. Eng. trans. *Basic Ecclesial Communities in Brazil.* Washington D.C.: Georgetown University Press, 1987.
Barreiro, A. "Raizes da consciência eclesial das CEBs". *Convergência* 158 (1982), pp. 602–09.
Boff, C. "Fisonomia das comunidades eclesiais de base". *Concilium* 164 (1981), pp. 72–79. Eng. ed. *Concilium 144, Tensions between the Churches of the First World and the Third World.*
—. "'E uma pedrinha soltou-se . . . ' – As bases do povo de Deus". *Revista Eclesiástica Brasileira* 42,168 (1982), pp. 659–87.
Boff, L. *Ecclesiogenesis: the Base Communities Reinvent the Church.* Maryknoll: Orbis, 1977, London: SCM Press, 1986.
—. *O caminhar da Igreja com os oprimidos.* Rio de Janeiro: Codecri, 1980.
Bruneau, T. C. *The Political Transformation of the Brazilian Catholic Church.* London and New York: Cambridge UP,1974.
—. *The Church in Brazil: The Politics of Religion.* Austin, Texas: University of Texas Press, 1982.
Demo, P. and Calsing, E. F. "Relatório de pesquisa sobre comunidades eclesiais de base". CNBB. *Comunidades: Igreja na base.* (Estudos da CNBB, 3) São Paulo: Paulinas, 1977, pp. 15–64.
Fernandes, L. *Como se faz uma comunidade eclesial de base.* Petrópolis: Vozes/IBASE, 1984.
—. "Gênese, dinámica e perspectiva das CEBs do Brasil". *Revista Eclesiástica Brasileira* 42, 167 (1982), pp. 456–63.
Gregory, A. "Dados preliminares sobre experiências de CEBs no Brasil. Uma visão sociográfica". Gregory, A. (ed.). *Comunidades eclesiais de base: utopia ou realidade.* Petrópolis: Vozes, 1973, pp. 46–64.
Guimarães, A. R. *Comunidades de base no Brasil.* Petrópolis: Vozes, 1978.
IBASE. *Pesquisa sobre CEBs – 5°Encontro Eclesial, Canindé CE.* Centro de Dados. 06/09/83. Projeto CEBs – Programa CEBP 1. Rio de Janeiro: IBASE, 1983 (duplicated).
Klein, L. F. *Comunidades eclesiais de base no Brasil; descrição fenomenológica, avaliação teológica e perspectivas pastorais.* MA dissertation. Rio de Janeiro: Theology Faculty, Pontifícia Universidade Católica, 1979.
Lesbaupin, Y. do A. *Mouvement populaire, Eglise catholique et politique au Brésil: l'apport des communautés ecclésiales urbaines de base aux mouvements populaires.* Doctoral thesis. Toulouse: Université de Toulouse-Le-Mirail, UER de Sciences Sociales, 1987.
Libânio, J. B. *Teologia da libertação; roteiro didático para um estudo.* São Paulo Loyola, 1987.
—. "Experiência das comunidades eclesiais de base no Brasil". Antoniazzi, A. and others. *CRB: dez anos de teologia.* Rio de Janeiro: CRB, 1982, pp. 113–38.
Mainwaring, S. *The Catholic Church and Politics in Brazil, 1916–1985.* Stanford, Ca.: Stanford UP, 1986.
Marins, J. "Comunidades eclesiais de base na América Latina". *Concilium* 104 (1975), pp. 20–29. Eng. ed. *Concilium 104, The Poor and the Church.*
Mesters, C. "O futuro do nosso passado". Various. *Uma Igrejaque nasce do povo.* Petrópolis: Vozes, 1975, pp. 120–200.

Oliveira, P. A. de. "As comunidades na caminhada contra a pobreza e a opressão". *SEDOC* 9, 95 (1976), pp. 286–95.
Perani, C. "A Igreja no Nordeste: breves notas histórico- críticas". *Cadernos do CEAS* 94 (1984), pp. 53–65.
Salém, H. (ed.). *A Igreja dos oprimidos*. São Paulo: Brasil Debates, 1981.
Souza, L. A. G. de. *A JUC: os estudantes cristãos e a política*. Petrópolis: Vozes, 1984.
Teixeira, F. L. C. *A gênese das CEBs no Brasil*. São Paulo: Paulinas, 1988.
Wanderley, L. E. W. *Educar para transformar: educação popular, Igreja católica e política no Movimento de Educação de Base*. Petrópolis: Vozes, 1984.

Chapter 24

CHRISTIANITY AND REVOLUTION
I. CUBA (1959–89)

Raúl Gómez Treto

1. INTRODUCTION

The Christian Church, and above all its Roman Catholic branch, has been present and survived in practically all cultures and social systems. It was founded to proclaim the "good news" of its liberation to the whole world, and, with a greater or lesser degree of "light and shadows," it has been doing so for the twenty centuries of its existence in the midst of the "darkness of the world," thanks to the Spirit with which it is infused by its head, who is Christ.

Since its body is made up of sinners, the Church has continued in its basic unity of faith, but torn apart by conflicts, both internal and in its relations with the world, produced by the sin of its members. These conflicts have sometimes related to ethnic, racial and local factors, sometimes to ideological – including theological – , philosophical, political and even economic circumstances. They have always been exacerbated in periods of social ferment or revolution, leading at times to internal schism, as happened in the Great Schism between the Western and Eastern churches, in England under Henry VIII and in other European countries due to Luther's protests and Calvin's reforms.

In Latin America, the Church went through periods of acute tension during the wars of independence, though this never produced an actual break as it had done earlier in Europe. It often came close to this, however, as in the cases of Frs Hidalgo and Morelos in the Mexican uprising of the early nineteenth century, or, to a lesser extent, those of Bishop Espada and Fr Varela a little later in Cuba, not to mention the hundred priests "unfaithful" to Spain during the Cuban war of independence at the end of the last century.

More recently in Cuba, during the war of national liberation (1956–8), there was a particular case: that of Fr Guillermo Sardiñas who, without totally breaking with the Church, rose to the rank of Commandant in the rebel army and stoically accepted repudiation by conservative elements in the Church.[1] The case of Fr Camilo Torres in Colombia is similar, and there are several more examples from Central America. We are, however, unlikely to see repeated in America the sad case of Joan of Arc, burned as a witch and later canonized when the political interests of the Holy See changed their age-old objectives.

The Socialist Revolution in Cuba, begun shortly after the popular victory of 1959, brought its attendant repercussions both within the churches – Catholic and other – and in their relations with the Cuban people and state. The fact that these disputes are gradually being resolved shows that they were not insuperable, that they were not of a nature that would necessarily be repeated in other, similar circumstances and, finally, that in this case at this time – and possibly in other parts of the world from now on – such conflicts are not any longer as serious or as brutal as those in medieval, modern and even contemporary Europe.

2. THE CASE OF CUBA

The experience of the Cuban people in these years of unfinished revolution and the part played by the Christian churches, basically the Catholic Church, are an example of how conflicts arising more from reciprocal prejudices, both hereditary and imported, than from genuinely evangelical and theological material and spiritual realities can be overcome. Taking these years stage by stage will illustrate this process of conflict followed by gradual *rapprochement*.

Stage 1: Discomfiture of the Church

The ecclesiastical hierarchy – both the Catholic, formed in the Spanish mould, and the Protestant, formed in the U.S. mould – as well as most of their respective clergy and pastors, assumed that the triumphant revolution would not affect church interests – which are not always the same thing as the churches' evangelizing mission. The fact that both church dignitaries and members had, to a greater or lesser extent, been involved – to the extent of heroism and even martyrdom in some cases – in the popular struggle for power, led the church leadership to suppose that ecclesiastical institutions would be safeguarded from any political, ideological or economic consequences. Those pre-conciliar churches failed to take account of the fact that the behaviour and image of the Church is determined not by its saints, but by its communities, and that in Cuba the institutional apparatus of the Church had been heavily compromised with the corrupt governments and privileged classes of earlier years, looking to them for the bulk of its material support.

The first legal and practical measures taken by the revolutionary government were designed to strip the dominant classes of their privileges and the means by which they unjustly exploited the people. There was no anti-religious or anti-clerical intent behind them, which did not prevent the churches from seeing themselves affected in their institutions, or indirectly through the effects on the wealthy sectors of society which had materially supported them. Soon spokespersons for the churches began to accuse the revolution of being communist – thereby echoing the imperialist campaign from the United States, where capitalism could not admit any form of revolution – and, consequently, accusing it of being atheist, anti-church and anti religion. In the social climate of the time, this was practically tantamount to labelling it immoral and diabolical, given the strictures against communism launched by Pius XII in the 1940s and 50s.

The National Catholic Congress, which took place in November 1959, was the most obvious demonstration of these conflicts. While large numbers of people supported the event in order to demonstrate the compatibility of their Christian faith, of varying degrees of purity or syncretism, with the revolutionary measures being taken for the benefit of the people, the doctrinal message and pastoral letters subsequently published were frankly populist, anti-communist and counter-revolutionary.[2] The initial discomfiture turned into distrust that was to lead to confrontation.

Stage 2: Church-State Confrontation (1961–2)

The attitude of the ecclesiastical institution – already well differentiated from that of the "believing" masses with their popular or "syncretic" religiosity, the product of the poor "evangelization" carried out in Cuba – in open opposition to the revolution, generated a reaction from the revolutionary government installed with the massive support of the people who had benefitted from its success: repression of all counter-revolutionary (anti-people) action, whatever source it came from, including the believing, Christian, Catholic sector. There was a saying at the time that the revolution was being made "with the army, without the army or against the army"; it could as well have been said – though it never was – that it was being made "with the church, without the church, or against the church."

These were the days when prominent lay figures in the Church, and some priests and religious, zealous for "ecclesiastical rights," joined and even led counter-revolutionary organizations that enjoyed no support among the people. Illustrative of this stage was the failed invasion of Girón beach (the "Bay of Pigs"), defeated by the army and the police with the help of popular militias in sixty-eight hours. Later, there was the "procession" of the Virgin of Charity, organized by the auxiliary Bishop of Santiago and parish priest of the diocesan sanctuary of the "Patroness of Cuba," Mgr E. Boza Masdival. This tried to go beyond the traditional parish boundary and create an unaccustomed "procession" through the streets of the city, only to be met with the opposition of the people who sensed its obvious politicization. The encounter left the legacy of the death of a young Catholic who was also a revolutionary militiaman.

The government's response was the immediate expulsion from Cuba of some 135 priests classified as foreign "falangists" (though not all were and others who were remained in the country). This action broke the counter-revolutionary network which was manipulating the clergy and the docile and reactionary elements of the laity.

Faced with the political defeat of the Catholic Church, the enemy of the Cuban people tried to manipulate other churches originating in the United States or Great Britain, but these attempts also failed a short while later.

Stage 3. Avoidance of Reality

Defeated politically, both Catholic and Protestant church apparatuses began on the one hand to withdraw into "ghettoes," and on the other to avoid or "flee from" reality and the country. More than one bishop, priest, sister and pastor counselled people to "save themselves from communism" and gave material assistance to encourage people to leave the country. They had "their feet on the island, but their heads in Miami or Madrid." In this way they contributed to the "brain drain" designed to defeat the revolution by robbing the country of talent.

After the "Bay of Pigs," the Catholic Church closed its seminaries and novitiates and sent its few seminarians and novices to finish their studies overseas. Some returned, though not all of these stayed in the country. Shortage of clergy forced some priests to take charge of four or even five parishes: out of eight hundred in the country, a little over 130 were expelled and 470 "left," leaving a mere two hundred. This campaign emptied the churches of their traditional faithful, but filled them with "non-regulars" seeking the help of the clergy to abandon the country and to receive recommendations that would help them to find privileges abroad.

Alongside this activity, there were those who, without leaving the Church, stayed in the country, "being people," helping in the positive side of the revolution, actively integrated into its organizations and institutions (except the Communist Party, which required a profession of atheism), from the standpoint of their Christian faith and in an exercise of that hoped-for and hope-giving "effective love" which Fr Camilo Torres was campaigning for in Colombia.

Several Cuban bishops went to the Second Vatican Council, but, apart from certain formal changes in the liturgy, the spirit of the Council failed to penetrate the Catholic community sufficiently to shake the Church out of its self-absorption and evasive tendencies.

At this time compulsory military service was brought in for all males over the age of sixteen. At first, mistrust of individuals of known opposition or apathy toward the revolution, or of anti-social tendencies, led to the creation of "Military Production Aid Units" to which many Christians were unjustly assigned, including some young priests (one of whom later became the present Archbishop of Havana, Mgr Jaime Ortega Alamino). This mistake was soon rectified and priests, pastors and seminarians are now not called to do military service. The Production brigades were replaced by the "Young Centenary Column" and later by the "Young Labour Army," militarized units doing heavy manual work on development projects, whose members could acquire social standing similar to that of the regular army.

Stage 4. Re-encounter. 1968–78

The CELAM Conference held in Medellín in 1968 provided the initial impetus for the Church in general to come out of its inclaustration and take stock of its missionary vocation to the service of society, of which it forms part.

Two pastoral letters from the Cuban bishops marked this progressive opening. The first was dated 20 April 1969, and dealt with the pressing subject of development. It spelt out the need for Cuban Christians to be involved in their country's efforts in this direction. The Catholic bishops declared themselves against the economic blockade imposed on Cuba by the United States and its allies, calling this unjust and in contravention of international morality.[3]

The second pastoral was dated 8 September 1969. Its subject was faith and atheism, and it recommended Catholic lay people not to stand aside from the social, economic and political life of the country, but to play a responsible part in secular organizations by virtue of their faith, love and hope, in accordance with their vocation, and always provided they were not required to apostasize from their faith. In this context it advised Catholics to approach their atheist companions with all the respect required by brotherly love and due to all by the fact that all share in the human condition.[4]

This new attitude of "re-encounter" of the church with the people surprised and disgusted its more conservative sectors, but it brought peace of mind to all those who had felt themselves to be under ecclesiastical interdict for having supported the revolution. For their part, the more recalcitrant atheists interpreted the Church's gesture as a new piece of "entryism" designed to distract the revolution from its aims. The revolutionary government and the Communist party leaders, however, publicly welcomed the gesture and called for moderation and mutual respect in the "ideological struggle." The speeches made by Fidel Castro in Chile in 1971 and Jamaica in 1974 on the necessary (long term) strategic alliance between Marxists and revolutionary Christians[5] are highly significant in this regard, as are the relevant resolutions of the First and Second Party Congresses.[6]

Stage 5. Dialogue. 1979–86

During this period exchanges with other churches, including those of the United States, multiplied. Likewise, high dignitaries from the Holy See and the World Council of Churches visited the Cuban churches and the country, where they were received by the highest authorities of the government, the state and the party.

Progressing along this line of re-encounter with the people in order to serve them honestly and disinterestedly – evangelically – as the only means of "reconciling" the church with God after its historical "shadows," from 1980 on the Catholic Church as a whole began a serious process of self-criticism and study of its real mission in Cuba. This "Cuban Church Reflection" was designed and carried out on all levels and in all parts of the Church. Its partial conclusions were finally drawn together in a working document which was to serve as the basis for the "National Cuban Church Meeting" (*Encuentro Nacional Eclesial Cubano – ENEC*) held in February 1986 as the culmination of this broad and deep process of reflection. It was also to serve as the launch pad for putting into practice, for the first time in the history of the country and its church, an overall pastoral strategy to be implemented in stages over the coming years.[7]

ENEC was made up of the bishops of Cuba and elected representatives from all levels and sectors of the church: priests, brothers, monks, lay people; men, women, young people; professionals, workers, peasants, and the like. Also invited were bishops from the United States, Latin America and Spain, together with a delegation from CELAM and, as Papal Legate, Cardinal Eduardo Pironio, President of the Pontifical Laity Commission, who brought greetings and a personal blessing from Pope John Paul II. Representatives of the Ecumenical Council (of evangelical churches) of Cuba, the revolutionary government and the Communist Party of Cuba were also present as observers.

This was, in effect, a landmark in the history of the Church and the country. It marked the point from which, with the support of the Ecumenical Council of Cuba and other Christian churches, the Catholic Church and the state set up something more than a dialogue: an honest and sincere quest for areas in which the two could collaborate, maintaining their separate and mutually respected identities, for the benefit of the people whom both institutions are called to serve. Fidel Castro's public, official and repeated praise for the work of religious sisters in the field of health and social work, setting them up as an example of the humanity and efficacity that all communists and other workers in Cuba should demonstrate, was a promising sign of the acceptance the renewed activity of the Church was finding at the highest levels in the party and the government.[6]

Stage 6. The future. (1987–)

The role played by the Christian churches – of all denominations and families – after ENEC will be strongly marked by the pastoral guidelines mapped out at that historic event, and at the same time by the actual needs of the country. Given the general approach of the socialist government, there is certainly no need for the church institution to mount a separate programme of "works of charity." The revolution has closed the yawning gap that existed – and still exists in other countries – between rich and poor: there are no rich people in the country now, but neither are there any poor. The Church's mission is that assigned it by the gospel brought up to date by Vatican II: to be salt of the earth, light of the world, soul of society.

In this context, the ethical formation of Christians takes on a new importance. They need to "project themselves," not in any spirit of proselytism, but through "contagion," force of example, into all the areas in which they can serve and stimulate their fellow workers. This is the aim of all the pastoral steps taken by the "post-ENEC" Church.

Significant pointers to this new situation are: first, the state authorization for foreign priests to come and work in the country, armed with the renewed evangelical spirit of the post-conciliar period; second, the need spelt out by Fidel Castro for several hundred sisters to come and work in Cuba on social projects, and eventually to direct them, by virtue of their experience, effectiveness and exemplary humanism.

3. CONCLUSION

The experiences and activities of the Christian Church during these three decades of revolutionary history of the Cuban people show that faith, like ideologies, can be traduced into absurd prejudices and dogmatizations which, instead of bringing liberation and peace, bring only conflicts foreign to its original guiding principles. In the case of Cuba, even the times of greatest tension were never as acute as those experienced by the Church at other periods and in other places over its long history. There were extremists on both sides, but also responsible individuals and groups who gradually brought harmony, understanding and mutual respect and opened the way for honest collaboration among different institutions in a spirit of mutual service to the people. The Cuban example illustrates both the "shadows" to be avoided and the "lights" which can help the people on their way to integral liberation. This is the mission of the Church, as it is that of the state. It is absurd – sinful, even – for the two authorities to oppose each other. They need to collaborate, with each doing what it is best suited to do.

NOTES

1. Y. Sardiñas, *El Sacerdote Comandante* (Havana, 1987); *idem*. 15-minute documentary produced by Cuban Institute for Art and Cinematography (Havana, 1960); *Boletín de las Provincias Eclesiásticas de la República de Cuba*, Year XLIII, Jan–Feb. 1960, nos. 1 & 2.

3. *Vida Cristiana*, supplement no. 327, Sunday 27 April 1969 (Havana).

4. Leaflet printed by the (Catholic) Bishops' Conference of Cuba, addressed to all priests and faithful and distributed the following Sunday.

5. Revolutionary Orientation Commission of the Central Committee of the Cuban Communist party, *Cuba-Chile* (Havana, 1972); also in *Fidel en Chile*, complete texts of his talks to the people (Santiago, 1972); and in *Granma* (official organ of the Central Committee of the Communist party of Cuba) 3 Nov. 1977, p. 2, reprinted by the Study Centre of the Ecumenical Council of Cuba for distribution on the Eighth National "Camilo Torres Day," celebrated in Havana on 24 Feb. 1978.

6. *Primer Congreso del Partido Comunista de Cuba: Tésis y Resoluciones* (Havana, 1976); *Plataforma Progamática del Partido Comunista de Cuba* (Havana. 1976); *II Congreso del PCC: Documentos y Discursos* (Havana, 1981).

7. *Encuentro Nacional Eclesial Cubano: Documento Final e Instrucción Pastoral de los Obispos* (printed in Rome, 1987).

8. *Juventud Rebelde* (official organ of the Young Communist Union, Havana) Thursday 5 July 1984, p.1; *Fidel y la Religión: Conversaciones con Frei Betto* (Havana, 1985).

SELECT BIBLIOGRAPHY

Betto, Frei. *Fidel and Religion: Castro Talks on Revolution and Religion with Frei Betto*. New York: Simon & Schuster, 1987.

Dewart, L. *Christianity and Revolution: The Lesson of Cuba*. New York: Herder & Herder, 1963.

Fernández, M. *Religión y Revolición en Cuba: Ceinticinco Años de Lucha Asteísta*. Miami-Caracas: Saeta Ediciones; Colección Realidades, 1984.

Gómez Treto, R. "The Church in Cuba after the Revolution." *International Christian Digest*, vol. 3, no. 7. Nashville, TN and Peterborough: Methodist Publishing House, Sep. 1989.

—. *La Iglesia Católica durante la Construcción del Socialismo en Cuba*. San José, Costa Rica: DEI, 1987. Eng. trans. *The Church and Socialism in Cuba*. Maryknoll, N.Y.: Orbis, 1988.

—. "La Iglesia en Cuba: Del Vaticano II al ENEC, pasando por Medellin y Puebla." Paper given at the Annual Assembly of CEHILA/CUBA, April 1988, in *Boletín no. 5*.

Janz, D. "Perspectives: Castro and the Rebirth of the Church in Cuba." *Cross Currents*, vol. XXXVIII, no. 4. Mercy College, N.Y.: Convergence, pp. 435–42.

Kirk, J. "From Counterrevolution to Modus Vivendi. The Church in Cuba, 1959–1984." Ed. S. Habelsky and J. Kirk, *Cuba: Twenty Five Years of Revolution*, 1959–1984. New York:

Stubbs, J. *Cuba: the Test of Time*. London: Latin America Bureau for Research and Action, 1989 (distributed in UK by Third World Publications, Birmingham; in USA by Monthly Review, N.Y.), pp. 22, 74, 113–4.

Tennant, W. "Cuba: the Church is Open." *America*, 24 Oct. 1987, pp. 266–9.

II: NICARAGUA (1979–90)
Angel Arnaiz Quintana

Although we are still very close to the ten years of Christian involvement in the Sandinista revolution, the intensity of the experience and its repercussions require an in-depth study. As Vice-President Sergio Ramírez said in Caracas on 28 June 1983: "The Sandinista revolution in Nicaragua arose as a historical response to a double situation: that of age-old injustice inside the country and and subjection to the imperial interests of the United States from outside. Both conditions, of injustice and domination, are closely woven into Nicaraguan history and into that of the Latin American continent. We can also state, therefore, that the Sandinista revolution is a historic Latin American response, or part of a response, to injustice and domination."

We have to judge the events and see our current situation from this viewpoint. A revolution means bringing about deep and rapid change in a society in favour of the impoverished majorities. The Sandinista revolution was a moderate one, led by the FSLN in the nationalist and popular spirit of Augusto César Sandino, who with an army composed of workers and peasants succeeded in expelling the U.S. Marines from the country in 1933, after a struggle lasting over six years. The following year, he was assassinated by those the United States had left behind in the country to look after their interests: Anastasio Somoza and his caucus, who were to maintain a bloody dictatorship, protected by successive U.S. administrations, for forty-five years. The principles informing the Sandinista revolution were political pluralism, a mixed economy, international non-alignment and representative and participatory democracy.

The Christians who participated actively in the revolution were mainly Catholics, since Protestants and Evangelicals were a small minority in 1979, though their numbers were to grow rapidly (see the statistical table at the end of section 3). Their Christianity was basically popular, theologically backward, though with very active and thinking minorities, drawn into the revolutionary process by a deeply Christian ethical and moral feeling, without at first becoming involved overmuch in theoretical discussion. They were concerned to do away with corruption and injustice, abuses of power and assassinations, to create a society in which the poor would have opportunities and their voice could be heard.

From January 1978 to February 1990, three stages of Christian participation in the revolutionary process can be distinguished:

(i) January 1978 – July 1990: Christian pluralism in the triumph of the revolution. The unity of the forces ranged against the Somoza dictatorship cannot hide the fact that Christians held a variety of positions in the struggle: there were Christians in all social classes of society, from the allies of Somoza through the middle classes dependent on him to the Sandinista guerrillas. Each sector reflected its Christian convictions in different ways, though a theological analysis of this would have to start from their practical actions and the words they used to support them. The fact that the Church embraced all classes became particularly evident at such a critcial juncture.

(ii) May 1980 – July 1986: Toward overall internal confrontation. The dynamic of the war imposed on Nicargua by conservative interests in the United States gradually polarized political attitudes inside the country and created strong tensions within the Church, reaching its height with the support expressed by some of the bishops for President Reagan's request to Congress to unfreeze a hundred million dollars of aid to the contra-revolutionary forces. This inspired the Nicaraguan Foreign Minister, the Maryknoll priest Miguel D'Escoto, to non-violent and prophetic protest actions that had a powerful impact inside the country and internationally. The "Low Intensity Conflict" promoted by the U.S. administration following their defeat in Vietnam involved destruction of economic centres and a huge propaganda apparatus, as well as the so-called "Polonization" of the Church, which consisted in creating a focus of opposition to Sandinismo based on church structures and built around the figure of Mgr Obando y Bravo, later to be appointed Cardinal.

(iii) July 1986 – February 1990: Politics of mediation and neo-Christendom. The wear and tear brought on by confrontation and the seriousness of the situation in Central America produced a change in the Vatican's attitude to Nicaragua. Despite difficulties, a line of dialogue and collaboration was established between the government and the Catholic hierarchy, though within the Catholic Church, those who supported the popular Sandinista process still had official support withdrawn from them. The Catholic Church promoted a line of dialogue in accordance with its institutional ambitions and the project of neo-Christendom it was trying to impose on the whole of Latin America.

(iv) February 1990– : Institutional presence in the new government. The longing for peace of a people bled by the contra war brought a coalition of parties created by the United States to power in the February 1990 election. The presence and influence of Cardinal Obando and those sectors of the Church identified with his political position in the new government are evident. The objectives of neo-Christendom will be at least partly achieved. The bishops of Nicaragua, as one theologian wrote earlier, in 1985, "not only failed to move beyond an antiquated view of the role of the Church in society, but remained faithful to their links with one particular social class, the bourgeoisie. So when the Nicaraguan bourgeoisie supported Somoza, the bishops supported Somoza; when the Nicaraguan bourgeoisie opposed Somoza, the bishops opposed Somoza; when the Nicaraguan bourgoisie sympathized with the Sandinistas, the bishops sympathized with the Sandinistas; when the bourgeoisie broke with the Sandinistas, the bishops broke with the Sandinistas too. Not only are they tied to a social class, but in effect the Bishops Conference of Nicaragua has acted, and especially is acting now, as a political party."[1] A new historical era began in Nicaragua in 1990.

Let us now look at each of these stages in greater detail.

1. JANUARY 1978 – MAY 1980: A DIVIDED CHURCH AND POLITICAL PLURALISM

The assassination of the newspaperman Pedro Joaquín Chamorro Cardenal on Somoza's orders raised the level of popular insurrection. The Sandinista Front started the final uprising in September 1978 and this triumphed on 19 July 1979. During this final uprising, while the dictator ordered the bombing of towns such as Estelí and León, the papal nuncio in Managua, Mgr Montalvo, drank toasts with him in the so-called National Festival. Other priests featured as chaplains in Somoza's National Guard, with officer rank. Many priests and nuns closed the doors of their houses, schools and convents at the height of the fighting to prevent combatants and wounded being brought in. And when the revolution triumphed, many left the country never to return.

Besides this Catholic Church identified with Somoza, there were Sandinista guerrillas and their families, large sectors of the population as a whole, and their leaders, who fought and organized for motives inspired wholly by faith. When the revolution triumphed on that 19 July, the people expressed their faith in thanksgiving, wore rosaries round their necks, attended vigils, made vows. . . . One month later, the men and women of the religious orders in Nicaragua issued a statement of support for the revolutionary process: "With immense joy we see a new period in Nicaraguan history being inaugurated . . . We all know the option the most conscientious Christians have made for the liberation of the poor. We have, at risk to our lives, taken part in the process that has led to victory."[2] Two priests, Francisco Luis Espinosa and Gaspar García Laviana, were among those who gave their lives in the struggle. Several more took part in the new "government of national reconstruction." These were the symbol of the massive Christian participation in the revolutionary process, a historical event of immense significance, unknown before then. Even the bishops, in a famous Pastoral Letter dated 17 November 1979, supported the process and viewed with some favour the sort of socialism that might be established in Nicaragua. The papal nuncio had been changed, and the current one had taken part in the changes in Algeria. Soon, however, he too was to be moved on.

The stance adopted by the bishops reflected that of the bourgeoisie: indecisive and wavering. The documents they produced in the months following the triumph of the revolution reflect this: on one hand support for the struggle in June 1979 and the November Pastoral Letter mentioned above; on the other, silences and attempts at compromise with the intervention of the U.S. embassy, as in the case of Mgr Obando, who was in Caracas with representatives of the traditional parties at the time of the triumph, trying to find a way of getting Somoza out of the country. At the end of July 1979, in the middle of the euphoria of successful revolution and the obvious deprivations it brought, they issued a Pastoral on the dangers and limitations of the moment.

In February 1980 the CELAM of López Trujillo instigated an international campaign of prayers for Nicaragua. Inside the country, it promoted studies, seminars and discussions as though there had never been any pastoral work done in Nicaragua, all on the most conservative lines, such as the lectures the theologian Boaventura Kloppenburg gave to bishops and priests. It looked as though López Trujillo wanted to be recognized in Rome as a champion of anti-communism, and had chosen Nicaragua as his platform. In effect, it earned him a cardinal's hat.[3]

In April and May 1980 a serious crisis upset the alliance existing among various factions in the government. Violeta Barrios de Chamorro, Pedro Joaquín's widow (now President) and the agro-exporter Alfonso Robelo, the representatives of the bourgeoisie, left the government of national reconstruction, trying thereby to provoke chaos in the revolutionary state, which they failed to achieve. Some of the communications media also took part in the crisis, such as the daily newspaper La Prensa, which led Pedro Joaquín Chamorro's chief remaining collaborators on the paper to walk out and start another paper, El Nuevo Diario. So these two, plus the official organ of the FSLN, Barricada, were all run by different members of the Chamorro family, an indication of the state of affairs in the country. In the midst of all this, the bishops issued a communiqué on 13 May requiring the priests who were members of the government to relinquish their posts, since they regarded the "state of exception" which allowed them to hold these posts under Canon Law as now over. Those involved replied that this "state of exception" was still in existence. The same document also de-commissioned several centres of theological study and pastoral work. This was the first intra-church conflict to appear in the wake of the revolution.

In March the great "literacy" campaign had opened, which in six months was to reduce illiteracy in the population from over 50 to 12 percent. Priests and nuns, many from schools, took part in this tremendous mobilization. The contacts they made with the extreme poverty in which much of the population lived made an enormous impression on them, to the extent that by the end of the campaign, many of them were questioning their way of life and the institution they were part of. Some were removed from their posts and even from Nicaragua, since they were seen as becoming "communists"; other more sensitive religious orders began or continued to station their members among the urban or rural poor.

The revolution was progressing, and each day that passed forced people to define their position in relation to it.

2. MAY 1980 – JULY 1986: "POLONIZATION" AND POLARIZATION OF THE CHURCH

The massive participation of Christians in a process of a deep change to the benefit of the poor majorities was viewed with alarm in power centres concerned with America. So an alternative project was devised, in which the institutional Church united around its chief representative was to become a bulwark of opposition to *Sandinismo*. So the "Polish model," to which Pope Woytila was so sympathetic, was reproduced. The weakness of the traditional parties was much strengthened by alliance with this church model.

The first step, in conjunction with other contestatory actions, was the removal of a number of priests and religious brothers and sisters from their pastoral appointments. They were either expelled directly, or indirectly, by means such as non-renewal of their contracts in parishes, institutes, schools and the like. Though several dioceses were affected, the process was most marked in Mgr Obando's archdiocese of Managua. Among tens of priests and religious whose removal he procured were the well-known cases of the Dominican Manuel Batalla, the diocesan priest Arias Caldera, the Franciscan Mauro Iacomelli, the Sisters of the Assumption of St Jude, the Carmelite Sisters of Chiliquistagua. . . . It is no exaggeration to speak of a real persecution within the Church, by some bishops, of those religious most closely identified with a progressive pastoral approach.

Faced with this turn of events, in October 1980 the Sandinista Front issued a famous document on the principles that guided its actions in the religious field, the first such by a revolutionary party in power. This recognized that Christians motivated by their faith had taken part in the process of change and were *de facto* members of the FSLN. It declared the principles of religious freedom, the lay nature of the state, and respect for the religious traditions of the people. Many in the Church were delighted by this declaration. The Bishops' Conference, however, pointed to totalitarianism, atheism, manipulation of the Church and other evils, in its response to the document. Anti-communism was, without further justification, held to be a legitimate weapon in destabilizing the established government.

In the meantime, evangelical and Protestant churches were continuing their process of penetrating the convulsed social fabric of Nicaragua. Broad sectors of the population came under the influence of Adventist or Latter-day churches. A huge campaign of the "Christ is coming. Be ready" type was spread across the country. This campaign coincided with the increase in contra activity in peasant zones in the north and centre of Nicaragua, which led people to see a correlation between the two. Other churches, those known as "mainstream," such as the Baptist, Lutheran and Anglican, adopted their own, often supportive, attitudes to the revolution.

In the Atlantic Coast region, which makes up half the country, sparsely populated and occupied by ethnic groups such as the Miskito and Sumo Indians, blacks and mulattos, religious influence on events was very pronounced. The native peoples mostly belong to the Moravian Church, the others to the Catholic Church, and their whole political, military, social and religious history has been largely *sui generis*. The Sandinista government, after some initial mistakes, responded with a Law of Autonomy of the Atlantic Coast which was exemplary in its recognition of the historic rights of the native peoples. Bishops, priests, pastors, religious brothers and sisters, delegates of the word and catechists have all played an often determining role in events that fashioned the course taken by "the Coast."

The campaign to "Polonize" the Church led to the disawoval of the broad Christian sector that supported the revolutionary process. It was accused of politicizing the gospel, manipulating the Church and being unfaithful to its legitimate pastors, i.e. the bishops, particularly Mgr Obando, and even of not being in communion with the Pope. It had formed itself into a "parallel church," its political opponents said, a popular church. Radio Católica de Nicaragua, controlled from the archdiocesan curia, spoke of "true Catholics," as opposed to those in the popular church. The alarm spread to Rome; a letter from Pope John Paul II dated 29 June 1982 spoke of the unity of the Church and the popular church, which, said the Pope, can have a double meaning: that already attributed to it or a meaning sanctified by tradition in the Church as making up the people of God.

Events were to reach a culmination with the announced visit of the Pope to Central America and in particular to Nicaragua. This was to set the seal on many recent tendencies. The contra war was growing in intensity: the day before the Pope visited Managua, a vigil was held over the corpses of seventeen young men killed in an ambush. The Pope was expected to talk of peace. There was a huge crowd: the government had mobilized all possible forms of transport to enable people to attend. When the crowd asked for peace and a prayer for the young men killed, the Pope spoke of the Church, of unity around the bishops and Mgr Obando. The shouts grew louder. It all ended with a general feeling of frustration in all quarters. The international news media saw it as a profanation and an insult to the Pope; Catholics were divided, some seeing it as Sandinista manipulation of the crowd, others as the Pope's failure to live up to the expectations aroused by his visit, because he had been badly briefed. What is certain is that on that 3 March 1983 an entire people had told the Pope something he was not used to hearing. The people had given voice and demanded to be heard, not just to listen.[4]

Popular faith was also affected by the controversy. This was of course purely political, since no one was discussing doctrinal or moral matters, although the opponents of the revolution often tried to shift the debate on to these grounds.

Rumours abounded, tensions mounted, there were crowded demonstrations while others simply abandoned their beliefs and practices, and meanwhile the advance of the revolutionary process and that of Protestant bodies changed matters profoundly. One significant event, for example, was what happened to a much-venerated image of Christ Crucified in Managua known as The Blood of Christ. The Capuchin fathers had been responsible for its veneration since 1916, but in Holy Week 1985, after the traditional Good Friday procession, it was taken without their permission to a different parish church. The archbishop did not want it looked after by members of the popular church, which he considered the Capuchins to be. Their protests to Rome were in vain.

In April 1985, Mgr Obando received a cardinal's hat in Rome. Before returning to Nicaragua, he said his first mass as a cardinal in Miami, where a large group of Somoza supporters and their allies were living in self-imposed exile, and many of them took part in this mass. Back in Nicaragua, he toured all the dioceses, encouraging strongly anti-Sandinista demonstrations in all of them.

The contra war was further escalated, and affected most of the country from the Honduran border in the north to the Costa Rican border in the south. The economic boycott imposed by the US administration was also strengthened. Fuel depots, cement works and other strategic points were bombed, ports mined and other terrorist activity increased. The numbers of dead, homeless, orphans, kidnap victims and maimed grew daily. The three million plus population of Nicaragua was being subjected to an infernal process of bloodshed and destruction. In July 1985, the Foreign Minister, Miguel D'Escoto, embarked on a long hunger strike in a parish church in Managua to draw attention and provoke a Christian response to this unjustified aggression. Thousands of Nicaraguans and Christians all over the the world joined with him.

The following February, faced with the continuance of the war, D'Escoto undertook a "Way of the Cross" from the Honduran border, source of most of the aggression, to Managua. This non-violent protest also had a great effect on the population, although the polarization of Nicaraguan society was by then an established fact, and many rejected his gesture. At the end of this Way of the Cross, mass was concelebrated in front of Managua cathedral, largely destroyed by the 1972 earthquake, by over seventy priests, a number which, taken with those who expressed their solidarity but were unable to come, represents about half the priests in the country, then a little over two hundred. D'Escoto himself spoke with a vigour that amazed everyone, in terms that recalled the Old Testament prophets. Strong things were said, including the suggestion that Cardinal Obando should cease saying mass, since he was an accomplice in the deaths that were taking place in Nicaragua.

It was actually at this time that Cardinal Obando and the Bishop of Juigalpa, Mgr Pablo Vega, went to Washington to support President Reagan's request to a divided Congress for a hundred million dollars in aid to the contras. Reagan himself acknowledged the importance of the bishops' presence for the furtherance of his plan. They rallied the Republican Party behind a scheme that divided public opinion in the United States, where pacifists and supporters of Nicaragua demonstrated against the war aims of the administration.

These events marked the maximum degree of confrontation, both by the anti-Sandinista church against the revolution, and within the Church itself, between those who supported and those who opposed the aims of the revolution.

3. JULY 1986 – FEBRUARY 1990: A POLICY OF MEDIATION

The damage done to the Church as well as the government by these confrontations, plus the overall concerns of the Catholic Church for America and the advice given to Rome, produced a shift in Vatican policy toward Nicaragua. The nuncio was changed again, with just one residence, in Managua. The new one was Paolo Giglio, fresh from important diplomatic relations with the national church of China, itself an indication of what his approach was likely to be.

In September 1986, church-state dialogue was re-opened, and despite various interruptions, this at least served to cover over the tensions. The number of bishops was also increased, from seven in 1979 to twelve ten years later. Though they had preserved outward unity, it was known that there were different viewpoints among them, and that the four Franciscans in particular were anxious to treat the government with greater respect.

At the end of 1986, the Iran-contra scandal broke in the United States, demonstrating the illegality of the administration's actions even in relation to the laws of the country. Some months earlier, the International Court of Justice in The Hague, the highest authority of its kind, had declared the contra war illegal according to international law. But neither one event nor the other prevented the continued flow of funds to carry on the war. One of the bombs financed by the Reagan government killed the Franciscan Tomás Zavaleta and one of his catechists, seriously wounding several other Franciscans and their companions. This was on 3 July 1987.

The same year saw the beginning of talks between the Central American presidents known as the Esquipulas agreement, aimed at ending all the wars in the region and especially that in Nicaragua. One of its provisions was the establishment of national commissions of reconciliation. President Daniel Ortega offered the presidency of the Nicaraguan commission to Cardinal Obando. It was in Nicaragua that most progress was made, and for a moment it looked as though agreement between the government and the contras would be reached. But once again, intervention by the United States, which boycotted the agreement, meant the continuance of the war. *Sandinismo*, in Washington's view, had to be eliminated; there could be no agreement or compromise with it. The U.S. ambassador to Nicaragua was even responsible for drawing up a plan to destabilize the government, known as the Melton plan. This was exposed in Mexican newspapers, and the government had no option but to expel him and various embassy officials from Nicaragua. The plan included a letter from the bishops alleging persecution, and this was published as planned. This worsened relations between Managua and Washington, and once more led to a cooling of church-state relations.

When the bishops made their *ad limina* visit to Rome in 1988, they protested their fidelity to the Pope and the Marian and eucharistic fervour of the Nicaraguan people, united with their legitimate pastors. The only fly in the ointment was a group of priests, religious, nuns and lay people "belligerently" trying to divide the Church. This according to Cardinal Obando. The practical result of this was that many pastoral agents, working with full permission of their superiors and in compliance with canonical requirements, failed to receive licenses to carry on their work, and those who declared themselves open to the Sandinista process were removed, either from office or from the country. This determined intra-church persecution was still operative in 1989.

At the end of ten years of Sandinista government, the growth statistics of the churches, according to government figures, were as follows:

	1979	1988	Growth	Growth %
CATHOLIC CHURCH				
Parishes	167	178	11	6
Diocesan clergy	144	167	23	16
Religious congregations	54	83	29	54
Male religious	149	272	123	83
Women religious	400	621	221	55
Seminaries	2	10	8	400
PROTESTANT (EVANGELICAL) CHURCHES				
Denominations	46	120	74	150
Pastors	1500	2000	500	34
Practising members (as % of population)	3.5	17.5	14	400

4. 1990: THE NEW GOVERNMENT AND ITS RELATIONS WITH THE CHURCH

The need for peace after the appalling bloodshed in relation to the size of the population and the physical destruction and economic collapse brought about by nine years of war, led to the U.S. alternative winning the day in the February 1990 elections, the cleanest in Nicaragua's history. The Cardinal's influence, and that of the Catholic Church in general, on the new government is evident. In this sense, we have the best scenario for the implantation of neo-Christendom, in which the Church legitimizes the civil power in exchange for assuring its position in society through benefits and privileges in the fields of communication, education, law and even finance.

There is still, however, a broad church sector remaining faithful to the liberation of the poor along lines closer to popular understanding and organization. Furthermore, social and cultural conditions have changed in Nicaragua over these ten years, and the sort of control possible in the past can no longer be exercised. There is also the growing membership of evangelical sects and Protestant churches, a major factor in some social groups. One way or another, the next months and years should see an increase in dynamism on the part of Christian groupings, despite the de-Christianization of some sectors of the population, who either have never been evangelized or have abandoned their faith on acount of the lack of witness provided by church representatives over the past ten years.

Translated from the Spanish by Paul Burns

NOTES

1. Frei Betto, interviewed in *Amanecer* 8 (Apr. 1982), p. 12. See also his *El compromiso cristiano con Nicaragua, Nicaruac* 5 (Apr. 1985).

2. *Barricada*, 19 Aug. 1979, p. 1. This daily paper, as well as *La Prensa* and *El Nuevo Diario*, the three national papers, have given extensive coverage to the religious dimension, and can provide the background to the data given here. See also the Select Bibliography below.

3. José María Vigil, *Nicaragua y los teólogos* (Mexico, 1987), pp 88–9, interview with Jose Comblin. See also the interview with Ernesto Bravo in *Amanecer* 10 (July 1982), p. 16.

4. IEPALA, *El Papa en Nicaragua* (Madrid, 1983). Contains ample documentation on the visit, including the vital document, classified "top secret," "How the Pope was briefed: the key document," pp, 161–76. Besides giving an idealized and very one-sided view of Nicaragua, this insists on the need to build up the figure of the then Bishop Obando, as well as giving the Polish example as a model on several points, such as asking for a Polish nuncio, or uniting around the primate, "as has been the case in Poland."

SELECT BIBLIOGRAPHY

Cabestrero, T. *Ministros de Dios, ministros del pueblo*. Bilbao: Desclée, 1983. Eng. trans. *Ministers of God, Ministers of the People*. Maryknoll, N.Y.: Orbis, 1986.

—. *Revolucionarios por el Evangelio*. Bilbao: Desclée, 1983. Eng. trans. *Revolutionaries for the Gospel*. Maryknoll, N.y.: Orbis, 1985.

Casaldáliga, P. *Nicaragua: combate y profecía*. Madrid: Misión Abierta, 1986.

Girardi, G. *Faith and Revolution in Nicaragua*. Maryknoll, N.Y.: Orbis, 1986.

—. *Sandinismo, marxismo, cristianismo: la confluencia*. Managua: Centro Antonio Valdivieso, 1987.

— and J. M. Vigil. *Nicaragua trinchera teológica*. Managua: Centro A. Valdivieso; Salamanca: Lóguez, 1987.

Ezcurra, A. M. *Agresión ideológica contra la revolución sandinista*. Mexico: Nuevomar-Claves, 1983.

Martínez, A. *Las sectas en Nicaragua*. Managua: Centro A. Valdivieso; San José: DEI, 1989.

Reviews. *Amanecer*. Managua: Centro A. Valdivieso; *Envío*. Managua: Instituto Histórico Centroamericano.

Various. *Fe cristiana y revolución sandinista en Nicaragua*. Managua: IHCA, 1979.

Chapter 25

THE CHURCH AND DEFENCE OF HUMAN RIGHTS

José Comblin

How can one sum up these last two decades in the history of the Church? I have chosen "human rights" as the theme which symbolizes the action of the Latin American Church in this period. For twenty years human rights gave the Church a *raison d'être* and a mission in the world. Now, at the beginning of the new decade, the mission of defending human rights has run out of steam. The Church is looking for a different definition in the midst of a society which is more puzzling than ever, and cannot find one. Can the "new evangelization" be anything more in Latin America than an appearance of programme covering a lack of direction?

The historical situation to which both Vatican II and Medellín were a response has disappeared very quickly. The majority of Latin American bishops had barely returned to their diocese, when they were faced with new situations.

Medellín sought to respond to the challenge of revolutionary vanguardism inspired by the Cuban model. The revolutionary vanguards were speedily eliminated. On the one hand, they suffered the repression of the dictatorships, but there was also something more serious: they realized that they were failing to interest the mass of the poor. They were cut off from the impoverished masses: how could they liberate them without their support or against their will?

Almost all Latin American countries went through a phase of military dictatorship following the programme of the doctrine of national security. These dictatorships fought against revolutionary movements, and also destroyed political and economic nationalism. They promoted a neo-liberal economic model, and sought integration into the geopolitical scheme of the United States.

In almost every country the local churches eventually resisted the terrorism practised by the military governments: they led the struggle for human rights in a number of countries and cooperated with other bodies in other countries.

After only a few years the military governments had run out of energy. They had ceased to receive encouragement from the metropolitan countries and their more perceptive leaders, such as General Golbery do Couto e Silva in Brazil, realized that the military could achieve the same ends without recourse to the dangerous expedient of directly exercising political power. Accordingly, the military did not ultimately oppose the return to democracy called for by the popular movements and the Church. The last military dictatorship fell in 1989 in Chile.

However, the return to democracy did not lead to the hoped-for mobilization of strong popular movements and a policy of social reforms capable of reversing the serious decline in the situation of the masses. The new democracies confirmed the neo-liberal models and further increased the injustices in the distribution of wealth. The masses in general elected conservative presidents for their charismatic qualities: Collor de Mello in Brazil, Menem in Argentina, Fujimori in Peru, Paz Estenssoro in Bolivia, and even Carlos Andrés Pérez in Venezuela.

Two years into the 1990s the diagnosis is as follows: failure of democracy, incapable of bringing about changes which are now more urgently needed than ever, failure of economic liberalism, which was responsible for the "lost decade" of the 1980s, and failure of socialism, dealt a mortal blow in 1973 in Chile. At present the remains of the left are searching for something new in the face of the collapse of the Soviet Union and its satellites. And now? Irrational popular rebellions? A new decade of paralysis? Who can say? No-one dares to proclaim the future. Twenty years ago everyone knew what was going to happen. But it didn't happen.

And the Church? First of all, there is a mass movement: the masses are leaving Catholicism for Pentecostal Protestantism. It is the most important religious movement since the sixteenth century. The Catholic Church is losing the masses almost without realizing the fact and without doing anything about it. It is totally powerless in the face of this mass phenomenon. Shackled by medieval structures, but unwilling and unable to change these structures, the Church looks on passively while its bases disintegrate. The Catholic hierarchy has lost all power of decision.

Rome is fighting against a non-existent modern world, and against a communism which died twenty years ago. Rome is fighting to recreate an extreme centralism which is dealing the mortal blow. The new Roman centralism is paralyzing the clergy at the time they most need creativity and freedom. But the Vatican's information network is made up of fanatics incapable of understanding the course of events.

The Medellín Church saw its plans and hopes for a Church of the poor frustrated by the military governments. Liberation was reduced to the most urgent task, the struggle for human rights. This struggle, however, while occupying the space of the struggle for liberation, was unable to produce a genuine liberation. The Medellín Church set up a Church of activists (base church communities, ministries to the poor) at the moment at which the masses were awakening. Today the masses are choosing Pentecostalism in its various forms. Even within the Catholic Church, the most rapidly growing movement is Catholic Charismatic Renewal. Hence the perplexity of bishops as they look forward into the 1990s, after two decades which gave the lie to all forecasts.

1. THE DECLINE OF THE REVOLUTIONARY VANGUARDS

The example of Cuba was convincing for much of the Catholic élite, those who could not accept the situation of "institutionalized violence" in Latin America (the phrase was used by the Medellín bishops' conference). The death of the Colombian priest Camilo Torres with the guerrillas in 1965 and the death of Che Guevara in Bolivia in 1967 did not dampen the enthusiasm. The revolutionaries refused to see the warnings embodied in these two deaths. On the contrary, the heroism was attractive, all the more if it ended in tragedy. The popularity of the Cuban model continued. It was at its height at the time of the bishops' conference at Medellín in 1968 (the Second Latin American Episcopal Conference).

In turn great Catholic leaders went to Cuba, being received with the greatest possible respect by Fidel Castro: first the Bishop of Cuernavaca, Sergio Mendes Arceo, then the Nicaraguan priest and poet Ernesto Cardenal, the Nicaraguan foreign minister and priest Miguel D'Escoto, the Brazilian Frei Betto, whose account of the visit, *Fidel and Religion* (1985) became a world bestseller. In 1971, during his visit to Allende's Chile, Fidel had had an interview with Chilean priests and had received a bible from the hands of Cardinal Silva. These were signs of a an increasingly rapid coming together. Ten years earlier this coming together could have had a decisive influence. Now it was too late.

In the context of Medellín, of the student movements of 1967–8 and the appearance of guerrilla movements in many Latin American countries, movements of "dissident" priests appeared in a number of countries (1968–9). They challenged both the church structure and the social structure: examples were "priests for the Third World" in Argentina, ONIS in Peru, the Golconda movement in Colombia, and less important groups in other countries. There were no such movements in Chile and Brazil. The countries in which there were such priests' movements went through, and are still going through, a more severe form of internal Church repression.

These movements were short-lived. They suffered repression from the police and the armed forces, some priests were killed, many were rejected by the hierarchy and many chose a process of secularization. Some joined guerrilla movements, but few, a tiny proportion.

In 1972 the guerrilla movements had been broken by the security apparatus in almost every country, for example, in Brazil, Peru, Bolivia and Uruguay, and the Colombian guerrillas had been neutralized. The revolutionaries' hopes turned to the Chile of Salvador Allende's Popular Unity (1970–3). In Chile young Christians were drawn to work with Popular Unity, within two parties which were small but important because they contained an intellectual élite, MAPU (1969) and the Christian Left (1971).

Catholic intellectuals and university students, especially those trained by Catholic Action, were irresistibly drawn to Marxism-Leninism. The prototype was *Açao Popular* ("Popular Action"), founded in 1962 in Brazil by former members of JUC (the university wing of Catholic Action). In 1976 *Açao Popular* decided to affiliate formally to the *Partido Comunista do Brasil*, a more revolutionary breakaway from the traditional communist party, the *Partido Comunista Brasileiro*.

In April 1972 in Santiago de Chile four hundred revolutionary priests and lay people attended the founding congress of the movement "Christians for Socialism". The military coup of 11 September 1973 in Chile dealt a mortal blow to Christians for Socialism. With Allende's regime there disappeared the dream of a democratic transition to socialism. Neither guerrilla war nor democracy, so what? The Latin American Left went into a deep crisis from which it has still not emerged.

It is true that there was one further tragic event in Argentina, so absurd that it appears surreal. Perón, the charismatic leader exiled since 1955, returned in

1972, engineered the election of his surrogate, Hector Campos, as President in 1973, forced him to resign and regained the presidency in 1973, but died a few months later, leaving the country in a state of total anarchy. Since 1972 two guerrilla movements, ERP and the Montoneros, had competed to win power. At the same time Perón himself had permitted the organization of ferocious repression: on 23 June 1973 three hundred young people who had gone to welcome Perón at Ezeiza airport were killed by firing squads while Perón was landing at the military airport of Morón. It was a portent of things to come. Isabel Perón, the widow of the leader, became President, but did nothing or chose to do nothing to check the repression. When the military took power in 1976, the guerrillas had already been defeated, but the new government was to use the guerrillas as pretext for wiping out all the youthful supporters of revolution: thirty thousand were tortured or disappeared. Among them were many young Catholics. It is not too much to say that the élite of young Catholics was wiped out in the repression directed against the guerrilla movements, whether they had been members of movements or simply sympathizers or suspected of being sympathizers. This happened above all in Brazil, Argentina, Uruguay, Peru and Colombia. It removed a whole generation, whose loss was to be felt later.

The survivors of this lost generation have now gone into the political parties of the new democracies. They are all converts to democracy and human rights. All long ago rejected the Soviet system and those who remain faithful to Marxism give it a content more symbolic than real. The real Marxist faithful are the old guard, who were already Marxists before the events of 1965–75.

There is, or appears to be, one exception to this development, Central America. In Central America the guerrillas reached their peak after their disappearance in South America. In Nicaragua the guerrilla movement had remained very limited until 1978. Then the excesses of Somoza's repression provoked a popular insurrection which eventually achieved victory on 19 July 1979. It was the first guerrilla victory since Cuba.

Nevertheless the conditions were already different. The Sandinista movement did not seek to apply a Marxist programme. Its popular base was narrow; it was provided with a base by the "popular church." In the Sandinista government there were three priest ministers and many convinced lay Christians. The Sandinista regime was made up to a large extent of Christians, and they exerted considerable influence on the regime.

Would Nicaragua be a new example for Latin America? In Nicaragua many people thought that El Salvador would go the same way. From 1976–7 violence increased. From 1980 El Salvador was in a state of civil war. Guatemala too has been in a state of civil war for almost twenty years. In the Salvadorean and Guatemalan revolutionary movements Christians occupy prominent positions. Many are refugees from a Christian Democracy which let them down.

The 1990 elections in Nicaragua, however, showed that that country too is tending to be reabsorbed into the so-called democratic system. For how long? The Salvadorean and Guatemalan guerrillas have been seeking negotiations, which in the case of El Salvador produced a peace agreement at the end of 1991. Similarly, the guerrilla movements in Colombia have been seeking negotiations. What has been hoped for since 1967–71 is coming to pass: the guerrilla road is being abandoned by the majority of left-wing groups, and also by Christians. There is still *Sendero Luminoso*, the Shining Path, which has been operating in Peru since 1980, followed by the Tupac-amaru movement, but Christians are not involved. For Catholics the cycle of the revolutionary vanguards has come to an end.

The hierarchical Church from the beginning rejected any rapprochement with the guerrilla movements. For ten years in Cuba there was no relationship of any sort with Fidel Castro's government; only in the 1970s was a degree of *de facto* tolerance achieved. Even today Catholics are excluded from political life and from the universities. Medellín rejected the solution of violent insurrection, but declared it comprehensible. It was the most that could be expected. Paul VI's sermons in Colombia in 1968 before Medellín had been much more trenchant. Toward the Latin American guerrillas Rome had always been intransigent. The reason was probably not so much rejection of violence as such, since in Nicaragua Pope John Paul II did not say a word in condemnation of the anti-Sandinista guerrillas; he had not before, nor did he later. A number of Nicaraguan bishops showed public support for the anti-Sandinista guerrillas. The Church's rejection is directed at left-wing movements, not at violence itself. Nevertheless, a few weeks before the Sandinista victory in 1979, the Nicaraguan bishops proclaimed the legitimacy of the popular insurrection which was already winning (2 June 1979).

The hierarchy's rejection applied not only to guerrilla socialism, but also to the democratic transition, as in the case of Chile. The hierarchy was expressing the views of Catholics. In Chile Catholics voted for the Right or the Christian Democrats. The bishops' sympathies tended toward Christian Democracy. The alliance with socialism was rejected in a document published within days of the 1973 military coup. Paul VI's shift toward "democratic" socialism in *Octagesima Adveniens* (1971) was generally well received in some lay circles, but was unpopular in the hierarchy or among the clergy in general. The bishops open to a socialist solution cannot have numbered more than ten in all of Latin America in the period of the Christians for Socialism movement. One of them was the Bishop of Cuernavaca (Mexico), Sergio Mendes Arceo, but everyone knew that Don Sergio was "atypical." He attended the Christians for Socialism congress in 1972, but his presence displeased the whole Chilean hierarchy.

The only place where greater openness toward socialism was shown was in Peru in 1971, in a preparatory document for the Roman synod. Coincidentally, the President of Peru at the time was General Velasco, and the military who held power were trying to implement a socialist programme.

Again in Nicaragua, after the Sandinista victory, the bishops published a statement recognizing a sort of socialism (17 November 1979), but from that date onwards the bishops' conference showed no further sign of conciliation. A few months later a new policy was established at the instigation of CELAM: the bishops chose confrontation.

2. THE CHURCH AND THE NATIONAL SECURITY MILITARY DICTATORSHIPS

From 1947, as part of the opening of the cold war, the United States adopted the doctrine of national security as the basis of its foreign policy. This was first and foremost a military doctrine, a doctrine about war. It was developed in military academies, basically in the U.S. National War College (1948). The idea is simple: We are in a total war. It is total because it involves all the nation's resources, because it involves time and space, total because all nations are involved in it. Very soon the strategists came to the conclusion that there would not be total, direct confrontation between the United States and the Soviet Union, but that the confrontation would take place in the Third World. In this field, ideological war was primary. It was imagined that the Soviet Union had achieved so many victories because of its ideological war.

In the American Panama Canal Zone the United States established military academies (including the College of the Americas) to teach thousands of Latin American army officers the doctrine of total war, national security, ideological war and the methods of conducting the war. For Latin America the doctrine included military takeovers of power in case of necessity. The doctrine asserted that Latin American democracies were too weak to fight against the communist ideological war.

Since ideological war occupied pride of place in the doctrine of national security, it was a matter of urgency to identify the enemy. The enemy were intellectual forces, among them the universities, the popular organizations and the Catholic Church. The military who seized power in Latin America between 1964 and 1976 were all converts to the doctrine of national security, and their programme was to apply the doctrine as taught in the United States (plus the French doctrine developed in the Algerian war). The only exceptions were the Peruvians and the Panamanians (1968), and General J. J. Torres in Bolivia (1970). The best pupils were the Argentines, the Uruguayans, the Brazilians, the Bolivians, the Paraguayans, the Chileans and the Central Americans.

The first national security military coup was staged in Brazil in 1964, and a second coup followed to stiffen the first in 1968 (Institutional Act No 5, which suspended the remaining public freedoms).

In 1968 there were nationalist military coups in Peru and Panama (Generals Velasco Alvarado and Omar Torrijos). These regimes did not come into conflict with the Church. In Bolivia General Banzer took power in 1971 and revealed himself a faithful follower of the doctrine. In Uruguay there were always civilian presidents, but the system was military. The national security doctrine was clearly dominant from 1973. In Chile the 1973 coup was carried out by the minority of the military trained in the North American doctrine. It was one of the harshest. In 1976 it was Argentina's turn: the regime of Generals Videla, then Viola and then Galtieri was the bloodiest of all. In Colombia there was no military coup, but in 1989 President Turbay gave the military all the powers of a national security system. Finally, in Central America the United States exercized a much more direct control over the armed forces. In the 1980s the doctrine of national security took the form of low-intensity warfare, but the methods established in the previous phase continued in use and gave the regimes instruments for an implacable repression (Somoza's Nicaragua and support for the contras, El Salvador, Guatemala, the invasion of Panama, and the *de facto* occupation of Honduras as a military base). In Paraguay the dictatorship of General Stroessner dated from 1954, but it adapted to circumstances and became as repressive as, if not more so than, the others. In

Ecuador the dictatorship was milder, but it became famous for the Riobamba episode, mentioned below.

In this period Vatican policy toward the Latin American military governments was defined by Cardinal Sebastian Baggio, president of the Pontifical Commission for Latin America. Baggio had been nuncio in Brazil during the early years of the military dictatorship. He was a loyal ally of the military and an equally constant adversary of the bishops who took a stand against the dictatorship. He was one of the most persistent enemies of Archbishop Helder Câmara. After Medellín Cardinal Samoré, the Holy See's representative at Medellín as the president of the Commission for Latin America, was sacked. He was held responsible for the excesses of Medellín; the Vatican immediately reacted against Medellín.

On 13 August 1976 a group of seventeen American bishops from eight different countries were arrested in Riobamba, Ecuador, and taken to a Quito barracks. There were four U.S. bishops, and the U.S. embassy protested, as did others. No protest came from the nuncio or from Cardinal Baggio, or from any representative of the Roman Curia. Quite the opposite: they forbade others to protest. Cardinal Baggio agreed. The nuncio of the time, Mgr Luigi Accogli, knew, agreed, and even insulted the detained bishops in the police barracks. The case attracted such comment in Ecuador that the nuncio was posted to Bangladesh.

CELAM's protest also carried little conviction. CELAM (the Latin American Episcopal Council) never condemned the doctrine of national security. During the whole period of military dictatorships CELAM never took a clear stand to defend the human rights violated with such excesses in so many countries.

In addition to this, the Latin American bishops who led the struggle for human rights in their countries were systematically disowned by Rome. Archbishop Helder Câmara (archbishop of Olinda and Recife from 1964 to 1984, exactly the period of the dictatorship) was persecuted by the Roman Curia and only survived through the personal confidence of Paul VI (who, however, did not dare to defend him publicly). In 1985 Helder Câmara was given a successor, Archbishop José Cardoso, whose mission was not only to undo the achievements of Dom Helder, but also to wipe out his memory. In Chile Cardinal Raul Silva led the resistance against General Pinochet, but met Roman opposition at every step. His appointed successor was the man Pinochet wanted. In Brazil, ever since he was appointed in 1970, Cardinal Paulo Evaristo Arns took the strongest possible stand in defence of human rights, not only in his diocese, but throughout Brazil and all over Latin America. He has received countless international awards in recognition of his fight for human rights. He has received countless honorary degrees on all continents. But both Rome and CELAM persecute him systematically. His diocese was divided into five sections in such a way as to deprive him of the poor areas, the idea being that he would thus lose his base of support. It can be said that almost all the bishops who have taken strong stands against the abuses of the military dictatorships were fought in Rome, were subjected to apostolic visitations, and, once they retired, were given successors with totally opposite views with the task of undoing all they had done.

At the time that Latin America entered the system of national security military dictatorships, there was a radical change in CELAM. Rome had not accepted Medellín. In the elections for the new leadership, held in Sucre in November 1972, the Holy See obliged the bishops to vote for its candidates. The pressure led to the election as president of the Argentine Archbishop Eduardo Pironio (later made a curial cardinal), and as general secretary of the young auxiliary bishop (ordained bishop only a year) of Bogotá, Alfonso López Trujillo (later to be archbishop of Medellín and cardinal). Alfonso López remained general secretary until 1979, and was then elected president. He abolished all the bodies and dismissed all the staff from the previous period, and made the institution an organ of personal power. From 1972 CELAM was a war machine directed against the theology of liberation, the base church communities, and particularly against the Brazilian bishops' conference.

In the individual bishops' conferences and among the clergy it is fair to say that the military coups were in general well received. The military were seen as saving the nation from an imminent communist invasion. However, the excesses of repression were so great and so arbitrary that a reaction took place in a number of episcopates. Catholics in general trusted the military. But there were so many victims that the crimes committed in the name of the anti-communist struggle could not be explained merely by individual lapses: there was a whole system at the root of the "internal war." Bishops were thus divided. Some placed themselves clearly alongside the military: among them were Dom Castro Mayer and Archbishop Sigaud in Brazil, Mgr Tortolo in Argentina, and the military bishops (leaders of the military chaplains) in general. In every country there were bishops favourable to the military and bishops who were critical, but the proportions varied greatly from country to country.

The bishops' conferences which overall supported the military were those of Argentina (the clearest case, only four or five dissidents out of sixty bishops), Uruguay, Colombia (a military dictatorship with a civilian president), Ecuador, El Salvador (one exception, Archbishop Oscar Romero, and his successor, Archbishop Rivera y Damas), and initially Guatemala. Those critical of the military included Brazil (except for a few individuals in a conference of 350 bishops), Chile (until new appointments swung the conference some way toward the military), Bolivia and Guatemala in recent years.

In Brazil the first condemnation of the doctrine of national security came from a text by Dom Cândido Padim published in 1968 as a preparation for Medellín. In 1964 the episcopal conference had hailed the military coup as a heroic act by the armed forces to save the country from communism. Archbishop Helder Câmara battled for seven years to change the attitudes of the Brazilian bishops, and in 1971 succeeded in changing the leadership. Dom Aloísio Lorscheider, first bishop of Santo Angelo in the southern state of Rio Grande do Sul, and from 1973 archbishop of Fortaleza in Ceará state in the North-East, was president for eight years and was succeeded by his cousin, Bishop Ivo Lorscheiter, of Santa Maria in Rio Grande do Sul, who was secretary for eight years and held the presidency for eight years. Dom Luciano Mendes de Almeida, archbishop of Mariana and formerly an auxiliary bishop in São Paulo, has been at the head of the Brazilian conference since 1987, after having been secretary for eight years. This was a period of twenty years of continuity, of declared independence vis à vis the dictatorship and overt struggle for human rights. Almost every year the conference published a document focusing on one or other aspect of the country's situation. The most striking was that of 1977: *Christian requirements for a political order.*

Locally three centres headed the struggle against the dictatorship's oppression. One was Recife with Archbishop Helder Câmara: in 1972 seventeen bishops and religious superiors published a manifesto, "I have heard the cries of my people," which received worldwide publicity. In the same year in the second centre, Goiânia, see of Archbishop Fernando Gomes (who died in 1985) there appeared another notable document, "The Marginalization of a People." The third centre is São Paulo. In 1975 the bishops of the state of São Paulo published "Thou shalt not oppress thy brother," to protest against the tortures and arbitrary actions of the dictatorship. In 1973 a group of bishops from Amazonia denounced the genocide inflicted on the Indians: "The Indian, doomed to die." In 1972 the Brazilian bishops' conference backed the establishment of CIMI (the Indigenist Missionary Council) to fight to defend the Indians, their land and their culture. Since then CIMI has supported hundreds of local struggles by indigenous tribes scattered right across Brazil.

Various justice and peace commissions, especially the National Commission and the São Paulo and Recife Commissions, took up the cause of the oppressed. Many bishops championed peasants driven off their land, Archbishop José Maria Pires of João Pessoa, Bishop Pedro Casaldáliga of São Félix do Araguaia, and generally the bishops of Amazonia, Maranhão and Mato Grosso.

In 1978 the National Secretariat for Justice and Non-Violence was founded in São Paulo. An international group of bishops met regularly to discuss social struggle by non-violent means. In 1982 a large number of bodies concerned with human rights held the First National Human Rights Meeting in Petrópolis.

An important initiative was taken by the Brazilian bishops' conference, at the suggestion of Dom Cândido Padim, in 1973, proposing the holding of an "International Conference for a Society Beyond Domination." The Brazilian conference had received the support of the bishops' conferences of the United States, Canada and France. The project had got as far as the setting up of a permanent secretariat in Paris, and the first meeting was planned for 1977 in Dakar. Rome forbade the meeting, and Cardinal Gantin toured the bishops' conferences to get them to withdraw their support.

In Chile, in the face of the horrendous violence of the military repression, immediately after the coup a Pro-Peace Committee was formed in Santiago with the aim of offering at least an attempt at support to all those persecuted. Gradually the methods of repression became known – systematic torture and the practice of "disappearing" detainees, who were held in secret detention centres by DINA, the political police, and then killed in secret. In 1975 the committee's work was taken over by Cardinal Raul Silva as a work of the diocese under the name "Vicariate of Solidarity." The guiding spirit of the Vicariate, as of the earlier Committee, was the priest Cristián Precht. His brilliant action at the forefront of the defence of human rights assured him a place on the military's death list; he was never made a bishop, although he was the real pastor of the diocese as vicar general in charge of pastoral work after the resignation of Cardinal Silva. The Vicariate of Solidarity became famous throughout the world for its courage. It dared to challenge Pinochet's absolutism. It is a safe assumption that the steadfast action of the Vicariate and of the bishops who supported it in their dioceses contributed to reducing the excesses of repressive violence: there were twenty times fewer victims than in Argentina, where the bishops refused ever to act publicly.

In Argentina the bishops as a body decided not to take any action which might irritate the military, or to utter any word which might displease them. It is said that they always consulted the generals about their doubts, the generals always said that nothing was wrong, and the bishops accepted the generals' denials. They shut the doors of their houses against the victims of repression. There were few exceptions. Only three stood up to the military: de Nevares (Neuquén), Hesayne (Viedma) and Novak (Quilmes).

When the Argentine architect, Adolfo Pérez Esquivel, after being arrested and tortured in abominable conditions for fourteen months for no reason, received the Nobel Peace Prize in 1980, the bishops' conference publicly dissociated itself from him and also rejected the international movement for non-violent action he founded, the "Peace and Justice Service" (SERPAJ), based in Rio de Janeiro.

Human rights work was done by members of other conferences, but in isolation. Among them were Archbishop Leonidas Proaño in Riobamba, Archbishop Sergio Mendes Arceo in Cuernavaca (Mexico), Bishops L. Bambarén and G. Schmidt, auxiliary bishops of Lima (Mgr Bambarén has since been moved to Chimbote). The most notable example was certainly that of Archbishop Oscar Romero, archbishop of San Salvador, in 1977. When he became archbishop, the violence of the paramilitary groups against all popular organizations was reaching a climax, eventually bringing about civil war in 1980 which continued until the end of 1991. El Salvador was the country in which the repression was most savage and took the highest toll, some 75,000, slaughtered by the armed forces and the death squads. Oscar Romero denounced all acts of violence and called for peace and justice with total frankness. He was killed by a crack gunman in the middle of mass on 24 March 1980.

Archbishop Romero was not the only victim of repression against all defenders of human rights. Bishop Enrique Angelelli of La Rioja in Argentina died on 4 August 1976 in a motor accident caused by the police. Earlier, an engineered accident in his light plane caused the death of Bishop Geraldo Valencia Cano of Buenaventura, Colombia. More than fifty priests were murdered for their action against human rights violations. Among the best known are Fr Carlos Mugica, a leader of the Argentine clergy and popular movements (11 May 1974), Fr João Bosco Penido Burnier, right-hand man of Bishop Pedro Casaldáliga in Brazil (12 October 1976), Fr Rutilio Grande, confidant of Archbishop Romero (12 March 1977). The lay leaders, activists, ministers of the word, community leaders and catechists who died for their fidelity to their mission are numbered in tens of thousands. Such martyrs are most numerous in Central America (Nicaragua 1977–9, El Salvador 1975–91,

Guatemala, continually). Also Argentina (1973–80), Uruguay (1972–6), Chile (1973–6), Paraguay (1970–6), and Colombia (continually), but there have also been martyrs in Mexico, Haiti, Bolivia, etc. The celebration of the martyrs has become an essential part of religious life in Latin America.

In 1979 the Latin American bishops' conference at Puebla condemned the doctrine of national security, but the hidden hand of Rome corrected the final text of the conclusions before publication, softening the terms of the condemnation: the military were once more protected in Rome. After these nuanced condemnations, the bishops' conferences of Argentina and Colombia could regard themselves as not referred to, and the others felt supported in their fight for resistance and redemocratization.

3. THE EMERGENCE OF THE "CHURCH OF THE POOR"

The option for the poor emphatically adopted in Medellín by the minority represented there ratified the new experiment of base church communities. The base communities had originated simultaneously, though in different forms, from the beginning of the 1960s in the North-East of Brazil (Pirambu in Ceará and São Paulo de Potengi in Rio Grande do Norte), in Panama (San Miguelito, a suburb of Panama City), and in Chile (the southern zone of Santiago). In Brazil the base communities were officially adopted by the bishops' conference in its five-year pastoral plan of 1965. After this ratification by Medellín they spread across the continent. In some cases they were officially adopted by the bishops' conferences (Chile 1970), and in others they were adopted by a number of dioceses within a country (Riobamba in Ecuador, the southern Andean region of Peru, Cajamarca, Chimbote and the suburbs of Lima, in turn by up to ten dioceses in Mexico). In other countries, such as Colombia, they developed against the wishes of the bishops.

Despite the developments of these twenty years since Medellín, however, few dioceses are totally organized on the basis of base communities: in Brazil Crateus, under Bishop Antônio Fragoso, São Félix do Araguaia under Bishop Pedro Casaldáliga, Volta Redonda under Bishop Waldir Calheiros, and Duque de Caxias under Bishop Mauro Morelli, as well as some poor areas of the dioceses of São Paulo now separated from the original trunk. In the great majority of dioceses, however, base communities are at least partially established. The Inter-Ecclesial Meetings of Base Communities have been important stages in the process: Vitória, 1975 and 1976, João Pessoa, 1978, Itaici, 1981, Canindé, 1983, Trindade, 1986, Duque de Caxias, 1989.

In Chile, although officially adopted by the national bishops' conference, base communities are established mainly in the poor areas of Santiago, where there are around a thousand, and Concepción. In the rural diocese, there is the name, but little content. In Peru the base communities are well established in the poor outskirts of Lima, and were in the southern part of the Andean region, especially until the accidental death of Archbishop Callejos of Cuzco (1982), in Cajamarca (Bishop José Dammert) and Chimbote. In Ecuador leaders of the movement included Archbishop Leonidas Proaño (who died in 1988) and Archbishop Luna of Cuenca. Nicaragua is a special case. In 1979 the base communities were almost non-existent. With the Sandinista victory they began to develop, but many of their members became involved in full-time work for the Sandinista government. The Pope's visit on 4 March 1983 reinforced the hostile attitude toward the Sandinista movement already adopted by the Nicaraguan bishops, with the encouragement of CELAM, and much of the clergy. Nevertheless the base community movement gained a new lease of life when it began to be more open to popular religion as a result of three events: the fast by Fr Miguel D'Escoto, the Nicaraguan foreign minister, from 7 July to 6 August 1985, Bishop Pedro Casaldáliga's visit to all the regions of Nicaragua from 28 July to 22 August 1985, and the great Way of the Cross, covering 326 kilometres between 14 and 28 February 1986, with the famous personal exhortation of Miguel D'Escoto to Cardinal Miguel Obando y Bravo, archbishop of Managua.

Another special case is Colombia. Although the bishops are without exception linked to the local oligarchies, part of the clergy continue to promote the idea of a church of the poor. After the dismantling of the priests' movement Golconda, the priests attached to the popular movement organized SAL (Priests for Latin America, until 1980), "Christians for Socialism" (1975-88), and from 1978 the journal *Solidaridad*. In 1982 they organized the first national meeting of base communities in Cundinamarca. The second was held in Bugá in 1984, the third in 1987 in Ditutama, Boyacá. In 1988 they organized in Bogotá a national ecumenical meeting "for life." All these activities were condemned by the bishops.

In Puebla the Pope had warned against the danger of a "popular church," detached from the hierarchy. After this the spokespersons of conservatism in the Church (the Brazilian Bishop Boaventura Kloppenburg, with the support of CELAM) denounced the existence of such a popular church within the base communities. For a number of years they made great play with the threat of a schismatic popular church, but in the end there was not even the shadow of a possible schism.

Apart from the base communities and the structures of the Church, Christians were present in many popular movements. In Brazil some thirty specialized "pastoral ministries" encouraged Christian presence in the popular movements (the Pastoral Land Commission, Ministry to Workers, to Fishing Communities, to Marginalized Women, to Young People, etc.). Catholics took an active part in the popular movements which reached their high point between 1978 and 1984 (the great metalworkers' strikes in the São Paulo industrial region, the movement against the high cost of living). They are increasingly involved in the trade unions grouped in the CUT federation founded in 1983.

In Chile the Vicariate for the Ministry to Workers developed rapidly after the coup, and has become the centre of operations of an even more effective ministry to the poor since a dialogue was opened with the socialists and communists who have always been in the majority in the working class. The journal *Pastoral Popular*, founded in the 1960s, has acquired a readership throughout Latin America.

In the Andean countries and Mexico and Guatemala, Christians have taken an active part in the new indigenous movements, and on many occasions have led them. In 1980 in São Paulo there was held the first ecumenical meeting on pastoral ministry to indigenous communities. On 20 December the first Black

Consciousness Day or Zumbi Day was celebrated in the Union of Palmares, in Alagoas, Brazil, the site of a famous community of escaped slaves (*quilombo*), led by Zumbi, who has since become a hero to black Brazilians. On this occasion Archbishop José Maria Pires, the black archbishop of João Pessoa, celebrated a specially composed *Quilombo Mass*, which included songs and dances of African origin. The mass was promptly banned by the Holy See after its second celebration in Recife on 22 November of the same year.

In this connection, the most striking phenomenon of the period was the participation of Catholics in the Sandinista Revolution, both in its insurrectional phase and in the period of Sandinista government (1979–90). The Sandinista ideology divided the Church. The bishops, led by Cardinal Obando y Bravo, became the leaders of the opposition, giving support and backing to the contra guerrillas, while part of the clergy and laity actively cooperated with the Sandinista government. The symbol of this cooperation was the presence of three priests in the government at ministerial level: Miguel D'Escoto, foreign minister and member of the Maryknoll Fathers, Ernesto Cardenal, minister of culture, ex-Cistercian and priest of the diocese of Managua, and Fernando Cardenal, minister of education and Jesuit. From 1981 onwards the bishops brought pressure to bear on the priests to abandon their ministerial posts. During his visit in 1983 the Pope publicly rebuked Ernesto Cardenal. The situation came to a head in 1984, when Fernando Cardenal was expelled from the Society of Jesus on 10 December. D'Escoto was never expelled from his congregation, though he refrained from public priestly activity.

In the 1980s all the dictatorships went through a process of redemocratization. The months before the restoration of civilian rule were generally a time of intense popular mobilization. The impression was created that the mass of the people was about to win control of its historic destiny; such an atmosphere existed in Brazil in 1984–5, in Argentina in 1983, in Chile in 1987–8, in Peru in 1980, and even in Mexico in 1987, when the PRI was threatened by the popular candidature of Cuauctemoc Cárdenas. With the return to a certain type of democracy, at least to the holding of elections, came immediate disillusionment and a massive abandonment of political activity by the popular movements. In this context the base communities have gone into crisis, like the popular movements: they are finding that they are unable to reach or influence the masses. The poor are increasingly turning to Pentecostalism, African religions or Indian traditions. The Church is losing control over the religion of the masses, and the whole strategy of liberating conscientization, which has been the basis of the programme of Medellín, is threatened with collapse.

4. THE "THEOLOGY OF LIBERATION"

The founders of the theology of liberation had already started writing before Medellín: Juan Luis Segundo (Uruguay, 1964), (Gustavo Gutiérrez, Peru, 1966), Hugo Assmann (Brazil, 1966). Nonetheless the name began to be used only in the context of Medellín. The first meeting on the subject was held in Bogotá in 1970. Gustavo Gutiérrez' book *A Theology of Liberation*, which gave the movement its manifesto, appeared in 1971. It is the classic synthesis, which was translated into every European language. A second edition appeared in 1988 with a new introduction to take account of subsequent developments.

In a first phase, which ended in 1973 with the Chilean coup, the theology of liberation started from a number of options: the use of dependency theory as a system of sociological categories, openness to a possible collaboration with Marxism, especially the Latin American version as exemplified by Mariátegui, an option for a radical transformation of society, rejection of the pure Cuban model of *foquismo* (small guerrilla nuclei to bring about revolution) espoused by Che Guevara and Camilo Torres (who studied with the authors of the theology of liberation and belongs to their generation), high regard for intellectual vanguards and intellectuals in general. In the initial phase the theologians worked primarily with student intellectuals. Later Segundo was to lament that liberation theology had abandoned its origins.

From 1972–3 the Brazilians Leonardo and Clodovis Boff and the Chilean Ronaldo Muñoz redirected liberation theology toward popular pastoral work and the base communities; that is, toward popular rather than intellectual work. This produced studies of popular religion. There were two important international meetings. At the El Escorial Congress in 1972 all the leading figures in liberation theology were present, along with theologians and sociologists from different schools. A meeting in Mexico in 1976 brought together the theologians of the first and second generations.

Argentina is outside the movement. At the beginning Lucio Gera and J. C. Scannone were among the founders, but soon felt that Argentina did not offer them a favourable climate. They founded a culturalist variant of liberation theology which was successful in CELAM: Gera was an official expert at Puebla, though the liberation theologians had been excluded.

A development became apparent during the 1970s which strengthened in the 1980s: liberation theology became increasingly less socio-political and more religious and ecclesial. After the resounding disaster of the Popular Unity government in Chile Latin American sociology fell silent. It no longer had a model to interpret developments. Marxism increasingly became a critique of Marxism.

From 1979 Central America became the centre of attention for intellectuals, including theologians. A new centre of liberation theology became the focus of attention: DEI in Costa Rica, with Franz Hinkelammert, Hugo Assmann (Mark 2) and Pablo Richard. The movement which encouraged a critique of religion and of the traditional Church intensified.

At the same time the theology of liberation began to expand beyond the borders of theology in the strict sense. In 1972 CEHILA (Commission for the Study of Latin American Church History) was founded with Enrique Dussel, an Argentine settled in Mexico, as coordinator. CEHILA is publishing a ten-volume series of the history of the Church in Latin America. It holds an annual symposium on themes of Church history, and publishes smaller collections. Enrique Dussel also launched the philosophy of liberation movement.

An Ecumenical Association of Third World Theologians (EATWOT) was founded in 1976. It held its first meeting in Dar-es-Salaam in that year, bringing together theologians from Latin America, Asia and Africa. The influence of Latin American liberation theologians is steadily growing among both Asian and African theologians, despite the differences in tradition. EATWOT met in 1977 in Accra, in 1979 in Sri-Lanka, in 1980 in São Paulo, in 1981 in New Delhi, in 1986 in Oaxtepec (Mexico). The organizer was the Chilean priest Sergio Torres, at the time in exile in New York. In 1980 in Brazil Carlos Mesters founded CEBI, an ecumenical centre for the study of the Bible, following a popular interpretation of the Bible along the lines of the option for the poor and the theology of liberation. In 1983 in Petrópolis, Brazil, the idea of a comprehensive (54-volume) collection of liberation theology was announced, to be published not only in Spanish and Portuguese but also in English, German, Italian and French. All the editions are in process of publication in whole or in part, despite official and financial constraints. In 1983 the idea of a biblical commentary along the same lines was launched, and the first volumes appeared in 1985. In Brazil the same group started the journal *Estudos Bíblicos*, with a first issue in 1985. In 1988 the journal *RIBLA* (Review of Latin American Biblical Interpretation) began publication, appearing simultaneously in Spanish and Portuguese. The DEI centre in San José, Costa Rica, has published the journal *Pasos* since 1985, and the Jesuits in San Salvador have been publishing the *Revista Latinoamericana de teología* since 1984.

Two men coordinated the fight against the theology of liberation, which began before the publication of the first books. In fact the fight began a day after Medellín. The most powerful enemy of the movement was, and is, Cardinal Alfonso López Trujillo, who was able to use all the facilities and prestige of his office in CELAM. In a first phase, in the 1970s, López Trujillo acted in concert with the Jesuit Roger Vekemans. Vekemans founded in 1971 in Bogotá a centre, CEDIAL, and a journal, *Tierra Nueva*, designed exclusively to combat liberation theology. Everything which later appeared in Roman documents can already be found in *Tierra Nueva* ten years earlier. Vekemans coordinated a powerful triangle Bogotá-Frankfurt-Rome, bringing together the German and Colombian episcopates with certain circles in Rome. He organized congresses and an extensive campaign of defamation. More recently López Trujillo has worked with Opus Dei to organize his campaigns. Opus was his collaborator in organizing the 1985 Los Andes meeting in Chile and at the Catholic University of Chile in Santiago in 1990.

The campaign was directed in particular against two men, Gustavo Gutiérrez and Leonardo Boff. After nearly fifteen years of denunciation the plotters succeeded in getting the Roman authorities to act.

In March 1983 Cardinal Ratzinger sent the Peruvian bishops ten observations about the theology of Gustavo Gutiérrez. The bishops deliberated for more than a year and were unable to reach agreement or a decision. They were summoned to Rome, but even there published a relatively moderate text with no condemnations but merely friendly exhortations. Still the Roman congregation indicated dissatisfaction. In subsequent years, as a result of a one-sided policy of episcopal appointments, the majority in the conference shifted and from 1988 new, relatively discreet discussions began between Gutiérrez, the bishops' conference and the Holy See. In 1990 the archbishop of Lima, Cardinal Landázuri, retired and Gutiérrez lost an important protector.

The trial of Leonardo Boff was prepared by public condemnations from the Commission for the Defence of the Faith in the archdiocese of Rio de Janeiro, the see of Cardinal Eugênio Sales, defender of orthodoxy in the Brazilian Church. The propositions condemned appeared in the book, *Church: Charism and Power*, published in 1981. After three years of accusations and denunciations in Brazil and abroad, Leonardo Boff was summoned to testify at the Congregation for the Defence of the Faith in Rome on 7 September 1984. The conclusions were sent to the theologian on 20 March, including a series of criticisms, which the writer accepted. Leonardo Boff was subjected to a period of "submissive silence," which lasted for about a year. Subsequently Leonardo Boff was subjected to various restrictions on his activities in the Franciscan Order connected with teaching and publishing.

During the same period Cardinal Ratzinger signed, on 6 August 1984, a very harsh Instruction "on some aspects of the theology of liberation," which presented the theology as the sum of all heresies and the greatest synthesis of heresy of all time. Liberation theology was simply identified with Marxism. European experts on Marxism had been summoned to write a document designed to cause fear. In Latin America liberation theologians unanimously said that they did not feel referred to because they did not recognize their theology in the picture presented by the Instruction. Two years later, on 22 March 1986, Cardinal Ratzinger published a second Instruction, "On Christian Freedom and Liberation," which was much more balanced and used many of the themes raised by liberation theology. The tension eased, especially because on 9 April 1986 the Pope sent a letter to the bishops of Brazil in which he said that "the theology of liberation is not only opportune, but also useful and necessary." The Pope gave the Brazilian bishops a special mission, to guide the development of this theology, not only in Brazil, but throughout Latin America.

Nevertheless nothing short of an Inquisition has been under way in Latin America. In May 1984 Cardinal Höffner, the archbishop of Cologne, went to visit the theology faculty in São Paulo to denounce the Marxism which – he knew in advance – was taught there. After this there was an Apostolic Visitation of all the seminaries of Brazil for the same purpose. The most visible result of this was the closure in 1989 of the Theological Institute in Recife (ITER) and of the North-East regional seminary, both institutions founded twenty years previously under the patronage of Archbishop Helder Câmara by the bishops of Brazil's North-East. Today liberation theology is a forbidden topic in nearly all the seminaries of Latin America: the circulation and reading of such books is forbidden, as is reference to the topic in lectures. Only in some Brazilian seminaries is the reading and exposition of this theology permitted. The Inquisition was never so effective in the past.

A later notorious episode in the witch-hunt against liberation theology was the banning, in April 1989, of the publication of the "Word-Life Project," a biblical refresher course for Latin American religious sponsored by the Latin American Conference of Religious (CLAR). On this occasion the Holy See interfered with the statutes of the organization and imposed a secretary general against the preferences of the members.

5. PUEBLA

CELAM prepared a general conference of Latin American bishops for the beginning of 1979 to condemn the theology of liberation and offer an alternative both to this theology and the Medellín programme. The result was, according to the commentators, "an away draw." The bishops sympathetic to liberation theology ensured that the conclusions of the conference renewed and repeated the themes of Medellín using the language of liberation and offering support to base communities. Nevertheless the assembly took very seriously the Pope's warnings in his opening address against a "parallel magisterium" and the "popular church," and his insistence on the need to affirm the truth about Christ, the Church and human beings. This was taken as referring to the base communities and the theology of liberation. In addition some texts drew their inspiration from the alternative theology of the Argentine-Uruguayan school, the theology of culture based on the ideas of the Argentines Lucio Gera and J.C. Scannone. Some chapters reflect "culturalist" inspiration and others a "liberationist" one. After Puebla, the whole line deriving from Medellín felt stimulated, but the other current also felt encouraged, and immediately afterwards was to receive the backing and publicity resulting from the campaign for a new evangelization promoted by John Paul II and the international movements.

6. JOHN PAUL II AND THE "NEW EVANGELIZATION"

The Pope has visited every country in Latin America and the Caribbean, except for the smaller Caribbean islands. In 1990 in Mexico he began a second series of visits. The most notable journeys were the first visit to Mexico, which coincided with the Puebla conference, with the result that the Pope's speeches were heavily quoted in its conclusions. Later, in 1980, came the long visit to Brazil, with a series of speeches interpreted as supporting the line of the bishops' conference. The most tragic was the visit to Nicaragua on 4 March 1983. The Pope took a clear stand against any collaboration with the Sandinista movement and clearly supported the systematic opposition led by the archbishop of Managua, which created a deep division in the Church. In 1986 in Chile the Pope's visit was the occasion for the first mass public expression of hostility to the Pinochet regime.

On 11 and 12 October 1984 in Santo Domingo, capital of the Dominican Republic, the Pope solemnly opened the celebrations of the Fifth Centenary of the conquest of Latin America with a nine-year novena. He called for a new evangelization, and has subsequently repeated that call at every opportunity.

The programme of the new evangelization has various elements. First, the Holy See has reinforced the movement for the restoration of "Tridentine" discipline, already initiated with the Sucre "coup" of 1972 in CELAM. This involves appointing bishops who will be primarily administrators and more concerned with internal discipline than with presence in the world, insistence on priestly vocations and on training according to the traditional model, and a return to discipline in liturgy, catechesis and organization.

This return to discipline is credited with achieving something which might possibly have occurred anyway: the seminaries, which emptied during the great youth crisis of 1967-72, have begun to fill up again to their previous levels.

Ordinations have increased, but within a generation do not hold out the prospect of a better priest-laity ratio than one for every ten thousand inhabitants in some countries, such as Brazil, or at best one for every five thousand. Certainly the problem labelled "shortage of priests" and highlighted in the 1950s seems still unsolved. Latin America's Catholic communities are going Protestant as they get used to liturgical celebrations without the eucharist.

The more the new evangelization has seemed to be a new movement, different from the one initiated in Medellín, the greater the enthusiasm shown for it by the international movements which began to develop strongly since 1970. Almost half of Opus Dei's seventy thousand members are in Latin America, where it has great penetration in the universities and seminaries, especially in Colombia, Peru, Chile, Venezuela and Mexico. Opus Dei has already provided more than ten bishops for Latin America, and all the signs are that this number will grow very fast. The "short course" or *cursillo* movement was already in existence, but has grown rapidly in this period. The Couples' Encounters with Christ are also taking off at dizzying speed. The Focolari movement already existed in the 1960s, but has grown and has hundreds of thousands of members at all levels. The Neo-Catechumenate movement is also present in almost all countries, and is the basis of pastoral work in many dioceses. The Comunione e Liberazione movement is present in every country. The founder, Luigi Giussani, organized a Latin American meeting, at least for the southern part of the continent, in Córdoba in 1986. The Italian magazine *30 Giorni* publishes editions in Portuguese and Spanish. Both the Focolari and Comunione e Liberazione run publishing houses in Latin America, where they have a great impact. The Schönstatt movement developed particularly in Chile, where it has already produced two bishops and has a strong presence in the universities. The main sociologist of the current Latin American Catholic Right, the Chilean Pedro Morandé, has links with Schönstatt; he has been an official adviser at almost all Church assemblies, including the Roman and Argentine synods.

These movements grew rapidly during the 1980s, but they are all far outweighed by the main force in present-day Latin American Catholicism, Catholic Charismatic Renewal. This movement has millions of members. It is by far the fastest growing movement, an avalanche comparable only with the sensational expansion of Protestant Pentecostalism. Charismatic renewal has taken responsibility for the Lumen 2000 project and for Evangelization 2000. It has an efficient infrastructure, and claims the unconditional support of its faithful. It is constant in its professions of loyalty to the hierarchy, but at the same time is difficult to integrate into diocesan pastoral plans unless the movement itself is the basis of pastoral work.

The lay movements are the most dynamic force in the Latin American Church, whether it be the more left-wing forces of the base communities or the more right-wing forces of the transnational movements. The clergy are becoming more and more bureaucratic, distributing sacraments and holding meetings, but losing contact with real people. The bishops hold meetings. The religious hold meetings. Evangelization is left to the laity.

Governments have returned to democracy once more, but these new democracies are totally unstable. Development has stagnated. There is no future in sight. The élites do not know what to do to maintain their privileges in an increasingly explosive situation. They are postponing reforms until society seems to be falling apart. The Church is facing a new challenge: poverty which has grown steadily for the last twenty years, almost complete urbanization, accounting for 75 percent of the population, which constitutes a huge sub-proletariat waiting for change, an economic situation with no hope and public authorities which are more semblances of power than real power. The powers of the First World are totally indifferent to the fate of human beings in a raw capitalism which thinks itself victorious. The hierarchical Church is silent, not knowing what to say. We are in a period in which the Church is active only at the base, in the invisible cells in which the poor construct the forms of the presence of the Kingdom of God in a world without meaning. All the evidence is that the Church of the clergy and the clerical powers will become less and less capable of saying anything which is not a repetition of the empty formulas of the past which no one listens to in a new culture. Evangelization will be carried out in the silence of the deep levels of the people: for a generation everything will happen in secret. The only other possibility is a sudden social explosion with incalculable consequences and on a scale which also cannot yet be forecast.

Translated from the Portuguese by Francis McDonagh

SELECT BIBLIOGRAPHY

The General Situation
de Arruda, A. *A escola superior de Guerra*. São Paulo: GRD, 2nd ed., 1983.
Bermúdez, L. *Guerra de baja intensidad: Reagan contra Centroamerica*. Mexico City: Siglo XXI, 2nd ed. 1989.
Bustamente, F., *et al. Democracia e fuerzas armadas en Sudamérica*. Quito: Cordes, 1988.
Cheresky, I., Chonchol, J. *Críse e transformação dos regimes autoritários*. São Paulo: Icone, 1986.
Lázara, S. *Poder militar, origen, apogeo y transición*. Buenos Aires: Legasa, 1989.
Stepan, A. *Os militares: da abertura à Nova República*. Rio de Janeiro, 3rd ed. 1986.

The Church
Azevedo, M. *Comunidades Eclesiais de Base e Inculturaçao da fé*. São Paulo: Loyola, 1986. Eng. trans. *Basic Ecclesial Communities in Brazil*. Washington D.C.: Georgetown University Press, 1987.
Berryman, P. *The Religious Roots of Rebellion. Christians in Central American Revolutions*. Maryknoll, N.Y.: Orbis, 1984.
Berryman, P. *Liberation Theology. The essential facts about the revolutionary movement in Latin America and beyond*. New York: Random House, 1987.
Cabestrero, T. *Ministros de Dios, Ministros del Pueblo*. Managua, 1982. Eng. trans. *Ministers of God, Ministers of the People*. Maryknoll, N.Y.: Orbis, London: Zed Press, 1983.
Brockmann, J. R. *The Word remains: A Life of Oscar Romero*. Maryknoll, N.Y.: Orbis, 1982.
Delgado, J. *Oscar A. Romero. Biografía*. Madrid: Paulinas, 1986.
Dussel, E. *De Medellín a Puebla. Una década de sangre y esperanza. 1968–1979*. Mexico City, 1979.
Escobar, J. *Persecución a la Iglesia en Chile (Martirologio 1973–1986)*. Santiago, 1986.
Henríquez, P. *El Salvador: Iglesia profética y cambio social*. San José: DEI, 1988.
Gibellini, R. *Il dibattito sulla Teologia de la Liberazione*. Brescia: Queriniana, 1986. Eng. trans. *The Liberation Theology Debate*. Maryknoll, N.Y.: Orbis, 1987.
Gomes Treto, R. *La Iglesia católica durante la construcción del socialismo en Cuba*. San José: DEI, 1987. Eng. trans. *The Church and Socialism in Cuba*. Maryknoll, N.Y.: Orbis, 1989.
Goldstein, H. *Paulo Evaristo Arns. Kardinal der Ausgebeuteten*.
Marins, J., *et al. Martírio. Memória perigosa na América Latina hoje*. São Paulo: Paulinas, 1984.
Mignone, E. F. *Iglesia y dictadura*. Buenos Aires, 1985.

Movimento Nacional de Direitos Humanos. *Roma Locuta. Documentos sobre o livro "Igreja: carisma e poder".* São Paulo, 1985.

Regan, D. *Church for Liberation. A Pastoral Portrait of the Church in Brazil.* Dublin: Dominican Publications, 1985.

Romano, R. *Brasil: Igreja contra Estado.* São Paulo, Kairos, 1972.

Krischke, P., and Mainwaring, S. *A Igrejas nas bases em tempo de transição (1974–1985).* Porto Alegre: LPM-CEDEC, 1986.

Dos obispos del Sur Andino: Luis Vallejos – Luis Dalle. En el corazón de su pueblo. Lima: CEP, 1982.

Leonidas Proaño: 25 años obispo de Riobamba. Lima: CEP, 1979.

Dossiê Colômbia urgente. São Paulo: SISAC, 1990.

Vigil, J.M. (ed.). *Nicaragua y los teólogos.* Mexico City: Siglo XXI, 1987.

SOURCES AND BIBLIOGRAPHY

Enrique Dussel and José A. G. Moreira

To conclude this joint work, we tackle the subject of sources for and bibliography of the history of the Church in Latin America. The reader is referred also to the Select Bibliographies at the end of respective chapters.

I. SOURCES

We divide these into two parts: unpublished and published, in order to give those embarking on a study of sources an overall view.[1]

1. UNPUBLISHED SOURCES

This does not pretend to be an exhaustive survey, but is designed to initiate the interested student into research on the Church in Latin America.

For the history of the Spanish-American Church in the colonial period, the major archive is in Spain, the *Archivo General de Indias* (AGI), held in the Palace of La Lonja in Seville. Church documents are mainly in the *Patronato* (194 files) and *Audiencias* (almost 19,000 files) sections, though all the other sections contain some pertinent material.[2] Also important is the Spanish *Archivo General* held in the Castle of Simancas in Castile,[3] which contains a mass of material on native peoples, as well as Pope Alexander VI's famous bull *Inter caeteras* of 3 May 1493. There are files on the Jesuits and the Inquisition in the *Archivo Histórico Nacional* in Madrid, and the National Library in Madrid also contains a lot of material on the history of the Church,[4] as do the libraries of the Royal Palace[5] and the Royal Academy of History, which contains the works of Juan Bautista Muñoz, the chronicler of the Indies. The library of the Escorial Palace[6] holds such works as Motolinia's *Historia* and the text of the Third Council of Lima; the Provincial Library of Toledo holds the "Colección Lorenzana," with the text of the Fourth Council of Mexico, amongst other documents.

In Portugal there are likewise many archives containing material for the history of the Church in Brazil and Maranhão. First, the *Arquivo Nacional da Torre do Tombo*,[7] containing collections of papal bulls, the archives of the *Ordem de Cristo*, the *Mesa da Consciência e Ordens*, the Holy Office, etc. The *Corpo Cronológico* corresponds in date to the *Patronato* section in the Archive of the Indies. Then, the *Arquivo Histórico Ultramarino*,[8] better researched for our purposes than the first, corresponding rather to the Seville archive as a whole for Brazil. Third, the Lisbon National Library, which holds the important "Coleçao Pombalina." Further material can be found in the libraries of the Palacio da Ajuda,[9] the Academy of Sciences, the Military Historical Archive, the public libraries of Oporto[10] and Evora and the archives of the Foreign Ministry and of Coimbra.

Still in Europe, there are also the archives in Rome. The Vatican Archive[11] has the *Regesta Vaticana* (with bulls up to 1605), the *Regesta Laterensia* (up to 1803) and, amongst others, the *Breves Laterenses* (1490–1800). (Two volumes of documents, covering the years 1493–1592, were published in 1992 – TRANS.)[11]. The Consistorial Archive (*Acta Cameranii*) contains most material relating to the appointment of bishops. The *Processi* contain documents relating to the "causes" (of beatification and canonization) of many Latin Americans. All the material documenting *ad limina* visits is also important. The

Congregation of Extra-ordinary Affairs also has abundant material, particularly relating to the Emancipation period, on which Pedro de Leturia is the main authority. The Congregation for the Evangelization of Peoples (*De Propaganda Fide*) also holds material from 1623.

Valuable too are the central archives of the various religious orders: Franciscans,[12] Jesuits,[13] Dominicans, Augustinians, etc. The archive of the Spanish Embassy to the Holy See keeps part of the material relating to the nomination of bishops and other dealings with the Vatican. The Vittorio Emmanuele National Library holds proceedings of the beatification causes of numerous Latin American saints: Francisco Solano, Juan Masías, Palafox y Mendoza, Mariana de Jesús, José de Anchieta, Martin of Porres, Peter Claver, Rose of Lima, Toribio de Mogrovejo, Sebastián de Aparicio. . . .

Latin America, as is to be expected, contains the bulk of archive material.[14]

Mexico City, despite earthquakes, is the richest source.[15] The National General Archive has series of files on the history of the Church, such as: Secular and regular Clergy (217 volumes); Hospitals, Indians, the Inquisition (1,702 volumes); Jesuits, Bishops, Archbishops, Holy Crusade, Churches and Convents, Universities (572 volumes). There are also archives of source material in the National Institute of Anthropology and History (INAH) and many others. The Town Hall Archive contains the *Actas Capitulares* from 1536 to the present. There are also conventual archives, part of which have been incorporated into government archives. All cathedrals and major parish churches have their own archives: the Ecclesiastical Archive of the Archdiocese of Guadalajara, the Palafox Library in Puebla, the libraries of Oaxaca, Durango, Zacatecas, and so on in virtually all States in the country. There are also Maya Indian archives in Chiapas, Ebtum (Yucatán), and San Pedro Yolox (Oaxaca).

The Caribbean is not good for archives: the humidity and termites rapidly do away with them. There is little to be found in the General Archive of the Nation or the Cathedral Archive (baptismal registers and acts of the church council) in the Dominican Republic.[16] The most important material is in the historical archive of the University of Río Piedras in Puerto Rico, and there are others such as the General State Archive and the Municipal Historical Archive. Arturo Dávila has reorganized the Cathedral Archive and Mario Rodríguez is working on parish archives.[17] The National Archive of Cuba contains some material, but little before the eighteenth century.[18] The Archdiocesan Archive of Havana and that of the Cathedral Chapter also contain valuable material.

The most important archive in Central America is the Central Government Archive of Guatemala,[19] with a section on church affairs containing numerous documents on the Royal Prerogative (1634–1820), missions, crusades, convents, etc. The Archdiocesan archive is in good condition and very rich, and there are archives of the Mission College of Christ Crucified and the Franciscan College. Other major collections are the National Archive of Costa Rica in San José, the National Archive of Nicaragua and that of the Curia of León. The National Archive of Honduras has little on the Church; the same is true of El Salvador, though there is something in the archive of the church Curia; there is virtually nothing in Panama.

In Colombia,[20] the major collection is now the National Archive, since the valuable archive of the Archdiocese of Santa Fe was burned in 1948. It contained files on Indians (78 volumes), Chaplaincies (26 volumes), Convents (78 volumes), and many others, such as Priests and Bishops, Colleges, etc., valuable for the study of church history.[21] Series of indexes to the various parts of the archive have been published. Elsewhere in the country there are important church archives, such as those of the Archdiocese of Popayán, the Franciscan Missionary College in Calí, etc.

In Venezuela, the National General Archive in Caracas has sections such as Papal Bulls, Tithes, Churches, Indians, Missions and Ecclesiastical Affairs. The Archdiocesan Archive of Caracas[22] has a lot of material, and the Archive of the Church Council contains the Acts of the Council from 1580 to the present. There are interesting Franciscan and parish records in Caracas, and also in the provinces, such as the Historical Archive of Zulia in Maracaibo and the Historical Archive of the Province of Mérida.

In Peru, as important as Mexico in church history, the documents have been through such vicissitudes that few have come down to us in comparison with the amount that should have done. There are documents in the National Archive, the National Library, the Foreign Office Library and above all in the archive of the Archdiocese of Lima,[23] which has dozens of files on the causes of Peruvian saints, among others, as well much on the popular history of the Church (under headings such as "*beaterios*," charitable works for poor Indians, brotherhoods, etc.). Other archives are to be found in the Convento de San Francisco (with abundant material on the history of the Franciscans in South America), the Discalced Carmelites' convent, those of La Merced and St Augustine, the Ecclesiastical Council (whose Acts began in 1575) and the Seminary of St Torobio de Mogrovejo.[24] In Cuzco there are the Historical Archive, which includes material on church history, the Archdiocesan Archive, the Chapter Archive, that of La Merced, the Franciscan archive, and others. Arequipa and Trujillo also have archdiocesan archives.

In Ecuador, the National Historical Archive is more important than the Municipal Archive of Quito,[25] and has documents from 1534. The Archdiocesan and Chapter archives of Quito are also useful, and there are good municipal archives in Ibarra, Ambato, Cuenca, Riobamba, Guayaquil and elsewhere.[26]

In Bolivia, the National Archive is in Sucre[27] and contains, for example, forty-one volumes on Mojos and Chiquitos. There is more to be found in the Chapter Archive in Sucre (documents from 1572), in Santa Cruz de la Sierra[28] and other cities in the interior, particularly Cochabamba.

Moving to the Southern Cone, the National General Archive of Argentina is the oldest in Latin America, dating from 1821, and contains useful material on subjects such as Tithes, the Jesuit Missions, etc.[29] The Archdiocesan Archive of Buenos Aires was largely burned in 1955; there is little in the Chapter Archive, some things in St Francis. In Córdoba the Historical and Archdiocesan Archives, both now well cared for, have interesting documents, as does the University Archive (from 1609, the date the Jesuit college in Santiago del Estero was founded). Mendoza and Santiago del Estero have General Provincial Archives; the latter also has a cathedral archive, as do Salta, Santa Fe and Corrientes. In Paraguay, the major archives are the National and that of the ecclesiastical curia.[30] Uruguay has the National Museum, with some useful material.[31] The National Archive of Chile contains documents on the Jesuits and the Inquisition, as well as the "Archivo Eyzaguirre." The "Sala Medina" in the National Library is devoted to the great historian of that name. The archdiocesan archive in the Curia begins in 1634; the Franciscan archive begins in 1553 and is very good. Work is being done on parish archives.[32]

The major collection in Brazil is the National Archive in Rio de Janeiro, which covers not only the colonial period but also the time when the Imperial Court was in Brazil. Sections include "Ecclesiastical," under Dealings with Portugal; Ecclesiastical Affairs (up to 1820 with documents on the *Mesa de Consciência e Ordens*, Brotherhoods, etc.). The archdiocesan archive of Rio has some 1600 documents, from 1575. In São Paulo there are the Public State Archive and the Municipal Archive, as well as the Archdiocesan one, though this has no sixteenth century documents, but begins in 1640. In Bahía there is a parish register from the seventeenth century and a metropolitan curial archive. There are archives too in Belém, Cuibá, Goiás, Olinda, and São Luis do Maranhão. Of sees established after the eighteenth century, the following possess archives: Aparecida, Campoinas, Curitiba, Diamantina, Florianópolis, Limoeiro do

Norte, Petrópolis and Sobral. There are also those of the religious orders: Benedictines, Carmelites, Franciscans.

For the present, there is no organized information in Latin America relating to Protestant archives and unpublished documents, nor a description of the contents of those archives that do exist. So researchers need to approach the headquarters of each Protestant church or society in each country, where they will usually find a denominational archive. In Mexico, for example, the Methodist Church has built up a historical archive and organized a society for the study of Methodism in the country. Besides these denominational archives, others have been created by the National Evangelical Councils established to promote ecumenism within Latin American Protestantism. These archives are based at the headquarters of each Council and contain much information relating to the interdenominational movement initiated by the Congress of Panama in 1916. The ecumenical movements that started in the 1960s have also collected their own archives, to be found in their respective headquarters. Lima has the archives of the Latin American Evangelical Commission for Christian Education (CELADEC) and the Latin American Union of Ecumenical Youth (ULAJE); part of the Church and Society in Latin America (ISAL) archives have been moved from Montevideo to Buenos Aires, the rest having been destroyed by the military regime in Uruguay; the archives of the Universal Federation of Student Christian Movements (FUMEC) are in Mexico City; the Coordinating Committee for Ecumenical Projects (COPEC) has bases in Puerto Rico and Mexico; the archives of the Movement for Evangelical Unity in Latin America (UNELAM) are scattered, with some collected in the central offices of the Latin American Council of Churches (CLAI) in Brazil.

Finally, the larger Protestant training colleges have libraries containing many national and regional evangelical journals: these are vital for research. Other sources of useful material are: the Higher Institute of Theological Studies (ISEDET) in Buenos Aires; the Evangelical Theology Faculty in Santiago in Chile; the Methodist and Presbyterian Colleges in Rio de Janeiro; the Baptist College in Recife; the Faculty of Lutheran Theology in São Leopoldo; the Biblical College of San José in Costa Rica; the Evangelical Theological College of Matanzas in Cuba; the Evangelical Theological College of Río Piedras in Puerto Rico; the Mexican Theological Community in Mexico City.

The most important sources of information on Latin American Protestantism, however, are outside the continent, in the United States and Europe. The archives of U.S. and European Missionary Societies should of course be consulted, particularly the Northern and Southern U.S. Methodists, the Northern and Southern U.S. Baptists, and the scores of Pentecostal denominations and groups. For the U.S. Presbyterian Church, the following published sources can be indicated:

> Montreal, N.C., Foundation for History of Presbyterian and Reformed Churches (Reports and Letters from Missions in Latin America).
> Nashville, Ten., Board of World Mission of the Presbyterian Church in the United States (Latin American Missions Files).
> Philadelphia, Pa., Presbyterian Historical Society (Letters from Latin America).
> Princeton, N.J., Princeton Theological Seminary (Robert Speer Papers).
> Washington, D.C., National Library of Congress, Manuscripts Division (Samuel G. Inman Papers).

All documents relating to Moravian missions in Latin America are held at the central offices of the Moravian Church in Hernhutt, Germany.

Finally, there are two archives that are essential to anyone researching into Latin American (and indeed world) Protestantism. One is the archive and library of the World Council of Churches in Geneva. These contain all documents relating to the ecumenical movement, which enable one to follow Latin American participation in the development of the links that have been established over the years. The other is the archive and library of the National Council of Churches (CCC-USA) in New York, which is of prime importance for studying Protestant missions in Latin America.

NOTES

1. See L. Gómez Canedo, *Los Archivos de la Historia de América*, vols I-II (Mexico City, 1961).
2. See J. Torre Revello, *El Archivo General de Indias de Sevilla* (Buenos Aires, 1929). There are other works on this archive by P. Torres Lanzas, G. Latorre, C. Bermúdez, and others.
3. For this and other Spanish archives see P. Torres Lanzas, *Guía histórica y descriptiva de los archivos, bibliotecas y museos arqueológicos de España* (Madrid, 1916). On Spain see *Guía de fuentes para la historia de Iberoamérica conservadas en España* (Madrid, 1966).
4. See J. Paz, *Catálogo de los manuscritos de América existentes en la Biblioteca Nacional* (Madrid, 1933).
5. See J. Domínguez Bordona, *Manuscritos de América* (Madrid, 1935).
6. See E. Zarco Cueva, *Catálogo de los manuscritos castellanos de la Real Biblioteca de El Escorial* (Madrid, 1929–34).
7. On this subject in general, see J. C. de Macedo Soares, *Fontes da História da Igreja Católica no Brasil* (São Paulo, 1954). On the Torre do Tombo, see P. A. de Azevedo and A. Baiano, *O archivo da Torre do Tombo* (Lisbon, 1905).
8. See E. Castro e Almeida, *Inventario dos Documentos relativos ao Brasil existentes no Archivo de Marinha e Ultramar de Lisboa* (Rio de Janeiro, vols. I-VIII, 1913–36).
9. See C. A. Ferreira, *Inventario dos manuscritos da Biblioteca da Ajuda riferentes a América do Sul* (Coimbra, 1946).
10. See the *Catálogo dos manuscritos ultramarinos da Biblioteca Publica do Porto* (Lisbon, 1938).
11. See Lajos Pastor, *Guida delle fonti per la storia dell'America latina negli Archivi della Santa Sede e negli Archivi ecclesiastici d'Italia* (Vatican City, 1970). [For documents from 1493–1592, see J. Metzler (ed.) *America Pontificia Primi Saeculi Evangelizationis 1493–1592* (Vatican City: Libreria Editrice Vaticana, 1992) – TRANS.]
12. See J. M. Pou y Martí, "Index Regestorum Familiae Ultramontane," *Archivum Franciscanum Historicum* (Florence, vols. XII-XX, 1919–27).
13. From whose archives the *Monumenta Historica Societatis Jesu* are in the course of publication, beginning with F. Zubillaga on Florida, E. Egaña on Peru and S. Leite on Brazil (part).
14. See R. R. Hill, *The National Archives of Latin America* (Cambridge, Mass., 1945); idem. "Ecclesiastical Archives in America," *Archivum* 3 (Paris, 1954), 135–44; J. P. Harrison, *Guide to Materials in Latin America in the National Archives* (Washington, vols. I-II, 1961–7).
15. See L. Medina Ascensio, *Archivos y bibliotecas eclesiásticas* (Mexico City, 1966); L. Gómez Canedo, "Archivos eclesiásticos de México," *Anuario de Bibliotecología, Archivología e Informática* 3 (Mexico, 1971); J. Specker, "Missionsgeschlichtliches Material," *Neue Zeitschrift für Missionswissenschaft* XXX (1974), 220ff.
16. See F. Sevillano Colom, "El Archivo Genral de la Nación y el servicio de microfilm de la UNESCO," *Boletín del Archivo General de la Nación* XXII (Santo Domingo, 1952), 205–25; H. Polanco Brito, "Archivos eclesiásticos de América Latina," *Boletín CEHILA* 16–17 (1979), 26–9.
17. On this subject see L. Hanke, "Ecclesiastical Archives of Latin America," *Boletín CEHILA* 16–17 (1979), 8–10.
18. See L. Marino Pérez, *Guide to the Material for American History in Cuban Archives* (Washington, 1907).
19. See R. Chamberlain, "Report on Colonial Materials in the Government Archives of Guatemala City," *Handbook of Latin American Studies* (Cambridge, 1936).
20 See R. Posada, "Los archivos eclesiásticos colombianos," *Revista de la Academia Colombiana de Historia Eclesiástica* I/2 (Medellín, 1966), 169–73.
21. See W. Graff, "Inventario de algunos archivos locales de Colombia y Cundinamarca," *Anuario Colombiano de Historia Social* 5 (Bogotá, 1970), 219–29.
22. See J. Suría, *Catálogo general del Archivo arquidiocesano de Caracas* (1964); M. Briceño Pewrozo, "Concentración de archivos eclesiásticos," *Memoria del I Congreso Venezolano de Historia Eclesiástica* (Caracas, 1970), pp. 259–61.
23. See R. Vargas Ugarte, El archivo arzobispal de Lima," *Handbook of Latin American Studies* (Cambridge, 1936).
24. See F. Barreda, "Libros parroquiales de ciudades del Perú," *Revista del Instituto Peruano de Investigaciones Genealógicas* 10 (1957), 79–85.
25. See J. H. Pazmiño, "Archivo arzobispal de Quito," *Boletín CEHILA* 16–17, 15–17.
26. See O. Romero Arteta, "Indice del Archivo de la Antigua Provincia de Quito de la Compañía de Jesús," *Boletín del Archivo Nacional de Historia* IX/14–15 (Quito, 1965), 180–91.
27. See J. de Zengoitia, "The National Archive and the National Library of Bolivia at Sucre," *The Hispanic American Historical Review* (1949), 17–28.
28. See C. López and F. Cajías, "Archivo de la catedral de Santa Cruz de la Sierra," *Boletín CEHILA* 16–17, 17–28.

29. J. C. Zuretti, "Documentos eclesiásticos de la época de la revolución existentes en el Archivo Central de la Nación," *Archivum* IV/1 (1960), 297–370; G. Furlong, "Diseños de carácter eclesiástico que se conservan en el Archivo Genral de la Nación," *Archivum* III/2 (1959), 303–37.

30. See H.F. Pérez, *Los Archivos de la Asunción en Paraguay* (Buenos Aires, 1923).

31. See *Revista Histórica* XV (Montevideo, 1944), 85–105.

32. See R. Díaz Vidal, *Revista de Estudios Históricos* 10 (Santiago, 1962). See also C. Morin, "Los libros parroquiales como fuente para la historia demográfica y social," *Historia Mexicana* 21/83 (1972), 398–418.

33. See M. R. da Cunha Rodrígues, "As fontes primárias existentes no Achivo da curia de São Paulo," *Revista Histórica da São Paulo* 66 (1966), 437ff; B. J. Barbosa, *Archivo Histórico da Venerável Ordem Terceira da Nossa Senhora do Monte do Carmo* (Rio de Janeiro, 1872).

2. PUBLISHED SOURCES

There follows a list of some published sources useful for the study of the history of the Church in Latin America.

AZEVEDO BAIAO, P.A. de. *O arquivo da Torre do Tombo*. Lisbon, 1905.n

BARREDA, F."Libros parroquiales de ciudades del Perú." *Revista el Instituto Peruano de Investigaciones Genealógicas*, 10 (1957) 79–85.

BRICEÑO PEROZO, M. "Concentración de archivos eclesiásticos." *Memoria del I Congreso Venezolano de Historia Eclesiástica*, Caracas, 1970, 259–61.

CASTRO E ALMEIDA, E. *Inventario dos Documentos relativos ao Brasil existentes no Arquivo da Marinha e Ultramar de Lisboa*. Rio, 1913–36, vols I-VIII.

"Catálogo de exposiçao da História do Brasil", clase VI: *Históría Eclesiástica. Annaes da Bibliotheca Nacional*, vol.9, 1881–2, 749–812.

Catálogo dos manuscritos ultramarinos da Biblioteca Pública do Porto. Lisbon, 1938.

Cedulario Americano del siglo XVII. Colección de disposiciones legales indianas desde 1680 a 1800 contenidas en los Cedularios del Archivo General de Indias. ed. A. Muro Orejón, Seville, 1956–69, I-II.

Cedulario Indiano Compiled by Diego Encinas. Reproduction of the single edition of 1596. Madrid: Cultura Hispánica, 1945–6, I-IV.

Colección de Cédulas Reales dirigidas a la Audiencia de Quito 1560–1660. Quito: Archivo Nacional, 1935, I-IX.

Colección de documentos históricos inéditos referentes al arzobispado de Guadalajara, Guadalajara: Francisco Orozco y Jiménez Dávila Garibai, 1922–7, I-VI.

Colección de documentos inéditos para la Historia de Colombia. Bogotá: Juan Friede, 1955–6, I-X.

Colección de documentos inéditos para la historia de España. Madrid: Impr. Viúda Clavero, 1864–95, I-CXII (See: Díaz Trechuelo, Ma.de L., "América . . . " *Colección de Documentos inéditos de España*, thematic, geographic and cosmological Catalogue in *Anuario de Estudios Americanos* (Seville), XXVII (1970) 641-732.

Colección de documentos inéditos para la Historia de Chile. Santiago: José T. Medina, 1883–1902, I-X.

Colección de documentos inéditos relativos al Descubrimiento, Conquista y Colonización de las Antiguas Posesiones de Ultramar (II Series). Madrid, 1885–1932, I-XXV. (See: Schäfer, Ernst, *Indice de la Colección de los Documentos Inéditos de Indias*. Madrid 1946–7, I-II).

Colección de documentos para la Historia de la Formación Social de Hispanoamérica (1493–1810). Madrid: Richard Konetzke, 1953–62, I-V.

Colección de documentos para la Historia de Costa Rica. San José-Barcelona: León Fernández, 1881–1902, I-X.

Colección de documentos para la Historia de Colombia (Period of Independence). Bogotá: Elías Ortiz S., 1966.

Colección de documentos para la Historia de la Iglesia en el Perú. Seville: Lisson Chaves, 1943–5, I-IV.

Colección de documentos para la Historia de México. Mexico City: J. García Icazbalceta, 1858–66, I-II.

Colección Muñóz. Documents compiled by doctor Juan B. Muñóz, kept in the Academia de Historia in Madrid.

Compendiosa relación de la cristiandad de Quito, by B. Regio, ed. C. García Goldaraz. Madrid, 1948.

Compendiosa descripción del Arzobispado de México hecha en 1570 y otros Documentos, Mexico City: L. García Pimentel, 1897, 461.

Cuerpo de Documentos del siglo XVI sobre Derechos de España. Mexico City: Lewis Hanke-Carlos Millares, 1943.

División y límites de los obispados de Cuzco, los reyes de Quito, in Museo Histórico (Quito), 41-42 (1962) 80–89.

Documentos para la Historia de la Iglesia colonial en Venezuela. Caracas: Guillermo Figuera, 1965, I-II, 397–488.

Documentos para la Historia colonial de los Andes venezolanos (XVII to XVIII centuries). Caracas: José A. de Armas Chitty, 1957, 320.

Documentos para la Historia Argentina. Cartas anuas de la provincia del Paraguay, Chile y Tucumán de la Compañía de Jesús. Buenos Aires: C.J. Leonhardt, 1904.

DOMINGUEZ BORDONA, J. *Manuscritos de América*. Madrid, 1935.

Études et Documents pour l'Histoire Missionnaire de l'Espagne et du Portugal. Louvain: Robert Ricard, 1931.

FERREIRA, C.A. *Inventario dos manuscritos da Biblioteca da Ajuda referentes à América do Sul*. Coimbra, 1946.

GOMEZ CANEDO, L. *Los Archivos de Historia de América*. Mexico City, 1961, vols I-II.

—. "Archivos eclesiásticos de México." *Anuario de Bibliotecología, Archivología e Informática* III. Mexico City, 1971.

HARRISON, J.P. *Guide to materials on Latin America in the National Archives.* Washington, 1961–7, vols I–II.

HILL, R.R. *The National Archives of Latin America.* Cambridge, Mass.: University of Cambridge, 1945.

—. "Ecclesiastical archives in Latin America." *Archivum* 4. Paris, 1954, 135–44.

LAJOS PASTOR. *Guida delle fonti per la storia dell'America latina negli Archivi della Santa Sede e negli Archivi ecclesiastici d'Italia.* Vatican City, 1970.

Leyes, Las . . . Nuevas (1542–1543), with transcription and notes by A. Muro Orejón. *Anuario de Estudios Americanos* II. Seville, 1945.

Leyes, Recopilación de . . . de los Reynos de las Indias. Madrid: Julián Paredes, 1681, I–IV. Inst. Cultura Hispánica, Madrid, I–III. See Schäfer, Ernst, *Las Rúbricas del Consejo Real y Supremos de Indias.* Seville, 1934.

LOPEZ, C.-CAJIAS, F. "Archivo de la catedral de Santa Cruz de la Sierra." *Boletín-CEHILA*, 16–17 (1979), 17–28.

MACEDO SOAREZ, J.D. de. *Fontes da História da Igreja Católica no Brasil.* São Paulo, 1954.

MEDINA ASCENCIO, L. *Archivos y bibliotecas eclesiásticas.* Mexico City, 1966.

NAUMAN, Ann K. *A Handbook of Latin American and Caribbean National Archives. Guía de los archivos nacionales de América Latina y el Caribe.* Detroit: Blaine Ethridge Books, 1983.

PAZMIÑO, J.H. "Archivo arzobispal de Quito." *Boletín-CEHILA*, 16–17 (1979), 15–17.

PAZ, J. *Catálogo de los manuscritos de América existentes en la Biblioteca Nacional.* Madrid, 1933.

POU y MARTI, J.M. "Index Regestorum Familiae Ultramontanae." *Archivum Franciscanum Historicum* XII–XX. Florence, 1919–27.

PUGA, Vasco de. *Cedulario de la Nueva España* (Facsimile of the original, Mexico 1563. Commemorative edition for the Twentieth Anniversary of the Centro de Estudios de Historia de México Condumex). Mexico City: Chimalistac, 1985.

ROMERO ARTETA, O. "Indice del archivo de la antigua provincia de Quito de la Compañía de Jesús." *Boletín del Archivo Nacional de Historia* IX/14–15 Quito, 1965, 180–191.

SPECKER, J. "Missionsgeschichtliches Material." *Neue Zeitschrift für Missionswissenschaft*, XXX (1974) 220ff.

SURIA, J. *Catálogo general del archivo arquidiocesano de Caracas.* Caracas, 1964.

TORRE REVELLO, J. *El Archivo General de Indias de Sevilla*, Buenos Aires, 1929. (There are works on the archive by Torres Lanzas, Germán Latorre, Cristóbal Bermúdez, et al.).

TORRES LANZAS, P. *Guía histórica y descriptiva de los archivos, bibliotecas y museos arqueológicos de España.* Madrid, 1916.

—. *Guía de fuentes para la historia de Iberoamérica conservadas en España.* Madrid, 1966.

TRUJILLO MENA, V. "Archivo arzobispal de Lima." *Boletín-CEHILA* 16–17 (1979) 15–17.

VARGAS UGARTE, R. "El archivo arzobispal de Lima." *Handbook of Latin American Studies.* Cambridge, Mass., 1936.

ZARCO CUEVA, E. *Catálogo de los manuscritos castellanos de la Real Biblioteca Nacional.* Madrid, 1933.

ZENGOITIA, J. de. "The National Archive and the National Library of Bolivia at Sucre." *The Hispanic American Historical Review* (1949), 649–76.

Roman Decisions and other Documents

Actas y documentos del Cabildo Eclesiástico de Buenos Aires,Buenos Aires: E.C. Actis, 1943–4.

Bulario de la Iglesia mejicana. Documentos relativos a erecciones, desmembraciones. . . . de diócesis mejicanas, Mexico City: J.García Gutiérrez, 1951.

Bullarium Diplomatum et Privilegiorum Sanctorum Romanorum Pontificum, publ. by Card. Gaude. Rome-Naples: A. Taurinorum, 1859–67, IV-XII.

Bullarum Patronatus Portugalliae Regnum in Ecclesiis Africae, Asie et Oceanieae. Bulas, Brevia, Epístolas . . . , Olisipone: Paiva Manso, 1868–79, I-IV.

Cartas do Brasil de Manoel da Nóbrega, Rio de Janeiro: Academia Brasileira, 1931.

Cartas, Informaçoes, Fragmentos históricos e Sermoes de José de Anchieta. Rio de Janeiro, Civilizaçao Brasileira, 1933.

Colección de Bulas, Breves y otros documentos relativos a la Iglesia de América y Filipinas, Brussels: Francisco J. Hernáez and Alfredo Vromant, 1879, I-II (reprinted Vaduz, USA: Karaus, 1964).

Colección de documentos históricos del Arzobispado de Santiago. 1. Cartas de los obispos al rey; 2. Cedulario. Santiago, 1919–23.

Compendio Bulario Indico, Seville: Baltasar de Tobar, I (1954), II (1966).

CORTES Y CARRAZ, P. *Descripción geográfico-moral de la diócesis de Goathemala . . .*, Prol. by A. Recinos. Guatemala, 1958, 302.

Documentos para la historia de la diócesis de Mérida. Caracas: Antonio R. Silva, archbishop of the diocese, 1927, I-V.

Documentos para la Historia de Nicaragua (Somoza Collection). Madrid: Juan Bravo, 1945–57, I-XVII.

Documentos inéditos del siglo XVI para la historia de México, Mexico City: Mariano Cuevas, 1914.

Documentos inéditos que ilustran los orígenes de los Obispados Carolense (1519), Tierra Florida (1520) y Yucatán (1561). ed. Sergio Méndez Arceo, *Revista de Historia de América* (Mexico City) 9 (1940), 31–61.

Documentos para la Historia de Arequipa. Arequipa: Victor de Barriaga, 1940.

ESPINOSA, Isidro Félix de. *Crónica de los Colegios de Propaganda Fide de la Nueva España*, por Fray. . . . New edition with notes and introduction by Lino Gómez Canedo, Washington, 1964.

JAN, J.M. (ed.), *Collecta pour l'histoire du diocèse du Cap-Haïtien.* Port-au-Prince, 1955, I-II, 367; 288.

—, *Port-au-Prince: documents pour l'histoire religieuse.* Port-au-Prince, 1956, 527.

LEVILLIER, Robert. *La organización de la Iglesia y Ordenes Religiosas en el Virreinato del Perú en el siglo XVI.* Madrid, 1919, I-II.

—. *Papeles eclesiásticos del Tucumán.* Madrid, 1929, I-II.

—. *Gobernantes del Perú. Cartas y otros documentos del siglo XVI.* Madrid, 1913-26, I-XII.

—. *Gobernación de Tucumán. Papeles de gobernantes en el siglo XVI.* Madrid, 1920.

Materiales para la Historia de la Cultura en Venezuela, 1523-1828: documentos del Archivo General de Indias de Sevilla. Comp. by Mario Dorta, Caracas, 1967.

Monumenta Brasiliae. Rome: Serafim Leite, 1956-60, I-IV.

Monumenta Centro-Americae Historica. Managua: Car-

los Molina Argüello, 1965, I.

Monumenta Floridae. Rome: Félix Zubillaga, 1946, I.

Monumenta Mexicana. Rome: Félix Zubillaga, 1956-8, I-II.

Monumenta Peruana. Rome: Antonio Egaña, 1954-8, I-II.

Nueva colección de documentos para la Historia de México. Mexico City: García Icazbalceta, 1886-92, I-V.

Obispo Mariano Martí. Documents relating to his pastoral visit to the diocese of Caracas (1771-1784). Preliminary study and coordination by Lino Gómez Canedo, Caracas, 1969, I-VII.

Raccolta di Concordati su materie ecclesiastiche tra la Santa Sede e le autorità civili. Rome: A. Mercati, 1919, I-XIX.

Provincial Councils and Diocesan Synods

Actas y Decretos del Concilio Plenario de la América Latina celebrado en Roma el año del Señor de MDCCCXCIV. Official trans., Rome, 1906.

Acta et Decreta Primi Concilii Provincialis Nova Carthagine in America Meridionali anno Domini MCMII et a sede Apostolica anno MCMIV examinati et recogniti. Mediolani, MCMV.

APARICIO, S. *Los Mercedarios en los Concilios Limenses,* Madrid, 1973.

—. "El influjo de Trento en los Concilios Limenses." *Revista Missionalia Hispánica* XXV (Madrid, 1969) 215-39.

BAYLE, C. "El Concilio de Trento en las Indias Españolas". *Revista Razón y Fe,* 131 (1945) 257-84.

Colección de cánones y de todos los concilios de la Iglesia de España y de América. Tejada y Ramiro, 1851-9, I-V.

Collectio Maxima Conciliorum Omnium Hispaniae et Novi Orbis. Rome: Card. J. Sáez de Aguirre, 1694, IV.

Concilio II Provincial Mexicano . . . . Ed. M. Galván Rivera, Barcelona, 1870.

Concilio Provincial Mexicano IV (1771). Printed by order of Rafael Sabas Camacho, third bishop of Querétaro, Querétaro, 1898.

Concilio Limense, Constituciones Synodales et alia utilia Monumenta . . . nunc denuo exarata studio et diligentia Doctoris D. Francisci de Montalvo. Pub. by J. Vannaci, Rome, 1684.

Concilios Limenses. Lima: R. Vargas Ugarte, 1951-1954, I-III.

Concilio Provincial de Charcas de 1629. Pub. by B. Velasco *Missionalia Hispanica* XXI (1964) 79-130.

Concilio Provincial de Santo Domingo (1622-1623). Pub. by C. de Armellada. *Missionalia Hispanica* XXVI (1970) 129-252.

Concilio Provincial Limense Segundo. Pub. by F. Mateos. *Missionalia Hispanica,* VII (1950) 209-296, 525-617.

Concilios Provinciales Primero, y Segundo, celebrados en la muy noble y muy leal Ciudad de México, presidiendo el illmo. y Rmo. Señor Dr.Fr. Alonso de Montufar, en los años 1555, y 1565. Dálos a luz el illmo. s.r.d. Francisco Antonio Lorenzana. Mexico City, 1769. Cf. the edition by J. Ramírez, Mexico City, 1943, I-II.

Conciliorum Sacrorum . . . Nova et Amplissima Collectio. Paris: J.D. Mansio, 1902-15, XXI-XLVII.

Constituciones Synodales del Arzobispado de los Reyes (1613). Celebrado por Bartolomé Lobo Guerrero, ed. por Francisco del Canto, Lima, 1614. (see: CIDOC, *Colección Fuentes, Serie Segunda: Sínodos diocesanos,* 11, Cuernavaca, 1970).

Constituciones Synodales del Arzobispado de los Reyes, por el Ilmo. Señor Dr. Feliciano de la Vega, obispo de la dicha ciudad de La Paz, del año 1638, printed by Geronymo de Contreras, 1639.

De Primo Concilio Plenario Brasiliensi (1939) eiusque decretis, Studium Historico. Rome: J.C. Knoll, 1967.

MATEOS, F. *Sínodos del obispo de Tucumán, fray Fernando de Trejo y Sanabria. Missionalia Hispanica* XXVII (1970) 257-340. *Sínodo de Santa Fe de 1556,* en G. Romero, *Juan de los Barrios,* 459-563.

MORERI, Luis (1643-80). *El gran diccionario histórico, o Miscellanea curiosa de la historia sagrada y profana . . . por Don Joseph de Miravel y Casadevarte . . . .* Paris and León: Hermanos de Tournes, 1753, 8 vols.

PEREZ PASTOR, F. *Diccionario portátil de los concilios, que contiene una suma de todos los concilios generales, nacionales, provinciales y particulares,* vols.1-2.

Primer Concilio de Quito (1570). Pub. by F. Mateos, *Missionalia Hispanica,* XXV (1968) 193-247.

Primer Concilio del Río de la Plata, en Asunción (1603). Publ. by F. Mateos, *Missionalia Hispanica* XXVI (1969) 157-359.

Sínodos de Tucumán de 1597, 1606 y 1607, en Papeles eclesiásticos del Tucumán. Pub. by R. Levillier, Madrid, 1926, I-II (see: *Sínodo de Quito de 1590,* en Vargas Ugarte, *Concilios Limenses II,* 150 (see: Vargas J.M., *Constituciones del Primer Sínodo de Quito,* Quito, 1945.

Sínodo de Asunción de 1603. Revista de la Biblioteca Pública de Buenos Aires IV (1882) 8-13.

Sínodos diocesanos de Santo Toribio de Mogrovejo, 1582-1604. CIDOC, Colección Fuentes, Serie Segunda: Sínodos diocesanos, 1, Cuernavaca, 1970.

Sínodo diocesano de Santiago de Chile, celebrado en 1626. Historia (Santiago) 3 (1964) 313-60.

Sínodos y Concilios chilenos (1584-?). Historia (Santiago) 3 (1964) 7-86.

Sínodo del Paraguay de 1631. Revista de la Biblioteca Pública de Buenos Aires IV (1882), 13–17.

Sínodo diocesano del Obispado de Puerto Rico . . . del año 1917. Puerto Rico, 1917.

Sínodo diocesano Santiago de Chile, 1688. CIDOC, *Colección Fuentes, Serie Segunda: Sínodos diocesanos,* 2, Cuernavaca, 1970 (see P. Lira Urquieta, *El*

Protestant Published Sources

Among Protestant published sources, we take, first, the acts and documents of the major missionary conferences held on the continent: the Congress of Panama (*Christian Work in Latin America, Panama Congress.* New York, 1917, 3 vols.) and the regional conferences that followed (*Regional Conferences in Latin America.* New York, 1917); the Congress of Montevideo (*Christian Work in Latin America, Montevideo Congress.* New York, 1925, 2 vols.) for South America, and the Havana Congress for the north of the continent (Gonzalo Báez Camargo, *Hacia la Revolución Religiosa en Hispanoamérica.* Mexico City, 1930; Samuel G. Inman, *Evangelicals at Havana.* New York, 1919). The papers given at the Havana Congress appear in a separate publication (*Ponencias para el Congreso Evangélico de La Habana.* Havana, 1929).

Evangelical conferences are: Buenos Aires, 1949 (*El Cristianismo evangélico en la América Latina, Informe y resoluciones de la primera conferencia evangélica latinoamericana.* Buenos Aires, 1949); Lima, 1961 (*Cristo: la esperanza para América Latina, Ponencias, Informes, Comentarios de la Segunda Conferencia Evangélica Latinoamericana.* Buenos Aires, 1962); Buenos Aires, 1969 (*Deudores al mundo. Tercera Conferencia Evangélica Latinoamericana.* Montevideo, 1969); Oaxtepec, 1978 (*Unidad y Misión en América Latina, Oaxtepec, 1978.* San José, Costa Rica, 1980). Also the First Latin American Conference on Evangelization, CLADE (*Acción en Cristo para un continente en crisis,* San José, 1970).

Next, we need to consider the documents of the great international missionary conferences, in particular the World Missionary Conference held in Edinburgh in 1910 (*World Missionary Conference, 1910,* Edinburgh-London, 9 vols.); the Jerusalem Assembly of the International Missionary Council in 1928 (*The Jerusalem Meeting of the International Missionary Council,* London, 1928, 6 vols.), the World Missionary Assembly in Tambaram, India, 1938 (*La Misión Mundial de la Iglesia. Informe oficial del Consejo Misionero Internacional,* Buenos Aires, 1939); as well as other reports of meetings of the International Missionary Council: Whitby, Canada, 1947; Willing-

Sínodo diocesano de 1763. Historia (Santiago) 8 (1969) 277–87.

VERA, Fortino H. *Apuntamientos históricos de los concilios provinciales mexicanos y privilegios de América. Estudios Previos al primer Concilio.* Mexico City, 1893.

—. *Concilios provinciales mexicanos,* Mexico City, 1893.

en, W. Germany, 1952; Achimota, Ghana 1957–8; Mexico City, 1963; Bangkok, 1972–3; and Melbourne, 1980.

Thirdly, there are the reports of meetings of Latin American ecumenical bodies: ULAJE (*Con Cristo un mundo nuevo. Congreso Latinoamericano de Juventudes Evangélicas.* Lima, 1942); ISAL (*Encuentro y desafío. Conclusiones y resoluciones de la Primera Consulta Evangélica Latinoamericana sobre Iglesia y Sociedad, realizada en Huampani.* Montevideo, 1961; *América hoy, acción de Dios y responsabilidad del hombre.* Montevideo, 1966; *América Latina, movilización popular y fe cristiana.* Montevideo, 1971).

Most reports of these ecumenical bodies have not been published and exist in photocopied form only: UNELAM has, though, published reports of two meetings: one on women in Latin America (*El rol de la mujer en la Iglesia y en la sociedad.* Montevideo, 1968); the other on the missionary presence on the continent (*Misioneros norteamericanos en América Latina, ¿ para qué?,* Montevideo, 1971).

Then there are the missionary conferences held in the United States by councils for mission work in Latin America (*Ecumenical Missionary Conference on Foreign Missions.* New York, 1902, 2 vols.; *Conference on Mission in Latin America.* New York, 1913), and the various denominational or interdenominational meetings held on the continent for specific reasons: *Informe oficial del Congreso Evangélico Centroamericano.* Guatemala City, 1941; *Consultation on Religious Liberty in Latin America.* New York, 1955; *The Listening Isles.* Puerto Rico-New York, 1957; *Christian Literature Program for Latin America.* Mexico City, 1941; *Informe de la Primera Asamblea Evangélica Interamericana de Obra Rural.* Mexico City, 1956; Carlos Gattinoni, *Vida y Misión de la Iglesia Metodista.* Buenos Aires, 1961; *Committee on Latin America.* Geneva, 1963.

Finally, the "Informes Anuales del Comité de Cooperación para América Latina" (CCLA) from 1916 to 1965, are held in the "Missionary Research Library" in New York, and the duplicated reports of the National Council of Churches of Christ are held at that body's headquarters in New York.

Lists of Bishops

ALEGRE, Francisco J. Various lists in *Historia de la Provincia de la Compañía de Jesús en Nueva España.* Roma 1956–60, I–IV.

ASCARAY, J. "Serie cronológica de los obispos de Quito". *Anales de la Universidad de Quito.* (Quito) 1892.

BRAVO UGARTE, J. *Diócesis y Obispos de la Iglesia Mexicana (1519–1939).* Mexico City, 1941.

DUSSEL, E. "Liste critique des évêques hispano-américains (1504–1620)." Appendix I in *Les*

évêques hispanoaméricains, défenseurs et évangelisateurs de l'indien (1504–1620). Wiesbaden, 1970, 228–49. Full version in *El episcopado latinoamericano defensor del indio (1504–1620).* Cuernavaca: CIDOC vols.I–IX, 1969–71. New edition in *El episcopado y la liberación de los pobres.* Mexico City: CRT, 1979.

FURLONG, G. *Diócesis y obispos de la Iglesia Argentina (1572–1942).* Buenos Aires, 1942.

GAMS, B. *Series Episcoporum Ecclesiae Catholicae.* Graz: Akademische Druck, 1957.

GARCIA BENITEZ, L. *Reseña histórica de los obispos que han regenteado la diócesis de Santa Marta (1534-1891)*. Bogotá, 1953, 663.

GULIK, G.-EUBEL. *Hierarchia Catholica-Medi et recentioris Aevi*. Regesburg: Schmitz Kallenberg, III, 1923.

MATEUS, A.E. Albuja. "El Obispado de Quito en el siglo XVI." *Missionalia Hispanica* XVIII (1961), 161-209.

MESANZA, A. *Obispos dominicos de América*, I, Einsiedeln, 1939.

"Nómina de obispos y arzobispos de Venezuela." *Crónica de Caracas* (Caracas) 45–46/9 (1960), 349–50.

NOBREGA, A. "Diócesis e bispos do Brasil" *Revista do Instituto Histórico e Geográfico Brasileiro* (Rio de Janeiro) 222 (1954) 3–328.

OVIEDO CAVADA, C. *Los obispos de Chile 1561–1978*. Santiago, 1979.

PACHECO, J.M. "Los primeros obispos de Cartagena (de 1534 a 1577)." *Revista Ecclesiastica Xaveriana* (Bogotá) VI (1956) 357–92.

PANIAGUA OLLER, A. *Episcopologio portorricense . . . Sínodo diocesano del Obispado de Puerto Rico . . . del año 1917, por el Ilmo. Obispo Guillermo A. Jones*.

Puerto Rico, 1917.

RESTREPO POSADA, J. *Arquidiócesis de Bogotá. Datos biográficos de sus prelados*. Bogotá, 1961, I-III (from 1564 to 1981).

RUIZ CAJAR, C. "La jerarquía eclesiástica en Panamá durante el siglo XVI." *Boletín de Historia y Antigüedades* (Bogotá) 47–48/2 (1955), 301-20.

SANABRIA MARTINEZ, V. *Episcopologio de la diócesis de Nicaragua y Costa Rica, 1531–1850*. San José, 1943.

SCHWALLER, R.F. "The Episcopal Succession in Spanish America, 1800–1850." *The Americas* (Washington) 3/24 (1968), 207–71.

UTRERA, C. de. "Episcopologio dominocpolitano." Section of nos 85 and 87 of *Boletín del Archivo General de la Nación* (Ciudad Trujillo) 1956, 56.

VALVERDE TELLEZ, E. *Bio-bibliografía eclesiástica mexicana (1821–1943)*, I-II (Obispos). Mexico City, 1949.

VARGAS UGARTE, R. "Episcopado de las diócesis del Virreinato del Perú desde los orígenes hasta mediados del siglo XVII." *Boletín del Instituto de Investigaciones Históricas* (Buenos Aires) XXIV (1940), 1–31.

II. BIBLIOGRAPHY

The Bibliography that follows is divided into two main sections: "Bibliographic Bibliography" and Bibliography proper. The second section is divided in turn into: (1) basic works dealing with the whole continent; (2) regional, following the division made in Part II of this volume.

1. BIBLIOGRAPHIC BIBLIOGRAPHY

General Works

"Bibliografía de la Historia de América (1965–1969)." *Revista de Historia de América* (Mexico City), 1953, 292.

Bibliografía Missionaria, by Rommerskirchen, Kowalsky, Metzler, Henkel (1965–1972). Pont. Bibliot. Miss. Prop. Fide, Rome, 1966–1973.

Bibliotheca Missionum, ed. Robert Streit-Dindinger, vol. I, *Grundlegender und Allgemeiner Teil*. Münster: Inter. Inst. für Missionswissenschaft Forschung, 1916; vols II-III, *Amerikanische Missionsliteratur (1493–1909)*. Aachen, 1924–1927; supplements, vols XXII-XXIII (1963–4); vols XXIV-XXVI, ed. J. Rommerskirchen-J. Metzler, with bibliography 1910–1960. Freiburg, 1967–8.

BISSAINTHE, Max. *Dictionnaire de Bibliographie haitienne*. Washington: Scarecrow Press, 1951.

BLANCHET, Paul. *Bibliographie haitienne: 1957–1967*. Port-au-Prince: Panorama, 1982.

BRAVO, Enrique R. *Bibliografía puertorriqueña selecta y anotada. An Annotated Selected Puerto Rican Bibliography*. New York: Urban Center of Columbia University, 1972.

BYRNE, Pamela R. and S.R. ONTIVEROS. *Women in the Third World: A Historical Bibliography*. Santa Barbara: ABC-Clio, 1986.

Cambridge Encyclopedia of Latin America and the Caribbean, Cambridge: Cambridge University Press, 1985.

CHAMBERS, Frances. *Haiti*. Oxford: Clio Press, 1983 (World Bibliographical Series n. 39).

CORTES CONDE, R. and S.J. STEIN (eds.). *Latin America: a Guide to Economic History, 1830–1930*. Berkeley: University of California Press, 1977.

Current Caribbean Bibliography. Port-of-Spain, Trinidad: Caribbean Commission, 1951- .

DEIROS, Pablo A. et.al. "Protestantismo en el Cono Sur: Argentina, Chile, Paraguay, Uruguay." *Para una Historia de la Evangelización en América Latina*. Barcelona: CEHILA, Editorial Nova Terra, 1977, 26–269.

Fichero bibliográfico Hispanoamericano. Termly catalogue of all books published in Spanish in the Americas. New York, 1961-.

FLORIDA, University of, Gainesville. Libraries. Technical Processes Department. *Caribbean Acquisitions: Material Acquired by the University of Florida, 1957/58-*, Gainesville, 1959-.

GEOGHEGAN, A. R. (comp.).*Obras de referencia de América Latina* (annotated selection of encyclopedias, dictionaries, bibliographies, biographical reports, catalogues, guides, annuals, indexes). Buenos Aires, 1965.

GRIFFIN, Ch. (ed.). *Latin America. A Guide to the Historical Literature.* Austin: Conference on Latin American History, 1971.

GROPP, A.E. (comp.). *A Bibliography of Latin American Bibliographies.* Metuchen, 1968.

Handbook of Latin American Studies, ed. Miron Burgin. Cambridge (Mass.), 1936–48, I-XI.

Handbook of Latin American Studies. Gainesville: University of Florida Press, 1935-.

Hispanic Foundation in the Library of Congress. Gainesville: University of Florida Press, 1980, vol. XVII.

Historiografía y Bibliografía Americanistas. Seville: Escuela de Estudios Hispanoamericanos, 1955-72.

Indice Histórico Español. Barcelona: University of Barcelona, 1953-.

INSTITUTE OF JAMAICA, Kingston, Library of. *Bibliography of the West Indies (Excluding Jamaica),* 1909. Reprint by Johnson Reprint Corp., New York, 1971.

—. West Indies Reference Library. *Catalog of the West Indies Reference Library,* 6 vols. Millwood, N.Y.: Kraus International, 1980.

KNASTER, Meri. *Women in Spanish America: An Annotated Bibliography from Pre-Conquest to Contemporary Times.* Boston: G.K. Hall, 1977.

LEVINE, Robert M. *Race and Ethnic Relations in Latin America and the Caribbean: An Historical Dictionary and Bibliography.* Metuchen, N.J.: Scarecrow Press, 1980.

MIAMI, University of. Cuban and Caribbean Library, *Catalog of the Cuban and Caribbean Library, University of Miami, Gables, Florida,* 6 vols. Boston: G.K. Hall, 1977.

NELSON, Wilton N. "Bosquejo y Bibliografía para una historia del protestantismo en América Latina." CEHILA, *Para una Historia de la Evangelización en América Latina.* Barcelona: Nova Terra, 1977.

New Catholic Encyclopedia. New York: McGraw-Hill, 1967-74.

PUERTO Rican Research and Resources Center. *The Puerto Ricans: An Annotated Bibliography.* New York: Bowker, 1973.

Revista Interamericana de Bibliografía. Washington, 1961-.

Revue d'Histoire Ecclesiastique, Bibliographie. Louvain: Université Catholique de Louvain, 1900-.

SANCHEZ ALONSO, B. *Fuentes de la Historia Española e Hispanoamericana.* Madrid, 1952, I-III.

SINCLAIR, J.A. *Protestantism in Latin America. A Bibliographical Guide.* Austin, 1967, 213.

TRASK, D.F., M.C. MEYER and R. TRASK. *Bibliography of United States-Latin American Relations Since 1810.* Lincoln: University of Nebraska Press, 1968.

VAN DER GRIJP, Klaus. "Protestantismo en Brasil." CEHILA, *Para una Historia de la Evangelización en América Latina.* Barcelona: Nova Terra, 1977, 230–48.

WILGUS, A.C. *Latin America in the Nineteenth Century. A Selected Bibliography of Books of Travel and Description Published in English.* Metuchen, N.J.: Scarecrow Press, 1973.

Historical Dictionaries

BORK, Albert W. and G. MAIER. *Historical Dictionary of Ecuador.* Metuchen, N.J.: Scarecrow Press, N.J., 1973.

BRIGGS, Donald C. and M. ALISKI. *Historical Dictionary of Mexico.* Metuchen, N.J.: Scarecrow Press, 1981.

CREEDMAN, Theodore S. *Historical Dictionary of Costa Rica.* Metuchen, N.J.: Scarecrow Press, 1977.

DAVIS, Robert H. *Historical Dictionary of Colombia,* Metuchen, N.J.: Scarecrow Press, 1977.

Diccionario Histórico Argentino, 6 vols. Buenos Aires: Ediciones Históricas Argentinas, 1953–4.

Dicionario de História do Brasil, moral e civismo. São Paulo: Melhoramentos, 4th ed., 1976.

Diccionario Porrúa de Historia, Biografía y Geografía, 2 vols. Mexico City: Porrúa, 4th ed., 1976.

FARR, Kenneth R. *Historical Dictionary of Puerto Rico and the U.S. Virgin Islands.* Metuchen, N. J.: Scarecrow Press, 1973.

FLEMION, Philip F. *Historical Dictionary of El Salvador.* Metuchen, N.J.: Scarecrow Press, 1972.

FUENTES, Jordi, et.al. *Diccionario Histórico de Chile.* Santiago: Editorial del Pacífico, 1978.

GASTMANN, Albert. *Historical Dictionary of the French and Netherlands Antilles.* Metuchen, N.J.: Scarecrow Press, 1973.

HEATH, Dwight B., *Historical Dictionary of Bolivia.* Metuchen, N.J.: Scarecrow Press, 1972.

KOLINSKI, Charles J. *Historical Dictionary of Paraguay.* Metuchen, N.J.: Scarecrow Press, 1973.

LEVINE, Robert M., *Historical Dictionary of Brazil.* Metuchen, N.J.: Scarecrow Press, 1979.

—. *Race and Ethnic Relations in Latin America and the Caribbean: An Historical Dictionary and Bibliography.* Metuchen, N.J.: Scarecrow Press, 1980.

LUX, William. *Historical Dictionary of the British Caribbean.* Metuchen, N.J.: Scarecrow Press, 1975.

MARTINEZ, Rufino. *Diccionario biográfico-histórico dominicano 1821–1930.* Santo Domingo: Universidad Autónoma de Santo Domingo, 1971.

MENDIBURU, Manuel de. *Diccionario Histórico-biográfico del Perú.* Lima: Enrique Palacios, 2nd. ed. 1931–5.

MEIER, Matt S. and F. RIVERA. *Dictionary of Mexican American History.* Westport, Conn.: Greenwood Press, 1981.

MEYER, Harvey K. *Historical Dictionary of Nicaragua.* Metuchen, N.J.: Scarecrow Press, 1972.

MOORE, Richard E. *Historical Dictionary of Guatemala.* Metuchen, N.J.: Scarecrow Press, 1967.

NUÑEZ, Benjamin. *Dictionary of Afro-Latin American Civilization.* Westport, Conn.: Greenwood Press, 1980, 525.

PERUSSE, Roland I. *Historical Dictionary of Haiti.*

Metuchen, N.J.: Scarecrow Press, 1977.
SAN CRISTOVAL, E. *Apéndice al Diccionario Histór-ico-biográfico del Perú.* Lima: Imp. Gil, 1935–8.

See also the bibliographies in: L. LOPETEGUI and F. ZUBILLAGA *Historia de la Iglesia en la América Española,* from the discovery to the early nineteenth century, Madrid, 1965, vol .I, XXIX-LIX; A. de EGAÑA, *ibid.,* vol II, at the beginning of each chapter; H.J. PRIEN, *Die Geschichte des Christentums in Lateinamerika,* Göttingen, 1978, 1188–1243. The

volumes of the *Historia General de la Iglesia en América Latina* published by CEHILA have a bibliography at the end of each volume devoted to their respective areas or countries.
On Protestantism, see: SINCLAIR, J.A., *Protestant-ism in Latin America. A Bibliographical Guide.* Pasadena, 1976; PRIEN, H.J., *Die Geschichte des Christentums in Lateinamerika.* Göttingen, 1978, 1188–1243; *Bibliogra-fía Teológica Comentada,* dir. by Bierzychudek, Buenos Aires, from 1973. Consult particularly sections: 1. Social Sciencies and 3. History of the Churches.

Statistical Bibliography

Anuario estadístico de América Latina. Statistical Yearbook for Latin America. New York-Santiago: United Nations, Economic Commission for Latin America, 1973-.
BEACH, H.-BURTON, J. *World Statistics of Mission-ary Societies,* New York, 1916.
DAMBORIENA, P. and E. DUSSEL. *Protestantismo en América Latina.* Freiburg: FERES, 1961.
EDMONSTON, Barry. *Population Research in Latin America and the Caribbean: A Reference Bibliography.* Ann Arbor: University Microfilms International, 1979.
GOYER, Doreen S. *The International Population Census Bibliography: Revision and Update, 1945–1977.* New York: Academic Press, 1980.

INTERCHURCH WORLD MOVEMENT OF NORTH AMERICA (ed.). *World Survey.* New York, 1920, 2 vols.
READ, W.-MONTERROSO, V.. *Latin American Church Growth.* Grand Rapids: Eerdmans, 1969.
Statistical Abstract of Latin America. Los Angeles: Center of Latin American Studies, University of California, 1955-.
TATUM, Charles M. *A Selected and Annotated Bibliography of Chicano Studies.* Lincoln Neb.: Society of Spanish and Spanish-American Stu-dies, 1979.
TAYLOR, Gl.-GOGGINS, W. *Protestant Missions in Latin America. A Statistical Survey.* Washington, 1961.

Cartographic Bibliography

AGI (Archivo General de Indias). The whole cartographic section, partly catalogued by Torres de Lanza. All the material found here can be used directly or indirectly for church history.
AMAYA TOPETE, J. *Atlas Mexicano de la Conquista.* Mexico City, 1958.
Atlante delle Missioni Cattoliche dipendenti dalla Sacra-Congregazione de "Propaganda Fide". Vatican City, 1947.
Atlas Missionum, a Sacra Congregatione de Propaganda Fide dependentium. Ed. G. Mödling. Vatican City, 1958.
BEACH, H. and C. FAHS. *World Missionary Atlas, containing a Directory of Missionary Societies, Classified Summaries of Statistics, Maps showing the Location of Mission Stations throughout the World, a Descriptive Account of the Principal Mission Lands, and Comprehensive Indices.* New York, 1925.
BEACH, Harlan. *A Geography and Atlas of Protestant Missions.* New York, 1903, 2 vols.
BLUME, Helmut. *The Caribbean Islands.* London: Longman, 1974.
BN (Bibliothèque National de Paris), section *Cartes et Plans du XVIe siècle.*
BUENO, Cosme. *Geografía del Perú Virreinal (1739)* Ed. Valcárcel, Lima 1951.
DENNIS, J., H. BEACH and Ch. FAHS. *World Atlas of Christian Missions, containing a Directory of Missionary Societies, a Classified Summary of Statistics, an Index of Mission Stations and Maps showing the Location of Mission Stations throughout the World.* New York, 1911.

DESPONT, J. *Nouvel Atlas des Missions.* Paris-Lyon, 1951.
DIETRICH-HAGEN-TERMER. *Nord und Mittel-amerika. Handbuch der Geog.Wiss..* Wildpark-Postdam, 1933.
EVANS, F.C. *The West Indies.* London: Cambridge University Press, 1973.
FREITAG, A. *Historicher Missionsatlas.* Steyl, 1959.
JIMENEZ, J. *Mapa Lingüístico del Norte y Centro América.* Mexico City: Instituto Panamericano de Geografía e Historia, 1936.
KLEMP, Egon (comp. and ed.). *America in Maps Dating from 1500 to 1856.* New York: Holmes & Meier, 1976.
LOPEZ DE VELASCO, J. *Geografía y Descripción de las Indias.* Zaragoza-Madrid, 1894.
MAULL-KUHN-TROLL. "Süd-Amerika in natura." *Handbuch der Geogr.Wiss..* 1930.
MEER, Frederic Van Der.*Atlas de la Civilisation Occidentale.* Amsterdam, 1951.
NEUHAUSTER, J. *Atlas der Katholischer Estmission.* Munich, 1932.
STIER-KIRSTEN. *Atlas zur Weltgeschichte.* Braun-schweig, 1956.
STREIT, C. *Atlas Hierarchicus.* Paderborn, 1929.
TOYNBEE, A. "Historical Atlas and Gazetteer." *A Study of History,* XI. London, 1959.
VAZQUEZ DE ESPINOSA, A. *Compendio y Descrip-ción de las Indias Occidentales (1630).* Washington: Smithsonian Institute, 1948.
VIDAL-LABLANCHE. *Atlas Historique et Géograph-ique.* Paris, 1951.

2. GENERAL BIBLIOGRAPHY

The overall history of the Church in Latin America has only recently been undertaken. Leandro Tormo tried to write a *Historia de la Iglesia en América Latina*, but managed only an Introduction to the subject of evangelizatcion (Vol I, Bogotá: FERES, 1962) and that of emancipation (Vol. II, 1963). L. Lopetegui, F. Zubillaga and A. Egaña published in 1965 and 1966 their *Historia de la Iglesia en la América española* (Madrid: BAC, vols. I-II) on the colonial period. Enrique Dussel's work, *Hipótesis para una Historia de la Iglesia en América Latina*, written in 1964 (published in 1967 in Barcelona by Estela), which went into its 7th Spanish edition in 1992, also translated into English (Grand Rapids: Eerdmans, 1981) and German (Mainz: Matthias Grünewald), was therefore the first to give a complete overview of the history of the Church in Latin America. The work of the Commission for Study of the History of the Church in Latin America (CEHILA), begun in 1973 in Quito, will complete the programme sketched out in the "hypothesis" of 1964. Its *Historia General de la Iglesia en América Latina* in ten volumes began publication in 1977. Hans-Jürgen Prien's *Die Geschichte des Christentums in Lateinamerika*, (Gottingen: Vandenhoeck und Ruprecht, 1978) marked a decisive step forward. Then various versions appeared in the Spanish editions of the European general histories of the Church (Frederick Pike, "La Iglesia en Latinoamérica," in *Nueva Historia de la Iglesia*, edited by Fliche-Martin (Valencia: EDICEP, vol. I complementary, 1981, pp.697–72); Felix Zubillaga, "Die Kirche in Lateinamerika," in *Handbuch der Kirchengeschichte*, edited by Hubert Jedin (Freiburg: Herder, vol. VII, 1979, pp.685–768; the Spanish edition, published by Herder, Barcelona, devotes a complete volume to the history of the Church in Latin America).

General Works

ACERBI, A. *La Chiesa nel tempo. Sguardi sui progetti di relazione tra chiesa e società civile negli ultimi cento anni*. Milan, 1979, 11–93.

ACTA et Documenta Concilio Oecumenico Vaticano II apparando. Series II, vol.II, parts VI-VII, Vatican City, 1960–1.

ACTAS y Decretos del Concilio Plenario de América Latina celebrado en Roma el año del Señor de MDCCCXCIX (1899). Rome, 1906.

ALBA, V. *Le Mouvement ouvrier en Amérique Latine*. Paris, 1953.

ALONSO, I. and G. GARRIDO, *La Iglesia en América Central y el Caribe*. Bogotá, 1962.

ANDRE-VINCENT, I. "Le Document de Puebla." *Esprit et Vie* (1979) 2, 395–400.

ANNUARIUM Statisticum. *Ecclesiae Catholicae Anno 1975*. Vatican City, 1976.

ANON. *Anuario de la Iglesia Católica. Cuba Isla - Diáspora*. Caracas.

—. "La crisis del centroamericanismo." *ECA* (1969), 417–21.

—. *La Gerarchia Cattolica*, Vatican City: Tip.Vaticana, 1899.

—. *La lucha de los católicos mexicanos*, Tanayona, 1926.

—. *La voz de los sin voz. La palabra viva de Monseñor Romero*. San Salvador, 1980.

—. *Rutilio Grande, Mártir de la Evangelización Rural en El Salvador*. 1978.

APPENDIX ad Concilium Plenarium Americae Latinae. Rome, 1900.

ARCOS, J. *El sindicalismo en América Latina*. Freiburg-Bogotá, 1960.

ARDAO, A. *Espiritualismo y positivismo en el Uruguay*. Buenos Aires, 1950.

AUPING, J. *The Relative Efficiency of Evangelical Nonviolence. The Influence of a Revival of Religion on the Abolition of Slavery in North America 1740-1865*. Rome, 1977.

AUZA, N. *Católicos y liberales en la generación del ochenta (Argentina)*. Buenos Aires, 1984.

AZEVEDO, Th. de. "O Catolicismo no Brasil." *Cadernos de Cultura* (Rio de Janeiro) 87, 1955.

BARBOSA, M., *A Igreja no Brasil*. Río de Janeiro, 1945.

BASTIAN, J.P. *Breve Historia del Protestantismo en América Latina*. Mexico City: CUPSA, 1986 (2nd ed., 1990).

BAUER, A.J. (comp.). *La iglesia en la economía de América Latina siglos XVI al XIX*. Mexico City: INAH, 1986, 500

BERNAL, L.C. "Política y Justicia." *Theologica Xaveriana* (Bogotá) 1976, 365–72.

BIGO, P. "Concepto Marxista y Concepto Cristiano del Conflicto de Clases." *Medellín* (Medellín) 1967, 36–49.

BORRAT, H. *La svolta. Chiesa e Politica tra Medellín e Puebla*. Assisi, 1979.

BROWN, L.C. "Mexican Church-State Relations." *A Journal of Church and State* (1964) 6, 202–22; (1966) 8, 214–33.

BRUNO, C. *Historia de la Iglesia en Argentina*. Buenos Aires, vol. I, 1960-.

CAMARA, H. *La Iglesia en el desarrollo de América Latina*. Madrid: Zero, 1965, 52.

CAMARGO, P. *Historia Eclesiástica do Brasil*. Petrópolis, 1965.

CAPRILE, G. *Il Sinodo dei Vescovi 1974*. Rome, 1971; 2 vols, Rome, 1972.

CARDENAL, R. *Historia de una esperanza. Vida de Rutilio Grande.* San Salvador: UCA Editores, 1985; 2nd ed., 1987.

CARDENAS, E. "Vida Religiosa y situaciones históricas." *CLAR. Perspectivas* 2. Bogotá, 1974.

CASSANO, G. *Il Cardinale Giovanni Cagliero (1838-1926).* 2 vols, Turin, 1936.

CASTRO, M. *León XIII, Colección Completa de las Encíclicas de S.S. León XIII en latín y castellano.* 2 vols, Valladolid, 1903.

CAVALLI, F. "Documenti Pontifici per la ripresa religiosa dell'America Latina." *La Civiltà Cattolica* (1965) III, 248–55.

CAVALLI, F. "I problemi del cattolicismo nell'America Latina." *La Civiltà Cattolica* (1965) III, 458–72.

CEDIAL (Centro de Estudios para el Desarrollo e Integración de América Latina). *Cristianos Latinoamericanos y Socialismo.* Bogotá, 1972.

CEHILA, ed. Enrique Dussel. *Historia General de la Iglesia en América Latina.* Vol. I/1: *Introducción General.* Salamanca: Sígueme, 1983; Vol. II/1: *Brasil (1500–1808).* Petrópolis-São Paulo: Vozes-Paulinas, (1977) 3rd ed. 1983; vol. II/2: *Brasil (séc.XIX).* Petrópolis-São Paulo: Vozes-Paulinas, 2nd ed. 1985; vol. V: *México.* Salamanca-Mexico: Sígueme-Paulinas, 1984; vol. VI: *Centroamérica.* Salamanca: Sígueme, 1985; vol. VII: *Colombia-Venezuela.* Salamanca: Sígueme, 1981; vol. VIII: *Perú, Bolivia y Ecuador.* Salamanca: Sígueme, 1987; vol. X: *Fronteras: A History of the Latin American Church in USA since 1513.* San Antonio: MACC, 1983.

—. *Para una Historia de la Iglesia en América Latina,* ed. E. Dussel. Barcelona: Nova Terra, 1975 (CEHILA, 1st Symposium).

—. *Bartolomé de las Casas (1474–1974) e Historia de la Iglesia en América Latina,* ed. E. Dussel. Barcelona: Nova Terra, 1976 (CEHILA, 2nd Symposium).

—. *Para una Historia de la Evangelización en América Latina,* ed. E. Dussel. Barcelona: Nova Terra, 1977 (CEHILA, 3rd Symposium).

—. "História da religiosidade popular na América Latina." ed. E. Hoornaert. *Revista de Cultura Vozes* (Petrópolis) LXXII/4 (May 1979) (CEHILA, 5th Symposium).

—. *La Iglesia Latinoamericana de Medellín a Puebla.* Bogotá: CEHILA-CODECAL, 1979 (CEHILA, 6th Symposium).

—. *Escravidão Negra e História da Igreja na América Latina e no Caribe,* ed. J.O. Beozzo. Petrópolis: Vozes, 1987.

—. *Das Reduções Latino-Americanas às Lutas Indígenas Atuais,* ed. E. Hoornaert. São Paulo: Paulinas, 1982 (CEHILA, 9th Symposium).

—. *Para uma História da Igreja na América Latina. O debate metodológico.* Petrópolis: Vozes, 1986 (CEHILA, 12th Symposium).

—. "Los archivos eclesiásticos en Latinoamérica," ed.Alfonso Alcalá. *Boletín CEHILA* 16–17 (Jan. 1979).

—. "Para una historia de los cristianismos en América Latina." *Cristianismo y Sociedad* 82 (Mexico City: ASEL, 1984).

—. "Penetración ideológica norteamericana y anti-yanquismo. Perspectiva histórica." *Cristianismo y Sociedad* 86 (1985).

CEJUDO VEGA, F. *El Primer Concilio Plenario en América Latina. Estudio Comparativo.* Mexico City, 1961.

CELAM. *Directorio Católico Latinoamericano.* Bogotá, 1968.

—. *Iglesia y religiosidad popular en América Latina*: I. Conclusiones; II. Ponencias y documento final. Bogotá, 1976.

—. *Liberación. Diálogos en el CELAM.* Bogotá, 1974.

—. *Reflexiones sobre Puebla.* Bogotá, 1980.

—. *Seminarios. Departamento de Ministerios Jerárquicos.* Bogotá, 1973.

—. "Libros auxiliares para la III Conferencia General del Episcopado Latinoamericano": I. *Iglesia y América Latina en cifras*; II. *La Iglesia y América Latina. Aportes Pastorales desde el CELAM,* 2 vols.; III. *Aportes Pastorales desde las Conferencias Episcopales*; IV. *Visión Pastoral de América Latina. Equipo de Reflexión del CELAM.* Bogotá, 1978.

—. *Socialismo y Socialismos en América Latina.* Bogotá, 1977.

CLARK, G. *The Coming Explosion in Latin America.* Mc Kay, 1962.

COMMISSION, Pontifical "Justitia et Pax." *La Iglesia y los derechos del hombre.* Working Document, no. 1. Vatican City, 1975.

COMMISSION, International Theological. "Declaration on Human Development and Christian Salvation" (Sep. 1977). A.T. Hennelly, ed., *Liberation Theology: A Documentary History.* Maryknoll, N.Y.: Orbis, 1990, 205–19.

CONFERENCIA GENERAL DEL EPISCOPADO LATINOAMERICANO, I, Rio de Janeiro, 1955. CELAM Archive.

CONFERENCIA GENERAL DEL EPISCOPADO LATINOAMERICANO, II, Medellín, 1968. *La Iglesia en la Actual Transformación de América Latina a la luz del Concilio*: vol.I. *Ponencias*; vol. II. *Conclusiones.* Bogotá, 1969. Eng. trans. *The Church in the Present-day Transformation of Latin America,* vol. 2. Washington, D.C.: USCC, 1970.

CONFERENCIA GENERAL DEL EPISCOPADO LATINOAMERICANO, III, Puebla, 1979. *La Evangelización en el Presente y en el Futuro de América Latina.* Bogotá, 1979. Eng. trans. J. Eagleson and P. Scharper, eds., *Puebla and Beyond.* Maryknoll, N.Y.: Orbis, 1980; also *Puebla.* Slough: St Paul; London: CIIR, 1980.

CONSIDINE, J. *Call for Forty Thousand.* New York, 1946.

—. *New Horizons in Latin America.* New York, 1958.

—. *The Church in the New Latin America.* Indiana: Notre Dame, 1964.

COTAPOS SILVA, C. *Historia Eclesiástica de Chile.* Santiago, 1925.

CRIVELLI, C. *Directorio Protestante de la América Latina.* Isola del Liri (Italy), 1933.

—. *Los protestantes y la América Latina.* Isola del Liri, 1931.

CROW, J.A. *The Epic of Latin America.* New York: Doubleday, 1946.

CUEVAS, M. *Historia de la Igleisa en México.* 5 vols, El Paso, 1928.

CHAMORRO, P.J. *Historia de la Federación de la América Central, 1823–1840.* Madrid, 1959.

CHAUMU, P. *Histoire de L'Amérique Latine* (Que sais-je? 361). Paris, 1979.

D'ANTONIO, F., F. PIKE et al. *Religión, Revolución y Reforma.* Barcelona: Herder, 1967.

DAMBORIENA, P. *El Protestantismo en América Latina.* 2 vols. Bogotá, 1962–3.

—. "Le péril protestant en Amérique Latine." *Documentation Catholique* (1955), 148ff.

DAMMERT BELLIDO, J. "¿Es aplicable la legislación canónica en América Latina?" *Revista Española de Derecho Canónico* (1962) 17, no. 50, 513–23.

—. "Un grave problema, la distancia." *Incunable* (Salamanca) 2, no. 905, 177.

DELOBELLE, A. *Las Universidades Católicas de América Latina [1963].* Cuernavaca: CIDOC, 1968, cuad.16.

DEWART, L. *Christianity and Revolution.* New York:: Herder & Herder, 1964.

DORNAS FILHO, J. *O Padroado e a Igreja Brasileira.* São Paulo, 1939.

DUCLERQ, M. *Crises et Combats de l'Église en Amérique Latine* Paris, 1979.

DUSSEL, E. *Desintegración de la Cristiandad colonial y liberación.* Salamanca: Sígueme, 1978. Eng. trans. Maryknoll, N.Y.: Orbis, 1985..

—. *De Medellín a Puebla: Una década de sangre y esperanza (1968–1979).* Mexico City: Centro de Estudios Ecuménicos, 1979.

—. *Hipótesis para una Historia de la Iglesia en América Latina.* Barcelona: Estela, 1967. Eng. trans. *A History of the Church in Latin America.* Grand Rapids: Eerdmans, 1981.

—. *Historia de la Iglesia en América Latina,* Barcelona: Estela, 1972, 7th ed. 1992.

—. *Los últimos 50 años (1930–1985) en la historia de la Iglesia en América Latina.* Bogotá: Indo-American Press Service, 1986.

—. *Hipótesis para una Historia de la Teología en América Latina.* Bogotá: Indo-American Press Service, 1989.

ECHEVERRIA, B. *La Iglesia en el Ecuador.* Quito, 1979.

ESTRADA MONROY, A. *Datos para la historia de Iglesia en Guatemala,* vol. III. Guatemala, 1979.

FELLMANN VELARDE, J. *Historia de Bolivia.* 2 vols., La Paz, 1970.

FERNANDEZ-SHAW, F. *La organización de los Estados Americanos.* Madrid, 1966.

FINOT, E. *Nueva Historia de Bolivia (Ensayo de interpretación sociológica).* La Paz, 1954.

FLICHE-MARTIN, ed. *Historia de la Igelsia,* vol. XXVI, 2, with Appendix: *Historia de la Iglesia Latinoamericana* [1914–1939], 453–691. Valencia: EDICEP, 1980.

GARCIA GUTIERREZ, J. *Acción Anticatólica en México.* Mexico City, 1956.

GHEDDO, P. et al. *Puebla, Una Chiesa per il duemila.* Milan, 1979.

GHEERBRANT. *La Iglesia Rebelde de América Latina.*

Mexico, 1970.

GIBBONS, W.J. "Basic Ecclesiastical Statistics for Latin America." World Horizon Reports, vols. 12 (1956), 24 (1958), 26 (1960). Ed. Maryknoll, reproduced in CONSIDINE, J. *New Horizons in Latin America.* New York, 1958, 327–36.

GIL, C. *Misión Política de la Iglesia.* Caracas, 1978.

GILLOW Z., Bp. *Reminiscencias del Illm. Sr. d. Eulogio Gillow Zavalza.* Los Angeles, 1920.

GOMEZ TAMAYO, D.M. *Desterrados ilustres o Confesores de Cristo.* Pasto (Colombia), 1942.

—. "La caída del presidente Estrada Cabrera." *ECA,* 1065, 52–8.

GRIGORIOU DE LOSADA, R. "Relaciones de Iglesia y Estado en Bolivia." *Simposio sudamericano-alemán sobre Iglesia y Estado.* Quito, 1980, 251ff.

GUERRA, F. *A questão religiosa do Segundo Imperio Brasileiro: Fundamentos Históricos.* Rio de Janeiro, 1952.

GUTIERREZ, G. *Teología de la Liberación,* Lima, 1971. Eng. trans. *A Theology of Liberation.* Maryknoll, N.Y.: Orbis; London: SCM Press, 1973, revised edition 1988.

—. *Teología desde el Reverso de la Historia.* Lima, 1977. Eng. trans. *The Power of the Poor in History.* Maryknoll, N.Y.: Orbis, 1980.

HALPERIN DONGHI, T. *Historia Contemporánea de América Latina.* Madrid, 1970.

HARDORY, J. *Las ciudades en América Latina.* Buenos Aires, 1972.

HERNANDEZ Y SANCHEZ-BARRA, M. *Tensiones Históricas Hispanoamericanas en el Siglo XX.* Madrid, 1961.

HERRERA RESTREPO, B. *Pastorales y Documentos.* Bogotá, 1898.

HOLLERAN, M.P. *Church and State in Guatemala.* New York, 1949.

HOURDIN, G. *A Cuba deux ans aprés: Les Catholiques devant l'imposture.* ICI, 137 (17 Feb. 1961), 13–26.

HOUTART, F. *La Iglesia Latinoamericana en la Hora del Concilio.* Freiburg-Bogotá, 1962.

—. and E. PIN. *L'Église à l'heure de l'Amérique Latine.* Tournai, 1965.

JARLOT, G. *Doctrine Pontificale et Histoire. L'enseignement social de Léon XIII, Pie X, et Benoît XV vu dans son ambiance historique (1878-1922).* Rome, 1964.

—. *Doctrine pontificale et Histoire. Pie XI (1922-1939).* Vol. II, Rome, 1973.

JEDIN, H. *Manual de Historia de la Iglesia,* vol.VIII. Barcelona: Herder, 1978.

JIMENEZ, R. *América Latina y el mundo desarrollado.* (Commented bibliography on dependence and imperialism. Bogotá, 1977.

JOHN PAUL II. *Mensaje a la Iglesia Latinoamericana* (BAC minor 52). Madrid 1979.

—. *Pronunciamentos do Papa no Brasil.* São Paulo: Conferencia Episcopal do Brasil, 1980.

JOVER, M. "Presencia de la Iglesia en una Sociedad en transformación revolucionaria: la experiencia cubana, ensayo de análisis prospectivo." *Exilio* (New York) year4, no .1, 218–53.

KLOPPENBURG, B. *A Maçonaria no Brasil.* Petrópolis, 1961.

—. "El Proceso de la Secularización en América Latina." *Medellín* (Medellín) 1976, 308–32.

—. *Iglesia Popular.* Bogotá, 1977.

—. "Movimientos Religiosos autónomos en América Latina." *Medellín* (Medellín) 1978, 156ff.

—. "Visión Pastoral de la realidad latinoamericana." *Medellín* (Medellín) 1980, 81ff.

KUBIS, A. *La Théologie du Martyre au 20e. Siècle.* Rome, 1969.

LARA Y TORRES, L. *Documentos para la historia de la persecución religiosa en México.* Mexico City, 1954.

LEGON, F. *Doctrina y ejercicio del Patronato nacional.* Buenos Aires, 1920.

LEPARGNEUR, P. "Laicat adulte, premier problème de l'Église en Amérique Latine." *Nouvelle Révue Théologique* (1961) 83, 1031–80.

LERNOUX, P. *Cry of the People.* New York, 1980.

—. *People of God. The Struggle for World Catholicism.* New York: Penguin, 1989.

LEVAGGI VEGA, U. "¿Qué es el CELAM?" *Agencia Católica de Informaciones de América Latina* (Lima) Sep.-Oct., 1980.

LOOR, W. *Eloy Alfaro,* 3 vols. Quito, 1947.

LOPEZ TRUJILLO, A. "Líneas Pastorales de la Iglesia en América Latina." *Medellín* (Medellin) 1979, 181–8.

LORA, C. de. *Estudio sociográfico de los Religiosos y Religiosas en América Latina* (CLAR, "Colección Perspectivas" n.2). Bogotá, 1971.

LORSCHEIDER, A. "Preparación de la III Conferencia General." *Medellín* (Medellín) 1978, 500–5.

LUZZI, J. "L'appel de l'Amérique Latine." *Nouvelle Révue Théologique* (1953) 8, 617–27.

—. "L'Amérique Latine a besoin de prêtres." *Ibid.,* (1955) 87, 822–48.

LLUBERES, A. "La Iglesia en las Antillas Españolas (1914-1939)." *Historia de la Iglesia* (FLICHE-MARTIN), XXVI, 2, 519–31.

MACEDO ACOSTA, A. de. *A questão religiosa no Brasil perante a Santa Sé . . . a Missão especial a Roma em 1873 à luz de Documentos públicos e inéditos* [. . .]. Lisbon, 1886.

MAGNET, A. "Bibliografía de tres revoluciones: México, Bolivia y Cuba." *Mensaje* 2, (Santiago de Chile) 1968, 652–66.

MALDONADO KARIM, A. *La misión educadora de la Iglesia [en América Latina].* Rome: Lateran University, 1969.

MARADEI, C. *Venezuela, su Iglesia y sus Gobiernos.* Caracas, 1978.

MARCILIO, M. L. (ed.). *A mulher pobre na história da Igreja latino-americana.* São Paulo: Paulinas, 1983 (CEHILA, 11th Symposium).

MARIA, J. *O Catolicismo no Brasil. Memoria histórica.* Rio de Janeiro, 1950.

MARINS J. et al. *Praxis de los Padres de América Latina. Los Documentos de las Conferencias episcopales de Medellín a Puebla.* Bogotá, 1978.

MARINS, J. "Reflexión Episcopal entre Medellín y Puebla." *Medellín* (1979), 316ff.

MASPERO, E. "Le Syndicalisme Chrétien en Amérique Latine." *ICI* (1961) 146, 17–28.

MATICORENA ESTRADA, M. "La Iglesia ante los problemas bolivianos." *Estudios Americanos* (Sevilla) 30, 1954.

MECHAN, J. Lloyd. *Church and State in Latin America: A History of Politico-Ecclesiastical Relations.* Chapel Hill, 1934, 2nd ed.1966.

MEDINA ASCENSIO, L. *Historia del Colegio Pío Latinoamericano. Roma 1858–1978.* Mexico City, 1979.

MERCATI, G. *Raccolta di Concordati.* I. Rome, 1919; II. Vatican City, 1954.

METHOL FERRÉ, A. *De Río a Puebla. Etapas históricas de la Iglesia en América Latina (1945-1980).* Bogotá, 1980.

MIRANDA, F. "La comunidad eclesial católica en la República del Ecuador." FLICHE-MARTIN. *Historia de la Iglesia* XXVI, 2, 589–603.

MONEST, J.E. *On les croyait Chrétiens.* Paris, 1969.

MONGE ALFARO, C. *Historia de Costa Rica.* San José, 1966.

MOORE, O.R. *A History of Latin America.* New York, 1956.

MORANDO, F. *Il primo Concilio Plenario Latinoamericano* (unpublished thesis). University of Rome, 1981.

MOREIRA-ALVES, M. *L'Église et la politique au Brésil.* Paris, 1974.

MORENO Y DIAZ, E. *Cartas Pastorales,* vol. I. Madrid 1908 [He was the bishop of Pasto, Colombia, beatified in 1975].

MÖRNER, M. *Historia Social Latinoamericana (Nuevos enfoques).* Caracas, 1979.

MUNERA, A. "Crónica de la II Conferencia del Episcopado Latinoamericano." *RJ* (1968) 2, 393–9.

MURRAY, J.C. "The Problem of State Religion." *Theological Studies* (1951) 12, 155–78.

NAVARRETE, F. *La masonería en la historia y en las leyes de México.* Mexico City, 1957.

NAVARRETE, H. *Por Dios y por la patria.* Mexico City, 1961.

NAVARRO, N. *Anales eclesiásticos venezolanos.* Caracas, 1951.

—. *Disquisición sobre el patronato eclesiástico en Venezuela.* Caracas, 1931.

—. *El Arzobispo Guevara y Guzmán Blanco.* Caracas, 1932.

—. *La Masonería en Venezuela.* Caracas, 2nd ed., 1979.

NOUEL, C. *Historia Eclesiástica de la Archidiócesis de Santo Domingo,* 3 vols. Rome-Santo Domingo, 1913-15.

PARSONS, W. *Mexican Martyrdom.* New York, 1936.

PATTEE, R. *El Catolicismo Contemporáneo en Hispanoamérica.* Buenos Aires, 1951.

—. and J.F. PARR. *Love Thy Neighbor.* Huntington-Indiana, 1951.

PAUL VI, *Il Viaggio di Paolo VI a Bogotá.* Vatican City 1968.

PEREYRA, C. *Historia de la América Española.* Madrid, 1925.

PÉREZ, R. *La Compañía de Jesús en Colombia y Centroamérica.* 3 vols. Valladolid, 1895–8.

PIKE, F. *The Conflict between Church and States in Latin America.* New York, 1967.

POBLETE TRONCOSO, M. *El movimiento obrero latinoamericano.* Mexico City, 1946.

PROMPER, W. "Priesternot in Lateinamerika." *The Americas* (1966) 22, 413–20.

QUILES, I. "Laicismo en Latinoamérica. *"Latino-américa* 1957. 150–3.

RICHARD, P. (ed.). *Materiales para una historia de la teología en América Latina.* San José: DEI-CEHILA 1981.

—. (ed.). *Raíces de la Teología Latinoamericana.* San José: DEI, (1985) 1987 (CEHILA, 8th Symposium).

—. *Death of Christendoms: Birth of the Church.* Maryknoll, N.Y.: Orbis, 1982.

ROGIER, L.J. et al. *Nueva Historia de la Iglesia.* 5 vols. Madrid, 1977.

ROMERO DE SOLIS, J.M. *El Porfiriato y la Iglesia de México* (doctoral thesis, ms). Rome, 1979].

—. *Iglesia y Clero en la Constitución política Mexicana de 1917* (licentiate thesis). Rome, 1979.

RUIZ GARCIA, E. *América Latina Hoy.* 2 vols, Madrid, 1971.

RYAN, E. *The Church in the South American Republics.* Westminster, Md.: 1943.

SALCEDO, C. *Biografía de Monseñor Luis Javier Muñoz, S.I., Arzobispo de Guatemala.* Medellín, 1940.

SANABRIA, V. *Bernardo Augusto Thiel, segundo obispo de Costa Rica.* San José, 1941.

SANCHEZ ESPEJO. *El Patronato en Venezuela.* Caracas, 2nd ed., 1955.

SANTINI, C. *De regio patronatu in Brasilia [. . .] 1514-189.* Porto Alegre, 1934.

SANTO ROSARIO, M.R., *O Cardeal Leme.* Rio de Janeiro, 1962.

SCHMIDT, A. "Panorama General de la Iglesia y sus Seminarios en América Latina." *Seminarios* (Salamanca) 5, 1959, 187–201].

SCHOOYANS, M. "La Conférence de Puebla. Un risque, un espoir." *Nouvelle Révue Théologique,* 1979, 640–75.

SCHUMACHER, P. *La Sociedad civil y cristiana según la doctrina de la Iglesia Romana.* Freiburg: Herder, 1900.

Seminaria Ecclesiae Catholicae. Vatican City, 1963.

SERRANO, J. "Brésil." *DHGE X.* Paris, 1938, col. 556–89.

SIERRA, V. *Historia de la Argentina.* Buenos Aires, 1956.

SILLIS, D. (dir.). "Enciclopedia Internacional de las Ciencias Sociales." *Iberoamérica* V. New York, 1968.

SIREAU, A. "La Crisis Religiosa en América Latina." *Latinoamérica,* 1955, 370–3.

SOARES LIMA, L. "Relaçoes entre a Igreja e o Estado no alvorecer da República Brasileira." *Estudos* (Oct.-Dec.) 1948, 51–70.

SOLARI, A.E. *Estudiantes y política en América Latina.* Caracas, 1968.

SORGE, B. "Puebla 1979: Un segno di Dio per tutta la Chiesa." *La Civiltà Cattolica* (1979) 2, 9–30.

SOBRINO, J. "Puebla. Serena afirmación de Medellín." *Christus* 1979, 45–55.

SUESS, P. (comp.). *Quema y Siembra. De la Conquista*

espiritual al descubrimiento de una nueva evangelización.* Quito: Abya-Yala, 1990.

TAPIE, V.-M. *Histoire de l'Amérique Latine au Siècle XIX.* Paris, 1945.

TEICHERT, P. *Revolución económica e industrialización en América Latina.* Mexico City, 1963.

TERAN DUTARI, J. *Simposio Sudamericano-Alemán sobre Iglesia y Estado,* ed. J. Terán Dutari. Quito, 1980.

TESTE, I. *Historia Eclesiástica de Cuba.* 3 vols, Madrid, 1969–73.

THIEL, B.A. *Datos Cronológicos para la Historia Eclesiástica de Costa Rica.* San José, 1896.

TOBAR DONOSO, J. *La Iglesia Ecuatoriana en el Siglo XIX.* 2 vols, Quito, 1934–6.

—. *La Iglesia Modeladora de la Nacionalidad.* Quito, 1953.

TORRUBIANO RIPOLL, J. *Los Concordatos de la Postguerra y la Constitución Civil de los Estados.* Madrid, 1931.

TOULAT, J. *Esperanza en América del Sur.* Barcelona, 1966.

TURNER, F. *Catholicism and Political Development in Latin America.* University of North Carolina, 1971.

VALADES, J.C. *El Porfirismo. Historia de un régimen.* 2 vols, Mexico City, 1941, 1948.

VALLIER, I. *Catolicismo, control social y modernización en América Latina.* Buenos Aires, 1971.

VARIOUS. *Les tâches de l'Église en Amérique Latine.* Freiburg, 1963.

—. *La Iglesia Nace en el Pueblo* (Colección Iglesia Nueva). Bogotá, 1979.

—. *La Iglesia en Centroamérica. Survey de la Compañía de Jesús sobre la Iglesia en Centroamérica.* San Salvador, 1969.

—. *El Sistema Interamericano. Estudio sobre su desarrollo y fortalecimiento.* Madrid, 1966.

—. "Revolución en América Latina." *Mensaje* (Santiago) 115, 1963.

VEKEMANS, R. *Teología de la Liberación y Cristianos por el Socialismo.* Bogotá, 1976.

VENTURA COROMINAS, C. *Historia de las Conferencias Interamericanas.* Buenos Aires, 1959.

VICENS VIVES, J. *Historia Social y Económica de España y América,* vol.V. Barcelona, 1959.

VIDAL, J.M. *El primer arzobispo de Montevideo, Dr Mariano Soler.* 2 vols, Montevideo, 1935.

VILANOVA, S.R. *Apuntamientos de Historia Patria Eclesiástica.* San Salvador, 1911.

WATTERS, M. *Historia de la Iglesia Católica en Venezuela.* Caracas, 1951.

WHITAKER, A.P. *Argentina. Transformación de un país y el flujo de inmigrantes 1880–1916.* Mexico City, 1966.

ZEA, L. *Dos etapas del pensamiento en Hispanoamérica: del romanticismo al positivismo.* Mexico City, 1949.

—. *América en la Historia.* Madrid, 1970.

ZURETTI, J.C. *Historia Eclesiástica Argentina.* Buenos Aires, 1945.

Regional Binliography

I. BRAZIL

a. General Works on the Church

AZEVEDO, T. de. *O catolicismo no Brasil.* Rio de Janeiro: Ministério de Educação e Cultura, 1955.

AZZI, R. *A Vida Religiosa no Brasil- Enfoques Históricos.* São Paulo: Paulinas, 1983.

BARBOSA, M. *A Igreja no Brasil. Notas para su história.* Rio de Janeiro, 1945.

BERTA LEITE. "História Eclesiástica do Brasil." *Anais do Instituto Histórico e Geográfico Brasileiro* (Rio de Janeiro), 1951, 207–59.

CEHILA *História da Igreja no Brasil*, História Geral da Igreja na América Latina (HGIAL) vol. II/1-4, Petrópolis-São Paulo: Vozes-Paulinas, 1977-.

—. *Navio Negreiro.* São Paulo: Paulinas, 1981.

CERIS. *Anuário Católico da Igreja do Brasil.* Rio de Janeiro, 1st ed., 1933.

DESROCHERS, G. and E. HOORNAERT (orgs.). *Padre Ibiapina e a Igreja dos pobres.* São Paulo: Paulinas, 1984.

HOORNAERT, E. *O cristianismo moreno no Brasil.* Petrópolis: Vozes, 1991.

—. *Crônica das casas de caridade fundadas pelo Padre Ibiapina.* São Paulo: Loyola, 1981.

—."A evangelização segundo a tradição guadalupana." REB 34, no. 135, Sept.1974, 524–45.

—. *Formação do catolicismo brasileiro, 1550–1800: ensaio de interpretação à partir dos oprimidos.* Petrópolis: Vozes, 1974.

—.*A Igreja no Brasil-Colõnia: 1550–1800.*, São Paulo: Brasiliense, 1992.

—. "Para uma História da Igreja no Brasil." *Revista Eclesiástica Brasileira* (REB), vol. 33, no. 129, Mar. 1973.

—. et.al. *Historia da Igreja no Brasil: ensaio de interpretação a partir do povo (primeira época).* Petrópolis: Vozes, 1977. (Vol. II/1 of HGIAL).

LUSTOSA, O. de F. *A Igreja Católica no Brasil e o regime republicano*, São Paulo: Loyola-CEPEHIB, 1990.

—. *Igreja e política no Brasil: do Partido Católico à L.E.C. (1874–1945).* São Paulo: Loyola-CEPEHIB, 1983.

—. *Reformistas na Igreja do Brasil Império.* São Paulo: USP, Faculdade de Filosofia, Letras e Ciências Humanas, 1977.

—. *Política e Igreja: o partido católico no Brasil, mito ou realidade?.* São Paulo: Paulinas, 1982.

—. *Reformismo da Igreja no Brasil Imperio: do celibato à caixa eclesiástica.* São Paulo: Loyola, 1985.

—. *Os bispos do Brasil e a Imprensa.* São Paulo: Loyola-CEPEHIB, 1983.

MONTENEGRO, J.A. de Souza. *Evolução do catolicismo no Brasil.* Petrópolis: Vozes, 1972.

MOURA, O.D., OSB. *Idéias Católicas no Brasil. Direções do pensamento católico no Brasil do século XX.* São Paulo: Convívio, 1978.

OLIVEIRA TORRES, J.C. de. *História das ideias religiosas no Brasil: a Igreja e a sociedade brasileira.* São Paulo, 1968.

PIRES, P.H. "Os construtores da História Eclesiástica no Brasil." REB 3 (Mar. 1943) 79–95.

PREZIA, B. and E. HOORNAERT. *Essa Terra tinha Dono.* São Paulo: CEHILA-Popular, CIMI, 1989.

REZENDE, M.V. *Não se pode servir a dois senhores.* Lins: Editora Todos Irmãos, 4th ed., 1985.

SILVA, S. da (org.). *A Igreja e a questão agrária no nordeste. Subsidios históricos.* São Paulo: Paulinas, 1986.

SILVEIRA CAMARGO, P.Fl. da. *História da Igreja no Brasil.* Petrópolis: Vozes, 1955.

SOUZA LIMA, L.G. de. *Evolução política dos Católicos e da Igreja no Brasil. Hipóteses para uma interpretação.* Petrópolis: Vozes, 1979.

SOUSA RANGEL, M.A. de. "Os reis de Portugal e a Igreja no Brasil." *Anais do Instituto Histórico e Geográfico Brasileiro* (Rio de Janeiro) 1951.

TONUCCI, P. *Quando os atabaques batem.* São Paulo: Paulinas 1984.

b. Evangelization (XVI-XVIIIc)

BATLLORI, M. *Bibliografía de Serafim Leite.* Rome, 1962.

Constituiçoes Primeiras do arcebispado da Bahia. Salvador, 1707.

LEITE, S. *História da Companhia de Jesus no Brasil*, vols I-X.

VARIOUS. *Conflito e Continuidade na sociedade brasileira.* Rio de Janeiro, 1970.

c. Church Organization (XVI-XVIIIc)

ALMEIDA, L.C. de. "Clero secular diocesano brasileiro setecentista." *Anais do Congresso Comemorativo do Bicentenário de transferência da Sede do Governo do Brasil da Cidade do Salvador para o Rio de Janeiro*, III (1967) 41–103.

AZZI, R. *O episcopado na história da Igreja do Brasil; Evangelização e Catequese (século XVI); A vida do clero no Brasil; Os leigos na vida religiosa do Brasil;* (unpublished investigations carried out at the Centro de Estatística Religiosa e Investigação Social (CERIS), Rio de Janeiro, 1967-9).

MATTOS, W. *Os carmelitas descalços na Bahia.* Salvador, 1964.

MUELLER, G. *História da Abadia de Salvador-Bahia.* Salvador, 1947.

VAN DER VAT, O. *Princípios da Igreja no Brasil.* Petrópolis, 1952.

d. Daily Religious Life (XVI-XVIIIc)

COMBLIN, J. "Para uma tipologia do catolicismo no Brasil." REB 28 (1968).

FREYRE, G. *Casa Grande e Senzala.* Buenos Aires, 1943.

HOORNAERT, E. "As relaçoes entre Igreja e Estado na Bahia colonial." REB 32 (1972) 275–308.

SALVADOR, J.G. *Cristãos-Novos, jesuitas e Inquisição. Aspectos da sua atuaçao nas Capitanias do Sul 1530-1680.* São Paulo, 1969.

e. The Church and Emancipation (XIXc)

CARDOZO, M. "Azeredo Coutinho e o fermento intelectual de sua época." *Conflito e continuidade na sociedade brasileira.* Rio de Janeiro, 1970.

DUARTE E SILVA, L. *O clero e a independência.* Rio de Janeiro, 1923.

ENNES, E. *Os autos crimes contra os réus eclesiásticos da conspiração de Minas Gerais.* Ouro Preto, 1952.
FRIEIRO, E. *O diabo na livraria do conego.* Itatiaia, 1956.
RODRIGUES, J.H. "O clero e a independência." REB 32 (1972) 309–26.

f. The Church and the New State (XXc to 1930)

CARTA PASTORAL por ocasião do centenário da Independência (1922). Petrópolis: Vozes, 1957.
COMBLIN, J. "Situação Histórica do Catolicismo no Brasil." REB 26 (1966) 574–601.
CONCILIUM PLENARIUM BRASILIENSE in urbe S.Sebastiani Fluminis Januarii Anno Domini MDCCCCXXXIX celebratum. Petrópolis: Vozes, 1939.
DAUPHINEE, B.A. *Church and Parliament in Brazil during the First Empire, 1823–1831.* Georgetown University, 1965.
GOVINI, H. *Laicato e ministério hierárquico na zona de colonização italiana no Rio Grande do Sul.* (Unpublished research carried out at CERIS, Rio de Janeiro, 1966.
PASTORAL COLETIVA dos Senhores Arcebispos e Bispos das Províncias Eclesiásticas de S. Sebastião do Rio de Janeiro, Mariana, S. Paulo, Cuiabá e Porto Alegre comunicando al clero e aos fiéis os resultados das Conferências Episcopais realizadas na cidade de Nova Friburgo de 12 a 17 de janeiro de 1915. Rio de Janeiro: Tipografia Martins de Araújo, 1915.
SILVEIRA, I. "As ordens religiosas e a legislação no primeiro império." REB, 1958, 970.
VIEIRA, A. "A maçonaria no Brasil." REB 1955, 627; 1956, 399.

g. Church Reorganization in the Liberal State (to 1930)

BOEHRER, G.C. "The Church and the Overthrow of the Brazilian Monarchy," *Hispanic American Historical Review* 48 (1969) 380–401.
—. "A Igreja no segundo reinado: 1840–1899," *Conflito e continuidade na sociedade brasileira.* Rio de Janeiro, 1970.
CARRATO, J.F. *As Minas Gerais e os primórdios do Caraça.* São Paulo, 1963.
—. *Igreja, Iluminismo e Escolas Mineiras Coloniais. Notas sobre a cultura da decadência mineira setecentista.* São Paulo, 1968.
DORNAS, J. *O Padroado e a Igreja brasileira.* São Paulo, 1938.
GABAGLIA, L.P.R., *O Cardeal Leme (1882–1942).* Rio de Janeiro, 1962.
MAGALHAES, B.de. "Dom Pedro II e a Igreja." *Rev. do Inst.Histórico* (1925) 98, vol. 152.
MENDES DE ALMEIDA, C. *Direito civil e eclesiástico brasileiro. Introdução, 1860–1873.*
Pastoral Collectiva dos Arcebispos e Bispos das Províncias Meridionais do Brasil, 1915.
RUBERT, A. "Os bispos do Brasil no Vaticano I." REB 103 (1969).
THORNTON, M.C. *The Church and Freemasonry in Brazil. A Study in Regalism.* Washington, 1948.
TRINDADE, R. *Archidiocese de Marianna. Subsídios para a sua história.* São Paulo, 1928.
VIOTTI, A. "Pio IX e o Brasil." REB 1963, 658.

h. Laity and Society (1930–1964)

FIGUEIREDO, J. de. *A questão social na filosofia de Farias Brito.* 1929; *Do nacionalismo na hora presente.* 1921; *A reaçao do bom senso.* 1922; *Literatura reacionaria.* 1924.
EREIRA DE QUEIROS, M.I. *Historia y etnología de los movimientos messiânicos.* Mexico City, 1969.
QUEIROS, M.V. de. *Messianismo e conflito social.* Rio de Janeiro, 1966.
DE KADT, E.J. *Catholic Radicals in Brazil.* London, 1979.
—. *The Catholic Church and Social Reform in Brazil.* New York, 1970.
GHEERBRANT, A. *L'Eglise rebelle d'Amerique Latine.* Paris, 1969.
GOMES DE SOUZA, L.A. *Brasil: confronto de duas geraçoes de cristãos.* Cuernavaca: CIDOC, 1966.

II. THE CARIBBEAN AREA

1. HAITI

BREATHETT, G. "Religions, protectionism and the Slave in Haiti." *Catholic Historical Review* (Washington) 55 (1969) 26–39.
BELLEGARDE, D. *Histoire du peuple haïtien (1492–1952).* Lausanne, 1953.
—. *Haïti et ses problèmes.* Montreal, 1941.
FAGG, J.E. *Cuba, Haiti and the Dominican Republic.* New York: Prentice-Hall, 1965.
ROBERT, P. *L'Eglise et la première République Noire.* Lampau-Guimiliale (France), 1964.
PATTEE, R. *Haiti.* Madrid, 1956.
PRICE-MARS, J. *De la préhistoire d'Afrique a l'histoire d'Haïti.* Port-au-Prince, 1962.
VERSCHVEREN, J. *La République d'Haïti.* Wetteren: Scaldis, 1948.

2. CUBA

AGRUPACION CATOLICA UNIVERSITARIA. BIP, *Encuesta sobre el sentimiento religioso del pueblo de Cuba.* Havana, 1954.
—. *¿Por qué reforma agraria?.* Havana, 1959.
ALVAREZ, C. (interviews) *Cuba. Testimonio cristiano, vivencia revolucionaria.* San José: DEI, 1990.
ALVAREZ MOLA, M.V. and P. MARTINEZ PEREZ. "Algo acerca del problema negro en Cuba hasta 1912." *Universidad de La Habana* (Havana) 179 (1966) 79–93.
AMIGO JANSEN, G. "Cuba." R. Patte, *El Catolicismo Contemporáneo en Hispanoamérica.* Buenos Aires, 1951.
—. "Informaciones francesas sobre Cuba." *Revista Javeriana* LXIV, (Bogotá) 317 (Aug. 1965), 222-33.
—. "El coraje de Cuba, ¿símbolo y llamado para la liberación de América Latina?" *ECA* (San Salvador, June 1968), 154–9.
Anuario de la Iglesia Católica, Cuba: Isla y Diáspora. Caracas, 1972.
Anuario de la Iglesia Católica, Cuba Diáspora, 1976, 1977, 1978 y 1981. Miami: Revista Ideal, 1976–81.
Anuario Pontificio. 1955 to 1982.

ASSMAN, H. *Habla Fidel Castro sobre los cristianos revolucionarios*. Montevideo: Tierra Nueva, 1972;

ARCE, L.A. de. "Apuntes exegéticos sobre el seminario de San Carlos y San Ambrosio." *Universidad de la Habana*. (Havana) 182 (1966) 7–56.

—. "Esbozo sinóptico de la filosofía del siglo XVIII en los conventos." *Universidad de la Habana*. (Havana) 183 (1967) 21–53.

BARNET, M. *Biografía de un cimarrón*. Barcelona, 1968.

Bohemia. (Havana) 18 Jan., 25 Feb., 5 April, 24 May, 30 May and 5 June, 1959.

Boletín Parroquial. Parroquia de Nuestra Señora de la Caridad. (Havana) 4 May, 7 July and 7 Dec., 1958.

BOZA MASVIDAL, E. *Voz en el destierro*. Miami: Revista Ideal, 1976.

—. "La Iglesia frente al comunismo ¿por qué una doble actitud?" *ECA* (San Salvador) 243, XXIII (Nov. 1968) 379–80.

BUNTIG, Aldo J. "La Iglesia en Cuba. Hacia una nueva frontera. Reflexiones de un testigo." *Revista del CIAS* (Buenos Aires) 193 (June 1970) 5–46.

CASTRO, F. *La Revolución Cubana. Escritos y discursos*. Buenos Aires: Palestra, n.d.

CEPEDA, R. (ed.). *La herencia misionera en Cuba*. San José: DEI, 1986, 248.

CELAM. *Boletín Informativo* 45 (July 1961).

CORWIN, A.F. *Spain and the Abolition of Slavery in Cuba, 1817–1886* Austin, 1967.

"Episcopado cubano. Apuntes histórico-críticos sobre la creación del obispado de la isla de Cuba y los obispos que ocuparon la mitra." *El Curioso Americano* (La Habana) año IV, época IV (Sept.-Dec. 1910), 131.

DEWART, L., *Christianity and Revolution*. New York: Herder & Herder, 1964.

FERNANDEZ, M. "La Iglesia en Cuba a los diez años de la Revolución." *Mensaje Iberoamericano* (Madrid) 42 (Apr. 1969) 10–13.

—. "La política religiosa cubana en tres documentos oficiales." *Mensaje Iberoamericano* (Madrid) 199 (May 1982), 6–14.

FROILAN DOMINGUEZ. "La situación de la Iglesia en Cuba." *Mensaje Iberoamericano* (Madrid) 199 (May 1982), 2–7.

FUNDACION "ANDRES VALDESPINO." *Valdespino, Cuba como pasión*. Hato Rey (Puerto Rico), n.d..

GOMEZ TRETO, R. *La Iglesia católica durante la construcción del socialismo en Cuba*. San José: CEHILA-DEI, 1987, 125.

—. *A Igreja e o Socialismo*. São Paulo: Paulinas, 1989.

GUERRA SANCHEZ, R. and PEREZ CABRERA, J.M. (eds.). *Historia de la Nación Cubana*. 10 vols., Havana, 1962, ff.

GUERRA Y SANCHEZ, R. *Manual de Historia de Cuba económica, social y política*. Havana, 2nd ed., 1962.

HAGEMAN, A. and WEATON, Ph. *Cuba. La Religión en la Revolución*. Buenos Aires: Granica, 1974.

HERNANDEZ, J.M. *ACU, Agrupación Católica Universitaria: Los primeros cincuenta años*. Miami: ACU, 1981.

JOVER, M. "Presencia de la Iglesia en una sociedad en transformación revolucionaria: la experiencia cubana. Ensayo de análisis prospectivo." *Exilio* (New York) (Winter 1969-Spring 1970), 218–23 and 302–13.

JUVENTUDES DE ACCION CATOLICA. "Historia de veinticinco años." *Memorias de las Bodas de Plata de las Juventudes de Acción Católica Cubana*. Havana, 1953.

LASAGA, J.I. "La Iglesia de Cuba en el proceso revolucionario." *Mensaje Iberoamericano*. (Madrid) 128 (June 1976), 2–9.

—. "La Iglesia cubana en el marco de la constitución socialista de 1976." *Anuario de la Iglesia Católica. Cuba Diáspora*. Miami: Revista Ideal, 1977, 10–20.

LEBROC, R.G. "Síntesis histórica de la Iglesia cubana." *Anuario de la Iglesia Católica. Cuba Isla y Diáspora*. (Caracas) UCE, 1972, 7–29.

LEISECA, J.M. *Apuntes para la histórica Eclesiástica de Cuba*. Havana, 1938.

MORENO FRAGINALS, M. "Iglesia e ingenio." *Revista de la Biblioteca Nacional José Martí* (Havana), V, nos. 1–4 (1963) 11–28.

PEREZ CABRERA, J.M. "En torno al primer obispo de Cuba." *Miss. Hispan.* (Madrid) XXIII (1966) 373–82.

PRO MUNDI VITA. *Cuba, Haití, República Dominicana. La Iglesia en dos de las grandes Antillas*. Dominican Republic: Impresos Obispado Santiago de los Caballeros, 1983.

RENES, C.G. "¿Revolución en la Iglesia o Iglesia en la Revolución?" *Mensaje Iberoamericano* (Madrid) 97 (Nov. 1973).

TESTE, I. *História Eclesiástica de Cuba*. Burgos-Barcelona, 1969–75, 5 vols.

TRIGO, P. "¿Giro en la política religiosa del P.C. cubano?" *Revista SIC* (Caracas) (Mar. 1981) and in *Mensaje Iberoamericano* (Madrid) 199 (May 1982) 15–17.

3. SANTO DOMINGO

INCHAUSTEGUI, J.M. *Historia dominicana*. Ciudad Trujillo, 1955, I-II.

LARRAZABAL BLANCO, C. *Los negros y la esclavitud en Santo Domingo*. Santo Domingo, 1967.

MARRERO ARISTY, R. *La República Dominicana. Origen y destino del pueblo cristiano más antiguo de América*. Ciudad Trujillo, 1957-8, I-II.

NOUEL, C. *Historia eclesiástica de la Arquidiócesis de Santo Domingo*. Rome-Santo Domingo, 1913-15, I-III.

PATTEE, R. *La República Dominicana*, Madrid, 1967.

POLANCO BRITO, H.E., " La Iglesia Católica y la primera constitución dominicana." *Clío* (Santo Domingo) XXXVIII, n.125 (1970).

RODRIGUEZ DEMORIZI, E. "Apuntes y documentos." *Clío* (Ciudad Trujillo) XXII, 101 (1954) 226-51.

TREMBLEY, W.A. "The Status of the Church in Saint-Domingue During the Last Years of the French Monarchy 1781–1793." *Caribbean Studies* (Rio Piedras) 1:1 (1961) 11–18.

UTRERA, C. "Los Sínodos del Arzobispado de Sto. Domingo." *Clío* (Ciudad Trujillo) XXII, 100 (1954) 141–62.

WIPFLER, W.L. *The Churches of the Dominican Republic in the Light of History.* Cuernavaca, 1968.

4. PUERTO RICO

BERBUSSE, E.J. "Aspects of Church-State relations in Puerto Rico, 1989–1900." *The Americas* (Washington) XIX, 3 (1962–3) 291–304.

CAMPO LACASA, C. *La Iglesia en Puerto Rico en el siglo XVIII.* Seville, 1963, 126.

—. "Las iglesias y conventos de Puerto Rico en el siglo XVIII." *Rev. del Inst. de Cultura Puertorriqueña* (San Juan de Puerto Rico) IV, 13 (1961) 14–19.

CRUZ MONCLOVA, L. *Historia de Puerto Rico (siglo XIX).* Madrid, 1952, 1957, I–II.

CUESTA MENDOZA, A. *Historia eclesiástica del Puerto Rico colonial.* Dominican Republic, 1948.

DAVILA, A. (ed.). *Las encíclicas sobre la revolución hispanoamericana y su divulgación en Puerto Rico (siglo XIX).* San Juan de Puerto Rico, 1965.

FERNANDEZ MENDEZ, E. "Las encomiendas y la esclavitud de los indios de Puerto Rico, 1508–1550." *Anuarios de Estudios Americanos* (Seville) 23 (1966) 377–443.

GERTRUDE, M.T. "History of the Seminary in Puerto Rico." *Horizontes,* Revista de la Universidad Católica de Puerto Rico (Ponce) 5:10 (1962) 66–78.

GOMEZ CANEDO, L. "Los franciscanos: las primitivas fundaciones de San Germán, Caparra y La Aguada." *Revista del Inst. de Cultura Puertorriqueña* (San Juan) 35 (1967) 33–40.

GUTIERREZ DEL ARROYO, I. *El reformismo ilustrado en Puerto Rico.* Mexico City, 1953.

—. "Itinerario de la 2da. Visita pastoral de su Ilma. el Dr. Juan Alejo de Arizmendi (1803–1914)." *Revista del Inst. de Cultura Puertorriqueña* (San Juan) (Oct.-Dec. 1960) 40–4.

—. "Juan Alejo de Arizmendi, 1er obispo puertorriqueño (1803–1814)." *Ibid.* 36–9.

LOPEZ DE SANTA ANA, A. *Los jesuitas en Puerto Rico de 1858 a 1886.* Santander, 1958.

PEREA, J.A.-PEREA, S. *Early Ecclesiastical History of Puerto Rico.* Caracas, 1929.

VIVAS MALDONADO, J.L., *Historia de Puerto Rico.* New York, 1960.

III. MEXICAN AREA

1. General Works on the Church

BAZANT, J. *Los bienes de la Iglesia en México, 1856-1875.* El Colegio de México, 1971.

BRAVO UGARTE, J. "Historia Religiosa." *Historia Mexicana* (Mexico City) XV, 58–9 (1965–6) 379–98. (Bibliographic record of published works on the history of the Mexican Church from 1940 to 1965).

—. *Diócesis y obispos de la Iglesia mexicana 1519-1965 con un apéndice de los representantes de la Santa Sede en México y viceversa.* Mexico City, 1965.

CARREÑO, A. M. *La Real y Pontificia Universidad de México, 1536-1865.* Mexico City, 1961.

—. *Don Fray Juan de Zumárraga. Primer obispo y arzopispo de México. Documentos inéditos publicados con una introducción y notas por . . . con la reproducción en facsimile de los documentos.* Mexico City: Porrúa, 1941.

CASO, A. *El pueblo del sol.* Mexico City: FCE, 1971.

CUEVAS, M. *Historia de la Iglesia en México.* Mexico City, 1952, I-V.

DAVILA, J.I. and S. CHAVEZ. *Colección de documentos relativos a la cuestión religiosa en Jalisco.* 2 vols. Guadalajara, 1920.

DAVILA GABIRI, J. *Apuntes para la historia de la Iglesia en Guadalajara.* Mexico City, 1958, 87.

Documentos Colectivos del Episcopado Mexicano, 1965-1975. Mexico City, 1977.

DOOLEY, F. P. *Los cristeros, Calles y el catolicismo mexicano.* Mexico City, 1976.

DUVERGER, Ch. *La Conversión de los Indios de la Nueva España.* Quito: Abya-Yala, 1990.

GARCIA CANTU, G. *El pensamiento de la reacción mexicana. Historia documental: 1810-1962.* Mexico City, 1965.

GARCIA GUTIERREZ, J. *Bulario de la Iglesia Mejicana.* Mexico City, 1954.

GARCIA PIMENTAL, L. (pub.). *Compendiosa descripción del Arzobispo de México hecha en 1570 y otros Documentos.* Mexico City, 1897.

GARIBAY, A.M. (ed.). *Teogonía e Historia de los. Mexicanos. Tres opúsculos del siglo XVI.* Mexico City: Porrúa, 1965.

GRANADOS ROLDAN, O. *La Iglesia católica mexicana como grupo de presión.* Mexico City: UNAM, 1981.

GUTIERREZ CASILLAS, J. *Historia de la Iglesia en México.* Mexico City: Porrúa, 1974.

KRICKEBER, W. *Mitos y leyendas de los aztecas, incas, mayas y muiscas.* Mexico City: FCE, 1975.

LAFAYE, J. *Quetzalcóatl y Guadalupe. La formación de la conciencia nacional en México.* Madrid: FCE, 1977.

LOPEZ AUSTIN, A. *Hombre-Dios. Religión y política en el mundo náhuatl.* Mexico City: UNAM, 1973.

MEDINA ASCENCIO, L. *Historia del Seminario de Montezuma. Sus precedentes, fundación y consolidación, 1910-1953.* Mexico City, 1962.

—. *Una pugna diplomática ante la Santa Sede: el restablecimiento del Episcopado Mexicano 1825-1831.* Mexico City: Porrúa, 1967.

MEDIZ BOLIO, A. (prol. and trans. from the Maya). *Libro de Chilam Balam de Chumayel.* Mexico City: UNAM, 1941.

MENDEZ PLANCARTE, G. (ed.) *Humanistas mexicanos del siglo XVI.* Mexico City: UNAM, 1946.

MIRANDA GODINEZ, F. *El Real Colegio de San Nicolás de Pátzcuaro.* Cuernavaca: CIDOC, 1967.

MORALES, F. *Clero y política en México, 1767-1845.* Mexico City, 1975.

MURRAY, P.V. *The Catholic Church in Mexico. Historical Essays for the General Reader (1519-1910).* Mexico City, 1965.

NAVARRETE, F. *La lucha entre el poder civil y el clero a la luz de la historia.* Mexico City, 1984.

OROZCO, F. and J. DAVILA GABIRI. *Colección de documentos históricos inéditos referentes al Arzobispado de Guadalajara.* Guadalajara, 1922-7, I-VI.

PASTOR, L. *Guida delle fonti per la Storia dell'America Latina*. Vatican City, 1970, 198ff.

PIÑA CHAN, R. *Quetzalcóatl. Serpiente emplumada*. Mexico City: FCE, 1977.

QUIRARTE, M. *El problema religioso en México*. Mexico City, 1967.

REGIS PLANCHET, F. *La cuestión religiosa en México*. Mexico City, 1956.

ROSA, M. de la, and C.REILLY (coords). *Religión y política en México*. Mexico City: Siglo XXI, 1985.

Secret Archive of the Vatican. *Archivo della Visita Apostolica nel Messico* (Mar. 1896-Feb. 1900) (Archivo Averardi).

SOSA, F. *Bibliografía de los Ilmos. Sres. Arzobispos de México. Desde la época colonial hasta nuestros días*. Mexico City, 1962, I-II.

STAPLES, A. *La iglesia en la primera república federal mexicana (1824–1835)*. El Colegio de México, 1982.

THOMPSON, E.J. *Historia y religión de los mayas*. Mexico City: Siglo XXI, 1975.

TORO, A. *La Iglesia y el Estado de México. Estudio sobre los conflictos entre el clero católico y los gobiernos mexicanos desde la independencia hasta nuestros días*. Mexico City, 1927 (facs. ed. 1975).

VALVERDE TELLEZ, E. *Bio-bibliografía eclesiástica mejicana*. 2 vols. Mexico City, 1949.

VILLASEÑOR, G. *Estado e Iglesia. El caso de la Educación*. Mexico City: Edicol, 1978.

ZIEGLER, A.W. "Kirche und Staat in Mexico." *Münchener Theologische Zeitschrift* (Munich) XXII (1971), 264-81.

Reviews: *Revista Eclesiástica Mexicana* (1919–1923, official organ of various dioceses); *Christus* (1936ff, official organ of various dioceses and the most important priestly review in Mexico to the present); *Contacto* (1962ff, organ of the Mexican Social Secretariat); *Iglesias* (1978ff, ecumenical organ linked to the National Centre for Social Communication); *Servir* (1964ff, organ of the CIRM); *Documentación e Información Católica (DIC)* (1973ff, weekly bulletin linked to the Mexican Bishops Conference).

b. *Missionary Congregations*

ASTRAIN, A. *Historia de la Compañía de Jesús en la asistencia de España*. Madrid, 1905–23.

ALEGRE, J. *Historia de la Cía. de Jesús. Memorias para la historia de la Provincia que tuvo la Cía. de Jesús en Nueva España*. Mexico City, 1940–4, I-II.

DAVILA Y ARRILLAGA, J. *Continuación de la historia de la Compañía de Jesús en Nueva España, del padre Francisco J. Alegre*. Puebla, 1888–9, I-II.

DECORME, G. *Historia de la Compañía de Jesús en la república mexicana durante el siglo XIX*. Guadalupe, 1914, 1921, I-II.

ESPINOSA, I.F. *Crónica de la provincia franciscana de los Apóstoles S. Pedro y S. Pablo de Michoacán*. Mexico City, 1945, 2nd ed.

PHELAN, John L. *El reino milenario de los franciscanos en el nuevo mundo*. Mexico City: UNAM, 1972.

LEON-PORTILLA, M. *Los franciscanos vistos por el hombre náhuatl. Testimonios indígenas del siglo XVI.*, Mexico City: UNAM, 1985.

ORDOÑEZ, P.P. "Las misiones franciscanas del

Nuevo Reino de León (1575–1715)." *Historia Mexicana* (Mexico City) 3 (1953) 102–12.

ULLOA, D. *Los predicadores divididos. Los dominicos en Nueva España, siglo XVI*. El Colegio de México, 1977.

c. *Evangelization*

BATY, R.M. "Las órdenes mendicantes y la aculturación religiosa a principios del México colonial." *América Indígena* (Mexico City) 28:1 (1968) 23–50.

BAUDOT, G. "La biblioteca de los evangelizadores de México. Un documento sobre Fray Juan de Gaona." *Historia Mexicana* (Mexico City) 27 (1968) 610-7.

FRANCH J.A. (ed.) *Bartolomé de las Casas. Obra Indigenista*. Madrid: Alianza Editorial, 1985.

GOMES MOREIRA, J.A. *Conquista y Conciencia Cristiana. El pensamiento indigenista y jurídico-teológico de Don Vasco de Quiroga (±565)*. Quito/Mexico City: Abya-Yala/CENAMI, 1990.

—. "Esclavitud y Evangelización Indígena en el siglo XVI. El pensamiento de Don Vasco de Quiroga." *Iglesia pueblos y culturas* (Quito) 21 (Apr.-June 1991), 7–33.

LEMOINE VILLICAÑA, E. "Un notable escrito póstumo del obispo de Michoacán, Fray Antonio de San Miguel, sobre la situación social, económica y eclesiástica de la Nueva España en 1804." *Boletín del Archivo General de la Nación* (Mexico City), 5:1 (1964) 5–66.

MEADE, J. "La evangelización de la Huasteca Tamaulipeca y la historia eclesiástica de la región." *Memorias de la Academia Mexicana de Historia* (Mexico City) XIV, n.3 (1955) 271–96; XIV, n.4 (1955) 331–69.

PALOMERA, E.J. *Fray Diego Valadés (OFM) evangelizador humanista de la Nueva España: su obra*. Mexico City, 1962.

PEÑALOSA, J.A. *La práctica religiosa en México. Siglo XVI. Asedios de sociología religiosa*. Mexico City, 1969.

RICARD, R. *La conquête spirituelle du Mexique. Essai sur l'apostolat et les méthodes missionnaires des Ordres mendiants en Nouvelle Espagne de 1523–1524 à 1572*. Paris, 1933.

—. "Reflexiones acerca de la evangelización de México por los misioneros españoles en el siglo XVI." *Revista de Indias* (Madrid) V (1944) 7–25.

VARIOUS. *Symposium. Fray Bartolomé de las Casas. Trascendencia de su obra y doctrina*. Mexico City: UNAM 1985.

VAZQUEZ VAZQUEZ, E. *Distribución geográfica de las órdenes religiosas en la Nueva España, siglo XVI*. Mexico City, 1965.

d. *The Church and Emancipation (XIXc)*

ALCALA, A. *Una pugna diplomática ante la Santa Sede: el restablecimento del Episcopado Mexicano 1825–1831*. Mexico City: Porrúa, 1967.

BAZANT, J. *Alienation of Church Wealth in Mexico. Social and economic aspects of the liberal revolution, 1856–1875*. Cambridge, 1971.

KNOWLTON, R.J. "Expropriation of Church Property in Nineteenth-century Mexico and Colombia:

a Comparison." *The Americas* (Washington) 25:4 (1969) 387–401.

MORALES, F. *Clero y política en México (1767–1834). Algunas ideas sobre la autoridad, la independencia y la reforma eclesiástica.* Mexico: SepSetentas, 1975.

QUIRIARTE, M. *El problema religioso en México.* Mexico City: IHAN, 1967.

RIVERA RAMIREZ, P. "México en el Concilio Vaticano I." *Memorias de la Academia Mexicana de Historia* (Mexico City) 18 (1959) 18–45.

SCHMITT, K.M. "Catholic adjustment to the secular state: the case of Mexico, 1867–1911." *Catholic Historical Review* 48:2 (1962) 182–204.

e. Church and Revolution (early XXc)

BAILEY, D.C. "Alvaro Obregon and anticlericalism in the 1910 revolution." *The Americas* (Washington) 26:2 (1969).

CAPISTRAN GARZA, R. *La Iglesia católica y la revolución mexicana: prontuario de ideas políticas.* Mexico City: Atisbos, 1964.

MICHELS, A.L. "The modification of the anticlerical nationalism of the Mexican Revolution by General Lázaro Cárdenas and its relationship to the Church-State détente in Mexico." *The Americas* (Washington) 26:1 (1969) 35–53.

OLIVERA SEDANO, A. *Aspectos del conflicto religioso de 1926 a 1929: sus antecedentes y sus consecuencias.* Mexico City, 1966.

QUIRK, R.E. "La religión y la revolución social en Méjico." W.V. D'ANTONIO-F.B.PIKE, *Religión, Revolución y Reforma.* Barcelona: Herder, 1967, 111–31.

RAMOS, R., ALSONSO, I., GARRE, D. *La Iglesia en México. Estructuras eclesiásticas.* Madrid, 1963.

ROMERO DE SOLIS, J.M. "Iglesia y revolución en México (1910–1940)." FLICHE-MARTIN. *Historia de la Iglesia,* XXVI, 2. Valencia, 1980, 465–505.

f. Biographies

BARQUIN Y RUIZ, A. *José de Jesús Manríquez y Zárate, gran defensor de la Iglesia.* Mexico City, 1952.

—. *José María González Valencia, arzobispo de Durango.* Mexico City, 1967.

BRAVO UGARTE, J. *Diócesis y obispos en la Iglesia Mexicana (1519–1965).* Mexico City, 1973.

CAMBEROS VIZCAINO, V. *Francisco el Grande: monseñor Francisco Orózco y Jiménez,* 2 vols. Mexico City, 1966.

CARREÑO, A.Ma. *El arzobispo de México (. . .) Pascual Díaz, S.I., el arzobispo mártir.* Mexico City, 1945.

—. *Monseñor Rafael Guízar y Valencia, el obispo santo, 1878–1938.* Mexico City, 1951.

GONZALEZ RAMIREZ, M. *La Iglesia Mexicana en cifras.* Mexico City, 1969.

HURTADO, A. *El cisma mexicano.* Mexico City, 1956.

MARQUEZ, O. *Monseñor Ibarra.* Mexico City, 1962.

MECHAN, J.L. *Church and State in Latin America.* Chapel Hill, 1966, esp. pp. 376–415.

PALAZZINI, G. "Pio XI e il Messico, la Spagna, el Portogallo." RIMOLDI, A., *Pio XI nel trentesimo della morte,* Milan, 1969, 623–57.

IV. CENTRAL AMERICAN REGION

1. REGIONAL

MELENDEZ, G. *Iglesia, cristianismo y religión en América Central: Resumen bibliográfico (1960-1988).* San José: DEI, 1988.

—. *Seeds of Promise. The Prophetic Church in Central America.* New York: Friendship Press, 1990.

RICHARD, P.-MELENDEZ, G. (eds.) *La Iglesia de los Pobres en América Central.* San José: DEI, 1982.

CEHILA. *Historia General de la Iglesia en América Latina,* Vol. VI: *América Central.* Salamanca: CEHILA-Sígueme, 1985 (see general bibliography and by countries, pp. 573–84).

2. GUATEMALA

BIERMANN, B. "Don Fray Juan Ramírez de Arellano, OP und sein Kampf gegen die Unterdrückung der Indianer." *Jahrbuch für Geschichte von Staat* (Cologne) IV (1967) 318–47.

—. "Der zwerte Missionsversuch bei den Choles in der Verapaz (1672–1676)." *Jahrbuch für Geschicte von Staat* (Cologne) II (1965) 245–56.

—. "Missionsgeschichte der Verapaz in Guatemala." *Jahrbuch für Geschichte von Staat* (Cologne) I (1964) 117–56.

CHEA, J.L. *Guatemala: la cruz fragmentada.* San José: DEI, 2nd ed., 1989.

MILLER, H.J. *La Iglesia católica y el estado en Guatemala.* Guatemala: Universidad de San Carlos, 1976.

MONDRAGON, R. *De indios y cristianos en Guatemala.* Mexico City: Claves Latinoamericanas (CECOPE), 1983.

PEREZ S.I., R., *La Compañía de Jesús en Colombia y Centro América después de su Restauración.* Valladolid, 1898.

SAENZ DE SANTAMARIA, C. "Un corte sociológico-religioso en la situación del indígena guatemalteco en la segunda mitad del siglo XVIII." *Eca* (San Salvador) XV, n.145 (1960) 12–22.

SAINTLU, A. "La Vera-Paz. Esprit évangélique et colonisation." Paris, 1968.

SAMANDU, L., H. SIEBERS and O.SIERRA. *Guatemala. Retos de la Iglesia católica en una sociedad en crisis.* , San José: DEI, 1990.

SHERMAN, W.L. "Abusos contra los indios de Guatemala 1602-1605 relaciones del obispo." *Caravelle* (Toulouse) 11 (1968) 5–28.

SOLANO PEREZ LILA, F. de. "Los libros del misionero en Guatemala (siglo XVIII)." *Mission. Hispanic* (Madrid) XX, n.60 (1963) 319–49.

—. "La espiritualidad del indio, Guatemala, siglo XVIII." *Mission. Hispanic* (Madrid) XXVII, n.79 (1970) 5–57.

TELETOR, C.N. *Síntesis biográfica del clero de Guatemala.* New York, 1949.

TOMO SANS, L. "Una protesta social-misionera del siglo XVIII." *Mission. Hispanau.* (Madrid) XVI, n.48 (1959) 363–77.

3. PANAMA

ARIZA, A.E. *Los dominicos en Panamá.* Bogotá, 1964.

CASTILLERO, R., E.J. *Breve Historia de la Iglesia Panameña.* Panama, 1965.

—. "El obispo Fray Tomás de Berlanga." *F.C.A.* (San Salvador) X, n.94 (1955) 264–69.

MEGA, P. *Compendio biográfico de los Ilmos. y Excmos. Monseñores obispos y arzobispos de Panamá. Reseña histórica* . . . . Panama, 1958.

OPASO BERNALES, A. *Panama. La Iglesia y la lucha de los pobres.* San José: DEI, 1988.

ROJAS ARRIETA, G. *Historia de los obispos de Panamá.* Panama, 1929.

RUIZ CAJAR, C. "Historia de las misiones en Panamá." *Revista de la Universidad de Madrid* (Madrid) VII, n.28 (1958) 488–98.

4. COSTA RICA

BLANCO SEGURA, R. *Historia eclesiástica de Costa Rica del descubrimiento a la erección de la diócesis 1502–1850.* San José, 1967.

—. "Obispos y arzobispos de Costa Rica." *Anales de Academia de Geografía e Historia de Costa Rica* (San José) (1966) 70–103.

—. "Cinco clérigos ilustres durante los años de la Independencia." *Anales de la Academia de Geografía e Historia de Costa Rica,* (San José) (1966) 24–33.

GONZALEZ, L.P. *El gobierno eclesiástico en Costa Rica durante el régimen colonial y la influencia de los sacerdotes en el desenvolvimiento religioso y cultural del país.* San José, 1957.

OPASO BERNALES, A. *Costa Rica. La Iglesia Católica y el Orden Social.* San José: DEI, 1987.

PICADO, M. *La iglesia costarricense entre Dios y el César.* San José: DEI, 2nd ed. 1991.

THIEL, B.A. "La Iglesia Católica en Costa Rica durante el siglo XIX." *Revista de Costa Rica en el siglo XIX* (San José) (1902).

VALVERDE, J. *Las sectas en Costa Rica. Pentecostalismo y conflicto social.* San José: DEI, 1990.

5. EL SALVADOR

CARDENAL, R. *El poder eclesiástico en el Salvador (1871–1931).* San Salvador: UCA, 1980.

—. *Historia de una esperanza. Vida de Rutilo Grande.* San Salvador: UCA, 1985.

COMISION DE DERECHOS HUMANOS DE EL SALVADOR. *La Iglesia en El Salvador.* Salamanca: Logues, 1982; 2nd ed., San Salvador: UCA, 1982.

GRISERI, A. "Labor de los religiosos en El Salvador." *ECA. Estudios Centroamericanos* (San Salvador) XVIII, 188 (1963) 386–91.

HENRIQUEZ, P. *El Salvador. Iglesia profética y cambio social.* San José: DEI, 1988.

LOPEZ JIMENEZ, R. *Mitras salvadoreñas.* San Salvador, 1960.

MELENDEZ CHAVARRI, C. *El presbítero don José M.Delgado en la forja de la nacionalidad centroamericana. Ensayo histórico.* San Salvador, 1962.

VILANOVA, S.R. *Apuntamientos de historia patria eclesiástica.* San Salvador, 1911.

6. NICARAGUA

CABESTRERO, T. *Ministros de Dios Ministros del Pueblo. Testimonio de tres sacerdotes en el gobierno revolucionario de Nicaragua.* Managua: Ministerio de Cultura, 1985. Eng. trans. *Ministers of God, Ministers of the People: Testimonies of faith from Nicaragua.* Maryknoll, N.Y.: Orbis, 1986.

GIRARDI, G. *Cristianos y marxistas en la revolución nicaragüense.* Mexico City: Ediciones Nuevo Mar, 1983. Eng. trans. *Faith and Revolution in Nicaragua: Convergence and Contradictions.* Maryknoll, N.Y.: Orbis, 1990.

GONZALEZ GARY, O. *Iglesia Católica y Revolución en Nicaragua.* Mexico City: Claves Latinoamericanas, 1986.

MARTINEZ, A. *Las sectas en Nicaragua. Oferta y demanda de salvación.* San José: DEI, 1989.

POCHET, R.M. and A. MARTINEZ. *Nicaragua. Iglesia, manipulación o profecía?.* San José: DEI, 1987.

7. HONDURAS

"Para la historia eclesiástica de Honduras." *Revista de la Sociedad de Geografía e Historia de Honduras* (Tegucigalpa) XXXVII, n.1–3 (1958) 27–32.

CARDENAL, R. *Acontecimientos sobresalientes de la Iglesia de Honduras, 1900–1962: primeros pasos para la elaboración de una historia.* Tegucigalpa, 1974.

BLANCO, G. and J. VALVERDE. *Honduras. Iglesia y cambio social.* San José: DEI, 2nd ed., 1990.

V. COLOMBIA-VENEZUELA REGION

1. COLOMBIA

a. General Works on the Church

"ACTA et Documenta Concilio Oecum.Vat apparando", series I (*Antepraeparatoria*), vol. II, part VII, *América Meridionalis.* Vatican City, 1961.

ALVAREZ, J. "La Iglesia Católica en Colombia." *Revista Javeriana (RJ)* I (1947), 102–194.

ANDRADE, V. "UTC, realidad católica." *RJ* I (1952), 98ff.

"Annuarium Statisticum Eccl. Catholicae." Vatican City, 1975.

ANON. *El Consejo de Bogotá y la cuestión religiosa. Debates acerca de la Universidad Javeriana y la Compañía de Jesús.* Bogotá, 1935.

BUILES, M.A. *Cartas Pastorales.* 3 vols., Medellín, 1964–5.

CADAVID, I. *Los fueros de la Iglesia ante el liberalismo y el conservatismo.* Medellín, 1956.

CAMACHO MONTOYA, G. *El Concordato ante la conciencia católica de Colombia.* Bogotá, 1942.

CAMACHO, P.P. *El régimen concordatario colombiano. Sociedad Colombiana de Abogados.* Bogotá, 1974.

CEHILA. *Historia General de la Iglesia en América Latina,* Vol. VII: *Colombia-Venezuela.* Salamanca: Sígueme, 1981.

CELAM. *Directorio católico latinoamericano.* Bogotá, 1968.

—. *Iglesia y América Latina en cifras. Auxiliar para la III Conferencia General del Episcopado Latinoamericano.* Bogotá, 1978.

Conferencias Episcopales de Colombia. vol. I: 1908-1953, Bogotá, 1954, vol. II: 1954-1960, Bogotá, 1962.

CONFERENCIA EPISCOPAL DE COLOMBIA. *Presentación del Nuevo Concordato.* (Updated ed.) Bogotá, 1975.

FERNANDEZ, J.M. and R. GRANADOS. *La obra civilizadora de la Iglesia en Colombia.* Bogotá, 1967.

CHEERBRANT, A. *La Iglesia rebelde de América Latina.* Mexico City, 1970.

GOMEZ HOYOS, R. *La Iglesia en Colombia.* Bogotá, 1955.

—. et al. *Iglesia y el Estado en Colombia: sus relaciones desde la Colonia hasta nuestros días.* Medellín, 1969.

HADDOX, B. *Sociedad y Religión en Colombia.* Bogotá, 1965.

MEJIA, J. *Diócesis y jerarcas de la Iglesia en Colombia.* Medellín, 1942.

PIEDRAHITA, J. *Historia de los Sínodos.* Medellín, 1966.

RESTREPO POSADA, J. *Genealogía episcopal de la jerarquía en los países que formaron la Gran Colombia 1513–1966.* Bogotá, 1968.

b. Missionary Congregations

BONILLA, V.D. *Siervos de Dios y amos de los indios. El Estado y la misión capuchina en el Putumayo.* Bogotá, 1969.

BOTERO RESTREPO, J. *El problema misional.* Medellín, 1948.

CROUS, P. "Los misioneros capuchinos y los indígenas del Putumayo." *Revista de la Academia de Historia Eclesiástica* (Medellín, 1968), 342ff.

FRIEDE, J. "Los franciscanos en el Nuevo Reino de Granada y el movimiento indigenista del siglo XVI." *Bulletin Hispanique* (Bordeaux) LX n.1 (1958) 5–29.

LORA, C.de. *Estudio sociográfico de los religiosos y religiosas en América Latina.* Bogotá: CLAR, 1971.

MESANZA, A. *Apuntes y Documentos sobre la Orden Dominicana en Colombia 1680–1930.* Caracas, 1936.

ORTEGA TORRES, S. *La obra salesiana de los lazaretos.* Bogotá, 1938.

PACHECO, J.M. *Los jesuitas en Colombia.* Bogotá, 1959–1962, I-II.

PEREZ GOMEZ, J. *Apuntes históricos de las misiones agustinianas en Colombia.* Bogotá, 1924.

ROBLEDO ARCILA, G. *Las misiones franciscanas en Colombia.* Bogot[AO], 1951.

—. *Apuntes históricos de la provincia franciscana en Colombia.* Bogotá, 1953.

ROBLEDO MEJIA, A. *Territorios misionales* Bogotá, 1973.

VARGAS, M.T. "Origen en Colombia de la Orden de los ermitaños recoletos descalzos de San Agustín." *Boletín de Historia y Antigüedades* (Bogotá) XLI (1954) 587ff.

c. Religion, Society and Culture (to mid XVIIIc)

MESA, C. "Manifestaciones Eucarísticas en la primitiva historia colombiana." *Revista de la Academia Colombiana de Historia Eclesiástica* (Medellín) (1970), 303–29.

GONZALEZ DAVILA, G. "Teatro eclesiástico de la primitiva iglesia de las Indias Occidentales, Santa Fe, Santa Marta, Cartagena y Popayan." *Boletín de Historia y Antigüedades* (Bogotá) XIII.

SALAZAR, J.A. *Los estudios eclesiásticos superiores en el Nuevo Reino de Granada (1563–1810).* Madrid, 1946.

TRIANA Y ANTOURUEZA, H. "El aspecto religioso en los gremios neogranadinos." *Boletín Cultural y Bibliográfico* (Bogotá) IX, n.2 (1966) 269–81.

d. Church Reorganization (early XIXc)

PINILLA, A.M. "Relaciones de Colombia con la Sta. Sede de 1810 a 1835." *Revista de la Academia Colombiana de Historia Eclesiástica* (Bogotá) 17–18 (1970) 29–40.

RESTREPO POSADA, J. *Arquidiócesis de Bogotá. Cabildos Eclesiásticos.* Bogotá, 1971, vol. IV.

—. "Provisores del arzobispado." *Boletín de Historia y Antigüedades* (Bogotá) LIV, n.627-29 (1967) 71–100.

ROMERO, M.G. "Participación del clero en la lucha por la independencia." *Boletín de Historia y Antigüedades* (Bogotá) XLIX, n.573-4 (1962) 325–44.

TISNESS, J.R.M. *Fray Ignacio Mariño, O.P., capellán general del ejército libertador.* Bogotá, 1963.

e. Church Life (late XIXc to present)

CARRASQUILLA, J.R. "Estudio sobre el Liberalismo" (written 1913). *RJ* II (1948), 79ff.

CONSIDINE, J. "Nuestra Casa de la Esquina." *RJ* I (1947), 213ff.

DEL CORRO, A. *Camilo Torres, un símbolo controvertido, 1962–1966.* Cuernavaca, 1968.

DIAZ JORDAN, J. *Diócesis de Garzon. Proceso histórico de pueblos y parroquias.* Neiva, 1959.

DUQUE BOTERO, G. *Apuntes para la historia del clero de Caldas.* Medellín, 1957.

EGUREN, J.A. *El derecho concordatario colombiano.* Bogotá, 1960.

—. "El Estado colombiano frente a la Iglesia Católica. Visión histórica del régimen concordatario en Colombia." *Revista de la Academia de Historia Eclesiástica* (Medellín 1970), 81ff.

GOMEZ, J. "El XXXIX Congreso Eucarístico Internacional: 192 horas de historia." *Revista de la Academia de Historia Eclesiástica* (Medellín 1968), 286ff.

GONZALEZ, F. "Iglesia Católica y partidos políticos en Colombia." *Revista de la Universidad de Medellín* (Medellín 1976), 87ff.

GONZALEZ, M.A. "Análisis de un Libro." *RJ* (1962), 296ff.

GONZALEZ QUINTANA, G. *El padre Campoamor: la obra y su espíritu.* Bogotá, 1941.

HOUTART, F. and G. PREZA. *Acción Cultural Popular. Sus principios y medios de acción. Consideraciones teológicas y sociológicas.* Bogotá, 1960.

JIMENEZ, G. *Sacerdote y cambio social.* Bogotá, 1967.

LOZANO TORRES, L. *Intervención del clero en la actividad política del Estado.* Bogotá, 1949.

MARINS, J. et al. *Praxis de los padres de América Latina. Los documentos de las conferencias episcopales de Medellín a Puebla (1968–1978).* Bogotá, 1978.

MARTINEZ CUESTA, A. *Beato Ezequiel Moreno. El camino del deber.* Rome, 1975.

MEJIA Y MEJIA, J.C. *Pasto, pastores y pastorales.* Bogotá, 1969, I-II.

MESA, C. *Autobiografía de la madre Laura de Santa Catalina.* Medellín, 1971.

MINISTERIO DE GOBIERNO DE COLOMBIA. *La cuestión de las religiones acatólicas en Colombia.* Bogotá, 1956.

OLANO, M.D. *Monseñor Builes.* Medellín, 1978.

OSPINA, E.P. "Diez años de vida católica en

Colombia." *RJ* (Bogotá) Nov. 1948.
—. *Las sectas protestantes en Colombia. Breve reseña histórica con un estudio especial de la llamada "persecución religiosa."* Bogotá, 1954.
—. "Perfil espiritual de Colombia." *Latinoamérica* (Mexico City) (1949) 118ff.
PEREZ, G., *El problema sacerdotal en Colombia.* Bogotá, 1962.
PEREZ, G. and I. WUST. *La Iglesia en Colombia. Estructuras eclesiásticas.* Freiburg-Madrid: FERES, 1961.
RESTREPO JARAMILLO, G. *El pensamiento conservador.* Medellín, 1936.
RESTREPO POSADA, J.M. *La Iglesia en dos momentos difíciles de la historia patria.* Bogotá, 1971.
RESTREPO URIBE, E. *El protestantismo en Colombia.* Bogotá, 1944.
RODRIGUEZ, F.J. *Educación católica y secularización en Colombia.* Bogotá, 1970.
SANTA TERESA, S. de. *Historia documentada de la Iglesia de Urabá y el Darién.* Bogotá, 1956-7, I-V.
SECRETARIADO PERMANENTE DEL EPISCOPADO COLOMBIANO (SPEC) in Bogotá. *La Iglesia ante el cambio.* 1969; *La justicia en el mundo: apostes de la Iglesia Colombiana para el Sínodo de 1971.* 1972; *Justicia y exigencias cristianas.* 1974; *La Evangelización.* 1974; *La Reforma Litúrgica.* 1975; *Documentos de Trabajo para la Conferencia de Puebla* (mimeo) 2 vols., 1978.
TORRES, C. *Cristianismo y Revolución. Prólogo, selecciones y notas.* Mexico City, 1970.
UPRIMMY. "¿Es inconstitucional, anacrónico y contrario al Vaticano II el Concordato de 1973?" *Foro Colombiano* (Bogotá) 63.
URIBE MISAS, A. *La libertad de enseñanza en Colombia.* Bogotá, 1962.
VARIOUS. "Iglesia y Estado en Colombia. Sus relaciones desde la colonia hasta nuestros días." *Revista de la Academia de Historia Eclesiástica* (Medellín) (1970).
VASQUEZ CARRIZOSA, A. *El Concordato de Colombia con la Santa Sede.* Bogotá: Ministerio de Relaciones Exteriores de Colombia, 1973.
VIDAL, R. *Crítica histórica al libro de Víctor Bonilla "Siervos de Dios y amos de los indios."* Pasto, 1970.
ZAPATA RESTREPO, M. *La Mitra Azul, Miguel Angel Builes, el hombre, el obispo, el caudillo.* Medellín, 1973.
ZULUAGA, F. *Estructuras eclesiásticas de Colombia.* Bogotá, 1971.

2. VENEZUELA

a. General Works on the Church

AYERRA XACINTO. *Los protestantes en Venezuela. Quiénes son? Qué hacen?.* Caracas: Trípode, 1980.
CEHILA. *Historia General de la Iglesia en América Latina,* vol. VII: *Colombia-Venezuela.* Salamanca: Sígueme, 1985.
CONFERENCIA EPISCOPAL VENEZOLANA. *Cartas, instrucciones y mensajes (1883–1977).* Caracas: UCAB, 1978.
COSTA GOMEZ, P. "Historia de la antigua diócesis de Coro." *Revista de Cultura del Estado de Falcon* (Coro) 25 (1965) 23- 33.

FELICE CARDOT, C. *Noticias para la historia de la diócesis de Barquisimeto.* Caracas, 1964.
GONZALEZ, E.A. *Epítome histórico de la diócesis de Calabozo.* Caracas: Escuelas Gráficas Salesianas, 1951.
GUEVARA CARRERA, J.M. *Apuntes para la historia de la diócesis de Guayana.* Caracas: Azteca, 1930.
MALDONADO, F.A. *Intento de periodicidad de la historia de la Iglesia en Venezuela.* Caracas, n.d.
MANZO NUÑEZ. *Diócesis de Valencia. Noticias sobre su erección. . . .* Caracas: Imprenta Nacional, 1975.
MARADEI, C. *Venezuela. Su Iglesia y sus gobiernos.* Caracas: Trípode, 1978.
NAVARRO, N. *Anales Eclesiásticos venezolanos.* Caracas: Tipografía Americana, 1951.
PELLIN, J.M. *Disquisitio iuridico-critica relationum actualium inter ecclesiam et Statum Venezuelensem.* Rome: Officium libri catholici, 1958.
PEREZ VILA, M. *Ensayo sobre las fuentes para la historia de la diócesis de Guayana durante los períodos de la colonia y la independencia.* Caracas, 1969.
PICON-FEBRES, G. *Datos para la historia de la Diócesis de Mérida.* Caracas, 1916.
REY, J. Del. *Aportes jesuíticos a la filología colonial venezolana,* 2 vols. Caracas: Universidad Católica Andrés Bello, 1971.
SANABRIA, A. "La antigua diócesis de Guayana." *Boletín de la Academia Nacional de la Historia* (Caracas) XLVII, n.187 (1964) 433–5.
SURIA, J. "El obispado de Barinas en 1803." *Boletín de la Academia Nacional de la Historia* (Caracas) XLVI, n.183 (1963) 475–85.
WATERS, M. *A History of the Church in Venezuela.* University of North Carolina, 1933.
—. *Telón de fondo de la Iglesia colonial en Venezuela.* Caracas, 1951.

b. Missionary Congregations

ARIZA, A.E. *Los dominicos en Venezuela.* Bogotá, 1971.
CARRILLO MORENO, J. *Pao de San Juan Bautista. Ciudad primogénita de Cojedes.* Caracas, 1962. (Capuchins).
CARROCERA, C. "Las misiones en Venezuela. Síntesis histórica." *Boletín de la Academia Nacional de la Historia* (Caracas) LIV n.215 (1971) 443–57. (Franciscans).
DEL REY FAJARDO, J. "Jesuítas criollos que trabajaron en las misiones llaneras." *Boletín de la Academia Nacional de la Historia* (Caracas) LIV, n.215 (1971) 458–88. (Jesuits).
—. *Bio-bibliografía de los Jesuítas en la Venezuela colonial.* Caracas: Universidad Católica "Andrés Bello", Instituto de Investigaciones Históricas, 1974.
GOMEZ CANEDO, L. "Los franciscanos en Guayana." *Boletín de la Academia Nacional de la Historia* (Caracas) XLIX, N.194 (1966) 224–8.

c. Evangelization

"El Padre Francisco de Caracas, capuchino, informa sobre la situación de los indios en el año 1813." *Boletín de la Academia Nacional de la Historia* (Caracas) 48–194 (1966) 293–308.
PERERA, A. "Doctrinas y curatos de la jurisdicción de Trujillo." *Boletín del Centro de Historia del Estado de Trujillo* (Trujillo) II, n.5 (1965) 55–61.

TAPIA, D. de. *Rezo cotidiano en lengua cumanagota.* Critical edition; preliminary study by Pablo Ojer. Caracas: Carmela Bentivenga, 1969.

UNCEIN TAMAYO, L.A. "Melchor Zapata de Rivadeneyra. Una empresa misionera en el siglo XVII." *Boletín de la Academia Nacional de la Historia* (Caracas) XLVII, n.185 (1964) 59–75.

d. Religion and Society (to XVIIIc)

ACOSTA SAIGNES, M. "Las cofradías coloniales y el folklore." *Cultura Universitaria* (Caracas) n.47 (1955) 79–102.

SURIA, J. "La primera cofradía de Caracas." *Boletín Histórico* (Caracas) 3 (1963) 28–39.

TROCONIS DE VERACOECHEA, E. *Las obras pías en la Iglesia colonial venezolana.* Caracas, 1971.

e. Religion and Politics (to mid-XIXc)

GRASES, P. "El 'Catecismo religioso-político' del doctor Juan Germán Roscio." *Revista Nacional de Cultura* (Caracas) XXVI, n.161 (1963) 289–306.

NAVARRO, N.E. *El Cabildo Metropolitano de Caracas y la guerra de la Emancipación.* Madrid, 1959, 1962.

NAVARRO, N.E. *Anales eclesiásticos venezolanos.* Caracas, 1951, 2nd ed.

—. *Desquisición sobre el Patronato eclesiástico en Venezuela.* Caracas, 1931.

BOLIVAR, Simón. *Obras completas.* Comp. and notes by Vicente Lecuna, Havana, 1950, I-III.

OCANDO YAMARTE, G. *Problemática eclesiástica venezolana 1830–1847.* Rome, Doctoral Thesis at the Pontifical Gregorian University, 1972–3, I-II.

RODRIGUEZ ITURBE, J. *Aportación al estudio de las relaciones entre la Iglesia y el Estado en Venezuela. De la ley de Patronato (1824) al Modus Vivendi (1964).* Caracas, 1971.

SURIA, J. *Iglesia y Estado 1810–1821.* Caracas, 1967.

VI. ANDEAN-INCA REGION

1. ECUADOR

a. General Works on the Church

ANNUALS: *La Iglesia Católica en el Ecuador.* Quito, 1949; *La Iglesia en el Ecuador.* Quito, 1963; *La Iglesia en el Ecuador.* Ambato, 1957;

ARIAS, L. *Diccionario biográfico del clero guayaquilense, 1820- 1970.* Guayaquil, 1970.

BERMEO, A. "Relaciones entre la Iglesia y el Estado en la República del Ecuador." *Cuadernos de Historia y Arqueología* (Guayaquil) 33 (1967) 34–135.

Boletin Eclesiástico. Quito, from 1896 to mid-XXc.

CEHILA. *Historia General de la Iglesia en América Latina,* vol. VIII: *Perú, Bolivia, Ecuador.* Salamanca: Sígueme, 1987.

"División y Límites de los Obispados de Cuzco, los Reyes y Quito." *Museo Histórico,* 41–42 (1962) 80–9.

GARCIA MORENO, G. *Escritos y Discursos,* 2 vols. Quito: M.M. Polit, 1923.

—. *Cartas de García Moreno,* 4 vols. Quito: W. Loor, n.d.

GRIGORIOU DE LOSADA, R. "Relaciones de Iglesia y Estado en Bolivia." *Simposio sudamericano-alemán sobre la Iglesia y el Estado.* Quito, 1980, 453–691.

HEREDIA, J.F. *La Consagración de la República del Ecuador al Sagrado Corazón de Jesús.* Quito, 1934.

—. *Notas bio-bibliográficas acerca de Manuel José Proaño, S.I..* Quito, 1935.

JOUAHEN, J. *Historia de la Compañía de Jesús en la antigua Provincia de Quito,* 2 vols., 1941 and1943.

—. *Los jesuitas y el oriente ecuatoriano* (under President García), Guayaquil, 1977.

LARREA, J.I. *La Iglesia y el Estado en el Ecuador.* Seville, 1974.

LOOR, W. *Los Jesuítas en el Ecuador, 1850–1852.* Quito, 1959.

—. *Mons. Arsenio Andrade Landázuri. Biografía.* Quito, 1970.

—. *Biografía del padre Julio María Matovelle.* Cuenca, n.d.

—. *José María Yerovi.* 2 vols, 1964 and 1968.

MIRANDA, F. "Aspectos de la realidad (político-religiosa) ecuatoriana." *Política Cristiana* Quito, 1951, 122–255.

—. *García Moreno y la Compañía de Jesús.* Quito, 1976.

—. "Las Religiosas del Buen Pastor." *Ensayos Pedagógicos y sociales.* Quito, 1955, 3–25.

—. "Mons Borja Yerovi y el Pensionado Elemental." *Ensayos Pedagógicos y Sociales.* Quito, 1955, 3–25.

MUÑOZ, E. *Vida del (Beato) Hermano Miguel.* Madrid, 1970.

MUÑOZ VEGA, Cardinal P., J.TERAN, J.M. VARGAS, G. CEVALLOS and J. TOBAR. *La Iglesia y el Estado en el Ecuador. Segundas Jornadas Teológicas.* Quito, 1976.

—., J. TERAN, J. LARREA and F. MIRANDA. *Simposio Sudamericano alemán, Iglesia-Estado.* Quito, 1980.

MONROY, J.L. *La Santísima Virgen de la Merced de Quito y su Santuario.* Quito, 1933.

"Pastorales y Documentos Coletivos del Episcopado Ecuatoriado de 1939 a 1979." *Iglesia-Ecuador, 1979.* Quito, 1979.

PORRAS, P.I. *Entre los Yumbos del Napo* (biography of Mgr Jorge Rossi). Quito, 1955.

REGIO, B. and C. GODARAZ (eds.). *Compendiosa relación de la cristiandad de Quito.* Madrid, 1948.

REYES, R.I. *La jerarquía eclesiástica del Ecuador y estadística de la Diócesis de Ibarra.* Quito, 1944.

ROMERO, O. (ed.). *Bibliografía de Aurelio Espinosa Pólit, S.I..* Quito, 1961.

—. "Bibliografía de Mons. José Félix Heredia." *Pensamiento Católico* (Quito) 14 (1945) 134-49.

RUEDA, M.V., J. GONZALEZ and J. TERAN, *Puebla. La Tercera Conferencia General del Episcopado Latinoamericano.* Quito: INEDES, 1979.

SANCHEZ, M.. *Textos de catedráticos jesuitas en Quito Colonial.* Quito, 1959.

TERAN, J., L. PROAÑO, E. RUBIANES and I. ROBALINOB. *Iglesia y fe en América Latina. Reflexiones desde el Ecuador.* Quito: INEDES, 1979.

TERENZIANI, E. *Cursos de Derecho Canónico y Legislación.* Quito, 1870–5.

—. *Programas de la Escuela Politécnica de Quito.* Quito, 1870–5.

TOBAR DONOSO, J. *La Iglesia, modeladora de la nacionalidad.* Quito, 1953.
—. *García Moreno y la Instrucción Pública.* Quito, 1940.
VARGAS, J.M. *La conquista espiritual del Imperio de los Incas.* Quito, 1948.
—. *Historia de la Iglesia en el Ecuador durante el Patronato Español.* Quito, 1962.
—. *Historia de la Provincia de Santa Catalina, de la Orden de Predicadores.* Quito, 1942.
—. *Federico González.* Quito, 1969.
VAZQUEZ, H. *Defensa de los intereses católicos en el Ecuador.* Cuenca, 1908.
ZAMBRANO, A. *Labor misionera en el Oriente* Quito, 1972.

b. Evangelization

ALBORNOZ, V.M. *Fray Vicente Solano: estudio biográfico crítico.* Cuenca, 1966, I–II.
ALBUJA MATEUS, A.E. *Doctrinas y parroquias del obispado de Quito en la 2da. mitad del siglo XVI.* Madrid, 1961.
-. *alig* "El obispado de Quito en el siglo XVI." *Missionalia Hispanica* (Madrid) XVIII, n.53 (1961) 161–209.
BANDIN HERMO, M. *El obispo de Quito don Alonso de la Peña Montenegro, 1546–1687,* ed. Fidel de Lejarza. Madrid, 1951.

c. Church and State (2nd half XIXc)

KING, W. "La Iglesia Ecuatoriana y las Relaciones con el Estado durante el gobierno de García Moreno." *Boletín de la Academia Nacional de Historia* (Quito) (1975) 125ff.
PATTEE, R. *Gabriel García Moreno y el Ecuador de su tiempo.* Mexico City, 1944..
ROBALINO DAVILA, L. *Orígenes del Ecuador de hoy. García Moreno.* Quito, 1948.
TOBAR, J. "El Primer Concordato Ecuatoriano." *Monografías Históricas* (Quito) (1938) 256-310.
—. *La Iglesia ecuatoriana en el siglo XIX.* Quito, 1934–5.

2. PERU

a. General Works on the Church

ANUARIO ECLESIASTICO DEL PERU 1947–74. Secretariado del Episcopado Peruano, Departamento de Estadística, Arzobispo de Lima, Perú.
ARMAS MEDINA, F. "La jerarquía eclesiástica peruana en la primera mitad del siglo XVII." *Anuario de Estudios Americanos* (Seville) XXII (1965) 673–703.
—. "Las propiedades de las órdenes religiosas y el problema de los diezmos en el virreinato peruano de la primera mitad del siglo XVII." *Anuario de Estudios Americanos* (Seville) XXIII (1966) 681–721.
—. *Cristianización del Perú (1532–1600).* Seville 1953.
CHAVES, L. (pub.). *Colección de documentos para la Historia de la Iglesia en el Perú,* 1943–5, I–IV.
LEVILLIER, R. *Organización de la Iglesia y órdenes religiosas en el Virreinato del Perú en el siglo XVI.* Madrid, 1919, I–II.
VARGAS UGARTE, R. *Historia de la Iglesia en el Perú.* Lima, 1953–62, I–V.

b. Missionary Congregations

BARRIAGA, V. de. *Los mercedarios en el Perú en el siglo XVI.* Rome, 1933.
VARGAS UGARTE, R. *Historia de la Compañía de Jesús en el Perú.* Burgos, I–IV.
VILLAREJO, A. *Los agustinos en el Perú, 1548–1965.* Lima, 1965.

c. Evangelization

ARMAS MEDINA, F. *Cristianización del Perú (1532-1600.* Seville, 1953.
CASTILLO ARROYO, J. *Catecismos peruanos en el siglo XVI.* Cuernavaca, 1966.
DUVIOLS, P. "El Inca Garcilaso de la Vega, intérprete humanista de la religión incaica." *Diógenes* (Buenos Aires) XI, n.47 (1969) 31–43.
—. *La lutte contre les religions autochtones dans le Pérou colonial. L'extirpation de l'idolatrie entre 1532 et 1660.* Lima, 1971.
MILLONES SANTA GADEA, L. "La 'idolatría de Santiago': un nuevo documento para el estudio de la evangelización del Perú." *Cuadernos del Seminario de Historia* (Lima) 7 (1964) 31–6.
MÖRNER, M. "La afortunada gestión de un misionero del Perú en Madrid en 1578." *Anuario de Estudios Americanos* (Seville) 19 (1962) 247–75.
WOLF, I. "Negersklaverei und Negerhandel in Hochperú (1545–1640)." *Jahrbuch für Geschichte von Staat* (Köln) I (1964) 157–86.

d. Religion and Society (to XVIIIc)

DESCOLA, J. *La vie quotidienne au Pérou au temps des espagnols 1720–1820.* Paris, 1962.
MACERA, P. *Iglesia y economía en el Perú del siglo XVIII.* Lima, 1963.
VELAZCO, O.B. "Situación de la diócesis del Cuzco en el 1er tercio del siglo XVIII." *Miss.Hispan.* (Madrid) XIX, n.57 (1962) 371–3.

e. Church and State (XIXc)

APARICIO, S. *Goyeneche ante las dificultades de la Iglesia en el Perú (1816–1872).* Rome, 1972.
PIKE, Fr.B. "Church and State in Peru and Chile since 1840: a Study in Contrast." *American Historical Review* (Washington) 73:1, (1967) 30–50.
—. "Heresy Real and Alleged in Peru: An Aspect of the Conservative Liberal Struggle, 1830–1875." *Hispanic American Historical Review* (Durham) 47 (1967) 50-74.
RAMALLO, J.M. "La guerra religiosa en el Alto Perú 1811-1813." *Actas del Congreso Internacional de Historia de América,* IV, Buenos Aires, 1966, 5: 299–322.
TIBESAR, A. "The Peruvian Church at the Time of Independence in the Light of Vatican II." *The Americas* (Washington) 26 (1970) 349–75.

3. BOLIVIA

a. General Works on the Church

AGUIRRE, J.M. *Obras Oratorias* (intr.H.VAZQUEZ). 3 vols., Cuenca, 1924.
ANUARIO ECLESIASTICO DE BOLIVIA para el año del Señor 1960. La Paz, 1960.

ANUARIO ECLESIASTICO DE BOLIVIA. Año 1964.
La Paz, 1964.
BRITO, E. *Las misiones salesianas.* Quito, 1935.
GARCIA QUINTANILLA, J. *Historia de la Iglesia en la Plata. La Iglesia durante la colonia (1553–1700),* I. Sucre, 1964.
—. *Historia de la Iglesia de los Charcas o La Plata. Templos, conventos, monasterios.* Sucre, 1963.
LOPEZ MENENDEZ, F. *Compendio de historia eclesiástica de Bolivia.* La Paz, 1965.
—. *El Arzobispado de Ntra.Sra. de la Paz.* La Paz, 1949.
OVANDO-SANZ, G. *El curato de la iglesia matriz de Potosí en 1807.* Potosí, 1960.
TABORGA, M. de los Santos. *Estudios históricos de Monseñor . . . Capítulos de la Historia de Bolivia.* Sucre, 1908.
VAZQUEZ MACHICADO, H. *Obispos y canónigos Tahures.* La Paz, 1938.

b. Religion and Society (XIXc)

CONDARCO MORALES, R. *Zárate, el temible Willka: historia de la rebelión indígena de 1899.* La Paz, 1965.
MONAST, J. *L'univers religieux des aymaras de Bolivie.* Cuernavaca: CIDOC, 1966.
PAREDES, R. *Ritos, supersticiones y supervivencias populares de Bolivia.* La Paz, 2nd ed., 1936.
VALENCIA VEGA, A. *El indio en la independencia.* La Paz, 1961.

VII. THE SOUTHERN CONE

1. ARGENTINA

a. General Works on the Church

ALAMEDA, J. *Argentina Católica.* Buenos Aires, 1935.
BEGH, R.Mc. *Catolicismo y cambio sociopolítico en la Argentina.* Buenos Aires: Itinerarium, 1984.
BRUNO, C. *Historia de la Iglesia en la Argentina.* 12 vols, Buenos Aires, 1966–1971, .
CARBIA, R. D. *Historia eclesiástica del Río de la Plata (1536–1810).* 2 vols, Buenos Aires, 1924.
FARREL, G. *Iglesia y Pueblo en Argentina.* Buenos Aires, 1976.
LEONHARDT, C.J. (pub.) *Documentos para la historia argentina. Cartas anuas de la Provincia del Paraguay, Chile y Tucuman de la Compañía de Jesús.* Buenos Aires, 1904.
METHOL FERRÉ, A. "La Iglesia en el Cono Sur." *Actualidad Pastoral* (Buenos Aires) 144 (1982) 150–225.
PATTE, R. *El catolicismo contemporáneo en Hispano América.* Fides, 1951.
SEGURA, J.J.A. *Historia eclesiástica de Entre Ríos.* Entre Ríos, 1964.
VERDAGUER, J.A. *Historia eclesiástica de Cuyo.* 2 vols, Milan 1931.
VERGARA, M.A. "Síntesis de la historia eclesiástica de Salta en la época colonial." *Investigaciones y Ensayos* (Buenos Aires) n.10 (1971) 351–78.
ZURETTI, J.C. *Nueva historia eclesiástica argentina.* Buenos Aires: Itinerarium, 1972.

b. Missionary Congregations

CANO, L. "San Francisco Solano y otros misioneros franciscanos de la Argentina en el siglo XVI." *Misiones Franciscanas* (Oñate) XLV, n.385 (1961) 18–26.
CARRASCO, J. *Ensayo histórico sobre la Orden Dominica Argentina.* Buenos Aires, 1924.
DE CORDOBA, A. *La orden franciscana en las Repúblicas del Plata.* Buenos Aires, 1934.
HERNANDEZ, R. *Cartas Misioneras. Reseña histórica, científica y descriptiva de las Misiones Argentinas.* Buenos Aires, 1887.
MASSA, L. *Historia de las misiones salesianas en la Pampa.* 2 vols, Buenos Aires, 1968.
MILLE, A. *La Orden de la Merced en la conquista del Perú, Chile y el Tucumán y su convento del antiguo Buenos Aires, 1518–1804.* Buenos Aires, 1958.
—. *Crónica de la Orden Franciscana en la conquista del Perú, Paraguay y el Tucumán y su convento del antiguo Buenos Aires, 1512–1800.* Buenos Aires, 1961.
—. *Itinerario de la Orden dominicana en la conquista del Perú, Chile, y el Tucumán y su convento del antiguo Buenos Aires 1516–1807,* Buenos Aires. 1964.
—. *Derrotero de la Compañía de Jesús en la conquista del Perú, Tucumán y Paraguay y sus iglesias del antiguo Buenos Aires, 1567–1768.* Buenos Aires, 1968.
PALACIO, E. de. *Los Mercedarios en la Argentina (1535-1754).* Buenos Aires, 1971.
PEREZ, R. *La Compañía de Jesús restaurada en la República Argentina, Chile, el Uruguay y el Brasil.* Barcelona, 1901.
UDAONDO, E. *Crónica histórica de la Venerable Orden Tercera de San Francisco en la República Argentina.* Buenos Aires, 1920.

c. Popular Catholicism

ACTIS, F.C. *Historia de la Parroquia de San Isidro y de su Santo Patrono 1730–1930.* Buenos Aires, n.d.
ACEVEDO, E.O. "Situación social y religiosa de Catamarca en 1770–1771." *Revista de Historia Americana y Argentina* (Mendoza) 2:3–4 (1958–9) 237–340.
CARRIZO, J.A. *Cancionero popular de Jujuy.* Tucumán, 1934.
—. *Cancionero popular de Tucumán.* Buenos Aires, 1937.
—. *Cancionero popular de Salta.* Buenos Aires, 1932.
—. *Antiguos santos populares argentinos (Cancioneros de Catamarca).* Buenos Aires, 1936.
DI LULLO, O. *Cancionero popular de Santiago del Estero.* Buenos Aires, 1940.
DUSSEL, E. and M.M. ESANDI. *El catolicismo popular en la Argentina.* Buenos Aires, 1970.
LARROUY, A. *Historia de Ntra. Sra. del Valle en el siglo XVII.* Buenos Aires, 1916.
TOMMASINI, G. *Los indios ocloyas y sus doctrineros en el siglo XVII.* Córdoba, 1933.
—. *La civilización cristiana del Chaco.* Buenos Aires, 1927.
TORRE REVELLO, J. *Los Santos Patrones de Buenos Aires y otros ensayos históricos.* Buenos Aires, 1937.

d. Religion and Politics (early XIXc)

ACEVEDO, E.O. "San Martín y el clero cuyano, opositor al nuevo régimen." *Cuarto Congreso Internacional de Historia de América* (Buenos Aires) IV (1966) 9-75.

—. "Sobre las relaciones entre el Estado y la Iglesia." *Trabajos y comunicaciones* (La Plata) n.18 (1968) 9-43.

BREDA, E.A. "Bibliografía histórica del Sesquicentenario de la Revolución de Mayo referente a la Iglesia." *Archivum* (Buenos Aires) V (1961) 322-30.

MONTI, D.P. *Las preocupaciones religiosas en los hombres de Mayo.* Buenos Aires, 1966.

MOYANO ALIAGA, A. "Heterodoxos de la primera hora., *Archivum* (Buenos Aires) V (1961) 252-62.

MUSEO HISTORICO NACIONAL. *El clero argentino de 1810 a 1830.* 2 vols, Buenos Aires, 1907.

SCHIMITT, K. "The Clergy and the Enlightenment in Latin America: An Analysis." *The Americas* (Washington) XV, n.4 (1959), 381-91.

VIDELA ESCALADA, F. (Intro. by). *Congreso de Tucumán. Actitudes. Decisiones. Hombres.* Buenos Aires, 1966.

e. Church-State Relations (to mid-XIXc)

GARCIA DE LOYDI, L. "El cabildo eclesiástico de Buenos Aires: su gravitación en la vida ciudadana." *Investigaciones y Ensayos* (Buenos Aires) 5 (July-Dec. 1968) 289-316.

RIO, M. "La Iglesia: su historia y sus relaciones con el Estado 1810-1928." LEVILLIER, R. (ed.) *Historia Argentina.* 5 vols, Buenos Aires, 1969.

TANZI, H. "Las relaciones de la Iglesia y el Estado en la época de Rosas." *Historia* (Buenos Aires) 9:30 (Jan.-Mar. 1963) 5-28.

TONDA, A. *La Iglesia argentina incomunicada con Roma, 1810-1858. Problemas, conflictos, soluciones.* Santa Fe, 1965.

f. Laity and Social Action (late XIXc)

AUZA, N.T. *Historia de los congresos católicos argentinos 1884-1921.* Cuernavaca, 1968.

FRIAS, F.G. *Escritos y discursos.* 4 vols, Buenos Aires, 1884.

GARRO, J.M. *Obras completas de J. Manuel Estrada.* Buenos Aires, 1899.

ORTIZ, A. *El Padre Esquiú, Obispo de Córdoba. Sus sermones. Discursos. Cartas pastorales. Oraciones fúnebres . . . .* Córdoba, 1883.

USHER, S. *100 Años de la Acción Católica en la Argentina 1831-1931.* Buenos Aires, 1957.

2. URUGUAY

a. General Works on the Church

MARTINEZ, G. *Función de la Iglesia en la cultura nacional.* Montevideo, 1966.

METHOL FERRÉ, A. *Las corrientes religiosas.* Montevideo, 1969.

SEGUNDO, J.L. *Función de la Iglesia en la realidad rioplatense.* Montevideo, 1962.

—. and P. RODE. *Presencia de la Iglesia.* Montevideo, 1969.

CENTRO DE ESTUDIOS CRISTIANOS. *Aspectos religiosos de la sociedad uruguaya.* Montevideo, 1965.

b. Church-state Relations (XIXc)

ARDAO, A. *Racionalismo y liberalismo en el Uruguay.* Montevideo, 1962.

FAVARO, E. *Dámaso Antonio Larrañaga.* Montevideo, 1950.

FURLONG, G. "La misión Muzi en Montevideo (1824-1825)." *Revista del Instituto Histórico y Geográfico del Uruguay* (Montevideo) XI (1934-5) 145-78; XIII (1937) 235-80.

LISIERO, D. "Iglesia y Estado del Uruguay en el lustro definitorio, 1859-1863." *Revista Histórica* (Montevideo) XLIII, 2nd Series (1972), 1-225.

PONS, L.A. *Biografía de D. Jacinto Vera y Durán.* Montevideo, 1905.

SECCO ILLA, J. *El Civismo Católico. Su primera etapa.* Montevideo, n.d.

TOME, E. *El Vicariato Apostólico de José Benito Lamas.* Montevideo, 1941.

VIDAL, J.Ma. *El primer arzobispo de Montevideo. Don Mariano Soler.* 2 vols, Montevideo, 1935.

3. PARAGUAY

a. General Works on the Church

ROA, M. *Breve reseña histórica de la Iglesia del Paraguay.* Buenos Aires, 1906.

ZINNY, A. "Cronología de los obispos de Paraguay." *Revista Nacional* (Buenos Aires) 1887.

b. Missions

BERGLAR, P. *Der 'Jesuitenstaat' in Paraguay.* Bonn, 1963.

HAUBERT, M. *La vie quotidienne au Paraguay sous les jésuites.* Paris, 1967.

—. "Indiens et jésuites au Paraguay: rencontre de deux messianismes." *Archives de Sociologie des Religions* (Paris) 27 (1969) 119-33.

LUGON, C. *La République des guaranis. Les jésuites au pouvoir.* Paris, 1970.

PLA, J. "Las misiones jesuíticas guaraníes." *Cuadernos Americanos* (Mexico City) XXII, n.2 (1963) 131-61.

4. CHILE

a. General Works on the Church

ALIAGA, F. *Itinerario histórico de los Círculos de Estudio a las comunidades de base.* Santiago: ESEJ, 1977.

—. *Historia de los movimientos apostólicos juveniles de Chile.* Santiago: ESEJ, 1973.

ALIAGA, F. and J. OSORIO. "Historia de la Iglesia en Chile." *Historia de la Iglesia.* Valencia: EDICEP, 1982.

ALIAGA, F. et al. *Documentos de la Conferencia Episcopal de Chile (1952-1977).* Santiago: ESEJ, 1979, 4 vols.

ARANCIBIA SALCEDO, R. *Diccionario biográfico del clero secular chileno, 1918-1969,* Santiago, 1969.

ARANEDA BRAVO, F. *Cien años del arzobispado de Santiago 1840-1940.* Santiago: Talleres Gráficos Casa del Niño, 1940.

—. *Breve historia de la Iglesia en Chile.* Santiago, 1968.
—. *Obispos, sacerdotes y frailes.* Santiago, 1962.
BIBLIOTECA CENTRAL DE LA PONTIFICIA UNIVERSIDAD CATOLICA DE CHILE. *Bibliografía eclesiástica chilena.* Santiago, 1959.
EYZAGUIRRE, J. *Historia eclesiástica, política y literaria de Chile.* Valparaíso, 1850.
GONZALEZ ESPEJO, F. *Cuatro decenios de historia eclesiástica de Chile.* Santiago, 1948.
HANISH ESPINDOLA, W. *Las vocaciones en Chile 1536-1850.* Cuernavaca, 1970.
PRIETO DEL RIO, L.F. *Diccionario biográfico del clero secular de Chile, 1535-1918.* Santiago, 1922.
SALINAS, M. *Historia del Pueblo de Dios en Chile. Evolución del cristianismo desde la perspectiva de los pobres.* Santiago: CEHILA, 1987.
SILVA COTAPOS, C. *Historia eclesiástica de Chile.* Santiago, 1925.
URRUTIA INFANTE, Z. *El Obispado de Concepción, 1567-1957.* Santiago, 1957.

b. Missionary Congregations

ENRICH, F. *Historia de la Cía. de Jesús en Chile.* 2 vols, Barcelona, 1891.
GAZULLA, P. *Los mercedarios en la independencia de Chile.* Santiago, 1958.
GUERNICA, J. de. *Historia del monasterio de Clarisas de Ntra.Sra. de la Victoria.* Santiago, 1944.
HANISCH, W. *Peumo, historia de una parroquia.* Santiago, 1963.
LAGOS, R. *Historia de las misiones del colegio de Chillan.* Barcelona, 1908.
MATURANA, V. *Historia de los agustinos en Chile.* Santiago, 1904.
MUÑOZ O. *Las monjas trinitarias de Concepción, 1570-1822.* Santiago, 1918.
OLIVARES, L. *La provincia franciscana de Chile de 1553 a 1700 y la defensa que hizo de los Indios.* Santiago, 1961.
PAMPLONA, I. de. *Historia de las misiones de los PP. Capuchinos en Chile y Argentina (1849-1911).* Santiago, 1911.
PEÑA OTAEGUIA, C. *Una crónica conventual: las agustinas de Santiago, 1574-1951.* Santiago, 1951.

c. Evangelization

ALIAGA ROJAS, F. "Las relación diocesana de la visita Ad Limina de 1609 del obispo de Santiago de Chile." *Historia* (Santiago) n.5 (1966) 105–69.
ARANGUIZ DONOSO, H. "Notas para el estudio de una parroquia rural del siglo XVIII: Pelarco, 1786 -1796." *Anales de la Facultad de Filosofía y Ciencias de la Educación* (1969) 37–42.
GONZALEZ POMES, M.I. *La encomienda indígena en Chile durante el siglo XVIII.* Santiago, 1966.
OLIVARES MOLINA, L. *La provincia franciscana de Chile de 1553 a 1700 y la defensa que hizo de los indios.* Santiago, 1961.
OROZ, R. "La evangelización de Chile, sus problemas lingüísticos y la política idiomática de la corona en el siglo XVI." *Boletín de la Academia Chilena de la Historia* (Santiago) XXIX, n.66 (1962) 5–37.

d. Social History (XVI-XVIIIc)

JARA, A. *Guerre et société au Chili: essai de sociologie coloniale.* Paris, 1961.
KORTH, E.H. *Spanish Policy in Colonial Chile.* Stanford, 1968.
SANCHEZ AGUILERA, V. *El pasado colonial.* Osorno, 1948.

e. Religion and Politics (early XIXc)

COLEMAN, W.J. *La restauración del episcopado chileno en 1828, según Fuentes Vaticanas.* Santiago, 1954.
COLLIER, S. *Ideas and politics of Chilean Independence 1808-1833.* London, 1967.
GONGORA, M. "Aspectos de la ilustración católica en el pensamiento y la vida eclesiástica chilena 1770-1814." *Historia* (Santiago) n. 8 (1969) 43–73.
—. "El pensamiento de Juan Egaña sobre la reforma eclesiástica: avance y repliegue de una ideología de la época de la Independencia." *Boletín de la Academia Chilena de Historia* (Santiago) 30:68 (1963) 30–53.
HANISCH, W. *El Catecismo político cristiano. Las ideas y la época: 1810.* Santiago, 1970.
RETAMAL FAVEREAU, J. "El cabildo eclesiástico de Santiago en los prolegómenos de la independencia de Chile." *Historia* (Santiago) n.6 (1967) 285–314.
—. "Un catecismo político de 1820." *Revista Chilena de Historia y Geografía* (Santiago) 132 (1964) 256–64.

f. Social Problems (XIXc)

ARANGUIZ DONOSO, H. "La situación de los trabajadores agrícolas en el siglo XIX." *Estudio de Historia de las Instituciones Políticas y Sociales* (Santiago) 2 (1967) 5–31.
RANDOLPH, J. *Las guerras de Arauco y la esclavitud.* Santiago, 1966.
SEGALI, R.M. "Las luchas de clase en las primeras décadas de la República de Chile, 1810–1846." *Anales de la Universidad de Chile* (Santiago) 201:125 (1962) 175–218.

g. Church and State (late XIXc)

CRUCHAGA TOCORNAL, M. *De las relaciones de la Iglesia y el Estado en Chile.* Madrid, 1929.
DONOSO, R. *Las ideas políticas en Chile.* Mexico City, 1946.
EDWARDS VIVES, A. *La fronda aristocrática.* Santiago, 1952.
ESTELLE, P. "El debate de 1865 sobre la libertad de cultos y de conciencia."*Estudio de Historia de las Instituciones Políticas y Sociales* (Santiago) 2 (1967) 181–225.
GONZALEZ ECHENIQUE, J. and J. RETAMAL FAVEREAU. "El gobierno chileno y el concepto misionero del estado, 1832–1861." *Historia* (Santiago) n.5 (1966) 197–214.
GUZMAN ROSALES, M. and M. VIO HENRIQUEZ. *Don Francisco de Paula Taforó y la vacancia arzobispal, 1878-1887.* Santiago, 1964.

h. Social History (XXc)

BARRIA SERON, J.I. *Los movimientos sociales de Chile desde 1910 hasta 1926: aspecto político y social.* Santiago, 1960.

CARO, J.M. "Orientaciones sociales señaladas por los Pontífices." *Revista Católica* (Santiago) 500 (1922).

—. *Entrevista a monseñor Caro realizada por Joaquín Blaya Allende.* Valparaíso: Editorial Auda, 1939.

—. "Pastoral sobre algunos problemas sociales." *Revista Católica* (Santiago) 938 (1948).

CASTILLO, L., A. SAEZ. and P. ROGERS. "Notas para un estudio de la historia del movimiento obrero en Chile." *Cuadernos de la Realidad Nacional* (Santiago) 4 (1970) 3–30.

CEDIAL. *Cristianos latinoamericanos y socialismo.* Bogotá, 1972.

CHILEAN BISHOPS. *Instrucciones pastorales acerca de los problemas sociales.* (Santiago) 52, 1949.

—. *Documentos del Episcopado. Chile 1970–1973.* Santiago: Ediciones Mundo, 1974.

—. *Documentos del Episcopado. Chile 1974–1982.* Santiago: Ediciones Mundo, 1982.

—. "Asamblea Plenaria: un camino cristiano." *El Mercurio* (Santiago) 17 Dec. 1983.

CRUCHAGA, M. *De las relaciones entre la Iglesia y el Estado en Chile.* Madrid, 1929.

CRUZAT, G. "Chile comienza a cambiar." *Mensaje* (Santiago) 137 (1965).

CUMPLIDO, F. "La Constitución de 1925 y el cambio social." *Mensaje* (Santiago) 250 (1976).

DONOSO, R. *Alessandri, agitador y demoledor: cincuenta años de historia política de Chile.* Mexico City, 1952–4, I-II.

VIII. THE CHURCH AMONG THE HISPANICS IN THE U.S.A.

BRONDER, S. E. *Social Justice & Church Authority: the Public Life of Archbishop Robert E.Lucey.* Temple University Press, 1982.

CASTAÑEDA, C.E. *Our Catholic Heritage in Texas (1519-1936).* 7 vols., New Arno Press, 1936–1958.

CEHILA (vol. coord. by M. SANDOVAL). *Fronteras. A History of the Latin American Church in the USA since 1513.* San Antonio: MACC, 1987 (vol. X of *Historia General de la Iglesia en América Latina*).

DECK, A.F. *The Second Wave. Hispanic Ministry and the Evangelization of Cultures.* Mahwah, N.J.: Paulist Press, 1989.

ELIZONDO, V. *Christianity and Culture: An Introduction to Pastoral Theology and Ministry for the Bicultural Community.* Huntington: Our Sunday Visitor, 1975.

FOGEL, D. *Junípero Serra, the Vatican, and Enslavement Theology.* San Francisco: Ism Press, 1988.

GEIGER, M. *Franciscan Missionaries in Hispanic California, 1769–1848; A Biographical Dictionary.* San Marino, CA.: Huntington Library, 1969.

HACKETT, S. *Dominican Women in Texas: From Ohio to Galveston and Beyond.* Houston: Sacred Heart Convent of Houston, 1986.

Journal of Texas Catholic History and Culture, The. Azle: Texas Catholic Historical Society, 1990-.

MARIA PICCOLO, F. *Informe del estado de la nueva cristiandad de California* (ed. E.J. Burrus). Madrid: Porrúa, 1962.

NATIONAL CONFERENCE OF CATHOLIC BISHOPS. *The Hispanic Presence, Challenge, and Commitment: A Pastoral Letter on Hispanic Ministry,* Dec. 12, 1983.

OFFICE OF PASTORAL RESEARCH. *Hispanics in New York: Religious, Cultural, and Social Experiences: A Study of Hispanics in the Archdiocese of New York.* New York: Archdiocese of New York, 1982.

PRIVETT, S.A. *The U.S. Catholic Church and its Hispanic Members: The Pastoral Vision of Archbishop Robert E.Lucey.* San Antonio: Trinity U. P., 1988.

SANDOVAL, M. *On the Move. A History of the Hispanic Church in the United States.* Maryknoll, N.Y.: Orbis, 1990.

INDEX

NOTES ON CONTRIBUTORS

ANGEL ARNAIZ is a Dominincan Friar, living in Nicaragua. A member of CEHILA, he is author of *Historia del Pueblo de Dios en Nicaragua* (1990).

JEAN-PIERRE BASTIAN is a Protestant, living in Mexico. He holds a doctorate in history from the Colegio de México and teaches history at the Universidad Autónoma Metropolitana in Mexico City. He is co-ordinator of the Protestant sphere for CEHILA, author of *Historia del Protestantismo en América Latina* (1990) and editor of *Protestantes, liberales y francmasones* (1990).

JOSE-OSCAR BEOZZO is a Catholic priest, living in Brazil. He holds a doctorate in sociology from Louvain University and lectures in history in São Paulo. A member of CEHILA, he is author of *Historia da Igreja no Brasil. Segunda Epoca* (1980), in CEHILA's multi-volume history of the Church in Latin America.

ANA MARIA BIDEGAIN was born in Uruguay and is Colombian by adoption. She holds a doctorate in history from Louvain and has taught at the University of the Andes and the National University of Colombia, besides being visiting professor at Notre Dame and Duke Universities in the U.S.A. and that of Alcalá in Spain. A Catholic, she works with ecumenical groups such as CEHILA and Kairos Europe. Her books include *Así actuaron los cristianos en la historia de América Latina* (1985) and *From Catholic Action to Liberation Theology: Historical Process of the Laity in Latin America in the Twentieth Century* (1985), as well the chapter "Women and Theology of Liberation" in *Through Her Eyes* (1990).

RODOLFO CARDENAL is a Jesuit priest, born in Nicaragua in 1950, now working at the Central American University in San Salvador. He holds an M.A. from the University of Austin, Texas, and a master's degree in theology completed in Spain. A member of CEHILA, he edited the volume on Central America in its General History (1985). His other works include *Rutilio Grande. Mártir de la evangelización rural en El Salvador* (1978), and (with others) *La voz de los sin voz. La palabra viva de Monseñor Romero* (1980) and *Church and Politics in Latin America*.

JOSE COMBLIN is Belgian by birth, living in Latin America since 1958. He holds a doctorate in theology from Louvain, and has lectured there and in Brazil. Hailed by Dom Helder Câmara as "a living example of the committed theologian," he was expelled from Brazil in 1972 for his commitment to the poor, but allowed back in 1980. He has since lived and worked in a poor peasant community in the North-East of the country. He has written over forty books of theology and social criticism, of which the most recent to appear in English are *The Holy Spirit and Liberation* (1989) and (in U.S.A) *Retrieving the Human/*(in U.K.) *Being Human: A Christian Anthropology* (1991).

FAUSTINO COUTO TEIXEIRA is a Catholic, living in Brazil. He works at the John XXIII Institute, researching sociology of religion.

MARGARITA DURAN is a Catholic, living in Paraguay. She holds a doctorate in history from the Catholic University of Asunción and is author of numerous works on the history of the Church in Paraguay.

ENRIQUE DUSSEL was born in Argentina in 1934. Forced to leave his native country for political reasons, he now lives in Mexico. He studied in Madrid, Paris and Mainz, and holds doctorates in philosophy and history. A founder member of CEHILA, he is now its president and general editor of its General History; he is also a committee member of the Third World Theology sector of the international theological review *Concilium*. His *Historia de la Iglesia en América Latina* is now in its seventh edition (1992) and works translated into English include *Philosophy of Liberation* and *Ethics and Community* (1988).

JOSE APARECIDO GOMES MOREIRA, born in 1951, is a Catholic born in Brazil. He holds a master's degree in history and ethno-history from the University of Mexico and is a member of CEHILA. Besides articles in books and reviews, he has published *Conquista y conciencia cristiana. El pensamiento indigenista y jurídico-teológico de Don Vasco de Quiroga* (1990).

RAUL GOMEZ TRETO was born in Cuba in 1932. A Catholic, he is legal adviser to the Cuban bishops, and author of *The Church and Socialism in Cuba* (1988).

EDUARDO HOORNAERT was born in Belgium in 1930 and now lives in Brazil. He studied classical philology and ancient history at Louvain, and theology at Bruges, and has held professorships in history in several institutes in Brazil. A founder member of CEHILA, he is responsible for its popular editions. He is author of *Formaçao do catolicismo no Brasil* (1974), *Historia da Igreja no Brasil. Primera epoca* (1977), *The Memory of the Christian People* (1989) and *O Cristianismo moreno no Brasil* (1991).

LAENNEC HURBON is a Catholic priest from Haiti. A doctor of sociology, he is a member of CNRS in Paris, and of CEHILA. He has published numerous works on the sociology of religion and the anthropology and history of Haiti and the Caribbean.

JEFFREY KLAIBER is a Jesuit priest, born in the United States in 1943 and now living in Peru. He holds a Ph.D. in history from the Catholic University of America and a master's degree in history from Loyola University, Chicago. He is currently Associate Professor of history at the Catholic University of Peru. His published works include *Religion and Revolution in Peru, 1824–1976* (1977), *Violencia y crisis de valores en el Perú* (1987) and *The Catholic Church in Peru, 1821–1985* (1992).

ARMANDO LAMPE was born in Aruba in the Caribbean in 1958 and is a Catholic priest of the diocese of the Dutch Antilles. He holds master's degrees in theology from the Catholic University of Nijmegen, in sociology from the Universidad Iberoamericana in Mexico City, and a Ph.D. in social sciences from the Free University of Amsterdam. Author of various articles and *Descubrir a Dios en el Caribe* (1991), he is currently pastor for the Antillean minorities in the Netherlands.

MANUEL MARZAL was born in Spain in 1931. He is a Jesuit priest, has lived in Peru since 1951 and is now a Peruvian citizen. He holds a master's degree in anthropology from the Universidad Iberoamericana in Mexico City and a doctorate in philosophy from the Universidad Católica in Quito, and is now senior lecturer in social sciences at the Pontificia Universidad Católica of Peru. He has published *Historia de la antropología indigenista: México y Peru* (1981), *La transformación religiosa peruana* (1983), *El sincretismo iberoamericano* (1985) and *Los caminos religiosos de los inmigrantes de la gran Lima* (1988).

JOHANNES MEIER was born in W. Germany in 1948 and is a Catholic priest. He holds a doctorate in theology from the University of Würzburg, where he lectures at the Institut für Historische Theologie. His historical works include *Der priestliche Dienst nach*

Johannes Gropper (1503–1559) (1977), "Philipp von Hutten (1511–1546), ein Fränkischer Ritter auf Conquistadorepfaden in Venezuela" (1988) and "Die Anfänge der Kirche auf den Karibischen Inseln ... 1511–1522 bis zur Mitte des 17 Jahrhunderts" in *Neue Zeitschrift für Missionswissenschaft* (1991).

MARIA ALICIA PUENTE was born in Mexico in 1936. She holds a master's degree in sociology from the Universidad Iberoamericana there, studied sociology of religion at Louvain, and gained a doctorate in social anthropology from the Centro de Investigaciones y Estudios Superiores en Antropología Social in Mexico. She is Mexican co-ordinator for CEHILA. Besides articles and conference papers, she has published *Hacia una historia mínima de la Iglesia en México* (1991).

MARIO RODRIGUEZ was born in Puerto Rico in 1950. A Dominican Friar, he holds a doctorate in history and lectures on Latin American church history at CEDOC and the Convent of St John of the Lateran in Cuba. He is author of *Bayamón: Notas para su historia* (1985), *Sínodo de San Juan de Puerto Rico de 1645* (1986) and *Fray Bartolomé de las Casas y la Teología de la Liberación* (1989).

RODOLFO DE ROUX was born in Colombia in 1945. He holds a degree in philosophy from Gallarte in Italy, a master's in theology from the Universidad Javeriana in Bogotá, and a doctorate from the Ecole de Hautes Etudes in Paris. He lectures at the Universidad Nacional Pedagógica in Bogotá, and has been a member of CEHILA since 1976, responsible for the volume on Colombia and Venezuela in its General History. Besides numerous articles, he has compiled an audio-visual course on the history of Christianity in Latin America, and is author of *Una Iglesia en estado de alerta. Funciones sociales y funcionamiento del catolicismo Colombiano (1930–1980)* (1983) and *Dos mundos enfrentados* (1990).

MAXIMILIANO SALINAS was born in Chile in 1952. He holds a doctorate in theology from the Pontifical University of Salamanca, and lectures in the social sciences faculty of the Universidad Academia de Humanismo Cristiano in Santiago. He has co-ordinated CEHILA's history of theology in Latin America, and his published works include "The Voices of Those who Spoke up for the Victims" in the *Concilium* Special Issue *1492–1992: The Voice of the Victims* (1990), *Historia del Pueblo de Dios en Chile* (1987) and *Canto a lo divino y religión del oprimido en Chile* (1991).

MOISES SANDOVAL was born in the United States in 1930. He holds a B.Sc. from Marquette University and a certificate in international reporting from Columbia. He is editor-at-large of the *Maryknoll* magazine, editor of *Revista Maryknoll* and CEHILA co-ordinator for Hispanics in the United States. He is author of *On the Move: A History of the Hispanic Church in the United States* (1990), editor of *Fronteras, A History of the Latin American Church in the U.S. since 1513* (1983) and *The Mexican Experience in the Church* (1983); he is also a member of the advisory commission and contributor to the forthcoming three-volume *The History of the Hispanic Church in the U.S. in the 20th Century*.

JUAN SCHOBINGER was born in Switzerland in 1928, moved to Argentina at the age of three and is now an Argentine citizen. A member of the Swiss Reformed Church of the Canton of Vaud, he holds a degree in history and a doctorate in philosophy from the Universidad Nacional of Buenos Aires. Since 1956 he has worked at the National University in Cuyo (Argentina) where he holds the chair of prehistoric archeology. His published works include: (with others) *La Momia del Cerro el Toro* (1966), *Prehistoria de Sudamérica* (1969, revised ed. 1988) and (with Carlos Gradin) *Cazadores de la Patagonia y agricultores Andinos: arte rupestre de la Argentina* (1985).